Falkus & Buller's

Freshwater
FISHING

Falkus & Buller's
Freshwater
FISHING

FRED BULLER & HUGH FALKUS

A book of tackles and techniques,
with some notes on various fish, fish recipes,
fishing safety and sundry
other matters

CRESSET PRESS

To Kathleen and Pauline

A Cresset Press Book
First published in 1975
Revised edition 1988
This edition published 1992

Copyright © Fred Buller and Hugh Falkus 1975, 1988
All rights reserved
ISBN 0 09 177107 2
Printed and bound by Thomson Press, India.

CONTENTS

Introduction 7

Part 1: The Fishes

Fish as Food 13

The Barbel 15
A British record barbel; Cooking the barbel

The Bleak 22
Cooking the bleak

The Bream 24
Cooking the bream

The Silver Bream 28

The Bullhead or Miller's Thumb 29

The Burbot 30
Cooking the burbot

The Carp 33
Determining age

The Crucian Carp 43
Cooking the carp

The Catfish 45
Cooking the catfish

The Charr 49
The habits of Windermere charr; Traditional Windermere charr fishing; Cooking the charr

The Chub 63
Cooking the chub

The Dace 68
Cooking the dace

The Eel 73
Eel fishing; Cooking the eel

The Flounder 88
Cooking the flounder

The Grayling 94
Cooking the grayling

The Gudgeon 99
Cooking the gudgeon

The Lampreys 103
The sea lamprey; The river lamprey, or lampern; The brook lamprey, or Planer's lamprey; Cooking the lamprey

The Loaches 108
The stone loach; The spined loach

The Minnow 110
Cooking the minnow

The Grey Mullets 113
Cooking the mullet

The Perch 116
Cooking the perch

The Pike 124
Pike in antiquity; Diet and appetite; Riddle of the Cepedian pike; Deformity; Age and fecundity; Senses and feeding habits; Deadbait fishing; Livebaiting; Fly fishing for pike; Cooking the pike

The Roach 165
Trotting; A roach-pole technique; A ledgering technique for Hampshire Avon roach; A swimfeeder technique on the Dorset Stour; Fly fishing for roach; Cooking the roach

The Rudd 181
Identification of rudd, roach, bream and their hybrids; Cooking the rudd

The Ruffe or Pope 190
Cooking the ruffe

The Atlantic Salmon 192
Salmon fishing; Waterside behaviour; Low water worm fishing; Prawn fishing; Shrimp fishing; Gillies; Cooking the salmon

The Shads 232
Allis shad; Twaite shad; Cooking the shad

The Three-spined Stickleback 235

The Sturgeon 237

The White Sturgeon 240
Cooking the sturgeon

The Tench 245
Cooking the tench

The Brown Trout 253
*Angling sportsmanship; Fly fishing –
historical; A trout stream; Dry-fly
fishing; Stillwater fly-fishing; Nymph
fishing; Casting the shooting head; Rise-
forms; Boat fishing; Acid rain – how to
overcome some problems; Acid rain
devastation; An angler's delight; Cooking
the trout*

The Sea Trout 298
*The angling approach; Sea Trout by
night; The Falkus finger-ring figure-of-
eight retrieve; Playing a sea trout;
Cooking the sea trout*

The Rainbow Trout 325

The Brook Trout 329

The Whitefishes 330
Houting; Vendace

The Zander 342
Cooking the Zander

Part 2: Tackle & Technique

Rods 347
*Origin and materials; Choice of rod; Rod-
rings; Rod-rests*

Reels 358
*Origin of the reel; The earliest fishing
reels; Notes on early English reels; The
multiplier; Nottingham type reels; The
fixed-spool reel*

Lines 378
*Putting line on a fixed-spool reel; Fly-
lines; Discarded nylon – a warning!*

Hooks 384
Hook design; Hook sizes

Knots 388

Swivels 395

Leads 396

Nets 399
Landing nets; Keepnets

Gags and disgorgers 405
*The Buller gag and Baker 'hookout'
disgorger*

Floats 408
*Design and function; Bite indicators;
Swing-tip historical*

Baits and Baiting 421
*Breadcrust; Breadcrumb; Worm; The
sliced-shanked bait-hook; The Stewart 3-
hook tackle; Maggots; Stewed hempseed;
Hemp and elderberry; Groundbaiting*

Ledgering 442
*Pierced-bullet ledger; Bomb-link ledger;
Variable shot-link ledger*

Float Fishing 445
*Fast water trotting; The lift method of
float fishing; The adjustable float-link
rig; Floating crust link rig*

Float-Ledgering, Laying-On and 454
Stret-Pegging

Paternostering 459
*Sliding bubble-float paternoster; Count de
Moira's beam paternoster; The standing
pike-paternoster*

Spinning 463
*Spinning historical; Artificial baits; The
McElrath deadbait (sprat) spinning mount;
Baits; Housing baits, plugs and spinners*

Plug Fishing 474
An afternoon with floating plug

Trolling and Trailing 479
*Trolling; Trailing; The downrigger; The
nose-cone trailing tackle*

Chance and Mischance 493
*Angling 'luck'; Twenty-six ways of losing
a fish*

Angling safety 501
*Wading; Emergency; Boat fishing
accidents; Removing hook from finger;
Rods and electricity*

Index 509

INTRODUCTION

Fishing is an unceasing expectation and
a perpetual disappointment.

Thomas de Quincey

This is a book of simple purpose. Our object has been to compile a few tested fishing rigs and methods, together with some notes on the fish themselves, which we hope may lead our readers towards a fuller appreciation of their sport.

It is not of course complete. Nor could it ever be, such is the complexity of angling and the speed of modern development. Tackle and technique are discussed weekly by a host of writers; any attempt at making a comprehensive survey of so much material would be absurd. We are conscious that even with revision at the moment of printing, certain aspects will seem dated a few years hence.

Nevertheless, for all its technical improvement, angling is basically the same as it was when *A Treatyse of Fysshynge wyth an Angle* appeared five hundred years ago. It is mainly the trappings that have changed. Compared with some of today's sophisticated rigs, those tackles described and illustrated in the *Treatyse* may seem quaint and far away; but the fishes are the same and the way we fish for them hasn't altered much – in some cases not at all. As some of the examples in this book endorse, there is still quite a lot to be learnt from our predecessors.

Anyone sceptical of this has only to consider the illustrations on page 465, which show the first known spoon-bait to have been a much more reliable hooker than its modern counterpart – a point that bait manufacturers could note with advantage!

And past values apply to other than tackle and method. In its attitude to angling, the *Treatyse* offers a dictum that could be blazoned on the banks of every salmon river today:

You must not use the aforesaid artful sport for covetousness merely for the increasing or saving of your money....!

In writing this book we have confined our comments mainly to aspects that gave us pleasure to discuss. Not least of these has been a glance at angling history, for the enjoyment of any sport is enriched by some knowledge of its background. As Dr J. J. Manley suggested in *Notes on Fish and Fishing* (1877):

Anglers should know something of angling literature; of the natural history of the fishes; of gastronomic merits and demerits and nomenclature, so that they shall not pursue their quarry as mere savages....

The book has been arranged in two parts. The second section deals mainly with fishing tackle and technique. The first takes a look at the fish themselves, placed alphabetically – except that, not being mere slaves to system, we have allowed the Silver Bream to follow the Common Bream; the Allis and Twaite Shads to come together under Shads; the Grey Mullets to meet under 'M'; the Brown Trout, Sea Trout, Rainbow Trout and Brook Trout to group themselves under 'T' for trout, and the Gwyniad, Powan, Pollan, Vendace and Skelly to share the general title *The Whitefishes*. That this section is prefaced with some remarks on 'fish as food' is because, historically, human association with fishes is founded on their culinary value, however much that relationship may have been subsumed by the sophistries and sentiment of anglers.

The text follows no particular pattern, being by turns didactic, lyrical and discursive. Its frequent use of quotation is not through any reluctance to write our own copy, but to acquaint the reader with some of the delights (and follies) to be found in angling literature; in particular, with authors who in addition to being fine anglers wrote with wit and charm – qualities seldom encountered in today's sporting press.

Finally, since we are aware that modern angling techniques result from experience accumulated over many centuries, that every angler owes a debt to others both past and present, we have done our best to trace the originators of the rigs and methods described and to give credit where it is due.

The Authors 1987

Figure 1: Bobbing for Eels is practised in a boat, with a large bunch of worms suspended by a strong cord from a pole or stout rod, in the following manner: first of all, you must procure a large quantity of worms, (marsh worms are best) and string them on worsted, by passing a needle through them from head to tail, until you have as many strung as will form a bunch as large as a good sized turnip, then fasten them on the line so that all the ends may hang level. In the middle is placed a piece of lead, of a conical form, which may be got at any of the fishing-tackle shops, made for the purpose; thus prepared, cast the baits into the water gently, let them sink to the bottom, and then keep raising them a few inches from the ground, and dropping them again, until you have a bite, which is easily perceived, as the Eel tugs very strongly: be as expert as possible, and at the same time as steady, in raising your line, so that your fish, in dropping off, may fall into the boat. Immense numbers are taken by this method. During the hot weather, fish in rather shoal water, and out of the stream.

T. F. Salter, *The London Anglers Guide* (1814)

ACKNOWLEDGEMENTS

For their very kind asssistance in the preparation of this book, our grateful thanks are due (in alphabetical order) to:

Bill Arnold, for permission to publish his recordings of acid rain, and his description of how to overcome acidity problems in a Cumbrian tarn.

David Beazley, for criticism of our bibliographical references and for items from his paper *Fishing Reels: A History,* published in the 1987 Summer edition of *The Flyfishers' Journal.*

Brian Clarke, for his splendid contribution on the 'Rise Forms' of feeding trout.

Ronald Coleby, most helpful of angling bibliophiles.

H. Claypool, for drawings of dace and gudgeon.

Joan Corp and Dr M. A. Newman of Vancouver B.C., for information and photographs of white sturgeon.

E. J. Crossman, for the use of the white sturgeon drawing taken from *Freshwater Fishes of Canada* (1973), and for help on the biology of the pike.

Editors of *The Field, Angling Times* and *Anglers' Mail,* for permission to reproduce various photographs.

Jan Eggers, for providing much interesting information about big fish in addition to several photographs.

A. Gibson, for his sturgeon photographs.

Linde Hardaker, the designer of this book, for her felicitous blending of photographs, drawings and text.

The late Sir Frederick Hoare, for the photograph of the two pike locked together in death.

Colin Howes, Assistant Keeper of Doncaster Museum, for sturgeon catch-records.

Ted Hughes, for allowing us to include extracts from his poem *Pike,* reprinted by permission of Faber and Faber Ltd from *Imperial* by Ted Hughes.

Jim Miller, chairman of Hardy Bros, for his generous invitations to fish various beats on the Tay and Tweed, and James Hardy of the same company, for help with details of early fishing-rod materials and for his notes on shooting-head fishing.

Dr Joseph Needham of The Needham Research Institute, for information about early Chinese reels.

North West Water Authority, for permission to print extracts from their Scientists Division Department.

Oxford Scientific Films, for the photograph of the stickleback.

Marion Paull, our publishing editor, for her unfailing enthusiasm and kindness.

Scientific Anglers, for permission to reproduce the drawings of casting the shooting head.

Roy Shaw, for his photographs of spawning grayling, and the pictures of trout-tails and minnows.

Günther Sturba, for the drawing taken from *Freshwater Fishes of the World* (1962).

Ken Sutton, for photographs and information on old British reels.

Fred J. Taylor and Frank Plum, for their company and humour at the waterside.

Dr H. Thirlaway, librarian of the Piscatorial Society, for permission to reproduce *An eel-bobber of Battersea*.

Alwyne Wheeler of the British Museum (Natural History), for his patient help in solving so many of our problems.

Phill Williams, for photographs of charr and Whitefish.

For their help with the manuscript along the way, we should also like to express our gratitude to: Dr Peter Behan, R. N. Booth, Des Elliott, the late Dr W. F. Frost, Michael Kendall, Moc Morgan and that other great Welsh sportsman Tim Thomas, together with our old friends Peter Thomas and the late Richard Walker.

Finally, the delightful engravings used as chapter headings for "The Fishes", were originally published in: P. Fisher's *The Angler's Souvenir* (1835); Mr and Mrs S. C. Hall's *The Book of The Thames* (1859); William Yarrell's *A History of British Fishes* (1841); Couch's *A History of the Fishes of the British Islands* (1862); The Rev. W. Houghton's *British Freshwater Fishes* (1884), and Francis Francis's *Sporting Sketches* (1878). To those distant craftsmen, now in Elysian fields, our grateful thanks.

Part One
The FISHES

Fishing, if I a fisher may protest,
Of pleasures is the sweet'st of sports the best,
Of exercises the most excellent,
Of recreations the most innocent,
But now the sport is marde, and wott ye why?
Fishes decrease, and fishers multiply.

Thomas Bastard, *Chresteleros,*
Seven Bookes of Epigrames (1598)

Figure 2: An oil painting – which includes gudgeon, dace, roach,
pike, perch and trout – by H. L. Rolfe (1850). Rolfe, who was one
of the greatest fish painters of all time, was commissioned to paint
a picture for Mr Mundella as a testimonial for sponsoring the Bill
protecting freshwater fishes by means of a close season. The Bill
became an Act of Parliament in 1878

... the austere, scrupulous regulations of the Romish Church have tended more than any other circumstances, to enhance the value, and increase the quantity of this species of food: so rigid was the precept upon this point, that in the year 1629, *Claude Guillon* was beheaded at *St Claude* in *Burgundy*, for eating a morsel of *Horseflesh* on a *Fish*-day.

The Rev. W. B. Daniel, *Rural Sports* (1801)

Figure 3: Thursday.
Tomorrow will be Friday, so we'll fish the stream today. (Painted by Dendy Sadler, 1880)

FISH *as* FOOD

And ete the olde fisshe, and leve the yonge,
Though they moore towgh be uppon the tonge.

But stynkkyng fisshe, and unsesonable,
Latte passe, and taake such as be able.

Piers of Fulham (*c*. 1400)

One of the rewards of fishing is that with few exceptions fish are good to eat. For centuries this has been taken for granted, but in ancient times it was the subject of much argument. The fathers of medicine recommended certain species of fish as being wholesome, and disparaged others as being very unwholesome. Unfortunately, when it came to deciding which species were good and which were bad, they were seldom in agreement. One old thinker divided fish into clean and unclean species by their habitat:

Those which keep near the rocks are easily digested, but not very nutritious. Those which haunt deep water are very nutritious, but upsetting to the internal economy.

He had it both ways.

On the grounds that some fish didn't get enough exercise, another early intellectual wrote:

All fish that standing pools frequent,
Do ever yield bad juice and nourishment.

This was an interesting point, since that great physician Xenocrates had stated emphatically:

The tail end of *all* fishes is the most wholesome part, on account of its being most frequently exercised.

But although the great medical minds of long ago disagreed over dietary values, they were united in prescribing fish – in one form or another – as a nostrum for most human ills and disorders.

If you were bitten by a mad dog, 'Pickled fish, applied topically', would be found 'sufficiently effectual'.

Toothache? Then, 'Rub your teeth with the brains of a dog-fish boiled in oil'. If your wife became hysterical, 'Lint greased with a dolphin's fat, and then ignited . . . ' proved instantly effective.

For easy deliverance in pregnancy, the ' . . . fragrance of burnt eel' took some beating; or, 'A torpedo fish, caught when the moon is in Libra and kept in the open air for three days before being placed in the patient's room' would be sure to do the trick. (In hot weather, one might think, it certainly would!)

Superfluous hair? There was a choice of depilatories. 'Tunny guts, fresh or pickled' were pretty good; or 'fish brains, applied with alum on the sixteenth day of the moon' – just as effective.

For carbuncles there was nothing better than 'burnt mullet mixed with honey'.

The best aphrodisiac? Fish every time. Fish, it seems, was an essential part of the wedding feast.

But to more recent times. In medieval England, fish was of great value, the pike in particular. Its price, as fixed by Edward I, was double that of salmon and more than ten times that of either turbot or cod. Even in the sixteenth century, a big pike fetched as much as a lamb, and a small pickerel was dearer than a fat capon.

According to Robert Howlett in *The Angler's Sure Guide* (1706), pike flesh was considered very medicinal:

The Croslike bone in his Head is given against the Falling-sickness; and his Flesh is so harmless and excellent, that it may be given to a sick Person. His Spawn and Row provoke both to Vomit and Stool, and are used for that Purpose; the Jaws calcin'd helps the Stone, cleanses and dries up Ulcers, old Sores and Hemorrhoids; the Teeth in Powder gives Ease in the Pleurisie; the Grease takes away Coughs in Children, by anointing the Feet therewith; the Gall taken inwardly, cures Agues; outwardly helps Spots and Dimness of the Eyes; the Heart eaten cures Fevers.

Both authors of this book can testify to the excellence of pike when properly cooked, but the chief reason for its popularity in medieval times is unlikely to have been its flavour, or even its value as a panacea. 'Days of abstinence', which occurred several times a week, made fish a necessity. Roads were bad; transport difficult and tedious. Saltwater species were not readily available to people living far inland. The pike was a large fish, obtainable nearly everywhere in any season. The demand for it is not surprising at a time when Fast Days numbered no fewer than a hundred and forty-five a year!

Religious festivals notwithstanding, there is no doubt that most species of freshwater fish were eagerly sought, and much care lavished on their preparation. Thus Izaak Walton wrote, with relish, of the carp (at the end of a complicated recipe which included marjoram, thyme, rosemary, parsley, onions, oysters, oranges, anchovies, claret and cloves):

... lay it with the broth, into the dish; and pour upon a quarter of a pound of the best fresh butter, melted, and beaten with half a dozen spoonfuls of the broth, the yolks of two or three eggs, and some of the herbs

shred. Garnish your dish with lemons, and serve it up. And much good do you.

Doubtless, the primary function of such elaborations was to conceal the muddy flavour. All the same, as Arthur Ransome said:

There are fashions in fish. It is possible in angling literature to watch, for example, the decline and fall of the pike from the eminence he once enjoyed. He was once for the angler 'my joy of all the scaly shoal' and when cooked 'too good' for any but those who fished for him 'or very honest men'. With the pike the other coarse fish have lost their kitchen reputations. Yet once upon a time a pike would be the chief dish at a banquet and many another fish now seldom cooked was valued as highly as trout or salmon. At the Assizes in Derby in 1613, the bill of fare included: '15 different sorts of fowl, among others young swans, knots, herns, bitterns, etc., three venison pasties appointed for every meal, 13 several sorts of sea-fish, 14 several sorts of freshwater fish, each appointed to be ordered a different way'.

In Britain today most coarse fishers return their catch. This is not surprising. Apart from the increasing popularity of angling and the resulting pressure on water space, tastes have changed with changing social conditions.

Besides, comparatively few modern British housewives would fancy, or have the time for, dressing pike or skinning eels; all the fish she needs are easy to cook and readily available. Nevertheless, many fishes seldom seen in the marketplace are valuable as food – indeed in less affluent societies they would be eaten with alacrity (and in many countries they are) – and since we feel that an effort should be made to keep one or two recipes in print we have added a selection to our notes on the various species.*

*In early March 1986, roach were on a Dumfries fishmonger's slab at 65p per lb.

The
BARBEL

Barbus barbus

In the great carp family, the Cyprinidae, there is a genus of fishes, *Barbus*, very rich in species. Of these, the mahseer of India, *Barbus tor*, is perhaps the best known. In Africa there are at least a hundred different species and four sub-species, only one of which is found in Britain: *Barbus barbus*.

The British barbel is mainly confined to one northern habitat centred on the Trent river system, and one southern habitat centred on the Thames. Southern barbel rivers include the Thames, Kennet, Lea, Colne, Wey, Loddon and Great Ouse. Northern barbel rivers include the Trent, Nidd, Wharfe, Ure, Swale, Dove and Derwent. It has, however, been successfully introduced to other rivers, notably the Severn, Wye, Medway, Wiltshire Avon, Hampshire Avon and Dorset Stour.

The barbel is distinguishable from all other British species by the presence of four barbules attached to the upper lip and jaw. These are organs of touch and taste. Whereas predatory fish and plankton-feeding fish rely mainly on visual aids in their search for food, touch and taste organs are used by most species that live

and feed on the bottom. Equipped with such organs, the barbel has adapted itself to bottom living in swift-flowing streams of deep rivers.

Although big strides have been made in modern fishing techniques, present-day barbel specialists are unlikely to catch the quantities of fish hooked by earlier anglers. During eight days on the River Trent an angler once caught three hundred barbel to his own rod, and individual catches of 97, 100 and 123 have been recorded in a day. Most of these old-timers pre-baited their swims – or had them baited by local professionals – with huge quantities of groundbait; as many as three or four thousand lobworms sometimes being used for this purpose!

Today, although such bags are probably long past, barbel fishing is enjoyed by more anglers than ever before. Since the last war two new techniques have emerged.

The first of these – a truly remarkable concept – was to groundbait a small patch of river bed very heavily with cooked hempseeds. This was done by means of a large baitdropper. A *size 6 hook* was then baited with one or two hempseeds! The tackle, with just sufficient weight to hold bottom, was ledgered *on top* of the groundbait seeds. The angler sat, rod in hand, waiting for a hungry barbel to find the little heap of hemp and suck up the two 'armed' hempseeds along with the decoy seeds.

We have nothing but admiration for the angler who conceived this astonishing method. He must have persevered, without the benefit of previous success, until such time as Stour barbel came to accept hempseeds as foodstuff. It was developed on the Throop Fishery of the Dorset Stour – and then banned by the riparian owners. In our opinion, quite unnecessarily.

The second technique was developed on the Royalty Fishery of the Hampshire Avon. It evolved from the traditional rolling-ledger method in which baits like breadcrust, breadcrumb, bran-paste, lobworms and bunches of maggots were fished (on sizes, 4, 6, or 8 hooks, tied to 6 or 7 BS lines) in fast swims that had been heavily groundbaited with large balls of bread-and-bran mixture. In time, small hooks (sizes 14 and 16) baited with single maggot on lines of 2–4 lb BS, replaced the traditional tackle. Very large quantities of maggots were used as groundbait, with the result that the barbel gradually became preoccupied maggot-feeders. Gen-erally, the maggots were delivered accurately into the quieter runs close to the bank by means of swimfeeder or baitdropper.

Another significant post-war development has been the discovery of several new baits. In some rivers barbel, like chub, will take lumps of sausage or luncheon-meat – and other items from the delicatessen store.

Apart from these new methods and baits there are, of course, the traditional laying-on, float-ledgering, ledgering and swimming-the-stream methods of catching barbel. These are the same as used for roach fishing, but with stronger tackle. A big barbel is a powerful fish and will break light tackle nearly every time if it reaches weed cover. If you find that 6 lb BS line is acceptable to the barbel, never use lighter.

It is always exciting to know that bigger fish haunt the water than ever seem to come out of it. One of Britain's most experienced skin divers once stated that the remains of the original supports for the old Chertsey Bridge held barbel of record size. Later, to prove his point to anglers sceptical of their existence, he used the age-old technique of 'tickling' to bring several of these monsters to the surface!

A BRITISH RECORD BARBEL

On 13 September 1934, Aylmer Tryon, then a novice coarse angler, was ledgering the Hampshire Avon from a moored boat with his father

Figure 4: Aylmer Tryon's barbel of 14 lb 6 oz caught on lobworm in the Royalty Water of the Hampshire Avon, 13 September 1934. The NASA rod-caught British record

Freshwater Fishing

the late G. C. Tryon and Mr Hayter, warden of the Christchurch Royalty Fishery. He was receiving instruction on barbel fishing from a parent who was one of the best all-round anglers of his time; indeed, although G. C. Tryon shared a trout beat on the Test with Sir Edward Grey, author of the classic *Fly Fishing*, his preference was for pike and barbel.

Aylmer remembers how perplexed he felt when his first catch – a 4 lb barbel, to him a splendidly large fish – was described by his companions as 'only a small one'. He recalls Hayter taking the fish some distance upstream before releasing it – 'so that it shouldn't disturb the swim'.

Minutes later, Aylmer hooked a second fish – which broke him. A misfortune which, in his own words, 'made me not at all popular with my companions'.

With a stronger gut leader fitted, he fished on,

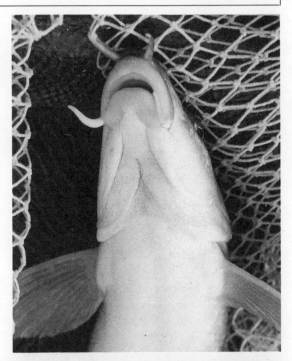

Figure 5: (*above*) The four barbules, two near the tip of the nose and a pair at the angle of the jaw, show the barbel to be exclusively a bottom feeder

Figure 6: (*right*) A three-ounce Avon barbel. Although F.B. was not wildly excited when he caught this tiny fish instead of the hoped-for ten pounder, he was encouraged to read that he had made one of 'the rarest of catches'! In *Coarse Fish* (1943) E. Marshall-Hardy writes: 'Very small barbel (gudgeon size) are unbelievably scarce. To the best of my knowledge I have not caught one in forty years' angling, and I have sought them diligently, for their rarity has always fascinated and mystified me.'

Figure 7: (*above*) Barbel, 12 lb 12 oz (top) and 10 lb 12 oz. This beautiful brace was taken from Ham Mill Pool on the River Kennet by W. Kelsey on 11 August 1894. The heavier fish measured $30\frac{1}{2}$ in. and the lighter $29\frac{1}{2}$ in. The fish are the property of the Piscatorial Society

Figure 8: (*right*) Barbel, $12\frac{1}{4}$ lb, caught on the River Kennet at Newbury in July, 1894, by R. C. Blundell of the Piscatorial Society

and soon his lobworm bait was taken by yet another fish. This was much heavier than the last, but although their attention was called, Hayter and Tryon senior failed to respond. 'They were amusing themselves trying to catch some large perch, clearly visible on that lovely sunny day, just downstream of the boat. However, when I mentioned that I thought I was into a salmon, they suddenly lost interest in the perch and showered me with advice on how to play it.'

Eventually the fish was netted. It proved to be a magnificent barbel: 14 lb 6 oz when weighed by Hayter at the Royalty Hut. This was confirmed when the fish was weighed again at a butcher's shop.

Knowing that a 16 lb 4 oz barbel had been foul-hooked by Roy Beddington when salmon fishing during the 1931 coarse-fish close season, the Tryons had no thought of their fish being in record class. Nevertheless it was sent to the taxidermists, J. Cooper & Sons, who set it up.

Subsequently the fish was recognized as the (equal) British record and is preserved at the home of the Tryon family in Wiltshire. Its modest captor, nowadays a great exponent of salmon and trout fishing, is still very much alive. He has one regret:

It was a pity my father didn't catch it. He had long dreamed of a big barbel. In fact, that was our reason for going to the Royalty.

Figure 9: The bridge pool on the Hampshire Avon at Ibsley. The two largest barbel landed in recent times came from the Hampshire Avon. Both were foul-hooked by salmon anglers. The larger fish, caught at Avon-Tyrell by Lady Rothes, weighed 17 lb. The other, taken by Mr C. Cassey from the bridge pool at Ibsley, weighed 16 lb 1 oz. This fish created considerable interest as members of the Prince of Wales Hanwell Club gathered round Colonel Crow, the famous bailiff of Lord Normanton's water at Ibsley, to see it weighed

Figure 11: (*right*) The mighty mahseer (a cousin of the barbel) is India's finest freshwater game fish. This one was caught near Bombay

Figure 10: Barbel 16 lb 1 oz. Foul-hooked in the bridge pool at Ibsley on 6 March 1960 by C. Cassey

---

The Barbel

Figure 12: A pair of spawning barbel. The female (darker of the two) having cut a redd in the gravel, is laying her eggs, while the male sheds milt to fertilize them. Roy Shaw, who took the picture, noted that female barbel are reluctant to spawn if too many males are in attendance

Cooking the Barbel

The barbel is a swete fysshe; but it is a quasy meete and a perylous, for mannys body.

Dame Juliana Berners (attrib.)
A Treatyse of Fysshynge wyth an Angle (1496)

Despite Dame Juliana's caveat, Michel Dur-borgel, in *La Pêche et les Poissons de Riviere*, offers the following:

BOILED BARBEL IN COURT BOUILLON
Court Bouillon
Parsley
Butter
Capers

But timorous *Barbels* will not taste the bit
Till with their tayles they haue vnhooked it,
And all the baytes the Fisher can deuise
Cannot beguile their warie jealousies.

Guillaume de Saluste du Bartas, *La Semaine* (1578)

Clean the fish and boil in court bouillon. Serve in a sauce made by reducing two cupfuls of the court bouillon, thickened with a nut of butter, some chopped parsley, and capers. If served cold, provide mayonnaise or vinaigrette sauce.

STUFFED BARBEL

Mushrooms
Hardboiled egg
Bechamel sauce

Clean and split the fish and stuff with chopped mushrooms and hardboiled egg. Cook in a fireproof dish and serve covered with white sauce.

From Mrs Beeton, the following:

BARBEAU

1–2 barbel, according to size
1 tablespn. salt
2 small onions, sliced
2 anchovies
2 tablespn. vinegar
juice of 1 lemon
Bouquet garni
Grated nutmeg to taste
Pinch of mace

Soak the fish in slightly salted water for 2–3 hr. Put into a fish-kettle or saucepan with warm water and the salt, and poach gently until done. Take 1 pt. of the water in which the fish was cooked and add to it the other ingredients. Simmer gently for about 15 min., then strain, and return to the saucepan. Put in the fish and let it heat gradually in the flavoured liquor.
4 helpings

And these from Auguste Escoffier:

YOUNG BARBEL MEUNIERE

Small barbel
Salt
Pepper
Flour
Butter
Lemon

Choose small fish. Make one or two incisions in the backs, salt and pepper, coat with flour and fry in butter. Arrange on a dish, with a squeeze of lemon. Add a few dabs of fresh butter to the butter left in the frying pan, and when it begins to bubble pour over the fish.

The barbell is soft and moist, of easy concoction, and very pleasant taste; of good nourishment, but somewhat muddy and excremental. The greater excel the lesser for meat, because their superfluous moisture is amended by age. The spawn of them is to be objected to as most offensive to the belly and stomach.

T. Venner: Of Fish. From *Via Recta ad Vitam Longam* (1650)

YOUNG BARBEL BAKED IN THE OVEN

Barbel
Salt
Pepper
Oil or melted butter

Choose fish of medium size. Make one or two incisions in the back, season and put into a fireproof dish, brush with oil or melted butter and cook in the oven.

For a more substantial dish, surround the fish with cubed potatoes and a little chopped onion. Season the vegetables and baste with a little oil or melted butter during the cooking process. Sprinkle with chopped parsley before serving.

YOUNG BARBEL WITH SHALLOTS AND MUSHROOMS

1–1½ lb barbel
Butter
Salt
Pepper
Chopped Parsley
2 shallots
Mushrooms
3–4 tablespoons breadcrumbs
1 wine glass white wine
Juice ½ lemon

Make one or two incisions in the fleshy part of the back of the fish and put into a well buttered fireproof dish. Add salt, pepper, parsley, chopped shallots and finely chopped mushrooms. Cover with the breadcrumbs. Add wine and lemon juice and cook in a slow oven, basting frequently.

The
BLEAK
Alburnus alburnus

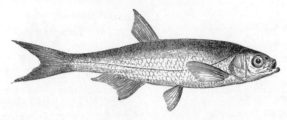

The Bleak or fresh Water Sprat, may be taken either at Mid-Water or the Top, with a Line called a Paternoster Line (viz.), a Line having six or eight small Hooks tied to single Hair-Links, and fixed within half a Foot of each other, and baited with Gentils, your Line having a Float of Quill.

Giles Jacob, *The Compleat Sportsman* (1718)

Although of little interest to the angler as a sport fish, the bleak deserves some notice. Dr J. J. Manley wrote about this and other small fish with great charm in *Notes on Fish and Fishing* (1877). He thought (as we do) that anglers should know something of angling literature; of the natural history of fishes; of gastronomic merits and demerits, and nomenclature – so that they should not '. . . pursue their quarry as mere savages'. His book was published a century ago, but it has a timeless appeal.

The bleak with its green-tinted back and glittering coat of scales was once the object of a commercial fishery supporting a French industry dating from 1656. A substance called 'nacre', derived from the bleak's scales, was used for the coating of imitation pearls (and still is in Eastern Europe). Four thousand bleak are required to produce four ounces of pearl essence!

The bleak is widely distributed throughout Europe north of the Alps and Pyrenees and eastwards to the Caspian basin. It is absent from Norway, Ireland, Scotland and the English Lake District. Its normal length is between five and six inches, exceptionally eight inches, making it scarcely worth the angler's attention.

Bleak tend to swim near the surface, and if the angler wishes to *avoid* catching them – as usually he does – he should fish with sufficient weight to take his bait through the shoal as quickly as possible. Before the cult of 'all-in' match angling, the Thames match angler would rid his swim of these little fish by throwing in a handful of casters (chrysalids), which floated away downsteam taking the bleak shoal with them.

O let me rather on the pleasant Brinke
Of *Tyne* and *Trent* possesse some dwelling-
   place;
Where I may see my Quill and Corke downe
   sink
With eager bit of *Barbill*, *Bleike*, or *Dace*:
And on the World and his Creator thinke,
While they proud *Thais* painted sheat imbrace.
   And with the fume of strong *Tobacco's*
   smoke,
   All quaffing round are ready for a choke.

John Dennys, *The Secrets of Angling* (1613)

Cooking the Bleak

Prior to the twentieth century, bleak were popular table fish. According to Cholmondeley-Pennell, bleak '... dressed and eaten like white-bait make a very good dish'. Another Victorian, Francis Francis, thought them '... very good eating when cooked in the way sprats are cooked'. A modern author, Alwyne Wheeler, thinks them 'palatable, if somewhat bony'.

Perch and pike, however, regard them highly. In consequence the bleak is an excellent bait for these freshwater predators.

FRIED BLEAK
3 doz. bleak
2 tablespoons flour
Salt
Pepper
$\frac{1}{4}$ pint cooking oil
Lemon wedges

Wash and dry the bleak thoroughly. Mix the flour with the seasoning. Dip the bleak in the flour and fry them quickly in the hot oil. Serve immediately with the lemon wedges.

BLEAK PASTE
Bleak
Butter
Salt
Pepper
Cayenne
Ground mace
Anchovy essence

Bake the bleak with a little butter in the oven. When cold, pull off the head, tails, backbone and skin. Place the flesh in a food processor, add the seasoning and spices and process until smooth. Place in small pots, add a dash of anchovy essence and pour over clarified butter.

The
BREAM
Abramis brama

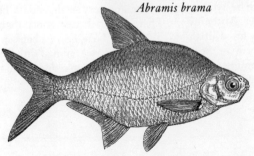

The Bream being at full growth is a large and stately fish, he will breed both in rivers and ponds, and where, if he likes the water and air, he will grow not only to be very large, but as fat as a hog.

Izaak Walton, *The Compleat Angler* (1653)

The bream is essentially a fish of lowland lakes and sluggish rivers. According to Alwyne Wheeler in *The Fishes of The British Isles and North-West Europe* (1969) it is always gregarious, and this propensity for shoaling goes a long way to explain its popularity with anglers: the arrival of one bream implies the presence of many others. The experienced match-angler is well aware of this and will attempt to hold a bream shoal within the confines of his swim by heavy groundbaiting.

But bream are great wanderers. Although they may be taken by the stone from a particular swim on one occasion, this in no way guarantees their appearance in that swim on any future occasion.

Were it not for anglers the adult bream would be almost entirely a bottom feeder, for its natural food is the flora and fauna of the bottom, which it obtains by grubbing in the mud or silt. When bream are feeding like this in a lake they will seldom take a bait that is not resting on the bottom. In these circumstances the angler is restricted to methods such as ledgering, float-ledgering and laying-on.

In rivers, however, when the angler's maggots, casters and particles of other forms of ground-bait are brought to a shoal by means of the current, bream may intercept these items. On such occasions they can be caught by 'swimming the stream' or by 'long-trotting'. Sometimes when bream can see these acceptable offerings drifting down from above, they will even move some away towards the surface to intercept them – and can then be taken 'on the drop'.

The 'big five' bream baits are lobworms, paste, pinched-crumb, and bunches of maggots or brandlings. The best fishing in some bream waters is to be had at night.

Although stillwater bream fishing is generally considered to be a sport of the summer and autumn months, many good bream are now taken in winter. F. B. has taken bream from Wilstone reservoir (a big-bream water at Tring) on a day when groundbait was used to free the float from newly formed ice. When the water temperature is low the slightest sign of a bite, be it registered on dough-bobbin, swingtip or float, should receive the angler's immediate attention.

Although the bream is a poor fighter it must be struck and played carefully when hooked on light tackle. This is particularly so in the swollen waters of flooded rivers, where the pressure of the stream increases the fish's resistance.

A perplexing aspect of bream fishing is the sudden disappearance of quality fish after several increasingly good seasons. The Tring complex of reservoirs in Hertfordshire, the most famous of all big-bream waters, provides an example of this. After producing a series of big bream during the period 1931–33 the reservoirs of Startops End and Marsworth offered nothing of note until the period 1938–40 when again they were responsible for many near-record and one new record fish. The best years for big fish were the years 1933 and 1940. In 1933 there were fish of 12 lb 14 oz, 12 lb, 11 lb 12 oz, 11 lb 11½ oz, 10 lb 15 oz, 10 lb 14 oz, 10 lb 12 oz, 10 lb 11 oz, 10 lb 9 oz, 10 lb 8 oz, 10 lb 8 oz, 10 lb 7 oz, 10 lb 4 oz, 10 lb 4 oz and 10 lb 3 oz. In 1934 not a single double-figure fish was taken.

The most notable catch was from Startops End on 31 July 1939, when Frank Bench of Coventry took bream of 8 lb, 9 lb, 10 lb, 11 lb, 12 lb, 12½ lb, and 12 lb 15 oz – which broke the previous record.

A few large fish survived to be caught during 1940, then once again these reservoirs lived on their reputations until the next double-figure bream was caught in 1945.

A probable explanation of the temporary disappearance of big bream may be found in a brief study of population dynamics. Although the stock of bream in any given water may consist of individuals varying from one to twelve or thirteen years old, each shoal usually consists of survivors from a certain year-class, i.e. fish surviving from one season's spawning. Due to death from various natural causes the number of fish in each succeeding year-class diminishes. As a result the population pattern of bream (like that of other fish) can be compared to the formation of stones in a pyramid.

The first-year fish, being the most numerous, are represented by the stones that make up the

---

Figure 13: Britain's sometime largest bream: 13 lb 12 oz found dead in Startops End Reservoir, Tring, on 19 November 1931. It was weighed two hours after being taken from the water; the weight verified by Dr Jordan, Curator of Tring Museum. The 50 pence piece on the tail fin gives an idea of the size of the bream's 'rudder'

Figure 14: (*top*) Common bream, a former British Record, caught in July 1970 by Will Gollins. This 11 lb 12 oz fish was the culmination of a programme of fishing by a group of anglers who caught several bream over 10 lb in a Shropshire mere

Figure 15: The photograph on the left above shows a bream fossil from the Likhvinsk inter-glacial deposits and the one on the right shows a modern bream. Permission to reproduce them was kindly given by Professor G. V. Nikolsky of Moscow University

base layer of the pyramid. Succeeding years are represented by the gradually diminishing numbers of stones that make up the succeeding layers. The last surviving fish in the oldest year-class is represented by the apex stone.

From this pattern of a progressively diminishing number of fish in each year-class we can see why large fish are comparatively rare. From time to time, however, one particular year-class survives in unusually large numbers. This flourishing year-class remains as a population bulge throughout the shoal-members' lifespan, and during the later years of its existence provides anglers with unusually good sport. When these fish have died, many years may elapse before replacement shoals of the same quality fish occur. During its tenancy the year-class of a population bulge represents such an enormous burden on the food supply that for a time subsequent year-classes are impoverished and diminished.

Cooking the Bream

The bream is considered of little consequence as food – at least in Britain. H. F. once breakfasted on fried bream while camping near the Broads ... he was very hungry! But for those who want to make what they can of it, here are three other recipes – for which we are grateful to *The Sporting Wife* by Barbara Hargreaves (2nd edition, 1971).

STUFFED BREAM
1 Bream, $1\frac{1}{2}$–2 lb
1 oz butter
Flour
1 tablespoonful lemon juice
Forcemeat
Salt and Pepper

Forcemeat
$\frac{1}{2}$ small onion, grated
1 oz grated cheese
2 oz sliced mushrooms
1 small cupful cooked rice
1 tablespoonful chopped chives
1 dessertspoonful chopped parsley
Grated lemon rind
Nutmeg
Cayenne pepper
1 oz butter
4 tablespoonsful cream
1 beaten egg
Salt and Pepper

Fry the onion and mushrooms in butter and mix the rice and cheese. Add all other ingredients and blend well. Put nearly all the butter in a fireproof dish. Stuff the fish with the forcemeat and place in the dish. Sprinkle with flour and seasoning and dot with the rest of the butter: then sprinkle with lemon juice. Cover the dish with greased paper or foil. Bake in a moderate oven for 40–50 minutes according to size of fish.

BREME À LA MODE DU PÊCHEUR
1 bream
Shallots
White wine
Butter
Breadcrumbs

Place the cleaned fish upon a bed of chopped shallots and breadcrumbs, in a fireproof dish, and cover the fish with the same mixture. Add the white wine and part of butter and cook in a medium oven for 25 minutes, adding wine and butter as needed to keep the fish moist.

BAKED BREAM
1 bream
Onion
Garlic
Lemon
Oil
Breadcrumbs

Clean the fish and remove head and fins. Score the sides. Chop onion and garlic and place in bottom of a fireproof dish. Slice a lemon thinly and put one slice in each of the scores. Lay the fish in the dish and squeeze the juice from any of the lemon that is left over on to the fish. Pour two tablespoonsful of oil over the fish and sprinkle with breadcrumbs. Cover with lid or foil and cook in a moderate oven for 30 minutes. Remove foil and leave the fish in the oven until the breadcrumbs are browned and the fish is cooked right through. Serve very hot.

In Europe the bream had, and indeed still has, some sort of reputation as a table fish. As Walton said: 'Though some do not, yet the French esteem this fish highly, and to that end have a proverb: "He that hath breams in his pond is able to bid his friend welcome."'

Well – maybe.

The SILVER BREAM

Blicca bjoerkna

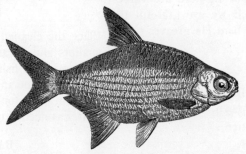

It was long doubted whether what was supposed to be a
second species of Bream in our lakes was truly distinct ...
Yet that they were believed to be distinct fishes in very early
times appears from the *Book of St Albans*, where Bremettis
are mentioned separately, as to be fished for with some
difference of baits; and that they are distinct fishes is now
generally admitted.

Jonathan Couch, *British Fishes* (Vol. 4, 1877)

The silver bream, also known as white bream or
breamflat, is widely distributed in lakes and slow-
running rivers throughout Europe north of the
Alps and Pyrenees and eastwards to the USSR.
It is absent from Norway and occurs in the
British Isles only in the eastern counties of
England, north of the Thames.

That two seperate species of bream exist was
recognized over five hundred years ago. Nevertheless, few anglers seem able to differentiate
between them. The following extract comes from
Fish and Fishing (1877) by Dr J. J. Manley:

The white bream is a fish hardly worth pen, ink and
paper. It seldom exceeds a pound in weight, and
though its colouring is pretty enough, being very
silvery, it is covered with an indescribably nasty slime,
something like starch, and almost as difficult to get
off the fingers as bird lime.

Manley was wrong. The silver bream is *not* a
slimy fish. What he described is, in fact, a small

common, bronze bream (*Abramis brama*). The
following points of recognition refer to the silver
bream:

1. It seldom exceeds ten inches in length.
2. It is not a slimy fish. As a result, its scales
readily become detached when handled.
3. It is a much more slender fish than the
common bream.
4. Its eye is noticeably larger.
5. With its silvery sides and green-tinted back,
it closely resembles the bleak in colouring.

It has been said that silver bream occur in the
Royalty Fishery on the Hampshire Avon, and
that common bream are absent from the Throop
fishery on the Dorset Stour, but Richard Walker
stated that all the bream he caught in the House-
pool on the Royalty were common bream and
roach/common bream hybrids from the Throop
Fishery, at Nettlebed.

The
BULLHEAD
_or_ MILLER'S THUMB
Cottus gobio

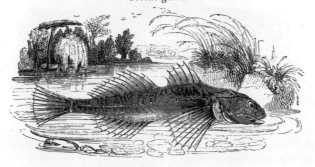

Notwithstanding the disgust which the form of the
Bull-head creates, the largest, when the heads are cut
off, are very delicious eating ...

The Rev. W. B. Daniel, _Rural Sports_ (1801)

This aggressive little fish grows to a length of
three to four inches. It is of no angling interest,
save that it may compete with other species for
food such as bottom-living invertebrates and fly
larvae. It lives a solitary life, fiercely defending
a small hole or crevice under rock or stones
from which it seldom emerges except at night. It
dislikes company, and emits a distinctive threat
call – a sharp 'barking' sound – when approached
too closely by another bullhead.

There is indisputable evidence that bullheads
are occasionally eaten by pike. Our friends at
Oxford Scientific Films, Peter Parks and Sean
Morris, took some remarkable film of a small
pike seizing a bullhead from its lair. The pike
had some difficulty in swallowing the bullhead
owing to its spiny nature, but eventually succeeded after regurgitating and then re-swal-
lowing. Altogether the meal lasted about half an
hour.

The
BURBOT

Lota lota

We Londoners very seldom see or hear of a burbolt*, and they are such a stupid and ugly fish that I cannot advise trouble to be taken with their dissemination, though doubtless they would thrive in many of our ponds and lakes ...

The flesh is said to be good, especially the liver when fried, but it is indigestible.

Frank Buckland, *The Natural History of British Fishes* (1881)

The burbot, pout, or eel-pout was once common in most of the East Anglian streams and although local in distribution, was not uncommon in the rivers of Durham, Yorkshire, Lincolnshire and Cambridgeshire. It is now very rare.

Anglers fortunate enough to catch one should not be put off by William Samuel, thought to be the author of *The Arte of Angling* (1577), who described the pout as 'an ill-favoured fish':

'Rather give me the carpe, than the poute ... for the head of the one is better than the liver of the other.' We can guess that the author was probably alluding to the ugliness of the pout's head (more particularly to its protruding lips) and to the excellent flavour of its liver, which was considered a great delicacy at that time. The ancients were no fools: modern science reveals that the pout's liver is rich in vitamin A.

---

*Nevertheless the burbot, or eel-pout, was being caught and sold in Britain before the Norman conquest ...

Magister: What trade are you acquainted with?
Piscator: I am a fisherman.
Magister: What do you get by your trade?
Piscator: Food, clothes and money.
Magister: How do you catch the fish?
Piscator: I go out in my boat, put forth my nets in the river, throw forth the hook and the baskets, and whatever they catch I take.
Magister: What do you do if the fish happen to be unclean?
Piscator: I throw out the unclean and take the clean ones to eat.

Magister: Where do you sell the fish?
Piscator: In the city.
Magister: Who buys them?
Piscator: The citizens. I am unable to catch as many as I can sell.
Magister: What kind of fish do you catch?
Piscator: Eels, pike, minnows, eel pouts, trout, and lampreys, and as many other kinds as swim in the river.
Magister: Why don't you fish in the sea?
Piscator: I do sometimes, but not often, because it is a long voyage to the sea.

From the earliest description of fishing in the English language. Colloquy written by Ælfric the Abbot (AD 980). Quoted in W. J. Turrell's *Ancient Angling Authors* (1910)

Figure 16: (*below*) A specimen of a British burbot (*Lota lota*), or 'eel pout', caught on a ledgered worm by the Rev. E. C. Alston in 1936 in the stream that runs out of Stamford Water near Thetford in Norfolk. One of his fishing companions at that time, the late W. Griggs, proprietor of the most famous of all fish taxidermist firms J. Cooper & Sons, later caught three of these little fishes

Figure 17: (*bottom*) According to the *Sunday Telegraph* (16.11.86) the last burbot caught on rod and line in British waters was believed to have been landed in 1969 on the River Ouse. In the early 1970s F. B. drove, via Napoleon's route to Moscow, to Poznan in Poland spurred on by the prospect of catching this rare fish. From Poznan he drove to an estate near the Baltic coast where he was taken by horse and carriage (see picture) to his burbot swim. Sadly he was not able to add the eel pout to his list of rare catches

Shakespeare, the most famous contemporary of William Samuel, also referred to the appearance of our little fish when he said: 'Like a misbehaved and sullen wench, Thou pout'st upon thy fortune and thy love.'

We can think of nothing more to say about the burbot. Although, as a boy, H. F. caught a number of eel-pouts in the sea, we have never caught one in fresh water and can offer no advice other than to go to Siberia where specimens of three feet or more have been recorded, according to Couch's *British Fishes* (1877). As food, however, the burbot is considered quite tasty, and overleaf are three simple recipes from Auguste Escoffier.

The Burbot

BURBOT MEUNIERE

Burbot
Salt
Pepper
Butter
Lemon juice

Slice the filleted fish, season with salt and pepper, coat with flour and fry in butter. Arrange on a serving dish, and spinkle with lemon juice. Add a few dabs of butter to the butter left in the frying pan, heat briskly and pour over the fish. *Note*: This may be accompanied by saute potatoes, puree of potatoes, plain boiled potatoes, spinach, sorrel, etc.

The same method is used for all fish cooked *à la meunière*. The flesh of the burbot, being rather firm, is excellent in stews, with peas, broad beans, potatoes, aubergines, baby marrows, etc.

BURBOT WITH TOMATOES AND WINE

1 lb burbot
Salt
Pepper
Flour
1 tablespoon finely chopped onion
3–4 tomatoes
Pinch chopped parsley
3–4 tablespoons white wine
$1\frac{1}{2}$ oz butter
Lemon juice

Slice filleted fish and season with salt and pepper. Coat with flour and arrange in a buttered saute pan. Add the onion, tomatoes, peeled, seeded and chopped, parsley and wine. Cook fairly quickly for about 15–20 minutes. Arrange fish on a serving dish. Add the butter and lemon juice to the sauce and pour over the fish.

PROVENÇAL STYLE BURBOT

1 lb burbot
Salt and Pepper
Flour
2 tablespoons finely chopped onion
4–5 tomatoes
Pinch chopped parsley
1 clove garlic
Pinch saffron
4–5 tablespoons olive oil
1 wine glass white wine
1 wine glass water
Toast

Fillet and prepare the fish as described for Burbot with tomatoes and wine and arrange in a saute pan. Add onion, tomatoes, peeled, seeded and chopped, parsley, garlic, and saffron. Pour over the oil, add white wine and the water. Cover and cook fairly quickly for 15–20 minutes. Arrange the scallops on slices of toast and pour sauce over them.

Provençal style burbot is also served with rice pilaf; in which case omit the toast.

The
CARP
Cyprinus carpio

It is common practice in *Holland* to keep *carp* alive for
three weeks or a month, by placing them in a *net*, well
wrapped up with *wet moss*, hanging them up in a cellar
or cool place, and feeding them with *bread* and *milk*.

The Rev. W. B. Daniel, *Rural Sports* (1801)

It is generally believed that the common carp
was introduced into Britain from the Continent
during the Middle Ages. In *A Treatyse of Fys-shynge wyth an Angle*, published in 1496, but
probably written sometime between 1406 and
1425, the author (supposedly Dame Juliana
Berners) wrote:

The Carpe is a deyntous fysshe: but there ben but
fewe in Englonde. And therefore I wryte the lasse of
hym.

A phrase that finds an interesting echo a hundred
years later in Leonard Mascall's *A Booke of
Fishing with Hooke and Line* (1590):

The Carpe also is a straunge and daintie fish to take,
his baites are not well knowne, for he hath not long
beene in this realme ... and because not knowing well
his cheefe baites in each moneth, I will write the lesse
of him.

All the more interesting, therefore, to learn from
Arthur Bryant's *The Age of Chivalry* that in
1248, John Pechum, an Oxford friar, when
created Archbishop of Canterbury, had to
provide for his enthronement feast (in addition
to many other items):

... 300 ling, 600 cod, 40 fresh salmon, 7 barrels of
salt salmon, 5 barrels of salt sturgeon, 600 fresh eels,
8,000 whelks, 100 pike, 400 tench, *100 carp* [our
italics], 800 bream, 1,400 lampreys, 200 large roach,
besides seals, porpoises and 'pophyns'!

If there were indeed 'but fewe' English carp
about at the beginning of the fifteenth century
the provision of a hundred for a thirteenth-century feast seems a pretty stiff order. How
Pechum solved his problem is not recorded, but
his enthronement seems to have been responsible
for the first mention of this fish in English
history.

Since its introduction, the carp has survived
in its preferred habitat of small lakes and certain
sections of a few slow-flowing rivers. Although
nowadays treated as a sport fish, it was originally
cultivated by members of religious orders, as one
of the fish foods which was allowable on the
numerous 'days of abstinence'.

Except for a few new colonies that have
become established as a result of fish making
good their escape from flooded ponds or stews,
all British carp populations appear to have been
man-made.

Figure 18: 'The Carpe is a deyntous fysshe: but there ben but fewe in Englonde.' The common carp (a misnomer if ever there was one), once the dainty of monks, is now, together with the varieties developed by pisciculturists, well distributed throughout Europe

Figure 19: 12 lb common carp, outwitted by Bill Keal

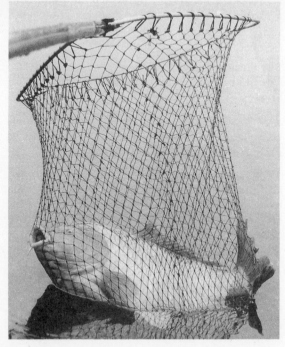

Carp spawn during the late spring or summer if and when the water temperature rises to 64–68°F. Because of their intolerance of low temperature at spawning time, carp living in water whose temperature in certain years does not reach the required level are unable to spawn. And, of course, this must occasionally happen in Britain.

Carp fishing, at least in temperate latitudes, is essentially a pursuit of the summer and autumn months. Although in mild winters sport may be obtained with fish that have not yet started their hibernation, winter carp fishing is undesirable.

Winter hibernation is characterized by a cessation, or at least a sharp reduction of food consumption, and a consequent fall in the level of metabolism. These combine to reduce the demand on the energy that has been accumulated in the carp's body in the form of fat deposits. Hibernation results from the fish's need to adapt to the absence of vegetating plants and to the relatively low oxygen content of the water during a period of ice cover. Even with minimal activity, an overwintering fish must be in good condition with sufficient reserves of fat if it is to survive. In an experiment, Kirpichnikov (1958) demonstrated that small carp with a 1.92 condition factor survived for only six days when kept at a temperature of 32°F, whereas those with a 2.40 to 2.50 condition factor survived for over forty days at the same temperature.[1] (See footnote on next page.)

Perhaps the problem of overwintering explains the failure of the common carp to penetrate our river systems. It is likely that extremely cold winters make demands on the fat reserves

Figure 20: Peter Thomas holding Richard Walker's 44 lb carp; from an original painting by Maurice Ingham

of river carp that prove fatal, in which case it is easy to understand why the best river carp fisheries are found in areas downstream of hot-water effluents.

That the common carp sustains itself in Great Britain rather uneasily is not surprising when one remembers that it is an exotic species 'planted' beyond its natural boundaries.[2]

In recent years, however, the carp's promotion to the status of major sport-fish has resulted in many attempts at starting new carp fisheries. The chief problem in a temperate climate is the difficulty of reconciling the carp's need for deep water in winter (so that it can escape the deoxygenated shallow water when ice cover is prolonged), with its need for very warm water during the breeding season (high temperature is only regularly achieved in water that warms quickly – i.e. *shallow* water). From this it can be seen that the ideal carp water is a shallow lake containing at least one sizeable pocket of deep water.

The carp is an extremely wary fish. So much so that until the 1940s the main problem in carp fishing was finding a line strong enough to hold such a powerful fish, yet fine enough to escape its suspicions. To the old school of carp fishermen this problem was insoluble – so they fished with light tackle and banked on their skill to land the fish. The result was that although many carp were hooked, few big ones reached the bank. Albert Buckley's record carp of 26 lb, caught in 1930 on 4X gut and a size 10 hook, represented the very pinnacle of achievement using the old methods. Today the record stands at 51 lb 6 oz (NASA record), and hardly a season passes without a 30-pounder being caught.

---

[1] The condition of a fish can be assessed by relating the ratio of its length to its weight. The larger the ratio the better the condition.

Thus: $\Omega = W100/L^3$

Where W is the weight of the fish: L is its length: Ω is the condition coefficient.

[2] The case of the crucian carp (page 43) is somewhat different. This species can actually survive freezing. From the evidence available – its tolerance of low temperatures, or low oxygen requirement, and the spread of habitat – there is every reason to suspect that the crucian carp is indigenous.

Twice, the carp shot off with such speed that the reel overran, checked and gave warning. On the fourth occasion one of the monsters made a direct run of thirty yards and then broke me, the fine gut cast parting above the float. There then occurred an incident that illustrates the uncanny nature of these fish. My float, lying out in the middle of the pond, turned and sailed slowly in again to my very feet, towed by the monster who then in some manner freed himself, thus returning me my tackle with a sardonic invitation to try again. No other fish is capable of putting so fine a point on irony.

Arthur Ransome, *Rod and Line* (1929)

From what has been said, a reader who has yet to try for carp might suspect that this fish is strong as well as cautious. He would be right. The strength of a carp is prodigious: its caution legendary. Nearly four hundred years ago, William Samuel, reputed author of the second known angling book in English, *The Arte of Angling* (1577), offered this timeless advice:

The best bait that ever I did know for the killing of Carpe, is, a quantitie of sufference, with a good deale of patience, and as much silence as may be possible, all these mingled together.

The modern carp angler uses a powerful rod, similar to the Hardy 'R. W.' Carp Rod; a monofilament line of 10-14 lb BS; and a size 8 or 10 straight-eyed hook tied direct to the mainline. He takes with him a landing net capable of enclosing a fifty-pounder, and an electric bite alarm, or a glowbobbin (see page 419). Leads and floats are seldom used, although the tackle described on page 453 is an excellent rig when the angler is fishing into the wind.

Margin-fishing with floating crust is a technique specially associated with carp. One of freshwater angling's biggest thrills is the sight of a big carp approaching and then sucking-in that piece of crust – a moment of palpitating excitement. But whatever method is used – and there are times when most of the methods described in this book are possible – *the tackle must be free-*

Figure 21: (*above*) Richard Walker playing a 31¼ lb carp in Redmire Pool, 1954, kneeling to keep out of sight of the fish

Figure 22: (*right*) The fish at the feet of the master

running. A carp *must* be allowed to take the bait and move off without feeling the slightest drag. This demands a fixed spool reel on which – until the moment of the strike – the bale arm is always left open.

Because carp fishing is a long, patient, waiting game, often most propitious during the hours of darkness, many carp fanatics pitch a tent and take their beds with them!

DETERMINING AGE

Scientists use one of three methods for determining the age of fish.
1. Scale reading
2. Otolith (ear bone) reading
3. Opercular (gill bone) reading
All three methods are based on the principle that a fish grows at a faster rate during the summer than it does during the winter, and that it *continues to grow throughout its life*.

Each year of growth produces a series of rings (or circuli) on a fish's scales and bones (unlike a tree, which produces one ring each year). During a period of quick summer-growth these rings are well spaced, whereas during a period of slow winter-growth the rings are close together and form what it known as a 'growth-check'.

Counting these checks (or annuli) is commonly the basis for determining the age of a fish. But in his book *Pike*, F.B. suggested that it was possible for a fish to go on living after it had stopped growing, and that this last phase of its life would not be recorded on its bones. Hoping that Richard Walker's then record carp might one day provide the necessary evidence, he wrote (in 1969):

Although scientists prefer to have an opercular bone for determining the age of a fish, this bone can only be obtained when the fish is dead. An alternative is to read a scale taken from a fish's shoulder

Figure 23: Scale from a five-year-old pike

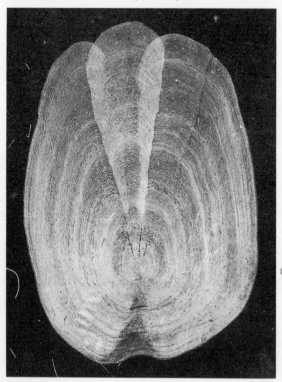

Figure 24: Opercular bone from a fifteen-year-old pike

Figure 25: Opercular bone from Walker's 44 lb carp

Freshwater Fishing

Figure 26: Mirror carp from Redmire Pool

This fish weighed 44 lb at time of capture (1952), when its scale reading indicated an age of 15 years. Nevertheless, Walker's fish has survived a further 16 years at the London Zoo and is still alive. This fish now weighs a lot less than it did when it was caught. In the circumstances we can hardly expect the scales or opercular bones to record the non-growing phase of its life. We expect the reading to indicate an age of 15 – but we know the fish to be at least 31 years old.

F. B. was right. After the carp's death in 1971, when it was 34 years old, he was able to obtain one of its opercular bones. A reading of this bone showed *no indication of the carp's last nineteen years of life*.

Note: It should be remembered that the carp in question was living in an unnatural environment, with limited space and fairly constant water temperature, incidence of light, and food availability. Until further research has been made, it would be unwise to apply this finding to fish living in natural conditions. It is, however, permissible to say that a fish can live *in certain circumstances* for a period of time without linear growth, and without recording this non-growing phase of life on its scales and bones.

One doesn't associate George Orwell with angling; least of all, perhaps, with carp.

But he wrote about it, vividly:

The pool was swarming with bream, small ones, about four to six inches long. Every now and again you'd see one of them turn half over and gleam reddy-brown under the water. There were pike there too, and they must have been big ones. You never saw them, but sometimes one that was basking among the weeds would turn over and plunge with a splash that was like a brick being bunged into the water. It was no use trying to catch them, though of course I always tried every time I went there. I tried them with dace and minnows I'd caught in the Thames and kept alive in a jam-jar, and even with a spinner made out of a bit of tin. But they were gorged with fish and wouldn't bite, and in any case they'd have broken any tackle I possessed. I never came back from the pool without at least a dozen small bream. Sometimes in the summer holidays I went there for a whole day, with my fishing-rod and a copy of *Chums* or the *Union Jack* or something, and a hunk of bread and cheese which Mother had wrapped up for me. And I've fished for hours and then lain in the grass hollow and read the *Union Jack*, and then the smell of my bread paste and the plop of a fish jumping somewhere would send me wild again, and I'd go back to the water and have another go, and so on all through a summer's day . . .

One afternoon the fish weren't biting and I began to explore . . . and I came to another pool which I had never known existed. It was a small pool not more than twenty yards wide, and rather dark because of the boughs that overhung it. But it was very clear water and immensely deep. I could see ten or fifteen feet down into it. I hung about for a bit, enjoying the dampness and the rotten boggy smell, the way a boy does. And then I saw something that almost made me jump out of my skin.

It was an enormous fish. I don't exaggerate when I say it was enormous. It was almost the length of my arm. It glided across the pool, deep under water, and then became a shadow and disappeared into the darker water on the other side. I felt as if a sword had gone through me. It was far the biggest fish I'd ever seen, dead or alive. I stood there without breathing, and in a moment another huge thick shape glided through the water, and then another and then two more close together. The pool was full of them . . .

It was a wonderful secret for a boy to have. There was the dark pool hidden away in the woods and the monstrous fish sailing around it – fish that had never been fished for and would grab the first bait you offered them. It was only a question of getting hold of a line strong enough to hold them. Already I'd made all the arrangements. I'd buy the tackle that would hold them if I had to steal the money out of the till. Somehow, God knew how, I'd get hold of half a crown and buy a length of silk salmon line and some thick gut or gimp and Number 5 hooks, and come back with cheese and gentles and paste and mealworms and brandlings and grasshoppers and every mortal bait a carp might look at. The very next Saturday afternoon I'd come back and try for them.

But as it happened I never went back. One never does go back. I never stole the money out of the till or bought the bit of salmon line or had a try for those carp. Almost immediately afterwards something turned up to prevent me, but if it hadn't been that it would have been something else. It's the way things happen.

I know, of course, that you think I'm exaggerating about the size of those fish. You think, probably, that they were just medium-sized fish (a foot long, say) and that they've swollen gradually in my memory. But it isn't so. People tell lies about the fish they've caught and still more about the fish that are hooked and get away, but I never caught any of these or even tried to catch them, and I've no motive for lying. I tell you they were enormous.

George Orwell, *Coming up for Air* (1939)

The mirror carp is the most esteemed member of the Cyprinus family. His flesh is superior in flavour to all the other six or seven varieties we have in Austria and elsewhere, and therefore he is called the *Rex cyprinorum*.

He is distinguished at the first glance from his relations by his strikingly few, but large and peculiarly-shaped golden lustred scales, which cover only one part of each side of the fish, usually set in two rows, leaving all the other parts bare or uncovered. Some specimens are possessed of three rows of scales; another variety presents only one row near the back, and is called 'saddle carp'. If they happen to have no scales at all they are called 'leather carp', and are much sought for . . . Mirror carp scaling from 5 to 12 lb are considered the best as table fish . . . one meets in the most parts of England with the opinion that the carp in general is a very bad eating . . . In this country not only 'poor bodies' are eating carp, also wealthy and rich people like it – people to whom the salmon, the trout, the great lake trout and the most delicious of the *genus Salmonidae*, the char – which abounds in our mountain lakes, and attains a weight of more than 15 lb – as well as all the finest saltwater fishes are no rarities . . . I do not mean to say that a carp in his best condition is as good as a fresh-run salmon or as a turbot – he is surely inferior to these and even other fishes; nevertheless, he is what one can say a very good eating, *provided he is in season, in good condition, and taken out from a not muddy, but comparatively clear water*.

Emil Weeger, Brünn, Austria, 29 December 1884 (From an article in *The Fishing Gazette*, 17 January 1885)

Figure 27: (*right*) F. B. photographed this successful Chinese angler when visiting China in 1986 to research early Chinese fishing reels. With a population of one billion, Chinese anglers play their part in the constant battle to keep the Chinese nation well fed. These common carp weighing near the legal top limit of 5 kilos of takeable fish, were caught in Kunming Lake in the grounds of the beautiful Summer Palace – an hour's drive north-west of Peking.

The common carp is highly prized as a table fish and is third in the table of merit, pike being the number one, closely followed by silver carp – a species closely related to the grass carp

In large rivers carp grow up to an enormous size. Some years ago I have seen in the Hungarian metropolis, in Pesth, one weighing 67 lb, and I know that in the lower Danube sometimes a great-grandfather is caught by the fisherman scaling upwards of 80 lb. In the Theis, Save, Draü, and other rivers 20 or 30-pounders are no rarities, and are frequently caught by rod and line. A friend of mine, captain of a Danube steamer, caught one weighing 46 lb with a piece of black dumpling on the hook, groundbaiting previously with boiled peas.

Emil Weeger (From an article in *The Fishing Gazette*, 17 January 1885)

Figure 28: (*below*) A partially scaled mirror carp. This picture reveals that Alfred Buckley's one-time record carp (see page 42) *was* a mirror carp, which is surely another way of saying that a carp with 'reduced' scaling *is* a mirror carp. Whereas a leather carp is scaleless and leather looking

Figure 29: The leather carp

It is unnaturall for the Carpe, Breame, Tench, or Roach to eat another raw fish, as it is for a sheep or a cow to eat raw flesh. The sharpe and devouring teeth in the Pike, Perch, Trought and Eele, are easily seene and perceived, but so are not the flat grinding teeth in the other kind of fish. Howbeit if you search diligently the head of the Carpe, Breame, or any other of that nature, and of any bignesse, when it is sodden you shall find two neather jawes, having in each jaw a row of flat teeth, like to the eye teeth in a man, and apt to grind and chew withall, with which two neather jawes they grind their meate against a certaine flat bone in the roofe of their mouth or upper part of their throte.

Certaine experiments concerning fish and fruite: practised by John Taverner, Gentleman, and by him published for the benefit of others (1600)

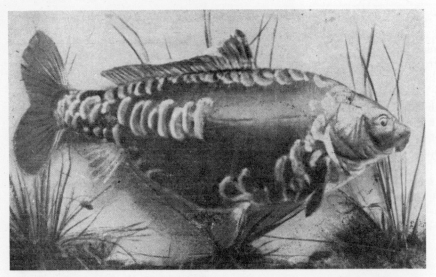

Figure 30: This photograph of the one-time record rod-caught carp caught by Alfred Buckley in Mapperley Reservoir on 24 July 1930 was published in the *Angler's News* (1 June 1946). The editor's comments in the caption to the photograph reveal how much the views of angling editors and presumably carp fishermen have changed in forty years:

'When some readers were recently interested in large carp and its varieties we said we would show this illustration again when we had space for it. According to our information the species of this fish is the common carp (*Cyprinus carpio*) and the fish itself has been variously referred to as a 'mirror carp' and as a 'leather carp' (artificially bred varieties of the carp). Artificial breeding can produce some wonderful monstrosities, as witness those from the common carp's cousin the goldfish. To our mind its appeal is on a par with that of any other ugly old animal – better to take it out of the water before it died of old age.'

The
CRUCIAN CARP
Carassius carassius

Pallas, in his *Zoographia*, mentions the Crucian Carp as inhabiting all the lakes and marshes of Russia and Siberia, and as yielding the inhabitants of those countries a delicious food. It is taken with nets in the vicinity of Jakutsk in the winter time, and is then quite torpid. The fishermen select the largest, and return the others into the water, where they revive on the advent of spring. Even when the lakes freeze to the bottom, it survives, and when a thaw comes issues from the mud, in which it had buried itself.

British Fishes by Yarrell

The crucian is a hardy fish, tolerant of both very cold water and water of comparatively low oxygen content. It can be distinguished from the common carp by the following means:

1. It lacks the barbules and is deeper in the body; its depth being equal to half its length.
2. It has an elevated convex dorsal fin, the trailing edge of which points to the base of the tail.
3. It has a characteristic humped back.

In favourable conditions it attains a length of ten to twelve inches and a weight of about two pounds. Exceptionally (in Europe) it grows to eighteen inches and a weight of seven pounds. The British record crucian carp (5 lb 10½ oz) was taken by G. Halls from a lake near King's Lynn, Norfolk, in 1976.

Crucian carp fishing is a summer and autumn sport. The bait should be fished on or near the bottom. All the usual roach baits (with the exception of hemp) can be tried with hope of success.

The crucian was reputedly caught in the Thames during the nineteenth century and is now said to be found in certain slow-flowing rivers of south-west England, but we have not had confirmation of this.

The Crucian Carp, according to J. Travis Jenkins in *The Fishes of The British Isles* (1925) 'is a bottom fish of the shallow-water regions of ponds or pools, and is one of the hardiest of fish. Not only can it be sent long distances out of water if packed in damp grass, but it will also bury itself in soft mud in the bottom of ponds, so that even if the pond is entirely dried up in summer the fish can survive.'

Cooking the Carp

WALTON'S CARP

Marjoram
Thyme
Parsley
Rosemary
Savoury
Onions
Pickled oysters
Anchovies
Claret wine
Salt
Cloves
Mace
Oranges
Lemons
Butter
3 egg yolks
1 carp

Take a carp and rub him clean with water and salt, but scale him not; then open him; and put him, with his blood and his liver, which you must save when you open him, into a small pot or kettle; then take sweet marjoram, thyme and parsley, of each half a handful, a sprig of rosemary, and another of savoury; bind them into two or three small bundles and put them in your Carp, with four or five whole onions, twenty pickled oysters, and three anchovies. Then pour upon your Carp as much claret wine as will only cover him; and season your claret well with salt, cloves and mace, and the rinds of oranges and lemons. That done, cover your pot and set it on a quick fire till it be sufficiently boiled. Then take out the Carp; and lay it with the broth, into the dish; and pour upon it a quarter of a pound of the best fresh butter, melted and beaten with half-a-dozen spoonfuls of the broth, the yolks of two or three eggs, and some of the herbs shred. Garnish your dish with lemons, and so serve up. And much good do you.

CARP DELICIOUS

A recipe by Manuel de la Friandaise (1796), cited in *The Sporting Wife*.

Handful of chopped sorrel
Bread
Shallots
Cream
Salt
Pepper
Garlic
Bayleaf
Plain flour
Chopped anchovies
Butter
Chopped chives
Parsley
3 hardboiled eggs
3 raw yolks
Thyme
Mushrooms
Capers
Fish stock
Lemon juice
Vinegar
1 carp

Put a handful of prepared, washed and chopped sorrel, a piece of butter, a piece of bread, chopped chives, parsley and shallots into a saucepan and simmer for ten minutes. Add some cream and simmer till mixed. Hardboil three eggs; chop the yolks and add to the mixture with three raw yolks, salt and black pepper. Stuff the cleaned carp with this mixture and sew it up; put the whole to marinate in oil seasoned with salt, pepper, chives, garlic, thyme and bayleaf. When ready, grill, basting with marinade.

Put chopped mushrooms in a saucepan and simmer in a little butter; let them cool and add a pinch of flour, capers, chopped anchovies, parsley, chives, shallots, butter, stock, salt and pepper. Cook gently and finish with a little lemon juice or a dash of vinegar.

Serve the carp on a hot dish with this sauce. From Izaak Walton's *The Compleat Angler*.

The
CATFISH

Silurus glanis

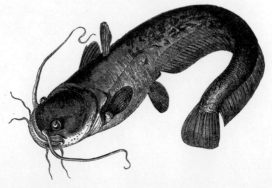

Another fish that would do well in this country is the Catfish (Pimelodus). It is a species of Silurus, also called the
Bullhead and Bull-pout. They are found in all the waters of
North America. In some places it is esteemed a great delicacy,
equal to an eel.

Frank Buckland, *The Natural History of British Fishes* (1881)

The European catfish, sometimes known as the 'wels', was introduced during the latter part of the last century into a number of British lakes including the lake complexes at Claydon in Buckinghamshire, Tring in Hertfordshire and Woburn Abbey in Bedfordshire. It has perpetuated itself in all three waters and at Claydon lake is regularly caught by a few specialist 'cat' anglers.

In suitable conditions the wels catfish can grow to a remarkable size. Specimens measuring $16\frac{1}{2}$ ft, weighing up to 660 lb and immensely strong have been recorded from the USSR. In Poland recently, a young angler who had tied his line to his wrist was pulled out of his boat by a catfish and drowned.

The catfish is an active night feeder and like most night feeding fishes possesses very small eyes. It has two long feelers (8 in. long for a 20 lb fish) on the top side of the jaw, and four small barbules ($\frac{1}{2}$ to 1 in) on the underside of the chin; these indicate its preference for bottom feeding.

Of all types of bottom (as its name implies) it prefers mud, for 'wels' derives from the German 'walzen' (English 'wallow') from its habit of wallowing in mud.

The wels is mainly a lake dweller, although it flourishes in the deep parts of large rivers. In eastern Europe the catfish spawns between May and July in the marshy areas of lakes. River catfish usually migrate upstream before or during a flood in order to spawn over suitable areas of flooded land.

> The world record rod-caught catfish (202 lb
> 6 oz) was hooked on a 6-inch roach livebait
> at 4 o'clock on a September afternoon – and
> landed in the dark five hours later – by Herr
> Krischker and his father who were fishing
> from the Rumanian side of the Danube
> delta.

Figure 31: This catfish, estimated weight 40–45 lb, was found in Marsworth Reservoir, *c.* 1934. Holding the fish are C. E. Double and T. Plumridge. This huge 'cat' was probably one of the seven small catfish put into Marsworth Reservoir many years before, which were probably descendants of the seventy catfish originally introduced into Woburn Abbey, from Germany, in 1880. Another huge catfish, estimated weight 50 lb, was found dead in Marsworth Reservoir, *c.* 1943

Three British anglers, R. Rolph, R. Blackmore and D. Cruickshank are specialist catfishers and we are indebted to them for guidance on cat-fishing techniques.

These three anglers prepare their swims by pre-baiting with freshwater mussels. Of all baits they have found mussel to be the most effective, although *continued* use of this bait has resulted in a drop-off in catches. Settled periods of warm, windless weather have been the most productive. Early in the season the period between dusk and 2 a.m. produces most bites, but as the season progresses feeding times become more irregular, with fish sometimes taking during the hours of daylight.

Their tackle has consisted of a carp rod and fixed spool reel with 10–12 lb BS nylon. Hooks, sizes 1 or 2, were used to lip-hook a variety of deadbaits: rudd, perch, roach and small bream. The angling method was ledgering – carp style – with balearm pickup left open to allow the 'cats' to run with the bait. Premature striking invariably resulted in failure to hook the fish.

By such methods these three anglers accounted for 38 catfish over 10 lb in three seasons. A remarkable achievement – and a just reward for their keenness and perseverance.

Note: Enthusiastic catfish-anglers may be interested to know that West African catfish can be caught on ledgered cubes of bar soap. These catfish often feed on palm nuts. Palm nuts are made into palm oil, which is used in soap manufacture. Hence this somewhat unusual bait!

Figure 32: (*above*) This picture taken in 1954 of a 282 lb catfish caught on a longline by commercial fishermen in Czechoslovakia gives some idea of the growth potential of Eastern Europe catfish. It was 8 ft 9 in long and the head alone weighed 88 lb (*Jan Eggers*)

Figure 33: (*right*) Wels catfish of 194 lb, over 7 ft in length, caught by Jan Stava in Vranou Reservoir, Czechoslovakia.

British anglers anxious to see catfish well established throughout the UK will look forward to the day when fish of this size can be landed – although the knowledge that big 'cats' consume large numbers of waterfowl may reduce the enthusiasm of riparian owners!

Whole rabbits are sometimes used as bait by anglers fishing Wilstone Reservoir, where big 'cats' are said to lurk. So far without success

Figure 34: In September 1981 F.B. was photographed fishing a noted deep hole, in the Manych River near Rostov-on-Don, said to be the home of the giant Som (catfish up to 400 lb). Alas, he failed to provide himself with the baits recommended by Arthur Ransome in *Rod and Line* (1929) viz 'huge lumps of meat, half-plucked ducks or hens or suckling pigs.'

Undaunted, he used large deadbaits and in an ecstasy of anticipation experienced two fast runs of long duration – both of which were, alas, abortive. But as a consolation he landed (in two days) twenty-four pike

Figure 35: Catfish are often described as having six whiskers. This description fits the American catfish, but not the European, the wels. The latter has two large feelers on the top side of the mouth, and four small barbules, $\frac{1}{2}$ in. to 1 in. long, underneath the chin.

Large catfish are known to be great eaters of wildfowl – large and small. This catfish, weighing 137 lb $11\frac{1}{2}$ oz, built its weight on fish and fowl – until it was caught on Ossiacher Lake in Austria. Photo courtesy of Herr Moser – Austria's most famous taxidermist

Cooking the Catfish

Although the prospect of eating catfish seems rather daunting, Alwyne Wheeler in *The Fishes of the British Isles and North-West Europe*, states that the wels is a valuable commercial fish in Russia, where the eggs are said to be used as a substitute for caviar or to adulterate genuine caviar. The Russians have a high opinion of catfish flesh (as have the Americans for their own species of catfish, *Amiurus lacustris*): indeed they find a use for the whole body since they process catfish skin into leather.

Freshwater Fishing

The
CHARR

Salvelinus alpinus

I have heard say that no man may discuss the salmon, in print, unless he has caught twelve of them for each year of his own life ... What the ruling on char may be I do not know, but I am confident that I now contravene it; for only once have I caught a char, and then he was only a very little one. But he was as beautiful as a butterfly.

Patrick Chalmers, *A Fisherman's Angles* (1931)

The charr* populations of the British Isles are a series of non-migratory, lake dwelling colonies of fishes belonging to the salmon family (Salmonidae). They are found in several deep lakes of the English Lake District and North Wales, and in many of the deep lakes in Scotland and Ireland.

Whether these charr populations represent a number of different species and sub-species (as classified by Tate Regan and other authorities) remains undetermined. The present taxonomic situation is one of considerable confusion. Until further studies have been completed it seems reasonable to consider the British and Irish charr as varieties of the charr found in alpine lakes of countries as widely separated as Greenland, Russia, Japan and North America.

In the arctic, the charr is migratory, and like salmon and sea trout is an anadromous fish (that is, the adult fish feeds in the sea, enters freshwater rivers to spawn and, in a few instances, returns to sea after breeding).

All lake-dwelling charr are probably descended from a migratory stock whose extensive habitat shrank to its present size some 11,500 years ago when, during the last ice age, the ice retreated north. It has been suggested that the migratory charr became a freshwater species as a result of being land-locked in lakes that formed behind terminal moraines when these were deposited by melting glaciers. It seems likely, however, that the evolution was more gradual, and that a true lake-dwelling variety came about as a result of certain migratory charr exploiting these lakes.

A similar instance of an anadromous fish adapting itself to freshwater is provided by the offspring of the coho salmon introduced into Lake Michigan. They seem to have accepted this new environment as a 'sea' feeding ground, and spawn in rivers which flow into the lake. As a result, a purely freshwater variety of the coho salmon has been established.

Adult lake charr in Britain average 10 in. to 12 in. in length; but in favourable conditions can attain 16 in. In the exceptional conditions of Lac Leman (Geneva), charr reach a length of 31 in.

---

* Although the spelling *char* is commonly used – and seems to be endemic in Ireland – we prefer the older form.

Figure 36: Windermere charr taken by F.B. on a deep trailing-rig.

and a weight of 22 lb. This size is similar to that recorded for the sea-fed migratory race of charr.

Charr usually live in deep water. Alwyne Wheeler in *The Fishes of the British Isles and North-West Europe*, records that Lac Leman charr are mostly found at depths of 100 ft to 230 ft, and sometimes as deep as 325 ft. R. P. Hardie in *Ferox and Char* (1940), his work on charr distribution in Scotland, quotes James Murray who, in enumerating the animals found in the 'abyssal' region of Loch Ness, mentions a small charr 'dredged from a depth of over 500 ft.' Charr are certainly abundant in the loch at depths down to 400 ft. (Were the existence of a 'monster' verified, and should it prove to be a fish-eater, charr could contribute largely to its diet!) The same writer was of the opinion that charr were the main diet of the mighty *Salmon-ferox*, and in his book traced the link between these fish. Studies at Konigsee Lake in Austria revealed

that charr were the staple food of large Konigsee trout.

In the main charr feed on planktonic crustacea, although insect larvae, shrimps, molluscs and small fish also feature in their diet.

THE HABITS OF WINDERMERE CHARR

The best known British charr are those of Lake Windermere, which were intensively studied by Dr W. E. Frost of the Freshwater Biological Association. Windermere holds two distinct charr populations: the *autumn* spawners and the *spring* spawners.

The autumn spawners breed on gravel shallows in 3 ft to 12 ft of water near the shore during November and December, whereas the spring spawners breed on stony ground in 50 ft to 70 ft of water during February and March. A small number of charr also run from the lake and spawn in the River Brathay.

By tagging charr on their breeding grounds it

has been established that autumn and spring fish remain true to their respective spawning times and places.

For many years the annual charr run up the River Brathay ceased, or was too small to be noticed. This situation prevailed for some time before and during the period when perch trapping (started 1939) and pike netting (started 1945) were in operation. After the removal of many tons of pike and perch the charr population increased, and since 1948 the annual charr run has again become a feature of the Brathay.

Figure 37: Two charr from Lough Melvin presented to the Piscatorial Society in 1866 by T. R. Sachs

Charr normally keep to the deeps and repair to the shallows only to spawn. For this reason they have few opportunities to feed on small fish, and their principal diet is plankton. When small fish also take to the deeps, however, the charr feed on them as greedily as do the trout, many charr having been seen to regurgitate small perch about an inch long. In a statement given before the Fishery Commissioners at Bowness in 1878, a Mr Jackson declared that he took a three-inch perch from a charr's stomach.

The year 1970 marked what seems to have been change in the traditional behaviour of Windermere charr. According to Albert Dixon,

The char fishing in Loch Doon has long been regarded as some of the best in Britain, for unlike those from other large char waters these fish can be caught all season on fly from the shore. Exquisitely coloured, they average nine or ten inches and occasionally reach a pound in weight. Since their isolation in the loch after the retreat of the glaciers the arctic char here, like those of other relict populations, have undergone some remarkable physical changes, developing the narrow tailstalks and swallow-tails of free-swimming shoalfish as well as the small mouths of plankton-feeders. The tiny crustaceans on which they mainly feed tinges their rich flesh a bright orange, and local people have always regarded char as delicacies. The only complaint to be heard about these delightful fish is that their shoals usually pass by too fast and too infrequently to allow an angler to take enough for a good meal.

Robin Ade, *Fisher in the Hills.*
A Season in Galloway (1985)

Figure 38: Loch Doon from the Rev. C. H. Dick's *Highways and Byways in Galloway & Carrick* (1916)

veteran Windermere charr fisherman, it was the first year he had ever been able to catch charr throughout the season without proceeding south of Red Knab – a point midway down the north basin.

Perhaps this change in charr behaviour can be linked with the change in the whole economy of Windermere. The oligotrophic state (poor in dissolved nutrient salts) of the majority of British mountain lakes, extending from the end of the ice-age, has now changed with relative rapidity in lakes where the human population has increased in the catchment area. Such lakes have been enriched by sewage and crop dressings to the point where they have become eutrophic in character (rich in dissolved nutrient salts). If the process continues at the same rate, lakes that were once ideally suited to members of the Salmonidae – brown trout, sea trout, salmon, charr and whitefish – will open themselves to members of the Cyprinidae: roach, bream, rudd and tench.

Windermere charr weigh from five ounces to about a pound. Larger fish are occasionally taken, but in a lifetime of fishing, Dixon has had only eight bigger charr. Of these the best was a cock fish of $1\frac{1}{4}$ lb. Although there are records of charr weighing up to 3 lb, $1\frac{1}{2}$ lb is an exceptional fish.

It is therefore interesting to note that T. Upton, of Sedbergh, introduced some $\frac{1}{2}$ lb Windermere charr into Lilleymere (a lake presumably rich in food) in the autumn of 1839. Two caught on a fly the following August weighed 2 lb apiece.

Following this demonstration of growth rate, it might be interesting to introduce charr fingerlings into one of the deeper and more fertile southern reservoirs.

Nowadays, although fishermen flood into the Lake District in their hundreds, only three boat crews regularly patrol the north basin of Windermere – home of the old method of plumbline fishing for charr. And yet – charr fishing on Windermere has never been better than it is today, something that can be said about no other naturally bred freshwater British sportfish.

TRADITIONAL WINDERMERE CHARR FISHING

The traditional method of catching Windermere charr has remained the same for at least 150 years, and bears testimony to the skill of the old professional charr-fishers. This skill has been handed down from father to son. Even today, descendants of the famous charr-fishing families still top the lists; among them the Nicholsons of Bowness and the Sproats of Ambleside.

In days gone by, on or about 12 May, twenty-five boats with their complement of fifty anglers would assemble off Waterhead in the North Basin where most of the charr were congregated. This meeting was called The Carnival, and good fishing was expected by all. As an old-time charr fisherman said: 'They'll take a flat-iron in May!' And May is still one of the best fishing months of the season.

Tackle

The basis of the traditional charr trailing-rig is a heavy lead, about $1\frac{1}{2}$ lb, cone-shaped in sections, and fashioned like a rudder to keep it from twisting. This lead hangs straight down from the boat like a plumbline – hence the phrase 'plumblining for charr'.

The lead is suspended at depth from a rod, or spreader, about 18 ft long. Formerly one-piece ash saplings were used, but nowadays one-piece East India canes are the most popular.

The 26 yards of mainline that connects the tip of the rod to the lead is a braided cotton, or cuttyhunk, between 60 and 80 lb BS, soaked in a mixture of lampblack and linseed oil. After a thorough soaking the line is hung out under cover for about three weeks to dry. This dressing helps to preserve cotton lines for a number of

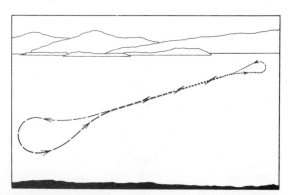

Figure 39. A typical repetitive course maintained by a charr fisherman once he has found taking fish
Figure 40: Albert Dixon fishing the north basin of Windermere

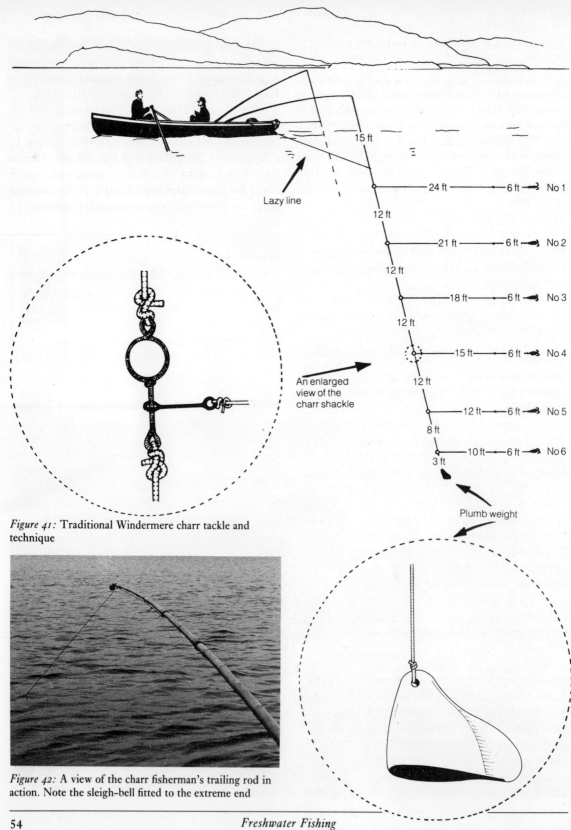

15 ft

Lazy line

24 ft — 6 ft → No 1

12 ft

21 ft — 6 ft → No 2

12 ft

18 ft — 6 ft → No 3

12 ft

An enlarged view of the charr shackle

15 ft — 6 ft → No 4

12 ft

12 ft — 6 ft → No 5

8 ft

10 ft — 6 ft → No 6

3 ft

Plumb weight

Figure 41: Traditional Windermere charr tackle and technique

Figure 42: A view of the charr fisherman's trailing rod in action. Note the sleigh-bell fitted to the extreme end

Figure 43: (right): Charr baits are kept highly polished since every glimmer of reflected light is needed in the deeps where sunlight barely penetrates. Baits are polished the night before use. Some fishermen even re-polish their baits during the lunch break. Like Irish trout fishermen on Lough Mask, Windermere charr fishermen traditionally meet and brew tea at certain places on the lake shore

years. It also stiffens the texture of the line and closes the braid, so that it becomes much easier to handle.

Six droppers are attached to the mainline. The top dropper is tied 15 ft from the rod tip; the second, third, fourth and fifth at intervals of 12 ft. The sixth and last dropper is tied 8 ft below the fifth dropper. The lead is attached 2 or 3 ft below the sixth dropper.

The droppers, which are not tied directly to the line but to a brass wire charr-shackle, vary in length. The top dropper is 24 ft long, with a 6 ft leader, making 30 ft in all. Each lower dropper, proceeding downwards, is three feet shorter than the previous one. This has the effect of making the baits fish vertically in line rather than in echelon.

The line used on the droppers is about 30 lb BS and dressed in the same manner as the mainline. The leader (nowadays) is 8 lb BS nylon, and incorporates three swivels: one at each end and one in the middle. The spinners are armed with a size 8 treble hook which is fastened to the terminal swivel by means of an oval link.

A set consisting of two 'sides' of charr tackle is carried in a case with three drawers. Two drawers are for the made-up tackle, and the other for various spares; leads, leader material, spinners and hooks. The drawers that contain the complete rig are fitted with a cork shoulder which ensures that the hooks can be seated without snarling.

This highly specialized rig, devised by generations of charr fishermen, cannot be purchased. Even the spinners are handmade. These are of two basic types: head spinners and tail spinners (tail spinners are preferred). All baits are made of thin sheet-metal. The finish can be plain silver or copper and silver (copper on one side and electroplated silver on the other); or brass and silver; or silver and gold-leaf.

Figure 44: Traditional charr tackle case

For generations, real gold was used in the making of charr baits – a thin gold strip which covered the side of a silver bait. Gold from a sovereign was preferred, and the instructions for using it are quite clear: 'The gold must be beaten out to the thickness of a butterfly wing.'

The old charr fishermen believed that gold from Australian sovereigns had some special charr-catching properties. The last fisherman to own genuine Australian gold baits is believed to have been the late Bruce Squires of Ambleside. These baits were so precious to him that after the 1940 season he never chanced them in the lake again where, as he said, 'Those terrible pike abound!'

Figure 45: In the United Kingdom the British associate ice-fishing with Eskimos, and do not realize how much of it is done in other countries. The fisherman in this picture has just caught a charr or a whitefish, having previously chopped himself a hole in the ice at the Lake of Bays, Ontario. Moscovite fishermen can't wait for the Moscow river to freeze so as to get at the fishing. But for the ban on aerial photography, F. B. would have taken a picture showing a panoramic view of ice-fishing activity during a recent landing approach to one of the Moscow airports. For the citizens of Leningrad, the winter freeze-up on Lake Ladoga sees them moving on to the ice for the annual family fish-catching/camping bonanza. All other northern and central European countries have winter ice-fishing and have developed special equipment, i.e. ice hole-borers and ultra-short rods, to facilitate the sport. (*Canadian National Railways*)

Technique

The lead is dropped over the side of the boat and allowed to sink until the first shackle is reached. The big half-inch ring on the shackle is then placed over the nail that projects upwards from the gunwale.

The sixth bait is tossed overboard, the dropper held until the bait is seen to be spinning freely, then released.

As soon as the boat's forward speed tensions the dropper, the shackle is lifted off the nail and the next section of mainline fed out until the next shackle is reached – and the process repeated. When the top shackle is reached, it is left on the nail until the line has been fastened to the rod tip.

A sleigh-bell which has been soldered on to two strips of springy wire is then bound on to the rod top. (Most charr fishermen leave this bell permanently fixed.)

The butt of the rod is now slotted into position and the top shackle released.

The charr often strikes a spinner without hooking itself, but the ringing of the bell caused by a well-hooked fish gives evidence of a proper strike. The angler now pulls on the lazy-line until he can reach the mainline. (One end of the lazy-line is attached to the mainline some two feet above the top shackle and the other end to a convenient brass screw-eye in the gunwale.)

Coiling the mainline and droppers neatly on the stern sheet he pulls up the mainline until the appropriate dropper is reached. This is placed over the nail. He can then pull in the dropper and net the fish.

The line must never be allowed to go slack when a fish is being brought up. Charr fishermen expect to land only three fish out of five, so that carelessness will lead to a much lower average.

The landing net should have the same dressing recommended for the lines. This helps to prevent treble hooks from penetrating the braid.

The skill in fishing single-handed is to keep the boat moving while the tackle is taken up and let out again. This is made possible by the design of Windermere boats. These are fitted with pin rowlocks to allow an angler to pull on each oar in turn with one hand (proprietors of South of England reservoirs, please note). The best trailing speed is between 1 and $1\frac{1}{2}$ m.p.h.

Charr may take a bait at any time of the day from first light until late evening. Sometimes fish are taken mostly on the top bait 15 to 20 ft down; sometimes on the lower baits – ranging from 15 ft to 70 ft. During hot weather, fish are seldom taken on the top two baits.

May and June are the peak months for charr fishing. At this time of the year the angler can expect any or all of his baits to catch fish. July is usually the poorest month, but in August and September the fish begin to take more freely

Figure 46: (*below*) Pin rowlocks. A necessity if the fisherman is to work the boat single-handed. Note the size of the net – an insurance against hooking a large brown trout

Figure 47: (*below right*) The rod is held in position by the two specially made fittings. It has been lifted out of the 'V'-shaped fitting to show how this is bolted on the gunwale. Note the lashing, which provides additional security

again. At this time of the season the bottom baits produce the bulk of the catch.

Year after year an individual bag of the season is directly related to the order of merit established among charr fishermen. Albert Dixon's explanation of this is rather surprising: 'I fish according to my diary.' That is to say he directs his boat (on a lake ten miles long and nearly a mile wide at its widest point) along the very same line that he followed on that date the previous year! There is an unwritten law which inhibits a charr fisherman from fishing along another man's line.

Formerly, some good trout were taken on charr tackle, but fewer are taken nowadays. It may be that the big Windermere trout (though never present in large numbers) have succumbed to the gill-nets used to reduce the pike population. Most trout taken on charr tackle are caught on the third bait from the top, about 40 ft below the surface. When a big trout is hooked the angler makes a long turn and comes downwind before attempting to land the fish.

So far as we know only two English lakes besides Windermere have been fished with Windermere plumbline charr tackle: Crummock and Coniston. In 1971, F. B. – with permission of Ireland's Inland Fisheries Trust – fished Lough Currane and Lough Mask for charr and trout with plumbline tackle of his own making as an experiment. Trailing on Mask during a two-day period of hot, dry weather when, according to all reports, the fishing was 'dead', he caught 13 trout. Ten were caught 60 ft down – confirming evidence of minimal surface activity during these difficult conditions.

Significantly, studies of Lough Mask by Patrick Fitzmaurice of the Inland Fisheries Trust, during 1968 and 1969, show that the oxygen content of the water at depths of up to 70 ft was never less than it was near the surface. Even at the greatest depth – 192 ft, the deepest sounding ever made on an Irish lough – the dissolved oxygen value never fell below five parts per million.

Because of this favourable oxygen profile, the trout and charr of Lough Mask have freedom to feed at greater depth than fish occupying deep lakes where the *thermocline* is of the classic pattern.

When the coldest part of the winter has passed, deep lakes in cold and temperate regions develop a uniform temperature from top to bottom (approximately 39–42°F). As the summer advances, the surface layer – unlike the lower layer which has no source of heat – absorbs heat

Figure 48: Albert Dixon, with charr 'rods' outside his boathouse

Freshwater Fishing

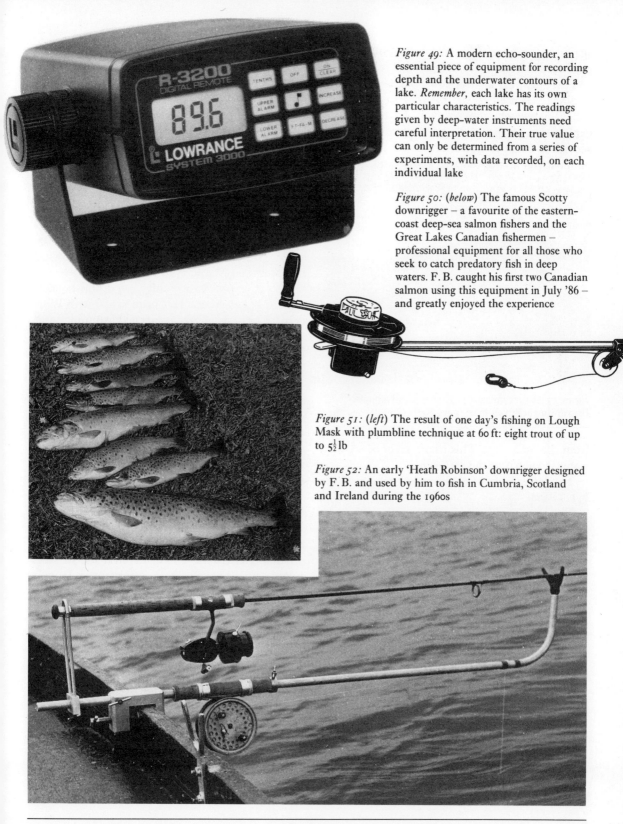

Figure 49: A modern echo-sounder, an essential piece of equipment for recording depth and the underwater contours of a lake. *Remember,* each lake has its own particular characteristics. The readings given by deep-water instruments need careful interpretation. Their true value can only be determined from a series of experiments, with data recorded, on each individual lake

Figure 50: (*below*) The famous Scotty downrigger – a favourite of the eastern-coast deep-sea salmon fishers and the Great Lakes Canadian fishermen – professional equipment for all those who seek to catch predatory fish in deep waters. F. B. caught his first two Canadian salmon using this equipment in July '86 – and greatly enjoyed the experience

Figure 51: (*left*) The result of one day's fishing on Lough Mask with plumbline technique at 60 ft: eight trout of up to $5\frac{1}{2}$ lb

Figure 52: An early 'Heath Robinson' downrigger designed by F. B. and used by him to fish in Cumbria, Scotland and Ireland during the 1960s

The Charr

Figure 53: A very unusual picture, possibly unique. British-caught brown trout (top), skelly (middle) and charr

from the sun's rays. This upper layer of warmed water is known as the *epilimnion*.

The lower layer of cold water is known as the *hypolimnion*.

The 'sandwich' in between these two layers – a region of rapidly dropping temperature – is known as the *thermocline*.

Since warm water is lighter than cold water it floats on top; so that during windy spells, when surface water is blown across a lake, the warm water of the epilimnion circulates independently (see figure 54).

Most living organisms in a temperature-stratified lake live in the warm epilimnion where the oxygen supply is constantly replenished from contact with the surface. All dead organisms, however, sink into the hypolimnion where the process of decay uses up the oxygen. Since there is no source from which this oxygen can be replenished, the hypolimnion gradually becomes more deoxygenated as the summer advances.

In *Life in Lakes and Rivers* (1961), Worthington and Macan record a typical example of summer depth of epilimnion and thermocline in Windermere, July 1948:

Epilimnion: o–30 ft
Thermocline: 33–50 ft

From this it can be seen that thermal stratification has a considerable effect on the activities of fish. American anglers have long been aware of this. As a result, echo-sounders and deepwater thermometers form a standard part of their fishing equipment.

An angler fishing a lake or loch from the bank might think that since he is casting into relatively shallow water (say 20 ft deep), he will always

Figure 54

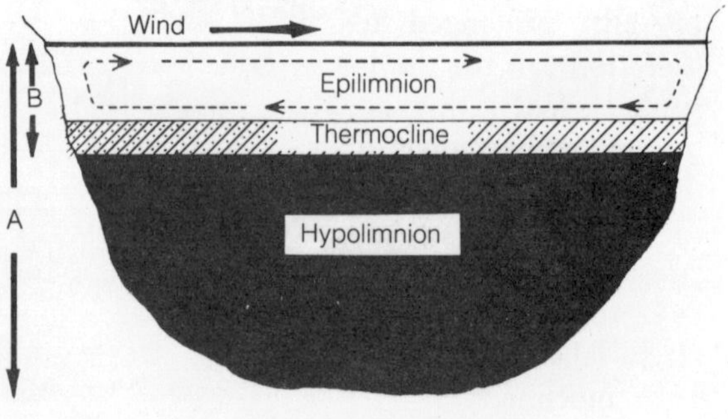

Freshwater Fishing

A B G
D E
C 80m F

75 m B
70 m H
65 m K
60 m H
55 m K
50 m L
5 m K
5 m H
5 m K

5 m L   9.5 m   M
10 m L   4.5 m   N
5 m L   4.5 m   O
5 m L   4.5 m   P
5 m L   4.5 m   Q
5 m L   4.5 m   R
1.5 m S

Figure 56: (*above*) Marryat-Interfly tackle

Figure 57: (*below*) David Beazley's reel

Figure 55: The 'multiple' charr-tackle illustrated in *The Fishing Gazette* of 25 January 1911: a revolving-drum variation of the Windermere charr rig, used during the last century on Lac Leman (Lake Geneva). When the bell rings, indicating a take, the mainline is wound on the right-hand side of the drum; the droppers, after being tensioned round a spike (see illustration) on the left-hand side. The bait trebles are embedded for safety in the cork rim.

be casting into the fish-holding epilimnion. He would be wrong. Although water stratifies horizontally, prolonged spells of wind from one direction can tilt the layers into the shape of a wedge. When this happens, the warm, oxygenated epilimnion is extra-deep on the lee shore of the lake, and the cold oxygen-starved hypolimnion reaches up towards the surface of the windward shore. It is mainly for this reason that, in summer, anglers should fish on the lee shore on all lakes that are subject to the formation of a thermocline.

In winter months the lee shore offers no such advantage. In autumn, as soon as the air temperature begins to fall, the epilimnion starts to cool down and with the advent of a gale is obliterated.

When he was alerted with the details of the ancient 'Multiple' charr-tackle, our friend David Beazley, who resides in Switzerland, responded to an invitation to 'sniff around' the fishermen's haunts of Lake Geneva, to see if this old charr-tackle was still in use.

He was not only able to affirm that it was –

but his purchase of a more modern variation (David collects reels) shown in the photograph indicates, when compared with the 4-inch spinning bait, its massive proportions.

Later F.B., through a business connection with a Swiss tackle distributor Marryat-Interfly, discovered that marketing charr-tackles is still part of their stock-in-trade. Indeed the illustration of the 'Swiss' system of deep water trailing for charr shown here decorates their current catalogue. Notice that the tackle allows baits to be fished down to 250 ft.

The only significant difference between Windermere and Geneva rigs is the strength of tackle, and bait size, the Swiss baits being much larger. This is because Windermere charr seldom weigh more than 1 lb, whereas Geneva charr have been known to weigh as much as 22 lb.

Note: Are these charr the fish referred to in *The Compleat Angler* in the following passage?

It is well known that in the Lake of Leman, the Lake of Geneva, there are trouts taken of three cubits long, as is affirmed by Gesner, a writer of good credit; and *Mercator* says, the Trouts that are taken in the Lake of Geneva, are a great part of the Merchandise of that famous city.

It is probable that these 'trouts' were big charr – like the huge 'lake trout' of North America (*Salvelinus namaycush*), which have been known to reach a weight of 102 lb.

Cooking the Charr

The charr is delicious to eat. H. F., who used to catch a few, enjoyed charr fried with a slice of bacon for breakfast. But by less philistine palates, this little fish has been praised for centuries as a potted delicacy. In 1769, Defoe wrote: 'It is a curious fish, and as a dainty, is potted and sent far and near by way of present.' Charr pies were once a favourite luxury. In 1662, Sir Daniel Fleming of Rydal, near Windermere, sent one to his aunt and duly noted in his account book: '... for the carriage of a charr-pie unto my Aunt Dudley at London. At 2d per lb, £0 6s. 0d.'

John Davy in *The Angler in the Lake District* (1857) gives a recipe for Potted Charr which he obtained from a 'worthy neighbour' who was 'so ... esteemed for higher qualities, that her portrait in her old age has been painted, paid for by a friendly subscription, and presented to her daughter.'

Here it is in her own words:

One dozen charr, dress and wipe with a dry cloth; strew a little salt in and over them, and let them lie all night; then wipe them with a dry cloth, and season with one ounce of white pepper, quarter of an ounce of cayenne, half an ounce of pounded cloves, and a little mace. Clarify two pounds of butter. Then put them with their backs down into a pot lined with paper; and then pour the butter over, and bake for four hours in a slow oven.

POTTED CHARR
(Old Windermere recipe)

Cook in the oven with the head on and when the eyes go white, then it is ready. Flake fish off the bones, mix into a paste with cream or white sauce, adding seasoning as required. Put into a pot and press down tight, then pour melted butter over the top and allow to set.

Figure 58: Charrs were potted in traditional decorative pots. Such pots as this one (shown side view) are now quite valuable

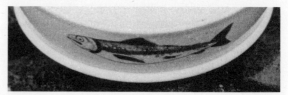

The
CHUB
Leuciscus cephalus

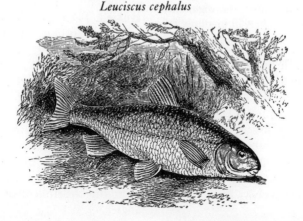

The chub, together with three sub-species, is widely distributed throughout mainland Europe except in the extreme north. Although in Great Britain the chub is absent from Ireland, West Wales, the Cornish peninsula and north of the Firth of Forth, it is nevertheless found throughout the rest of the United Kingdom.

Very occasionally the chub flourishes in stillwaters, but clean running water is its usual habitat. The spawning time is May, June or July, when the water temperature has reached about 59°F.

The chub's diet is catholic, and the range of baits that an angler may usefully take with him grows with the reading of every book. From just a few authors we have culled the following:

Worms of every sort; frogs; insect larvae; flies of all descriptions (live and artificial); water weeds; spinners; plugs; grasshoppers; slugs; crayfish; breadpaste; dough; crust; crumb; cheese; cheese-paste; wheat; barley; hemp; elderberry; cherries; sultanas; raisins; maggots; caterpillars; bullock's brains; pith from the backbone of an ox; wasp grubs; bacon rind; snails; withey grubs; shrimps (sea or freshwater); dock grubs; greaves; bumble bees; cockchafers; bullheads; minnows; caddis grub; beetles; water bugs; algae; macaroni; small water voles; small eels; gudgeon; small dace; prides; roachlets; young chub; cooked ham and sausage!

In a swim where a gamekeeper friend habitually discarded rabbit paunches, E. Marshall-Hardy caught many fine chub on pieces of rabbit gut.

The chub's habit of bold biting endears him to the angler, even though a highly developed sense of self-preservation makes him difficult to approach. There is a passage in *The Compleat Angler* describing these seemingly paradoxical traits in the chub's character:

… a Chub is the fearfullest of fishes …

But

… he will infallibly take the bait.

The same passage also provides an unsurpassed description of dapping:

Go to the same hole in which I caught my Chub, where in most holidays you will find a dozen or twenty Chevens floating near the top of the water. Get two or three grasshoppers as you go over the meadow, and get secretly behind the tree, and stand as free from motion as is possible. Then put a grasshopper on your hook, and let your hook hang a quarter of a yard short of the water, to which end you must rest your rod on some bough of the tree. But it is likely the Chubs will sink down towards the bottom of the water at the first shadow of your rod, for a Chub is the fearfullest of fishes, and will do so if but a bird flies over him, and makes the least shadow on the water; but they will presently rise up to the top again, and there lie soaring till some shadow affrights them again. I say when they lie upon the top of the water, look out the best Chub, which you, setting yourself in a fit place, may very easily see, and move your rod as softly as a snail moves, to that Chub you intend to catch; let your bait fall gently upon the water three or four inches before him, and he will infallibly take the bait.

Dapping apart, perhaps the deadliest method for catching chub is with an artificial fly. Some idea of its effectiveness can be gleaned from the following account. Sir Hugh Lucas-Tooth, owner of the Hampshire Avon fishing at Burgate, allowed three crack angling clubs to fish his water for many years – both to enjoy good sport and to rid his section of the river of as many coarse fish as possible. In consequence, many tons of coarse fish were caught and removed to other waters. In all that time only a few chub of over four pounds were taken by bait-fishing, whereas during the same period Sir Hugh caught many heavier chub on fly.

For chub fly-fishing, special big bushy lures are tied. There is no attempt to imitate any insect one may expect to find floating on the water but, rather, something that comes to the water by way of mishap – a fat moth, for example. Not that a chub will ignore an olive or sedge (or their artificials) if these are the best on offer, but on the whole the chub is an economical feeder who prefers to eat well rather than often.

When appropriate, the deadliest of all bait-fishing methods is unquestionably long-trotting. This removes the bait so far downstream that even the 'fearfullest of fishes' cannot see the angler.

The best ploy for ensuring continued sport with chub is *resting the swim*. If several fish are taken in quick succession the angler is well advised to move on for a time and fish another spot. If this is not possible, we suggest a walk downriver for half-an-hour or so while the swim recovers. It seems paradoxical that a reduction in fishing time leads to bigger catches, but this is certainly true when chub are the quarry.

Figure 59: The chub – 'skelly' to the Scots and Cumbrians (but not to be confused with the Houting variant from the Lake District, see 'skelly' page 336). Although a fine sporting fish, the chub is often persecuted where it shares water with fish of higher economic value such as trout and salmon. The 3 lb chub below was caught in that most famous of all trout streams: the Test. Note the perfect shape and immaculate scaling of a fish that has fed well and never been inside a keepnet

Freshwater Fishing

Figure 60: (*right*) The late Richard Walker with a chub

Figure 61: (*below*) Mrs Louie Thompson of Sheffield, with a magnificent 6 lb chub. The background of vegetation provided good cover while the fish was being played

Figure 62: (*bottom*) Although there are many points of identification between small chub and dace, a simple one is the shape of the anal fin. In the dace the free edge of the anal fin is concave. In the chub (as shown in this photograph) the free edge is convex

Viator: How kill you the chevin?
Piscator: He will bite very well at a minnow, the great red worm, the white worm in the dead ash, the grasshopper, the young unhaired mouse, the black snail, slit in the back that her grease may hang out, the hornet, the great bear worm in a swift stream or at a mill-tail with heavy gears, the marrow in the ridge-bone of a loin of veal, yea, and rather than fail, at a piece of bacon, I mean the fat.

Viator: I have heard say that he will not stick to bite at a frog.
Piscator: I know not that, but this I tell you, you must stand close, for he hath a quick eye and will fly like an arrow out of a bow to his den or hole, which he is never far from. Your line must be strong and your hook well hardened.

Attrib: William Samuel,
The Arte of Angling (1577)

The Chub

'Sir, I'm proud to say, that, sir, I caught, sir, that chub, sir.'

'I congratulate you. What a noble fish!'

'Yes, sir. I've never been man enough to get such another, sir. It is the biggest fish, sir, that has been seen in the Lee ever since, sir; and that is ten years ago, sir! I will show you the hook with which I hooked him, sir.'

With that, he opened one of the aforesaid closets, and then unlocked a compartment in it, about five feet high. It was, I found, his *sanctum sanctorum*. On the shelf were lying, in the nicest order, some portentous black pocket-books, enclosing cases that, I found, contained, on bamboo frames, twelve lines in each, of hair and Indian hurl, alternately, like the flats and sharps of a piano, and galore of shots, from number one downwards, in as many divisions of the sliding centre-bit; and side by side lay floats of all sizes, some green and red, some red green, some yellow and red, and some red and yellow;

together with sundry and divers plumbing machines, kill-devils, minnow-tackle, spring snap-hooks, nets, and kettles for live baits, fishing-panniers, landing-nets, worm-bags, and boxes for gentles and other uses.

He thought he had now produced the desired effect, and said – 'Now, sir, I will show you, sir, the hook, sir.' He opened a shagreen-cased snap-box, and produced the trophy with the air of a hero, and that self-consciousness of superiority that deeds of fame and glory justify …

As he was speaking, several persons … bustled in, and showed by their deference how much they appreciated the high 'eminence' to which 'merit' had raised him; and in a short time the house swarmed with fishers. He seemed perfectly known to them all; and in fact it was easy to see that he was the Apollo, the *arbiter ludorum*, the oracle of the temple.

Thomas Medwin, *The Angler in Wales, or Days and Nights of Sportsmen* (1834)

Freshwater Fishing

Figure 63: (*left*) F. B., under the watchful eye of the photographer, the late Richard Walker – who was writing and illustrating an article for an angling newspaper – is expected to land the chub copy-book style

Figure 64: 5 lb and 4 lb chub taken by F. B. on the River Test

Cruising down the Severn, we had moored our canoe under some bushes in a secluded spot to take our mid-day rest. Presently we saw two men in coracles coming down the river. They stopped opposite us and commenced to net the river. They played out their net in a semi-circle, and then, beating the water with their paddles, they closed in and with their coracles side by side, handed the net in.

It was a caution to see the fish they had caught. Roach, pike and dace; in half an hour they caught a great number; great chub of five pounds and one of nine pounds in weight.

The Angler's Souvenir (1877), quoted by A. Courtney Williams in *Angling Diversions* (1945)

Among big British chub on record is a $10\frac{1}{2}$ lb monster from the River Crane; this was caught on live minnow by W. Cockburn in 1875. Another is a fish of $8\frac{1}{2}$ lb caught by D. Deekes in the River Rother. On the Continent chub have been caught up to a weight of 18 lb, and some anglers are confident that a few British waters hold fish almost as big. The Hampshire Avon; the Wye; the Dorset Stour; the Annan and the Great Ouse are rivers likely to hold a record chub. Mr Harding, master-fisherman of the Dorset Stour who fished the Blandford stretch almost every day of his life between the wars, maintained that the biggest chub in Britain lived below the weir in the grounds of Bryanston School.

Cooking the Chub

His burnished gold outside hides a miserable interior. He is neither fish, flesh, nor good red herring. He is to all intents and purposes, save in appearance, what the French call him, *un villain*, that is, downright chaw-bacon, or clod-hopper. Though M. A. Soyer, of the Reform Club should condescend to dress him, I doubt whether he would make him fit to appear at any dinner table.

So much for the chub's table qualities as evaluated by Edward Fitzgibbon in *A Handbook of Angling* (1847). Nor was Izaak Walton's opinion much higher:

The chub … is objected against, not only for being full of small forked bones, dispersed through all his body, but that he eats waterfish, and that the flesh of him is not firm, but short and tasteless.

Nevertheless, *The Compleat Angler* includes a recipe for this much maligned fish, and for readers who feel they can face it we offer the possibility of 'roast chub'.

First scale him, and then wash him clean, and then take out his guts; and to that end make the hole as little and as near to his gills as you may conveniently, and especially make clean his throat from the grass and weeds that are usually in it, for if that be not very clean, it will make him to taste very sour. Having so done, put some sweet herbs into his belly; and then tie him with two or three splinters to a spit, and roast him, basted often with vinegar, or rather ver-juice and butter, with good store of salt mixed with it.

The
DACE

Leuciscus leuciscus

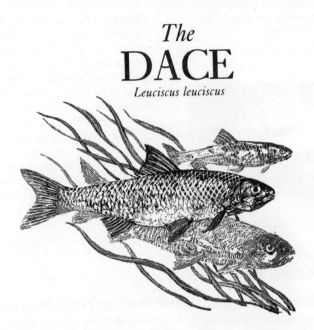

Except in Norway where it is confined to one area, the dace is widely distributed throughout Europe north of the Alps and the Pyrenees. It inhabits most British rivers except those in Cornwall, west Wales and Scotland. In the Lake District it is found only in the River Eden. In Ireland it was accidentally introduced when an English pike angler's livebait can tipped over! Since then it has become established in the Cork Blackwater system.

During the eighteenth and nineteenth centuries, Lancashire anglers were thought to be blessed with a species unique to that county: the 'graining' – a belief shared by the eminent naturalist William Yarrell. This was discounted by Tate Regan, and the graining turned out to be none other than the dace.

Since the dace is generally associated with clear, fairly fast-running rivers and streams, some anglers may wonder why it fails to exploit the higher waters of these rivers, as do trout, sea trout, grayling and salmon. The reason is that unlike the eggs of the Salmonidae, which are buried in gravel by the females and thus gain protection during spates, dace eggs are laid on water-plants of the type seldom found high up

in spate streams, where, anyway, they would be in danger of getting swept off by the current.

Dace usually spawn in February and March although, after a severe winter, spawning may be delayed until April or May. During the spawning period the head and body of the male dace is covered with white tubercles and the fish becomes very rough to the touch.

The biggest bags of dace are likely to be made in February and March, when the shoals migrate upstream from the deeps into shallow spawning areas. The record match bag of 251 dace weighing 64 lb, caught by F. B. in the Hampshire Avon on 10 March 1957, probably consisted of fish that had assembled in this way prior to spawning.

During November, December and January, dace are likely to be found in the deeper runs. At other times, if not disturbed, they move into relatively shallow water. At all times they tend to haunt gravelly runs, whether fast, slow, shallow or deep. When in very shallow runs, dace are easily frightened into deep water if groundbait other than the lightest sprinkling of maggots or casters is thrown to them.

In streams and small rivers the best way to prepare a dace swim is to wade out some fifteen or twenty yards above the fish and send a cloud of mud and silt downstream, together with a sprinkling of maggots. The angler can achieve this by stirring the bottom with his feet – an alternative to *raking* the bottom, which is the traditional method of small stream dace fishing.

Although not large in stature the dace gives a good account of itself on fine tackle. It can be caught on almost any of the small-fish baits with almost any method save livebaiting – although even this reservation must be discarded if one accepts the Rev. W. B. Daniel's claim to have caught dace '. . . upwards of a pound weight upon night lines baited with minnow for eels'. (But perhaps Daniel made the common error of confusing the dace with the chub, see page 65.)

The average-sized dace is a free-rising fish capable of testing the reflexes of the best fly-fisherman. Its rejection of fly or bait is often far too quick for the contemplative angler. Indeed, when hempseed is used as bait only a lightning strike has any chance of success.*

Large dace – upwards of nine inches – are more deliberate biters. As Hugh Sheringham

wrote: 'All fish become rather more dignified in their behaviour when they get bigger'!

Although the rod-caught record is 1 lb 8 oz 5dr, few anglers have caught dace of over a pound. The record fish was taken by R. W. Humphrey on the River Wylye in September 1932. Hugh Sheringham caught five that weighed over a pound apiece, all on fly – which is some indication of how successful this method can be.

Between 1898 and 1900 E. Steinhart caught eight dace of one pound or over from the River Beane at Waterford Marsh, Hertfordshire – an astonishing performance. Nevertheless, the all-time dace champion must surely be W. H. Clarke of Barnham, Norfolk, for during twenty-five years' fishing on the Little Ouse near Thetford he landed forty-two dace weighing over the pound! His best fish (1 lb 3½ oz) was caught in the summer of 1958. Had it been taken during the following winter it could well have weighed an extra two ounces.

---

* Even though the pain has eased after sixty years, H. F. – who at the age of ten considered himself a master angler – can still recall the frustrations and chagrin of an afternoon spent beside a Thames weirpool trying to hook dace on hempseed.

Figure 65: Dace 1 lb 3¼ oz, 1 lb 2 oz, 1 lb 1½ oz, 1 lb 1¼ oz, 1 lb 1 oz, 1 lb ½ oz, 1 lb and 1 lb (photographed by permission of A. G. Davies, Curator of the Hertford Museum)

DACE,
MATTHEWS, in the Beane, at Hertford, Oct. 19th 1899, Wgt 1lb 4ozs

Figure 66: Dace, 1 lb 4 oz, taken from the Beane in 1899 by A. R. Matthews. This fish held the rod-caught record until 1905 (photographed by permission of the Piscatorial Society)

The most famous English waters for big dace are the Kennet; the Kennet and Avon Canal; the Hampshire Avon; the Wiltshire Wylye; the Test; the Usk; the Dorset Stour; the Bedfordshire Ivel, and the Hertfordshire rivers Rib, Gade and Beane. A. R. Matthews, in *How to Catch Coarse Fish* (1921), wrote a delightful account of catching dace in the Beane – a story so interesting and vivid that we include it for the enjoyment of our readers:

The little River Beane was to be seen some time before we reached the eventful spot, its serpentine course being plainly discernible through the many old pollards and alders growing upon its banks. Just before my visit refreshing rains had been experienced, but in not sufficient volume to put any land water into the Beane, and we found that river not only on the bright side, but rather slow-running.

Nothing daunted, I jointed my roach-pole, put on a brand new line and hook length and a very old favourite float, and having nicked on a good bunch of gentles, made my initial cast. The swim was in a bend, and my friend walking well above me, now produced his box of gentles and used them for ground-bait. Just then, too, I saw a man walking across the field with a rake over his shoulder, and motioning him to hurry on, and pointing to a certain piece of water about 30 yards from where I was crouched on a camp stool, my friend rejoined me telling me that, as the water was not naturally coloured it would have to be made so artificially, and when I next looked upstream the man I had seen with the rake was already at work with that implement. The local mill now also began to work, and no sooner had the stream received impetus than down went the float. I promptly responded, felt a heavy drag, saw the glittering sides of an immense dace, and – then the line came back! My feelings under such circumstances can be better imagined than described, and, knowing that I must have disturbed the fish, I suggested a walk, and off downstream my friend and I tramped, leaving the man plying the rake stealthily.

When we returned to the spot the water was showing a nice colour and had risen, and there was quite a fast stream running. 'Now look out,' I thought, 'no bungling or missing fish this time!' My friend again stole above the swim with the groundbaiting gentles, and I had not had more than five swims down when the float disappeared in a slanting position. Once more I struck, and found I had hooked another splendid dace. The fish ran upstream and then started boring, but the whalebone-spliced top piece on my rod had very fortunately plenty of 'give' in it, and the fish was soon in mid-water. 'A beauty indeed,' exclaimed my friend, as the next moment he slipped skilfully my V-shaped landing net under the dace and lifted it on to the bank. It certainly was the largest dace I had ever seen alive out of a river, and on my friend's steelyards it weighed 1 lb $\frac{1}{2}$oz good ... He next measured the fish, its dimensions being: length 13 in., girth 8 in. The man with the rake (who I ascertained as a clever old angler himself) had noted my bent rod, and had further heard the splashing in the water and seen the dace netted, came up to admire it, while, what with the sight of the notable fish and the congratulations of my friend, my readers can better imagine than I can describe my feelings. I had caught a fish which thousands of anglers had never been able to secure, and it was a very proud moment for me, indeed, I can tell you.

Giving the swim another rest, I restarted operations in the course of half-an-hour, and found the faithful raker still at his post. For the third time my friend resorted to his gentle-box, and once more in went the 'groundbait' all alive-O! There was now a beautiful stream, and my friend prophesied that I would catch further dace. And, what was more thrilling to me, that I might get a larger dace than the one lying in the grass at the side of the hedge! But, strange to say, I fished for quite a quarter of an hour without the slightest sign of a dace bite. It then occurred to me to try a red worm, and when I had baited I fished a different part of the swim where, the water and stream having increased in height and pace, a little 'boily' eddy had been created.

Once or twice did the float go round and round the swim quietly, and then – such a lovely bite! I was on the fish in a second with one of those clean strikes that extract from the pole a kind of 'tung', and was soon doing battle with another monster of the dace tribe. First up and then downstream the fish rushed, now across it, now back in a vain endeavour to reach a bunch of lily roots at my feet.

'I don't think he's quite as large as the first,' I

remarked to my friend – I had not obtained a clear view of the fish then – but I promptly a bit later recalled the words, and when I gazed at the fish in the dripping landing-net, I felt I could scarcely believe my eyes.

'Now you've done something,' exclaimed my friend, as he put the fish on the steelyards.

'Bigger? Here! Wait a minute! Good gracious! You lucky beggar! Why, it weighs 1 lb 4 oz!'

'And don't it bump the weight, too', chimed in the old man with the rake. 'If that ain't the champion dace,' he added, 'I never seed such a dace, and I have had werry near 50 years of dodging about the river and seed millions of big daces.'

The dimensions of this fish, as taken on the bank by my friend, were: length $13\frac{1}{2}$in., girth $8\frac{1}{2}$in. It was a shapely, elegant-looking fish, and beautiful in colouring.

Cooking the Dace

On the preparation of a dace J. J. Manley remarked 'perhaps the more you disguise it the better'. Nevertheless he records the following old Thames-side recipe:

Without scaling the fish, lay him on a grid-iron, over a slow fire, and strew on him a little flour; when he begins to grow brown, make a slit not more than skin deep, in his back from head to tail, and lay him on again; when he is broiled enough, his skin, scales and all, will peel off, and leave the flesh, which will have become very firm, perfectly clean, then open the belly, and take out the inside, and use anchovy and butter for sauce.

DACE BOUILLABAISSE

From Maurice Wiggin, *Troubled Waters* (1960)

I don't say it is quite the English thing, don't
know if it really goes perfectly with beer and tea
and a cold climate. Doubt if it does. But a good
freshwater bouillabaisse is quite a thing to try.
As the poet said:

> A freshwater bouillabaisse
> Includes dace.
> Even if you can't spell it
> You can smell it.

You can indeed. But I wouldn't say it really and
truly has to include dace – a bit of poetic licence,
please – though you can chuck 'em in if you have
them handy. Everything helps – except bream,
of course. Bream are *persona non grata* in this as
in everything else. Talk about *slime*. But almost
anything else goes – perch, roach, gudgeon pre-
eminently, dace, rudd, ruffe, eels, even minnows
if you can stoop so low. Pike, bleak, and even
chub if you are very pushed. I wouldn't personally include carp in anything, but some
would. In fact carp are considered a delicacy by
many.

I think the first fact about a freshwater bouillabaisse is *the more the merrier*. The more mixed
the bag, the more intriguing the final flavour. Or
flavours. Cut them all up, fairly small, some
smaller than others. You need a couple of pounds
for a fair sitting. Then get busy on the trimmings.
With a couple of pounds of fish, give or take half
a pound, you will need two goodish onions,
which you should slice; four tomatoes, skinned
and crushed; a clove of garlic; a bay leaf; a pinch
of saffron; parsley and fennel; and enough olive
oil to cover the pieces of fish.

If you can't stand olive oil, try your luck with
something else. I think the general technique is
this, more or less ... You put the firmer, solider

Dace are by no means to be scorned as table
fish. How could they fail to be sweet eating,
when their own tastes are so pellucid and
aerial? A fine dish of them fried in delicate
fats, as soon as the happy angler comes
home, makes a royal banquet, with a suspicion of vinegar, a little cress, and some
brown bread and butter. You could not do
better, believe me, if they were troutlets
which hissed and spat in the pan. A little
white wine – Chablis shall we say – goes
well with them. Indeed, there is a proper
vintage for every kind of fish that swims, but
to enlarge upon this theme would be either
to speak to ears too gross to understand it,
or else it would be to insult the fine spirits
to whom this knowledge is native and
instinctive.

Charles Marson, *Super Flumina* (1906)

bits of fish, and all the trimmings into the pan
and pour in enough olive oil just to cover the
fish. You *then* pour boiling water over the whole
lot and cook fairly furiously for five minutes.
You must cook this lot very fast. Then you add
the softer fish flesh, *and* a glass of white wine,
and boil the lot hard for seven minutes more.

To serve, pour off the liquid into soup bowls
containing pieces of bread; whether fresh or
toasted, I leave it to you. Put the fish flesh into
a dish and sprinkle with parsley. Serve both at
once, the liquid and the flesh, and let joy be
unrestrained. It may well be so, provided you
have also put on the table generous quantities of
white wine, the best you can buy. Failing that,
I suppose, beer of the lighter sorts, or stout. I
have eaten this dish with stout. Or after stout.
I'm not sure that I'd face it all – the labour, the
complexity, the smells – without something to
drink.

The
EEL
Anguilla anguilla

The eel, as is well known, will live a long time out of water. This habit is of the greatest service to him, as sometimes it is necessary for him to migrate from place to place by an overland route.

Frank Buckland, *The Natural History of British Fishes* (1881)

There are those who denigrate the eel. Indeed, is any fish so badly treated? For many an angler reeling in that slimy, twisting knot, one look is enough: with his scissors he snips the leader and bends to his tackle-bag to repair the damage – leaving the eel to writhe among the rushes, wrapped in nylon with a hook in its gullet.

No creature should be so barbarously treated.

The eel is as fascinating in its habits as those other migratory fishes: salmon and sea trout. It has a history which is second to none. Besides, whether fried, stewed or smoked, it is delicious to eat. That enchanting writer Arthur Ransome knew its gastronomic value. Of a day when after big carp, he writes: 'Four times the baits were taken by eels, landed amid anathemas, tempered by the thought of next day's breakfast.' Catch *him* cutting them adrift!

The angler who is ignorant of the eel's table qualities is a fool. But the angler who leaves an eel writhing with a hook in its stomach is worse than a fool. It is hoped that the following notes will enlighten such an unfeeling oaf, and encourage him to treat this remarkable animal with more respect.

The eel, it seems, was the first fish to achieve the dignity of a name. A distinction it fully deserves: few other fish have been so highly praised or so highly prized. Certainly no fish has been the subject of more scientific controversy and conjecture. Indeed, the story of this quiet, mysterious creature is touched with a strange wonder and romance; a story not untinged with humour.

As an eighteenth-century writer put it:

There is a greater variety in the eel than in any other fish of the river, and it is not yet determined how to treat them, whether as a fish or as a reptile. Some who have no good will to them, put them as no better than a species of serpent and will call them water snakes.

Of course, not everyone has been in sympathy with this animal. Even to-day not everyone is deeply conscious of the eel and the riddle of its life cycle – which for so many centuries remained unsolved. Many people, unmoved by the mystery of its birth, have treated it as a fresh-water vermin, dismissing it as a slimy creature; an 'invigorated putrefaction'.

But not the ancient Greeks.

To them it was 'The King of Fish; the white-

Figure 67: An eel swimming, from *Fishing* (1904)

Figure 68: An eel moving overland

skinned Nymph; a goddess, all clothed in beet' –
with which, on beech leaves, it was often served.
And, highest of all honours: 'The Helen of the
Feast'.

The Greeks were inordinately fond of eels.
They paid vast sums of money for the luxury of
eating them – while the voluptuous Sybarites
were so addicted that all persons catching eels
were exempt from paying taxes and tributes.

By some of the more credulous, the eel was
considered a prophylactic, preventing all kinds
of maladies; a panacea; a tonic for the voice. The
smoke of burnt eel was said to ease the pangs of
childbirth; whereas the fragrance of it, cooking,
restored the sense of smell to a dead man.

By the Boeotians it was thought worthy of
sacrificial offering to the gods.

Agatharchides of Knidos relates:

The largest eels from Lake Copais are sacrificed by
the Boeotians, who crown them like human victims
and, after sprinkling them with meal, offer prayers
over them.

The Boeotians were proverbially stupid; but the

Freshwater Fishing

Egyptians went even further in their adoration of the eel. To them it was sacred – apropos of which, Antiphanes makes an ironic comparison between the value of a god and the exorbitant prices paid for an eel in Athens:

They say that the Egyptians are clever in that they rank the eel equal to a god; but in reality it is held in esteem and value far higher than gods, for them we can propitiate with a prayer or two, while to get even a smell of an eel at Athens we have to spend 12 drachmae or more!

To the Athenians, a dish of eels was the greatest of all delicacies. There was simply nothing to touch it. As one of them lamented: 'When you are dead, you cannot then eat eels!'

But for all these panegyrics, no one knew where the eels came from or how they bred. The supply of eels seemed inexhaustible – and yet, no eel had ever been observed to spawn.

This is not surprising for, as we know to-day, the European eel does not originate in European waters. Together with its close relative the American eel, it breeds thousands of miles away in the depths of the Sargasso Sea, outside the Gulf of Mexico.

From the Sargasso Sea, the eel larva starts off in the springtime as a tiny leaf-shaped creature called a leptocephalus, which drifts north-eastwards with the Gulf Stream. Three years later it turns up on our shores as an elver, or miniature eel: a slender creature about three inches long.

Practically no piece of freshwater is without its complement of eels, and each year a new stock arrives. During April and May the elvers enter our estuaries in vast numbers and make their way up towards their destinations in river, stream, lake, pond and mere. From then on, the eel lives in freshwater until, finally, it returns to sea.

That, very briefly, is the life-story of the eel. But until the present century little of this was known, and the riddle of the eel's breeding-cycle was the subject of continuous debate. From Aristotle onwards, pretty well every zoologist and fishing writer produced a theory. Aristotle himself records the first really important observation:

Some fish leave the sea to go to the pool and rivers. The eel, on the contrary, leaves them to go down to the sea.

But as eels had never been found with ova or milt inside them, and were seemingly lacking in generative organs, he thought they came from inside the earth:

They form spontaneously. In mud.

Oppian, on the other hand, thought that little eels came from eel slime:

Eels are not to be hindered by mechanical difficulties; and it is amusing to trace the means to which they have recourse in passing over barriers that might seem inaccessible to their efforts. It was at a time when a moderate but rapid stream had from dry weather become a small cascade, that the only way of ascent was up the declivity of a perpendicular rock, from which on one side hung some moss and herbage into the water below. When these Eels in succession came to this place they moved about rapidly near where the stream fell down from above, and presently disappeared; when looking more closely it was seen that on one side of the projecting rock they had crept among the fibres of the moss that hung downward, and were moving upwards with wriggling motion, like worms . . .

It was amusing to observe that it would sometimes happen that a head would be thrust out into the current, where observation shewed that it ran by too strong to be encountered, and then it was withdrawn to seek a more favourable spot; while others venturing thus too far were washed down the current, and had the labour to go over again. On one occasion while watching this continued succession of Eels, a Flounder made two attempts to stem this downward current, but these efforts were without success.

Jonathan Couch,
A History of British Fishes (1862–65)

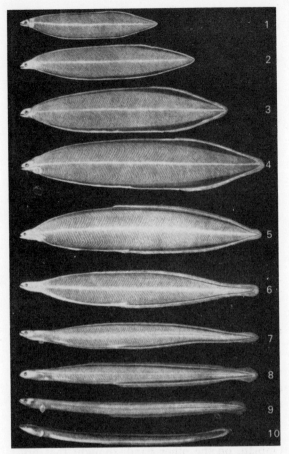

Strange the formation of the eely race,
That knows no sex, yet loves the close embrace.
Their folded lengths they round each other
   twine,
Twist amorous knots, and slimy bodies join;
Till the close strife brings off a frothy juice,
The seed that must the wriggling kind produce.
That genial bed impregnates all the heap,
And little eelets soon begin to creep.

In Pliny's opinion eels were sexless – being neither male nor female:

They have no other mode of procreation than by rubbing themselves against rocks – and their scrapings come to life.

Other thinkers attributed the birth of eels to the dew of May mornings; the hair of horses; the gills of fishes, and to various forms of 'spontaneous generation'. Izaak Walton summed it up in *The Compleat Angler*:

Most men differ about their breeding. Some say they are bred by generation as other fish do; and others, that they breed as some worms do, of mud, as rats and mice, and many other living creatures, by the sun's heat, or out of the putrefaction of the earth, and divers other ways. And others say, that eels growing old breed other eels out of the corruption of their own age. And others say that as pearls are made of glutinous dew drops, which are condensed by the sun's heat, so eels are bred of a particular dew, falling in the months of May or June on the banks of some particular ponds or rivers – adapted by nature for that end – which in a few days are by the sun's heat turned into eels: and some of the ancients have called the eels that are thus bred, the offspring of Jove.

Figure 69: The development of the European eel (after Murray and Hjørt). 1–5 The leaf-shaped *leptocephali* increasing in size during their long journey eastwards across the Atlantic. 6–8 Stages in metamorphosis from *leptocephalus* to glass-eel. 9 Glass-eel. 10 Elver

A poor naturalist, whatever his charm as a writer, old Izaak fell into the common trap of drawing false conclusions from data equally false:

But that eels may be bred as some worms, and some kinds of bees and wasps are, either of dew, or out of the corruption of the earth, seems to be made probable by the barnacles and the young goslings bred by the sun's heat, and the rotten planks of an old ship and hatched of trees.

It is known today that there is only one species of European eel: *Anguilla anguilla*. But its change of shape and colouring – notably the change

from yellow belly to silver belly which takes place shortly before its return to sea – led early observers to believe that there were several different species. And so, error was heaped on error. As Izaak Walton explained, each of these supposedly different species was thought to breed in a different way:

Let me tell you that some curious searchers into the nature of fish observe that there be several kinds of eels, as the silver eel, and green or greenish eel, with which the river of Thames abounds . . . and a blackish eel, whose head is more flat and bigger than ordinary eels: and also an eel whose fins are reddish – These several kinds of eels are, say some, diversely bred, as namely: out of the corruption of the earth, and some by dew and other ways . . . and yet it is affirmed by some for a certain, that the silver eel is bred not by spawning as other fish do, but that her brood come alive from her, being then little live eels no bigger nor longer than a pin: and I have had too many testimonies of this to doubt the truth of it myself, and if I thought it needful I might prove it, but I think it needless.

Izaak's belief in the spontaneous generation of silver eels is hardly surprising in an age when the study of natural history rested on such shaky foundations. Consider his views on the pro-creation of pike:

'Tis not to be doubted, but that they are bred of a weed called Pickerel Weed, unless learned Gesner is much mistaken, for he says: this weed and other glutinous matter with the help of the sun's heat in some particular months, do become pikes.

A century or so later, we were little further forward. In *The Fisherman: or The Art of Angling made Easy*, Guiniad Charfy* observed:

* Charfy was a pseudonym. The book was compiled by George Smeeton, printer, of St Martin's Lane, London, and published by J. Dixwell *c.* 1800. The second edition was published by J. Smeeton *c.* 1815. It is a verbatim appropriation of *The Complete Fisherman*, written by James Saunders and published in 1724.

Figure 70: Alan Dart's 8 lb 10 oz eel caught on dace deadbait in Hunstrete Lake, Gloucestershire, 1969 *Angling Times*

Others dispute their generation, and tell us they are produced not by any spawn, or ova, but by the slime of the earth, impregnated by the heat of the sun; so that they will have them to be only an invigorated corruption and putrefaction. These and many other nasty notions these squeamish people have about eels, in order to help their stomachs to loathe them, or at least to justify a pretended aversion to them.

But, after all, the eel, let him be engendered how he may, it is a very good, rich, nourishing and wholesome fish, when well digested, but is not so proper for weak and indisposed stomachs. They distinguish them into several sorts, but we generally know more than two, namely, the Silver Eel, and the Black Eel; and these seem to be of no specific difference in kind, only as the water is less clear or muddy in which they are nourished. The eel has this property that although they breed in rivers, yet as they grow bigger, those of them that remove and go down the stream never attempt to go back again, and those that reach into the sea, never return, but continue there till they die, or till they grow to an extraordinary size, and are then called Congers.

That Congers were simply overgrown freshwater eels was a common belief at the time. But reference to the seaward movement of eels recalls Izaak Walton's brilliant non sequitur:

It is said that eels that are bred in rivers that relate to the sea, return to the fresh water when once they have tasted the salt water; and I do the more easily believe this, because I am certain that powdered beef is a most excellent bait to catch an eel.*

Gradually, as the years went by, a little light began to dawn. The Rev. W. Richardson, writing in 1793, was of the opinion that eels descending a river went down to the sea to breed. Of the Cumberland Derwent, he remarks: 'The young eels come up the river in April, in size about the thickness of a common knitting needle.'

He was right. But naturalists in this country were lagging far behind those on the Continent. That adult eels disappeared into the sea, and young eels came out of it had been noted in Italy a century earlier by Francesco Redi, a gentleman of Tuscany:

I can affirm, following my long observations, that each year with the first August rains, and by night when it is dark and cloudy, the eels begin to descend from the lakes and rivers in compact groups towards the sea. Here, the female lays her eggs from which, after a variable time depending on the rigours of the sea, hatch elvers or young eels, which then ascend the fresh waters by way of the estuaries.

This very important and accurate piece of original observation was published in Italy in 1684. But in this country, as late as 1862, in the *Origin of the Silver Eel* – a work based on 'observations extending over 60 years' – we find Mr D. Cairncross blithely asserting:

The progenitor of the silver eel is a small beetle. Of this, I feel fully satisfied in my own mind, from a rigid and extensive comparison of its structure and habits with those of other insects.

Even the famous Frank Buckland, in his *Familiar History of British Fishes*, writes:

There are three or four distinct species of the freshwater eel inhabiting this country. It is, strictly speaking, a fresh-water fish, and undoubtedly remains all the year in ponds, and breeds there; but when following its natural instinct, it migrates towards the sea in autumn and lives in the brackish waters at the mouths of rivers.

On the subject of breeding he seems rather confused, for he also says:

The old eels run down the rivers in the autumn and deposit their ova. It is a disputed point whether the parent eels ever return up rivers. My own opinion is that they do.

Referring to elvers, he says:

Some argue that they are the spawn of the Conger. This is, of course, ridiculous. There can be no doubt that they are the young of fresh-water eels – I should think these little fish to be about a week or ten days old.

Well, he was about three years out. Regarding the birth of eels, he records a remarkable observation:

The roe of the eel is exceedingly minute, and is often taken to be simply fat. I once, and once only, found some young eels hatching out; this was on the rocks near the entrance of the harbour at Guernsey.

---

* 'Powdered' beef was beef cured with powdered salt. Perhaps it was the salty flavour that Izaak thought the eels found irresistible!

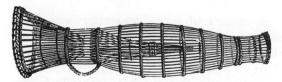

Figure 71: A Wicker Eel Trap, advertised in Farlow's catalogue of 1930, 'The bait – worms, fresh or saltwater mussels with the shells crushed, small fish and many kinds of offal e.g. rabbit guts – is put in at the small end of the basket which is then closed with the cap provided, and the trap covered with sacking. The bait may be enclosed in a special receptacle of woven or perforated material, and should be changed frequently. The basket can be weighted with a brick or piece of iron and should have a stout cord attached for recovery and placed in the stream where the eels are known to run. The large inverted neck of the basket prevents any eels secured escaping from the trap.'

Figure 72: Modern fish and eel trap, 3 ft. 9 in. × 12 in. (16 in. diameter at mouth of funnel). It is held open by stout locking struts, but can be collapsed flat for carrying

Buckland's little eels were almost certainly parasitic worms. The first recorded capture of an immature eel, before it had reached the elver stage, was made by a German scientist in the Straits of Messina in 1856. But, not realizing that the strange leaf-like little creature he had found was a young eel, he named it *Leptocephalus brevirostris* – or Short-snouted thinhead.

That this *Leptocephalus brevirostris* was in fact the larva of the eel was discovered by two Italian scientists in 1896. But it was not until some years later that the eels' spawning ground in the Sargasso Sea was located – a classic piece of research carried out by a young Danish marine biologist, Johannes Schmidt, who published his findings in 1921.

Figure 73: Eel bucks on Magpie Island from *Fishing* (1904) '... Most eels are caught on a *rising water*, on a falling very few indeed. A dark, quiet night is the best, and if it is the first freshet after a long drought in September and October, the quantity taken at times is very large indeed.'

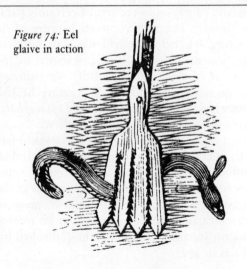

Figure 74: Eel glaive in action

There is also a practice adopted for killing eels ... that of spearing for them ... and this is so extensively practised, that when the rushes grow up, there is a regular flotilla of spearmen. A man stands on his bundle, poking before him with his long-handled spear. When he takes an eel, he bites its head between his teeth, and then strings it up with a needle on a long cord. Anything so hideous as the appearance of these fellows, their faces begrimed with blood and dirt, can hardly be imagined.

O'Gorman, *The Practice of Angling* Vol. 1 (1845)

Figure 75: Eel spears (or 'glaives')

By means of intensive netting with fine-meshed nets in the North Atlantic, and examining haul after haul, he was able to draw up a chart showing that the *leptocephali* that he caught became progressively smaller and smaller in size as he approached the Sargasso Sea – where he found the smallest larvae of all. It is from this far-off Atlantic birthplace that the tiny eels set off with the Gulf Stream on their three-year eastward drift, during the latter stages of which occurs the metamorphosis from *leptocephalus* to elver. The elvers reach our shores in the late spring and early summer. Then comes the determined thrust into river and stream as millions of little eels fight their way up towards the freshwater destinations where they will spend their lives.

St. John, in his *Wild Sports of the Highlands* (1846), writes of elvers running up the Findhorn:

I was much interested one day in May in watching the thousands of small eels which were making their way up the river. It was some distance from the mouth, and where the stream, confined by a narrow rocky channel, ran with great strength. Nevertheless, these little eels persevered in swimming against the stream. When they came to a fall, where they could not possibly ascend, they wriggled out of the water, and gliding along the rock close to the edge where the stone was constantly wet from the splashing and spray of the fall, they made their way up till they got above the difficulty and then again slipping into the water, they continued their course.

For several hours there was a continued succession of these little fish going up in the same way; and for more than a week, the same thing was to be seen every day. The perseverance they displayed was very great, for frequently, although washed back several times, an eel would always continue its efforts till it managed to ascend.

As the Polish biologist Opuszynski observed, nothing it seems can stop them:

Their urge to undertake this journey is unconquerable. They are not deterred by any obstacle such as sluice or waterfall. They have been seen mounting a vertical wall. Even the bodies of the elvers which die in doing so and adhere to the wall, serve as a kind of rung for succeeding elvers.

Freshwater Fishing

Figure 76: A nineteeth-century illustration from *Sport with Gun and Rod* by A.M. Mayer (1883)

The illustration shows a North American variation of eel-spearing viz:

'In the early spring when the shallows of Eel Bay or other sheets of water of the same kind become free from ice, the water, not being deep, becomes warm much more quickly than elsewhere, and here the half-frozen fish congregate in great quantities. The professional fisherman in the bow of the boat holds a spear, in shape like a trident, but with an alternate sharp iron prong between each barbed shaft, the whole fixed upon a long, firm handle. Immediately upon seeing a fish, he darts this gig at him, fixing the barb so effectually in his victim that to strike is to capture him. The weapon used is called a jaw-spear, from its peculiar form, being a jaw-shaped piece of wood, with a sharp iron barb firmly fixed in the angle, against which the eels are forced and pinned fast until they are safely landed in the boat.'

From data recorded by Dr Winifred Frost at Windermere it transpires that the male eel stays in fresh water for seven to nine years, the female for ten to twelve years – although in one exceptional case, a stay of nineteen years has been recorded. Almost invariably the mature female eel is larger than the male. Female silver eels – that is, eels on the point of seaward migration – average about one pound, while the males average three to four ounces and very rarely exceed eighteen inches in length. Large eels are almost certainly females.* The British rod-caught record stands at 11 lb 2 oz – although many larger eels caught by other methods have been recorded.

Richardson mentions eels upwards of 9 lb from Ullswater, and John Watson, in his *English Lake District Fisheries* (1899), refers to a 9 lb eel from Windermere. Buckland lists one of $8\frac{3}{4}$ lb from the pond of Dutford Mill, and another of 9 lb from the River Arun. And there are stories of a huge eel captured in the River Kennet. On the subject of a 36 lb eel taken from the River Ouse near Denver Sluice, Buckland says:

The man who secured it left for Cambridge with his prize, and obtained upwards of three pounds by showing it. I cannot help thinking this eel must have been a Conger.

* In very few other British species is the mature male smaller than the female. One exception is the pike (*Esox lucius*). Pike spawn while moving forward and are known to adopt an eye-to-eye orientation during the spawning act (see *Pike*, F. Buller, 1971). It is interesting to consider the possibility that this disparity in size of eels may indicate that the eel, too, is a mobile spawner.

Figure 77: Roy Shaw landing a good-sized eel

And he was surely right. He also has a droll account of a large eel taken from the Serpentine when the lake was cleaned out in 1869:

It was a fine specimen, and weighed over 6 lb. A cast of it is now in my museum. This eel was served up for dinner by my assistant, who stuffed it. It made the whole family ill for some hours.

After their long years in fresh water, the eels return to sea. In preparation for this migration, the snouts of both sexes become more pointed; the eyes enlarge; the back darkens and the belly changes from yellow to silver. Then, on some (usually) stormy night, the European eels begin to nose their way seawards towards their distant spawning ground.

At least, they go to sea; this much is certain. But little more is known. As Leon Bertin says in his biological study of the eel, published in 1956:

The eels virtually disappear once they have reached the sea, and we are almost completely in the dark concerning the tremendous journey of many thousands of miles which they accomplish in their passage to the Sargasso Sea.

Do they, in fact, ever reach the Sargasso? It has been suggested that the European eel is not equipped for such a journey, and that European stocks derive from the American eel, which might provide larvae for both American and European waters. But recent research by an American group of biologists from Wisconsin, using differences in mitochondrial DNA* proves that this is not the case. Although no-one knows whether American and European eel populations

* DNA (Diribo Nucleic Acid) is the 'blueprint' for all life processes. Most DNA is in the nucleus of each cell, but a small amount is in the mitochondria – tiny structures in the cell cytoplasm, which are mainly concerned with energy production in the cell. It turns out that an individual mitochondria DNA (m.DNA) is inherited from the mother.

share geographically separate breeding areas in the Sargasso Sea, it is now certain that the European eels *do* make the journey to the breeding grounds.

The eel's migrational body changes take about six months to complete, and their journey seawards begins during late summer and autumn. But migrating eels seldom move down river if there is a glimmer of light. They are creatures of darkness, tending to travel only on cloudy nights, usually when the river is rising. As Buckland observed:

The darker and stormier the night, the greater the exodus.

And nearly a hundred years earlier, referring to silver eels descending from Ullswater, Richardson noted:

Immense quantities of silver eels are taken in August, September and October, in nets at Eel-Stank, about half-a-mile down the River Eamont. In five or six hours, eight or ten horse loads have been caught; but such large quantities only on the darkest and stormiest nights. The largest eels commonly go last; some have weighed upwards of 9 lb. It is worthy of remark that they scarcely stir if the moon peeps out, or when there is lightning; the fishermen even think the light of a candle prevents their motion.

Not so far-fetched as it may seem, that candle-light. Hanging a piece of glowing turf over the gap while they emptied their nets in the darkness, was an old Irish eel-fishermen's dodge to prevent eels running past before the nets had been reset.

Figure 78: Head of a big silver eel *Roy Shaw*

Whether migrating eels ever wriggle overland during any stage of their journey from fresh water to the sea has been the subject of much controversy. Buckland writes:

There is no doubt indeed that eels occasionally quit the water and travel during the night over the moist meadows.

But some people are sceptical. Reliable eye-witness accounts are few, and very little evidence is available. Of great interest, therefore, is the following description written by an experienced angler and naturalist well known to H. F. who, while trout fishing one evening, witnessed an extraordinary overland migration of silver eels to the River Petterill near the village of Greystoke in Cumbria; a movement made all the more remarkable by the fact that it happened in bright moonlight:

It was a warm, damp autumn evening with a low mist over the river.

The sky was clear, with a full moon and very few clouds. The river was at normal height. Between 11 p.m. and midnight, while walking from one part of the river to another, I saw a moving, shimmering mass in the moonlight.

As I approached this mass I saw that it was a stream of silver eels, none of which was more than about a foot long. They kept moving steadily forward through the long wet meadow grass and were not halted by my walking among them; in fact, several of them passed over my waders. I followed them to the river and saw them dropping into the water from a steep bank about four feet high. The movement lasted for perhaps five minutes and must have involved several hundred eels.

Three very interesting points emerge from this account. First, the *size* of the eels. None was more than about a foot long – which indicates a mass migration of *males*. Secondly, the moonlight. That eels should move at all on a bright moonlit night – let alone overland – is remarkable. And thirdly, the quantity of eels involved.

Joscelyn Lane, in *Lake and Loch Fishing for Trout* (1955), also gives an excellent first-hand account:

Apparently there is still some difference of opinion among anglers as to whether eels can travel overland

From *The Chronicles of the Houghton Fishing Club*, 13 July 1849*

This evening four eels were seen at the edge of a weed, taking small gnats on the surface of the water.

(F. B. writes: 'I once witnessed a similar happening on the River Test below Romsey one hot late summer afternoon. The eels were rising very close to the bank in water twelve to eighteen inches deep.')

From *The Chronicles of the Houghton Fishing Club*, 1894*

A curious eel, spotted all over with yellow, was taken and sent to Dr Gunther of the British Museum, who pronounced it to be a semi-albino; adding: 'Perfect albinoes, of which I have seen numerous specimens, are uniformly lemon – or orange-yellow'.

*Published in 1908 by Sir Herbert Maxwell

when migrating or are restricted to following streams and rivulets. As luck would have it, I once came upon quite a large colony of eels just about to set out on their trans-Atlantic trek. I was in a car at the time on my way to Ichenor for a day's sailing in the estuary. There had been a few showers, and not far from the town the car was held up by a wide column of eels crossing the road. I got out to investigate and found they were coming along a deep ditch on the right-hand side of the road from a spot about twenty yards higher up, where they could be seen wriggling through the grass of an adjoining field on their way down to the ditch. On returning to the car I found that the eels were still crossing the road and streaming along the bottom of a ditch on the opposite side for some thirty yards, where I lost sight of them as the ditch diverged from the road. By the time I got back to the car again the tail of the procession had passed. There was no water in either of these ditches, along which several hundreds of eels must have travelled while I was there. Unfortunately I was not well acquainted with the countryside, nor, much to my regret, had I time to discover the source of the migration.

These extremely valuable eye-witness accounts affirm not only that migrating silver eels can travel overland, but that they will do so together in large numbers – sometimes even in bright moonlight!

There is no biological reason why the eel *shouldn't* move overland if it wishes. In water, three-fifths of an eel's oxygen uptake is through the skin. The carbon dioxide excretion in water is mainly through the gills; but in air, ten-elevenths of this excretion is through the skin. Experiments have shown that at a temperature of about 64°F (16°C), an eel out of water can take up as much oxygen when its mouth and gill openings are closed as when they are open and the gills able to function. Thus in damp conditions, such as long, dew-wet grass, with a temperature of around 64°F, an eel by breathing through its skin can stay alive out of water for a considerable time. As Bertin remarks:

There are pools which do not communicate directly or indirectly with any river. What happens to the silver eels of these pools? In the first place, they do all try to go. It is then that they are seen wandering at night in the damp meadows, profiting by their resistance to asphyxiation and desiccation.

Altogether, a very remarkable animal, the eel, and worthy of the angler's respect.

Finally, in the words of Izaak Walton:

Gesner quotes Venerable Bede to say that in England there is an island called Ely, by reason of the innumerable number of eels that breed in it.

On the subject of which, that seventeenth-century cleric, Thomas Fuller, observed:

It is said that when the priests of this part of the country would still retain their wives in spite of what Pope and Monks could do to the contrary, their wives and children were miraculously turned into eels. I consider it a lie.

Never mind what he considered. Next time you see an eel, reflect that what you are looking at is a creature whose fantastic life-cycle remained for centuries an unsolved riddle that is still not fully solved even today; a creature for whom the Greeks beggared themselves, and the Sybarites escaped their taxes; a tonic for the voice; a panacea; a Boeotian sacrifice; an Egyptian god. And perhaps, even, the descendant of some incontinent priest!

EEL FISHING

Bobbing or babbing for eels is pictured and described in the introduction. Guiniad Charfy mentions these early eighteenth-century methods of hooking them:

Catholic in his tastes, the eel may be caught with divers baits, namely, powdered Beef, Garden Worms, or Lobs, Minnows, Hen's or Chicken's Guts, Fish Garbage, etc., but their best bait is a small kind of Lamprey, called a Pride.... The Ledger Bait and Lying on the Grabble are the Methods chiefly in use in angling for these fish. He bites best in a fall of rain, in windy or gloomy weather and after a thunderstorm.

Charfy's 'Ledger Bait' was very different from what is known as ledgering today (see page 442). Of passing interest, however, is his description of Lying on the Grabble:

Figure 79: This eel met its death when it choked on a water vole. The vole's right leg can be seen poking out of one of the eel's gills. The proprietor of the Lamb and Flag Inn at Welney had no knowledge of the provenance of the photograph when he showed it to F.B. in 1974, but the 'locals' felt sure that the eel was found dead on the banks of the adjoining waterway – the Delph

Above the hook a cut Shot is to be fixed ... and next to this a small bored Bullet; thus the bullet will be prevented from slipping, and the hook Link have liberty to play in the water.

A recognizable outline of one of our modern ledgering techniques. After observing that eels 'are generally catched at Night' and 'seldom stir in the daytime unless by force', he mentions a method of bringing them out in daylight by 'mud-raking'. This, of course, works as well today as it did in the eighteenth century – or indeed as it did over two thousand years ago, when Aristophanes' sausage-seller outbawled Cleon:

Yes, it is with you as with the eel-catchers; when the lake is still, they do not take anything, but if they stir up the mud, they do. So it is with you, when you disturb the State.

To all this we have very little to add. For catching eels, float, ledger and even fly tackle (at night) can be used successfully. And boiled shrimp is an excellent bait.

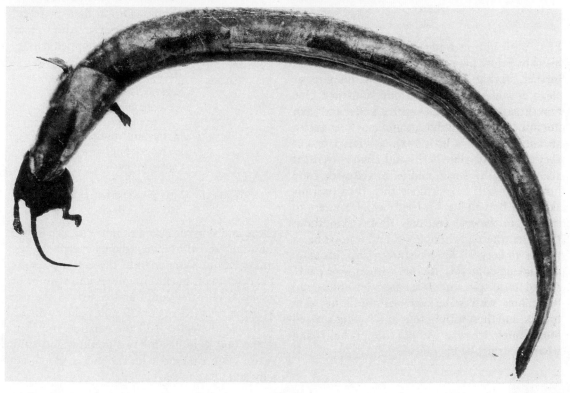

HOW TO HANDLE
AND SKIN AN EEL

What fisshe is slipperer than an ele?
Ffor whan thow hym grippist and wenest
    wele
Too haue hym siker right as the list,
Than faylist thou off hym, he is owte of
    thy fyst . . .

Piers of Fulham, Manuscript poem (c. 1400)

An eel will live for a long time out of water and if it is to be killed this should be done as quickly and humanely as possible. But to jab with a knife at a wriggling eel frequently results in injury to the angler. The eel should be stunned before any attempt is made to kill it.

With the grip shown in the picture, hold the eel with three fingers. This is the only grip that will overcome the eel's sliminess. If you happen to have some sand or a dry newspaper handy, roll the eel in it first: contact with dry sand or paper makes an eel more quiescent.

To stun an eel, hold it as shown and strike its tail (the portion just downwards of the vent) hard against a rock; or hit it with your priest.

Kill the eel by severing the vertebrae in the neck. If you wish to skin the eel, *don't cut off its head*. A headless eel is more difficult to skin.

Cooking the Eel

ROAST EEL

From Izaak Walton, *The Compleat Angler*

Sweet herbs
Anchovy
Nutmeg
Butter
Salt

First wash him in water and salt; then pull off his skin below his vent or navel, and not much further; having done that, take out his guts as clean as you can, but wash him not; then give him three or four scotches with a knife; and then put into his belly and those scotches, sweet herbs, an anchovy, and a little nutmeg grated or cut very small; and your herbs and anchovies must also be cut very small, and be mixed with good butter and salt: having done this, then pull his skin over him all but his head, which you are to cut off, to the end you may tie his skin about that part where his head grew, and it must be so tied as to keep all his moisture within his skin: and having done this, tie him with tape or packthread to a spit, and roast him leisurely, and baste him with water and salt until his skin breaks, and then with butter: and having roasted him enough, let what was put into his belly, and what his drips, be his sauce.

GRILLED EEL

Flour or breadcrumbs
Tomato sauce
Lemon slices
Chopped parsley

Cut the eel into chunks. Dip in flour or breadcrumbs, and grill or fry. Serve with tomato sauce, or with lemon slices and chopped parsley.

JELLIED EEL

Several 2 lb eels
1 large onion
1 bay leaf
1 tablespoonful vinegar
2 oz gelatine
1 sprig of parsley
2 pints of cold water
Whites of 2 eggs plus crushed egg shells
Salt and pepper

Clean and skin the eels. Put into a saucepan with the water and all the ingredients except the eggs and gelatine. Simmer until the eels are tender. Take out the fish, cut into pieces and remove the bones. Strain the liquid and return to the pan. Add the crushed egg shells and lightly whisked whites of the eggs. Add the gelatine and bring to the boil. Simmer for two minutes and strain again. Line a mould with the pieces of eel, add jelly and leave to set.

Figure 80: Four stages in skinning an eel

1. Clench the live eel firmly under the middle finger. Stun it by striking it by the tail. Sever the neck vertebrae: *do not* cut off the head

2. Tie a string round the neck of the eel and fasten to a nail. Using a razor blade or very sharp knife slice the skin right round the neck. Be careful not to cut too far into the neck. *Note*: A cotton work-glove is useful for handling eels

3. Grasp the edge of the cut skin with a pair of pliers and pull the skin right off over the tail

4. Skinned eel with skin held alongside

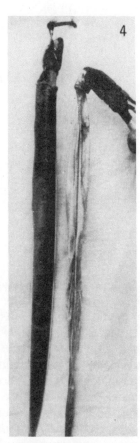

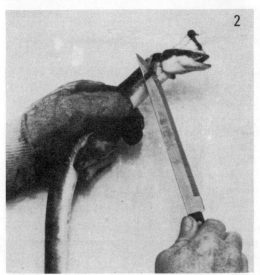

Figure 81: Referring to our description of skinning an eel in the first edition of *Falkus & Buller's Freshwater Fishing*, Fred Buller's friend, William Blake of Totnes, wrote to him, 'Incidentally, I skin an eel by simply pushing a small meat (game-size) hook through its head and hooking it onto the cold-water tap! It is less trouble than tying around the head with a string and moreover there is a constant stream of cold water. The rest of the operation I do as you describe. In my young days country people used the skins as boot-laces. "Never break," they said.' Here is a photograph of one of Mr Blake's boot-laces

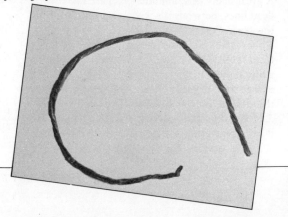

The
FLOUNDER
Platichthys flesus

The flounder, or fluke, flourishes in brackish water, its denser populations being found in estuaries and that noted sea of low salinity, the Baltic. Since it is the only European flatfish capable of living for a time in freshwater, the identity of any flatfish caught in rivers or lakes is never in doubt. It can, indeed, totally adapt to freshwater. In 1934, after the dyke enclosing the Dutch Zuider Zee was completed, land-locked flounders acclimatized to the gradual desalination and now breed in what has become a freshwater lake: Yesselmeer.

Linnaeus suggested that the name 'flounder' probably derives from the Swedish 'fludra' – a reference to its manner of swimming very close to the bottom. It certainly feeds at ground level – on tiny worms, shellfish and crustaceans found in estuary mudflats and shared with shelducks, oystercatchers, redshanks, dunlins and other waders: *Nereis diversi-colour*, *Hydrobia ulvae*, *Macoma baltica* and *Corophium volutator*.

For a species that does not usually breed in freshwater, some flounders migrate surprisingly long distances up-river and are frequently caught by anglers ledgering for other species. This movement from the sea into freshwater takes place in early summer; the fish returning to sea in autumn. Spawning takes place between February and June in depths of fifteen to thirty fathoms.

The flounder is commonly greyish-olive in colour, occasionally mottled with brown, but it can vary from nearly yellow (sand colour) to almost black (mud). Small orange spots similar

---

A great many eels, flounders etc, are taken with dead lines, between Blackwall and Old Ford, in the several creeks round Bromley, West-Ham, Abbey-Mills and Stratford, where the tide flows from the River Thames ... Loop the hooks on a line about a foot apart; close to every hook put a large shot, or piece of lead, to keep the bait on the ground, as every hook must lie at the bottom. ... Flounders and Eels seldom take a bait unless it lies on the ground: the best bait is a red worm. ... It is astonishing how great a number of

Flounders are caught by this method of fishing ... particularly from an hour after high water till the tide is quite run out; you may begin to use dead lines in April, and meet sport until November.

T. F. Salter, *The Angler's Guide* – Or Complete London Angler, Containing the Whole Art of Angling As Practised in The River Thames and Lea. And Other Waters Twenty Miles Round London, Founded on Actual Experience: With the Art of Trolling For Jack or Pike (1814) ('I write from experience, not from books arrange.')

to those on the plaice are sometimes present. As Tate Regan says:

Like most flatfish the Flounder is able to change colour according to the nature of the ground, and the resemblance to the sand, gravel or mud on which it lies is so perfect that it is almost impossible to see the fish unless it moves.

Commenting on this in his book *A History of British Fishes*, Yarrel thought it: '... a beautiful instance of the design employed for the preservation of species'.

Although the flounder is not so highly esteemed as a table fish as the plaice (*Pleuronecteo platessa*) or that other delicious little inshore flatfish the dab (*Limanda limanda*), it certainly equals them as a sportfish. It grows to a length of twenty inches and six pounds in weight and can be caught on rod-and-line, mainly in river estuaries. The present British record, taken off Fowey, Cornwall, in 1956 by A. G. L. Cobbledick, weighed 5 lb 11½ oz.

Common angling methods are paternostering and ledgering with, say, 12 lb BS line and leads of not more than 2 oz. But the flounder responds well to a baited spoon fished on float tackle. This ingenious method, popularized by the late P. Garrard in *Sea Angling with Baited Spoon* (1960), exploits the adult flounder's greedy response to a tiny flatfish swimming past trailing a worm too big to swallow!

The rig consists of two swivels separately linked to a split-ring to which a 2½ in. spoon is also attached. the mainline is connected to the front swivel; a ragworm-baited hook to the other swivel with a 5 in. nylon link that allows the bait to trail about 3 inches behind the spoon, which is painted white to simulate the underside of a flatfish. It is usually fished in shallow water from a boat, with a lightish spinning rod. We recommend the use of a 'float-link' rig, page 449.

Figure 82: This flounder is either poised to strike at a food morsel or about to dart forward leaving behind a characteristic sand cloud

Figure 83: Richard Walker with a flounder caught twelve miles from the sea while he was fishing with F. B. in Loch Lomond. In 1965, F. B. caught several flounders twenty-five miles from saltwater when roach-fishing the Tweed at Sprouston. H. F. has seen them in the Tweed even further upstream – just below the cauld at Kelso. Three examples from our own experience of the surprising distances flounders sometimes travel upriver when there are no major obstructions

Drifting with the tide and casting across and up-current seems to induce most takes, but slow trailing upstream, or shore-casting from jetties or breakwaters is also effective.

The first mention of a baited-spoon technique was in *Sea Fishing* (1934), edited by A. E. Cooper, of which chapter thirty-two entitled 'The Flounder' was contributed by Garrard. In it he described bait and spoon fishing, stating that it had been used for several years.

H. F. writes: 'It had indeed. In 1925, as a small boy, I caught flounders on a bare fly-spoon while fishing with my father in an Essex creek. Subsequently, using light float-tackle, we landed many flatties and bass on spoons baited with ragworm or soft crab – a very sporting and successful method, which we greatly enjoyed. (Cf. *The Stolen Years*, Witherby, 1965.)'

Figure 84: Flounder in sand. Only eyes and branchial openings are visible

Figure 85: Flounder's resting place uncovered at low tide. Redshank prints nearby

Cooking the Flounder

These big flat fish are, according to Mrs Beeton, when sufficiently large, very good grilled for breakfast on a gridiron in front of the fire with a little butter rubbed over. Small plaice are good when cooked in the same manner or under a hot griller. Flounders may also be dipped in beaten egg, then in seasoned breadcrumbs and fried in hot fat, then dished on a folded napkin with fried parsley. They may, alternatively, be poached gently for about 5 minutes in salted water to which a little vinegar has been added; if boiled fast they will break. They should be served with a good fish sauce. (From Sheila Hutchins, *English Recipes and Others* (1969))

Figure 86: Postures adopted by flounder as it makes a feeding hole and sorts its food from the mud

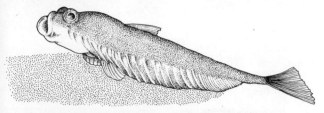

1. Supported by its fins, the fish shuffles across a stretch of tidal flats on the hunt for food

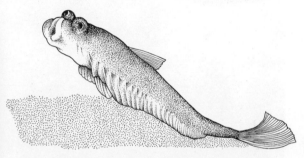

2. At a chosen spot it tilts sharply upwards

3. Then, arching its body, it sucks in a mouthful of mud

4. The food items in the mouthful are extracted by the flounder's gill rakers and the sifted mud blown out through the lower branchial aperture. After which the fish moves on towards another snack, leaving a trail of feeding holes behind it

---

The Flounder

Freshwater Fishing

This recipe, originally by Mrs Glasse, was much copied in other eighteenth-century cookery books:

Line a well-buttered pie-dish with thinly rolled puff pastry and prick the bottom with a fork to prevent it from rising. Then lay lumps of butter all over it. Poach your fish in salted water till tender, keep this cooking water, while skinning and boning the fish, seasoning this with salt and pepper to your mind.

Boil the fish bones, heads and skins in the water the fish was cooked in, with some parsley, a small piece of horseradish and the thinly pared rind of half a lemon, and a crust of bread. Boil the fish liquor to reduce it until there is just enough for the pie. Then strain it through a sieve on to the fish and butter. Cover the whole with a lid of thinly rolled puff pastry. Pinch the sides together to seal it well. Brush the pastry with egg or milk. Bake for about 35 minutes in a pre-heated hot oven (400°F *Mark* 6) for the first 15 minutes to raise the pastry, then reduce the heat to moderate (350°F *Mark* 4) for the remaining cooking time. (From Sheila Hutchins, *English Recipes and Others* (1969))

FLOUNDERS
From Mrs Beeton's *Family Cookery* (1963)

3–4 flounders
½ carrot
½ turnip
1 slice parsnip
Water *or* fish stock
1 small onion
1 small bunch herbs
6 peppercorns
Salt parsley

Cut the carrot, turnip and parsnip into very fine strips and cook till tender in slightly salted water or fish stock. Trim the fish and place in a deep saute-pan, with the onion cut up in slices, the bunch of herbs and peppercorns. Add a little salt and pour on sufficient water to cover the fish well. Bring to the boil and cook gently for about 10 min. Lift out the fish and place in a deep entrée dish, sprinkle over the shredded cooked vegetables and some finely chopped parsley, add a little of the fish liquor and serve.
3–4 helpings.

The
GRAYLING

Thymallus thymallus

The long, brownish dorsal fin is beautifully marked with stripes of darker hue. The adipose fin is velvety in texture. The head and back are deep purple, while the sides are a riot of purple, blue and copper, with here and there a tinge of pink and palest blue.... Trout may be called handsome – grayling are beautiful fish.

E. Marshall-Hardy. *Coarse Fish* (1943)

The grayling, like its cousins the trout and salmon, belongs to the Salmonoidei, a sub-order of fishes that have existed since the beginning of the Eocene period 70 million years ago. Of the seven characteristics that distinguish Salmonoid fishes from other groups of fishes, two are familiar to anglers: the adipose fin and pyloric caeca – worm-like appendages attached to the gut. The characteristic that distinguishes the grayling from all other Salmonoids is the possession of a large, dappled, sail-like dorsal fin.

The grayling has a wide distribution in the rivers of Britain and Northern Europe principally because of its introduction to waters where previously it never existed. Prior to widespread introduction it was confined to a few east-flowing rivers. It does not occur in Ireland.

In the upper reaches of most clean and unpolluted rivers, where water turbulence and high rate of fall are typical features, the trout reigns supreme. Conversely, in the middle reaches of slower rivers and where glides, shallows and deeps alternate, the grayling seem to have a decided advantage over the trout. Provided there

is an abundant weed growth, the middle reaches are also favoured by chub and dace, although these fishes extend even farther downstream than the grayling.

Not surprisingly, where the habitats of several species overlap, some species will suffer due to competition for food and spawning areas. A probable explanation for the separate niches enjoyed by the trout and the grayling lies in the different spawning techniques. Trout eggs are buried in gravel by the parent fish and are thus protected from the force of the current, whereas grayling eggs are merely 'dropped' on the gravel bottom and in consequence would be more likely to be swept away by the currents of headwater streams.

In Britain, grayling rarely attain a weight of 4 lb, although grayling of twice this weight have been recorded from northern Scandinavia. The British record rod-caught grayling (4 lb 9 oz) was caught in 1883 by Dr T. Sanctuary on the River Wylye. Other large grayling include a 4 lb 4 oz fish from the River Itchen and three more, each over 4 lb, taken from the River Test in 1905. A

Figure 88: Grayling, 2 lb 9 oz, taken from the River Test on shotlink ledger by F. B.

fine bag of heavy grayling – 15 weighing 30 lb – was taken by H. J. Mordaunt, also from the River Test. Other big-grayling rivers include: Itchen, Hampshire Avon, Driffield Beck, Driffield Canal, Chess, Kennet and Dove.

The grayling's large dorsal fin, reminiscent of the fin of the sailfish, is used in a unique way. At spawning time – usually May or June – the cock fish wraps his fin over the back of the hen. This behaviour stimulates the hen grayling to oviposit while keeping the cockfish 'on station' or, in scientific language, 'properly orientated', so that its milt is accurately deposited.

The grayling's eye is different from that of any other native fish, its pupil being pear-shaped. Writers have suggested that this may account for the grayling's curious behaviour when it rises to take a fly at the surface. During a hatch, trout and most other surface-feeding fish either feed in shallow water or, if in deep water, 'keep station' a few inches below the surface. Not the grayling. It keeps station near the bottom, rises almost perpendicularly to take a fly and then returns to its lie with the celerity of a dive-bomber.

There is yet another facet of the grayling's behaviour; when hooked it often gyrates like a propeller. This manoeuvre does nothing to inspire an angler's confidence. He knows from experience that any but a well-hooked fish will quickly regain its freedom.

Figure 89: (*above*) In March and April the grayling of the Driffield Canal congregate on the spawning shallows

Figure 91: (*below*) Material from the spawning site, sand, fine gravel and snail shells

Figure 90: In as little as six inches of water the males, who are mostly larger, and noticeably darker than the females, perform their courtship ceremonies and shepherd the ripe females into position. Pairs of competing males frequently clash in a flurry of spray. Shaw says: 'At times several battles are enacted simultaneously and large dorsals cleave the water side by side'

Figure 92: (above) Clouds of gravel fly as a female (darkest of the three) cuts a redd in the gravel, and two males fertilize the eggs

Figure 93: (right) Although grayling frequently share a habitat with trout they occupy a different niche, and although it is often said that grayling flourish to the detriment of trout, it is sometimes forgotten that trout can sometimes flourish to the detriment of grayling. As the grayling's eggs are dropped a brown trout moves in to take them

It had a deceptive because only superficial likeness to a pool in another river that I happened to know very well. As a result I started to fish it at the wrong place and so scared grayling instead of catching them.

As I moved off with only half or less than half the grayling I ought to have taken from that pool, I knew that I had failed and badly failed to meet the true test of a fisherman, which is, that he shall be able to catch his share of fish in water that he is fishing for the first time.

Arthur Ransome, *Rod and Line* (1929)

One of the pleasantest ways to catch a grayling is with the artificial fly. Trout fly-fishing pundits argue amicably about which is the most sporting technique. Fortunately, no purist dogma has attached itself to the grayling. A fisherman need feel no guilt in following his inclination to fish 'up' or 'down' with either wet or dry flies.

Fishing the cockspur worm on float tackle is the classic style of the Yorkshireman – who fishes happily in the knowledge that this method will interest fewer spawning or ill-conditioned trout than that of the maggot angler with his liberal dosings of maggot groundbait.

F. B., who has enjoyed grayling fishing for most of his life, obtains great pleasure when he 'works up' a swim with groundbait in the traditional style of the roach-fisherman. For this style of fishing – long-trotting – he fishes a single maggot, or sometimes two maggots, on a short-shanked, size 10, spade-end hook and prefers to use a 4-inch fluted float rather than the traditional grayling float.

He has found the shot link-ledger method excellent for covering swims that vary in depth and has taken his largest grayling on this rig – including three of over 2 lb (best 2 lb 9 oz), all from swims of the same character, six to eight feet deep and close to the bank.

Grayling are obliging fish: they seem to feed for a period even during the coldest weather, sometimes on days when the river seems dead where other species are concerned. In autumn they tend to form into shoals, and the best time for catching them is in the darkening.

Compared with the trout, which has received considerable attention from scientists, the grayling has been largely neglected. Roy Shaw, the Yorkshire naturalist, however, has done much to redress this, having spent a great deal of time observing and photographing the grayling's spawning behaviour. We are grateful to him for permission to reproduce the splendid pictures on the preceding pages.

Cooking the Grayling

The grayling, besides offering good sport for nine months of the year, is an excellent fish for the table. Indeed the flesh of the grayling, taken in season (it comes in with the pheasant in October), is more predictably good than that of the trout. Before cooking grayling it is advisable to remove the scales.

BAKED GRAYLING

1 grayling
Salt and pepper
Butter

Clean and wash the fish. Dry it well, place it in a baking dish in which a little butter has been previously melted. Season with salt and pepper, cover with a greased paper, and bake gently from 25 to 35 minutes, basting occasionally. Or wrap the fish in greaseproof paper and bake in a tin. (From J. P. Moreton & W. A. Hunter, *Fisherman's Manual* (1932))

GRILLED GRAYLING

1 grayling
Olive oil
Salt and pepper
Lemon

Anoint them with olive oil, season with salt and pepper and grill for seven to ten minutes. A squeeze of lemon will prove a pleasant addition when the fish is served. (From E. Marshall-Hardy, *Coarse Fish*)

The
GUDGEON
Gobio gobio

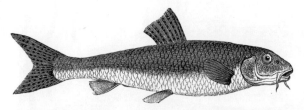

Gudgeon-fishing! . . . I maintain to be, *par excellence*,
the sport of the poet and the philosopher.

H. Cholmondeley-Pennell

The British record rod-caught gudgeon weighed 4 oz 4 dr. But in spite of its diminutive size, the 'toothsome morsel', as Dr J. J. Manley wrote, 'is well worth a Note all to himself'.

Since it feeds at ground the gudgeon lives close to the bottom and prefers a depth of from three to six feet in a stream just strong enough to keep a gravelly or sandy bottom lightly scoured. Although its natural habitat is running water, it sometimes flourishes and breeds when introduced into stillwaters.

For gudgeon fishing, a size 14 or 16 hook is tied on a $1\frac{1}{2}$–2 lb line, with a float big enough to support at least 4 BB shots. This will enable the leads to get the bait right down to the river bed at the *head* of the swim. The fishing depth should be adjusted so that the bait 'trips' along the

bottom. Given time, a gudgeon is capable of swallowing a sizeable worm, but a *small* bait – whether a pellet of paste, a pinch of bread, a maggot or a piece of worm – is more effective since it allows an immediate strike.

Experienced gudgeon anglers, realizing that gudgeon soon satisfy their appetites, do no groundbaiting. Instead, they disturb the gravel at the head of the swim with a huge rake. The gudgeon's exploitation of a newly raked swim can be compared to the seagull's exploitation of fresh plough.

Victorian and Edwardian professional Thames fishermen who took out gudgeon-fishing parties called this practice of raking, 'scratching their backs'. By these means, presumably, gudgeon were so easily caught that the *Oxford*

I shall mention the best places for Thames angling from London Bridge to Chelsea.

If the air is cold and raw, the wind high, the water rough, or if the weather is wet, it is totally useless to angle in the Thames.

The best places for pitching a boat for angling in the Thames, are about one hundred and fifty yards from York Stairs; the Savoy, Somerset House, Dorset Stairs, Black-Friars Stairs; the Dung-warf near Water-Lane, Trig Stairs and

Essex Stairs. On Surrey side, Falcon Stairs; Barge Houses; Cuper's vulgo Cupid Stairs; the Windmill and Lambeth.

At and about Windsor is a vast variety of all sorts of fish; but if a man be found angling in another's water, (without leave) he is fined very high by the court of that town, if he only catches a single gudgeon.

Thomas Best,
A Concise Treatise on the Art of Angling (1787)

Dictionary defines the gudgeon as 'A gullible person ... One that will swallow anything'. Jonathan Swift defined a (human) gudgeon as 'A person easily cheated and ensnared'. The poet John Gay went further:

> What gudgeons are we men,
> Every woman's easy prey!
> Though we've felt the hook, again
> We bite, and then betray.

Gudgeon fishing was once regarded as a social grace and some gallants even went so far as to claim that ladies made better gudgeon-fishers than men; their light touch, it was thought, fitted them for the delicate strike – the merest twist of the wrist – required to hook a gudgeon. Edmund Waller, however, was a realist. 'Beware of lady gudgeon-fishers', he warned:

> The Ladies angling in the chrystal lake,
> Feast on the waters with the prey they take;
> At once victorious, with their lines and eyes,
> They make the fishes and the men their prize.

Dr J. J. Manley, pointing out the dangers of taking women to the river bank, noted that 'Many a heart has been irretrievably lost when gudgeon fishing.'

Figure 94: The adult gudgeon is often mistaken for an immature barbel. This is surprising since the barbel can be recognized at a glance by its four barbules on lip and upper jaw. The gudgeon has only two – at the angle of the mouth. Research carried out on the River Mole by Stott, Elsdon and Johnson (1962), proved that some gudgeon possess a strong homing instinct. After a number of gudgeon had been transferred as far as one third of a mile upstream or downstream, over 50% of those recaptured had returned to the home range within two or three weeks

On the other hand, according to H. T. Sheringham, there was an occasion when gudgeon caused the irretrievable loss of a bride:

The Rev. George Harvest, of Thames Ditton, was one of the most absent men of his time; he was a lover of good eating, almost to gluttony; and was further remarkable as a great fisherman.... In his youth he was contracted to a daughter of the Bishop of London; but on his wedding day, being gudgeon fishing, 'he overstayed the canonical hour; and the lady, justly offended at his neglect, broke off the match'.

There is a calmness about the narrative which carries conviction. Is there anything more remarkable in the annals of gudgeon-fishing?

From *The Fishing Gazette* (10 April 1920)

Cooking the Gudgeon

'Let me say that, in my humble opinion, however mean a fish the gudgeon may be thought whereon to exercise the angler's skill, he is worthy of all commendation as a fish for the angler's table, and indeed the board of the most fastidious *gourmet*. There are few freshwater fish worth the salt with which they must be eaten, if eaten at all, but oesophagistically I am enthusiastic about our *Gobio fluviatilis*. The ancients highly prized it. Galen places it in a conspicuous position among edible fish, both for the delicacy and sweetness of its taste and its digestibility,' wrote J. J. Manley in *Fish and Fishing* (1877).

Figure 95: Strephon and Phyllis. After the engraving by J. R. Smith

Figure 96: (*below*) This engraving entitled 'Gudgeon Fishing, or He's Fairly Hook'd' by T. Wilson (1771) after a drawing by A. Walker is reproduced by courtesy of the executors of the late Mr Arthur Gilbey

The Gudgeon

Now this is another little fish that deserves better of anglers than he gets. True, he stays small – a two-ounce gudgeon is good, and three ounces is enormous – but he has a number of virtues. First, he will go on biting on the hottest day, when everything in the river seems to have called it a day and gone to sleep.... Secondly, the gudgeon is the most undemanding of fish – he will go on biting even when you are standing in the river with your feet in the middle of a shoal of him. Thirdly, he is delicious eating.... But it seems to have been forgotten, and you hear more curses than praise when an angler has happened to get among a mob of these drab-looking little fish. If only they would accept their luck, catch a panful, and try them fried in breadcrumbs, they might change their tune.

Maurice Wiggin,
Fishing for Beginners (1958)

In a gastronomic point of view, gobio gives precedence to none: a fry of fat gudgeon, eaten piping hot, with a squeeze of lemon-juice, is a dish 'to set before a king', and as superior to anything that Greenwich or Blackwall can produce, as Mouet's champagne is to gooseberry pop. John Williamson, gent, who seems to have had a keen eye to the good things of this life, commends the gudgeon 'for a fish of an excellent nourishment, easy of digestion, *and increasing good blood*'. Nay, even as a cure for desperate diseases, the gudgeon is not without his encomiasts; for Dr Brookes says, in his *History of Fishes*, that he 'is thought good for consumption, *and by many swallowed alive*'; though it is to be presumed that the fish so disposed of were not of the same size as the four from Uxbridge, to which the doctor refers, immediately afterwards as 'weighing a pound' each.

H. Cholmondeley-Pennell, *Fishing Gossip, or Stray Leaves from the Note-books of Several Anglers* (1866)

'The whole matter is one of extreme simplicity, just as boiling a potato, grilling a chop, or making melted butter; and hence, perhaps, the very general failure. To the wives of professional Thames fishermen it seems specially to have been given to master the art of cooking gudgeon successfully. The chief secret, as with the cooking of all coarse freshwater fish, is to allow the gudgeon, after being cleaned, to become dry and almost hard by exposure to sun and wind. The next important point is the quick and delicate manipulation to which he should be subjected in the frying-pan, as he becomes encrusted with egg and breadcrumbs; but a verbal description of this could not be given even by the most learned and versatile author of a most exhaustive cookery book. It is a question of fine and dexterous *touch*, and the operator could hardly say more of his performance than Dr Lynn says of his tricks, "And that's how it's done".'

The LAMPREYS

The Sea Lamprey (*Petromyzon marinus*)
The River Lamprey, or Lampern (*Lampetra fluviatilis*)
The Brook, or Planer's Lamprey (*Lampetra planeri*)

There are three species of lampreys. All spawn in freshwater, and all spend their first five to eight years in freshwater. During this period of their lives – when they are non-parasitic – they are called 'prides'.

Prides are blind, toothless, and bear little resemblance to their parents. As larvae they live in the mud or sand at the bottom of a pool somewhere downstream of the natal site, where they feed on organic matter and detritus.

When adult, all three species are jawless, eel-like fishes with round suctorial mouths. All spawn in gravelly streams or rivers, clearing a place in the gravel to deposit their eggs.

The strength of the lamprey's mouth is prodigious.

Both sexes unite in preparing the ground for spawning at the bottom of the river, by excavating a trench; and as in doing this it shall happen that stones of considerable size may be in the way, the mouth is employed in the labour of grasping and removing them.... A stone of the weight of two pounds has been known to be thus carried ... and on the authority of a fisherman that stones of even ten or twelve pounds have been turned over.

Thompson in his *Natural History of Ireland* (1849–56)

This behaviour is confirmed by the naturalist Sir William Jardine:

The manner in which the Common (sea) Lamprey and the Lamperns form their spawning beds is very curious. They are not furnished with an elongation of the jaw but the want is supplied by their sucker-like mouth, by which they individually remove each stone. Their power is immense.

All three species die shortly after spawning.

THE SEA LAMPREY

After its metamorphosis to its adult form – which takes place after six to eight years – it migrates to sea. Here it attacks a wide range of fishes, including cod, haddock, salmon and basking shark. Its powerful sucking apparatus causes death to the less robust species.

When the breadth of the open mouth is brought into contact with the surface of a fish on which the lamprey has laid hold, by producing a vacuum, these roughly-pointed teeth are brought forward in a manner to be able to act on it by a circular motion, and a limited space on the skin of the captive prey is thus rasped into a pulp and swallowed, so that a hole is made which may perhaps penetrate to the bones, and from the torture of which the utmost energy of exertion by the victim cannot deliver it.

Jonathan Couch, *A History of the Fishes of the British Islands*
(1862–65)

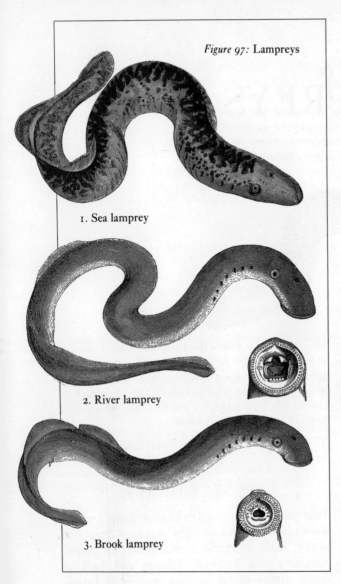

Figure 97: Lampreys

1. Sea lamprey

2. River lamprey

3. Brook lamprey

The eel may be caught with divers baits ... but their best bait is a small kind of Lamprey, called a Pride.

Guiniad Charfy, *The Fisherman*

4. Pride

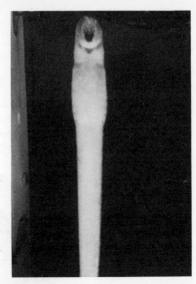

Figure 98: Recently spawned sea lamprey (3 lb) taken dead from the Cumbrian Esk

Sea lampreys grow to three feet in length and a weight of five or six pounds. After a sea life of one to two years they return to freshwater to spawn.

THE RIVER LAMPREY, OR LAMPERN

This species is smaller than the sea lamprey, reaching a maximum length of about twenty inches. The prides undergo a metamorphosis when they are about five inches long and then migrate to salt water. Although little is known about their marine life, it is thought that river lampreys do not move far out to sea. They stay in salt water for about a year, and are parasitic, feeding on the blood and body tissues of their hosts – mainly estuarine species.

According to Tate Regan, a number of river lampreys:

... reside permanently in freshwater, while the rest, like the sea lamprey, spend the greater part of their adult life in the sea and enter the rivers chiefly in order to spawn.

Loch Lomond swarms with river lampreys, which attack sea trout and powan. Perhaps in such a large stretch of water the lampreys use the loch as the 'sea', and its feeder streams as spawning rivers. Henry Lamond, one of Loch Lomond's greatest chroniclers and fishermen, found lampreys spawning in the lower reaches of the Luss Water. He also recorded the finding of lampreys on sea trout netted from the loch, but never on any netted from the River Leven (Loch Lomond's outflow) or in the Clyde estuary.

The late Andrew Colquhoun of Luss held an unusual record – the capture of a lamprey on a fly. Lamond quotes the incident in his book, *Loch Lomond* (1931):

In striking a rising sea-trout on one occasion, he missed the sea-trout but hooked and landed its attendant lamprey!

THE BROOK LAMPREY, OR PLANER'S LAMPREY

The brook lamprey differs in three respects from the others:

1. It spends its entire life in freshwater, usually in the headwaters of the stream.
2. It is non-parasitic, using its suctorial disc for holding on to stones.
3. The adult does not feed. It spawns in the year it matures.

The brook lamprey is seldom larger than eight inches in length. It is renowned as a hookbait for chub, perch, pike and eels.

With lovers 'twas of old the fashion
By presents to convey their passion:
No matter what the gift they sent,
The lady saw that love was meant.

Why then send lampreys? fie, for shame!
'Twill set a virgin's blood on flame.
This to fifteen a proper gift!
It might lend sixty-five a lift.

I know your maiden aunt will scold,
And think my present somewhat bold.
I see her lift her hands and eyes.

'What eat it, niece; eat Spanish flies!
Lamprey's a most immodest diet:
You'll neither wake nor sleep in quiet.

'The shepherdess, who lives on salad,
To cool her youth, controls her palate;
Should Dian's maids turn liqu'rish livers,
And of huge lampreys rob the rivers,
Then all beside each glade and visto,
You'd see nymphs lying like Calisto.

'The man who meant to heat your blood,
Needs not himself such vicious food –'

In this, I own, your aunt is clear,
I sent you what I well might spare:
For when I see you (without joking),
Your eyes, lips, breasts are so provoking,
They set my heart more cock-a-hoop,
Than could whole seas of craw-fish soup.

John Gay, 'To a Young Lady
with Some Lampreys' (*Poems*, 1720)

Figure 99: Lampern fishing at Teddington Lock, 1871

Severn, Trent and Thames were all valuable lampern fisheries. Fishing was mainly at night with nets and baskets. According to a Report of a Parliamentary Commission, a Victorian Thames fisherman caught a hundred and twenty thousand lamperns worth £400 during a single winter. It was from Teddington that Dutch fishermen bought lamperns to bait their long-lines for cod and turbot.

In his *Salmon Fishery report* (1878), Frank Buckland said of the Trent fishery:

A considerable trade exists on the Trent in the supply of lamperns, which are used as bait for the deep-sea fishermen, as many as 3,000 have been taken in one night at Newark.... The fish are sent alive in wicker baskets to Great Grimsby and other ports, but it is necessary that a man should go with them and keep stirring them all the time.

Figure 100: Lamprey and lampern from *The Book of the Thames* by Mr and Mrs S. C. Hall (Arthur Hall, Virtue and Co., 1859)

Cooking the Lamprey

The Lamprey is a sea fish.... It is reckoned a great delicacy either when potted or stewed, but is said to occasion surfeits; a fatal instance of this occurred to Henry I.

The Rev W. B. Daniel, *Rural Sports* (1801)

Here, for the curious, are two recipes:

BAKED LAMPREY

1 medium-sized lamprey
Suet farce
1 egg
Breadcrumbs
Fat for basting
Anchovy sauce, or any other fish sauce preferred
1 lemon
Butter
Salt

Rub the fish well with salt, wash it in warm water, and remove the cartilage and strings which run down the back. Fill the body with the prepared farce, sew it up securely, and fasten round two or three thicknesses of buttered or greased paper. Cover the fish with hot water, boil gently for 20 minutes, then drain and dry well. Put it into a baking dish in which a little butter or fat has been previously melted, and baste well. Bake gently for about half-an-hour, basting frequently, then strip off the skin, brush the fish over with beaten egg, and coat it lightly with breadcrumbs. Bake the fish for about ten minutes longer, or until nicely browned, then serve it garnished with sliced lemon, and send the sauce to table in a tureen.

STEWED LAMPREY

1 medium-sized lamprey
$\frac{3}{4}$ pint of stock or water
1 glass of port or sherry
1 oz of butter
1 oz of flour
1 lemon sliced
1 teaspoonful of lemon-juice
2 small onions sliced
2 or 3 mushrooms, or 6 button mushrooms
1 bay-leaf
Salt and pepper

Wash thoroughly in salted warm water, remove the head, tail and fins, and cut the fish across into two-inch lengths. Bring the stock or water to boiling point, put in the fish with the bay-leaf and necessary seasoning, and simmer gently for three-quarters of an hour. Meanwhile melt the butter in another saucepan, fry the onion slightly then add the flour, and fry slowly until well browned. When the fish has stewed one hour, pour the liquor from it over the prepared butter and flour, stir until boiling, then put in the mushrooms, wine and lemon-juice. Place the fish in the prepared sauce, simmer gently for half an hour longer, serve with the sauce strained over, and garnish with slices of lemon.

Slender his shape, his length a cubit ends;
No beauteous spot the gloomy race
    commends;
An Eel-like clinging kind of dusky looks;
His jaws display tenacious rows of hooks;
But in strange power the puny fish excels,
Beyond the boasted art of magic spells.

Oppian

The LOACHES

Cobitidae

The fish called Loches, and the other called Millers-
thumbes or Culles, they always feede in the bottome
of brookes, and rivers. They are fish holesome to be
eaten of feeble persons having an ague, or other sick-
nesse.

Leonard Mascall, *A Booke of Fishing with Hooke and Line* (1590)

Because loach are small fishes and because they are seldom fished for they are rarely featured in angling books or discussed in the angling press. Diminutive they may be but they do not deserve this neglect.

So sensitive are loach to changes in atmospheric pressure that by means of their restless behaviour (it is claimed) they can give up to 24 hours notice of an approaching thunderstorm. This sensitivity to atmospheric pressure – probably linked to changes in the amount of dissolved oxygen caused by changes in pressure – may be the key to the loach's behaviour, but it is not the whole story.

Uniquely in the physiology of British fishes, a loach uses its intestine as an auxilliary organ of respiration. Experiments have shown that when a loach dashes to the surface to take in a bubble of air (the air is swallowed, passed through the intestine and out through the anus) the air so taken is changed just as if it had been breathed.[1] Intestinal respiration has evolved in the loach to enable it to survive in stagnant pools, in over-warmed pools and even in nearly dried-up pools.[2]

The restless behaviour of loach was observed by the ancients; indeed the very name 'loach'

from the French 'loche' (Izaak Walton used this spelling) is derived from locher: to fidget. The ancients also averred that the loach 'seems always to be either spawning or in roe' so it acquired a reputation for its 'wondrous fecundity'. As one of Shakespeare's characters remarks: 'Your chimney lie breeds fleas like a loach.'

THE STONE LOACH
(*Cobitis barbatula*)

As its name implies, the stone loach is the one found (during daylight hours) hiding under stones. It has six barbules (two long and four short) or 'beards' as its specific name *barbatula* implies. It grows to a maximum length of about

[1] According to analysis the air contained less oxygen and more carbon dioxide.

[2] The frequency with which loach need to come to the surface to ingest air bubbles obviously varies with the amount of dissolved oxygen contained in the water. An experiment showed that in well oxygenated water at 41°F loach respired entirely by means of their gills, but when the temperature of the same water was raised to 50°F (thereby driving off some of the dissolved oxygen) the loach swallowed a single air bubble every 2 hours; at 59°F it swallowed 5 bubbles, at 70°F 10 bubbles, per hour.

5 inches or as Izaak Walton put it: 'groweth not to be above a finger long.'

The stone loach is nocturnal in habit, only leaving the shelter of stones or weed to forage after dark, which is why it is seldom caught on other than very dull days. Not surprisingly, therefore, loach are of small interest to the angler except as competitors with the young of other species for food, and as food for larger species. Mr R. Lawson, Fisheries Officer of the Piscatorial Society, who keeps records of the stomach contents of pike taken from a River Kennet trout fishery, found stones in the stomach of a $2\frac{1}{2}$lb pike together with unidentifiable fish remains. F. B. suggested that these remains were likely to be those of either a bullhead or a loach, since one would expect a pike to pick up occasional stones when attacking either of these bottom-haunting species. Strange to relate, the next pike examined had stones in its stomach – together with a stone loach!

In Ireland the stone loach (prior to c. 1810 a 'secret bait') was widely and successfully used on trailing rigs for the big lake trout (*Salmo ferox*). Victorian anglers were very enthusiastic about loach as bait. But as a changing economy forced many fishermen to catch their own loaches, trailing with loach bait died out.

The stone loach

THE SPINED LOACH
(*Cobitis taenia*)

Mainly inhabiting central and eastern counties of England in slow-flowing or stagnant water with a sandy or muddy bottom, the spined loach has two features that distinguish it from the stone loach: all six barbules are short and of equal length and its tail-fin is well-rounded (convex), whereas the stone loach has two long barbules and four short barbules as well as a tail-fin that is slightly concave. Adult spined loach grow to about $5\frac{1}{2}$ inches.

The spined loach is rarely observed because, unlike the stone loach, it prefers a deep-water habitat. The spines from which it takes its name are situated on each side of the head, just below the eye. By projecting these spines sideways and outwards, the loach can 'lock' itself in its burrow – a hole in silk weed, mud or sand, from which it seldom emerges except to feed. This locking device prevents larger fishes from sucking the loach from its lair.

The spined loach

The
MINNOW
Phoxinus phoxinus

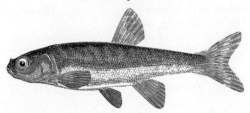

Shall remain!
Hear you this Triton of the minnows? Mark you
His absolute 'shall'?

Coriolanus

The minnow, typical of clean streams, rivers and occasionally lakes, is a member of the carp family: a slim, silvery, small-scaled fish, seldom exceeding four inches in length. The colour varies with the locality. Back and sides are usually olive green fading to yellow on the belly. The flanks are blotched with dark rounded markings that fuse into an irregular stripe.

With the exception of the Scottish Highlands and the extreme west of Ireland, it is distributed widely throughout Britain, Europe and eastwards through the USSR as far as the Amur River on the Chinese border.

Anglers view the minnow chiefly as a baitfish, since it features in the diet of (among others) pike, perch, chub, trout and eels, but it can be caught with fragments of worm or paste fished on tiny hooks.

Though so diminutive in size, the minnow may be compared, for the excellency of its taste, to some of the most famed fish. They are usually full of spawn all the summer, (for they breed often) during which time, particularly on hot days, they will very eagerly bite all day long, and afford great sport to youths and others that like to angle for them. You should have three or four very small hooks baited with the smallest red worm you can get, or a bit of one; and a small quill float.

Samuel Taylor, *Angling In All Its Branches* (1800)

The minnow spawns in shallow water on sand and gravel banks between the months of May and July, when the male fish becomes brilliantly coloured with white tubercules on its head. Spawning brings minnows together in vast shoals, making them easy prey to netsmen on the Continent, where the fish is still regarded as a delicacy.

Figure 102: The value of the minnow as a lure for trout is to some extent lessened by the difficulty of procuring them. In places and circumstances most favourable to their use, it is sometimes impossible to get them, and we have frequently found the capture of minnows much more difficult than the capture of the trout when we had got them. (From W. C. Stewart, *The Practical Angler* (1857))

(Roy Shaw)

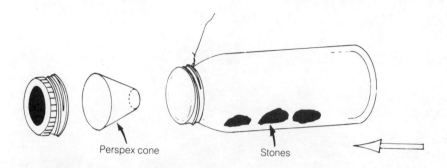

Perspex cone   Stones

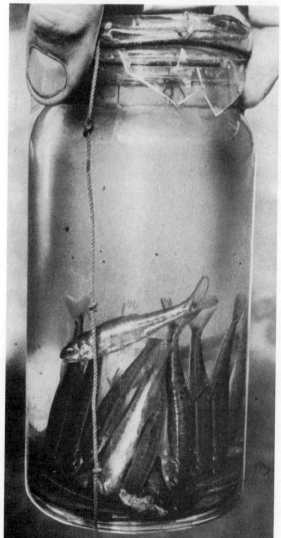

Figure 103: (*above*) Fit a transparent perspex or celluloid cone in the neck of a Kilner jar. Bait the trap with bread, add a few stones to weight the trap, fill with water and place on the bed of the stream, making sure that the entrance hole points down-stream

Figure 104: (*left*) Minnows taken in a Kilner trap. *Edwin Grant*/The Angler's Mail

Figure 105: (*below*) The wine-bottle trap. Make a cut below the apex in the bottom of a clear wine-bottle so as to leave a hole about an inch in diameter. Tie a piece of muslin over the neck of the bottle. The muslin allows easy filling of the bottle when it is placed in the water and provides a means of releasing captive minnows. Bait with pieces of bread and set the trap with the tapered entrance hole pointing downstream.

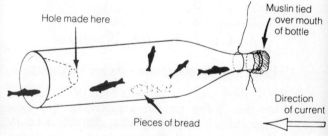

Hole made here

Muslin tied over mouth of bottle

Pieces of bread

Direction of current

16 June Coming back from Church caught a minnow with my hands. I ate minnow.

The Very Rev. Patrick Murray Smythe,
The Diary of an All-Round Angler

The Minnow

Figure 106: This picture of a tightly packed shoal of minnows was taken on the upper reaches of Yorkshire's River Hull. The shoal extended several yards along the river's edge, beyond which lay three pike of 10 lb or more (*Roy Shaw*)

Cooking the Minnow

Fried like whitebait, minnows are very tasty.

Toss them gently in seasoned flour, this is easier if the flour is first put into a paper bag. Fry them immediately in very hot oil or fat, a handful at a time. Drain on crumpled absorbent paper. Serve dusted with cayenne pepper and wedges of lemon, as well as slices of brown bread and butter.

(Old recipe)

On 16 September 1394, William of Wykeham, founder of Winchester College, gave a dinner for two hundred people including the King and Queen, 'feasting them with many kinds of fish together with seven gallons of minnows'. A Winchester tradition that seems to have been maintained . . .

When at Winchester, I used to pickle minnows with vinegar and spice, and keep them in pickle bottles. They were capital eating, especially when, as a 'junior', I was not over-fed and had to look out for what extra 'grub' I could get hold of.

Frank Buckland, *A Familiar History of British Fishes* (1873)

Izaak Walton favoured minnow-tansie:

Being washed well in salt, and their heads cut off, and their guts taken out and not washed after, they prove excellent for that use; that is, being fried with yolks of eggs, the flowers of cowslips, and of primroses, and a little tansie; thus used they make a dainty dish of meat.

The
GREY
MULLETS

Mugilidae

Thick-lipped (*Mugil labrosus*)
Thin-lipped (*Mugil capito*)

Apart from the rare 'golden' mullet, these are the species of grey mullet (in no way related to the red mullet) found in North Western Europe. They are mainly estuarine fish, moving in and out with the tide, often penetrating well upriver into freshwater in summer and autumn, seemingly migrating offshore to hibernate in deeper, warmer water during winter and (in British waters) spawning in spring.

The two species are readily distinguished by the thickness of the upper lip: very swollen and wide in the case of the thick-lipped mullet; thin and narrow in the thin-lipped. Food consists mainly of diatoms and algae, but small crustaceans and gasteropod molluscs are also taken by the bigger fish, which can attain a weight of over 10 lb.

A fine sporting fish, the mullet can be caught in the brackish estuarine water and lower freshwater reaches of many rivers and is particularly suited to the tackle and technique of the coarse-fish angler. The thin-lipped variety has a greater tolerance of freshwater than the thick-lipped, but is far less common in Britain, being found almost entirely on the south coast along the Sussex, Hampshire, Dorset and West Country coastline. It can be hooked on maggots or ragworm, and good catches have been recorded on ragworm-baited, fast rotating, red-bodied spoons. The 2 gm Jenspin is said to be the best.

Thick-lipped mullet are notoriously difficult to hook. Years ago, H. F. had some success in estuarine water with roach-type tackle and tiny hooks baited with tail of ragworm, minuscule cubes of bacon fat, banana or breadcrust, fished sometimes deep but more often near to the surface (see figure 107).

Note: The bow-wave of mullet cruising through the shallows and swirling as they come in with the tide, is well known to most anglers who fish

The mullet, or grey mullet, is popular on account of its fine fighting qualities and its excellence as a dish. But he is not so easy to capture as whitebait. . . . Like so many other fish, the mullet prefers southern waters, and is a very wary fish, being highly suspicious of the angler's bait, for the sudden appearance and even existence of which the average mullet sees no plausible reason.

Alan d'Egville, *Calling all Sea-Fishers* (1950)

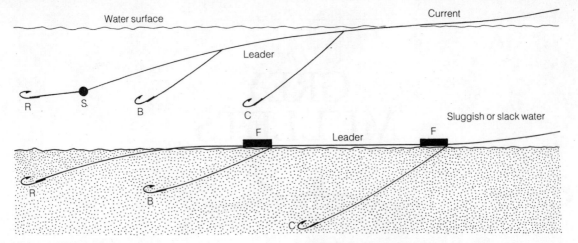

Figure 107: H. F.'s mullet rig

Leader: 10–12 ft of 2–4 lb BS monofilament

Hooks: Size 18–20

Baits:
R   Tail of ragworm
B   Bacon fat or banana
C   Breadcrust
S: Split-shot
F: Tiny floats. Pieces of matchstick or slivers of cork

In anything of a current one or more split-shots will be needed to keep the baits an inch or two beneath the surface. In sluggish water no weight is used. The leader is greased save for the last foot or two and the droppers, with tiny floats positioned to keep the dropper baits near the surface (the tail bait can be allowed to fish deeper). The line is twitched from time to time to give the baits slight movement.

When bank fishing – preferably from a promontory or jetty – a long roach-type rod is necessary. Boat fishing is much easier; a shorter rod can be used and the baits allowed to drift well away downstream.

Whatever his location, the angler must be neither seen nor heard. Mullet are extremely shy and *a stealthy approach is essential*.

Figure 108: Thick-lipped mullet   Thin-lipped mullet

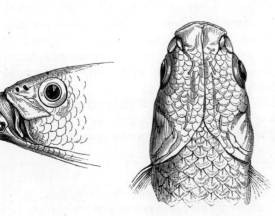

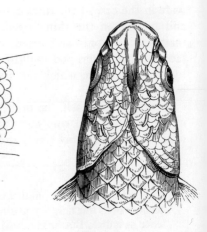

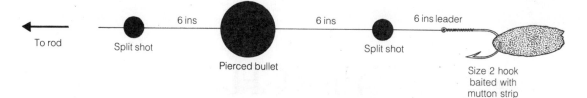

Figure 109: Falkland Islands bolt rig for mullet. Mullet to 50 lb are caught from the shore on rod and line by Falkland Islanders using the 'Bolt Rig'. When hooked, a mullet goes to ground and clings to the bottom. To save time, the islander cuts his line, ties it to a stake (which is driven in for that purpose) and returns to collect both line and stranded fish at low tide. Meanwhile, he ties on a replacement rig and continues fishing. After a number of fish have been hooked and recovered, the various lengths of line need to be rejoined. Three-inch ends are left on the knots to help them run more freely. A mullet fisherman's line can be heard 'singing' when he casts, as these knot-ends ping out through the rod rings.

in river estuaries. In this they resemble and are often confused with incoming sea trout. Indeed, they have been dubbed 'the fool's sea trout', for many a fly has been cast over them unsuccessfully by anglers making this mistake!

Cooking the Mullet

However they are cooked, mullet are excellent eating. The following recipes are recommended:

At Penzance, grey mullet after being scaled are divided in the middle, just covered with cold water and softly boiled with the addition of branches of parsley, pepper and salt, until the flesh of the back parts easily from the bone. Clotted cream, minced parsley and lemon juice are then added to the sauce, and the mullet are dished with the heads and tails laid even to the thick parts of the back where the fish were cut asunder.

Eliza Acton, *Modern Cookery for Private Families* (1845)

GREY MULLET – POACHED AND BAKED

Poach in salted water and serve with a sauce suitable for salmon, trout or turbot.

Small mullet are cooked *à la meunière* and grilled (US broiled). They may also be put on a baking dish, seasoned with salt and pepper, sprinkled with oil, coated with breadcrumbs and cooked in the oven.

Before cooking, make one or two incisions in the back of the fish. Serve with *maître d'hôtel* or anchovy butter or bearnaise or remoulde sauce.

GREY MULLET ROE (*Boutargue de mulet*)

This is much appreciated by the Italians. The roe is cut into slices as thinly as possible and sprinkled with olive oil and lemon juice. In season, fresh figs are served with it.

The nutritive properties of botargo are almost identical with those of caviar.

Auguste Escoffier, *Ma Cuisine* (1934)

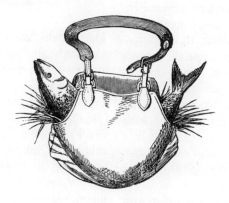

The
PERCH
Perca fluviatilis

Note the strong prickly dorsal spines. As many a young
angler has learnt through painful experience, the proper
way to hold a perch is to stroke back these dorsal spines
with one hand before securing the fish with the other.
From T. F. Salter, *The Angler's Guide* (8th edition, 1833)

The perch is widely distributed across the northern temperate parts of Asia and Europe, although absent from northern Scotland, northern Scandinavia, Spain and southern Italy. It spawns in April or May; the female laying her spawn on strands of weed or on sunken objects such as tree branches or roots.

Unlike most other European freshwater fishes it can survive in a body of water containing no other species of fish. Nikolsky, in *The Ecology of Fishes* (1963), states that adult perch, although not able to sustain themselves by feeding directly on plankton, nevertheless live at its expense by feeding on their own plankton-eating young. This habit is thought to explain those populations of stunted perch that exist in various lakes. When one season's crop of perch survives in great abundance, it can dominate as a year-class for up to fifteen years (see pages 25–26 for a discussion of the same phenomenon with regard to bream populations).

Perch are usually found in shoals of the same age group, the males outnumbering the females by ratios of up to 9 to 1.

A bold biter, the perch has been popular with generations of anglers; many a novice has been grateful for its attention when other species proved more reticent.

This was the fish of my childhood – and I suspect yours – this was the fish I began on, the first fish I ever caught. Perhaps it is the first fish to all men, perhaps all men get the same thrill as I do whenever I see a perch, perhaps their minds go back as mine does to that first day, that first tremendous thrill as the float bobbed and I pulled hard and there on the hook kicked a striped green fish with a silver tummy and red fins.

Brian Vesey-Fitzgerald, *The Hampshire Avon* (1950)

The perch bait *par excellence* is the worm. Although all species of worms will tempt a hungry perch, the two largest British species, the lobworm and the blue-headed lobworm (see page 427), are best for large perch. In *Rural Sports* (1801), the Rev. W. B. Daniel suggests using '... small lobworms which have no knot'. But this is simply the famous 'maiden lob' of early angling literature: in reality an immature lobworm – neither male nor female, since worms are hermaphrodites, having both male and female

Freshwater Fishing

reproductive organs. Live minnows and gudgeon are also excellent baits for perch.

Although Pennant lists an 8 lb perch from the Serpentine (Daniel records 9 lb for the same fish) and mentions another 8-pounder taken from Dagenham Breach, and Colonel Thornton describes the catching of a 7 lb 3 oz Loch Lomond perch, a 2-pounder represents a handsome catch for most anglers. A 3-pounder is considered a very good fish, whereas a 4-pounder is the peak of most anglers' expectations. In Britain, few anglers have landed a perch over 5 lb.

There are two angling methods that, although not exclusive to perch fishing, are distinctly associated with it:

1. Sink-and-draw, used with worm bait.
2. Paternoster, baited with worm or minnow.

Both methods display the bait a foot or so off the bottom, which is where the perch normally expects to dine.

In winter, particularly, big perch haunt the proximity of underwater ridges, or any place where there is a sudden discontinuity of depth; such places providing suitable cover for the sudden pounce which is characteristic of the hunting perch.

Spinning is a good method of taking perch but suffers from one drawback: the need to use a fairly heavy mainline and a wire leader in case

---

Perch like noise, and are fond of music, which attracts them to the surface. One of my sons (now I hope happy) assured me that he saw a vast shoal of them appear over water, attracted by the sound of bag-pipes when a Scotch regiment were marching over a neighbouring bridge, and that they remained there until the sound died away in the distance.

How much superior the ear of perch to that of Paganini, who, on hearing the Scotch pipe, prostrated himself on the floor, declaring that it must have been invented by the devil.

O'Gorman, *The Practice of Angling* Vol. 2 (1845)

---

a pike should be hooked. Unless wire is used, a pike is likely to bite through the nylon monofilament line and escape with a spinner in its mouth.

The perch prefers a bait that is spinning evenly rather than wobbling. The most deadly spinner is made with a mother-of-pearl spinning blade.

Perch will take an artificial fly or lure, retrieved with the same irregular jerk – or sink-and-draw action – used for mackerel 'feathering'. This sink-and-draw action can also be applied to a spinning bait, often proving effective after a perch has followed a bait without taking it. In these circumstances the spinner is allowed to sink close to the bottom, given a jerk and then let fall again. If this is repeated, the perch may finally be provoked into taking.

Figure 110: The photograph on the left shows a perch fossil from the Likhvinsk inter-glacial deposits and the one on the right shows a modern perch. These photographs are reproduced by permission of Professor G. V. Nikolsky of Moscow University

Figure 111: This fine picture of a perch about to be netted as four boat occupants look on, entitled 'A Party Angling', was published in 1789; after a mezzotint by G. Mordland, engraved by G. Keating. (Reproduction by courtesy of Walter T. Spencer)

Using this method, F. B. once hooked three 2-pound Hampshire Avon perch that previously had refused his fly-spoon after following it close into the bank.

Perch are free takers, but even so the loss of one hooked fish back to the shoal usually heralds the end of sport for a time so far as that particular shoal is concerned. J. H. R. Bazley, England's finest-ever match fisherman, suggests that the fear communicated by a broken-free perch to the rest of the shoal is one of panic, which causes a 'stampede', and is not to be confused with an awareness or suspicion of the angler's presence:

Immediately the fish is hooked, the others follow it about. When the hook comes away, the fortunate fish swims off full tilt – goodness knows where – and the others dovetail behind it, so that when the next bait is dropped in, there are no perch to take it. Sometimes a perch which has regained its liberty does not dash away any great distance, but after a swim round, comes back to the original spot, when the fish bite just as freely as if they had received no warning of what might be in store for them.

Every so often one hears about a fishing experience which, in retrospect, assumes a dream-like quality. An example is the following account of an astonishing season with giant perch, for which we are most grateful to Gerry Hughes, sometime features editor of *The Angler's Mail*:

When the perch fishing in our club pit really hit peak form it was 'fantastic'. In the course of one short season Brazier's Pit, an old gravel site near Nazeing in Essex, roughly an acre in size, produced at least six perch of over 4 lb, and three-pounders by the score.

The pit was square in shape, with tall trees overhanging one bank. The other three sides were bordered by hedges. The water was up to about ten feet in depth, going to 16 feet in places. When the club first took it over, a few years prior to this wonderful season, it was thought to hold very few fish, and since it looked right for carp, several hundred were put in.

We knew nothing about the stock of perch until the opening of the season. Then, within a few weeks, some hairy stories began to circulate.

Knowing how rumours build up, particularly over the size of fish, I ignored them for a couple of weeks. Then came an accidental meeting with another club member, who told of an astonishing experience the previous Sunday. He was watching a fellow angler playing a big perch, when, a few yards from the bank, the fish suddenly stopped coming in. Through the clear water he saw what appeared to be *two* perch on the end of the line, one holding the other by the tail. Eventually the bigger fish released its hold and the perch that had taken the minnow livebait was netted – it weighed $2\frac{3}{4}$ lb!

That story convinced me that I should investigate immediately. The most successful bait, it seemed, was live minnow, or a bunch of minnows, fished on float tackle. I hadn't time to catch any on my first visit, so had to make do with lobworms. When I got to the water, soon after dawn, I found at least 20 other members already there. When the sun came up the perch fed ravenously on their minnow baits. Most of the fish caught were round the 1 lb mark or under; but at midday word got round that a big one had been caught by a teenager fishing under the overhanging trees on the far bank, and with the sun now blazing down and the perch ignoring my lobworm I wandered round to have a look.

Yes, said the lad, he had caught a big perch several hours before. It had taken two minnows floatfished, just a few yards from the bank, at a spot where the water was deepest. Then he pulled up his keepnet and showed me the most impressive fish I have ever seen in my life.

Its spiky dorsal was raised like the crest on an angry dragon, its eyes were like marbles and it had a mouth like a small bucket. Weighed on a set of accurate scales it went 4 lb 10 oz and it made every big fish I had ever seen look like small fry.

With shaking hands I went back to my rod but very little was caught during that hot, sultry afternoon. Then, just before sunset something else happened that made me tremble as I watched.

As the air temperature dropped, shoals of bleak slashed on the surface, chased by some very large perch. The perch were so determined to get their evening meal that on occasion huge dorsals, and mouths like teacups came clear of the water.

On my next visit I stopped at the river – only half a mile from the pit – and caught a dozen bleak. These were hastily transported in a canvas bucket and transferred to my keepnet, once I arrived. Only four survived the journey but I knew I was in with a better chance than on my previous visit.

I tackled up with a large balsa-bodied Avon trotting-float, liphooked a big bleak on a size 6 spade-end, and with other anglers arriving in steady numbers, cast out as far as I could to avoid bankside disturbance.

Just five minutes later the float vanished. It didn't wobble or dip, it just vanished, and line poured off the spool of my reel, which had been left with the bale arm open.

I took a deep breath, lifted the rod from the rests, closed the pickup and struck. There was a mighty plunge on the end of the line. The perch made several strong rushes out in the depths and then began to give ground. I brought it in close enough to see its

Figure 112: 4 lb perch caught by R. Weston of Bletchley, Bucks, on 4 lb line and size 12 hook. At time of going to press this fine perch is a record for Wilstone Reservoir

dim, shadowy shape when everything went slack, and I reeled in an empty hook.

An hour later, with a fresh bait in the same spot, the float vanished again. It went down so fast you could almost hear the 'pop'. Once more I had the perch within a few yards of the bank when the hook came away. One of the bleak had died in the keepnet so I put the sole survivor on the hook and cast out again. 'This time,' I thought, 'I'll give the perch plenty of time before striking.'

The next bite was just like the other two. Down went the float with line pouring off the spool. This time I counted to ten, then picked up the rod, and struck. There was a violent plunging at the other end and I really bent the rod into that fish.

But it seemed that the bleak I was using were a shade too big for the perch to manage comfortably. This time I got the bait back – without a scale left on it. It must have lodged across the perch's mouth.

Two days later I had a phone call saying that a 4 lb 6 oz perch had been taken on a fly spoon, so I was there again the following weekend. I took along a friend, John Piper, who was keen on perch fishing, and gave him the swim where I'd had the three stupendous runs on the previous Sunday.

Thinking I would try for either perch or carp, I baited up with a very big lobworm, and dropped an Arlesey-bomb ledger rig on to a gravel bar that rose to within five feet of the surface about twenty feet out. As I put the rod on its rests, with the bale arm of the reel still open, I noticed that line was still trickling over the lip of the spool. Then the rod tip bounced and the trickle of line became a rush.

I struck immediately and my first thought was that I was into a carp. The fish ran to my left, changed its mind and doubled back, circled round and kited in towards the bank down to my right. There matters came to a halt for lying upside down in the water was a large thorn bush, presumably uprooted from the hedge the previous winter. It made safe sanctuary for whatever was on the end of my 4 lb line.

I put the rod back in the rest and opened the bale arm hoping that if left to its own devices the carp would swim out again. Ten minutes later it hadn't budged so I wandered along to John Piper. I asked if he would give me some assistance. 'It's a small carp,' I said as I explained the situation.

But it wasn't. When we got back I closed the bale arm, lifted the rod and there, just below the surface, was a huge perch, my worm hanging from the corner of its jaw. Miraculously it had untangled itself from the underwater branches and within a minute or two it was safely in the landing net.

Piper, a very experienced angler, was speechless. By far the biggest perch he had ever seen, and certainly the biggest I had ever caught. 4 lb 5 oz – the fish of a lifetime.

I remember little else about that day. In the evening, the bleak shoals fled for their lives once again as the big perch chased them, but I don't think I caught another fish.

Figure 113: F. B. found this beautiful engraving of two perch in an old scrap book inscribed 'Gilliat Hatfield 1881'. It would appear that J. W. Warren made the engraving from an original painting or drawing by A. Cooper R.A. It was published by R. Ackermann for the proprietors of the *New Sporting Magazine* in 1833

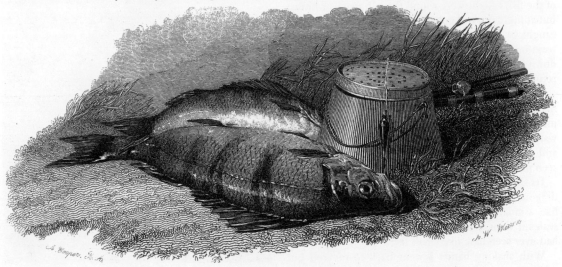

Freshwater Fishing

Two weeks later another friend of mine 'twitched' a lobworm slowly along the bottom, close by the bankside and landed a perch of 4 lb 6 oz. Before the season ended several more were reported and there were whispers of others, their captors preferring to keep quiet.

Sadly, the fishing went down after that. We must have caught it at its very peak. The following year the size of the fish fell off rapidly and the year after that sport was almost non-existent, except with carp.

We had just that one astonishing season. But I shall never forget it. I'll never see perch fishing like it again.

Figure 115: The engraving of the perch opposite depicts an early livebait can (*c.* 1830). The two bait-cans in this picture are older still – possibly late eighteenth century or early nineteenth century. These antique cans belonged to the late J. Milbourn of Carlisle and were photographed by the authors in 1972. Close inspection reveals that the 1830s can had a handle like the later nineteenth-century bait-cans, whereas the earlier cans were carried by means of a shoulder strap and were profiled to fit the waist. The change from sling-carried bait-cans to hand-carried cans may be reflected in the use of the term bait-kettle, rather than bait-can, since kettles have handles

Figure 114: Hanningfield Reservoir perch (two-pounders) taken on fly by Peter Thomas and F. B.

Figure 116: Nineteenth-century bait-cans

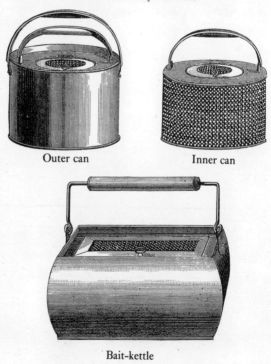

Outer can

Inner can

Bait-kettle

The Perch

Figure 117: Four-pound perch are a rarity in Britain but not so in Sweden. This one, caught by Arne Broman on a lobworm, weighed 4lb 4oz (*Jan Eggers*)

Figure 118: A shoal of perch. (*Seaphot Service*)

Cooking the Perch

AT THE LAKESIDE
Perch
Butter
Salt and pepper

Take each perch separately, merely wiping him dry – not cutting or scraping him in the least, as that would break the skin and let out his juices; then take a piece of paper, and wet it in the lake and roll the perch in it, in three or four folds. Screw up the ends and thrust perch, paper and all, into the embers. In five to ten minutes your fish is cooked. Rake him out; take off the charred paper, and carefully remove his scales which will come off *en masse*; rub the white succulent side with butter, pepper and salt to taste; make an incision along the backbone and flake off all the firm white flesh; turn the carcass over and serve the other side of the fish in the same way; throw away the bones and interior and eat the remainder. It is a dish for a king, or an angler. A salmon or big trout may be filleted and served in the same way, or roasted upon skewers. (From Francis Francis, *A Month in the West* (1886))

FRIED PERCH
4 perch
Eggs
Breadcrumbs
Frying-fat
Salt, pepper and flour

Scale, clean, wash and dry the fish thoroughly. Sprinkle with salt and pepper, dredge well with flour, brush over with beaten egg, and cover with breadcrumbs. Have ready some hot fat, fry the fish until nicely browned, drain well, and serve with anchovy, shrimp, or melted butter sauce. (From *Mrs Beeton's Every-Day Cookery*)

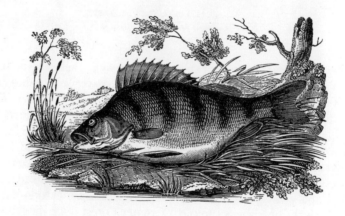

PIKE
Esox lucius

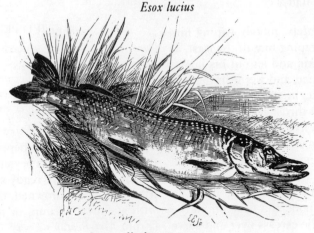

I saw, dimly,
Once a big pike rush,
And small fish fly like splinters.

D. H. Lawrence, 'Fish' from
Birds, Beasts and Flowers (1920–23)

There are six living species which represent the genus *Esocidae* (the Pikes and Pickerels), in the order *Clupeiformes*. The three larger species (the Pikes) consist of the pike, *Esox lucius*, known in America as the northern pike; the muskellunge, *Esox musquinongy*; and the Amur pike, *Esox reicherti*. The three smaller species (the Pickerels) are the chain pickerel, *Esox niger*; the redfin pickerel, *Esox americanus*; and the grass pickerel, *Esox vermiculatus*. *Esox lucius* is the only species found in the British Isles, and it occurs in stillwaters and the slower-moving parts of many rivers throughout England, Scotland, Wales and Ireland.

PIKE IN ANTIQUITY

Judging by the evidence of fossils, the pike, *Esox lucius*, is almost identical with its ancient and extinct forebear, *Esox lepidotus*, which lived during the Upper Miocene period. Fossils of *Esox lepidotus*, believed to be about 20 million years old, have been found in deposits at Oeningen in Baden. Fossils of *Esox papyraceus*, an even older pike (about thirty million years old), have been found in the lignites of Rott, near Bonn, in Germany. The fossils of *Esox lucius* found in Britain have come from the Cromer Forest beds at West Runton, in Norfolk. According to modern carbon-dating methods, the Cromer Forest flourished during an inter-glacial period just over 500,000 years ago. At that time, much ocean water was combined in glaciers; accordingly, sea levels were slightly lower than they are today. Even now, when tides are exceptionally low, fossilized tree stumps of the old Cromer Forest can still be seen. The pike of long ago would have lived in lakes and rivers within the forest area.

During the passage of time freshwater fishes showed remarkable stability in their physical character. Photographs kindly sent to us by

Professor G. V. Nikolsky of Moscow University illustrate a bream on page 26 and a perch fossil on page 117 from the Likhvinsk inter-glacial deposits.

The pike fossil on page 126 was found in the Upper Miocene deposits (about 20 million years old) at ●Oeningen in Baden, Germany. The appearance of this ancient pike, *Esox lepidotus*, bears a remarkable similarity to the modern pike, *Esox lucius*.

The oldest Esox yet, some 60 million years old, was recently found in Canadian Eocene deposits and was reported in the *Canadian Journal of Earth Sciences* in 1980. The fossil *Esox tiemani* (named in honour of its discoverer B. Tieman) was noticed when an access road to an oil well was being cut.

The 'new' oldest known pike fossil once again demonstrates the unchanging physical character

of the Esocidae – with an antiquity nearly three times older than previously recorded.

DIET AND APPETITE

Before considering the various pike tackles and techniques it is worthwhile studying the means by which pike satisfy their appetites. When an angler knows what pike feed on, and understands how they locate, select and capture their prey, he will fish with a much greater chance of success.

The pike is a fish of catholic tastes. Waterfowl, chickens, frogs, rats, mice, voles, puppies, kittens and many other species have been known to pass through those cavernous jaws, but although it will grab any creature it can swallow, the pike is mainly a fish eater. It is this aspect of its diet which is responsible for its age-old reputation as a relentless killer.

'He murders all he meets with,' wrote Richard Franck, over 300 years ago.

From his fierce looks the frightened trembling fry,
To holes and sedgy pits for safety fly.

Figure 119: The head of the famous Dowdeswell pike. This fish was found dead in Dowdeswell Reservoir, near Cheltenham, in 1896. Its weight was recorded as 60 lb

Figure 120: (top) Fossil pike (*Esox lepidotus*) *British Museum*

(*above*) A close look at the stomach area of the fossil *Esox tiemani* (see arrow) reveals the backbone of its last victim swallowed just before the pike's sudden death some 60 million years ago. The authors are grateful to Dr Peter Forey of the Department of Palaeontology, British Museum (Natural History) for this information

Figure 122: (right) Fossil pike teeth (*Esox lucius*) from the Cromer Forest beds at West Runton, Norfolk (*British Museum*)

Ever since the first pike-fishing story was told there have been accounts of the pike's enormous gluttony, of a cunning, rapacious monster unequalled in ferocity, a veritable fish of blood.

Though the salmon is called the King of Fresh-water Fish, yet the Pike is, and the more justly, styled the King of the Fresh-water. ... Nor is he barely king of the river, but, as a monarch, that makes by arbitrary power, and delights in the blood of his subjects, he becomes the tyrant thereof; for justly may he be said to be the terror of the watery people.

So wrote an eighteenth-century angler, whose summing-up of the general regard for pike was echoed by another writer 100 years later:

The pike is a systematic and professional marauder; he respects not his own kith and kin; he prowls up and down seeking what he may devour.

Dramatic stuff. But the reference to cannibalism is certainly true. Dr E. D. Toner, investigating the food of Lough Mask pike, reported the finding of 13 small pike among 323 fish taken from the stomachs of larger pike.

Alfred Jardine wrote of an incident witnessed on Loch Tay in 1870. Two pike were found together, one fish having the head of the other jammed inside its jaws. They were gaffed by a boatman and sent, undivided in death, to the great Frank Buckland – who made a cast of them for his fish museum. Together, they weighed 19 lb, an example of gluttony indeed. But there are many similar examples as our pictures on page 129 show.

The pike's gastronomic excesses do not end with the eating of its own kind.

A list of further victims is given by another in the long line of angling writers:

Shrouded from observation in his solitary retreat, he follows with his eye the shoals of fish that wander heedlessly along; he marks the water rat swimming in his burrow; the ducklings paddling among the water weeds, the dabchick and the moorhen swimming leisurely on the surface; he selects his victim, and like a tiger springing from the jungle he rushes forth, seldom missing his aim, there is a sudden swirl and splash; circle after circle forms on the surface of the water, and all is still in an instant.

And nigh this toppling reed, still as the dead
The great pike lies, the murderous patriarch
Watching the waterpit sheer-shelving dark,
Where through the plash his lithe bright vassals thread.

The rose-finned roach and bluish bream
And staring ruffe steal up the stream
Hard by their glutted tyrant, now
Still as a sunken bough.

He on the sandbank lies,
Sunning himself long hours
With stony gorgon eyes;
Westward the hot sun lowers.

Edmund Blunden, *The Pike*

There is no doubt that ducks and other wildfowl feature in the pike's diet. Jardine writes of a visit to Sonning-on-Thames where the landlord of his hostelry informed him of a pike which had swallowed, one by one, twelve from a brood of fifteen half-grown ducks. Jardine witnessed the demise of yet another of the brood, before setting out to fish with a gudgeon-baited paternoster. The pike was duly caught. It weighed 15 lb, and inside it Jardine found 'the recently swallowed duck with its feathers scarcely rumpled'.

But how often do such incidents occur?

Dr Michael Kennedy, of the Inland Fisheries Trust, Dublin, states that birds are seldom discovered among the stomach contents of Irish pike. It seems that by the time Irish pike attain a weight of two pounds and over, they are almost exclusively fish eaters.

Dr Winifred Frost found rodent remains inside Windermere pike on only one occasion; and a solitary duckling – in a Blenham Tarn pike.

That *Esox* is a rapacious glutton has been stated in unequivocal terms by nearly every pike angler who has obeyed the urge to write about his sport. Typical of this view was an estimate (published by Cholmondeley-Pennell in 1865)

The pike has long been known for its eager and almost indiscriminate appetite, accompanied with great boldness in all that relates to the satisfying of its cravings; and numerous stories illustrative of this are recorded in books of natural history.

The naturalist, Jonston, quotes Rondeletius as saying that a friend of his had stopped on the border of the Rhone that his mule might drink, when a pike seized the animal by the lower lip, and held it so fast, that as the animal started backward the fish was lifted out of the water and secured. Another of these fishes was known to have seized the foot of a young woman as she held it naked in a pond.

A more modern instance of similar ferocity is given from Mr Pennell's *Angler Naturalist*, as quoted in the *Athenaeum*:

'A young gentleman, aged fifteen, went with three other boys to bathe in Inglemere Pond, near Ascot racecourse, in June, 1856: he walked gently into the water to about the depth of four feet, when he spread out his hands to attempt to swim; instantly a large fish came up and took his hand into his mouth as far as the wrist, but finding he could not swallow it, relinquished his hold, and the boy turning round, prepared for a hasty retreat out of the pond; his companions who saw it also scrambled out as fast as possible.

He had scarcely turned himself round when the fish came up behind him, and immediately seized his other hand crosswise, inflicting some very deep wounds on the back of it; the boy raised his first bitten and still bleeding arm, and struck the monster a hard blow on the head, when the fish disappeared. Seven wounds were dressed on one hand, and so great was the pain the next day, that the lad fainted twice; the little finger was bitten through the nail, and it was more than six weeks before it was well. A few days after this occurrence one of the woodmen was walking by the side of the pond, when he saw something white floating. It was found to be a large Pike in a dying state, and he brought it to the shore, and the boy at once recognised his antagonist. The fish appeared to have been a long time in the agonies of death, and the body was very lean and curved like a bow. It measured forty-one inches, and died the next day. There can be no doubt the fish was in a state of complete starvation. If well fed, it is probable it might have weighed from thirty to forty pounds.'

In Dr Crull's *Present State of Muscovy* (1698), mention is made of a pike that, when taken, was found to have an infant child in its stomach.

Jonathan Couch, *A History of British Fishes* (1862–65)

which suggested that a pike was capable of consuming twice its own weight of fish in a week. By this reckoning, the yearly food consumption of a 10 lb pike would be roughly 1,040 lb. Many freshwater anglers would accept this figure as being a reasonable assessment of the pike's annual depredations.

And they would be wrong.

From experiments conducted by Dr L. Johnson of the Freshwater Biological Association on Lake Windermere, it may be adduced that a 10 lb pike can be kept alive on an annual food intake of only 14 lb of fish. This amount of food will not permit any increase in the pike's weight, but it will keep the pike alive. Similarly, a 10 lb pike, offered as much as it can eat, will show a normal yearly growth increment while con-

suming as little as 35 lb of small fish.

These experiments were made on captive pike. But even so, it seems likely that the annual food intake of a pike living in its natural habitat is not more than five to six times its own weight. This means that in one year a 10 lb pike consumes 50–60 lb of food. Almost 1,000 lb less than Cholmondeley-Pennell's estimate!

William Kendall, an American, was the first writer to take a more favourable view of pike:

It is beginning to be recognized that there are still places for them in both the human and natural economy ... there have been waters in which some pike and other fishes have lived in reciprocal counterpoise from time immemorial, notwithstanding the condemned characteristic voracity of the pike.

With a sag belly and the grin it was born with.
And indeed they spare nobody.
Two, six pounds each, over two feet long,
High and dry and dead in the willow-herb –

One jammed past its gills down the other's
    gullet:
The outside eye stared: as a vice locks –
The same iron in this eye
Though its film shrank in death.

Ted Hughes, from Pike

Figure 123: (top) The two pike in this remarkable picture –
which was given to us by Sir Frederick Hoare – were
found dead in Staines South Reservoir in April 1972.
Each fish was about 2 ft 6 in. long and weighed just over
6 lb. The attacking fish had its jaws extended to their limit
and since a pike's mouth contains a large number of sharp
backward-facing teeth it was quite unable to release its
prey. As a result, both fish died

Figure 124: (middle) These pike found 'locked together in
death' were cased by a taxidermist

Figure 125: (bottom) A case of the 'Union Jack'. This
photograph was published in the *Fishing Gazette* on 17
April 1920. The pike together weighed 13 lb and were
found on the shore of Loch Tay, near Killin

Figure 126: F. B. pike fishing on a Lincolnshire lake (*Sunday Times*)

With regard to this 'condemned characteristic voracity', Dr Johnson's research has revealed some interesting facts. In its ability to turn food into body maintenance and growth, the pike compares favourably with certain species; for instance, plaice and trout.

This turning of food into maintenance and growth is known as the 'gross conversion rate'. This, for the pike, is 3.41. In simple terms it means that to maintain life and increase its body weight by one pound, a pike must eat 3.41 lb of food. To do likewise, a plaice must consume 5 lb of food, and a trout 7.1 lb.

From these figures it is evident that, compared with some of the other fishes, nature has equipped the pike with a gut which functions with great economy, a fact not appreciated by Walton when he pronounced:

All pikes that live long prove chargeable to their keepers, because their life is maintained by the death of so many other fish.

On the contrary, the pike, with its gross conversion rate of only 3.41, seems to be a most reasonable fellow, unlike the 7.1 trout, who murders all he meets with!

RIDDLE OF THE CEPEDIAN PIKE

The curious old engraving (1808) depicting common pike and 'Cepedian' pike had been in Fred Buller's possession for many years. It had belonged to R. B. Marston (1851–1926), editor of *The Fishing Gazette*, and had been given to F. B. by Marston's granddaughter, Patricia Walker. One day in a moment of inspiration he placed a newly received picture of a fossil bone-pike upside down beside the Cepedian pike. To his astonishment it was an almost perfect match. F. B. writes as follows:

I had never heard of a Cepedian pike and the picture had long puzzled me. Was it possible that this enigmatic fish, which had defied taxonomists for nearly

two centuries, was no other than an upside down portrait of a bone-pike? I immediately set to work to find out.

First I had to trace the title of the book from which the page carrying the engraving was torn …

Alwyne Wheeler eventually found the original engraving in Volume 5 of George Shaw's *General Zoology Pisces* (1804). Shaw, it seems, was a colourful figure who had worked for the British Museum. Not only had he muddled the Cepedian pike's classification

Figure 127: The bone-pike (*top*) from Messel has been placed upside down so that it can be compared to the 'Cepedian' pike (*middle*) that was printed upside down. Note that each has a rounded caudal fin with ten rays. Note, too, the similar patterns of ganoid (armoured) scales – features that contrast with those of the common pike (*bottom*)

Cepedian pike

Common pike

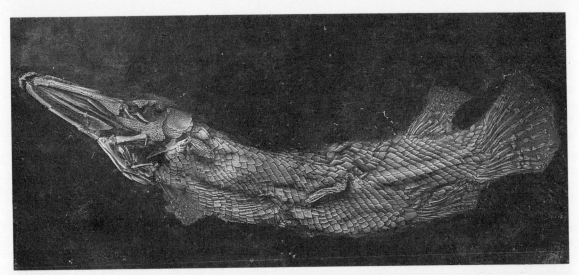

Figure 128

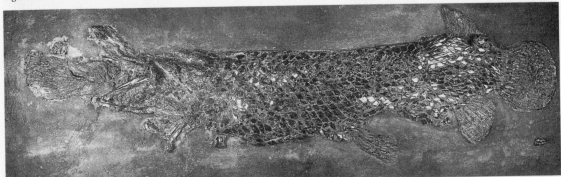

Figure 129

Figure 130

Freshwater Fishing

when describing it as *Esox cepedianus*, but, both in his own and in a subsequent book, he had allowed its picture to be printed upside down!

The 'Cepedian' was surely, Wheeler thought, a bone- or gar-pike – one of several species still surviving in fresh estuarine waters of America, from Costa Rica to Quebec. The word 'Cepedian' he felt sure was a corruption of LaCépède (1756–1826), the famous eighteenth-century French naturalist and taxonomist.

Figure 128: (*opposite*) Bone-pike (a form of gar-pike) *Atractosteus strausi* (LaCépède) from a quarry at Messel between Darmstadt and Frankfurt-on-Main, once the site of a primitive freshwater lake. So far, only five fossilized predator species from Messel have been identified, and no roach-like or carp-like fishes – although two members of the perch family have been found: *Palaeoperca* and *Amphiperca*, and a salmon-like fish: Thaumaturas. Freshwater gars are quite distinct from the pikes (*Esox*), but the common characteristic of having dorsal, anal and caudal fins in a cluster at the tail-end of the body, together with long, heavily armoured jaws and a long body, has been a successful design for a number of widely differentiated genera of fishes. Such a predator has the necessary thrust to achieve fast acceleration and high speed over short distances – tactics that suggest an ambushing rôle, but gained at the expense of sustained swimming at medium speeds. That pike are sometimes swept out to sea by floods and unable to colonize spate rivers illustrates this disability. (H. F. notes that pike from tarns in the catchment area of the Cumberland Esk occasionally take up residence in the river, where they flourish at the expense of salmon and trout parr. After each minor flood on this spate river, such pike are usually found to have dropped downstream into lower pools and, eventually, after a big flood, are seen no more)

Figure 129: A fifty-million-year-old bone-pike that choked to death on an outsize meal before being preserved, along with its victim, in the lignites or 'brown coal' deposits laid down during the Eocene period. Pike species have shown little change in their feeding habits! The victim is a bowfin (*Amia*). Note the up-curved tail-end section of its spinal column, together with the tail's covering of thin scales, a combination unique among fishes. The bowfin's modern counterparts are found only in the freshwaters of eastern North America

Figure 130: Fossil of a bowfin (*Amia*) from the Messel deposits, showing the up-curved spine. Modern relatives of the bowfin are found in the eastern freshwaters of North America. The location of these, and of related species in fossil form from the ancient Messel freshwater lake, points to the existence in former times of a land bridge between Europe and the American continent

DEFORMITY

In February 1971 Mr David Mason caught a remarkable pike in the River Witham. It was only $38\frac{1}{2}$ in. long, yet it weighed 30 lb! There can be no doubt that it weighed at least 30 lb since four competent witnesses, including Mr Albert Ibbotson, secretary of the Yorkshire Specimen Group, were present at the weighing-in. Nevertheless, some anglers found it impossible to believe that a pike measuring a mere $38\frac{1}{2}$ in. could weigh as much as 30 lb. They were partly justified in their criticism since it turned out that the length measurement had been taken 'from the tip of the pike's nose to the stub of the tail, instead of the cleft'. In order to compute the probable true length of this pike it is necessary to add a further 2 inches to the original measurement – making $40\frac{1}{2}$ in. in all.

It can be argued that even $40\frac{1}{2}$ in. is still very short for such a heavy pike. According to Mona's scale a $40\frac{1}{2}$ in. pike in good condition should weigh only 20–21 lb, while F. B.'s scale indicates an approximate weight of no more than 26 lb.* A *possible* explanation of the unusual length/weight ratio of this fish is that it possessed a shortened vertebral column. Due to a deformity known as 'coalesced vertebrae', a fish of normal weight will have a shortened body length. Such a fish has a sawn-off appearance – as if the tail were attached to the body without the tapered 'wrist' associated with most fishes. (See X-ray photograph on page 134.)

Mr Albert Ibbotson, writing to the *Angling Times*, gave measurements taken from other pike caught from the River Witham in the area where the controversial pike was caught. Two sets of these measurements are appended for comparison with the measurements of Mason's pike.

Mason's pike (after adjustment): $40\frac{1}{2}$ in. length, 23 in. girth, 30 lb weight; Pike 2: 36 in. length, 30 in. girth, 32 lb weight; Pike 3: 42 in. length, 23 in. girth, 33 lb weight.

* As F. B. points out in his book *Pike*, in *special circumstances* a $40\frac{1}{2}$ in. pike could weigh *more* than 30 lb. But in the case of Mason's pike these circumstances did not exist since the fish was not fully ripe with spawn nor had it just swallowed the largest food item that it was capable of swallowing.

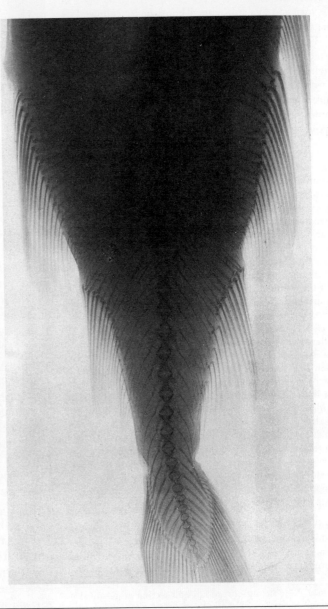

Figure 131: A pike from the River Witham: 27½ lb, caught by Deryck Naylor of Sheffield. This pike, which took a herring bait ledgered with float tackle, has the characteristic look of fish with coalesced vertebrae (*Angling News Services*). An X-ray photograph (*right*) shows coalesced vertebrae (*British Museum*)

These figures come from a reliable witness, and it seems likely that the River Witham contains a local race of pike suffering (quite happily it appears) from a congenital deformity – coalesced vertebrae.

Many of the roach that inhabited the River Lea near Hertford in the 1950s displayed a similar characteristic.

AGE AND FECUNDITY

It is not only the pike's gastronomic excesses that have been exaggerated. Most early writers were in error when they speculated on the number of years that pike will live. In 1653, Walton published the story of the 267-year-old Mannheim pike. His predecessor, Sir Francis

A pond I fished, fifty yards across,
Whose lilies and muscular tench
Had outlasted every visible stone
Of the monastery that planted them –

Stilled legendary depth:
It was as deep as England. It held
Pike too immense to stir, so immense and
    old
That past nightfall I dared not cast

But silently cast and fished
With the hair frozen on my head
For what might move, for what eye might
    move.
The still splashes on the dark pond.

Owls hushing the floating woods
Frail on my ear against the dream
Darkness beneath night's darkness had
    fixed,
That rose slowly towards me, watching.

Ted Hughes, from *Pike*

Bacon, in *A History of Life and Death* (1623), wrote: '… forty years is likely to be a maximum'. A century later, Pennant referred to a 90-year-old pike.

The Victorian naturalist, Frank Buckland, was the first writer to produce some facts. He describes the taking of a pike from a Windsor Park lake 12 years after it had been introduced as a $1\frac{1}{2}$-pounder. It weighed 35 lb, and by Buckland's calculation was 14 years old.

Dr Kennedy has given us details of the pike's amazingly rapid growth rate in Ireland's great limestone loughs. Some incidental determinations are as follows:

$50\frac{1}{2}$ lb female pike netted from Lough Mask in 1966 age 8 years +.

41 lb female pike netted from Lough Mask in 1966 age 8 years +.

36 lb female pike netted from Lough Cloone in 1963 age 8 years +.

Dr Winifred Frost, who has developed an accurate method of reading the age of pike from their opercular (gill cover) bones, has also given us some incidental determinations. These are:

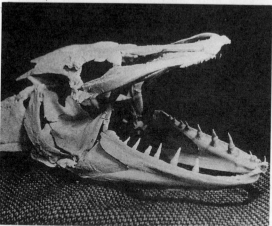

Figure 132: (*top*) On 12 October 1986 Lothar Louis, from Buhl in Germany, caught this magnificent 55 lb $1\frac{3}{4}$ oz pike spinning with a 20-gram spoon. This mighty fish $53\frac{1}{2}$ in. long, which will probably be recognized as the new world-record rod-caught pike since it was properly weighed on butcher's scales in front of many witnesses, was taken from a gravel pit belonging to the Grefern Angling Club

Figure 133: The skull of a 52 lb pike

35 lb female pike netted from Windermere in 1960 age 14 years.

33¼ lb female pike netted from Windermere in 1960 age 18 years.

The former was the heaviest pike taken from the lake during 25 years of netting operations, and the latter was the oldest pike taken during the same period.

William Giles, who has read the scales of many Norfolk pike for the Norfolk river authority, tells us that he has never known a pike to be older than about eighteen years.

Determining a pike's age from an opercular bone is more reliable than scale reading. Dr Frost's method is as follows:

Remove the left operculum from the dead pike with a scalpel or knife. Soak it in hot water and then clean off the skin with a cloth. To improve its 'reading' quality, keep the bone in storage for a month or two. View the bone by reflected light, on a dark background, under a low-power microscope.

Seasonal differences in the pike's rate of growth affect the bone structure of the operculum, so that reflected light, and to some extent transmitted light, gives the bone the appearance of being made up from a series of concentric bands, differing in their degree of whiteness from the white matrix of the background. A count of these growth checks (annuli) gives the age of the pike. Some caution is necessary if six or more annuli are counted, since a brown glutinous tissue usually obscures at least one annulus near the point of attachment.

It will have been noted that of the big pike netted from Loughs Mask, Cloone, and Windermere, all five were female. This is not surprising. Male pike rarely exceed 10 lb in weight. The largest male pike taken in Ireland during many years of gill-netting weighed 14 lb. The largest taken in a sample of 7,000 Windermere pike weighed 12½ lb. In three generations, the largest to pass through the hands of the London taxidermists, John Cooper and Sons, weighed 12 lb.

Reports of 20 and 30 lb male pike can be discounted. All 'male' pike of this size have been wrongly sexed. Various organs within the female's body cavity are sometimes mistaken for

By this the Pike, cleane wearied underneath
A willow lies and pants (if Fishes breath)
Wherewith the Angler gently puls him to him
And, lest his hast might happen to undoe him,
Lays downe his rod, then takes his line in hand
And, by degrees getting the Fishe to land.

William Browne, *Britannia's Pastorals* (1613)

male glands – a mistake usually made during the early stages of ovary development.

So far as we are aware, no scientist has attempted to explain why male pike are unable to match the growth rate and ultimate size of female pike. Having studied an account of the spawning behaviour of pike (Fabricius and Gustafson, 1956), it occurs to us that, historically, male body length may have been an important factor in the process of natural selection. Our reasons are these:

During the spawning act, male and female pike *move forward together*. While moving, the male pike is accurately located beside the female by means of eye to eye orientation. The natural displacement of water caused by both fish moving forward causes a current to flow in the opposite direction. If the male were bigger than the female, its vent would be positioned to the rear of the female's vent and its milt cloud would be *swept away* from the falling eggs, rather than over them. Thus, spawning acts would tend to be unsuccessful. As a result, smaller and shorter-bodied male pike would tend to become the more successful progenitors.

Although most pike spawn for the first time in their second or third year, it seems that size rather than age is the determining factor. Usually, pike spawn in relatively shallow water. Lake pike prefer sheltered bays within the 12-foot contour. They tend to use the same spawning sites year after year, and these are likely to

Figure 134: (right) '. . . then takes his line in hand'

Freshwater Fishing

The Pike

Figure 135: Grahame Parson of Horton, Berkshire, with a fine 35 lb English pike caught in December 1982 (*Angling Times*)

be near their normal feeding grounds. Exceptionally, pike have been known to travel up to five miles from their spawning sites.

The fecundity of pike is legendary. Buckland counted 595,200 eggs in the ovaries of a 32 lb pike. Frost and Kipling found that the weight of the female gonads, expressed as a percentage of the total bodyweight, increases from 2% in August to 7% in October, 10% in November, 12% in December, 14% in January, 15% in February, and when fully ripe, prior to spawning, to as much as 20%.

In May 1905, *The Field* reported the gaffing of a spent 48 lb female pike from one of the inlets of Lough Corrib. It was thought that, prior to spawning, this pike must have weighed about 60 lb! An astonishing figure, but there is every reason to believe it.

Esox lucius, like all the pikes and pickerels (with the exception of the Amur) strikes at its prey from ambush. The Amur pike – named after its native valley which lies between Russia and China – is the one species endowed with an instinct to hunt in open water.

The pike's hunting technique of striking from ambush is helped by its coloration: dark olive-green when viewed from above, lighter green and mottled when viewed from the side, and white when viewed from below. This colour combination is an excellent camouflage and enables a pike to lurk unseen in a green jungle of weeds and lily pads, until an unsuspecting victim has moved within range of its powerful dash.

SENSES AND FEEDING HABITS

A pike's awareness of a bait, and ability to locate it, can be achieved only by the use of one or more of three senses: sight, smell and hearing.

If an angler suspects which of these senses he is appealing to on any occasion, he should be able to present his bait with a good deal more confidence than he has felt hitherto.

A pike tends to use the minimum of effort in hunting its food. Its eyes are set high in the head and provide an extensive field of vision forwards and upwards. Many of its attacks on other fish are made from ambush. Once a prey fish swims into the striking zone, even if it is a wary and speedy trout, it has little chance of eluding the pike's short but powerful dash from the bottom.

The pike, then, is well equipped to hunt by sight. But it is certainly not vision that plays the *major* part in the pike's feeding routine. The netting of a totally blind but otherwise healthy pike in Lake Windermere proved that pike can obtain sufficient food by the use of senses other than sight.

Is it possible to evaluate the degree with which the pike's different senses are used for the purpose of getting a meal? One thing is certain,

a livebait has a much greater chance of being taken than a freely swimming fish of the same size and species. Is the attraction of a livebait simply visual, or does a pike become aware of the bait's presence through some emitted sound or scent? Does a tethered livebait cause distress signals (vibrations), which are picked up by the pike's listening equipment? Does it emit a fear substance, which a pike homes on by sense of smell? Is it merely a display of physical distress that catches a pike's eye?

Vigorous livebaits are more effective than ailing ones. Perhaps their signals are more vigorous, and extend over a greater range.

Like other fishes, pike don't possess hearing organs similar to mammals. The 'ear' seems to be used mainly as a balancing device. Nevertheless, many species of fish emit underwater sounds. The meaning of these sounds is not yet known, but it seems reasonable to suppose that they have some specific function and that in some way they can be understood by other fishes.

What is beyond doubt is that most species of fish are extremely sensitive to vibrations. And the pike is no exception. If a bait is cast so that it falls a little way behind a stationary pike, the pike may swim away – presumably frightened – or it may *turn round and face the bait*. Both reactions demonstrate the pike's ability to 'hear',

Figure 136: Young pike have quite different markings from mature pike – striped rather than dappled. This natural camouflage helps to protect the little fish from hungry adults by making them less conspicuous among reed stems and where the light values are high, i.e. in the marginal weedy areas where small pike feed

but the latter indicates that the pike's sense of 'hearing' may sometimes help it to locate its prey.

But what of ledgered deadbaits? They emit no vibrations, and yet deadbaits fished stationary on the bottom are extremely effective. Why? The answer is almost certainly – smell.

The sense of smell in most fishes is exceptionally acute. It has been demonstrated that salmon, returning from the sea to spawn in freshwater, detect their 'home' rivers by scent. The ability of sharks and other sea fishes to follow a scent trail is equally well established: as a result, the rubby-dubby bag has become a valuable item of sea-angling equipment. During the breeding season, a male pike is able to track down a female by sense of smell. And although, as yet, no one has produced scientific proof, it is almost certain that pike are able to locate their prey by the same means.

Since there is little doubt that a deadbait gives off a stronger scent than a livebait, it seems probable that pike approach deadbait as a result of picking up the trail of this scent in the same way that a shark picks up and follows the scent of the rubby-dubby – although, needless to say, over a very much shorter range.

This may explain why, in locations that permit satisfactory presentation, deadbait often proves more successful than livebait.

DEADBAIT FISHING

Although new methods and tackles are claimed from time to time, most of them are simply rediscoveries (a notable example is the swing-tip). Deadbaiting is no exception. Several anglers since the last war claim to have invented deadbait ledgering, and not a few claim to have been first to do so with herrings. But the ledgered herring was being used five hundred years ago. The following description is transcribed from *A Treatyse of Fysshynge wyth an Angle*:

Take a codling hook, and take a roach or a fresh herring, and a wire with an hole in the end, and put it in at the mouth, and out at the tail, down by the ridge of the fresh herring; and then put the hook in after, and draw the hook into the cheek of the fresh herring; then put a plumb of lead upon your line a yard long from your hook, and a float in midway between; and cast it in a pit where the pike useth, and this is the best and most surest craft of taking the pike.

For centuries, however, stationary deadbaits were little used until, in post-war years, Fred J. Taylor developed improved rigs for this technique. From his writings a new school of pike fishing grew up, so that today stationary deadbait fishing is once again a major method in the pike angler's repertoire.

The fish was evidently a huge one; the chance of tempting him to be caught *secundum artem* was *nil*. Tizard earnestly assured me his master was most anxious to have a large pike for the table – and so – I yielded to the tempter. ... The boat glides noiselessly down to the unconscious esox and now the gaff is steadily but surely stretched over the spot where the leviathan's shoulder is likely to be, giving him an imaginary length of about four feet ... whish! There was a rapid stroke, a plunge, and with a rush sufficient to upset a whaleboat the stricken monster dashed for the bottom of the river, at that point at least twenty feet deep.

It was an exciting moment. I found myself being incontinently pulled over the boat's side, which was taking in water freely and clutched at the nearest available support, which happened to be the seat of the keeper's corduroy nether garments. It came bodily away in my grasp. At this juncture, nothing I believe, could have saved the boat from capsizing, if the gaff, yielding to the excessive strain, had not first twisted in the socket, and then straightened out, thus, of course, releasing the enemy who, though struck deep, may, I would fain hope, have yet survived in the indefensible attack upon him *contra bonos mores* and lived on to attain a still greater age and yet vaster breadth of tail.

Tizard, the keeper, was the only one who did not laugh heartily, but on a hint that we should contribute to his next tailor's bill his countenance assumed its wonted serenity.

H. Cholmondeley-Pennell, *Fishing, Pike and Other Coarse Fish* (1885)

Figure 137: This 25½ lb Lough Mask pike was taken by
F. B. on about his tenth cast of the morning. He and his
boat companion, William Blake, fished on with great
expectations but in the event only one more pike (small)
was caught.

This common angling experience should be classified as
the 'this is the day' syndrome

For preference, herring deadbaits should be
ledgered on leadless tackle over a hard, weed-
free bottom. Unlike herring, whose bladders are
collapsed, roach and rudd sink slowly and are
superior baits when fished over weed or soft
mud.

Cast the bait close to a margin or weed bed.
Open the reel bale-arm and allow the pike to
make its first run unimpeded. Tighten on the
fish at the start of the second run.

Deadbait fishing, more particularly herring
deadbait fishing, accounts for many big pike.
Most anglers would agree that the sample of
pike it catches is better than that produced by
spinning.

Herring as a bait has obvious advantages. It
is useful to be able to buy supplies of bait in
advance of a fishing trip. Herring also provides

an opportunity to pre-bait; and, for those with
an experimental turn of mind, to locate pike by
means of hookless search-trimmers.

The Loch Lomond rig

There are few lakes in Britain so beautiful as
Loch Lomond and few that hold such big pike.
An angler fishing Lomond is always in with a
chance of hooking a 40- or even a 50-pounder.
His tackle demands special attention.

Five feet of 30 lb BS wire leader is essential.
This length reduces the chance of a pike's teeth
making contact with the nylon line, should the
leader take a turn or two round the pike's body.
The wire should be a dull bronze colour – simply
because most anglers fish less confidently with a
bright reflective wire.

A size 1 or 1/0 treble is fastened to one end of
the leader, and a loop is whip-finished at the
other end. If preferred, two trebles can be used
some 4 in. or 5 in. apart (see F. J. Taylor's tackle).

One arm of the treble is hooked through the
fleshy tail of the bait. If two trebles are in use,
the upper treble is hooked in the tail; the lower
treble just forward of the pectoral fin.

Figure 139: (*left*) 'The float above the herring suddenly bobbed under, came up, laid flat for a second, then sailed away ... the big pike slowly yielded to the constant pressure, and I was gradually able to pump it close to the bank, where it surfaced ... it looked huge! My knees shook. "It's a big-un, Dan," someone said. "Could be a record," I replied in an unfamiliar voice ....' It was, nearly, for it weighed $39\frac{1}{2}$ lb, within half a pound of equalling the record (in 1983). Such was Norwich water bailiff Dan Leary's experience when he caught the fish of a lifetime from Lyng gravel pit on 29 December 1983

Figure 138: (*left*) Winter pike fishing near Tulla, Co. Clare
Figure 140: Lough Mask pike netted in March 1957, by the Inland Fisheries Trust. Weight: 46 lb. Length: 45 in. Holding the fish is Dr Michael Kennedy, one of the Trust's scientists

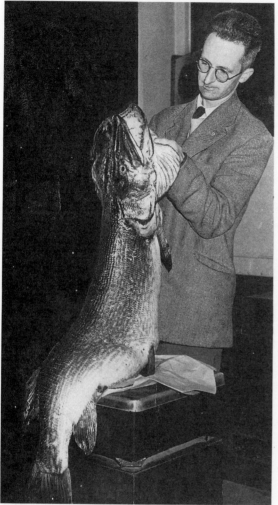

A 6 in. celluloid sliding float is preferred for its streamlined shape. A stop-knot (see figure 141) is fitted above the float. This is best tied with a 6 in. slip of 35 lb nylon. If necessary, a small-bored bead can be placed between stop-knot and float. This allows a less bulky stop-knot to be effective.

A Catherine barrel-lead is used because the line runs through it freely. The lead is stopped by a swanshot pinched on the wire. This sliding lead enables a pike to take the deadbait away without hindrance. In other than a strong wind, no lead need be used in shallow water, under, say, five feet deep.

Pilot floats are optional. They are sometimes necessary with monofil mainline to prevent the

Figure 141: Float-ledgering with the Loch Lomond pike rig

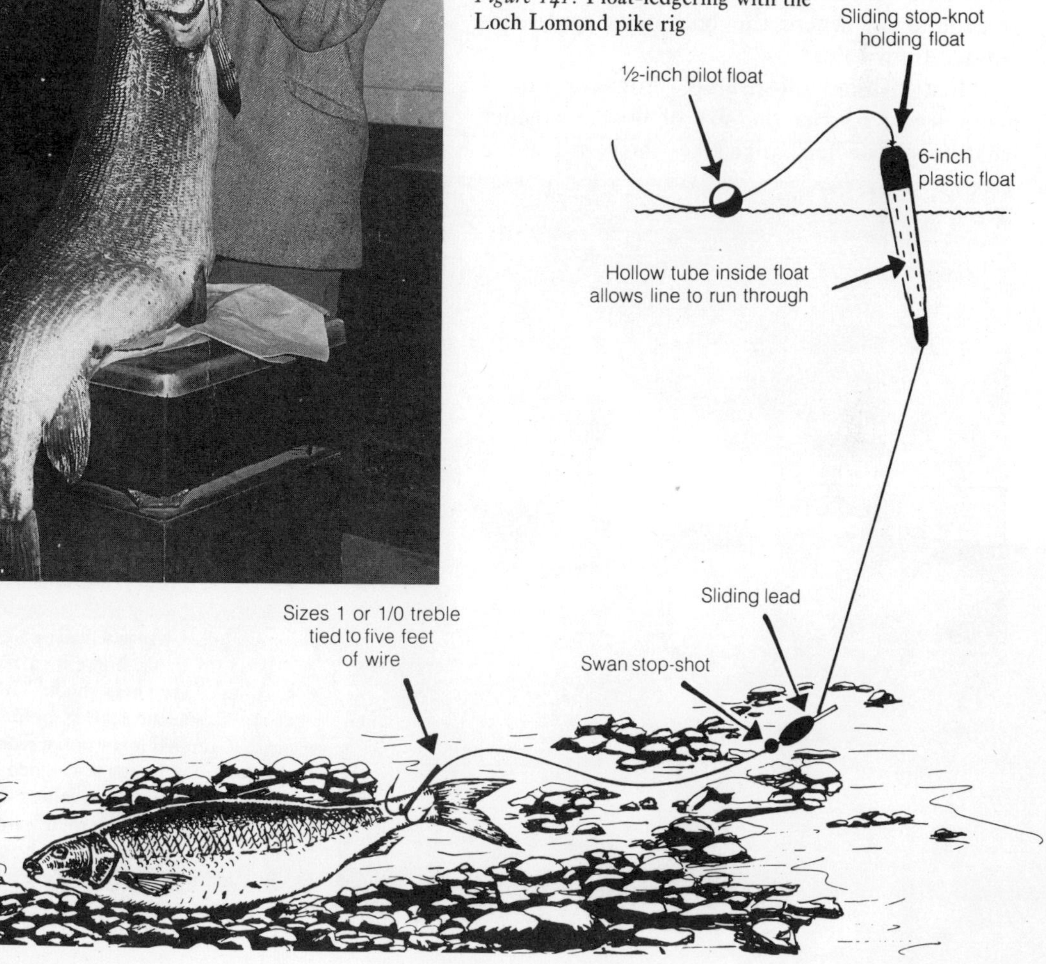

Sliding stop-knot holding float
½-inch pilot float
6-inch plastic float
Hollow tube inside float allows line to run through
Sliding lead
Sizes 1 or 1/0 treble tied to five feet of wire
Swan stop-shot

line from sinking, but several half-inch pilots are better than one large one. Better still, because of its good floatability, is a mainline of 30 lb *braided* nylon, used without pilots.

Note: Braided nylon must be fastened to the leader swivel or loop with a hangman's jam knot (see page 394). Any other knot may result in line strangulation. This could lose an angler the fish of a lifetime, as it did F. B.: a huge Loch Lomond pike, estimated by four experienced observers to be not less than 45 to 50 lb!

A note on pike floats

Although for hundreds of years livebaiting has been a popular method of catching pike, many modern anglers prefer the use of deadbait. They are losing little thereby. Fishing a deadbait can be just as successful, sometimes more so – either at ground or, where the bottom is foul, suspended from a float.

When fishing off-ground, however, it is necessary to restrict the size of float. Consider what happens when a pike takes the bait. Having struck from ambush, usually from below, and seized its 'prey', a pike does one of two things: it either swims slowly off towards safe cover or, pulling the float under as it does so, sinks back to the place from which it struck, lying there for a time, quite motionless. It is now very delicately balanced, and the pull of too big a float may lift the head of a small pike towards the surface. A heavy pike is unlikely to be moved in this way, but the buoyancy of an over-sized float is almost certain to increase rather than allay its suspicions.

As a general rule, if an angler sees his float resurface after a take and the bait released undamaged, he can be sure that the float is too big.

Figure 142: Germany once had, in the Rhine, the biggest run of Atlantic salmon of any country on earth – now they have none. By way of compensating, Germany treats the pike as her finest game fish. It is not surprising, therefore, considering the scope afforded by the lakes and rivers of Central and Eastern Europe, that German pike anglers have caught more big pike than any other nationals in the Northern Hemisphere. Joseph Schrädler and his father took this giant pike from Schliersee in Bavaria

Freshwater Fishing

Glaslough – the best preserved big pike lough in Ireland

A fishing cottage in the west of Ireland: a spot where host and guests when enjoying 'a good crack' tend to stay up late in front of a turf fire and consume much of the golden liquid

(left) John Lafferty, with a 19 lb Loch Lomond pike, caught off Balmaha with livebait

Often enough salmon fishing in January and February – laughably called 'spring fishing' – means frozen fingers; legs blue from wading in icy water; line freezing in the rod rings; floating blocks of ice or snow brought down by the current, alternating with dreams of big fish and an evening warm-up in a hot bath with a glass of grog. Here the authors pose at lunchtime with their morning's catch taken on big sunk fly and spinner. Notice the netmarks on two of the fish

Right: Since so many photographs of the catch (and captor) prove to be disappointing not only because of obvious technical reasons (camera shake, bad focusing, etc), but because of bad composition, it is pleasing to see a photograph without these defects. Florence Miller seen here with a fresh-run 18-pounder caught on a Toby would no doubt wish that photographs of her two best salmon both exceeding 30 lb were equally as good

Tailing a salmon by hand. The back of the angler's hand points towards the fish's head. Pressure is exerted by thumb and index finger only; the other fingers curl loosely round the tail. Peter Thomas lands a fine fresh-run summer salmon from the Wye

Figure 143: Peter Thomas and Fred Buller fishing 'Morgan's Bay', Loch Lomond, in 1967

Here in 1945, Tommy Morgan caught the biggest British pike of the twentieth century: 47 lb 11 oz.

In the same spot, shortly after taking this picture, F.B. hooked and lost a pike that may well have been even bigger than Morgan's – the mainline broke just above the leader swivel.

Dick Walker told H.F. later: 'It was the biggest freshwater fish I have ever seen.' Walker repeated this statement in *Angling Times* 10.8.77: 'I am prepared to swear an affidavit to the effect that this pike was by far the largest I have ever seen and that in my judgement it could not have weighed less than 50 lb. In fact I think it weighed a great deal more.' Ken Taylor, who also had a clear view of the fish when it came alongside the boat, stated: 'If my life depended on a guess, I would put it at 50 lb.'

Later, F.B. wrote in *Pike and the Pike Angler* (1981):

My old friends Harry Britton and Jackie Thompson put me on to the big pike that lived in the bay. They saw it frequently and wanted me to catch it and I failed. The 'big fellah', for that is what they called it, was never seen again.

... or was it?

In 1987 there was a remarkable sequel to this story. In response to an article on F.B.'s pike-fishing experiences by Brian Clarke in *The Sunday Times* of 25 January, Mr Charles Docherty of Boston Spa, Yorkshire, wrote:

Dear Mr Clarke,

I have just read your article on Mr Fred Buller about the pike which he lost.

It may just be coincidence but back in 1967 I was walking on the shores of Loch Lomond, just below Balmaha, towards the mouth of the River Endrick, where I came across the partial remains of a monster Pike.

The fish had drowned.

The fish had been securely hooked in the scissors but the wire trace with swivel was wrapped around the snout preventing the fish from breathing.

It was clearly a very large fish although the birds etc. had reduced its size considerably.

I recovered the wire trace but unfortunately it has disappeared with the passage of time.

Perhaps you would be good enough to let Mr Buller have this information which might throw some light on the one that got away!

Yours sincerely
Charles M. Docherty

Deadbait flights and mounts

The terms 'flight' and 'mount' are often confused. There is, however, an important distinction. A 'flight' is an arrangement of hooks that will put a curve in a bait, and so cause it to revolve when drawn through the water. A spinning 'mount' uses means other than a curve (vanes etc.) to induce the bait to spin or wobble.

Most of the traditional flights and mounts have not been marketed in recent years. The reason is not because they are wanting in appeal to fish or fishermen, but because of the harsh modern commercial climate that demands a reduction in tackle items.

An example is the Bromley-Pennell flight (see figure 144). It can easily be made up with alasticum wire. The curiously shaped 'holding' hook is a normal hook straightened out and trimmed with pliers. The lip hook is put on after the wire has been pushed through the gill cover and out through the mouth. It is secured in the correct position by a few turns of wire on the shank, before being pulled through both lips of the bait. Should extra casting weight be needed, a barrel lead is pushed down the throat of the bait before the lip hook is fitted. Cholmondeley-Pennell had this to say about the preparation of an eel-bait:

I have used fresh eel-bait dressed in a great many different fashions, from the whole eel (where the latter is not above seven or eight inches long), to six inches or so of the tail cut off a larger specimen. In this case the eel from which the bait is taken, is best rather small, and should not, for ordinary river and lake spinning, exceed a foot in length (9 in. better). For great lochs, like L. Corrib where pike are scarce and run sometimes to an extraordinary size, larger eels may be used with advantage. The most perfect eel-tail bait for pike spinning is, I consider, one about 7 inches long, made from an eel of say, three-quarters of a foot, an artificial head – which is more durable than the natural head – being formed out of the turned-back skin. This turned-back skin, besides being so much stronger by being doubled, has a blue colour which looks thoroughly fish-like in the water, and has apparently an appetising effect on the pike's taste.

In forming the head, skin the eel backwards towards the tail as far as the point where the bait is to commence, trimming off the flesh round the spinal bone 'cone-shaped'. Then tie the skin tightly round, close above the bone, and cut it off to within about an inch and a half of the ligature, turning the flap then downwards again, towards the tail. The pin-hook will eventually pass through both the turned down flap and the under-skin, and keep the flap fixed.

Figure 144: Eel-tail bait mounted on the original Bromley-Pennell flight. On Corrib, H. Cholmondeley-Pennell, fishing the eel-tail, hooked – and lost – the largest pike he contacted during his lifetime

Figure 145: A fine 38½ lb Irish pike caught on a deadbait flight *c.* 1875 by Thomas Moor, the father of Frank Moor (of Purdey hammergun fame) – one of the best shots of the modern era

Figure 146: Drop-minnow aerial flight. A bait can be fitted without the aid of a baiting needle. The spiked lead is pushed down the throat of a dead minnow and a single hook from each of the two forward trebles is pressed into the minnow to provide the necessary grip

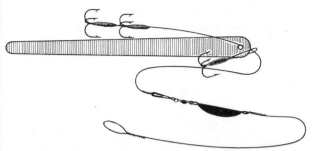

Figure 147: Martin's deadbait flight. 'Trent Otter', that great all-round coarse angler, J. W. Martin, writing in 1906, reckoned there was no better flight on which to fish a deadbait. He found that it not only caught a lot of pike, but held up well to long sessions of casting that caused most other baits to disintegrate. This tackle is a development of the old Trent flight, where two trebles (size 4 or 6) are fitted close together on a 16 in. length of wire. With the aid of a baiting needle the wire is threaded completely through the bait from the vent to the mouth and the hooks pulled up until the first treble buries itself in the vent, leaving the second treble to hand underneath the fish towards the tail. The wire is then passed through the eye of the tapered strip of zinc ($4\frac{1}{2}$–6 in. long, $\frac{3}{8}$ in. wide, tapering to $\frac{1}{8}$ in.). Then the zinc strip is pushed down the throat of the deadbait – dace, roach, bleak or sprat – until it emerges at the tail end, where half an inch of the strip is bent back to grip the bait at the root of the tail. Finally, the loose-looped treble is dropped into position. *Note:* The zinc strip should always be a little longer than the bait, which should not exceed $2\frac{1}{2}$ oz in weight

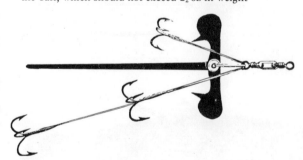

Figure 148: The Archer deadbait spinning mount

Wobbling

Unlike a bait that revolves with a regular action when retrieved, a wobbling bait is not intended to spin and its progress is irregular.

Wobbling is mostly confined to deadbait fishing, when the bait is twitched or jerked by the dropping and lifting of the rod-top, or by an irregular winding of the reel, or both; but some artificial baits can also be fished with a wobbling action, e.g. a kidney bar-spoon, and long-blade spoons such as the Toby.

Wobbled deadbaits are usually fished head first, i.e. in the head-up position prior to the cast. If the bait is reversed so that it hangs head down, the mode of fishing is the classic trolling style (see page 479).

LIVEBAITING

Although some anglers are convinced that pike never eat tench, these fish have been found in pike stomachs on many occasions, and one may hazard a guess that they didn't get there by accident. A taxidermist has recorded taking several tench of between 2 and 3 lb each from the stomachs of three 20-pounders. Nevertheless, we can find no reference to an angler having used them successfully as livebait, and have never done so ourselves.

Loch anglers seldom use perch as livebaits. This could be a mistake. A loch pike seems to prefer trout, roach or whitefish when it can get them, but there is no doubt that perch are eaten in large numbers.

Although dace and gudgeon have always been popular livebaits, it is a good plan to fish with a bait that is fairly selective: say, a roach or chub of not less than $\frac{3}{4}$ lb. This size tends to select pike upwards of 6 or 7 lb, and if properly presented is large enough to tempt the really big pike.

Saddle tackles

Salter's tackle (see figure 149) was one of the first saddle tackles, invented early in the nineteenth century. His instructions are as follows:

Take two hooks of the size No. 3, and tie each of them to about an inch-and-a-quarter of twisted wire; then take a hook, of the size No. 8, and about ten inches of gimp; put one end of the gimp to the wire that the aforesaid hooks are tied to; lay the hook No. 8 on the wire and gimp, and tie the whole very securely together; then make a loop at the other end of the gimp, and the whole is ready to receive the bait. To bait this snap; act as follows: take a proper-sized live Gudgeon, Roach, or Dace, and run the small hook through the flesh just under the back fin, and let the two large hooks hang one on each side of the bait-fish, and all is complete. When a Jack seizes your bait, and runs off, strike smartly, and you will seldom fail hooking him.

Salter's tackle was the precursor of a number of livebait saddle tackles. The last to be marketed was the 'Mullins', which survived until after the 1939–45 war. The lower hooks were kept in position by an elastic band.

According to Charles Marson in *Super Flumina* (1905), it was the Duke of Wellington who first tried elastic as a means of securing a livebait. Marson's attempts to emulate the Iron Duke stimulated this classic grizzle:

Out of humble imitation of him I have lost many valuable and rare dace, until his memory becomes odious to me.

Marson preferred a variation of Salter's original saddle tackle:

The bait wears a brace of triangles as an ass wears a pannier; but a single hook is caught in the back fin. The girth prevents the gear from breaking loose at the cast; and the enemy has a choice of seven hooks.

Seven! In spite of this armament, however, just the one hook secures the bait. As Marson pointed out: 'we know that the fewer pricks given to the bait the better both for mercy and business'.

Figure 149: Salter's saddle tackle (*The Angler's Guide*)

For over a century pike livebaiters have invented many types of livebait tackles including the Bickerdyke (figure 150) but only one – Jardine's snap tackle – is still in production (figure 151). In its earlier form Jardine's tackle was not adjustable (see figure 152 (a))

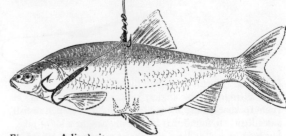

Figure 150 A livebait tackle of some repute, the 'Bickerdyke'

Figure 151: Snap tackle

Figure 152: (a) Mr Jardine's perfected snap tackle for pike fishing (b) Livebait snap (c) Paternoster snap

(a)

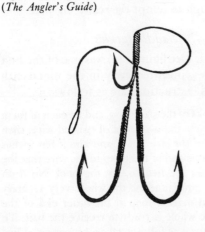

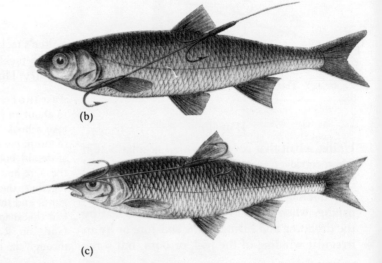

(b)

(c)

Freshwater Fishing

Figure 153: These drawings illustrate four ways of using a Universal snap tackle

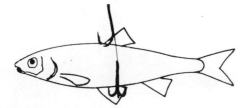

Livebait in still water

Livebait in running water

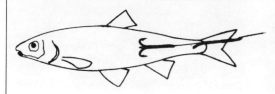

Deadbaiting with whole fish

Deadbaiting with half fish

By experiment over many years F. B. established the relationship between the size of the holding hook (which supports the bait) and the treble (which hooks the quarry). These combinations are listed below.

No. 1 Single with No. 4 treble (large)
No. 2 Single with No. 6 treble (medium)
No. 4 Single with No. 8 treble (small)
No. 6 Single with No. 10 treble (extra small)

The Universal snap tackle

Like many other contemporary pike anglers F. B. has experimented with a design for an improved snap tackle and the one that he found to cover all his needs, he called, not unnaturally, the *Universal* Snap Tackle. The tackle is based on a discovery he made many years ago when he found that a deadbait could be held much more securely during periods of long casting if a single hook of the *Beak* type was used as the 'holding' hook of the tackle. The Beak type of hook has a curved-in point which for some obscure reason is more efficient at gripping the bait.

Figure 154: Although the basic pattern has been copied, as has the name, genuine Universal snap tackles have hand-made oblique-eyed black lacquered treble hooks matched with similarly finished, curved-point singles forged by Britain's most famous hook maker

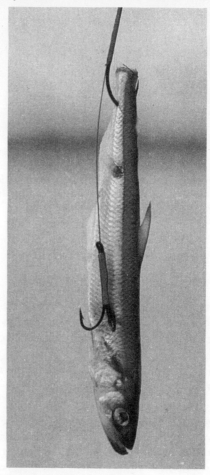

Figure 155: This early print (*c.* 1805) of a gentleman pike-fisher being assisted by his liveried servant shows that livebaiting (see the livebait can, the float-rigged tackle and the line attached to a Nottingham reel) was an established style of pike fishing nearly 200 years ago

FLY FISHING FOR PIKE

Anglers who associate fly fishing for pike only with the late Victorians may be surprised to learn that, although not widely used, the method was being discussed well over three hundred years ago. In the second edition of *The Experienc'd Angler*, Robert Venables wrote:

I know some do angle for Bream and Pike with artificial flies, but I judge the labour lost, and the knowledge a needless curiosity; those fish being taken much easier, especially the Pike, by other wayes ...

Most of the eighteenth-century writers mentioned the idea, but although (in *The Angler's Sure Guide*, 1706) Robert Howlett wrote: 'I have been assured the Pike will take the great long Salmon-flie', it wasn't until Samuel Taylor's *Angling in All Its Branches* (1800), that we meet an author who had actually caught pike on the fly – one, moreover, who published a pike-fly dressing:

The fly must be made upon a double hook formed of one piece of wire fastened to a good link of gimp. It must be composed of very gaudy materials; such as Pheasant's, Peacock's or Mallard's feathers, with the brown and softest part of Bear's fur, the reddish part of that of a squirrel, with a little yellow mohair for the body. The head is formed of a little fur, some gold twist, and two small black or blue beads for the eyes. The body must be made rough, full and round; the wings not parted, but to stand upright on the back, and some smaller feathers continued thence all down the back, to the end of the tail; so that where

An armful of unruly rods; torture from an over-burdened shoulder bag and the hand-severing weight of a water-filled bait kettle carried along during the seemingly endless trudge down the sucking bog of an approach road is a trial soon forgotten the moment the angler catches sight of the water. As he reaches its edge, the unimpeded fresh smelling wind, now some few degrees cooler, presses against his frame and his pulse quickens. Once wriggled out of his festooning gear, he stands up seemingly weightless. Now he can hear the lapping waves and the hiss of the bowing reed stems, but above all he can hear the welcoming knock and gurgle of the boat as it chafes the jetty. He is impatient to be afloat and try for a big pike.

Fred Buller from *Pike and The Pike Angler*

Figure 156: The lapping waves, the bowing reed stems, the boat, the jetty and somewhere – a big pike?

you finish, they may be left a little longer than the hook, and the whole to be about the size of a Wren. In this manner I make this sort of fly, which will often take Pike when other baits avail nothing; it is chiefly used in dark and windy days; and you must move the fly quick when in the water, to keep it on the surface if possible. There are several sorts of these flies to be had at the fishing-tackle shops both in town and country, as well as of the hooks and tackle before described, and all others for use, completely fitted up to the sportsman's hand.

A year later, the Rev. W. B. Daniel published Taylor's description of the pike-fly dressing in his book *Rural Sports*. He also mentioned the capture of a monster 72 lb pike in Loch Ken: 'with a common fly made of the Peacock's feather'.

By the mid-nineteenth century the method had become generally accepted. Edward Fitzgibbon, in *A Handbook of Angling* (1847), wrote:

I have seen nondescript large gaudy flies kill pike well, and Mr Blacker, of Dean Street, Soho, is the best dresser of them I know. An imitation of the sand-martin or swallow, dressed by means of feathers on a large hook, will prove an attractive bait.

In the same year, Thomas Tod Stoddart, in *The Angler's Companion*, had this to say:

With regard to fly-fishing for pike, I used to practise it, many years ago, with tolerable success on dull and windy days, in a shallow loch in Fife. ... Flies ought to be big and gaudy, the wings formed each of the eye of a peacock's tail-feather, the body plentifully bedizened with dyed wool, bright hackles, and tinsels. Bead-eyes, also, are held in estimation, and gimp or wire arming is of course essential.

Figure 157: F. B. standing in William Blake's 'garden' at Salthouse Bay, Lough Corrib, Co. Mayo, with a $25\frac{1}{2}$ lb pike that he caught on a spoon. Bill did everything he could to help F. B. catch one as big (or bigger) as his own biggest – a $36\frac{1}{2}$-pounder – but so far without success

George Rooper in *Thames and Tweed* (*c.* 1870) thought that pike flies were taken for waterfowl:

We have little doubt that the so-called fly used in fishing for pike is taken by that voracious monster for a newly-hatched moorhen, dabchick, or duck, for which he has a decided predilection, clearing off, one by one, a whole brood of the twittering, unconscious, helpless victims. No doubt the increase of waterfowl is greatly kept in check by the ravages of the pike.

One of the first anglers to catch pike on fly in significant numbers by design rather than accident was Lord Gage, in his lake at Firle, near Lewes. Knox's *Game Birds and Wild Fowl; their Friends and their Foes* (1850) states that Lord Gage constructed:

... artificial birds – rather than flies – varying from the size of a wren to that of a young duck, and composed of all manner of gaudy feathers, silk, and tinsel ... when this bait is worked a little under the surface – just as they play a salmon fly on the Shannon – its movements appear exceedingly like those of a young water-fowl when diving.

Even when Gage was fishing on the Test he evidently preferred to fly-fish for pike for we find an entry in *The Chronicles of Houghton Fishing Club*:

On 15 March, 1848, Lord Gage came down to fish the Peat Pits, and on 16th and 17th caught 14 jack weighing 83 lb 9 oz with a small red fly, ribbed yellow and gold.

Just two years before Gage caught his fine bag of pike on fly, the Houghton Fishing Club's *Annual Report* published an analysis of fish caught during the season:

By members – 99 Trout weighing 201 lb 14 oz – average weight 2 lb $\frac{2}{3}$ oz; 73 Grayling weighing 129 lb 13 oz – average weight 1 lb 11 oz
By keepers – eels weighing 1,511 lb and 345 jack weighing $360\frac{1}{2}$ lb

This catch indicates that some of the most valuable water on the River Test was producing between three and four pike and about 20 eels for every rod-caught trout. It also indicates what has been re-discovered since – that if you cull pike selectively, i.e. kill the big ones, then small pike proliferate.

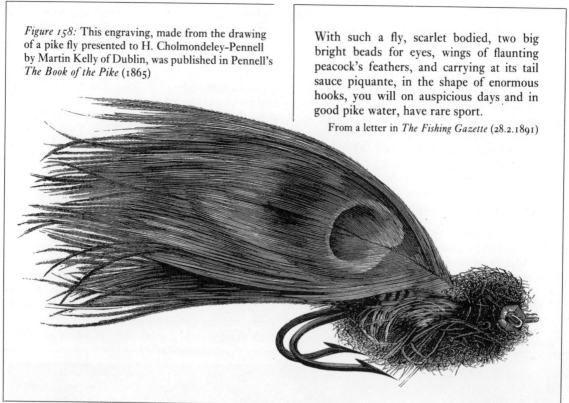

Figure 158: This engraving, made from the drawing of a pike fly presented to H. Cholmondeley-Pennell by Martin Kelly of Dublin, was published in Pennell's *The Book of the Pike* (1865)

With such a fly, scarlet bodied, two big bright beads for eyes, wings of flaunting peacock's feathers, and carrying at its tail sauce piquante, in the shape of enormous hooks, you will on auspicious days and in good pike water, have rare sport.

From a letter in *The Fishing Gazette* (28.2.1891)

John Bickerdyke in *The Book of the All-Round Angler* (1888) also described what he thought the pike fly represented:

In Lough Derg, on hot days, when the pike lay near the surface, I have known them take a fly well, even where the water was very deep. An old Irish fisherman of Banagher told me that a fly made out of the tail of a brown calf was very killing, and that he had taken many fish on such a one in a weedy backwater of the Shannon. Only the tip of the tail is used. It no doubt represents a rat. Pike probably take the usual pike-fly for a bird.

By the latter part of the nineteenth century pike-fly fishing was well established. The following account is from *The Field*, 1889:

It was getting on in September, the trout fishing in both the lochs, Tummel and Rannoch, was practically over, and friend Tommy and I were not of the fortunate ones who had a grouse moor in the neighbourhood. We had spent the entire summer trout fishing, from the inns of Tummel, Tummel Bridge and Kinloch Rannoch; but even after such a spell of

Figure 159: Alternative dressings of the old-fashioned pike fly

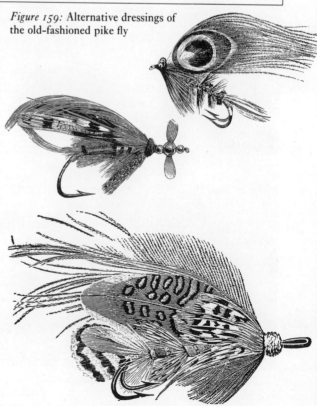

it, we were loth to leave that lovely country, and return to smoky London town. One evening we were reluctantly discussing this ultimate necessity, when somebody happened to say 'Why don't you have a go at the pike on Loch Chon before you leave?' Why not, indeed? ...

My spinning gear was at an end, and so I certainly concluded was my sport; but a thought struck me. A year or two before I had been presented with a marvellous insect, a thing of beauty, a work of art indeed, which I had been told was a pike fly. In its wing was no inconsiderable portion of the tail of a peacock, with wool of various shades which, along with hackles of gorgeous hue and a foot or two of the very broadest tinsel that formed its body, would have stuffed a moderate-sized pillow. But the leading features of this remarkable insect were its eyes, formed of two enormous glass beads, and calculated, as I thought, to strike terror into the breast of any fish which caught sight of it; even phlegmatic Donald fetched a longer breath, and took an even larger pinch of snuff when he saw it. As, however, it was the only thing in the shape of bait I had left, I cast it with a mighty effort on the bosom of the waters. It arrived with a terrific splash, but two seconds had not elapsed before it was grabbed from below the surface.

My insect proved altogether a great success. Mounted on strong gimp, it defied the best efforts of the Loch Chon pike, and at the end of a good day's sport it retired triumphant, after numerous fights, into its own proper recess in a tin box, with the loss of only one eye.

About six o'clock I foregathered with Tommy. On reckoning up our joint bag we found that we had killed fifty-two fish, weighing in the aggregate 236 lb, a very fair day's work on such a piece of water, as we both thought, and a good share of which had fallen to my much laughed at fly.

Figure 160: Ted Trueblood's bucktail fly (*top*). Ted, former associate editor of *Field & Stream*, tied this pike fly (approximately 6 in. long) with black and white bucktail. The middle and lower flies (one white and the other yellow) are based on Keys tarpon streamer flies but instead of being tied with bucktail as the Keys flies are, they are dressed on a long shank hook with a 'Palmer style' neck hackle and a streamer with six cock hackles. The finished length is approximately 5 in.

Figure 161: Fly fishing for pike in Norfolk. According to a correspondent writing in *The Field* 24 July 1865, the pike-fly was in frequent use in the Norfolk Broads and would attract good pike at a time when natural baits would 'tempt nothing over 6 lb'

Closer to modern times, Major G. L. Ashley Dodd gave his own dressing for a pike fly in *A Fisherman's Log* (1929):

I have a wonderful creature I once tied by the waterside, and on which I have caught a good many pike at one time or another. Its body is half a claret cork whipped round with red and yellow wool (taken from a rug in a farmhouse); hackle a piece of emu feather which came out of the guid wife's hat, and two peacock's 'eyes', as wings, reluctantly given up by a peacock after a stern chase. The tying silk used was a bit of unravelled string off my packet of sandwiches, which string I had waxed with the cobbler's wax I always carry.

From the *Fishing Gazette*, 1883

The curious incident depicted represents a scene from real life, and the following description is by Mr H. Band, who witnessed it. Mr B. was fishing in the Mulde, near Castle Zschepplin. He says:

'A few paces below me I noticed three young sand-martins perched on a bough which over-hung the water. They could hardly fly, and the old ones were fluttering about them. My float lay motionless on the surface. Suddenly there was a tremendous splash in the water directly down under the withie bough, which swung up and down. One bird was still on the bough, and another, after fluttering about a little, again settled down on it. I looked on in amazement;

the waves, caused by the splash, spread over the river, the surface became smooth and still again, but one bird was missing.

A bite at my line recalled my attention to fishing; but presently there was another splash under the bough, which swayed about again – the other bird was missing, and now only one remained, balancing itself with difficulty on the swinging branch. That the thief was a pike was quite evident. I stuck my rod-butt into the soft bank, and quietly approached the spot, soon finding a convenient place from which to rec-onnoitre. Steadily I watched for a long time. The final dash of the pike occurred so violently, so suddenly – and this time from the side where I had been sitting – that I could only get an instant's view of what had happened. The third sand-martin was gone. The swaying bough grew still again, and all was over.

Figure 162: Pike and sand-martins

In the late summer months and fine days in autumn, when the deeps are curled by a fine breeze, pike are to be taken very pleasantly by means of a fly. The best imitation is a very large one of a dragon fly.... An imitation of the sand-martin or swallow, dressed by means of feathers on a large hook, will prove an attractive bait for pike in the seasons last mentioned.

'Ephemera' (Edward Fitzgibbon),
A Handbook of Angling (1847)

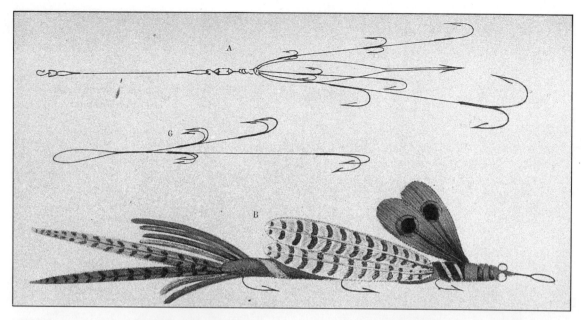

Among others who have re-discovered fly-fishing for pike are the Buckinghamshire brothers, F. J. and K. Taylor, who usually fish from a boat and retrieve their big streamer flies with a slow jerky motion. In late summer and autumn months they fish shallow weedy areas of lakes with a floating or sink-tip line, but concede that fast-sinking lines would be essential for fishing deep waters – especially during the winter season. They use leaders with specially strengthened foot-long tips of 20 lb BS nylon or 'Thin-Troll' wire.

Figure 163: (*left*) The Taylor brothers' pike flies

Figure 164: Pike fly (14 in.) from *Fly-Fishing in Salt and Fresh Water* (1851). The illustration is in colour, and instructions are given to load the fly with lead to give it 'casting weight'!

The following list of big pike caught on fly gives an idea of how successful this method can be.

The magnificent 36-pounder caught in 1981 was hooked by design and not by accident! Peter Thomsett wrote us a letter about it:

I would like to say that it was pike I was after on that day as opposed to trout. I've always had this thing about taking a pike on fly and I think that Grafham is one of the best places to do just that.

BIG PIKE CAUGHT ON FLY

Weight	Captor	Location	Country	Month	Year	Reference
36 lb 10 oz	Peter Thomsett	Grafham Res.	England	Oct	1981	*Angling Times*
30 lb	Not known	Lough Erne	Ireland	Feb	1878	Alfred Jardine's letter in *Fishing Gazette* 23.4.1904
28 lb	Frank Childs	River Dee	Scotland			Personal letter from captor
27½ lb	Lord Home, Kt.	Loch at Coldstream	Scotland	Nov		Personal communication
27 lb	Not known	Lough at Parsonstown	Ireland		1890	Letter in *Fishing Gazette* 28.2.1891

We made our way to the tower streaming our lines over the side of the boat, drifting without the aid of a drogue. On the very first drift, passing the tower to our left and with about 30 yards of line out I had a take, a sharp stab followed by a heavy draw on the rod. I struck and felt a fish kick. All went solid for a moment but then I realized the fish was moving steadily with us (in much the same way, I understand, as salmon anglers walk their fish but in this case with the boat doing the work). After a few minutes I gained some line and the fish surfaced about 20 yards from the boat lying there for a moment before diving for the bottom on a powerful run which made the centrepin really buzz.

After another five minutes or so it surfaced again, this time coming alongside the boat before tearing off once more. The thing uppermost in my mind was the

Figure 165: This magnificently marked 44 lb 1½ oz pike was caught by Willem Engelgeer while zander fishing in a canal near Amsterdam, November 1985. Anyone wishing to fish this water – said to be the best zander and pike fishing in Holland, and all within five miles of the city – is recommended to go in October or November (*Jan Eggers*)

danger of the fish chafing through the leader. I then asked my companion to throw out the drogue to slow our drift, the boat moving steadily in stiff wind. It was then a case of steady pressure.

This fish was, to say the least, very obliging, Mike netting it first go. The trouble came when he tried to lift it and found he couldn't. I lent a hand to get it over the side. When we laid it on the floorboards and opened the mesh we were both absolutely dumbstruck at the sight of such a superb pike.

Cooking the Pike

The Victorians, it seems, cared little for pike as food, even though Victorian writers concocted numerous recipes. In her *Dictionary of Cookery* (1872), Mrs Beeton offers the following:

PIKE – A LA GENEVESE

4 or 5 lb pike sliced $1\frac{1}{2}''$ thick
2 chopped shallots
Parsley
Bunch of herbs
2 bay leaves
2 carrots
Ground mace
Pepper and salt
4 tablespoonsful madeira or sherry
$\frac{1}{2}$ pint white stock
Flour
Butter
1 teaspoonful essence of anchovies
Juice of a lemon
Cayenne pepper

Rub the bottom of a stewpan over with butter, and put in the shallots, herbs, bay leaves, carrots, mace and seasoning; stir them for ten minutes over a clear fire, and add the madeira or sherry; simmer gently half an hour, and strain through a sieve over the fish, which stews in this gravy. As soon as the fish is sufficiently cooked take away all the liquor, except a little to keep the pike moist, and put it into another stewpan; add the stock, thicken with butter and flour, and put lemon juice, cayenne and salt, lay the pike on a hot dish, pour over it part of the sauce, and serve the remainder in a tureen. Time, $1\frac{1}{4}$ hours. Sufficient for six or eight persons.

The French regarded the pike in a very different light. In 1898, Georges Auguste Escoffier, unquestionably one of the greatest chefs the world has ever known, frequently called the 'King of Chefs and the Chef of Kings', began writing notes for a book which was to become the classic work on French cuisine: *A Guide to Modern Cookery*.

Since Escoffier is regarded as the *doyen* of *haute cuisine*, anglers may be interested in his *Quenelles de Brochet à la Lyonnaise* – the details of which we are happy to provide.

1 lb pike meat
1 lb beef kidney fat
1 lb frangipane panada
4 egg whites

Pound separately 1 lb of the meat of pike, cleared of all skin and bones, and 1 lb of the fat of kidney of beef, very dry, cleaned, and cut into small pieces. If desired, half the weight of the fat of kidney of beef may be replaced by $\frac{1}{2}$ lb of beef marrow.

Put the pounded meat of the pike and the kidney fat on separate plates. Now pound 1 lb frangipane panada and add thereto, little by little, the whites of 4 little eggs. Put the pike meat and the fat back in the mortar, and finely pound the whole until a fine smooth paste is obtained. Rub the latter through a sieve; put the resulting puree in a basin, and work it well with a wooden spoon in order to smooth it.

Of the Pike. His Names, Nature, Size, Age and Vertue

The Pike is a melancholy Fish, swims by himself and lives alone. His Flesh is very Midicinal: The Croslike bone in his Head is given against the Falling-sickness; and his Flesh is so harmless and excellent, that it may be given to a sick Person. His Spawn and Row provoke both to Vomit and Stool, and are used for that Purpose; the jaws cacin'd helps the Stone, cleanses and dries up Ulcers, old Sores and Hemorrhoids; the Teeth in Powder gives ease in the Pleurisie, the grease takes away Coughs in Children, by anointing the Feet therewith; the Gall taken inwardly, cures Agues; outwardly helps Spots and Dimness of the Eyes; the Heart eaten cures Fevers.

Robert Howlett from *The Angler's Sure Guide: or Angling Improved* (1706)

With this forcemeat, mould some quenelles with a spoon and poach them in salted water.

If these quenelles are to be served with an ordinary fish sauce, put them into it as soon as they are poached and drained, and simmer them in it for 10 minutes that they may swell.

If the sauce intended for them is to be thickened with egg yolks and buttered at the last moment, put them into a saucepan with a few tablespoons of fumet, and simmer them as directed in the case of an ordinary fish sauce, taking care to keep the saucepan well covered that the concentrated steam may assist the swelling of the quenelles. In this case they are added to the sauce at the last moment.

N.B. Slices of truffle may always be added to the sauce. The quenelles are dished either in a silver timbale, in a shallow timbale crust, or in a fine vol-au-vent crust, in accordance with the arrangement of the menu.

FRANGIPANE PANADA

4 oz sifted flour
4 egg yolks
Salt and pepper
Nutmeg
3 oz melted butter
$\frac{1}{2}$ pint milk

Put into a stewpan 4 oz sifted flour, the yolks of 4 eggs, a little salt, pepper and nutmeg. Now add by degrees 3 oz melted butter and dilute with $\frac{1}{2}$ pint boiled milk. Pass through a strainer, stir over the fire until the boil is reached; set to cook for five minutes whilst gently wielding the whisk. Lightly butter the surface of the panada in order to avoid its drying while it cools.

And now a recipe from a well-known British sportsman:

1 pike
1 lb beef suet
1 lb grated bread
Salt and pepper
Nutmeg
Shredded lemon peel
Thyme
Chopped anchovies
Egg yolks
Lemon juice

Sauce

1 pint of beef gravy
1 pint shrimps
$\frac{1}{2}$ pint stewed mushrooms
A quart of stewed oysters
Wineglass of port
1 lb melted butter

I suppose that the usual way to cook pike is to bake it. That is quite a job, but the result can be delicious. First of all you must scale the fish and then dry it carefully with a clean towel. Then you need a pound of beef suet and a pound of grated bread, and mix and season with salt, pepper and nutmeg; work into this some shredded lemon peel and some thyme and some chopped anchovies and the yolk of eggs (three eggs to an eight-pound fish), and then squeeze lemon juice over the whole, and place it in the stomach of the fish. Sew the fish up, and bake in an oven until the skin cracks. And now you need a sauce. This sauce is the real secret of baked pike. And the best sauce is compounded thus: a pint of beef gravy, a pint of skinned shrimps, half a pint of stewed mushrooms, a quart of stewed oysters, a wineglass full of port; mix this into a pound of melted butter. Now take the thread out of your pike, pour the sauce over him, and enjoy yourself.

But the best way of all, in my opinion, to cook pike is this: Clean and scale your fish, and then boil or parboil it and then bone it: cut the white flakes of flesh into strips of an inch or so, and fry them in bread crumbs (if you have an egg so much the better). That served hot with a lemon, if possible, and thin bread and butter is a dish for a king. (From Brian Vesey-Fitzgerald, *The Hampshire Avon* (1950))

Figure 166: F. B.'s biggest pike was $47\frac{1}{4}$ in. long. It weighed 32 lb. Tomorrow perhaps he will catch one 50 in. long that will be as fat as a pig. Thank goodness for *tomorrow* – that quintessential day which generates optimism for all anglers.

In ancient Greece they knew all that went on in an angler's mind – or at least Theocritus did when he wrote: 'In sleep, dogs dream of (hunting) bears, and of (large sized) fish dream I'

The Pike

And, lastly, Pike Fishcakes:

Since there is no pleasure in munching a mouthful of bones, a pike should be filleted before any attempt is made to cook it. Although difficult to describe, this operation is very easy to perform.

Two knives are required: one pointed, the other broad. Place the pike belly down on a table. Press the point of the gutting (or pointed) knife into the pike's back at the rear of the skull, and make a cut about an inch deep along one side of the backbone until the cut passes alongside and beyond the dorsal fin as shown in illustration (a). Repeat.the same stroke on the other side of the backbone (the cuts should be about $\frac{1}{8}$ in. apart), which will bring the blade past and beyond the other side of the dorsal fin. In (b), the backbone is just revealed. Lay the pike on its side, and with the same knife make a cut down the body immediately behind the gill-cover, and another a few inches forward of the tail fin (see the position of the knives in (c)). Still using the same knife, slit open the belly from the vent until both cuts are reached.

Lay the pike on its side with its back towards you and place the broad flat knife in the uppermost cut (one of the two cuts made along the backbone); draw the knife gently from end to end in a flowing motion; the blade follows the ribs until the whole side falls away complete as shown in (d).

Note: Wearing a cotton gardening glove helps when cleaning very slippery fish, like pike.

The late J. St John, well known to Berkshire sportsmen, used to take numbers of pike in the Loddon with the end of a calf's tail tied to a triangle. He occasionally used a squirrel's tail. The latter I have tried with some success. No doubt these baits are taken for rats. They should be drawn along the surface at a fair speed.

Anon (*c*. 1901)

Turn the pike over, still with its back towards you, and repeat the same operation until the other side falls away. Cut out the ventral fins with the gutting knife, as shown in (e). Now grip the thin end of the fillet, after laying it down on the table, and proceed to cut through the flesh down to the skin, changing the angle of the knife so as to make it run almost parallel to the skin, but taking care not to cut through the skin (f). The unusable remains, except for the skin and ventral fins, are left intact (g). Once the fillets are isolated and washed, hold them up for a minute to drain; then place them on a large plate and sprinkle with a fine layer of salt. Two or three hours' salting is sufficient if the pike is to be cooked the same day. Otherwise, place the salted fillets in a refrigerator.

Figure 167 (*right*): Filleting a pike

As the year advances from winter, a pike's food requirements increase. They become nearly double in late spring, and reach a maximum in June. Although temperature is significant, daylight is the main factor governing a pike's food intake. From this it might be thought that late June/July should provide an angler with his best sport. This could well be the case in large lochs; but not in smaller shallower waters, where weed cover is profuse. The pike's technique of attacking from ambush is most successful in conditions of abundant weed, and in this situation fewer hungry pike are available to the angler.

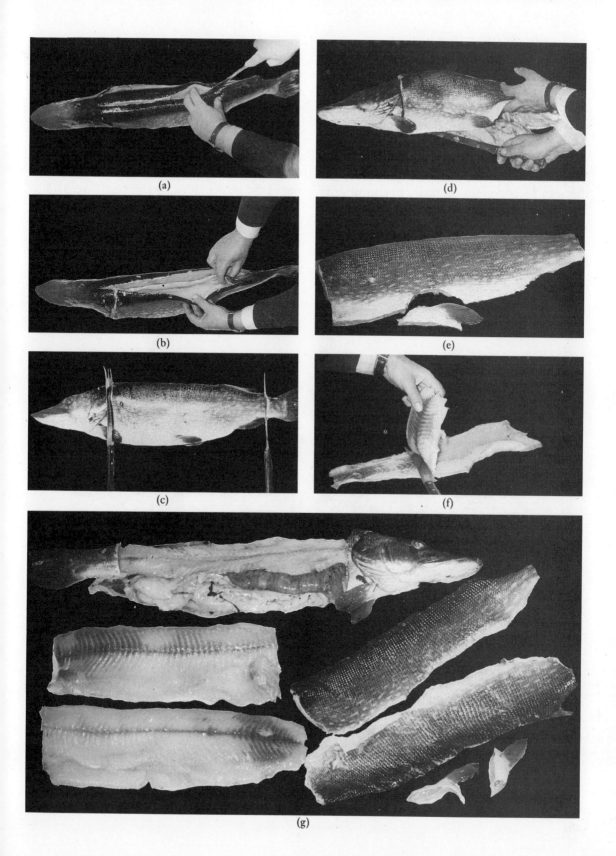

(a)

(b)

(c)

(d)

(e)

(f)

(g)

COOKING THE FISHCAKES

Pike fillets
Mashed potatoes
Parsley
Breadcrumbs

Boil the fillets for ten minutes; drain off and mash. Mix the cooked fish with an equal amount of boiled, mashed potato; sprinkle with parsley. Shape the fish/potato mash into fish cakes and dip into breadcrumbs or flour. Fry until crisp and brown. Serve with a knob of butter on each fish-cake.

Izaak Walton said of pike: 'This dish of meat is too good for any but Anglers, or very honest men.' After eating five of these fish cakes, suggests F. B., contemplate Walton's statement and consider whether even honest men should qualify for such a feast.

Choosing a pike for the table

In the first edition of *The Driffield Angler* (1806) the author Alexander Mackintosh, speaking of the ideal culinary weight for pike, said:

They are in season from the beginning of May till spawning time; the flesh is firm, dry and sweet; from seven to twelve pounds are the best fish, and under three they are watery and insipid.

Figure 168: 'Pike fishing at Killaloe' (Lough Derg, Ireland)
from *The Illustrated Sporting and Dramatic News*
(21 November 1891)

The
ROACH
Rutilus rutilus

There is a large class of anglers who confine their attention exclusively to this branch of fishing; they are never tempted to try any other, and I have fancied more than once that they rather prided themselves on the fact. But there is one thing certain; a successful roach fisherman stands on the very highest rung of the angling ladder.

'Trent Otter' (J. W. Martin)

The roach, in common with the bream, the dace, the tench and many other freshwater species, is a member of the carp family (Cyprinidae). Although absent from Norway and other high regions, including those of Scotland and Wales, it is generally distributed throughout the temperate parts of Western and Central Europe, and Eastern Europe as far as the USSR. According to the celebrated ichthyologist, Tate Regan, it is also found in Russian Turkestan and throughout Siberia.

It is not thought to be indigenous to Ireland. Alwyne Wheeler remarks that the only native Irish freshwater fish are sticklebacks, eels and shads. It has, however, established itself in the Foyle and Erne systems of Northern Ireland, and the Blackwater and Shannon of southern Ireland. In October 1970, an angler took a match-record bag of roach (64 lb 7½ oz) from the Erne below Belturbet, just five years after the first appearance of roach in that river.

The true home of British roach is in the sluggish waters of England's eastern rivers where the land is low-lying, but colonies have established themselves as far north as Loch Lomond and Teith in Scotland and, more recently, in Esthwaite Tarn in the English Lake District.

The penetration of roach to these higher areas seems to be linked with the changes that have occurred in some mountain lakes due to eutrophication – a process of becoming richer in dissolved nutrient salts.

The roach is a shoal fish and tends to swim in a shoal throughout its life: a point of considerable importance to the angler. A roach shoal usually consists of fish that have collected together soon after hatching, and subsequently kept together; although when shoals are reduced in size by natural hazards some mixing is noticeable, particularly in small waters.

The roach has no mouth teeth. Instead, it possesses throat or pharyngeal teeth, a feature of all cyprinids. These throat teeth enable the roach to crush food particles against a hard plate attached to the basal part of the skull.

Every roach angler must at some time or other have suffered the indignity of retrieving a bunch of maggot skins whose contents were sucked 'dry' without so much as a warning tremble of the float! This is the work of pharyngeal teeth.

Roach are omnivorous, subsisting on a mixed diet of animal and plant life. Adult roach find most of their food on or near the bottom – or, as bygone writers put it, 'at ground'. Their animal diet has been found to include the larvae of midges (Chironomids), caddis (Trichoptera),

mayflies (Ephemeroptera), as well as invertebrates such as shrimps (Gammarus), snails (Mollusca), and the water louse (Asellus). Their plant diet includes filamentous algae and some of the higher plants. Roach also feed on the pupae of many insects both in midwater and at sub-surface levels. During spells of warm weather they will take flies at the surface.

Anglers contribute enormously to the diet of roach. Literally tons of groundbait, both animal and vegetable, are thrown into heavily fished waters – and eaten by the fish.

Roach reach their peak condition in winter. During this period their ovaries and testes develop in weight, until by late spring the eggs and milt are ripe for spawning. By this time, male roach have developed numerous white conical tubercles on the head, the fin rays, and even on the scales. They are now noticeably rough to the touch. As the Rev. W. B. Daniel put it in *Rural Sports* (1801): 'They feel like the rough side of an oyster shell'.

Figure 169: A brace of roach from stillwater (Molesey Reservoir), including the former British Record roach, 3 lb 14 oz, caught by W. Penney on 6 September 1938

Spawning is carried out in the weedy shallows when the water temperature reaches about 59°F (15°C). The eggs adhere to the vegetation and usually hatch within nine to twelve days. After spawning, river roach migrate to the streamy runs. The reason for this migration has yet to be established.

In a favourite habitat with good feeding, roach commonly grow to a weight of 2 lb. A weight of 4 lb is likely to be the upper limit, but even in extremely favourable conditions such a weight is a rarity.

Since the roach is not highly regarded as a table fish, its economic value is low, except in those European countries that have no access to a supply of fresh sea fish. Where freshwater fish are prized for food, there is usually a long record of fish cultivation.

A great deal is known about the roach in Czechoslovakia, where written records of fish cultivation go back to the eleventh and twelfth centuries, and about 96% of all marketable fish is supplied from freshwater fish farms.

Most countries try to benefit from the study and application of advanced agricultural techniques. It is sad to record that although United Kingdom authorities should be looking to countries like Czechoslovakia for guidance in the techniques of coarse fish cultivation, they are not doing so. On the subject of coarse fish culture, Britain is truly backward. Where else, when dealing with the problems of poor fishing, would people transfer roach – netted from one water where they are unwanted, to another water – without thought for the infertile conditions of that new water, or of the limitations of its productive capacity, or the fate of the freshly introduced inmates? And the roach is by no means the only species to suffer such treatment.

If the importance of a fish species depended not on its commercial value but on the number of anglers who derived pleasure from catching it, the roach would deserve special consideration. No British record is so coveted as that of the biggest rod-caught roach: it is Britain's most popular sport-fish, giving enjoyment to more anglers than any other species. 'The successful roach fisher,' writes Denys Watkins Pitchford,

'is an artist. His tackle is fine, his "strike" is delicate and true, as swift and polished as the action of the fly fisher. He casts beautifully with unerring aim.' It was not always thus.

By contrast to present-day enthusiasm, Guiniad Charfy, writing two hundred years ago, thought roach:

Notorious for their simplicity and being easily taken. When they are hooked you have no more trouble with them; and therefore they are called the Water Sheep, being so mild and so ready to yield.

It must be conceded that the roach is not the most furious of fighters. Further, that small roach are exceedingly easy to catch. But the catching of *big* roach is altogether another matter. Specimen-roach fishing is as difficult as small-roach fishing is easy: it demands considerable skill and places an angler high in any piscatorial order of merit.

Roach angling methods are common to practically every branch of freshwater fishing: ledgering, rolling ledger, float-ledgering, laying-on, lift-fishing, stret-pegging, trotting, long-trotting, poling, fly fishing with artificials both wet and dry, dapping with the natural insect, all are skilled techniques. The angler who has mastered these and can consistently catch big roach is capable of catching anything.

The methods are studied in principle elsewhere in this book; but, as with all angling methods, they admit of infinite adjustment to meet the challenge of ever-changing conditions at the waterside. It is the ability to recognize and supply the need for some subtle variation in technique that singles out the expert angler from the rest.

TROTTING

In running water the most popular method of catching roach is swimming the stream, or 'trotting'. From a stretch of river the angler selects a swim of a dozen yards or so, and in doing this makes use of a long-established principle: fish are not evenly spread out along a water-course but, for reasons of safety, comfort and food availability, concentrated in certain pockets.

After judicious groundbaiting (see page 436) the angler begins his routine of casting to the head of the swim, just a little upstream of him, and retrieving from the downstream end. All seemingly straightforward. But during his day's fishing, our expert will almost certainly make many alterations in attempting to satisfy the changing demands of the fish. Some of these adjustments may be very slight indeed, but all of them significant to the total weight of his catch. For example, he may:

1. Change the hook size.

2. Try a different bait.

3. Vary the fishing depth by increasing or decreasing the distance between float and hook.

Figure 170: Trotting: an expert in action. Dave Steuart brings a fine roach to the net

4. Substitute a float carrying more weight to make the bait sink faster, or a float carrying less weight to allow the bait to sink more slowly.

5. Trot at longer range, by standing twenty or thirty yards upstream of the fish. (In clear water, roach are extremely shy.)

6. Change his rod. The longer the range at which roach are hooked, the greater the strain imposed on tackle by the strike. Because of this, and because heavier floats with more weight are normally used, a stronger, more supple rod is more efficient for this type of fishing.

The Roach

Figure 171: We make no excuse for re-using this sequence of photographs depicting the late Richard Walker using an old-fashioned roach-pole because the effective use of a pole in certain fishing situations, regardless of the material used for the pole's construction, never seems to change

A ROACH-POLE TECHNIQUE

Practitioners of the old River Thames and River Lea roach-poling tradition are being joined by a steady flow of new pole-fishing enthusiasts. This enthusiasm for pole-fishing is inspired by the example of Continental (mostly French) anglers, who use this technique so successfully in international competition.

Although it would be unwise to consider the roach-pole technique the complete answer to a match fisherman's problems, we must concede that the fixed-float, long-pole technique is deadly when fish are feeding in deep water.

To float-fish such water demands a sliding float, resulting in a considerable loss of hooking efficiency due to slack line. This loss is greatest at maximum range and depth, when the line is bent at full 90° to the float.

The strike achieves its greatest efficiency when the rod-tip is directly above the float.

The length of a roach-pole enables an angler to float-fish, float-ledger, or lay-on effectively in water otherwise held to be a swing-tip or ledger swim.

Tackling up

Baiting – with boiled wheat

Now – wait for it

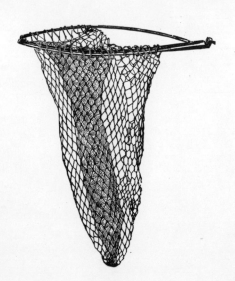

Got him!

Keep out of sight and let the net do the work

Lift the fish straight up with the minimum disturbance

A nice catch of medium roach

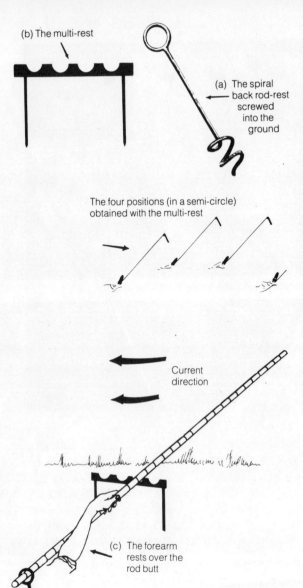

(b) The multi-rest

(a) The spiral back rod-rest screwed into the ground

The four positions (in a semi-circle) obtained with the multi-rest

Current direction

(c) The forearm rests over the rod butt

Because of the powerful lever action of any long rod, it has always been difficult to make full use of the exceptional length of a roach-pole. If an attempt is made to hold most of the rod out over the water, ordinary rod-rests get pulled out of the ground. An ingenious back rod-rest (figure 172 (a)) eliminates this problem. Used in conjunction with a multiple front rod-rest 172 (b) several spots in a swim can be searched with a laying-on or float-ledger technique. With these items, some twenty feet of a twenty-four-foot roach-pole can be made to overhang the river.

Figure 172 (c) illustrates how the forearm is used to counteract the leverage of the rod at the moment of striking. Experienced 'polers', swimming the stream from a sitting position, make use of knee and thigh to augment the support of the forearm: the thigh is moved in unison with the arm as the rod follows the float from head to tail of the swim. With some of the newer super-lightweight carbon poles, this extra support is unnecessary.

Figure 172: (left) Back rod-rest invented by R. Crosbie of the Harlesden Angling Society

Figure 174 (right): Roach-poling by a sluice on the River Thames at Hurley, 1811 style. The pole appears to be over 20 ft long (*Messrs Walter T. Spencer*)

Figure 173: (below) The most modern 'pole' is made from a composite of carbon and boron and it is made in lengths of up to 40 ft. and currently (1987) costs twice as much as the most expensive salmon fly rod, i.e. some £600. *Note:* See page 508 for special warning for owners of such rods

A LEDGERING TECHNIQUE FOR HAMPSHIRE AVON ROACH

Although the rolling ledger is a well-established and effective method of fishing the lower Hampshire Avon, it is often less rewarding when used on the middle Avon. After trying many variations on the theme, in the course of which he reluctantly discarded the often invaluable swimfeeder, F. B. began to think that ledgering in these waters took second place to float-fishing.

A walk down the river bank early one morning, on a day favourable for seeing fish, made him think again. In that low clear water he saw many shoals of large roach lying close to the bank. So long as these fish remained undisturbed they concentrated in swims along a line between the flowing water and the dead water at the edge (see figure 175). Moreover, a chance conversation with a very successful Avon roach fisher revealed that a number of three-pound roach had been taken after dark very close to the bank.

Generally speaking, deep water provides security for fish and, as a consequence, can be searched by them for food at any time of the day or night. On the other hand, shallow water, particularly the shallow strip close to the bank, provides no sense of security except at night, or during floods, or when the water is completely undisturbed. As a result, shallow waters can be cropped only when one or more of these special conditions obtain.

Because they are seldom visited, these shallow areas must offer better feeding and so become a great attraction. Water-borne food particles temporarily coming to rest somewhere in areas where streamy water fades into slack, add to this attraction.

To fish a ledgered bait into such an area, however, is anything but straightforward. Apart from the difficulty of pinpointing the shoal without alarming it, Avon roach in particular are very sensitive to splash – perhaps due to the absence of boat traffic – so that a direct cast frightens them back into the faster and deeper water. After experiment, the following technique was evolved. Of all methods used for catching large roach from the Hampshire Avon, this has proved the most deadly.

Because of its sensitivity and flexibility, use a medium fly rod for this type of fishing rather than the usual Avon-type rod. The latter is not needed because a long line is never fished.

The most important item of tackle is an ultra-light casting weight – an $\frac{1}{8}$ oz, or $\frac{1}{4}$ oz Arlesey Bomb.

Tackle-up well back from the water's edge and approach the head of the swim with great care.

Take portions from the inside of a new loaf, wetted and pressed sufficiently to sink, and release them quietly into the run with the aid of a landing net.

Cast a little more than halfway across the river at an angle of 45° downstream.

As soon as the lead enters the water, hold the rod high and let the current swing lead and crust-baited hook round in an arc.

With a normal winter flow, and such a light weight, the terminal tackle scarcely touches bottom. Holding the rod high helps to speed up the swing round. This ensures that the bread will not become fully saturated and part company with the hook before coming to rest.

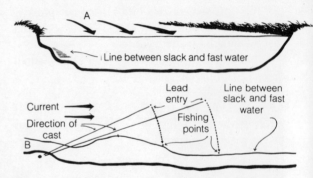

Figure 175: Fishing at ground provides a better chance of coming to terms with large roach. The big fish are inclined to feed on the bottom. Small fish tend to search for food particles in suspension

Provided you have not chosen to fish an outside bend of the river, the baited hook should now be resting in an area where the current fades into slack water (see figure 175).

Put the rod in a rest at right-angles to the direction of the flow, and fit a natural dough-bobbin bite-indicator to the line (figure 176). An alternative lay-out for the bite indicator is shown in figure 177.

Remember: the utmost caution is necessary if the fish are to remain unfrightened. Indeed, it is well to emulate the trout fly fisherman – and *kneel.*

Disturbance caused by catching one or two roach will necessitate a move of three or four yards downstream. At once repeat the ground-baiting process.

Figure 176: A swimfeeder technique for roach

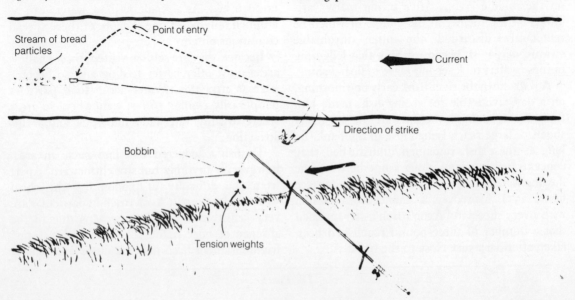

This time expect the bites to come quickly, for the first groundbaiting will have activated roach throughout the swim.

Because roach, even big roach, have small mouths compared with most other fish, it is advisable to use very small pieces of crust on a size 10 Mackenzie (or other fine, round-bend) hook. Although bites are just as frequent on bigger pieces of crust, fewer fish are hooked.

All roach over a pound are exciting to play on a light fly-rod. When hooked, big roach give a characteristic bump-bump sensation quite different from that of the occasional rogue chub, which tends to make a sudden dart.

Use crust from the top corners of an under-baked tin loaf. The rest can be broken up into small pieces and added sparingly to the crumb groundbait. Never use secondary groundbaits such as bran or cloud. Unlike their lesser brethren, big roach don't feed on one kind of groundbait and take another kind of hookbait – unless, of course, they are very hungry.

Crust is the deadliest of all baits for big Avon roach or, indeed, for big roach anywhere.

Although it is true that big roach are sometimes caught on maggots, most maggot-fishing anglers will have to catch many hundreds of small roach before they tighten on a two-pounder.

Big roach are usually the last to start feeding. Don't spoil your chance of catching them by trying to liven things up in the meantime. Small roach well on the feed are easily caught, but the disturbance caused by hooking and landing them one after another puts the big chaps down. So – be patient.

Figure 177 (c) shows an enlarged view of a modern doughbobbin bite indicator. The Beta-light contained within the body of the indicator enables an angler to see a bite in total darkness just as well as in daylight.

Figure 177 (d) shows a Beta-light fitted to a float.

Luminous float: Glow-worm inside a swan-quill float.

Howlett

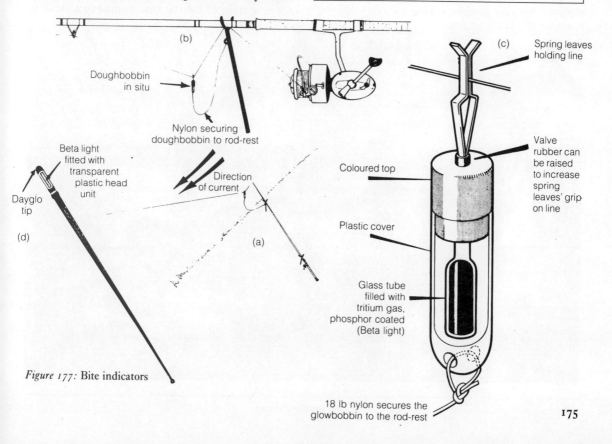

Figure 177: Bite indicators

A SWIMFEEDER TECHNIQUE ON THE DORSET STOUR

Sometimes in the written word and often in the minds of anglers, the Dorset Stour is coupled with the Hampshire Avon. But although it holds the same species of fish, and although it drains a neighbouring watershed before entering the sea as one with the Avon, the Stour demands a separate understanding. It has a greater variation of mood and character. The upper and middle reaches in particular have sections of lazy, muddy-bottomed deeps, frequently alternating with gravelly shallows. There is less urgency in the stream.

This slower current is essentially the difference between the two rivers.

Many anglers who have enjoyed success on the Avon find themselves in difficulty when they fish the Stour. A bag of chub is commonplace on the Avon; on the middle and upper Stour it is a rarity. So is the heavy mixed bag of fish taken by any one method and any one bait. Each of the many Stour species has its own special needs, and the roach is no exception.

If you wish to catch roach, you must fish for roach. But first you must locate them.

To this end the Stour is an accommodating river. In times of low water it displays its fish temptingly for all to see. A careful drift in a boat on a summer's day will reveal a host of fishes, likely to cause tackle-fumbling excitement even to the steadiest of anglers.

As you walk the bank you may notice the absence of roach from certain likely-looking stretches but find them here and there in unexpected 'pockets'. Usually they lie in the deeper runs, in the permanent open water of bridge pools and mill pools where they find their much-needed security. Such places often hold their own local shoals of roach – big, educated and hard to catch.

When the water is crystal clear and you are able to find and lay siege to a shoal of good roach, use fine, floatless and sometimes weightless tackle: a style of fishing that demands a stealthy

Figure 178: Six big roach caught in Hornsey Mere between the wars and set up after capture. They are all over 2 lb; the largest $2\frac{3}{4}$ lb and 11 years old (*Roy Shaw*)

Figure 179: Ranunculus on the Dorset Stour

approach, sometimes even a belly-crawl. If success follows, the pleasure comes not so much from the bag of fish, whatever its size, but from the manner of its taking.

In the tinted streams of autumn and winter, when the quarry can no longer be seen, roach can be expected to occupy the first substantial deeps beyond a stretch of shallows. Now you are fishing 'blind', and your technique must be changed accordingly.

Start fishing about eight yards above a known roach swim and, if the river is narrow, contrive to fish from the shallow side into the deep. This is important, since it is in the deepest part of a swim that fish find maximum security – and you must not be too close to them.

For groundbait, tear up two new loaves into hook-size pieces. These should be kept in a screw-lid sweetshop bottle to retain their original freshness.

Fill a swimfeeder straight from the bottle in the manner of the pipe smoker who fills his pipe from a pouch. But press gently; fresh crust and crumb will grip easily on the inside of the feeder.

The hookbait should be taken from the corners of a fresh, underbaked tin loaf, also kept fresh in a sealed container.

Let the loaded feeder hang clear while you bait a size 10 round-bend hook. Do this by biting off an irregular piece of crust, say about $\frac{5}{8}$ in. x $\frac{3}{8}$ in. x $\frac{3}{8}$ in., and pulling the hook right through the bait until the barb is exposed on the opposite side.

A light, medium length, all-action rod is used to put the swimfeeder and bait approximately 30° downstream of an imaginary line drawn straight across the river. Cast accurately to a chosen point each time, and let the stream take the feeder round in an arc on a tight line until it settles. Allow the contents of the feeder to soak for a few seconds; then make a long forearm strike to clear the feeder.

Repeat the process at least a dozen times. This will ensure that the river bed is carpeted with pieces of bread indistinguishable from the hookbait. When roach start to feed they invariably work upstream to the food source, and if your crust-baited hook is lying nicely among many similar pieces of crust it will cause the downfall of even the most suspicious roach.

A light, supple rod is essential for this style of ledgering, since it helps you to achieve slowly accelerated and accurate casts. Slow acceleration prevents the groundbait from being flung out of the feeder during casting. Even more important is the ability of the rod to function as an efficient shock absorber. Clumsy splashes will frighten the fish. Slow the feeder down just before it hits the water by trapping line coming off the spool.

Monofilament of 5 lb BS as the mainline is about right, with a 3 lb hook-link.

The distance between the feeder and the bottom eye of a three-way swivel should remain at fourteen inches.

The length between hook and swivel can be varied to suit conditions, but 3 ft is usual. These proportions ensure that when pieces of groundbait are washed out of the feeder by the current, they lay a trail downstream directly over the hookbait.

On most Stour roach swims it is possible to use a bite indicator. The most sensitive type is one that incorporates the doughbobbin principle. This signals a warning tremble and provides a biting fish with at least a foot of slack line. This slack is important, for it allows time for a bite to develop and gives the angler a chance to 'read' the bite. Recommended, is a clip 'Dobob', painted in contrasting colours, so that it can be seen regardless of the background. When necessary, weight is added to the bottom compartment. Suitably weighted, the 'Dobob' just counteracts the pull of the stream and gives the line the right amount of sag.

With this style of ledgering, the rod should be set up at right-angles to the line so that a sideways strike has immediate effect. If you ledger, as

Figure 180: For most British roach anglers such a beautiful specimen as this would be the catch of the year

some anglers do, with the rod pointing straight down the line, quick hook penetration is unlikely, since the line cannot be recovered at the same speed as the rodtip until the latter has been raised through 90°. Simple geometry illustrates the point. In practice, having the rod correctly angled means that it points 30° upstream, while the line points 60° downstream.

Resist the temptation to ginger up proceedings by using maggots. Maggots encourage the small fish. If these are caught in numbers, the suspicions of the big roach will be aroused.

Using the method just described, F. B. has caught some very good bags of large roach:

On one memorable occasion even the smallest capture weighed 1 lb 7 oz, and the best was well over 2 lb. On this particular day I resisted the temptation to use maggots, even though my companions were using them successfully to catch numbers of fine roach. My pleasure came later that evening.... There is only one sight better than a good bag of fine quality roach: a better bag of even finer quality roach!

FLY-FISHING FOR ROACH

There are times and places, both much commoner than many anglers suppose, which offer splendid chances of taking roach on the fly – a method that sometimes proves more successful than any other. Our old friend Richard Walker was very fond of roach fly-fishing and once, in conversation, we recorded his views on it:

In very hot weather, shoals of roach may rise to the surface and then they can be caught with a dry-fly. J. W. Dunne's dressing for the black gnat being a very successful fly, though there are times when really big roach will rise to a much larger fly. I have caught roach between one and two pounds on sedge imitations tied on hooks as large as size 10, and once or twice on artificial daddy-long-legs on size 10 longshank hooks.

It is much more common to find roach catchable with a sunk fly, however, and there are two outstandingly successful patterns, both nymphs. One is the Pheasant Tail; the other a little olive nymph with its abdomen ribbed with the narrowest gauge flat gold tinsel. Sixteen is the most useful size, though sometimes a size 14 is taken readily.

I have caught literally hundreds of good roach on

From first appearing of the rising Sunne,
Till nine of clocke low under water best
The fish will bite, and then from nine to noone,
From noone to foure they doe refraine and rest,
From foure again till Phoebus swift hath runne,
His daily course, and setteth in the West:
But at the flie aloft they use to bite,
All summer long from nine till it be night.

John Dennys, *Secrets of Angling*

one or other of these nymph patterns from many different rivers and lakes; from the Hampshire Avon to the Tweed; from south-country gravel pits to Loch Lomond. By introducing more or less fine copper wire into the dressing, the nymph can be made to fish at almost any desired depth. The secret of success in using it is to let it sink as far as conditions demand, then to retrieve it slowly and steadily without any jerks, being prepared to strike instantly if the slightest pluck or check is felt.

It is advantageous to use a knotless tapered leader down to 4X or 5X ($3\frac{3}{4}$ lb–$2\frac{1}{2}$ lb BS) at the point, because roach will often nip at the knots in an ordinary leader.

I don't suggest for a moment that fly-fishing will ever supersede the usual methods of roach fishing, such as trotting, ledgering, laying-on, lift-method and stret-pegging. But I do say that the roach fisher who doesn't possess and has not learned to use a fly rod is handicapped. He will miss many opportunities of catching roach that could have been taken in satisfactory numbers with fly-fishing equipment – as well as the very deep pleasure that the use of a fly-rod offers.

Roach fly-fishing doesn't necessarily involve the use of artificial flies. At times a small hook about size 16, tied to the end of a fine leader, baited with a single maggot and cast with a fly rod, will catch roach after roach, often in hot weather and gin-clear water where the splash of the lightest float tackle or ledger lead would scare the fish.

I also believe that up to the present we have only touched the fringe of the possibilities that fly-fishing can offer for roach and, indeed, other coarse fish, and that the angler who experiments will find exploration of these possibilities quite fascinating.

Cooking the Roach

H. F., who has tried, suggests that roach are just eatable if carefully filleted, dipped in milk, rolled in flour, fried in butter and served with slices of lemon.

Unfortunately, no writers that we have read give instructions for coping with the tiny, needle-sharp bones with which roach (and most other coarse species) abound. There seems no alternative to picking them out one by one, either before the fish is served or between each mouthful. Even Mrs Beeton has ducked this one!

The following two receipes are from Mrs E. M. Walker's *The Sportsman's Cookbook* (1978):

BAKED ROACH

3 lb (1½ kg) whole fish
Butter
Shallots or onion
Parsley
Salt and pepper
¼ pt (150 ml) dry white wine
¼ pt (150 ml) double cream

Butter generously an ovenproof dish and cover the base with chopped onions or shallots. Scatter over them parsley, salt and pepper, lay in the fish and dot with butter. Cover and bake in a fairly hot oven (400°F, 200°C, gas mark 6) for 15 minutes. Add the white wine, put back in the oven for a few minutes, then pour over sufficient cream to cover and cook for another 5 minutes before serving. *Serves 6.*

Tench is also good cooked in this way.

> ... a blank fishing day does not necessarily mean an unenjoyable (or uneventful) one ... to capture something of the calm philosophy of Izaak Walton is just as important as the ability to kill a large number of fish.
>
> A. Courtney Williams, *Angling Diversions* (1945)

BOILED ROACH

Put in a stewpan 1 quart (1 litre) of water with ¼ pint (150 ml) vinegar, salt, pepper, a *bouquet garni* and a tablespoon of grated horseradish. Bring to the boil, put in the fish, turn down heat and simmer 15-20 minutes. Serve with a sauce (either onion or caper would be good).

Caper Sauce
Add 2 tablespoons capers, a tablespoon of chopped parsley and a little vinegar. *Serve with fish.*

Onion Sauce
Add 2 large onions, boiled till tender, drained and chopped finely. (French chefs grate the onion raw and cook with the *béchamel* sauce.) *Serve with boiled fish.*

The
RUDD
Scardinius Erythrophthalmus

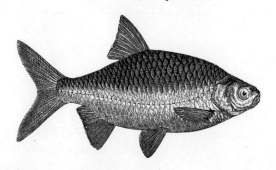

The rudd is a roach-like fish capable of attaining a weight of over 4 lb. It occurs mostly in ponds, but occasionally in sluggish rivers like the Great Ouse. Noted rudd waters are the Norfolk Broads and Slapton Ley in Devonshire.

With the exception of the Iberian peninsula, it is irregularly but extensively distributed throughout Central Europe and through Central Asia eastwards to Siberia. It is absent from Scotland but widely distributed and very abundant in Ireland.

Our description of the rudd as 'roach-like',
and that of the anonymous poet who called it:

... a kind of Roach all tinged with gold,
Strong, broad and thick, most lovely to behold.

have been chosen deliberately for two reasons:

First, because they are apposite.

Secondly, because they illustrate the difficulty many anglers face when trying to differentiate between roach and rudd and, even greater, the difficulty of differentiating between roach/rudd hybrids and their parents.

Confusion between roach and rudd has for long existed. Even the rudd's specific name is founded on error – perpetuated by so eminent an angler as H. Cholmondeley-Pennell who, in *The Fisherman's Magazine* (Vol. 1, 1864) wrote of the rudd:

'From these peculiarities of colouring it is unnecessary to say that it derives its name. The specific name, *erythrophthalmus* (from the Greek *erythros*, red, and *ophthalmos*, the eye) has also a similar origin.'

In Walton's time the rudd, or 'red-eye'* as it was often called, was thought to be a bastard
roach – the product of mixing the eggs and milt of two different species: roach and bream. T. F. Salter in *The Angler's Guide* (1833) states:

'I have no doubt that the fish called a Rudd is a true Roach, but a little altered in shape, by being put into ponds not congenial to their habits and nature.'

Even today, the rudd of Ireland are often known locally as 'roach'.

* The red-eye is a misnomer. It is the roach that has an iris of deep red, whereas the iris of the rudd is a brassy yellow

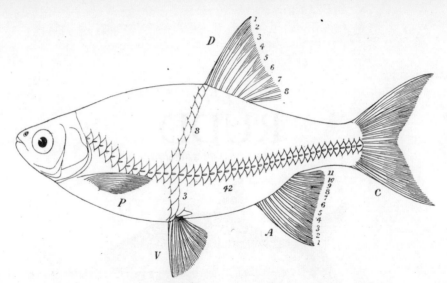

Figure 181: Rudd, showing the posterior position of the dorsal fin (D) with 8 branched rays, the anal (A) with 11 branched rays, the deep body, the depth twice and $\frac{3}{5}$ in the total length without caudal fin (C), and the large size of the scales, of which there are 42 in the lateral line, 8 between the dorsal fin and the lateral line, and 3 between the latter and the base of the ventral fin (V). The object of this figure is to explain how the fin-rays and scales should be counted in making use of the above key or synopsis. The pectoral fin is marked P

Although the famous nineteenth-century ichthyologist, Yarrell, dismissed the possibility of *hybrid* fishes, they are now known to be common. Indeed, the former 'authenticated' British Rod-Caught Record roach (the record was shared) was thought by some authorities to be a roach/rudd hybrid!

The rudd prefers a weedy habitat. Its feeding habits are very similar to those of the roach, but in warm sunny weather it rises even more readily to the fly. Some of the best-ever bags of rudd have been taken by fly fishermen. John Bickerdyke once took twenty-nine rudd weighing up to 3 lb from Lough Derg, all on fly.

Some idea of the opportunities that fall to the fly fisherman are evident in the catch made during a day in June 1906, by R. L. White and R. C. Hardy Corfe, who landed 170 lb of rudd from Ravensthorpe Reservoir, Northamptonshire. Most of the fish were caught on the dry-fly, and the bag included many fish weighing from 2 lb to 2½ lb.

H. T. Sheringham, who loved the rudd, wrote of it in his splendid book, *Coarse Fishing*:

Were it as common as the chub it would be one of the most popular and sought after fishes, for it bites heartily and fights with power.

Sheringham, a great all-rounder, recommended the following flies:

Wet patterns: Alder, Palmer, Coachman (all dressed as for chub fishing with the small white kid tag).

Dry patterns: Wickham's Fancy, Coachman, Black Gnat, Soldier Palmer and Red Tag.

Marshall-Hardy held strong views on the best times for catching rudd. He believed that rudd were most active when water temperatures were high. Accordingly, in high summer he preferred to fish during early morning and late evening. His favourite time was a still evening after a blazing hot day.

Most roach bait-fishing methods are suitable for rudd, but it should be remembered that the best rudd fishing is in weedy, reed or rush-fringed lakes and meres where bank fishing is often very difficult and where the water is far better fished by boat. Rudd, however, are very wary of an approaching boat. An angler should anchor well upwind and be prepared for a twenty-yard downwind cast into the rudd swim.

The bait fisherman should groundbait with floating materials such as unsqueezed bread-mush and crusts that will bring rudd to the surface. A small self-cocking float set about 18 in.

above the hook (size 8 or 10) provides the casting weight that will carry the bait (floating crust or slow-sinking crumb) up to the reed bed or rushes close to which the fish are likely to be feeding.

Figure 182: The former record rod-caught rudd of 4½lb (top) and the other of 4¼lb were taken on the same astonishing day by the late Rev. E. C. Alston at Ringmere near Thetford in June 1933. Altogether, Alston landed 30 fish including five rudd of over 4 lb each! A light breeze kept blowing his float back towards him. He had groundbaited with bread and bran, but all the rudd took small redworms suspended two feet below the float which drifted back in four feet of water.

These fish were survivors of a stock of small rudd he had introduced to Ringmere in 1929 when the lake had re-flooded after being dried up. The rudd, together with some tench, roach and pike, had come from nearby Stamford Water – a lake beyond the reach of modern anglers, since it lies in what is now a tank-testing area. Ringmere itself, alas, no longer exists: the water table has been lowered through water abstraction.

Alston's record was broken on 28 September 1986 when Mr D. Webb caught a 4 lb 10 oz rudd on a lure when fly fishing for fry-feeding trout (or were they fry-feeding rudd?) on Pitsford Reservoir. The fish was verified as a true rudd by Mr Alwyne Wheeler of the British Museum (Natural History)

Margin fishing is a comparatively new method of angling for rudd. Richard Walker admitted that success with this method came by accident when he caught rudd on tackle designed for carp. The use of suitably scaled-down tackle – 4 lb BS line and a size 10 hook – later proved that carp-style margin-fishing was an excellent method for taking rudd.

Another good method, which is also very exciting, is described in *Still Water Angling* (1953):

Where a boat is available, or the fish can be covered from the bank, a deadly way of fishing is to use a fly-rod with a hook-to-nylon instead of a fly, carrying a bunch of six or eight gentles. Get out as long a line as you can comfortably. It must be well-greased and so should all but the last link of the cast. Strike on seeing the line pulled along the surface. Groundbait can take the form of crusts of bread anchored to the bottom, or you can throw in loose crusts and follow them down-wind in a boat, keeping as far away as you can.*

* Marshall-Hardy's method of anchoring crusts is still a very good one. 'Bread buoys' are made by filling ladies' hair-nets with dry crusts which act as a float. The buoys are tied to lengths of nylon and anchored close to the reeds or lily pads with lead weights.

Caught by the E.C. Alston a ... the largest on the record for British Isles

The Rudd

As a sporting fish the rudd has long been neglected. Recently, however, a few groups of highly competent anglers have taken a renewed interest in the species. Parties have enjoyed very successful rudd-fishing trips to Ireland, and some Lancastrians have experienced considerable success with rudd in the Lake District, ledgering Esthwaite Lake mainly at night. This, they have found, is more productive than day fishing, with the months of September and October better than the generally accepted 'rudd-biting' months of June, July and August.

IDENTIFICATION OF RUDD, ROACH, BREAM AND THEIR HYBRIDS

Rudd, roach and bream are closely related species; the closeness of that relationship being exemplified by their ability to hybridize.

The best-known hybrid of the animal world is the mule – offspring of a male ass and a mare. A mule is incapable of reproducing its kind. Similarly, the hybrids of roach/rudd, roach/bream and rudd/bream cannot breed successfully with their own or any other hybrids. It is for this reason that our waters are not teeming with these in-between fishes; it explains why hybrids never supplant the parent species.

There are, of course, many other hybrids: chub/bleak, dace/bleak, dace/rudd, roach/bleak, roach/bream, roach/silver bream, rudd/silver bream, rudd/bleak, bream/silver bream, carp/crucian carp, have all been recorded.

Hybrids are not given scientific names; but first generation hybrids, like those listed above, are known as F_1 hybrids of two named parent species.

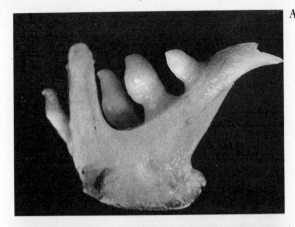

A

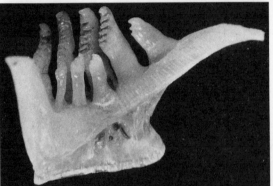

B

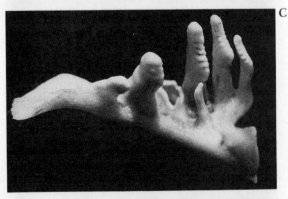

C

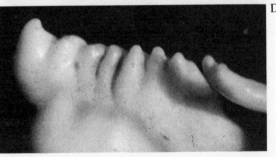

D

Figure 183: Pharyngeal teeth ('fingerprints' of identity).
A. Roach: one row; 5 or 6 teeth each side; *smooth edges*
B. Rudd: two rows. Back row, 5 teeth each side, *serrated edges*; front row, 3 smaller teeth each side, *serrated edges*
C. Roach/rudd hybrid: two rows. Back row, 5 slightly serrated teeth each side; front row, 3 smaller serrated teeth each side. (Note the broken main row tooth. Broken pharyngeal teeth regenerate.)
D. Close-up of the serrations of the roach/rudd hybrid. These are absent in the true roach but present in the true rudd

Although little research other than routine taxonomic work has been done on fish hybridism in Britain, American and Canadian scientists have shown that whereas the hybrids of species belonging to the Esocidae (the pikes) cannot reproduce their own kind, they can in certain instances become successful parents when back-crossed with one or other of the original parent species.

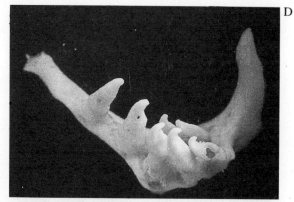

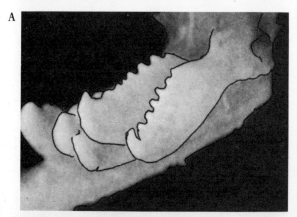

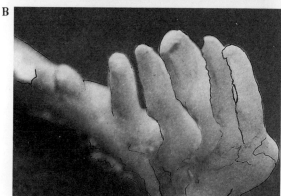

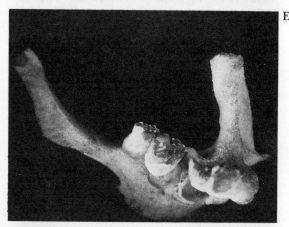

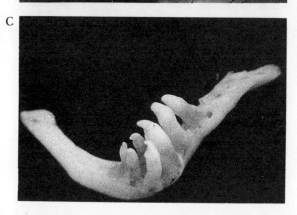

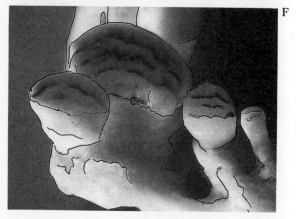

Figure 184: Pharyngeal teeth of other common cyprinids.
A. Common bream: single row long curling teeth
B. Roach/bream: mild serrations compared with bream
C. Barbel: characteristic triple row of teeth
D. Chub: two rows
E. Tench: one row
F. Carp: showing characteristic coral-like grinding surfaces

But if wild second generation (F$_2$) cyprinid hybrids exist in Britain, they are as yet unrecorded. For anglers, the problem so far as rudd, roach and bream are concerned is the identification of these species and the hybrids that can result. To reduce controversies of this nature we suggest identification by the supreme authority – the British Museum (Natural History). Only there does one find full facilities for the work of fish identification: trained staff, and a unique collection of specimens, including hybrids.

One of the invariable questions asked when a record claim is made on behalf of a roach, or a crucian carp, is whether the roach is a true roach or a hybrid between a roach and a bream; or whether the crucian carp is a true crucian or a hybrid between a crucian carp and a common carp. (There are many other cyprinid hybrids, but these are either less common or do not become the subject of a record claim.)

It has always been supposed that hybrids occur when spawn accidentally mixes on the spawning grounds. In North America, however, it has been demonstrated that natural hybrids have resulted from the deliberate mating of the male of one species with the female of another. So far as the UK is concerned, it is known that the male rudd sometimes mixes with a spawning female of another species with *apparent deliberation*.

Shoaling cyprinids such as rudd, roach, dace and bream have been noticed frequently to hybridize when there is a shortage of suitable weed. In the absence of an abundant weed growth there is competition for spawning sites, so that spawning shoals of different species get mixed up on the available sites. As a result, sperm from one species may well accidentally fertilize the ova from another.

The fact that hybrids are rare or non-existent in some waters, even where many cyprinid species share the habitat, may be due to ample spawning accommodation; or it may be due to the various species attaining ripeness at different times.

That different species of fish become active spawners at different temperatures is another

Figure 185: Head of common bream

Head of rudd/common bream hybrid. Note projecting lower lip

Anal fin of common bream

Anal fin of rudd/common bream hybrid

Freshwater Fishing

factor favouring the production of pure-bred fishes. According to Wheeler, in *The Fishes of the British Isles and North West Europe*, common bream favour a temperature of 59°F (15°C) whereas roach and rudd prefer a temperature of 64°F (18°C).

Roach/rudd hybrid

Identification of the roach/rudd hybrid has defeated all but the most experienced and practised observers. Richard Walker, who did a great deal of work in this field, used pharyngeal (throat) teeth to establish positive identification. It is not possible to distinguish between roach, rudd or roach/rudd hybrids by means of scale counts or fin ray counts alone because of the overlap in numbers. For example, the count of branched rays in the anal fin, according to Tate Regan, are as follows:

Roach: 9–12
Rudd: 10–13
Hybrid: 11

Pharyngeal teeth are the 'fingerprints' of identity to the taxonomic detective. If pharyngeals are not available (e.g. when fish are returned alive to the water) it is not possible to identify a true roach, or a true rudd, or a hybrid roach/rudd by reference to any *single* distinguishing characteristic. *True identity can be decided only by an accumulation of evidence.* The characteristic differences are summarized as follows:

1. *Position of the dorsal fin*
Roach The dorsal fin originates *slightly behind* a line raised from the frontal end of the base of the pelvic fins at right-angles to a line drawn from the centre of the fish's eye to the fork of its tail.
Rudd The dorsal fin originates *well behind* a line raised from the frontal end of the base of the pelvic fins.
Hybrid The dorsal fin originates midway between the points of origin specified for the roach and the rudd.

Figure 186: Photograph of the rudd, the roach and the roach/rudd F_1 hybrid showing how the position of the dorsal fin, relative to the root of the pelvic fin, varies in the three fishes. The close-up views of the head give the juxtaposition of the lips

Freshwater Fishing

2. *The juxtaposition of the lips*

Roach Upper lip protrudes slightly beyond lower lip (semi-ventral mouth).

Rudd Lower lip protrudes beyond upper lip (dorsal mouth).

Hybrid Lips are level (terminal mouth).

3. *Abdominal keel*

Roach Keel non-existent. A section through the body immediately in front of the frontal ray of the anal fin is oval.

Rudd The section through the body is pointed.

Hybrid The section through the body is pointed.

Note: This keel is very clear to an experienced observer.

4. *Colour*

Roach A young fish has an overall silvery tinge in its scales. An older fish is shot with coppery reflections when turned in the light. The fins are crimson. The iris of the eye is red.

Rudd The scales have a polished brassy or bronze tinge about them. The fins are tinted yellow. The iris of the eye is yellow.

Hybrid The scales have a brassy tinge reminiscent of the true rudd. The fins are tinted orange. The iris of the eye is orange.

Roach/common bream hybrid

This hybrid, often called the Pomeranian bream, is found in practically all waters containing the parent species, and in some locations is frequently caught. F. B. has taken many from the canal at Slough and the River Cam above Cambridge. Provided no rudd are present to complicate matters, a ray count of the anal fin will identify this hybrid, which has the appearance of a rather deep roach.

Number of rays in anal fin:

    Roach 9–12

    Bream 23–29

    Hybrid 15–19

In addition, the abdominal keel of the hybrid is not very pronounced. The upper lip protrudes slightly beyond lower lip.

Rudd/common bream hybrid

This hybrid differs from the roach/common bream hybrid in the same way that the rudd does from the roach: the body is deeper; the lower lip projects slightly; and the abdominal keel is well defined – as one might expect when both parents are well keeled.

Number of rays in anal fin:

    Rudd 10–13

    Bream 23–29

    Hybrid 15–18

Note: Although the foregoing notes are only a very brief study of hybridization, we hope they may encourage our reader to follow up the developments of future research into this complex subject.

Cooking the Rudd

Of the few who have tasted this fish, fewer still speak kindly of its flavour. There are not many recipes, either. However, here is one recommended by Anthony Bridges.

Fillet the fish, then cover the fillets with plenty of eggs and breadcrumbs and fry them over a brisk fire until thoroughly browned. Then pour over them a gravy made thus:

After removing the fillets, lay the bone and trimmings in a stewpan with two shallots and a small bunch of parsley, stew them for one hour, and strain the liquor, which add to the following sauce. Put 2 oz of butter over the fire; when melted, add the above liquor, and also one tablespoon of flour, one teaspoonful of soy, one dessertspoonful of anchovy, one of Worcestershire sauce, and a little salt.

But watch those bones!

Figure 187: A rudd lough in Co. Clare

The
RUFFE
or POPE

Gymnocephalus cernus

The pope annoys the perch-fisher more than the bleak annoys
the roach-fisher. Pope are chiefly remarkable for an appetite
which cannot be appeased and for never growing any bigger.
They could not be any smaller.

H. T. Sheringham, *Fishing: Its Cause, Treatment and Cure*
(1925)

The name 'Ruffe' or 'Ruff', a variant of 'rough',
alludes to this fish's prickly scales. 'Pope' is of
unknown origin, although according to one authority it is connected with the barbarous practice
of pressing a ruffe's spiky dorsal fin into a piece
of cork before releasing the fish, so that it would
die a lingering death – a ritual ascribed to the
anti-Papists of Tudor Britain who, wishing to
express their hatred of the Pope, sent little Pope
substitutes sailing to their deaths from starvation.

The ruffe seldom grows to a length of more
than seven inches. It is closely related to the
perch, proof of which exists in the form of
perch/ruffe hybrids. These hybrids (F_1), like the
hybrids between two different pike species,
cannot breed *inter se*, but are fertile when back-
crossed with either parent species to produce F_2
hybrids.

During the late 1960s, when the perch in the
Metropolitan Barn Elms Reservoir died from an
epidemic of perch-ulcer, ruffe also died in their
thousands. Due to this disease the ruffe has
almost disappeared from many southern waters.

The ruffe is at home in stillwaters or slow-
flowing rivers and, like the perch, shoals readily.
Like the perch it is a bold biter – an unpopular
habit, since it invariably pouches the angler's
bait, making it difficult to unhook. The ruffe's
notorious appetite is mentioned in the second
angling book ever published in English:

The Arte of Angling, attrib. William Samuel (1577)

He is the grossest at his bite of any fish that biteth,
and is taken with the red worm on the ground, and
where he lieth, there is he commonly alone. . . . I have
been well content to deal with them, for this property
they have, as is seen among the wicked; that though
they see their fellows perish never so fast, yet will
they not be warned, so that you shall have them as
long as one is left, especially a little before a rain or
in the bite time. And if you close some small worms

Figure 188

in a ball of old black dung or earth, and cast it in where you angle for them, you shall have the better sport, for at that will they lie like little hogs.

Many anglers complain that if a swim produces ruffe it is unlikely to produce anything else, and try to avoid this little fish. But were fashions to change, anglers might think differently, since the ruffe has a high culinary reputation: its flesh is white, succulent and easily digested.

But surely an wholesome fish! ... There cannot be a better, and chiefly for a sick body. I count him better than either gudgeon or perch, for he eateth faster and pleasanter.

(Attrib. William Samuel)

Cooking the Ruffe

Although in days gone by every kind of freshwater fish was eaten, some species were preferred to others. The ruffe, it seems was high on the list. The opinion of its table qualities expressed in *A Treatyse of Fysshynge wyth an Angle* (1496) was unequivocal:

The ruf is a ryght an holsom fysshe:

The author of *The Arte of Angling* (1577) described it in equally glowing terms:

There can not be a better, and chiefly for a sicke body, I count him better than either goodgin or perch.

Two hundred years later, Richard Brookes in the fourth edition of *The Art of Angling* (1774), described the ruffe as:

Second to none for the Delicasy of the Taste.

In the last century the epicurean Dr J. J. Manley was more precise:

... like the gudgeon, his flesh is firm and sweet,

Yarrell, in the third edition of *British Fishes* (1859), agreed with Manley:

though it seldom exceeds six or seven inches in length, its flesh is considered excellent.

Unfortunately we have been unable to trace a recipe for cooking this little fish and suggest, simply, that you treat it as you would its closest relative – the perch.

The
ATLANTIC
SALMON

Salmo salar

Sir Joseph Bankes it has been said, attempted to produce
lobsters from fleas, but failed; and, in a rage, exclaimed –
'Fleas are not lobsters, damn their souls!' I hope the Scotch
breeders will fare better, and not have to exclaim – 'Par are
not salmon, damn their souls!'

O'Gorman, *The Practice of Angling* (Vol. 2, 1845)

It is generally agreed that the several species of
salmon, both Pacific and Atlantic, came from a
common ancestor about half a million years ago.
Whether this ancestor originated in fresh or salt
water is uncertain. Biological evidence favours
fresh, since most members of the Salmonidae are
unable to breed in salt water.

The Atlantic salmon's life-cycle starts when
the eggs are laid during winter in the gravel bed
of some well-oxygenated and fairly fast-flowing
stream. An egg takes between three and four
months to hatch, and the product – known as an
alevin – is a tiny translucent creature with an
umbilical sac hanging below its throat.

During the alevin stage the little salmon lives
on the contents of its yolk sac, which contains
upwards of a month's rations. When the yolk sac
has been absorbed the alevin wriggles out of the
gravel as a fry.

Now forced to fend for itself it hunts actively
for food, gradually acquiring a form of camouflage in the shape of dark 'finger-marks' along its
sides. At this stage it is known as a parr and, in
looks, is very similar to a small brown trout.

Parr feed on fly larvae, tiny crustaceans and
other forms of life, depending on the food supply
available. In turn they are preyed on by a host
of enemies. Among many others, kingfishers,
herons, mink, otters, cormorants, mergansers,

Figure 189: Van Voorst's tinted drawing of a salmonid
showing the characteristic parr marks, published in 1839

goosanders, pike, perch, chub, eels and other coarse fish have all been known to take their share of immature salmon. The salmon's cousin, the brown trout, is undoubtedly one of its worst enemies. This is not only because of direct predation, but because predation *threat* impairs the diet selection of young salmon and reduces their rate of feeding.

When the parr is anything between one and four or five years old – usually two – certain physiological changes take place to fit it for a new environment, and during May or June, as a slender, fork-tailed, silvery little fish about six inches long, now known as a smolt, it migrates to salt water.

It is interesting that recent research has shown a dramatic difference in parr behaviour within a similar age group. Certain parr switch off feeding in autumn, while their siblings continue. Thus, some fish consume barely a maintenance ration, while the rest feed at a rate that maximises their growth. These better fish migrate to sea the following summer, whereas the others (which

Make not a daily practice (which is nothing else but a profession) of any recreation, lest your immoderate love and delight therein, bring a cross with it, and blast all your content and pleasure in the same.

Colonel Robert Venables, *The Experienc'd Angler* (1662)

don't restart their feeding until the end of March) remain in the river for at least another year.

Having reached the river estuary, the young salmon encounter further enemies: herring-gulls, shags, pollack, bass, coalfish, congers and many more. But they hurry on towards the rich feeding grounds of the open sea. And they go there in order to grow.

They grow quickly. By the end of their first year at sea they are twenty to thirty times their original weight, although after this their growth rate lessens. Some salmon return to freshwater as grilse – fish of roughly 3 lb to 10 lb that have stayed little over a year at sea. Some return as 'maiden' salmon after a sea life of two or more years. Some may even return, after an absence

Figure 190: Salmon, H. L. Rolfe, 1865

Figure 191: The 'fly only' rule on the River Tweed allows fishing only by this method when the nets are off during the first fortnight of the season and again after 15 September. Many good bags are taken on fly especially in the autumn when the river has its biggest runs. The photograph shows a catch made on 5 November that does not include one coloured or even partially coloured fish

of four years, as 40-pounders; indeed several years may separate the homecoming of fish that left the river together. But at whatever age they return whether as grilse after one winter at sea, or as maiden salmon of two sea years or longer, return they must, since they cannot spawn in salt water. And on their way back towards their destined rivers they stop feeding.

Recapture of tagged fish indicates that salmon returning to Britain move in from the Atlantic at many points, swimming close inshore up or down the coast until they reach their river estuaries. Although a small percentage (Nature's insurance policy) find their way into strange rivers, the majority return to spawn in the rivers of their birth. It is not known exactly how a salmon navigates from the distant ocean to the coast, although recent research suggests that a magnetic indicator in the front of the head is mainly responsible; but experiments have established beyond doubt that it selects its parent river by the particular *odour* of that river. Salmon have an almost unbelievably acute sense of smell.

Having stopped feeding, the returning salmon bring their rations with them and enter their rivers with sufficient reserves in their tissues to sustain them for upwards of twelve months.

Not all salmon, of course, endure so long a period of fasting. There is no month of the year during which, in some British river, fresh salmon are not running; and whereas those that arrive in winter and early spring wait many months before spawning, others spawn only a short time after their late autumn or early winter arrival.

Salmon run upstream according to water temperature, light intensity (movement is slight in bright sunlight) and the height of the river. Maximum movement occurs when the water level has fallen (after a rise) to roughly a third of the spate. It is at this time – apart from the first few inches of the rise – that angling chances are at their best.

Extremes of water temperature limit salmon migration upriver. Although fish may enter a river at temperatures as low as 34°F, they will not negotiate obstacles and run far upstream until the temperature is over 40°F. When summer temperatures rise above 68°F, movement is again inhibited and salmon lie doggo in the deeper pools. Air temperature seems to play no part in salmon migration. Provided light intensity and water levels are congenial, it is water temperature alone that affects their movement.*

During the long migration upstream towards the spawning redds, driven by their ripening sexual urge, salmon force their way past the most formidable obstacles. And what they cannot

Figure 192: Diagram of a salmon showing the various fins, lateral line, operculum and prae-operculum, maxillary and prae-maxillary, and branchiostegal rays (*top*).
Anatomy of a salmonid (*bottom*)

* For further data concerning running and taking behaviour see H.F.'s *Salmon Fishing* (H. F. and G. Witherby).

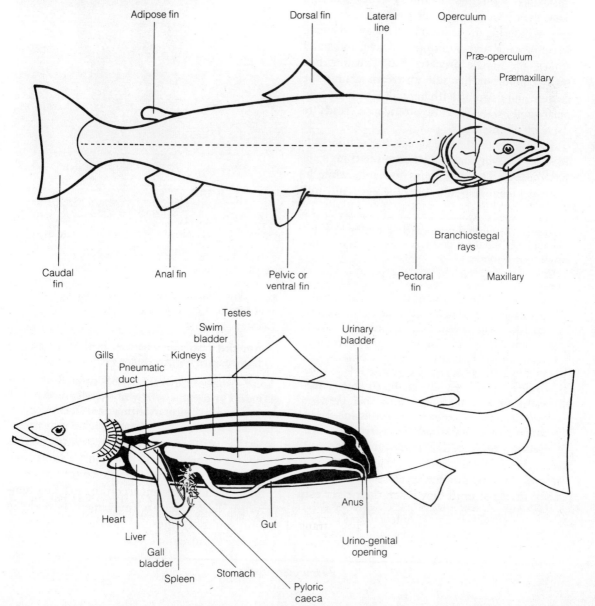

swim over, they jump. Their leaping has often been exaggerated, but fact is sufficiently dramatic: a perpendicular jump of twelve feet has been measured over the Orrin Falls in Scotland.

By November many of the fish have arrived in or close to those parts of the river, or feeder streams, where they are going to mate. And from then until, usually, about the end of January, most of the spawning takes place.

With the last leaves drifting overhead, the salmon's silver streamlined beauty has vanished. The females are dark, almost black, with bulging bellies; the males rust-red, their heads ugly and misshapen with huge pointed 'kypes' curving from their lower jaws. After a period of exploratory wandering in a stretch of clean, shallow, streamy water with a bottom of gravel and small stones, the female prepares the spawning bed by swimming on her side upstream against the current and flapping with her tail. The male fish, meanwhile, waits in close attendance, ready to drive off all intruders.

Eventually the female signals her readiness to mate by pressing hard down into the trough she has formed. The male joins her and, while he quivers violently beside her, the eggs and milt

Figure 193: The 27 lb autumn-caught fish taken by F. B. shows the ugly head and the kyped lower jaw of the ready-to-spawn male salmon

So much has been said of the breeding of fish, particularly of salmon, that I did not think any occasion could occur to call forth any observations of mine: but I have, within a short time, seen extracts from a treatise, by a Scotchman, on this subject, and in this treatise it is gravely asserted, first, that salmon breed with a fish called par; next, that salmon do not become what we call fry the first season they are produced, but rather have a kind of tadpole existence the first spring, and, in fact, do not attain the shape of fry till the second spring.

Now, to my mind, these are monstrous doctrines and, I think, incapable of being proved.... As to what par may be, I know not – it is possible that fish of different kinds, when closely confined, may produce an odd breed of some kind; but it must be somewhat like the breeding of cats and badgers in the Caves of Blarney:

> And there are caves where no daylight enters,
> But cats and badgers do for ever breed.

Since writing the above, I have discovered what is meant by par; they are what we call gravelin, and we suppose them to be produced from some part of the pea of the salmon which had been imperfect, or been carried away without due impregnation....

I regret to find that some of my most particular friends are imbued with what I call 'the tadpole heresy'. For my part, nothing but the evidence of my senses will persuade me.

O'Gorman, *The Practice of Angling* (Vol. 2, 1845)

are extruded almost simultaneously. Afterwards the male swims away some little distance downstream, while the female, by going a yard or so above the bed, covers the fertilized eggs with gravel by vigorous flapping movements of her tail, the dislodged stones being carried into place by the current.

Several more sequences may be carried out before the female has deposited all her eggs. Nature prepares for huge losses. A hen fish carries between 700 and 800 eggs per pound of her body weight.

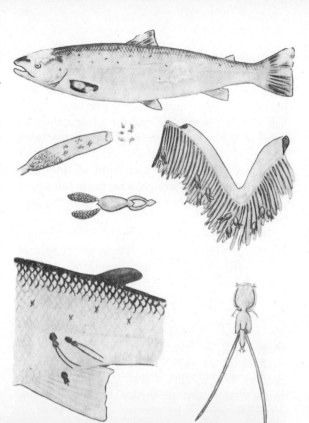

Figure 194: Parasites of the salmon: (*top*) salmon with parasite fungus, *Saprolegnia*; (*centre, above left*) reproductive tip of a fungus filament, discharging spores (greatly enlarged); (*centre, below left*) gill-maggot (enlarged); (*centre right*) gill-maggots attached to gill; (*bottom left*) sea lice attached above anal fin of salmon; (*bottom right*) a female sea louse (enlarged)

Figure 195: These salmon caught by F. B. on the River Tay in late September demonstrate the typical silhouettes of a cock (27 lb) and a hen fish (18½ lb) some two or three months before spawning

In spite of his efforts to protect his nuptials, the cock salmon sometimes fails to do so. It has been found that up to 75 per cent of male parr become sexually mature. These precocious little fish will often slip in behind the adult males and fertilize the eggs themselves! This remarkable fact may illustrate another aspect of Nature's insurance, since a parr's ejection of milt goes deep into the gravel trough, whereas in the strong current some of the adult's milt may get dispersed.

By the time spawning is finished the fish are emaciated and very weak. These spent fish, or 'kelts', are little more than two-thirds of their original weight. Their hollow-flanked and ragged-finned bodies are often smothered in fungus; the once juicy pink flesh is pale and flaccid. Only comparatively few fish survive. Of these, most, surprisingly, are females, and those that regain the rich feeding grounds of the sea recover their condition very quickly. Strangely, those that return to freshwater for a second spawning have a fat content as high as or, in some cases, even higher than that of virgin fish.

The proportion of salmon that survive for a third spawning is very small indeed. Only an exceptional fish returns to spawn a fourth time.

Figure 196: Pike, when they have the opportunity, are very destructive of young game fish. This photograph, taken in 1933 and published in the *Fishing Gazette* of 19 October 1935, shows twenty salmon and sea trout smolts taken from the stomach of a 6 lb pike trapped in Redewater, Northumberland

It is significant that surviving kelts don't all leave a river together even when seemingly able to do so, but over a period that may extend into several months. Here again, as with the staggered arrival of incoming fish, Nature tries to insure against the possibility of total loss.

But even Nature's ingenuity cannot prevail against the effects of human pollution. Three hundred years ago, Izaak Walton wrote:

There is no better salmon than in England; and that although some of our northern rivers have salmon as fat and as large as the River Thames, yet none are of so excellent a taste.

In 1816 the Thames had an exceptional run of salmon, which fetched only threepence a pound in Billingsgate market. Twenty years later the Thames salmon had all but vanished. For the next hundred and fifty years, London's river – an open sewer, like so many other rivers ruined by the Industrial Revolution – was a national disgrace.

As a result of the recent drive against pollution the Thames is once again clean enough to permit a run of migratory fish. Already, a number of salmon and sea trout have been caught on rod and line. According to Thames Water, over five hundred salmon ran into the river during 1986. And the Thames is not alone; a number of other British rivers have become cleaner during the past few years. It is an encouraging story and shows what could be done for all Europe's polluted North Sea and Atlantic seaboard rivers.

Freshwater Fishing

Figure 197: In the Gorge d'Enfer, at Les Eyzies, in the Dordogne, is a little shelter: Abri de Poisson, so named because it contains this relief carving of a salmon – one of the earliest records of pre-historic association between salmon and man. It was probably the invention of the flint-tipped spear, the bow and arrow and the bone harpoon that enabled early man to get on terms with the migrating salmon. *Note:* Are the indentations chiselled above the dorsal fin an early list of 'kills'? If so, this could be the first recorded attempt at a game diary!

Figure 198: Fresh run salmon whose stay in freshwater has been counted in hours rather than days have a faint pink bloom over their scales, the effect of which is to enhance the silver beauty of their bodies. Here, H. F. and Jim Miller hold up the morning's catch of three River Tay springers

Alas, although a Department of the Environment report shows that Britain's rivers have been improving since 1958 and that during the first half of the 1980s three thousand and twenty-eight miles of water have become cleaner, three thousand five hundred and six miles have become filthier, marking an abrupt reversal.

The Observer of 4 January 1987 comments:

There are two main causes of the reversal: spending on sewage treatment fell by more than a half between 1974 and 1981 and is only slowly increasing again.

Secondly, agriculture has emerged as a major polluter. Since 1979 water pollution incidents from farms – mainly leaking silage and slurry – have increased by 250 per cent.

Hitherto clean rural rivers are now joining such traditionally dirty waterways as the Mersey and Weaver, the Aire and Calder, the Don and Rother, the Tees and the Tame, all of which run through major industrial areas. The report cites deterioration of the River Cherwell near Banbury, the Cut near Windsor, the River Thame near Aylesbury, the River Wellow near Bath and the River Parrett in Somerset. And many small rivers throughout the country are shown to be seriously polluted. Much of the upper River Tywi in South Wales, once among the cleanest water category, has become the second most polluted because of the effects of acid rain. [See page 287.]

The essential river requirements of salmon and sea trout are water containing sufficient oxygen; pH above 5.6, and ready access to suitable spawning redds. Most fish return from the sea to spawn in their natal rivers. But not all. Each year a small but vital number find their way to strange rivers. Quite apart from fresh stocks introduced by fishery biologists, these wanderers would explore and eventually re-stock every barren river if not repelled by the disgusting outflow of filth.

Are we all so poor in spirit that we must continue to deny *Salmo* the encouragement of clean water?

Salmon and sea trout migration is reduced when the river's pH falls below about 5.5

Freshly fertilized salmonid eggs and newly hatched alevins are known to be more sensitive to low pH and low calcium concentrations than during the later stages of the life-cycle.

Coarse fish have less tolerance of acidity than game fish. Experiments with roach and perch eggs have shown their lower limits of tolerance to be pH 5.5 and 4.7 respectively. Atlantic salmon eggs are unable to hatch at pH 4.5

Figure 199: Three big fish: 48 lb, 40 lb, 30 lb, taken on Norway's River Aarø

Freshwater Fishing

Figure 200: Part of the Sprouston/Hendersyde beat showing a Tweed boatman manoeuvring his boat down what is for the uninitiated an invisible line along which fish lie. The boatman's skill becomes more apparent once it is realized that this line of salmon lies is not fixed but one that moves to the right or the left with the changing height of the water and/or the force of the stream.

The skilful dropping down of the boat, so as to allow the fly to fish at the right depth in the right spots, from the head of the pool to the pool tail may take an hour to cover with a big double-handed fly rod and even longer to back up.

Those who have fished this pool have enjoyed the privilege (whether or not they know it) of fishing one of the longest and most productive Atlantic salmon *fly-fishing* pools in the world. Over the years the McElrath family (father and two sons) have been prominent in providing this essential boatman's knowledge and skill

Tenth century river pollution

In a fascinating article in the *New Scientist* (6
November 1986), Terence O'Connor, research
fellow at the department of biology, University
of York, makes the point that river pollution is
not confined to recent times:

Much of the thrust of biology over the past 25 years
has concerned the place of humans in the ecosystem,
and their impact on it. Environmental archaeology
provides an opportunity to extend this investigation
beyond the confines of the present day by recon-
structing human ecology and behaviour in circumstances that no longer exist.

We can also examine the influence of people on
the landscape over long periods of time. To take a
straightforward example, the people of York have
always taken fish from the River Ouse which flows
through the city. By monitoring changes in the composition of the species of freshwater fish found in
archaeological deposits over the past 1900 years or

Figure 201: This 75½ lb salmon, measuring 63¼ in. long –
the longest Atlantic salmon ever recorded – was netted
near Hougsund, south of the Drammen River, in the
summer of 1925 (*Norman Weatherall*)

so, we have found a marked shift from clean-water species, such as salmon and grayling, to species such as roach and perch, which are more tolerant of grime, at around the time in the 10th century when the Viking town underwent rapid development. The Vikings' pollution of the river was probably not on the scale that modern York can achieve, but it seems to have been enough to have brought about a considerable change in the populations of fish. There is a similar shift in freshwater molluscs around this period as well, from species requiring well-oxygenated water to less demanding species. The conclusion that a 'low technology' 10th-century town could be a significant source of river pollution was unexpected, even contentious.

SALMON FISHING

When we think about it, the catching of a salmon on rod and line seems highly improbable, whether with natural bait or an artificial lure such as spinner or 'fly'. After all, why on earth should anyone expect to hook a fish that has no appetite? But that in effect is the problem confronting every salmon angler; for what he is trying to do is to catch a fish that is not hungry; that while lying in the river waiting to spawn, lives on the fat stored in its tissues and has no need of food. As already mentioned, a salmon returns from the sea and enters a river with sufficient nourishment to sustain it for over twelve months, in addition to providing for its developing spawn. It makes little or no effort to search for food, being content to lie where it is in some congenial resting-place where it can enjoy some well-oxygenated water. In consequence of this the angler finds the salmon a very difficult fish to catch. Indeed, what seems remarkable is that he catches one at all. Often, of course, he doesn't!

Nevertheless, he will catch one sooner or later, if he persists, because, surprisingly, there are times when salmon will react to and take various baits or lures – sometimes quite avidly.

Nobody knows for certain why they behave in this unexpected manner. It is quite possible that the research into salmon behaviour being started as we go to press may come up with the answer; but in the meantime the angler must be content with theory.

From a number of theories that have been propounded, the most attractive and plausible is that the salmon takes from *habit* – the feeding habit formed during its life at sea; and, perhaps, during its earlier river life as a parr; a habit triggered-off by the sight of something which is, or seems to be, alive. It is also possible that curiosity or irritation or (particularly near spawning time) aggression plays a part.

But whatever the reasons for it may be, the experienced angler has learned that a salmon's reaction to any sort of lure is based mainly on the prevailing temperature and height of the water. It is on these that his choice of lure and method of fishing it will depend.

He knows that in early spring he may fail to catch fish because his lure is too small, and in summer he may fail because his lure is too big. When the water temperature is low – as it is in early spring or late autumn – he will fish with a quick-sinking line and a large sunk lure, two to four inches long or even longer. And when the water temperature rises with warmer weather into the high forties (F), he changes to a small lure an inch or so in length, and often less, fished close to the surface. Indeed, if the air temperature is much higher than the water temperature he may do so in conditions of, say, $45°$–$48°F$. He has learned this from experience. He

---

Were I to select the professions among the members of which I have met the best men, and the most skilful anglers, I would certainly name the army and the law. I mean the highest branch of the latter; as for the attorneys, with many honourable exceptions, they are an incorrigible race. Indeed I have rarely seen any of them who could angle at all, perhaps, only one; and he was a sinister biped (left-handed). They are, for the most part, devoted to worldly gain; and, as Giles Daxon used to say, will never give a direct answer to a question.

Few merchants are good anglers.

O'Gorman, *The Practice of Angling* (Vol. 2, 1845)

Figure 202: Most anglers take a camera with them in the knowledge that a photographic record of a good fish will bring back fond memories. This picture of a New Brunswick angler with a catch taken from the Mirimichi River is an example of a finely composed picture

doesn't know the reasons for it, and at best it is only a rough guide.

Nevertheless, it is a guide that will help him to catch fish. There is a large element of luck in salmon fishing; it contains no certainties and, if he persists, the beginner is always in with a chance; but the veteran angler will catch more fish in the long run simply because in addition to his ration of luck he has the knowledge born of experience.

Choice and presentation of the small fly

In this illogical sport of salmon fishing – which consists of offering a meal to fish that are not hungry – it is obviously important for an angler to bolster his confidence, for only if he is confident in what he is doing will he persist, and persistence is essential. But what confidence can anyone have in any fly and method of presenting it that have not been chosen for some particular reason, be it fact or fancy?

Certain colours are sometimes recommended on the grounds that they enable a fish to see the fly better, and that brightly coloured flies will therefore result in more offers.

This is very doubtful. Salmon have excellent vision. They may refuse a fly for a number of reasons, but an inability to see it – even in spate water – is unlikely to be among them.

Theories have been advanced concerning colour and light. Some pundits advocate a bright fly for a bright day and a dull fly for a dull day; whereas others prefer a dull fly on a bright day and a bright fly on a dull day. Does it really make any difference? The angler who ignores colour and fishes nothing but a plain all-black stoat's tail seems to catch his share of fish.

It is probable (and we say this because we have done it) that if you select any one pattern of fly that, for whatever reason, gives you confidence, and fish it in varying sizes and degrees of dressing throughout the season, you will do as well as you would had you a host of patterns to choose from. Indeed, you are likely to do better, since you will not waste time wondering which pattern to choose, or whether what you have is really the best one for that particular moment.

Figure 204: Four more 'spring' salmon taken on fly from the Sprouston beat on Tweed. The smiling captors photographed by their gillie, Norman McElrath, are F. B. and 'Jock' Bruce Gardyne

Figure 203: Fresh-run 17-pounder just landed. Sprouston beat, River Tweed

The most important point to consider when choosing a fly, we suggest, is the depth at which you want it to swim. A fish may take a fly that is swimming at a certain depth, but refuse the same fly if it is swimming higher or lower. In summer, a salmon will sometimes take a fly that is swimming on or almost on the surface but, more usually, will simply swirl at it. If the fly is swimming too deep the fish tends to ignore it. As a broad generalisation, the ideal depth for fishing the small fly is about four inches.

A slender, lightly dressed fly will sink faster than a bushy dressing on a similar hook. And since weight usually decreases as the size of the hook diminishes, a lightly dressed size 8 may fish at the same depth as, say, a bushy size 6 on the same length of leader on the same fly-line in the same current. Dressing, then, is important, although not for the reasons usually ascribed. What *is* of primary importance in a fly dressing is neither the colour nor the material, it is the *quantity*.

So – it is sensible to start by choosing flies with dressings that will suit a certain size of hook and allow it to swim at the depth you wish in the water you are going to fish.

It is helpful to remember that (in addition to water temperature) the size of a fly depends on the height of the river. The higher the water the stronger the current and, therefore, the larger the fly. Conversely, the lower the river the slacker the current and the smaller the fly – until in conditions of extreme summer low, with high water temperature, you will probably be fishing a fly as small as size 12, or even 14.

Choice of fly line

There is a range of floating and sinking lines that will serve for any type of water. Each pool on each river has its own characteristics, and a salmon fisherman should choose the line or lines that will suit the particular water he is going to fish at the time of year he will be fishing it.

Whether he fishes a big fly or a small fly depends on the air and water temperatures. As a rough guide, the big fly is fished when the water temperature is *below* 48–50°F. The small fly when the water temperature is *above* 48–50°F. But the air temperature too is important. When the air is warmer than the water the small fly is always in with a chance, even with a water temperature as low as 42–44°F. When the air is appreciably colder than the water, the big fly will take fish even when the water temperature is 52–54°F. Generally speaking, however, the small fly is fished from mid-April to late autumn.

Very much the same applies to salmon spinning: deep down near the bottom with a big lure

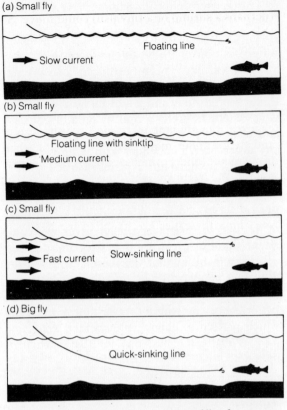

Figure 205: (a), (b) and (c) show choice of line for summer small-fly fishing, the object being to fish the fly at an average depth of four inches irrespective of current speed. For early spring and autumn fishing (d) a big fly is fished deep on fully sunk line

in early spring and autumn. High up near the surface with a small lure in summer.

But will any one selected size suit all the water in any particular pool? Possibly not. The current varies from a fast run-in to a slack or slackish middle and a streamy tail. To give yourself the best chance of attracting a fish at every cast, you may need to make at least one change of fly: starting perhaps with a size 4 or 6 in the neck; changing to a size 8 or 10 in the middle, and changing again to a size 6 in the tail. As already indicated, when the water in that pool has dropped to near drought level, you may find it expedient to fish it through with sizes 10, 14, and 12.

Since the speed at which a fly is fished relates roughly to its size, it is wise to present it no faster than the creature it is supposed to represent (perhaps a shrimp or a tiny fish) could move. So that correct presentation means controlling fly depth and speed all the way down the pool, and only by careful study of the water can you decide how to do this. Which is where 'water sense' takes over.

Note the strength of the current and where it changes; the amount of ripple (line-tip, leader and fly go under more readily in a ripple than in a smooth glide; which is important, because unless you are purposely intending to riffle the fly in the surface film, you should avoid letting it skid across the lies). Observe the spots where you think these lies are likely to be; the swirl and eddy that occur near sunken rocks – which themselves often form lies for salmon. Most important, study that narrow strip of moderate water between current and slack on the inside bend of a pool. Almost without exception these strips of water provide taking lies for salmon.

As you 'read' the water (and bear in mind the water temperature) an idea of fly size and dressing will take shape. And as you progress

Figure 206: Angler at B1 casts to B1. When the line is dragged into a curve by the current it can be switched over ('mended') to help control the speed and depth of the fly. But this is only possible with a floating line. By now, a sinking line will have gone under. Angler at A2 casts to B2 with a sinking line. As the line comes down on the water _before it has time to start sinking_ he rolls his rod over and creates an upstream curve by shooting extra line.

This is the technique for all sunk-line fishing when strength of current makes mending obligatory. It can of course be used with floating line as well, and often is

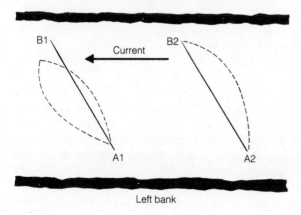

down the pool it soon becomes evident how often (if at all) you will need to change the fly in sympathy with the current. The depth at which a fly will swim depends on current strength, weight and dressing of fly, and type of fly-line. A rough guide for choice of fly-line is as follows:

Sluggish to medium strength water: floating line.
Medium to fast current: floating line with sink-tip.
Fast current: slow-sinking line.

If there is anyone alive who can unfailingly predict when salmon will or will not take, we can only say that we have never met him.

During the summer there is a better chance of catching a salmon on the small fly if the air temperature is higher than the water temperature; when the air is cold the fish usually tend to stay down. But sometimes they will show a determined reluctance to rise to a fly even on what seems to be the perfect day. And what salmon fisherman hasn't been surprised to hook a fish on some seemingly hopeless day when he was only casting for the fun of it?

Surely it is this very uncertainty that lends the sport of salmon fishing such fascination and charm. It provides a limitless field of speculation, and the beginner is justified in feeling that he is always in with a chance.

Now to the fly itself. From your box a multitude of variegated lures look up at you. Which one to choose?

Well, you have examined and read the water. A floating line has been fitted to the rod and you intend to use three yards of leader. You have a clear picture of fly size and amount of dressing, so already your choice has been considerably narrowed.

Next, the pattern of fly. Light or dark? Take a look at the sky. If you believe in bright flies for bright days, or whatever, select only those that seem to fit your particular bill. This reduces the number still further. From the remainder consider only those whose hairs or feather fibres are soft and flexible; which when the fly moves through the water will tend to flicker and give it life. A straggly, chewed-looking fly is more life-like and attractive than something neat and stiff and 'overstuffed'.

You have now whittled your choice down to perhaps three or four possibles. Close your eyes and pick one out.

And what have you come up with? A rather battered size 6 Blue Charm. And a very good fly, too.

It all boils down to the inescapable fact that there is no substitute for experience when it comes to choice of fly. Even so, however promising the fly, what really matters is how you present it to the fish.

Figure 207: A comfortable way of holding a long salmon rod while fishing out a cast

Angle of presentation

Since the object of summer fly-fishing for salmon is to present a small lure ($\frac{3}{8}$ in.-$1\frac{1}{4}$ in.) at a depth of about four inches, and a speed of between, say, one and a half and three m.p.h., it follows that the angle at which the fly is cast depends largely on the strength of current.

In slack water (figure 208(a)) the fly is cast square to the bank and line is stripped in to give the fly movement. This is how a fly has to be fished on some pools in conditions of dead low water. A modern floating line is used.

The ability to catch a fish in these circumstances is one of the skills that separate the expert salmon angler from the rest.

In a sluggish current (figure 208(b)) the fly is cast at a slightly more acute angle. This means

Figure 208: The diagrams show a salmon lying in the same position relative to the bank, but in water varying from dead slack to very fast. The angler is casting from point 'A'. In each case he is using a small summer fly ranging in length from $\frac{3}{8}$ in. in the slack water, to $1\frac{1}{4}$ in. in the fast water. His length of leader remains the same: 9 ft

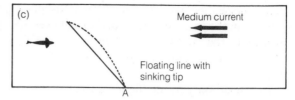

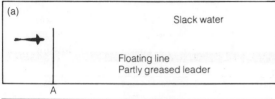

(a)   Slack water

Floating line
Partly greased leader

A

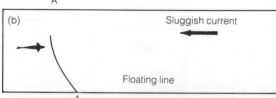

(b)   Sluggish current

Floating line

A

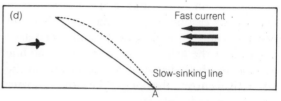

(c)   Medium current

Floating line with
sinking tip

A

(d)   Fast current

Slow-sinking line

A

Figure 209: Salmon fishing in low water conditions. Having cast, H. F. raises his rod point to form a belly of slack line. This slack helps to cushion any 'snatch' that may occur as a fish takes, and prevents the fly from being pulled out of the fish's mouth

that a longer line will have to be cast. No mend is made in the line. Instead, a belly is allowed to form, and the current is used to swing the fly over the fish. The angler is still fishing a floating line.

In a medium current (figure 208(c)) the cast is made at an even more acute angle, which necessitates casting an even longer line. Now, in order to control the fly's depth and speed as it passes over the fish, a mend is made in the line as soon as a belly has formed. According to the strength of current the line will be either a floater or a floater with sink-tip.

In a fast current (figure 208(d)) the angler must go further upstream and cast a longer line still, mending as soon as the cast is completed, shooting an extra yard or two of line as he does so. In water of this strength, a sink-tip may not be sufficient to fish the fly deep enough, in which case a slow-sinking line is used.

It will be seen that (as in figure 208(a)) the fish could easily be covered by casting more squarely. But to do so is usually fruitless since the fly cannot be prevented from fishing at excessive speed. Occasionally, however, a fly cast *upstream* in a strong current, and stripped back downstream over the salmon's head, will be grabbed. But we have found that this type of snatch take often results in a poorly hooked fish.

Note: Mending a line should be done only in rippled water where it is unlikely to cause disturbance. On the smooth glassy surface of a pool tail giving low water in summer, it will do more harm than good.

In these circumstances there is no alternative to throwing a long line from as far upstream as possible. Or, better, leaving that stretch of shallow glide until dusk shadows the pool.

Effective casting range

Although there is a considerable element of luck in salmon fishing, some anglers catch many more fish than others. Their success is not due mainly to good fortune. It derives from attention to detail – which reduces reliance on the element of luck.

1. By using water sense and intuition.

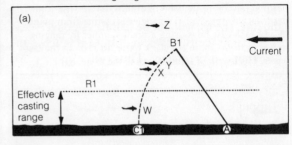

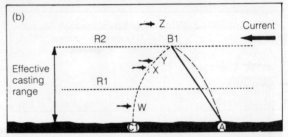

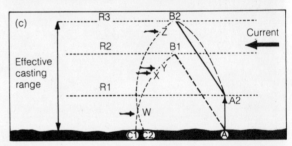

Figure 210: The increase in *effective casting range* in (b) and (c) has been exaggerated for the sake of clarity. It is the principle of the thing that matters. Once the novice salmon-angler appreciates the simple point that his lure is effective only when it is fishing at the correct depth and speed, he will start to catch many more salmon

2. Making a stealthy approach to the riverside. Concealment. Taking care not to cause vibration or shadow.

3. Using well balanced tackle, suitable for the water in question.

4. Correct choice and presentation of a lure.

5. Ability to wade stealthily, and deep.

6. Ability to cast and effectively control a long line. Factors 1 to 5 being equal, the angler who consistently achieves the greatest effective casting range will catch the most fish.

In figure 210(a), an angler at A casts to B1. His fly swings round on the arc B1, C1. It covers three fish: Y, X and W. Owing to the speed of the current, however, with its resultant drag on the line, the fly will not be fishing effectively (i.e. at the right depth and speed) until it reaches the horizontal dotted line. Thus, although he has cast to B1, the angler's effective casting range is only the distance between R1 and the bank. Although the fly has passed over salmon Y and X, it has not done so in a manner that would induce them to take. The only fish that is being effectively covered is the salmon at W.

In figure 210(b), the angler casts again to

Figure 211: More 'spring' fishing. F. B. playing a salmon on the lower reaches of the River Test

B1. This time, however, he mends his line. His effective casting range is now between R2 and the bank. A considerable advantage has been gained, since he can now effectively cover two extra salmon, Y and X.

In figure 210(c), the angler wades out to A2 and casts again, this time to B2. Again he mends his line correctly. His fly now traverses the arc B2, C2, and he can cover the salmon at Z.

By long casting, mending and wading, he can, therefore, effectively cover all four fish. *Note:* If he starts by wading out to A2 and casting to B2 in order to cover the fish at Z, he will over-cast the fish at X and Y.

To wade straight into a pool and start off by casting as far as possible across the river is a very common mistake. Always fish the nearer water first.

There is a further point of interest in figure 210(c). If the angler at A2 fishes his cast right out towards the point C2, by moving his rod across to his left as far as he can reach, and leading the fly inshore, he can also cover the fish at W.

When an angler is wading deep, he should always fish a cast right out in this manner. Many opportunities of catching fish are missed because when the fly is straight downstream, at the dangle, it is retrieved and cast again.

Hooking a salmon

According to our observation a salmon usually takes a fly in one of three ways (see figure 212).
a. It will rise from its lie, move forwards and upwards to intercept the fly, take the fly in its mouth and sink back to its lie without turning. This fish is hooked in the right-hand side of the mouth when the angler is casting from the left bank (and *vice versa*).
b. It will rise to intercept and take the fly, turn against the direction in which the fly is travelling, and describe a circle as it returns to its lie. When the angler is casting from the left bank this fish, too, is hooked in the right-hand side of the mouth. Like the fish in (a), it is usually well hooked.
c. Occasionally a salmon will turn in the same direction as that in which the fly is travelling and,

---

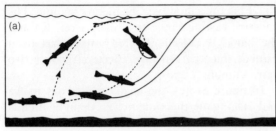

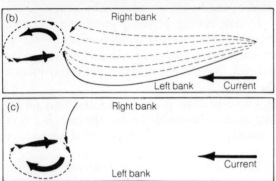

Figure 212: Hooking a salmon

Why violate a fish of such beauty by sticking a meat hook into it?

The time to approach a salmon and take it from the water is when it is lying on its side, exhausted. If a gaff is to be used, that is the time to use it, not before. But if the fish is beaten this is seldom necessary. Nature has equipped the salmon with a 'wrist' above its tail by which it may be lifted, and to land a fish by hand like this is in every way more satisfactory. The fish is undamaged, and any danger of the leader being broken by a hasty gaff stroke is avoided.

There are two golden rules when playing a salmon (which, for that matter, apply to all other species): never let him see you, and never force him. Keep well away from the water and don't try to bring him in too soon. Sometimes a fish allows itself to be brought close in during the

having taken the fly, circle away downstream. Unlike the fish in (a) and (b) it will have the fly in the left side of its mouth when the angler is on the left bank (and *vice versa*). In our experience the fish that takes like this is poorly hooked. Indeed, what often happens is that it runs out a few yards of line – and then comes off.

Note: Salmon will occasionally chase a fly for many yards across a pool before taking it (in the same way that a prawn or spinner is sometimes chased), but as often as not they turn away at the last moment.

Playing and landing a salmon

Unless you are a very experienced salmon fisherman, do not carry a gaff. Many are the fish that would be landed but for its inexpert use.

A gaff is of value in places where it is impossible to beach a fish or bring its nose in close to the side; where a strong back-eddy and a high bank make tailing difficult; when fishing from a boat; or when the line is caught on some obstruction and the fish, although beaten, cannot be brought closer to hand. In nearly every case a large net is preferable.

Figure 213: This fresh run autumn salmon was taken on fly from one of the River Tweed's most famous pools – the Bridge pool at Kelso. Over the centuries thousands of anglers have stepped out of a boat and stood on this patch of grass to play a salmon

Figure 214: This picture could be captioned – *The U-boats of the salmon river – their last docking*

Since we know that pike are very destructive of salmon stock (see figure 196) it follows that pike-infested salmon rivers would improve if the pike populations were eliminated.

Here we come to the crux of the problem since with all the established pike-killing methods there is no known selective method of eliminating an entire population.

The pike in this picture were taken from the Kirkcudbrightshire Dee (which drains Loch Ken), as part of a determined long-term programme of making it possible for more salmon smolts to reach the sea.

Predictably, this programme has been a failure. The result of reducing the population of big pike in a natural pike population has allowed smaller pike to proliferate alarmingly (large and medium pike regulate the numbers of smaller pike by preying on them). Large numbers of small pike (a half-pound pike will make a meal of a smolt) are now so prolific in the Dee that there are few 'gaps in the line' through which the smolts can pass as they allow the current to carry them backwards towards the sea.

Notwithstanding its historic ability to produce (in 1774) Britain's biggest pike, the Kenmure monster of 72 lb, the River Dee is now only a shadow of what it was – although to be fair there are other reasons besides pike predation that have contributed to its decline.

initial stages of the fight. This apparent submission is quite usual and may be described as the danger time. At this moment, far from lunging at him with net or gaff, you should take special precaution to remain out of sight. *The fish is only dimly aware of what is happening*, but once he sees you and becomes frightened, he will resist to the limit of his strength. There are exceptions, of course, but a frightened fish will fight far longer than the fish that never sees you. Provided they have not been scared, many salmon abandon the struggle quite quickly – especially if they have been treated to a 'walking' session up the pool.

It is advisable to 'walk' a fish (whether salmon or trout) whenever you are in a position to do so. It takes the heart out of the fish and, by reducing his resistance, shortens the fight. 'Walking' can sometimes prevent a fish from running into a snag; it may also prevent a fish from rejoining and scaring other members of a shoal.

The moment a fish is hooked, turn away and begin to walk upstream. The rod is held steady with the butt set firmly against the body, the point at an angle of about 45° to the water and at right-angles to the river. No attempt is made to pull him along, or indeed to bully him.

In response to the first gentle pressure, the fish either comes with you or he doesn't. If your move is made soon enough he usually does, but there is no question of trying to force him.

When he comes forward his weight on the line is scarcely felt, for he swims steadily upstream, urged on by the slight belly of line which forms between him and the rod, and only the drag of the line through the water is felt.

If a steady progress is maintained upstream the fish will follow quietly. He will often, in fact, gain ground, so that by the time a previously selected landing place is reached he is somewhere out in the middle of the river and conveniently opposite the rod. You are now in the best place for playing the fish and bringing matters to a conclusion. Indeed, if he has been 'walked' far, most of the playing has been done.

Stay where you are and keep well back from the water. If there is a background of foliage behind you so much the better.

> Young Salmons under a quarter of a yard long, have tender mouths,* so they are apt to break their hold: to obviate which inconvenience, I have known some that use to fasten two hooks together, in like manner as some double Pike hooks lately used in Trowling are made, not with the points opposite to one another, but about a quarter of a Circle from each other, and on them they make their Flie, that if one Hook break hold, the other may not fail
>
> Colonel Robert Venables, *The Experienc'd Angler*
> (fourth edition, 1676)
>
> ---
>
> * These sound like sea trout. The softness of mouth of a fresh-run sea trout is discussed on p. 321.

In the case of a big fish hooked on light tackle, it pays if you can walk him up and down a number of times. It is surprising how docile he will become and, provided he doesn't see you, how easily he can be landed.

In still water a big fish can (so to speak) be 'walked' by rowing the boat gently and steadily in one direction.

Remember: A fish cannot be 'walked' if:
1. You try to bully him.
2. He gets frightened.

As already explained, a hooked fish is not necessarily frightened. What *does* frighten a fish is the glimpse of human beings on the bank. So when playing a fish, *keep out of sight*. And, what is more, *insist that your gillie does the same*.

Wherever there is a place convenient for beaching a salmon no landing tackle of any sort is necessary. The exact landing spot is selected before fishing starts. When the salmon is beaten it is drawn ashore at this place – not by reeling in, but by walking backwards.

When the fish is lying on its side with its head aground the fight is ended and you can relax. The fish will not move again. To close matters, approach the salmon from downstream, reeling in as you go. Then, keeping a good length of line out by holding the rod at arm's length inshore, take the wrist of the tail firmly with thumb and forefinger, the back of the hand uppermost and pointing towards the head. First, push the fish forward up the shore clear of the water, then pick it up. It is a very simple operation.

The following excerpt from the second known English fishing book, *The Arte of Angling* (1577), shows Piscator to be an angler of rare perception.

Viator: ... May a man take a stool and sit down on the ground by you?
Piscator: Yea, so that you sit not over near the water.
Viator: Nay, I trow, I will sit far enough off for slipping in.
Piscator: I do not mean therefor, but I would not have you sit so that the fish may see either your shadow, your face, or any part of you.
Viator: And why? Are they so quick of sight?
Piscator: Look, what they lack in hearing, it is supplied into them in seeing chiefly....
Viator: Well, now I am set, may I then talk and not hinder your fishing?
Piscator: Spare not, but not too loud.
Viator: Do the fish then hear?
Piscator: No, you may talk, whoop, or hallo and never stir them, but I would not gladly by your loud talking that either some bungler, idle person, or jester might resort unto us....

In spite of the natural reluctance of salmon and sea trout to take a lure, failure to do so is by no means always their fault. Many an angler would improve his catch if he cultivated a more stealthy approach.

Thumping along against the skyline; rattling about on rocks in nailed waders; a noisy descent of a shingle bank; poking the bottom with iron-shod wading, splashing the water of a smooth pool tail by unskilful casting, fishing with sun or moon behind him, so that his shadow and the shadow of his rod precede him down a pool ... none of this is likely to be helpful. Fish are frightened by the sudden movement of shadow *across* the water. When the sun is behind an angler, shadow is thrown by the angler himself or the movement of his rod. This can frighten fish long before his lure reaches them.

A very elementary example of stealth – in this case, avoidance of shadow – is illustrated in figure 215.

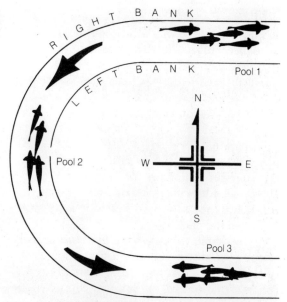

Figure 215: Avoidance of shadow

An angler who is allowed to fish from the left bank only, has three taking stretches at his disposal during a day's fishing. In order to minimize the risk of disturbance he should start in the morning on Pool 3, while the sun moves from east to south. Then, at mid-day and during the afternoon, when the sun is moving from south to west, he should fish Pool 2. In the evening, with the sun in the west, he can move to Pool 1.

The sea trout night fly-fisherman should make a similar approach during conditions of bright moonlight.

And let your garments Russet be or gray,
Of colour darke, and hardest to discry:
That with the Raine or weather will away,
And least offend the fearefull Fishes eye:
John Dennys, *The Secrets of Angling* (1613)

'Tis not so wide as a church-door,' he reflected with Mercutio, 'but 'twill suffice – if I can only land him.'
John Buchan, *John MacNab* (1925)

Figure 216: (*above*) *Salmon Fishing* after a drawing by Francis Barlow, engraved by W. Hollar circa 1650. The fishermen are wearing what appear to be waterproofed (leather?) waders (*Messrs. Walter T. Spencer*)

Figure 217: This 61 lb salmon was caught on a fly in Low Shaw Pool on the Deveron by Mrs Morison on 21 October 1924. It was 53 in. long and had a girth of 33 in. It took a $1\frac{1}{4}$ in. Brown Wing Killer fly. Two of the smaller fish in the picture each weighed 16 lb (*W. Keith Rollo*)

Freshwater Fishing

Figure 218: Miss G. W. Ballantine and her 64 lb British Record rod-caught salmon which she took from the Glendelvine beat on the River Tay, 7 October 1922

WATERSIDE BEHAVIOUR

No matter whether you are fishing a fly or spinner, don't go in halfway down a pool, look round at the angler above in feigned surprise and say: 'Oh, sorry! Didn't see you. You don't mind if I have a dip in, now I'm here, do you?'

This doesn't fool anybody.

The fisherman above does mind, whatever he may say. Having started first he has the right to fish down the pool first. If you want to fish it too, wait either until he has fished it out, or until he gives you the nod to start.

And again, if you are fishing spinner from one bank with a fisherman opposite fishing fly, wait for him to get a reasonable distance down the pool. He will find it disconcerting to have your piece of ironmongery hooking his line or flying around his ears. If his fly hooked you in the back of the neck you would be the first to whine – but he can't cast as far across the river as you can.

You may think we exaggerate. We don't. On much ticket and association water today, no matter what methods are being used, angling manners are appalling. Plop, plop, plop – in go those spinners, not a yard away. Worm or fly fishermen, behaving just as badly, push in ahead without even as much as 'By your leave'!

And while we are on the subject of thoughtless and selfish behaviour, who are the faceless anglers who leave the waterside littered with empty tins, beer bottles, plastic bags, food wrappings, cigarette cartons and, worst of all, discarded nylon? Some river banks are draped with the stuff – an enduring threat to wildlife (see page 382).

The result of an unstealthy approach to angling is twofold:
1. It affects the fish; so that no matter how skilfully a fly is cast no fish is going to take it.
2. It affects the angler. If he behaves in an insensitive manner he is unlikely to recognize and interpret the subtle signals constantly relayed by wind, weather, light, temperature and water; signals he should be relying on to tell him when and how to vary his tactics.

Anyone who wants to become a good angler should study the basic elements of hunting. When he has learned to think and act like a hunter he will no longer worry about being a good angler. Already, he has become one.

But not, one hopes, to the detriment of his manners.

> It is the birds and other creatures peculiar to the water that render fly-fishing so pleasant. Were they all destroyed and nothing left but mere fish, one might as well stand and angle in a stone cattle-trough.
>
> Richard Jefferies

Figure 219: Poaching implements. Salmon leisters from the Border country

Figure 220: (*below*) Curiously enough, an instrument remarkably like a leister – the *bâton fourchie* – was used in otter hunting during medieval times. Our illustration is from *Livre de Chasse*, most famous of all hunting treatises, written by Gaston de Foix, a fourteenth-century feudal lord of the Pyrenees. The following passage comes from *Sport in Art* (second edition, 1920) by W. A. Baillie-Grohman.

'Otter-hunting, as Gaston writes, required "Great Mastery", it required "lyners" and four experienced huntsmen, and he considered that it was a very fine chase … the *bâton fourchie*, as we see, carried still three iron prongs, while in later centuries the two-pronged iron came into use.' Gaston de Foix's exploits were recorded by the medieval chronicler Jean Froissart; he died, it seems, in 1391 of apoplexy after a day-long bear hunt

Cy apres deuise comment on doit chalaer et prendre la loutre.

LOW WATER WORM FISHING

During summer, in conditions of low water and high temperature, salmon (and sea trout) often lie in fast, shallow, broken runs and glides no more than two or three feet deep. That they do so is almost certainly because of the increased oxygenation* of this type of water.

In these conditions a worm offers an angler the best chance of success since it can be fished with less disturbance than any other method.

The object is to present the worm in such a way that it behaves as naturally as possible, drifting with the current without drag or hindrance. A fixed-spool reel can of course be used for the job, but in these fast, shallow runs the most suitable tackle is a centre-pin. A light 10–11 ft single-handed rod should be used with a centre-pin reel holding up to 200 yards of 16–20 lb BS monofilament nylon. On the end of this mainline is tied a small swivel, and on the other end of the swivel a 3 ft leader of much lighter nylon. On the end of the leader is either a Stewart tackle (three hooks in tandem) or a single hook (see page 431).

As we have witnessed on numerous occasions, a salmon frequently touches a worm a number of times before taking it inside its mouth. It is when a fish is toying with a bait in this fashion that the advantage of the centre-pin reel becomes

---

Figure 221: The 'Dee' Otter: This aid to the salmon fisherman who spins for his fish and leaves a small fortune in spinners on the river bottom each season, was developed by Willie Hogg of Castle Douglas. Particularly keen on sea trout and salmon fishing, Hogg was a fine all-round angler who fished the Kirkcudbrightshire Dee.

This 'Dee' otter (as the pictures show) is very simple and easily made. It consists of a wooden disc with a slit in it and two lead weights. A thick rubber band fits over the slit. When the otter is used to rescue a snagged spinner, the rubber band is slipped along the edge of the wooden disc so that the line can pass along the slit (between the two lead weights) into the centre hole.

The rubber band is then replaced to prevent the otter coming off the line, which can now run freely through the hole.

As the rod is raised the otter slides down the line and is worked into the current by pulling on the line from slightly upstream of the snag.

---

*Or it may be because it requires less muscular activity for a salmon to breathe in fast rather than in slow running water – so that increased oxygen intake comes from more water passing over the gills.

The Atlantic Salmon

Figure 222: Question: Given that the list of countries which enjoy a run of the Atlantic salmon *Salmo salar* is small – where do you think this photograph depicting a fresh caught fish and a team of oxen was taken?
Answer: Canada – somewhere near the Medway river in Nova Scotia

apparent. Time and again the worm must cover exactly the same spot. This is difficult to accomplish with anything but a reel which has the exact length of line already stripped off.

Cast from a position that is roughly at right-angles to, or just above, the lie you wish to cover. Drop the worm a sufficient distance upstream for it to sink within two or three inches of the bottom by the time it reaches the fish. This distance depends on the depth of water and strength of current.

Whenever possible, dispense with extra weight. If the current is very strong, a swanshot or a twist or two of lead wire can be put on the leader about 18 inches above the worm. But always use as little as you can.

When a fish is lying in fast, shallow water and takes the worm opposite to or just below the rod, the Stewart tackle is the best. In quiet water towards the tail of a deep pool, a fish will take as the worm floats slowly past or bumps gently round in front of it. Here, a single hook is preferable.

Tackles are very easy to make. Home-made worming tackles, if properly tied, are more reliable than most shop tackles. This is because the 'bought' tackle is made up with eyeless hooks. Even when the tackle is new an eyeless hook whipped to the leader is liable to 'draw'. When the whipping on the hook shank becomes frayed the hook will certainly 'draw' and we have known more salmon hooked on worm lost for this reason than any other (except striking too quickly!). We recommend the use of eyed-hooks tied with the Stewart tackle knot shown on page 391.

It is true that the Stewart is a sort of snap tackle. But when the bait suddenly stops on its passage downstream, don't jerk it. It may have snagged, and a jerk may simply increase the hold. Wait. If it is a fish, you will feel a slight 'grating' sensation.

All the time the worm is fishing try to gauge exactly where it is and what it is doing. Guide it over or round rocks. (This is where a long rod is so useful.) If the worm is heading for an unavoidable snag, retrieve it and cast again.

Hold the line between the fingers of the non-casting hand, and learn to detect the difference between the touch of a rock and a salmon which may 'nudge' the bait several times before actually taking it. Always 'feel' a line with wetted fingers. Fingertips are more sensitive wet than dry.

Don't expect salmon to be lying behind rocks that are close to the surface or partly exposed. There is too much turbulence. Fish only lie behind rocks that have a smooth flow of water over them; even then, they usually lie on top. Fish lie in front of rocks, beside rocks or between rocks in a steady glide, seldom behind them.

Don't start by fishing the distant water. Always fish the lies close to your own bank before casting further out.

Many of the fish are lying in water only two or three feet deep. Much of it will be wadeable. *But don't wade in too far.* Worming fast shallows is quite different from fly fishing deep runs and pools. In a pool, a fish disturbed by a wading angler may soon return to its lie but in a

> Those anglers who despise worm-fishing as a thing so simple as to be quite unworthy of their attention, would quickly discover their mistake if brought to a small clear water on a warm sunny day in June or July.
>
> W. C. Stewart, *The Practical Angler* (1857)

shallow run it will not.

Keep a supply of spare tackles in your pocket ready tied and wound on frames. If a tackle snags on the bottom, don't wade out to free it. Break it and tie on another. Tackles are expendable. You are bound to lose a lot of hooks in shallow, rocky water. But if you stumble about among the lies, you will simply drive the fish away.

Don't be in too much of a hurry. Fish slowly and carefully. You cannot over-fish a salmon lie – *provided you fish properly*. Although you have covered a salmon a number of times unsuccessfully, it may take later – if you haven't walked on top of it!

Presenting a worm (1) (see figure 223 (a))

The angler stands just upstream of the lie and casts to B. The worm sinks as it washes down with the current between B and C. AC is shorter than AB, so that the angler must shorten line as the worm comes downstream, by drawing in with the non-casting hand over the forefinger of the hand holding the rod.

Note. If the angler stands too far upstream of the fish it is difficult to prevent drag. Too far downstream, and the worm will not precede the line.

Regardless of what comes naturally, the most successful anglers are those who have developed their water-sense: that ability to examine a stretch of fishing and decide unerringly where fish are likely to be lying.

By those fortunate enough to have the opportunity, water-sense begins to be absorbed during childhood. To the late starter it is not so easily acquired, and books alone are of little help. There is simply no substitute for experience at the waterside, preferably in the company of a top-class fisherman.

It is like learning a new language. Gradually, what has seemed meaningless becomes significant, and certain spots will stand out as being more attractive than others. Aided by water-sense, the novice will find himself taking salmon and sea trout with the upstream-worm from water which, previously, he would have walked past without a second glance.

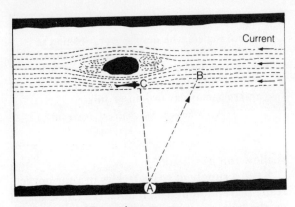

Figure 223 (a): Presenting a worm

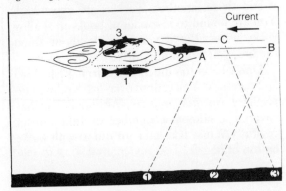

Figure 223 (b): Presenting a worm

Presenting a worm (2) (see figure 223 (b))

The order in which to fish three possible salmon lies by a rock.

1. Cast to point A for No. 1, the nearest fish, first. This operation, if unsuccessful, will not disturb the other lies.

2. Move upstream and fish for No. 2, by casting to point B.

3. No. 3 is an extremely difficult fish to catch – except from the opposite bank. Move still further upstream and cast downstream to point C, letting go some slack line. If the fish refuses the worm, guide the line over the rock by holding the rod at arm's length above your head. When fishing lies of this nature, a long, light rod is a great advantage.

Presenting a worm (3) (see figure 223 (c))

Ten salmon lying in a stretch of fast, shallow, clear, broken water. The tops of the rocks are

very close to or above the surface. None of the fish would be visible to an observer on the bank. Only by using his water-sense, by 'reading' the stretch, could an angler decide where the fish were lying.

Before starting to fish water of this sort, time should always be spent in careful examination: snags and probable lies being memorized.

Very seldom is such water fished straight down from top to bottom, or straight up from bottom to top. The angler should move about, now up, now down, according to the particular lie he wishes to cover. The order in which the lies are fished is of great importance.

In our imaginary piece of water, lies 1, 2 and 3 should be fished first. Then lies 4, 5 and 6. After this, the farther lies can be fished, 7 and 8.

The fish lying at 9 is virtually uncatchable (except from the opposite bank) unless the angler wades well in above lie 2. But if he does this he will certainly frighten away the fish lying at 1 and 2, which, if they have already refused the worm but remain undisturbed, may take later in the day. In addition, he is almost certain to get snagged on the long rock. This fish is best left alone.

There is, however, a good chance of covering 10 satisfactorily. It is now safe for the angler to wade, since he is well below the fish in lie 3. He can turn a long and difficult cast into a relatively easy one.

Of a number of salmon at any particular moment, only one or two (if any) may be taking fish. Obviously the more fish the angler covers correctly, the more chance he has of covering a taker. Although every salmon refuses his worm the first time he fishes the water, he may very well hook one later in the day – provided he has not frightened it out of its lie.

Presenting a worm (4) (see figure 223 (d))

A method of fishing the moving worm in deep water is to cast well upstream with a swanshot or twist of lead wire on the leader. The worm is allowed to sink, then to swing slowly round in front of the fish just off the bottom. It can work well in a pool where fish are lying in front of a steeply rising tail.

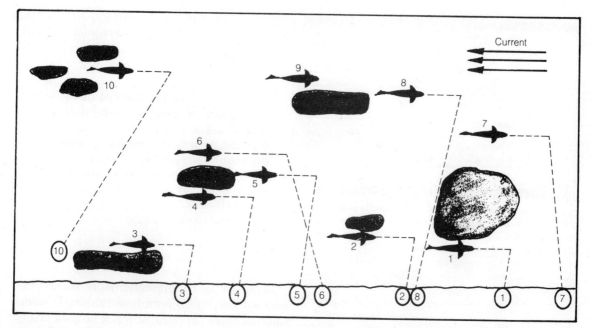

Figure 223 (c): Presenting a worm

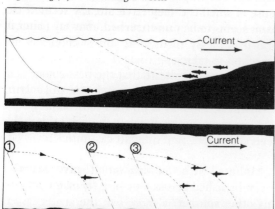

Figure 223 (d): Presenting a worm

Figure 223 (e): Prawn mount with vane

Figure 223 (f): Without vane

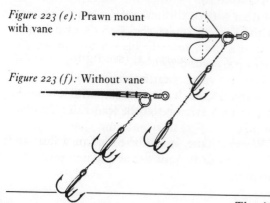

Salmon often nudge a worm more than once before taking it. The angler must *keep in touch* and try to 'feel' the worm during every moment of the cast: as it drifts downstream he must first draw in some line with the non-casting hand, then let it slip again at just the right speed as the bait travels past him towards the tail of the pool. *Note*: If the bottom is rough, a link-ledger rig is advisable (see page 444).

PRAWN FISHING

Most aspects of salmon fishing have received lavish attention from other writers and we have no wish to cover ground already combed bare. There are, however, a few behavioural points that have not been fully explained: for instance, the vexed question of the salmon and the prawn.

In general, the prawn is not an 'in' lure. Many writers have considered it and, almost without exception, condemned it. Some, throwing up their hands in horror, have denounced it as being harmful, and even 'unsporting'; a method quite beyond the pale.

We do not share this view. We think that the harmful effects of prawn fishing have been greatly exaggerated; we also think that far from

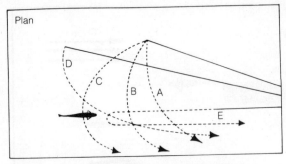

Figure 224 (a): Each cast over a known lie should be different. A fish can sometimes be induced to take if a prawn it has already seen and refused suddenly behaves differently. A, B, C, D, and E show ways of presenting a prawn with or without spinning vane. The various paths of the prawn are shown in plan view

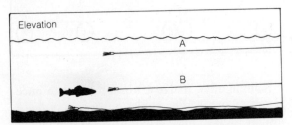

Figure 224 (b): A salmon will sometimes rise to a prawn fished near to the surface as shown in A. More often, however, it takes a prawn that is fished deep (B).

being an 'unsporting' method (whatever that may mean) it is a skilful and fascinating technique, especially in low clear water when both prawn and salmon can be seen during every moment of the encounter.

H. F., who has observed salmon behaviour in clear water rivers over many years, writes:

Although I have often been told that a prawn will sometimes empty a salmon pool I have never witnessed it. Time and time again I have watched the reactions of salmon to a prawn, but never once have I seen a salmon actually leave a pool.

We do not of course suggest that it never happens (the behaviour of migratory fishes varies from river to river). But if it *does* happen (and there is evidence that it does) it is only very occasional. In our experience the prawn does comparatively little harm and although it is by no means always successful, there are times when it can serve the angler well.

Being without inhibitions, H. F. has experimented with boiled prawns of different colours, painting them (in the absence of suitable dyes) with dabs of oil pigment. Although the salmon's sense of smell is extremely acute, the scent of oil paint seems to be no deterrent. A freshly painted prawn is messy to use, but the salmon has no objection to taking it.

Experiments indicate that the best colour is a rich magenta. The second most successful colour seems to be the boiled prawn's natural pink.

A prawn can be presented to a salmon in several ways:

1. Mounted with spinning vane (figure 223 (e)), it can be fished across a pool in the same way as any other spinner.
2. Without vane (figure 223 (f) and figure 225), it can be fished across a pool like a fly, or by sink-and-draw.
3. Either with or without vane, it can be let down on the current under the angler's own bank a yard at a time, brought back a foot or so, and then slowly withdrawn.
4. Without vane, it can be drift-lined.
5. Without vane, it can be left motionless on the bottom for a salmon to pick up – like a deadbait for pike.
6. Without vane, it can be fished on a float and allowed to drift unimpeded down a pool from top to tail.

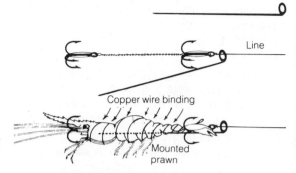

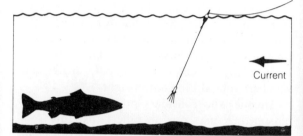

Figure 225: Home-made prawn mount

Figure 226: Float fishing with a prawn

A salmon reacts to a prawn as follows:

1. It remains in its lie and ignores the prawn.
2. It shows signs of agitation as the prawn approaches, eventually abandoning its lie and darting off, often leaping further up or down the pool. (It is probably this behaviour that has given rise to some of the hair-raising stories about salmon fleeing from a pool.) The salmon does not often stay away from its lie for very long – usually, from two to five minutes.
3. It swims up as though to intercept the prawn, but turns away without touching it and returns to its lie.
4. It sucks the prawn into its mouth and immediately blows it out again, leaving no mark on it.
5. It takes the prawn with the very front of its mouth and gives it a little nip, removing a tiny piece from the back, or the eggs from the belly.

Figure 228: Salmon often 'toy' with a prawn or a shrimp. The picture shows a female shrimp (fished by H. F.) with the head nipped off and the eggs sucked out – on successive casts. Fish behaving in this way are very difficult to catch

Figure 227: The list of the famous who also fish is prodigious. Welsh rugby fans will readily recognize this fisherman standing in the River Teviot above Junction Pool holding two salmon. If there is a fish to be caught, this man will catch it. Fly-fishing for salmon and sea trout is now – dare we say it – the great love of his life

At other times, it contrives to shave off the whiskers and sometimes part of the head as cleanly as if they had been cut by a razor.

6. It takes the prawn in its mouth, crushes it, and then blows it out again.

7. It takes the prawn fiercely (sometimes halfway down its throat), either by grabbing it as it swings past or by sucking it up off the bottom.

Figure 229: A stationary prawn positioned just on the edge of the salmon's backward vision (see dotted lines) will sometimes induce a savage take

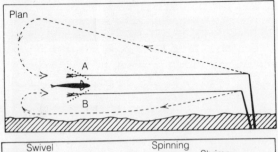

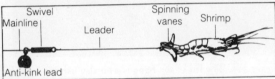

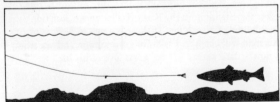

Figure 230: Spinning a shrimp (*above*) and rolling-ledger (*below*)

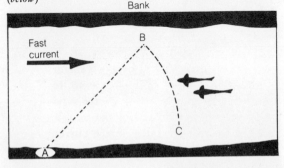

8. It chases the length or width of a pool to grab a prawn.

Probably the most effective way of fishing a prawn is to let it drift unchecked through a pool, suspended from a float (figure 226). But the most exciting method is in low clear water, when the prawn is drift-lined (with no float, and the very minimum of lead) to a particular fish, and both prawn and salmon are kept in view.

Sometimes, if the prawn can be swung round well below a salmon, then manoeuvred upstream into the position shown in figure 229 and left to lie there, the salmon, after a few minutes of increasing agitation, will suddenly turn and make a ferocious grab at it. A most exciting moment for the angler and anyone else who happens to be watching. Needless to say, both angler and watchers should keep out of sight.

Anyone who considers prawn fishing to be 'unsporting' may care to reflect that this low-water technique demands a very high degree of angling skill.

There is, however, one all-important aspect of prawn fishing. Whatever one's opinion may be, it is not the effect of the prawn on the fish that matters, it is the effect on other fishermen.

No sportsman should wittingly spoil someone else's pleasure. If your companions think that prawn will interfere with their chances of catching salmon, don't fish it. If the rules of the beat forbid prawn, observe them. It is a question of good manners. Always, when fishing as a guest, enquire first before using prawn.

SHRIMP FISHING

The shrimp is fished in clear water mainly during the summer months. Like a sunk fly, it should be presented fairly close to the bottom and as slowly as possible. All the prawn fishing methods can be used to present a shrimp.

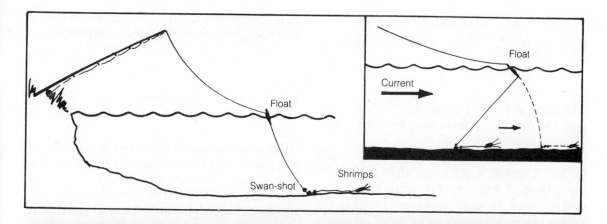

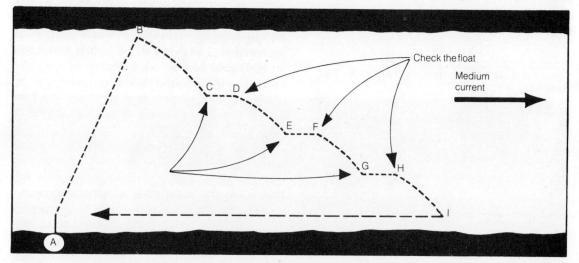

Figure 231: Stret-pegging

Spinning is not the most productive method but is practical, since it can be used in water which – owing to an uneven bottom – prohibits the use of rolling-ledger or stret-pegging.

Provided the river has a bed of fine gravel where fish are lying, the rolling-ledger is a good method of presenting shrimp in fast water. The angler casts (figure 230) from A to B and fishes the shrimp across the noses of the fish on the arc BC. The lead should be heavy enough to bump slowly round, thereby controlling the speed of the swing – with the shrimp 'swimming' an inch or two off the bottom. The use of a long rod assists in controlling speed.

To fish the shrimp too fast and with too short a rod is a common mistake. In strong water a long line should be cast from well upstream. This will lessen the angle BAC and help to slow down the speed of the swing.

When the shrimp stops, tighten.

Although, like rolling-ledgers, it can be used only when the bottom is suitable, stret-pegging is a very effective way of fishing a shrimp.

An angler (figure 231) at A casts to B and allows the shrimp to swing round as slowly as possible to C. At this point line is released so that the float drifts down on the current to D. The float is then checked, which allows the shrimp to wing round to E. And so on – until the shrimp finishes up in slack water under the angler's bank at I via E–G and H. (For other notes on stret-pegging, see page 457.)

The Atlantic Salmon

GILLIES

Gillie: Attendant on a Highland chief; one who attends on a sportsman. Gael. *gille* lad, servant.

The Oxford English Dictionary of Etymology (1966)

The gillie, as a type, reminds us of the little girl with the curl. When he is good he is very, very good – but when he is bad . . .

He is not often very, very good. Why should he be? The job is no holier than any other. Nevertheless, whatever his qualifications, at modern rates he is an expensive item on the salmon angler's account. The rates are fairly standard, but although there is little variation in cost there is considerable variation in value. At

Figure 232: F. B. with two springers from Stanley beat, River Tay

Figure 233: (*right*) F. B. holding a 'mended' Loch Ken salmon kelt. Such fish, although silvery in appearance, may weigh only a fraction of their pre-spawning weight. The 26 lb autumn Tweed salmon (inset) is, on the other hand, well coloured and not much short of its 'fresh run' weight

his best a gillie is priceless. At his worst he is a pest.

There are certain services you should expect, and assistance when wading is one of them. For a strong and healthy young gillie to sit idly on the bank smoking, as many do, while you stumble about trying to fish down unfamiliar water, is not part of the deal. As H. F. can endorse from his own experience of gillying (as an impecunious writer many years ago), most inexperienced anglers are not at their best when struggling to cast across a wide pool with the current swirling round their bottoms.

A good gillie should have his breast waders handy and be prepared to wade at your elbow if you require him to do so. If you are sensible you will, for to wade beside you is the duty of any gillie worth the name. But the true value of the really good gillie is not merely a willingness to wade, or shoulder your bag, or row the boat. It is the ability to give good advice: the advice of an expert who knows his water and something about the behaviour of the fish it holds.

Besides having a thorough knowledge of the contours of the river bottom and the varying depths throughout each pool, he should know the ways of the river itself with its swirls and eddies – and the effect they will have on your lure. He should know every important salmon lie in the beat and how the 'taking strips' alter according to the water height. It is this expert professional knowledge that (hopefully) you pay for when you employ him. If he really does know his stuff you should pay him well; not least because, quite simply, it is a good investment!

If you are wise you will not let the gillie (or anyone else, for that matter) set up your tackle and tie on your lure. *Always* do this for yourself. Only then will you be sure that the reel is firmly attached, the line correctly threaded, and the leader and lure securely tied. Similarly, you should seldom permit anyone else to land your fish for you. All too frequently are fish lost because some eager helper cranes forward at the water's edge, or even wades in, ready to swipe at the earliest opportunity!

In fairness to whoever your companion may be, you should be responsible for preparing your tackle and landing your fish. Then, if a knot slips, or the reel drops off while a fish is running, or a hasty gaff or net stroke knocks off the fish or breaks the leader ... you have only yourself to blame. It is better that way.

Cooking the Salmon

FRESH SALMON STEAKS

1 salmon 6–12 lb
Chopped parsley
Unsalted butter
Olive oil, 1 teaspoonful per steak
Slices of cucumber in the skin
Salt and black pepper

Cut the salmon into steaks $1\frac{1}{4}$–$1\frac{1}{2}$ inches thick. Sprinkle with salt and pepper. Melt butter. Add steaks and simmer gently. Turn steaks after about five minutes (or when slightly brown). Place steaks on a hot dish.

Clean pan. Fry the sliced cucumber in fresh butter. Pour over the steaks.

Note: Sliced cucumber in vinegar or soured cream is delicious with most salmon dishes.

Figure 234: A traditional Dunkeld whisky pot

SALMON KEDGEREE

1 lb poached salmon
$\frac{1}{4}$ lb rice
4 tablespoonsful butter
2 hardboiled eggs
Salted water
Salt and black pepper
$\frac{1}{2}$ pint hot cream sauce

Cook rice in boiling salted water until tender. Drain and keep warm. Flake fish, removing bones and skin. Melt butter in saucepan; add fish and sauté gently. Add $\frac{1}{4}$ pint fresh cream to 1 pint Bechamel sauce and bring to boiling point. Add a few drops of lemon juice.

Finely chop whites of hardboiled eggs and combine with rice and fish. Season to taste with salt and black pepper. Fold in hot cream sauce. Serve with yolks of hardboiled eggs, pressed through a sieve or finely chopped, sprinkled over the top.

POACHED SALMON

Clean fish and place in a fish kettle with salt and a dash of vinegar or a squeeze of lemon juice.

Cover with boiling water and simmer until the flesh can be separated easily from the bone (approximately 10 minutes per lb).

If the fish is to be eaten hot, drain and serve with shrimp sauce, sliced cucumber and brown bread and butter.

If it is to be eaten cold, leave it in the liquor. Serve with mayonnaise, lemon and salad.

The SHADS
Clupeidae

ALLIS SHAD
(*Alosa alosa*)

The shads, both members of the herring family, deserve our attention because not only do they migrate from sea to spawn in freshwater, but they can be caught (locally) on rod and line. The allis shad, less common than the twaite, usually has a single dark spot on the shoulder immediately behind the gills. It grows to a weight of about 8 lb, and runs up the Rivers Severn, Wye and Shannon. Spawning takes place in April or May, after which the adults return to sea while the young spend up to two years in the river.

Figure 235: Allis shad

TWAITE SHAD
(*Alosa fallax*)

The twaite shad is distinguished by a series of six or seven dark round spots along its flanks. It spawns rather later than the allis shad and grows only to a weight of about 3 lb. Prior to the pollution of the Thames, twaite shads used to arrive in the lower reaches in large numbers between May and July. Shad-netting sites were opposite the Millbank Prison and just above Putney Bridge.

Figure 236: Twaite shad

Figure 237: Twaite shad, top and middle. Allis shad, bottom. All caught on a fly-spoon by Phill Williams fishing the lower reaches of the Severn

Whitebait, too, ran into the Thames estuary in large numbers and during the early nineteenth century their parentage was disputed. Because of the prolific quantities caught during May and June, it was argued that whitebait were young twaite shad – but since shad were plentiful in the Severn and whitebait were not, the matter remained unresolved!

Allis and twaite shad are occasionally caught at sea by whiffing*; in freshwater by worm fishing, or on the fly-rod with fly-spoons or red and white flies.

* Whiffing: A sea-fishing method with a weighted hand-line to which half-a-dozen or so red, white, blue, green, orange or red-feathered hooks are attached on short droppers at intervals of about a yard, and fished at varying depth with a sink-and-draw action. Among the many species caught in this way are mackerel, garfish, bass, pollack and shad.

The earliest mention of the (allis) shad seems to be in John Dennys's *The Secrets of Angling* (published posthumously in 1613):

'The *Perch*, the *Tench*, and *Eele*, doe rather bite at great red worms in Field or Garden bred,
And with this bayte hath often taken bin
The *Shad*, that in the Spring time commeth in,
The *Peele**, the *Tweat*†, the *Botling*‡, and the rest,
With many more, that in the deepe doth lye of
Avon, *Uske*, or *Severne* and of *Wye*.'

A contemporary of Shakespeare, 'Glorious' John – as he was dubbed by those who admired his writing – lived in Gloucestershire within reach of the rivers mentioned in *The Secrets of Angling*

* Peele: sea trout   † Tweat: twaite (shad)   ‡ Botling: chub

Cooking the Shad

The flesh of allis shad, although bony, is said to be very good but better when taken from freshwater rather than salt. Ausonius pronounced the flesh notoriously unfit for any other tables than those of the common people: 'Who does not know those frizzing, sputtering fish on every poor man's grate.'

In *A History of The Fishes of The British Islands* (1877) Couch tells us that:

Once the shad runs into the river a change of quality is soon effected.... The Severn has long possessed the character of affording shads of a high degree of excellence where seventy or 80 dozen have been caught in a night ... for the shad is a shy and timid fish, and might not be easily enclosed in a net by day.

Pennant, too, esteemed the Severn shad: 'a very delicate fish; about the time of its first appearance. In April or May, it sells dearer than salmon.'

GRILLED SHAD

If it is to be served whole, choose a shad weighing $1-1\frac{1}{4}$ lb. *For the marinade*

Olive oil	Small sprig thyme
Lemon juice	1 bay leaf
1 sprig parsley	Salt and pepper

Clean the fish thoroughly, and make one or two deep incisions in the fleshy part of the back. Cover fish with marinade and leave for about 1 hour. Then grill gently for about 30 minutes, basting occasionally with a little oil or butter.

Serve with *maître-d'hôtel* butter, anchovy butter, bearnaise sauce, or with sorrel cooked in butter, bound with egg yolk and cream and seasoned with salt and pepper.

If the shad is rather big it can be cooked whole in the oven, in which case sprinkle lightly with breadcrumbs and baste with oil from time to time during the cooking.

If it is to be served in slices, cut the slices about $\frac{1}{4}$ inch thick; season with salt and pepper, marinate as described and then grill.

One day I witnessed a very strange thing. It was evening and the beach was forsaken.... A gentleman, followed by a big dog, came down to the beach and stood at a distance of forty or fifty yards from me, while the dog bounded forward over the flat, slippery rocks and through pools of water until he came to my side, and sitting on the edge of the rock began gazing intently down at the water.

He was a big, shaggy, round-headed animal, with a greyish coat with some patches of light reddish colour on it; what his breed was I cannot say, but he looked somewhat like a sheep-dog or an otter hound. Suddenly he plunged in, quite vanishing from sight, but quickly reappeared with a big shad in his jaws.

Climbing on to the rock he dropped the fish, which he had not appeared to have injured much, as it began floundering about in an exceedingly lively manner. I was astonished and looked back at the dog's master; but there he stood in the same place, smoking and paying no attention to what his animal was doing.

Again the dog plunged in and brought out a second big fish and dropped it on the flat rock, and again and again he dived, until there were five big shads all floundering about on the wet rock and likely soon to be washed back into the water.

The shad is a common fish in the Plata and the best to eat of all its fishes, resembling the salmon in its rich flavour, and is eagerly watched for when it comes up from the sea by the Buenos Aires fishermen, just as our fishermen watch for mackerel on our coasts. But on this evening the beach was deserted by everyone, watcher included, and the fish came and swarmed along the rocks, and there was no one to catch them – not even some poor hungry idler to pounce and carry off the five fishes the dog had captured. One by one I saw them washed back into the water, and presently the dog, hearing his master whistling him, bounded away.

W. H. Hudson,
Far Away and Long Ago

The
THREE-SPINED
STICKLEBACK
Gasterosteus aculeatus

The three-spined stickleback, or tiddler, is one of the most widespread, prolific and (behaviourally) most interesting of all North European freshwater fishes. Although some populations live and breed wholly in freshwater, others are anadromous – breeding in freshwater, migrating to sea, and then returning to freshwater to spawn. Yet others are wholly marine. (Its relative, the ten-spined stickleback *Gasterosteus pungitius*, is much less tolerant of salinity.)

This fascinating little fish grows to a length of 2–4 inches. Having studied its behaviour both in Britain and on the Continent, H. F. is tempted to write at length about it. He desists, since the

Most anglers will confess that they were first entered into the sport by fishing for sticklebacks, which abound in all the ponds and ditches in the neighbourhood of London, they are also very common in canals, especially in the Regent's Park Canal. In the summer-time, thousands of little boys go out fishing for 'tittlers', their apparatus consisting of a stick, a piece of thread, and a short piece of worm tied in the middle without any hook; if expert, they sometimes pull out two at a time in this way. The fashion is to take them home in pickle-bottles; and the boys generally sell them, sometimes getting as much as sixpence a bottleful. I always encourage these boys, as the little urchins are thus taken out of the London streets, and have a chance of learning a little natural history.

Frank Buckland, *A Familiar History of British Fishes*
(1873)

subject is of little direct interest to the angler, but encourages any readers interested in fish behaviour to pursue the matter for themselves.

Recommended reading: *Territory in the Three-Spined Stickleback (Gasterosteus aculeatus L.) An Experimental Study in Intraspecific Competition,* J. van den Assem; Leiden, E. J. Brill (1967). Also, the appropriate passages in *Animal Behav-*

Figure 238: Sticklebacks swim in a series of little bursts punctuated by stops and much fin-fanning. This strange mode of locomotion coupled with eyes which are much too big for their bodies give the impression that sticklebacks are very intense and deliberate

iour, Niko Tinbergen; Life Nature Library (1965).

Freshwater Fishing

The
STURGEON
Acipenser sturio

There was caught in a stake net, near Findhorn, Scotland, a sturgeon, eight feet six inches, long, three in width and weighing two hundred and three pounds.

Barrow's *Worcester Journal* (July 1833)

Only one species of this primitive family of fishes concerns us: the anadromous common, or green sturgeon. It is found in Western European rivers – and like all sturgeons of the Northern Hemisphere (there are some twenty-three species) is immediately recognizable by its tapering body armoured with rows of scutes (bony plates), an elongated barbuled snout and a tail-fin that leans to one side.

Adult sturgeon enter rivers in early spring to spawn – notably in the French Dordogne and Garonne rivers; the Gaudalquiver in Spain; Lake Ladoga in the USSR and rivers flowing into the Baltic, Black, Caspian and Mediterranean seas.

Dispersed members of these European populations are occasionally caught in Britain, more frequently in the rivers Severn, Trent, Parret, Usk, Wye and formerly in the Thames, but are said not to spawn in these rivers. Tagged specimens of a related North American species have been known to travel long distances – some may even travel to European waters. In *A History of The Fishes of The British Islands* (1862–65) Couch described the sturgeon as a fish 'which wanders widely from the principal haunts of its race'.

Sturgeon commonly grow to about 11 ft in length and according to Thomas Pennant in *British Zoology Vol 3* (1812), the heaviest to be taken from British waters weighed 460 lb.

Historically, because of their comparative rarity, British-caught sturgeon, especially those from the Thames within the jurisdiction of the Lord Mayor of London, are judged to be 'royal fish'.

William Yarrell in *A History of British Fishes* (1841) states that sturgeon were exclusively reserved for the table of Henry the First. But

Sturgeon occasionally come up the Thames, but they were never numerous in this river. Provision was made in ancient Acts excepting them from the vulgar fate of other fish, and in the instructions to the City water-bailiffs for the time being, orders were issued that the sturgeon 'was not to be secreted', and that all royal fishes taken within the jurisdiction of the Lord Mayor of London, as namely, whales, sturgeons, porpoises, and such like, should be made known, and the name and names of all such persons as shall take them shall be sent in to the Lord Mayor of London for the time being. The sturgeon therefore is always, when taken, sent direct to grace the table of majesty.

Charles Dickens, *A Dictionary of the Thames* (1880)

according to Couch (see above) an account of London, written by Fitz-Stephen in the twelfth century, suggests that a dish of sturgeon could be obtained readily at a hostelry in the City.

Preparation of caviare from sturgeon roe has long supported a large Russian industry on the Black and Caspian Seas and elsewhere:

The river Zongouska, in Siberia, abounds in sturgeons. The inhabitants of the neighbourhood sell a great quantity yearly to D'Illmsk, D'Leniseisk, and D'Irhoutsk. The most favourable time for fishing is when the river is gently frozen. They make use of a rod or pole, about four or five feet long, at the extremity of which they fix an iron, with two branches curved or bent, but round about half a foot from each other, and a sharp point coming out between the branches. When they fish, they break the ice, and put the rod into the holes, at the deepest places, until they have found the sturgeons. As soon as they have found the fish, they go into the branches, two at a time, (that is, two in each branch), until the whole are caught. They take at a time from two to three hundred. If any are injured, and blood issues from the wound, the fishing immediately ceases, as the fish all leave the place.

Gmelin, *Voyage en Siberie, Vol. 1*

Among several sturgeon caught in the lower reaches of the Welsh rivers Towy and Teifi was one of 320 lb, netted in shallow water in June 1896. And an even bigger one of 388 lb in July 1933. This fish, foul-hooked in the head by a salmon angler, is said to have been killed with a rock and dragged out on ropes after it had stranded itself.

Figure 239: This 200 lb sturgeon, now on view at the Doncaster Museum, was taken from the River Don near Doncaster *c.* 1872. According to the museum's records, most Yorkshire sturgeons were netted at sea or found washed ashore. Some in estuarine waters were killed by paddles or boat propellers; those well inland and perhaps halted by locks or weirs, were speared, harpooned with pitchforks, shot or beaten with sticks. Out of ninety sturgeons on record, only one had taken a bait. This was mentioned by W. J. Clarke in the *Naturalist* of 1936, '23 January 1936, a small sturgeon measuring 4 ft in length was caught (off Scarborough) on a baited hook on a long line and is the only instance with which I am acquainted where one of these fish has been captured in such a way. The bait taken was a Dahlia Anemone'

In *Natural History of British Fishes* (1881) Frank Buckland recorded:

'A very large sturgeon caught in the salmon draft net at Llandogo a few miles above Chepstow. It measured 9 ft 6 in. and 3 ft 1 in. in girth and weighed 392 lb. The fish contained 27 lb of caviar.'

A distinguished lawyer friend advised Buckland that the Duke of Beaufort (who owned the fishery at Chepstow) had no claim on the fish since by an unrepealed act of Edward II:

'The King shall have the wreck of the sea throughout the realm, whales and great sturgeon taken in the sea or elsewhere in the realm except in certain places privileged by the King.'

Three large sturgeons taken in the river Nyn, near Peterborough. One at Allerton mill, seven feet nine inches in length, weighed one hundred and twenty-three pounds. Another at Castor mill, was eight feet two inches in length, and three feet in width. Another was five feet nine inches long.

Morton's *Natural History of Staffordshire*

In the year 1829, a large sturgeon was caught and landed at Bushley Meadows; it was seven feet in length, two feet ten inches in girth, and weighed one hundred and twenty pounds.

Dr Hasting's *Natural History of Worcestershire*

This river (Medway) was formerly well stored with salmon and sturgeon. The Bishop of Rochester derived a valuable part of his revenue from the fishing for sturgeon. One was caught near Maidstone, in 1774, that was seven feet long, and weighed one hundred and sixty pounds.

Supplement to Daniel's *Rural Sports* (1813)

Figure 240: Head of a sturgeon. The mouth, which is ventral and can project as a short tube, is used for sucking up food rooted from the sea bed by the snout and detected with the sensitive barbules. The sturgeon, which is an anadromous fish, stops feeding while ascending a river to its spawning grounds. The adults return to sea immediately after spawning. The eggs are sticky and adhere to stones or plants. They hatch in three to seven days at water temperatures of 57–66°F. The young sturgeons remain in the river or estuary for up to three years

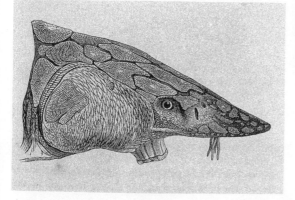

Figure 241: An example of a fish – however much modified – that has retained the essential characteristics of its remote ancestors

The Sturgeon

The
WHITE
STURGEON

Acipenser transmontanus

Sturgeon Eggs – The fishery of the Caspian sea, about
the mouth of the Volga, is of the highest importance.
Amongst the great variety of fish in which this river
abounds, the sturgeon is not the least considerable.
Its eggs afford what the Russians call ikari, and the
Italians caviar.

P. H. Bruce – quoted in *Piscatorial Reminiscences and Gleanings*
by Thomas Boosey (1835)

Unlike the common sturgeon of European waters
the Pacific white sturgeon of the North American
continent is a sport-fish. In one big river system
alone, some 20,000 lb of these fish are caught
annually on rod and line.

In 1977, Mr Garnet Ginther, fishing in Canada's mighty Fraser River at Dewdney, near
Mission, caught a 710 lb white sturgeon.* From
an examination of one of its fin bone sections, its
year of birth was reckoned to be *c.* 1845!

Compared with some sturgeons, however,
Garnet Ginther's fish was only middle-aged. In
the early 1950s, Mr Hank Watts of Vancouver
caught a 200 year old Fraser River sturgeon weighing 1871 lb in a gill-net at Westminster. When

young, that sturgeon would have fattened on supplies of chironomids, sculpins, lampreys and crayfish in those far-off days before the French
Revolution!

Until 1982, when the trade was banned, large
quantities of white sturgeon were exported to
China. China and Russia, the greatest consumers
of caviare and sturgeon flesh, also have a species
that grows big – up to a recorded 2,200 lb. But
this, seemingly, is short-lived and short-bodied –
about 80 years old and 15 feet in length.

Figure 242: This photograph (*right*) of 'a living relic of the
Earth's past', published in a British Columbian
newspaper, the *Sun*, on 18 October 1961, shows an 871 lb
white sturgeon caught in a gill-net by Henry Watts of
Port Mann on the Fraser River. Another big sturgeon
weighing 811 lb was gill-netted in the Fraser by Leo
Patterson in the same year. The picture (*far right*) shows
Patterson standing by the big fish and holding a 3-foot
'juvenile' sturgeon or rather a 'teenager' since such a
sturgeon would be about 14 years old.* (*Don Leblanc*)

* This would be a great age for most species of freshwater fish.

---

* Garnet Ginther's sturgeon was caught on eel bait from an 18 ft
boat. The fish towed Garnet and his boat for over forty-five
minutes, but his heavy cane rod and 200 lb BS line eventually
brought it under control. It died four days later, having been
transported alive to the Vancouver Aquarium. The body was put
in embalming fluid for anatomical studies by scientists of the
Zoology Department of the University of British Columbia.

Freshwater Fishing

Forth upon the Gitche Gumee,
On the shining Big-Sea-Water,
With his fishing-line of cedar,
Of the twisted bark of cedar,
Forth to catch the sturgeon Nahma,
Mishe-Nahma, King of Fishes,
In his birch-canoe exulting
All alone went Hiawatha.

'Take my bait,' cried Hiawatha,
Down into the depths beneath him,
'Take my bait, O Sturgeon, Nahma!
Come up from below the water,
Let us see which is the stronger!'
And he dropped his line of cedar
Through the clear, transparent water,
Waited vainly for an answer,
Long sat waiting for an answer,
And repeating loud and louder,
'Take my bait, O King of Fishes!'
　Quiet lay the sturgeon, Nahma,
Fanning slowly in the water,
Looking up at Hiawatha,
Listening to his call and clamour,
His unnecessary tumult,
Till he wearied of the shouting . . .

And the mighty sturgeon, Nahma,
Said to Ugudwash, the sun-fish,
To the bream, with scales of crimson,
'Take the bait of this great boaster,
Break the line of Hiawatha!'

Slowly upward, wavering, gleaming,
Rose the Ugudwash, the sun-fish,
Seized the line of Hiawatha,
Swung with all his weight upon it,
Made a whirlpool in the water . . .

But when Hiawatha saw him
Slowly rising through the water,
Lifting up his disc refulgent,
Loud he shouted in derision,
'Esa! Esa! shame upon you!
You are Ugudwash, the sun-fish,
You are not the fish I wanted,
You are not the King of Fishes!'
　Slowly downward, wavering, gleaming,
Sank the Ugudwash, the sun-fish,
And again the sturgeon, Nahma,
Heard the shout of Hiawatha,
Heard his challenge of defiance,
The unnecessary tumult,
Ringing far across the water,
　From the white sand of the bottom
Up he rose with angry gesture,
Quivering in each nerve and fibre,
Clashing all his plates of armour,
Gleaming bright with all his war-paint;
In his wrath he darted upward,
Flashing leaped into the sunshine,
Opened his great jaws, and swallowed
Both canoe and Hiawatha.

Henry Wadsworth Longfellow,
The Song of Hiawatha (Canto VIII, 1855)

According to Bart McDowell in *Journey Across Russia* (1977), the Russians catch the giant Kaluga sturgeon on Rye bread bait in places where an angler may be plagued with 'a mosquito that seems large enough for a taxidermist'!

A few years ago it was reported that Russian scientists had compounded an artificial caviare said to be indistinguishable from the real thing. Such is the demand for this expensive food that the vast capital outlay required for this scientific undertaking was said to have been justified.

Figure 243: This 8 ft 10½ in. sturgeon weighing 273 lb was caught by a trawler from the North Sea in July 1985. (*Fisch und Fang*)

Cooking the Sturgeon

Charles Dickens in *A Dictionary of the Thames* (1880) states that:

The flesh of the sturgeon is looked upon with suspicion little short of aversion by some persons, but it, according to the parts submitted to the operations of the cook, may be rendered into the choicest of dishes – one portion simulating the tenderest of veal, another that of the sapid succulence of chicken, and a third establishing its reputation to a claim to most of the gastronomic virtues of the flesh of many acceptable fish in combination. The great chefs, Francatelli and Ude, used to aver that there were one hundred different ways of rendering sturgeon fit for an emperor; and Soyer would boast that he had added two more methods of its culinary preparation to those apparently exhaustive receipts.

In early Rome *Acipenser* was third in the list of popular fishes, accorded the high honour of being served, crowned, at banquets to the music of flutes and pipes and borne by slaves likewise crowned. Pliny records that by many of the cognoscenti its flavour was considered the best of all.

Figure 244: This 294 lb sturgeon was captured at Mepal Bridge by C. Waters in July 1907. The young lady seen in the picture is still alive (1987) and remembers helping the men with the fish (*Tony Gibson*)

> *Caviar.* The roe of the sturgeon, etc., pressed and salted, and eaten as a relish; . . . caviar is generally unpalatable to those who have not acquired a taste for it.
>
> *Shorter O.E.D.*
>
> The play, I remember, pleased not the million; 'twas caviar to the general.
>
> *Hamlet*

The capture of this rare and elusive fish, according to Aelian, became the occasion of great rejoicing; the crew of the successful boat being crowned with wreaths and welcomed by flute-players. Cicero tells the story of Pontius's anxiety when he hears that Scipio, who has been presented with an *Acipenser* (*piscis . . . in primis nobilis*), proposes to serve it at a feast to which he has invited everyone who saluted him: 'Do you know what you are about?' Pontius asks Scipio. 'Lo! this is a fish fit only for a few choice palates!'

Unfortunately, notes on how this fish was prepared for those great Republican banquets are in short supply. But here are some more recent recipes:

The preparation of caviare (or 'kavia') as described by Thomas Shirley in *The Angler's Museum*, 1784:

'They take sturgeon's spawn and free it from the little fibres by which it is connected, and wash it in white wine or vinegar, afterwards spreading it upon a table to dry; then they put it into a vessel and salt it, breaking the spawn with their hands, not with a pestle; this done, they put it in a fine canvas bag, that the liquor may drain from it; last of all, they put it into a

tub, with a hole in the bottom, that if there be any more moisture still remaining, it may run out; then they press it down, and cover it close for use.'

Lest the prospect of this feast encouraged his readers to reach for their rods, Shirley added a cautionary note:

'The common way of killing sturgeon is with a harping-iron [barbed spear] for they take no bait; and when they feed they rout in the mud with their snouts like hogs.'

ROAST STURGEON

Cleanse the fish, bone and skin it; make a nice veal-stuffing and fill it in the part where the bones came from. Roll it in buttered paper, bind it up firmly with tape like a fillet of veal, and roast in a Dutch oven before a clear fire. Serve with good brown gravy or plain melted butter (English Butter Sauce). Time about one hour. Seasonable from April to September.

BAKED STURGEON

2 lb sturgeon
Salt and pepper
1 small bunch of herbs
Juice of $\frac{1}{2}$ lemon
$\frac{1}{2}$ pt white wine
$\frac{1}{4}$ lb butter

Clean the fish thoroughly and skin it. Lay the fish in a large fireproof dish, sprinkle over the seasoning and herbs very finely minced, and moisten with the lemon juice and wine. Place the butter in small pieces over the whole of the fish, put into a moderate oven (350°F Gas Mark 4) for about 30–40 minutes and baste frequently. Bake until brown, then serve with its own gravy.

STURGEON CUTLETS

$1\frac{1}{2}$ lb sturgeon
$\frac{1}{2}$ teasp. finely chopped parsley
$\frac{1}{4}$ teasp. finely grated lemon rind
Egg and breadcrumbs
Salt and pepper
Fat for frying

Cut the fish into thin slices, flatten them with a heavy knife and trim them into shape. Add the parsley and lemon rind to the breadcrumbs, and season with salt and pepper. Brush over with beaten egg, coat carefully with the seasoned breadcrumbs, and fry in hot fat until cooked and lightly browned on both sides. Drain free from fat, and serve with piquant or tomato sauce.

Cooking time – about 10 minutes

The
TENCH
Tinca tinca

In every Tench's head there are two little stones which foreign physicians make great use of, but he is not commended for wholesome meat, though there be very much use made of them for outward application. Rondeletius says, that at his being at Rome, he saw a great cure done by applying a Tench to the feet of a very sick man.

Izaak Walton, *The Compleat Angler* (5th Ed. 1676)

The tench is a member of the carp family, and like the carp has a wide distribution in Asia, Europe and Britain – Scotland and the Cornish peninsula apart.

Although tench are pre-eminently fish of still waters, Alwyne Wheeler describes them as occurring occasionally 'in the lower reaches of rivers, most often in backwaters'. He is right. Even the River Test – because of its fast current a most uncharacteristic environment – holds tench in backwaters below Romsey. And in *Fish and Fishing* (1877) Dr J. J. Manley states that he netted five tench averaging over 5 lb from a backwater in the lower reaches of the Hampshire Avon, another fast-flowing river.

Although the colour of tench varies with the locality, green is the characteristic colour. An exotic variety of tench, the golden tench, occasionally reported in the angling press, may be descendants of golden tench successfully bred and distributed by a Mr Burr of Aldermaston Park, Reading, from two given to him by Frank Buckland in 1862.

Tench usually spawn in June, although the necessary combination of ripeness, and an optimum spawning temperature of 64°F, may advance or retard the spawning act by a month or more. The fecundity of tench is prodigious. According to Gunther, 297,000 eggs have been taken from one female.

To anglers and non-anglers alike, the tench is famous for its rôle as physician to other fishes – more particularly to the pike.

A Tench is a good fyssh; and heelith all mannere of other fysshe that ben hurt yf they maye come to hym.

Attrib: Dame Juliana Berners, *A Treatyse of Fysshynge wyth an Angle* (1496)

A cork float with a crimson tip is very necessary to proper angling for tench; it supplies the one touch of colour that is wanting in the landscape and it is a satisfying thing to look upon. A severely practical mind might argue that it is as visible to the fish as to the fisherman, and might suggest a fragment of porcupine quill as being less ostentatious, but however one regards it, tench fishing is a lengthy occupation, and must be approached with leisurely mind. The sordid yearning for bites should not be put in the balance against artistic effect. Besides, it may be said of tench more emphatically than of most other fish; if they are going to feed they are and if they are not, they most certainly are not. As a rule they are not, and their feelings are therefore not so important as the angler's. In this canal at any rate, their feelings receive but the scantiest consideration. Evening by evening the villagers come forth, each armed with a beanpole to which is attached a stout window cord, the bung of a beer cask, and a huge hook on the stoutest gimp. A lobworm is affixed to the hook and flung with much force and splashing into

some little opening among the weeds, where it remains until night draws down her veil. The villagers sit in a contemplative row under this ancient grey wall, which once enclosed a grange fortressed against unquiet times. But now all is peace, and the cooing of doves in the garden trees has replaced the clash of arms. About once a week the villagers have a bite; a beanpole is lifted by stalwart arms; and a two-pound tench is summarily brought to the bank; but for the most part evening's solemn stillness is undisturbed by rude conflict. This is not surprising. Apart from the uncompromising nature of the tackle, there are other reasons against success. The canal here is one solid mass of weed. No barge has passed this way for years, and so there is no object in keeping the channel clear in summer. If the angler wishes to fish, he must clear a space for himself with the end of his beanpole. Hence it comes that the villagers angle in two feet of water not more than six feet away from the bank, while the tench live secure out of reach.

H. T. Sheringham, *An Angler's Hours* (1905)

Generations of anglers believed that a tench has the power to heal wounded fish, if they rub against its slime. Walton wrote:

The tyrant pike will not be a wolf to his physician, but forbears to devour him though he be never so hungry.

Here, Walton was wrong (see page 147). But that tench are extremely hardy fish is undoubtedly true; that they escape the ravages of the commoner fish diseases and fin rot is also probable.

As J. J. Manley states:

It has long been said that the tench, unlike other fish, is free from liability to all diseases; and certainly when carefully observing the freshwater fish at the Westminster Aquarium soon after it was opened, I noticed that tench alone seemed perfectly free from that un-natural coating of slimy excrescence which more or less affected the other fish, and so sorely puzzled the ichthyologists of the Aquarium. But whether this freedom from disease, presuming the fact established, is to be attributed to the natural slime on the tench, and whether this really has the

healing virtue so long credited to it, may be questioned.

That the perch has been seen to rub itself against the tench is beyond question. Dr Tate Regan, Britain's most famous ichthyologist, wrote in *British Freshwater Fishes* (1911):

My friend, the late Dr Bowdler Sharpe, told me that one day in May he stood on the bridge over the lake at Avington and watched a large Tench lying in the water below; a shoal of Perch swam up and lay round and above the Tench and appeared to be rubbing against him; on being disturbed they swam back under the bridge, but soon repaired again to the Tench and repeated this manoeuvre several times. The meaning of this is obscure, but there can be little doubt that observation of similar incidents has led to belief in the healing powers of the Tench.

Tench appear to be resistant to quite severe pollution and deoxygenation. Indeed it is probable that tench are the last fish to die whenever these diabolical twins of human ingenuity intensify their choking grasp. The largest tench that

F. B. has ever seen, fish of between 8 and 10 lb, were on Mr Pierpoint Morgan's estate near Watford. These were the progeny of tench that had survived a wartime pollution of the upper Colne where all other species of fish were killed. Later, in 1953, the estate keeper picked up an $8\frac{1}{2}$ lb tench which had grounded itself in some shallows.

According to most authors, tench hibernate during periods of cold weather by burying themselves in the mud. This view finds support in *A Treatyse of Fysshynge wyth an Angle*:

He is the most parte of the yere in the mudde. And he styryth moost in Iune and Iuly: and in other seasons but lytyll. He is an evyll byter.

Proof of this hibernating behaviour is still wanting. However, unlike most other fish, tench can certainly survive in wet mud during periods of drought. In *The Book of The All-Round Angler* (1888), John Bickerdyke gives a personal experience:

In my youthful days I used to fish a small farm horse-pond, which, though shallow and muddy, contained many tench over 1 lb in weight. One summer the pond all but dried up, and some gypsies nearly cleared it of tench by means of hay rakes, literally raking the fish out of the mud.

This ability to endure droughts is a very useful survival characteristic for a species inhabiting outlying ponds and lakes where the possibility of reinforcement from river colonies is remote.

Tench are attracted by the same variety of baits as most other members of the carp family. For the *best* bait we would be hard put to choose between breadflake, crust, marshworms and

Figure 245: This 11 lb 9¼ oz tench was found in Colonel Thornton's lake at Thornville Royal, Yorkshire, when the lake was drained in 1801. It measured 2 ft 9 in. from eye to fork and had a girth of 27 in. A diseased tench weighing 12 lb 8 oz was caught by R. Blaber in the River Kennet in 1951. This fish was suffering from dropsy and would have weighed much less had it been in good health

maggots. *A Treatyse of Fysshynge wyth an Angle* offers the following:

His Baytes ben thyse. For all the yere browne breede tostyd with hony in lyknesse of a butteryd loof: and the grete redde worme. And as for cheyf take the blacke blood in the herte of a shepe and floure and hony. And tempre theym all togyder somdeale softer then paast: and annoynt therwyth the redde worme: bothe for this fysshe and for other. And they woll byte muche the better therat at all tymes.

Izaak Walton reckoned that the tench, '... inclines very much to any paste with which tar is mixt'. In support of which, R. B. Marston, editor of *The Fishing Gazette* (most famous of all angling magazines), once had a very good day's fishing from a freshly tarred punt. He reported:

I felt certain then that the tench had been attracted to the spot by fresh tar, and proved it on other occasions, not invariably, but often enough to feel sure that there was no doubt about it.

Figure 246: A 7 lb tench – one-time equal record – caught by the Rev. E. C. Alston from Ringmere at Wretham, Norfolk, on 8 July 1933

The Rev. W. B. Daniel felt the same:

The only aid the Compiler has ever experienced from any application *whatever* to the bait, has been by dipping the worm in *Tar* when fishing for Tench.

Although we find a dissenter in John Whitney, who mentions tar in his book *The Genteel Recreation: or, the Pleasure of Angling* (1700):

A worm well scour'd without the help of stinking tar,
That was her bait and that was best by far,
Tho to my cost I've try'd and certain know,
That Tarr's strong stench hath little here to do,
But kill the worm, but I confess that fishes smell,
Or that my apprehension is but ill,
For I have seen them to my flote and Lead repair,
And gently touch them with insulting care.

Traditionally the best times to fish for tench are early morning and late evening. F. B. has noticed that tench fishing improved considerably when the water was well down – a condition that sometimes ruins sport with other fishes. He has caught exceptionally good bags of tench of a beautiful golden olive colour from Elstree Reservoir when the water level was very low; but with the water at a normal height he often fished a season through without catching a single tench.

TENCH
Caught by Rev E C Alston at Wretham 8th July 1933, Weight 7 lbs, record for British Isles.

Similar behaviour by Elstree tench was noticed by J. J. Manley in the 1870s when he wrote:

... and a year or two ago, when the water was very low at Elstree Reservoir, a large number were taken of between 3 lb and 4 lb.

Although groundbaiting is an important aid to successful tench fishing, *heavy* groundbaiting is not conducive to good sport. The successful tench angler usually prepares his swim *gradually*, over several days, before attempting to fish. Hugh Sheringham summed it up:

The longer and more regularly you bait a pitch before actually fishing it, the more likely are you to catch something when you do begin.

Most tench swims are in, or close to, weeds. Before groundbaiting in very weedy water it is

Figure 247: The current record rod-caught tench is an almost unbelievable 12 lb 8 oz! It was taken by Alan Wilson on sweetcorn bait in Tring Reservoir during the summer of 1985 (*Angling Times*)

necessary to clear a patch, or patches, about four yards square. Tench frequently advertise their presence in a groundbaited swim by releasing a series of tiny bubbles.

As with all fish, the best methods of catching tench depend to a large extent on the conditions found at the waterside. Ledgering is a good method, provided tackle of suitable strength is used. Tench are powerful fish and usually found close to tackle-breaking weeds. (The beginner should remember that only a fool boasts of being broken by a fish, good anglers being ashamed of such incompetence.)

When float fishing is appropriate, the 'lift' method (see page 447) is usually the most effective, particularly in swims close to the bank. In *Tench* (1971), Fred J. Taylor describes how he and his brothers developed this tench fishing technique:

The lift method, as we began to call it, became our basic tench-fishing rig. We soon learned that it was essential to place the rod in a rest after the line was tightened up and to *leave* it there. We fell into the trap of picking up the rod in readiness to strike at the first sign of a 'touch' many times in the beginning, but we found that it was fatal to do so. The moment the rod was taken up, the float keeled over and the rig became ineffective. We had to discipline ourselves to pick up the rod and strike in one continuous movement. We had to practise, practise, practise, but we were soon able to do it blindfold or without taking our eyes off the float. At times one of us would be otherwise occupied and looking somewhere else when the other would simply say 'strike!' Without looking or checking we grabbed the rod, struck and caught many fish by word of command . . . !

We have our few inches of peacock quill attached at the bottom end only to the reel line by a wide tight-fitting float cap.

What do we mean by wide? About three-eighths of an inch.

What do we mean by tight-fitting? So tight that to slide the float up or down the line without first wetting it will cause enough heat literally to melt the line and break it!

Why does it have to be so tight? Because the float setting in lift-method fishing is critical and continual striking tends to pull the line through a loose-fitting float cap and alter the depth.

How is a lift-float tackle set? So that the float lies flat while the shot remains on the bottom but cocks nicely as the tackle is drawn taut. This means that the float has to be set a little deeper than the water and the simplest and undoubtedly the most accurate way of doing this is to decide on the size of shot to be used first and trim the float accordingly. With all other float-fishing methods the shot is chosen to suit the float. With the lift method the float is trimmed to suit the shot.

How is it trimmed? With a sharp knife, or better still, scissors, a little at a time until the weight of the shot causes it to sink slowly.

Why does it have to sink? Because this is the only way you can get a *correct* depth setting in a water where the bottom varies. If the tackle is set too shallow the float will be pulled under and should be slid up until it lies flat on the surface. If it does not cock as soon as the tackle is tightened, the setting is too deep and the float must be lowered. The difference between too deep and too shallow is not a big one but the rig will fish so much better if it is correctly adjusted.

In the summerhouse swim we often find ourselves chasing bubbles. That is to say, the tench bubbles appeared on the surface here, there and everywhere in the swim at different times. Often, to drop a bait in the middle of a patch of bubbles meant the catching of a fish, but it was important that we should have the depth setting correct each time because a different line of cast often meant that we were fishing in water a few inches deeper or shallower than previously. The sinking lift-float soon gave us the necessary information regarding depth and the rig was quickly adjusted to suit the new condition.

For the greater part of the time it was sufficient to set the shot about two inches from the hook and to strike immediately the float lay flat, but there were times when it was necessary to use a little more finesse. It was sometimes essential to set the shot only one inch from the hook and make the strike while the float was actually in the process of lifting in the water. When you consider, as I have already described, that the rod was never held, but always remained in rests, and that the rod had to be picked up and the strike made during that brief split second, it will be seen that our reflexes became highly developed.

Figure 248: A fine Lincolnshire $5\frac{1}{2}$lb tench caught by F. J. Taylor

Although the tench appears in *A Treatyse of Fysshynge wyth an Angle* it is seldom mentioned by many of the other old angling writers. According to Couch in *British Fishes* (1862), this was due to its lack of esteem as a table fish. But was Couch right? Sheila Hutchins in *English Recipes as they appear in Eighteenth- and Nineteenth-century Cookery Books* (1967) writes: 'Tench used to be esteemed in this country as a delicious and wholesome food ...' and quotes as an example the Tench and Eel Pie. O'Gorman, too, speaks well of them. In *The Practice of Angling* (Vol. 2, 1845) he writes:

They are a firm and good fish to eat; some cooks stew them in wine, but they are by no means bad with parsley and butter. I have seen several tench from six to eight pounds weight; but there is no great value set on them here; and in summer a large one may be had for two or three pence.

TENCH À LA POULETTE

1 tench
$\frac{1}{2}$ litre white wine
1 oz flour
2 oz butter
Bouquet garni
Salt and pepper

Cook the cleaned fish in court bouillon and remove the skin. Cut into small pieces. Make a roux with the butter and flour and add the wine. Let this cook for ten minutes, gently stirring with a wooden spoon. Add the pieces of fish, the bouquet garni, and the seasoning, and let it simmer gently for 10 minutes more. Then blend into this two beaten egg yolks. Remove the bouquet garni. Garnish with chopped parsley and serve hot.

Figure 249: A recent find of a bag of tench caught in low-water conditions by James Bendall from Elstree Reservoir in 1874 perfectly illustrates J. J. Manley's remarks (page 249). This beautiful case of fish – now the property of F. B. – was thrown out by the brewers when the famous Fisheries Inn beside Elstree Reservoir was rebuilt. Such important ornaments of the history of angling – and there are many in Britain today – should be preserved in a national sporting museum

TENCH AND EEL PIE

Those tench caught in very muddy weedy water do, however, taste brackish. To prevent this the fish may be soaked in salt and water and then in a solution of vinegar and water before scaling and boning it. The best way to scale tench is to form the fish into the shape of an S and instead of scraping it from the tail to the head like other fish, scrape upwards from the belly to the back with an oyster knife, the scales running that way. Take out the gills, which are always muddy, open the belly, take out the inside and wash it clean.

2 tench
2 eels
2 onions
Faggot (bundle) of herbs
4 blades of mace
3 anchovies
Salt and pepper
Chopped parsley
6 hardboiled egg yolks
Puff pastry

Having cleaned and boned 2 tench, skin and bone 2 eels and cut them into pieces 2 inches long. Leave the sides of the tench whole. Put the bones into a stew-pan with 2 onions, a faggot of herbs, 4 blades of mace, 3 anchovies, $1\frac{1}{2}$ pints of water and salt and pepper at pleasure. Let them simmer gently for 1 hour then strain off the liquor, put it to cool and skim off the fat. Lay the tench and eels in a pie-dish, and between each layer put seasoning, a teaspoonful of chopped parsley and 6 hardboiled egg yolks. Pour in part

> The tench is unwholesome. Hard of concoction, unpleasant of taste, noisome to the stomach, and filleth the body with gross slimey humour. Notwithstanding, it is meat fit for labouring men.
>
> T. Venner: Of Fish. From *Via Recta ad Vitam Longam* (1650)

of the strained liquor, cover the top with puff pastry and bake for $\frac{1}{2}$ hour or rather more. The oven should be rather quick. [*A modern oven should be pre-heated (400°F Mark 6) for the first 10 minutes then reduce heat to moderate (350°F Mark 4) for the rest of the cooking time.*] When done, heat the remainder of the liquid, which pour into the pie. Quantities may be halved for a smaller pie of more modern and modest proportions.

STUFFED TENCH

1 tench
Breadcrumbs
Hardboiled egg
White wine
Chopped parsley
Chopped mushrooms

Split and clean the fish and stuff with a mixture of mushroom, egg, breadcrumbs and parsley. Place in a fireproof dish and cook in oven for 30 minutes, basting frequently with white wine.

The
BROWN
TROUT

Salmo trutta fario

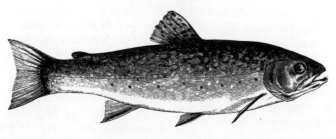

There are trout in my river whose attitude,
Is one of the blackest ingratitude;
Though I offer them duns,
Most superior ones,
They maintain a persistent Black Gnatitude

Anon

It was once the custom to refer to the brown trout as *Salmo fario*, and the sea trout as *Salmo trutta*. This, although seemingly unscientific, had the merit of clarity. Today, on the grounds that there is no discernible physiological difference, taxonomists classify both brown trout and sea trout as *Salmo trutta*. This is irritating. Although there may be no difference in the way non-migratory and migratory trout are built, there is an enormous difference in the way they behave. This disparity in behaviour demands separate identification. Above all else it is essential that a writer should make his meaning clear. To discuss the behaviour of a trout (*Salmo trutta*) meaning either brown trout or sea trout is absurd. With a respect for science, but a greater respect for clarity of expression, we recommend the following classifications:

Brown trout: *Salmo trutta fario*
Sea trout: *Salmo trutta trutta*

It will avoid much confusion.

The brown trout (*Salmo trutta fario*) is found almost everywhere. Indigenous to Europe, North Africa and North West Asia, it has been successfully introduced into most outposts of civilization, including Australia, New Zealand, Tasmania, Middle and South Africa, India, North and South America and Vancouver Island. The criteria necessary for its survival (apart from an adequate food supply) are suitable conditions of water temperature and oxygenation.

Like all its close relatives in the sub-order of fishes known as the *Salmonidae* it possesses seven characteristic taxonomic features. The only two which need concern us here are those familiar to all trout fishermen: the adipose fin, and the pyloric caeca, those worm-like appendages attached to the gut, which help to secrete digestive juices. For the adipose fin no particular function is known.

Salmo trutta fario has such a variation of size and colour that one eminent nineteenth-century ichthyologist described ten different species in Britain alone. This multiplicity of species is now discredited. A pity in a way, since they had such lovely names: for instance, *Salmo orcadensis* (the Orkney sea trout); *Salmo ferox* (the great lake trout); *Salmo stomachicus* (the gillaroo), and *Salmo nigripinnis* (the Welsh black-finned trout). It was the great taxonomist, Tate Regan, who first grouped all of these together, and added a load of other so-called species from the Continent.

But whatever their nomenclature trout are now the world's favourite game fish. In Britain, although roach attract more anglers, trout undoubtedly attract more words. About no other species has such a wealth of writing accumulated, some of it the most beautiful and memorable in angling literature.

There is not a lovelier sight (*pace* Ramsbury and Hurstbourne Priors in buttercup time) in England than Blagdon from the Butcombe end at sundown, with the tiny town straggling up the steep hillside like a Bavarian village, the red roofs of the houses peeping out of the thick orchards (with never a Methodist Chapel to shock the artist's eye) and the evening sunlight setting the windows of the old church aglow and flushing with purple pink the glassy surface of the lake. There is a stillness here that belongs to no other valley. You can hear the 'plop' of the big trout far out, half a mile away. You can talk to your friend across the water without ever raising your voice, and hear the scream of his reel in the blackness, and Blagdon is seven miles round, and he may be half the length of the lake from you.

But the dominant impression in my mind is of the lovely colour of the evening light upon the valley as you face it looking east. It has a crimson velvet glow which hangs like Aurora on the meadows and makes the shores and the scolloped hills burn with fires. It is Devonshire clay here, and the whole landscape warms pink and deepens to purple black as the sun sinks lower.

I know, too, that there was once a witch in the valley, and that they drowned her when they let the water in; and one night as I grope my way home in the dark I shall stumble on Hansel and Gretel asleep on the grass in a mist of white angels, with the myriad million stars of the milky way and the golden lights of Blagdon shining on their heads and winking in the watery glass at their feet.

Harry Plunkett Greene,
Where the Bright Waters Meet (1924)

One wet but amusing morning was occupied in playing to the gallery, not of set purpose indeed, but unwillingly.

The gallery consisted of Fairford bridge, and it was occupied at starting only by the youngest inhabitant, who could not get his head over the parapet, and therefore did not matter. . . .

It took me quite a long time to insinuate the fly under the bridge at all, and the youngest inhabitant was reinforced by several of his friends before the feat was accomplished.

Their rather cynical amusement was turned to respectful exclamations when the ginger quill rose hooked and landed one of the three-quarter pounders. The fame of this capture got abroad probably, for the gallery began to fill up, and the next fish was landed more or less in the public eye. Then misfortunes began. A fish was hooked, played for a little and lost. The fly hit itself against the bridge several times in succession. After that a really fine cast sent it right into the depths of the bridge. A 'plop' louder than any followed, the tightened fly provoked a heavy plunge, and the fly came right away. Of course, the frequent dashing against the bridge had broken the barb. A new fly was put on and promptly lost in the chestnut trees behind. Pity began to be expressed on the faces of the spectators. Interest was admissible, admiration was tolerable and even grateful, but pity was too much and could only be avoided by flight.

H. T. Sheringham,
An Open Creel (1910)

ANGLING SPORTSMANSHIP

Of all British fish species the trout is the most accommodating. It is tasty, easy to catch, fights well and can be taken on a wide variety of baits and lures by almost every known method of angling. Of all methods, however, fly-fishing is the most graceful. (And it must be stressed that both authors of this book are fanatical fly-fishermen.)

Unfortunately, by over-enthusiastic devotees and others who follow blindly in their wake, fly-fishing has also been described as being the most 'sporting' method; other methods being considered less 'sporting' or, sometimes, even 'unsporting'. This is a pity, since it has created a form of snobbery: a sense of false values.

In modern angling literature the terms 'sporting' and 'unsporting' are in constant use. They are words that flow easily from the tongue and from the pen. But what do they mean? There are many legal, but widely differing, methods of

Figure 250: The River Thames is a mixed fishery that has always produced a few really splendid trout. The best known exponent of Thames trout fishing is the late A. E. Hobbs, who caught this handsome fish in 1912, weight 8 lb 2 oz

angling; is it reasonable to suppose that some are more creditable than others?

We think not. And since it seems to us that an analysis of angling 'sportsmanship' is long overdue, we propose, briefly, to discuss the matter and try to arrive at a satisfactory definition of the word: 'sporting'.

Most anglers go fishing to enjoy themselves. Whatever their secondary motives – to catch a meal; to win a prize; to impress their wives or friends – their primary object is pleasure. Each angler has his favourite method or methods of fishing – perhaps because he enjoys handling the tackles involved, or because they are best suited to his temperament, or (most probably) because he finds that they catch him more fish. Whatever the reason, however, provided he does not interfere with another angler's pleasure, he should be free to catch fish by any legal method he chooses, and be thought neither more nor less of a 'sportsman' in consequence.

But all too often anglers are not free to fish as they choose. Occasionally this is due to exigency; more frequently, however, some of the methods anglers would like to use are forbidden simply because they are considered 'unsporting'.

How has this come about?

The Brown Trout

Figure 251: F. B. believes that Corrib trout are best tasting of all British and Irish trout. (H. F. disagrees. For him, spate stream sea trout are the best.) These three Corrib trout, two of which are three-pounders, fell to F. B.'s rod on Corrib in May 1982

First of all, the biggest mistake any angler can make is to be too successful. The 'Brotherhood of the Angle' – a concept much beloved of angling writers of a bygone age (may they rest in peace) – is unfortunately a myth. Human frailty exists in all men, whether they are financiers or phil-anderers, artists or anglers. And in angling, as in business, art or love, jealousy is seldom absent. Regrettable though it may be, some anglers cannot bear to see another angler catching more fish than they are catching themselves. And if his success derives from the use of an unusual method – even though it be merely a variation on an old theme – the presumptuous innovator can be sure that the 'sporting' aspects of his method will soon come under attack. Indeed, on some fisheries the objectors, if they make sufficient fuss, may even succeed in getting the method banned.

It is pointless to rail at such behaviour. The grizzlers have always existed and will always exist, and one would be naive to think that any-thing can be done to change them. Nevertheless, although they cannot be changed, they can and should be controlled. But they seldom are.

On some of the large waters open to the public, provided that a suitable limit is imposed, that *all* fish caught are counted as part of the limit *and that each method is confined to its own particular*

Figure 252: A reservoir trout angler casting into the breeze on Grafham Water. Tackle: 11 yards of No. 8 quick-sinking shooting-head line, needle-knotted to 100 yards of 20 lb BS monofilament mainline. The line-bucket, slung in front, holds the slack line that accumulates as nymph or lure is worked in at varying speed towards the rod

Freshwater Fishing

The Brown Trout

area, it is absurd to object to any technique on the grounds that it is too successful. If a trout angler possessed of some new magic can take his limit in half an hour, why on earth shouldn't he, if that is what gives him pleasure? Is another angler, using a more conventional method, to be congratulated simply because he takes longer to achieve a similar catch?

It is worth observing that the right fly, properly fished, is often the most killing lure of all; so that if angling methods are to be banned because they are too deadly, then fly-fishing should be one of the first!

But for one reason or another the lists of forbidden fishing methods grow, and one of angling's supreme pleasures – experimentation by trying other methods when one method fails – is diminished in consequence.

Those noodles who condemn such methods as fishing a static fly, 'side-casting', spinning, casting a shooting-head, or fly-trailing from a boat, seem to have forgotten *why* people want to go fishing. If anglers enjoy trailing their flies instead of waggling their rods about, why in heaven's name shouldn't they trail them? What harm is it doing, and to whom? If they enjoy casting 40 yards to catch fish instead of catching them at their feet (see page 271), why shouldn't they be allowed their shooting-heads and line-rafts? If they get pleasure from fishing a static fly, or dapping, or float-fishing, or ledgering for that matter, let them do it. *Give them their own clearly marked areas to do it in.* Then they will not interfere with anyone else, and no one will interfere with them. In other words, everyone will enjoy his fishing to the full. And that, surely, is what the 'sport' of fishing is supposed to be about.

It is of course quite impossible to please everybody, and we hasten to point out that the attitude of some anglers leaves one with a feeling of stunned incredulity. The following gem is taken from a letter written by Richard Walker to Tom Rawling.

Just how competitive some of these chaps are was well illustrated by an incident in the fishing lodge at Hanningfield a couple of years ago, when the bag limit was increased from six to ten fish temporarily.

Two chaps were talking about this, both of them condemning bitterly the increase in the bag limit. When I asked them what they were grizzling about, one replied: 'Why, it makes it nearly twice as hard to take your limit'!

There are, it is true, a few places run by enlightened men who have their values right and the benefit to the angler firmly at heart, but their example is all too seldom followed. Many fisheries are clogged with pettifogging restrictions bred from the notion that certain methods of fishing are more 'sporting' than others, and that, in consequence, certain species of fish should be caught only in certain ways.

A freak example of this is the salmon beat restricted to 'fly only' – as though there were some special merit in fishing for salmon with a feather as opposed to, say, a float. It seems to be a direct hangover from the concept, equally weird, that it is more 'sporting' to catch a trout on wet-fly than on spinner; or on dry-fly than on wet-fly – upstream rather than downstream.

On what grounds can such claims be made? Are these supposedly superior methods more difficult? More humane? Less obstructive to other anglers? Casting a fly is in every sense a highly rewarding method of fishing for salmon; but very often in conditions of low, clear water, to fish the worm is not only more effective – since, for one reason, it causes less disturbance than fly or spinner – it is more difficult. (Indeed, the dexterity involved in low-water worming suggests that some of the more vociferous 'fly-only' men may be trying to make a virtue of necessity!)

Much the same may be said of those anglers who, whatever the water conditions, use nothing but a spinner – priding themselves on being better 'sportsmen' than those who fish the prawn, although entirely without experience of fishing this much maligned bait.

The case of the dry-fly fisherman is also worth attention. The dry-fly men use a floating artificial because they derive more satisfaction from catching a trout on a close imitation of the fly on the water than on a 'chuck-and-chance-it' fly, or a spinner, or any other bait or lure. It entails

Figure 253: Corrib trout

stealth and observation, and at least an elementary knowledge of entomology, a subject which is in itself fascinating.

In their enthusiasm, however, some of them make the mistake of thinking that their method of catching a trout is more sporting than any other. When one considers the wealth of literature surrounding this branch of angling, the view is hardly surprising. Nevertheless, it is quite illogical.

With an irony that the banned and frustrated reservoir fly-trailer may appreciate, this 'holier-than-thou' attitude is based on a curious fallacy. The dry-fly, which gradually became popular during the latter part of the nineteenth century, was acclaimed not because it was considered more 'sporting' than the wet-fly, or the blow-line, but because it was more practical. As that growing band of Victorian fly-fishermen soon discovered, it caught more fish.

By the end of the nineteenth century the method had become firmly established and the very words 'fly-fishing' began to exert a strange influence. Irrespective of the species to be caught, the fly-rod became the 'sporting' tool of the middle and upper class angler who tended to regard anything else as being slightly suspect. Spinning tackle (other than for pike and salmon), ledger tackle and the humble float stayed mostly with the artisan on a somewhat lower level.

There were, of course, anglers who realized only too clearly the absurdity of such artificial distinctions; men of understanding and experience, such as that fine writer, Hugh Sheringham, who summed it all up so well during his address to the Piscatorial Society in 1909:

We may individually prefer one form of fishing to another, but collectively we despise none, if only it aims at the capture of good fish in a manner that befits the good sportsman.

As we get older our habits tend to get set, and it may be that we do not *all* retain the fine careless rapture of youth over the catching of any fish in any way. But it is certain that a keen angler is at heart an all-round angler, sympathizing with all branches of the sport, even though he does not practise them. Personally, I would counsel a man who wanted to get the most out of his fishing life never to outgrow or give up the variety of its interests, to keep his roach rod in action as well as his split cane, to remember that what gave him so much joy in youth may still give him joy in middle age.

This is as true today as it was then. All the same, there are many anglers who, seemingly ignorant of the history of fly-fishing, harbour vague notions of fly 'purity' and couple it with the ultimate in terms of 'sportsmanship'.

This strange cult, which has survived two world wars and exists today, appears in the most unexpected quarters. It is responsible for those innocents who speak disparagingly of 'wet' fly or lure fishing, or spinning, or ledgering, or trotting, or trailing; who think that 'coarse' fishing is really coarse; who question whether the use of a maggot on a fly at night is a 'sporting' way of killing sea trout. (If we are to equate what is 'sporting' with what is humane, the sea trout should be killed as quickly as possible. For this purpose a small bomb is ideal. But the pleasure in freshwater fishing comes from hunting with rod and line. Obviously, we must compromise in our definition of what is 'sporting'.)

Like the killing of any other animal the killing of a fish is a matter of individual conscience

---

WATER SENSE

The shaping hand of evolution that once fashioned man as a hunter has gradually adapted him to a new way of living. Even so, eleven thousand years of farming, manufacturing, trading and other substitute activities, have not succeeded entirely in eradicating his hunting instinct – the urge to stalk and kill his prey, be it fur, feather or fin. So that although the newcomer to angling is sometimes perplexed to find that he harbours an urge to hunt, such a desire is not really surprising.

Nor is it surprising that some persons, however eager, remain forever duffers, while others (in whom the hunting instinct is more strongly developed) quickly become accomplished anglers.

---

which every fisherman must rationalize. *A dead fish remains a dead fish however it is killed.* To suppose that there is more merit in killing it on an unadorned fly rather than on a fly with a maggot attached is as ridiculous as supposing that simply because a fly-rod is involved, the use of fly-maggot is any more creditable than the use of a worm, or a dock-grub, or a shrimp, or a sand-eel, or a spinner, or any other legitimate lure fished with a fixed-spool reel.

Clearly, all legal methods of angling are of equal merit. The vice or virtue in any form of fishing lies *not in the method but in the man.* It is the way a method is used; the way an angler behaves that can be termed 'sporting' or 'unsporting'.

Before starting to fish, an angler should ask himself two questions:

1. Am I interfering with the fishery or with a fellow angler's pleasure?
2. Am I giving myself a reasonable chance of landing a fish if I hook one?

If the answer to the first question is 'No', and to the second 'Yes', then by our definition the angler is a sportsman – whatever method he may be using.

Figure 254: Sharing a rod

For two anglers to share a rod is the most civilized approach to the sport of salmon or trout fishing, and can be applied equally well to certain aspects of coarse fishing. Gillying for the other man when it is his turn to hold the rod allows an angler to relax and observe what is going on around him. This is of particular importance to the novice. In addition to learning the 'dos' and 'don'ts' of angling technique from an experienced companion, he will acquire some understanding of his environment. Time spent in observation of the water and its wild life is never wasted.

What is 'a reasonable chance of landing a fish'? Every angler must answer that for himself, but he will not find it difficult if he accepts the following dictum:

To be broken by a fish is an angling disgrace. It is almost always the angler's fault.

However, although all methods are of equal merit, all tackles are *not*. Here, bearing in mind our humane/sporting compromise, there is a distinct division.

The use of tackle that is too thick is unprofitable but not unsporting. The use of tackle that is too thin, while equally unprofitable, undoubtedly *is* unsporting. A fish will simply refuse the former, but swim away towing the latter.

The angler who boasts of fishing fine 'to give the fish a chance' exposes himself as being stupid, and insensitive to the fate of the animal he hunts, since his notion of 'sportsmanship' is to allow the fish a vastly better chance of escaping with a hook in its throat and a length of line trailing behind it.

The *sportsman* knows that if he uses tackle too weak he is likely to be broken. If he uses tackle too strong he is unlikely to hook a fish. His compromise is to use tackle that will enable him to attract, hook and land a fish *in the conditions existing at the time*.

Thus: by our definition, *sporting* tackle (whether fly, float, ledger, spinning, trailing, trolling or trotting) is that which gives an angler the best chance of hooking *and landing* a fish.

This, we think, echoes Sheringham's words, and '... aims at the capture of good fish in the manner that befits the good sportsman'.

It is sad to report that attempts have been made to introduce into Britain an American system of assessing the merit of a catch. This system encourages an angler to fish for big fish with light tackle: the heavier the fish, the lighter the line, the greater the merit.

> When you have taken a grete fysshe, undo the maw and what ye find therein, make that your bayte, for it is your beste.
>
> *A Treatyse of Fysshynge wyth an Angle* (1496)

Such thinking can only help to bring angling into disrepute. A growing number of people in Britain today are becoming opposed to field sports, angling included. To provide these antis with a case so obvious as the American system is an act of folly. If those anglers advocating such a system must raise their voices, let them make clear that they speak for themselves alone. Better still, let them take fresh thought and shut up altogether.

FLY-FISHING – HISTORICAL

Five hundred years ago, *A Treatyse of Fysshynge wyth an Angle* mentioned 'A lyne of one or two herys, batyd with a flye'. It also referred to fishing with a dubbed hook – meaning the simulation of an insect rather than the insect itself.

But this wasn't the first reference to fly-fishing. The Roman poet Martial, born in AD 43, spoke of fish being taken on a fly – although whether he meant a natural or an artificial is not clear.

The first writer who specifically mentioned fishing with an *artificial* fly was Aelian, in his book of Natural History, *c.* AD 200.

I have heard of a Macedonian way of catching fish, and it is this: between Beroea and Thessalonica runs a river called the Astraeus, and in it there are fish with speckled skins.... These fish feed on a fly peculiar to the country, which hovers on the river. When a fish observes a fly on the surface it swims quietly up and gulps the fly down. Now, although the fishermen know of this, they do not use these flies as bait....

(Note the use of the word 'bait'. Obviously, dapping was no mystery 1,200 years before the *Treatyse*.)

They do not use these flies as bait, for if a man's hand touch them they lose their natural colour, their wings wither, and they become unfit food for the fish. But the fishermen get the better of the fish by their fisherman's craft. They fasten red wool round a hook, and fix on to the wool two feathers which grow under a cock's wattles, and which in colour are like wax. Their rod is six feet long, and their line is the same length. They throw their snare, and the fish attracted and maddened by the colour, come straight at it – thinking from the pretty sight to get a dainty mouthful.

Well – unquestionably, those fellows were using an artificial fly. And it is interesting that by their choice of red wool they thought the fish were colour conscious. Aelian seems to have been in no doubt that the fish were 'attracted and maddened' by the colour.

To what degree fish can distinguish colour is still uncertain, but most fish, except the shark, can see some colour. Examination of the nerve cells has shown that the shark's eye lacks colour-discriminating visual cones, and has only visual rods which distinguish between light and dark. The eyes of all other tested fishes possess both rods and cones.

But although, as Aelian implied, the discovery of colour vision in fishes is old hat, fly-fishing techniques have come a long way since those far-off Macedonian days of the six-foot rod and horsehair line.

A TROUT STREAM

To a casual observer a trout stream seems empty and lifeless, save for an occasional hatch of fly appearing mysteriously above the surface, or the rare glint of a fish. But underneath the surface,

Figure 255: Crawling about like a snake in the grass was *de rigueur* even in 1832 as this oil painting '*May Fly Fishing*' by William Jones exemplifies (*The executors of Arthur N. Gilbey's collection*)

among the stones on the bottom and the weed beds, the water is teeming with life: a host of tiny creatures, each of them going through its various metamorphoses in sympathy with the season.

The trout react immediately to every change in this flux of underwater life, and the knowledgeable fisherman reacts in turn. His understanding of insect growth and behaviour guides him in his choice of fly. Much of his success – certainly his pleasure – comes from a study of freshwater insects and the plants that harbour them, for they control the behaviour of the fish that rely on them for food.

At times during a hatch of duns, trout, often large, may be seen questing about near the surface in mid-stream and taking the nymphs which are ascending from the river-bed, generally breaking or 'humping' the surface when they effect a capture. And occasionally trout, when in the height of condition, may be observed

One of the first members to use a single-handed rod and to stalk his fish used to relate how Mr Martin Tucker Smith, seeing him one day crawling on his knees, called out: 'Why are you crawling about like a snake in the grass? Why don't you stand up and fish like a man?'

Chronicles of the Houghton Fishing Club (1908)

The Brown Trout

hovering in the fastest part of the stream, not moving from one spot, and intercepting just below the surface the nymphs on their way to hatch, and at times doing so without breaking the surface.

It will thus be seen that the occasions most favourable to the angler fishing to individual selected fish are those when the fish is taking the mature and, for the moment, practically inert nymph, on its way to hatch.

As a matter of fact, it does not seem to have been realized for many years after the advent of the dry-fly, what a large proportion of the rising trout under banks, and indeed in the open (other than bulging), is to nymphs on their way to the surface to hatch, with the result that many a fish so rising has been vainly hammered by anglers with floating flies.

DRY-FLY FISHING

The belief that dry-fly fishing was invented to make the capture of a trout more difficult is amusing but fallacious; the cult eventually ousted other methods for the simple reason that on the rivers concerned it proved the easiest and most successful means of fly-fishing yet discovered.

In fact, it was not a discovery but a natural progression. As early as 1676, Charles Cotton had described the basic principles of the dry-fly, as applied to fishing with a blow line. He made it quite clear that the fly, natural or artificial, should be fished *at the top of the water.*

Presentation in those days depended almost entirely on wind direction. The great advance in the art of dry-fly fishing came with the invention of tackle that permitted an angler to cast a fly without the aid of the wind. Indeed, under the new order, wind, instead of being a necessity, became an impediment.

The fundamental skills required for fishing the dry-fly are an ability to cast a fly without drag, and to recognize the natural fly on the water. The avoidance of drag is obtained by casting a loose line and by intelligent selection of the spot from which to cast.

Recognition and imitation of the fly on the water is not as difficult as it sounds.

Normal identification of insects at the riverside is of type, not of species, and this is all the angler needs for his purposes. For instance, it would be pointless to separate the few different types of Pale Wateries native to the Test into their various species, for they may all be represented by the same artificial. In like fashion, the six or seven Olives can be represented by two or three patterns, and the scores of Sedges by the same number.

Some confusion might arise at dusk, when the fishing is fast and furious and the fly in demand not easily determined. At such times a long-handled plankton net can provide a solution, for with it one can lift off an insect floating down and match it with an artificial from stock. The plankton net may profitably be used at any time of the day to capture insect specimens for later study. And it is no overstatement to suggest that this can lead to a pastime as fascinating as the fishing itself.

The valley – at all times a thing of pure delight – is perhaps at its best in the dusk. Now mystery and suggestiveness take the place of clear colour and bold outline and strong shadow. The river shines pale here and there among the formless meadows. The willows are like grey ghosts trooping down to drink....

I think that the crunch of brogues sounds oddly pleasant in the dusk; I am sure it is different from the harsh grind they set up under a strong sun. Do they at memory's moment, soften their voice for memory's sake? Do they hush themselves in sympathy with the soundlessness of the feet which tread the road by the fisherman's side? For each evening as I leave the mill for my walk home through the twilight along this Clere river I am joined always by one silent pair of brogues, and I think I go more slowly than I might (for I have every reason to hurry) because they lag a little, and because I know that I shall never hear them again.

William Caine, *Fish, Fishing and Fishermen* (1927)

Figure 256: Mr Denis Bridge, fishing a Test carrier with weighted nymph on floating line. Many artificial nymphs of today bear little resemblance to the natural insect. Some – like those pioneered by the late Major Oliver Kite – are simply different sizes of bare hook with copper wire wound round the shank just below the eye. Trout can often be induced to take such an unlikely artificial when it is moved rather faster than the speed of a real nymph. The reason for this may be that the faster speed helps to conceal the true nature of the lure, or, as Richard Walker suggested, it may be due to 'attraction through exaggeration'. Many animal species are attracted by exaggeration, e.g. a herring-gull will incubate an oversized dummy egg in preference to its own; the oversized gape of the young cuckoo so stimulates the feeding responses of a small song-bird that it continues to feed this huge interloper seemingly oblivious of the loss of its own ejected chicks; males of a certain species of butterfly prefer an artificial female four times the natural size, whose wings flap ten times faster. And there are many other examples. Of course, one can think of numerous examples in angling when exaggeration does *not* attract. Nevertheless, it is an interesting hypothesis which offers the thoughtful angler a fascinating new line of experiment and research

Figure 257: After death, the beauty of brown trout is sometimes enhanced whereas with rainbow trout it is seldom the case. Rainbows like these – caught by Mr Bridge and his friend – can be seen to have darkened in colour (note contrast where the grass has been sticking to their sides)

Permaflote

During the late 1960s, being acutely conscious of the shortcomings of the various waterproofing liquids sold for keeping dry-flies dry, Dick Walker began experimenting with a view to producing something better. He was assisted by Arnold Neave, of Hitchin.

Eventually, they arrived at a formula whose waterproofing qualities were greatly superior to anything previously tried.

The result is Permaflote – in our opinion the best dry-fly floatant ever produced. A fly dressed with Permaflote is unsinkable.

The following instructions for tying mayflies were sent by Dick in a letter to F. B. The new

Figure 258: This photograph of a big Lough Mask trout was sent to F. B. by David Beazley and the following note describes the good fortune (skill really) of Desmond Elliott. Needless to say all three have fished together for years.

Dear Fred, I'm not sure if you want to see this, but just in case – it's a picture of that lousy metal-dragging b . . . . . Elliott holding up some manky old deformed throw-back of a trout he didn't b . . . . . well deserve. You're a nice bloke 'cos you never catch . . . . all.

Regards, David

One of the great joys of fishing (and shooting) is the companionship. Ribaldry, leg-pulling and good humour help make an accommodation for the frequent unevenness of a day's sport which may otherwise tend to exasperate

Figure 259: Surveying Lough Corrib from the road above. A blazing hot day, cloudless sky and dead calm water: not hopeful conditions for fly-fishing. Nevertheless, artificial mayfly dipped in Permaflote accounted for five good trout with another lost. This may not sound dramatic; but the weather was such that six dapping boats came in with only one trout between them. Permaflote rendered the fly unsinkable and on this occasion it could be fished at much greater range than the natural insect. Furthermore, it could be made to move on the surface without dipping under

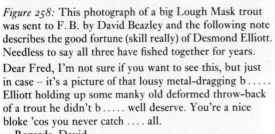

'soak-up' dressings take advantage of this advance in the technology of waterproofing fly-dressing materials.

Here are the mayfly patterns complete with tying instructions. I expect the flies will get rather flattened in the post but you can easily restore them by holding them in steam from a boiling kettle.

You will see that I have used two different kinds of material for the sub-imago body and I honestly don't think it makes much difference, if any, as far as the preference of the fish is concerned, but I think the feather fibre soaks up more 'Permaflote' and you might therefore find it better. However, a professional fly dresser might very well take the opposite view, since the raffine body is somewhat easier to tie, though it must be wound on while thoroughly damp.

You will probably find that these four patterns will cope with practically any situations you might discover.

1. Nymph

Hook: No. 10 or No. 8 long shank down-eyed. Not ultra-fine wire. Tails: short, pheasant tail fibres. The butts are used to make the two dark bands near the rear end of the abdomen.
Body and thorax: cream ostrich herl, 7 or 8 strands to make a fat body. Wing cases and legs: pheasant tail.
Weightings: tie in 3 or 4 layers of lead foil on hook shank before commencing the dressing.

2. Sub-imago (dun)

Hook: as nymph.
Tails: Pheasant tail, butts used to make dark bands.
Body: very pale buff turkey tail fibres, plenty so as to produce a fairly fat body.
Wings: two broad cock hackle points, dyed green, set upright.
Hackles: one brown partridge, one pale ginger cock.

3. Imago (spinner)

Hook: as above.
Tails: pheasant tail dyed sepia.

Body: ivory coloured turkey tail fibres, fat.
Wings: rusty badger cock hackle points tied flat.
Hackle: dark natural red cock.

4. Special mayfly for heavy hatches

Hook: as before.
Body: as sub-imago.
Hackles: one speckled duck feather, rather long in fibre, one green-dyed cock hackle, one hot orange hackle, shorter in fibre than the others.
Tails: pheasant tail.

5. Alternative

Body of sub-imago can be pale straw-coloured raffine ribbed with pale brown silk, instead of feather fibre.

STILLWATER FLY-FISHING

There have always been arguments among fly-fishers about whether the choice of fly pattern or the manner of presentation is more important, but few would disagree with the view that the correct fly, correctly presented, is likeliest to catch trout.

In reservoir trout fishing, working each pattern in the right way is of great importance. When imitations of actual insects are in use, there is no better way of learning how to fish them than careful observation of the insect. Make your artificial move as nearly as possible in the same way as the real insect.

For example, sedge flies of the larger kinds scuttle along the surface after hatching. After moving a few feet they stop and rest. Pull your floating imitation along the surface. You may have to pull faster than the real insect to make it rise on its hackles and skim along nicely. Do this by raising the rod from horizontal to about 50° to the surface of the water, pulling the line with the left hand at the same time. Then lower the

---

Almost everyone is now-a-days a 'piscator'. The *Fanatico*, about Easter, goes off as busy as the cockney on his *n*unter, when bound to Epping. He generally takes a great many things, and kills a few fish. The old angler takes a few things, and kills a great many fish.... When fish are well fed is the time to see who is, and who is not, an angler. About ninety in a hundred fancy themselves anglers. About one in a hundred *is* an angler. About ten in a hundred throw the hatchet better than a fly.

Peter Hawker, *Instructions to Young Sportsmen* (1816)

Figure 260: Richard Walker fishing with a 'leaded' nymph at Avington in May 1977

rod and recover the slack. Takes may come during the pull or the pause. Repeat until it is time to re-cast.

Midge pupae hang just below the surface. Unless there is bright sunlight, grease the leader to within an inch of the fly. Cast, and move the fly in jerks with long pauses.

A corixa swims up to the surface steadily. Let the artificial corixa sink nearly to the bottom, then bring it up in a long slow pull. When it is near the surface, give it plenty of time to sink again.

Ephemerid nymphs of stillwater flies like the Lake Olive, Pond Olive, Sepia Dun and Claret Dun move in short darts near the bottom and over weed beds until their time comes to hatch, when they swim steadily up to the surface. When no flies are seen hatching and trout are not visible, fish the artificial nymphs deep with short jerks. If flies are hatching, let the artificial sink deep, then draw it up steadily.

Fancy flies fall into two classes, those that are fished fast and those that are fished slowly. The Black and Peacock Spider is one that kills best when fished slowly, either in very slow draws or in tiny jerks. The popular Worm Fly should be retrieved slowly and steadily; the Barney Google in short slow pulls.

Streamlined versions of old favourites like Peter Ross, Dunkeld and Butcher should be drawn quite quickly, as should more modern dressings like the Sweeney Todd and other hair-wings. Sometimes it pays to draw these flies as fast through the water as can be easily managed and this is certainly true of what are usually called 'Lures', i.e. multihook streamers. However, when moving any of these flies fast or at medium pace, it often pays to vary the retrieve with pauses of about five seconds. Often, when re-commencing the retrieve, a trout will be found to have taken the fly. Strike firmly when this happens.

Polystickles and other fry-flies should be fished to move in the same way as sticklebacks and coarse-fish fry; small darts, pauses and occasional long pulls. A smooth steady retrieve is not desirable, though it does succeed occasion-ally.

The kind of line chosen plays an important part in the behaviour of the fly. For slow-moving imitations of insects the floating line is usually necessary, and to fish deep a long ungreased leader is needed, with plenty of time being given to allow the fly to sink. Floating lines may also be used to fish fancy flies, lures and Polystickles, casting crosswind and allowing the line to be blown round in a bow, towing the fly along just below the surface. Otherwise these flies are best fished on sinking lines. The faster you want to move the fly and the deeper you want to fish it, the faster sinking should be your line. Big hairwing flies and multi-hook lures will often catch trout, when used with an ultra-high density line, in conditions where other combinations of line and fly would fail.

Above all, the stillwater trout fisher should avoid acquiring a stereotyped style of retrieve. Instead, it should be capable of almost infinite variation. It may take as long as five minutes to retrieve some of the slow-fished flies, less than twenty seconds to retrieve some that need fast movement.

Time allowed for sinking is important and in this, a watch with a second hand helps. If you want to fish near the bottom, keep adding to the sinking time you allow your fly, until you actually touch bottom. Then subtract a few seconds from the time allowance on subsequent casts.

Remember there are nearly always more trout feeding near the bottom than anywhere else. By all means fish at the surface or close below, if you see many trout moving there, but if not, fish really deep. It is not unknown for trout to feed at midwater, but it is certainly uncommon. Flies near the surface or near the bottom account for many more trout than those fished at inter-mediate depths.

Think well before deciding which line, which fly and which kind of retrieve are most likely to succeed in the conditions you find, and then give your choice plenty of time to prove itself. Changing flies, lines and depths every few minutes will catch few trout; but when a change is quite obviously necessary, don't be too lazy to change not only the fly, but, if necessary, the line and leader as well.

NYMPH FISHING

Figure 261 (a) shows a technique of nymph fishing with a floating line and a split-shot on the leader. (A dropper can be used if required, above the split-shot.)

Although not easy to cast, this sink-and-draw style of fly-fishing – in reality nothing more than a form of old-fashioned trolling – is sometimes a highly successful ploy which can be tried when no trout are showing on or near the surface. Weather conditions: dull, windy, cold. Falling barometer. Poor hatch of fly.

Nymphs are very sensitive to weather con-ditions. A sudden change of temperature and barometric pressure may induce a hatch of fly or cause a hatch to cease with equal rapidity. On a sunny day, when the weather is soft and warm with a rising barometer, flies are likely to hatch. The following method of fishing nymph is preferable under these conditions (see Figure 261(b)).

The nymph is cast to B and allowed to sink to the bottom. A turn or two of fine wire round the hook shank will assist quick sinking. The nymph should be drawn up towards the surface with a steady continuous movement, to simulate the hatching insect.

Figure 261: (*below*) Nymph fishing
Figure 262: (*bottom*) Sedge fishing: plan view of water surface

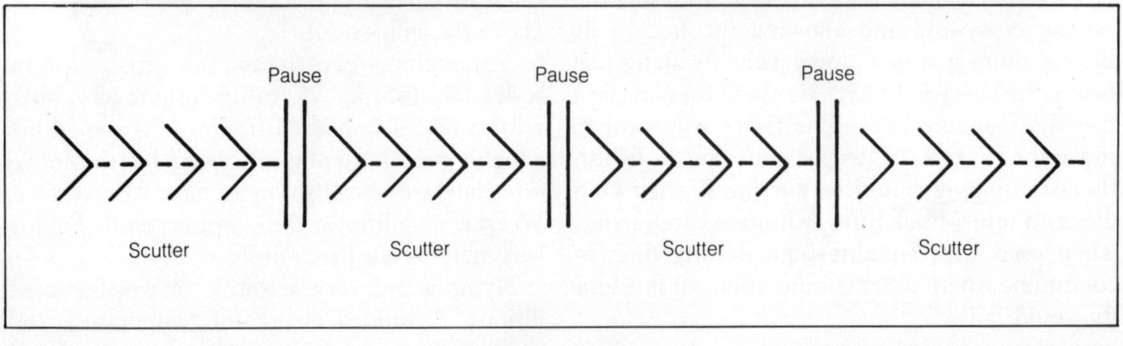

Sedge fishing at dusk – causing a wake

After hatching, large sedges tend to move across the surface of the water leaving a V-shaped wake. It is not a continuous movement. A sedge will scutter for a few feet, then stop and rest.

The artificial fly should be worked across the surface in a way that simulates this behaviour. Scutter, pause. Scutter, pause. Scutter, pause. (Figure 262). Trout may take when the fly is moving or while it is at rest, but the best taking time is just as it starts to move forward again after a period of rest.

The fly should be worked right in almost to the angler's legs. In the half-light, trout will sometimes take only a rod's length away.

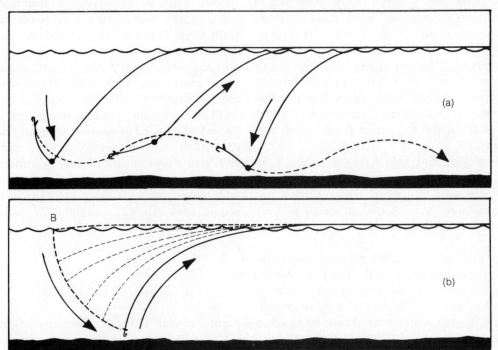

Freshwater Fishing

CASTING THE SHOOTING-HEAD

That this method of fishing has acquired a bad name is because it tends to be badly performed and grossly overdone. The fault lies not with the cast but with the caster. Inexperienced anglers, believing that fish feed only at the limit of casting range, strive to throw longer and longer lines and, because they *are* inexperienced, they don't do it very well.

Shooting-head tackle is simply a means of presenting a long line when this happens to be necessary. Frequently it is *not* necessary. Casting, say forty yards out, together with the deep wading that usually accompanies it, is often counter-productive. Poorly done it drives the fish farther and farther out – fish that otherwise would be feeding in the shallows close inshore.

Having made that point, we can go on to say that a competent caster can lay a shooting-head as lightly on the water as any other type of line, and that if he uses it well it is a valuable weapon in his armoury.

Level or double-tapered lines can be cast only so far. The length of line which can be shot is limited, so is the length which can be false cast. With a weight-forward line the back cast is always the same length, no matter how far forward the cast goes. Only the heavy belly portion is false cast; the rear taper will be just outside the rod tip but the weight concentrated in the first 30 ft of line, and because the shooting-line is smaller in diameter, much more line can be shot.

The shooting-head is really only a sophisticated weight-forward line with the shooting-line replaced by monofilament, which is lighter and shoots easily through the rod rings.

Other things being equal, the faster a fly is started on its way, the further it will go. Consequently, the knack of distance casting is primarily one of imparting maximum velocity to the line.

Figure 263: Casting the shooting-head (*Scientific Anglers*)

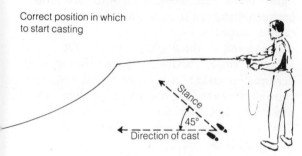

Correct position in which to start casting

Stance

45°

Direction of cast

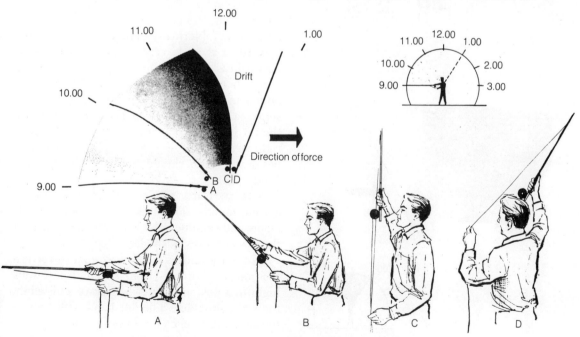

12.00

11.00

1.00

Drift

10.00

Direction of force

9.00

B C D A

11.00 12.00 1.00
10.00 2.00
9.00 3.00

A   B   C   D

MAKING THE BACK CAST

Position of rod and line at conclusion of good back cast

As the line straightens on back cast, raise left hand holding line so it will be in position for start of forward cast

THE FORWARD CAST

C   B   A

11.00   1.00   1.00

Rod tipped forward   Steady acceleration   Start

Direction of force

C B   A

11.00 12.00 1.00
10.00   2.00
9.00   3.00

To do this the technique must be altered and the double-haul method of casting employed. This means that velocity is achieved by pulling the line with the left hand as the rod reaches maximum speed in both the back and forward casts.

Only with monofilament and shooting-head line can full potential be realized.

The best position for a right-hand caster is with the feet comfortably separated and angled somewhat to the right of the direction he intends to cast. This will put the left foot forward, making it easier to watch the back cast over his shoulder.

False cast in the usual way until the backing knot is out of reel. Now strip off 25 or 30 ft of monofil. If you find it kinked from being wound tightly on the reel, straighten it with hard pulls – between hands, 4 ft at a time. Continue false casting until the knot is about 3 ft beyond the end ring and let the line fall on the water.

Next, since making a good fishing cast depends on making a good back cast first, let's concentrate on it. The back cast movement, when picking up line from the water, is up and back. This means up and back with rod and arm, not merely with the rod.

(Following a false cast, with the line higher out in front, the back cast is more a horizontal movement. Normally angled only slightly upward, it is made very much the same as the forward cast, save in the opposite direction.)

Reach out towards your extended line with both hands at waist height, backing up a few steps to remove slack if necessary. The rod should be pointed straight down the line, the right wrist cocked downward. The left hand, out beside the reel, should hold the shooting-line firmly.

Now start arm and rod up and back, accelerating rapidly. The back cast is made with the elbow and shoulder; the wrist remains locked in the position previously described.

As the rod moves from horizontal to vertical, the rod hand moves from out in front, waist high, to a position somewhat above and behind the right shoulder. The left hand, still holding the shooting-line, comes towards the body.

By the time the rod reaches the eleven o'clock position, the line will be coming towards you in the air. Bring the shoulder into play to move the entire rod back about 18 in. At the same time, pivot the elbow until the rod is vertical and stop it dead. The stop is accomplished by tensing forearm, wrist, and hand, then relaxing them instantly.

During the final movement of the rod, pull the line sharply with your hand. This is the first half of the double-haul. It will send the line singing out behind. Now let the rod drift back to one o'clock. Raise your left hand, still clutching the line tightly, up near your right shoulder.

With a perfect back cast, you will feel the line tug against the rod. When all the line is out straight behind, start the forward cast. The rod, in one o'clock position, is behind your shoulder. Push it forward briskly, still in this position. Push it as far forward as you can reach. Then, and not before, tip it ahead, faster and faster, pushing on the grip with your thumb.

Simultaneously with this movement, which is called the 'turnover', pull the line sharply with your left hand. The combination of turnover and left-hand pull gives the line the greatest possible velocity. Precisely at the completion of both, with the rod approximately at ten o'clock, stop it dead by tensing the muscles, then relaxing them. Release the monofil.

The shooting taper – well named – will shoot out like a bullet. The monofil will hit the reel with a jerk, and it will be obvious that you would have cast much farther, had you stripped off more line in the first place.

Don't do it! In fly casting, like every other activity requiring co-ordination, form is all important. Practise until you can make a perfect back cast every time, watching it over your shoulder. Practise moving the entire rod, and the double-haul. And let the forward cast come up hard against the reel.

But practise only a few minutes at a time. Weary muscles don't respond. Instead of working steadily for an hour, sit down occasionally and analyse what you are attempting to do. Accomplishment is easier with understanding.

A narrow arc of rod rotation results in the line going out in a shallow U-shaped loop essential for both distance and accuracy. A wide arc in which the rod is swung from 9.30 to 2.30 makes a deep loop with which distance is impossible and accuracy a matter of luck.

In addition, making sure the line is straight before starting the forward cast eliminates popping off flies and snapping the line like a whiplash. No fly line can long endure this punishment, yet many anglers ask their lines to do it by holding the butt in one position and swinging the tip farther and farther as they strive futilely for more distance. And since a rod brought too far back inevitably drives the line into the ground, they start the forward cast before the back cast has straightened. This causes the snapping that ruins their lines.

Now, after several practice sessions in which you moved the entire rod, making perfect, high-level back casts and forward casts that came up hard against the reel, you are ready to strip off more line and cast farther. And here – we can predict with certainty because we've watched it hundreds of times – you are going to fall flat. Instead of releasing one of the perfect false casts you have been making – and watching your fly sail out 100 ft – you are going to put a little extra muscle into the final effort.

So instead of sailing out fast and high, your fly will come to a halt and fall about 60 ft away. Why? Because you temporarily forgot form and relied, instead, on brute strength.

Remember form – fast, straight back cast; fast, straight forward cast; moving the entire rod, turning it over and pulling the line simultaneously at the conclusion of both. And hold to a narrow arc of rod rotation, even though the butt may move six feet and the tip much farther.

Have a friend watch and tell you when you bring the rod back too far – a much more common error than tipping it too far ahead, although you may do that, too. Remember – narrow arc, shallow loop and more distance; wide arc, deep loop and less distance. Move the entire rod, accelerating from fast to faster on both the back and forward casts.

Once you get the hang of casting a deep or shallow loop at will, you will be able to angle either the back or forward cast up or down as you see fit. And you will realize that the line can move only in a straight line – the line in which force is applied. Left, right, up or down, it goes only where the rod sends it.

Knowing this, you will be able to tilt the arc of rod movement to control the angle of your cast. And you will soon discover that for maximum distance on a calm day, or with the wind, your forward cast must be angled slightly upward, just as a rifle barrel must be angled well above the horizontal to send its bullet to maximum range. To do this, of course, the back cast must be aimed slightly lower. Conversely, when you are casting against the wind, you will get the best distance by aiming the forward cast lower and holding the back cast high.

Now for some errors you are bound to make. The first is what is known as 'creep'. Instead of keeping the rod far back in the one o'clock position until the back cast pulls against it, you begin to edge it forward as soon as the back cast is made. As a result, when you start to make the forward cast you can use only half the rod movement, apply only half the energy, and your cast goes only half as far.

Another very common error, the cause of so-called 'wind-knots' in the leader, is tipping the rod forward before you push it ahead. Bring the rod, in one o'clock position, from behind your shoulder to as far forward as you can reach, accelerating rapidly, then tip it over towards the target.

You may find yourself hauling line too soon. For maximum line speed, and distance, the haul must be made simultaneously with greatest tip speed. This is during the final, fastest rod movement of both the back and forward casts.

You will also forget that the back cast requires just as much power and takes just as long to straighten as a forward cast of equal length. Watch your back cast. When the back cast is perfect, the forward cast makes itself.

Don't lower your hand as you bring the butt of the rod forward on the fishing cast. Instead, keep it high, as though you were pushing a

I state this solemnly. I have never had quite that hushed feeling about the trout anywhere else. And we all felt it. Then one night there was a terrific strike, my rod bent in the dark; it bent, it bent, it bent. ... For you could not allow the fish to run into the rapids immediately below. And then it straightened out. The line came back empty. The fly was gone. I climbed up the bank by the church with the feeling that I was not meant to catch any more fish below the feet of St. Christopher painted on its walls.

I never did.

Negley Farson, *Going Fishing* (1942)

weight along a shoulder-high shelf. Remember, for long casts the force must be applied to the line in a single plane. To do this, the rod butt must also move in one plane.

And finally, as you begin to gain proficiency and can make cast after cast of more than 100 ft, you will discover that after you have fished awhile your casts get shorter. Try as you will, you can't improve them. This happens to all of us. We try too hard. We begin to rely on strength rather than correct form. Relax and use less muscle. As if by magic, your fly will sail out 20 ft farther on the next attempt.

One of the most common faults seen around the English reservoir banks is the undue amount of false casting. As soon as a good back cast has been achieved, the forward delivery should be made. Often anglers go on and on false casting, becoming more and more tired, and shoot the line following a very ragged back cast.

The static fly

That trout will occasionally pick up a fly that is lying on the bottom is well known. Many anglers have cast out their lines and rested their rods while taking a drink, or eating their lunch, and then found that a trout has obligingly attached itself. Only recently however has it been realized that sometimes it pays to fish a static fly deliberately.

The method is very simple. You cast out, a

shooting-head of sinking line, and allow everything to fall to the bottom. If fishing from a boat
you must be anchored, and cast far enough to
allow all the fly-line to lie on the bottom – that
is, have at least six or seven yards of monofil
backing beyond the top rod-ring.

It is important to choose the right place. The
criteria to observe are:
1. The penetration of light
2. The nature of the bottom

The static fly does best on a bottom of gravel
or sand, where there is little or no weed growth,
in depths of from 8 to 15 ft. Short of careful
investigation of depth and weed growth, it often
pays to try a static fly in parts of a lake where large
numbers of sedge flies are seen to be hatching.

The pattern of fly seems relatively unimportant. Trout can be caught on imitations of
midge pupae, sedge pupae and the nymphs of
dragonflies and water beetles, as well as on
Muddler Minnows, Polystickles and Rasputins,
and even on traditional dressings like Invicta,
Dunkeld and Butcher and, doubtless, many
others. Given such catholicity on the part of the
trout one may do well to use a fly that has mechanical advantages and there are two dressings
that are particularly successful: the Rasputin and
the Fore-and-aft Glowstickle.

The Rasputin has a body of fine-textured
expanded polyethylene and is therefore buoyant.
It is fished on a Hi-D fly-line (fast sinker) with
a very short leader. We have succeeded with as
little as four inches; twelve inches is the limit.

The Fore-and-aft Glowstickle can be fished
on a normal length of leader. This makes it more
convenient to use if the static-fly is given a short
trial as a change from normal fly-fishing. It consists of a cigar-shaped body made of luminous
plastic strip wound over an underbody of floss,
with a pale buff or cream cock hackle, long in
fibre, wound at both head and tail. The hackles
support the fly when it has sunk and prevent the
hook point from catching bottom debris.

Other fore-and-aft dressings in which luminous plastic is replaced by a body of peacock
herl, pheasant tail fibres or white polythene strip,
also succeed.

The main value of the static method is its

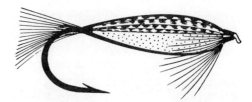

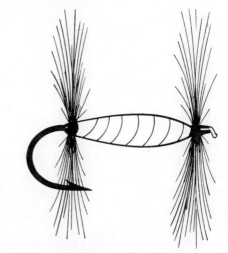

Figure 264: Rasputin

Figure 265: Fore-and-aft Glowstickle

ability to catch large brown trout that have
become almost exclusively bottom feeders.
These fish are seldom caught by surface or near-
surface fishing. To hook them with the static
fly adds an extra fillip to more conventional
methods.

It is true of fly-fishing, more perhaps than
of any other branch of angling, that no
sooner have you made a flat statement than
you have to qualify it.

Maurice Wiggin

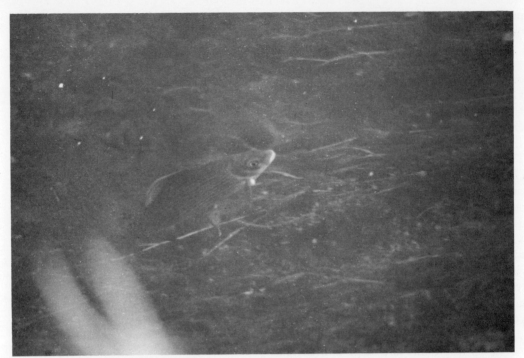

Figure 266 (a): A grayling drifts upwards in a precise and leisurely way, to intercept a small spinner trapped in the surface film (the fly is the small brown smudge just in front of its nose). This kind of behaviour – as one would expect – produces only a small surface disturbance accompanied by an audible sipping noise. The noise is created because the fish cannot avoid sucking in a little air as it takes down the fly

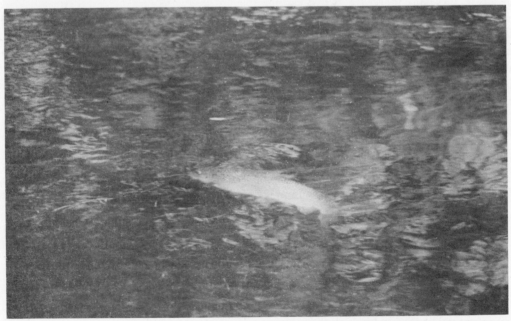

Figure 266 (b): A trout hurling itself at a hatching sedge (again, the fly is visible just in front of the fish's nose). It is obvious why fish feeding on hatching sedges tend to produce violent rise-forms! As in the previous picture the eye of the fish is fixed absolutely on the natural fly it is about to take

Figure 266(c): The typical removal of a small olive dun from the surface

RISE-FORMS

In his classic book *The Pursuit of Stillwater Trout* (1975), our friend Brian Clarke published some fascinating observations on the rise-forms of feeding trout. Here, specially written for our book, are his thoughts on the subject, perfectly illustrated by three of his own photographs, two of which are hitherto unpublished.

The route to consistent success in angling is the same route that provides success in all forms of hunting:

1. Knowledge of the quarry through observation
2. Ability to translate that observed behaviour into appropriate technique

In the case of a feeding trout – whether in river or lake – 'observed technique' usually means a rise-form; and 'appropriate technique' means presenting the fish with something like the creature it is expecting to see, where, when and how it expects to see it.

By and large, anglers have suffered a rather hard time when presented with information on rise-forms. Almost always they have been given a list of separate facts or one-off circumstances which have had to be learned by heart because there has been no clear linkage between them.

'Now the trout will cause the water to bulge; now its back will show; now it will do something else. When it is bulging, do this. . . . When it is head-and-tailing, do that. . . .'

Knowledge has been made available, yes, but all too often there has been a missing ingredient – *understanding*.

The problem of interpreting a rise-form becomes very much simpler once the *behaviour of the fish* and the *resulting rise-form* are seen as a logical process of cause and effect.

The trout, like any other creature in the wild, does not expend energy uselessly. It moves quickly only when it *needs* to; otherwise it moves slowly. (There are a few exceptions – such as competitive feeding when a small amount of a particularly stimulating food-form appears – but such exceptions merely prove the rule.)

In general it can be said that a feeding fish will move quickly only when pursuing something which is itself moving quickly; and that it will move slowly when taking, say, a snail. In other words there is a direct relationship between the movement of the fish and the movement of the creature it is attempting to catch and eat.

But there is also, of course, a direct relationship between the speed of the trout and the force with which it displaces the water around it. If the trout is moving quickly, then the water will be displaced violently. If it is moving slowly, then the water will be displaced gently.

So, we can see that there is a direct relationship between the movement of whatever creature the trout is intent upon eating, and the displacement of water entailed in its capture: *food and rise-form are directly related*.

Thus, by using his powers of observation and deduction (elementary nature detective work, as described in several films and books by Hugh Falkus), the angler can set aside the entomological roulette he has played hitherto; and put behind him, too, his wild-eyed speculation at the fly-vice. Provided he is prepared to learn a little about the creatures trout eat – especially where they live and how they move – he can watch any particular rise-form and relate it to the trout's speed and manner of movement. He can, furthermore, relate the trout's movement to the speeds of movement of the small group of insects known to be about at the time, and their approximate positions in and on the water.

As a result, he not only knows which artificials he should be wetting, but where he should be fishing them and how they should be moved.

'Boils', or swirls, on the surface *but not breaking it* are clearly the product of a fish moving quickly fairly near the top – probably to fast-moving or awkwardly moving nymphs and pupae a foot or so down. Sedge and midge pupae and olive nymphs all fall into this category; but time of year and time of day narrow the range of possibilities.

Trout movements that break the surface violently are likely to be to large, live insects like adult sedges on the surface, or sedge pupae swimming immediately beneath the surface, the momentum of the eager fish simply carrying it through the surface film to create the disturbance the angler sees.

Gentler movements at the surface in which the fish's neb shows, are likely to be to small duns or terrestrials – and so is head-and-tailing when the neb shows. Head-and-tailing in which the mouth does *not* break the surface is certainly to creatures trapped immediately beneath the surface film (why else would only the back of the fish show?). On lakes, the most common insects that cause this kind of rise-form are midge pupae hanging below the surface film, waiting to hatch. On rivers, the answer is likely to be inert olive nymphs also preparing to hatch or, on some rivers in the late evening or early morning, the dead spinners of some species of olives drifting down beneath the surface film after their underwater egg-laying odysseys are over.

A fish that is taking flies with an audible sipping noise – always accompanied by only a tiny movement of water – is one taking dead or dying flies trapped in the surface film, and there is absolutely no need to consider a fly in any other circumstance.

Note: 1. We know the fly is in the surface film because the sipping noise is clearly a sharp intake of air, and it is only at the surface that the fish can take in that air.

2. We know that the fly is trapped because, when faced with a prey that cannot escape, the trout's movements are confident and leisurely; there is no need to hurry.

All of the observations on rise-forms described above are true for both rivers and stillwaters, except that on rivers the turbulence and current can make rise-forms in general more difficult to see. (There is a side-issue here: fish in rivers drift backwards and upwards on the current to intercept flies, so they actually lie *upstream* of the place where the rise-form is seen. And the angler should take account of this when making a cast.)

On lakes, the presence of fish can be deduced even when no such distinct rises can be seen or noises heard. In flat calms the appearance of a *contortion* in an otherwise steady reflection in the surface can be the sign of a fish swimming just beneath the film, or the residue of a deep-down 'boil' caused by a fish taking a nymph or pupa. So, too, can the appearance of *unsteady dark patches* in an area of water reflecting light, or *winking light patches* appearing in a water area that is reflecting shade.

Even in rippled lake water, the presence of feeding fish can be detected without sounds or clear rise-forms. Typically, *small oases or calm patches* will appear in the ripple, indicating that a fish has turned violently a little way down and sent an upthrust of water to the surface, the effect being to flatten or stun the wavelets. Also in rippled water, *cross-ripple patterns* will sometimes appear, suggesting that the back of a fish has broken the surface unseen.

And that's about it.

Mind you, it takes practice, a lot of practice to get it right. Don't believe that the interpretation of rise-forms is a clinical business divined with mathematical precision. It isn't! On the day, with a stiff wind blowing in your teeth, water on the move and a mass of reflections, it can all be a lot less apparent than it is from the pages of a book being read in an armchair. But the *principle* it is based on is sound. It provides an angler faced with difficult fish that most satisfying of all starting points: an intelligent basis for action.

With experience it will certainly help him to catch more fish. Perhaps what is more important still will be his increased pleasure in catching them.

BOAT FISHING

Conventional methods of fishing from a boat on large lakes and reservoirs mostly involve drifting. It is usual to fish two or three flies, though on waters such as Loch Leven, it is common to use as many as four. On southern reservoirs, most anglers content themselves with two. With traditional fly patterns, a favourite team consists of Peter Ross at point, Mallard and Claret in the middle and Butcher on the bob. On southern reservoirs, especially in the evening, an Invicta can be tried at point and a Red Midge Pupa higher up the leader.

The most common method is to drift with the boat's beam at right-angles to the direction of the wind, the drift rate being slowed by means of a drogue. The anglers sit facing downwind,

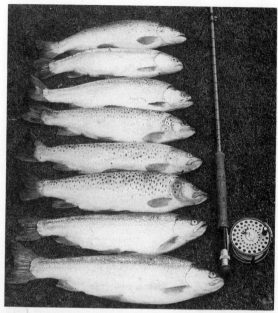

Figure 267: Eight fine brown and rainbow trout taken by F. B. from Grafham on a built-cane rod with thirty yards of *Kingfisher* line. A reminder that successful reservoir trout fishing – far from being dependent on carbon-fibre rods and shooting-heads – dates back to the late nineteenth century, when a cane rod and silk line reigned supreme

Figure 268: Gerry Berth-Jones with a Lough Mask trout

The Brown Trout

Figure 269: Lough Mask

casting ahead, and retrieving at a rate that allows them to keep in touch with their flies.

The retrieve is usually terminated by raising the rod and causing the nearest fly, the 'bob', to dance on the surface for a few seconds. The longer the rod, the lighter the line, the longer this can be made to happen. Since long casting is not necessary a combination of long rod and light line has advantages.

But straight downwind casting is not very efficient, as it covers less water, gives the fish (which tend to head upwind) an unattractive view of the flies, and increases the tendency to pull the fly out of a fish's mouth. It is better to cast at an angle to the direction of drift, so that the flies are drawn partly across the wind.

This can be done rather better if the boat drifts with its fore and aft axis in line with the wind direction and its occupants casting on opposite sides. This technique is a very old one and used to be known as 'fishing the fall'. With sinking lines, deep fishing is improved if the anglers cast across and slightly downwind and then allow the boat to 'drift through', so that the flies are caused to swing cross wind and inwards behind the boat. Of course, floating lines can be used in the same way, and the method is especially suitable for fishing hairwing and streamer flies of fairly large size.

Most of the earlier works on lake and loch fishing advise drifting over water not more than 8–12 ft deep. This may be good advice where natural lakes are concerned, but it is far from true of reservoirs, where trout are often to be found feeding in water up to 70 ft or more in depth. The best opportunities usually occur when there is a moderate breeze and what are known as 'slicks' – long 'lanes' of calm, oily-looking water in line with the direction of the wind and with rippled water on either side. Trout are found in the calm water close to the ripple or on the edge of the ripple itself. When they are feeding on midge or sedge pupae their rises are easily seen, and casts can be made to individual fish.

In such conditions it often pays to abandon drifting, drop anchor and let the fish move upwind towards the boat. Sedge or midge pupae are the fly patterns most often required, but at times floating sedges or crane-fly imitations can be deadly, as can imitations of ants, beetles, black gnats, hawthorn flies, drone flies and other creatures that may be blown on to the water.

When ephemerid flies such as pond olives and lake olives are seen hatching, the appropriate nymph can be tied on the point with an imitation of the winged dun on the dropper. The dry-fly is much neglected by stillwater trout-fishers, but it is well worth keeping a few daddy-long-legs, big sedges, and drone flies in one's box, and using them whenever fish are seen eating the natural insects on the surface.

Fishing from a boat in a considerable wind and wave can be very productive. The movement of the boat makes it difficult to keep in touch with the flies, but the wave effect on the line moves them even when the angler is out of touch.

The secret is to fish with a short line and tighten whenever you see the slightest sign of a fish even within several yards of where you think the flies are. You sometimes get a side view of a trout in a wave, as if it were in a glass case. Assume that any trout you see has your fly in its mouth, and tighten at once. You may be surprised to find how often you have hooked the fish.

For really rough water a fairly large worm fly on the point and a smallish red or black midge pupa on the dropper make a good combination.

A method which can be very effective at times is to cast a tandem lure as far as possible, and strip it back at high speed. The same applies to

Figure 270: A 13 lb 7 oz Lough Mask trout caught by Des Elliott in 1976

trailing a lure behind a moving boat. But although such methods are certainly not unsporting they can become very dull, since little skill is required to fish them. We suggest therefore that the novice angler keeps them in reserve and uses them only when more interesting methods fail.

Cross-wind fly-fishing

This is a method of stillwater fly-fishing from a boat for brown trout, rainbow trout, sea trout and salmon. Success at this type of fishing depends almost entirely on the way the boat is handled.

Stillwater trout fishermen usually fish two to a boat and manage without the services of a professional gillie. Almost invariably they restrict themselves to drifting downwind or casting from the boat at anchor – methods which permit both of them to fish at the same time. We suggest that angling companions who are prepared to think in terms of the total 'boat-catch' rather than their individual catches, should try taking it in turns to handle the boat so that cross-wind fishing can be practised. It is the deadliest of all stillwater fly-fishing methods. Needless to say, both sinking-line and floating-line techniques should be tried.

The usual method of fly-fishing from a boat in stillwater is to motor or row to the upwind end of a fishing area and then drift straight downwind (figure 271). The flies are cast ahead of the drifting boat and worked back towards the angler. An oar is used only to keep the boat broadside to the wind, or to avoid shallows.

A very much more profitable method is to fish to and fro along a zig-zag path across wind (figures 272 and 273). The course of the boat varies in relation to the shore according to the wind direction.

Note: The lee shore of a lake is nearly always the most productive.

When two rods are fishing (figure 273), the stern rod (A) should fish with a sinking line and cast as far as possible to B. As the boat moves forward across the wind he allows his line to sink, until (from position O) he fishes his flies round the arc CD.

The bow rod uses a floating line and casts a shorter distance to F, then concentrates on keeping his bob-fly skimming along the trough of the waves to G; the tail-fly fishing just under the surface.

When a 'hot-spot' is reached, the boat is held in position for a time so that the area can be thoroughly covered.

It is essential that the oarsman should know the best fishing areas and be able to manoeuvre the boat at just the right speed; checking and holding it in position when a 'hot-spot' is reached. For fishing these 'hot-spots' it is better to keep to the oars rather than drop anchor, since skilful handling can keep the boat on station, broadside to the wind.

Dapping

This was probably the earliest form of fly-fishing. Dangling an insect on the surface of the water would have been as effective two thousand years ago as it is today, although the first description of it (in English) seems not to have been until 1620 in the *William Lauson-edited* second edition of John Dennys's *The Secrets of Angling*.

Lauson named this method 'bushing', since the fly was fished with a short line on the surface – or 'crust' as he called it – from the concealment of bushes. 'Bushing' was called 'daping' by Izaak Walton. This became 'dibbing' and, eventually, 'dapping'.

After centuries of comparative neglect, dapping is now becoming rather more popular. This is largely due to the improvement in tackle. Modern dapping rods are very light for their length (16–18 ft) and made in telescopic form. They can be swiftly mounted ready for use, but carried in a boat conveniently 'closed down' and out of the way until congenial wind conditions prevail. In addition to ultra-light and responsive floss lines, the improvement in efficiency of modern fly floatant makes it practical for the dapper to use artificial flies: mayfly, daddy etc., rather than the natural insects, which sometimes take hours to collect. These improvements have so widened the appeal of dapping that many dedicated wet-fly fishermen on the Irish loughs have added a dapping outfit to their tackle, as have some of the most ardent reservoir trout fishers.

Besides providing an additional method of boat fishing, dapping is a good way to accommodate an extra 'rod' should three people wish to share the boat rather than the customary two.

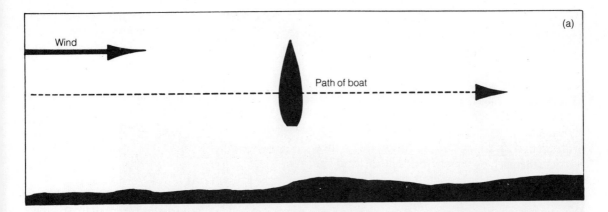

Wind

Path of boat

(a)

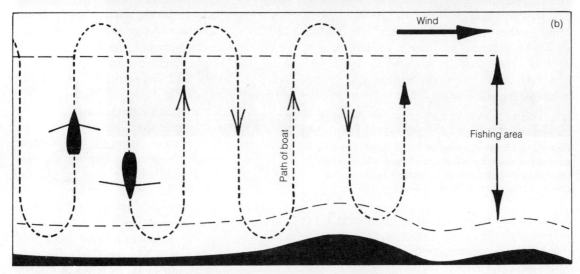

Wind

(b)

Path of boat

Fishing area

Figure 271: (top)
Figure 272: (above)
Figure 273: (right)

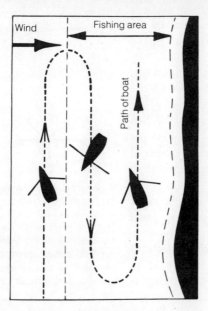

Wind

Fishing area

Path of boat

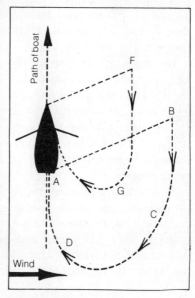

Path of boat

F

B

A

G

C

D

Wind

Figure 274: Dapping ground on Lough Mask; the word ground has more than a little significance when you see the rock-strewn shores and rock-strewn outcrops that appear even in the middle of the lough

Since no casting is required, young or inexperienced anglers gain experience, plus the possible bonus of catching the best fish of the day.

Women, of whatever angling experience, make very successful dappers, seeming to have a natural ability to keep their eyes focused on their fly and, when a fish eventually takes it, the composure to delay the strike.

In dapping, the strike is all-important. Delayed until the fish has turned down with the fly, it is executed with *a fast upward stroke of the whole arm* – not just with wrist or forearm. When a long line is being fished, the sideways or straight-back-over-the-shoulder wristy strikes of the wet-fly fishermen result in far fewer fish being hooked.

Although the dapping method can be used throughout the trout fishing season, local dappers tend to concentrate on mayfly time (parts of May and June), and during parts of August and September when the 'daddy' is on the water. In Ireland, where most dapping is

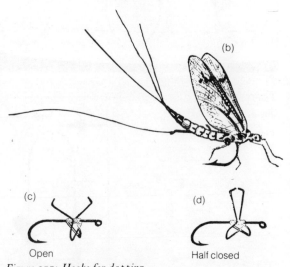

Figure 275: Hooks for dapping
(a) Single hook, size 10—12 shows a tiny bristle fastened to the shank with a few turns of fine tying silk
(b) The point of the hook is pushed through the side of the thorax until the bristle emerges and secures the fly
(c) The 'Arbro' spring clip dapping hook – permits the mounting of a live insect (mayfly, daddy-long-legs or grasshopper) without injury

Open   Half closed

done, mayfly time sees dappers out in force. Visiting anglers, whose holidays are limited, should remember that whereas on any one lough the best of the rise – be it to dun or spinner – is over in about three weeks, loughs whose mayflies hatch earlier or later can extend the season over two months or more.

The seasonal pattern of mayfly hatch generally progresses from south to north and from east to west. Thus the midland loughs have earlier hatches than those of the west; and of the big western loughs the southernmost, Lough Derg, has an earlier hatch than Lough Corrib. Corrib, in turn, has an earlier hatch than Lough Mask.

An exception is Lough Carra, to the northeast of Mask. Carra has a much earlier hatch than Mask, being shallower and warming up more quickly.

Figure 276: Dapping

We feel sure that although most experienced trout anglers would agree that the wet-fly catches more trout during a season, they would concede that trout caught on the dap are of larger average weight. Another point in support of dapping is that a big grasshopper or a bunch of daddies will bring good trout up from deeper water when no flies are hatching.

The Murrough – an artificial representing a large sedge – is a most effective dapping fly. Indeed, the most successful Lough Mask dapper of our acquaintance uses nothing but this pattern and the Green Peter.

During many years of fishing Mask, Corrib and Conn, F. B. has found an electric outboard a most useful dapping aid, since it enables him to negotiate the ins-and-outs of a broken shoreline without the assistance of a gillie. Shorelines (not forgetting those surrounding islands) are often the most productive dapping areas. Every shift of wind makes a different shoreline fishable, and

The grasshopper has attracted many trout anglers but none more famous than the subject of a note by Major F. Powell Hopkins, in his *Fishing Experiences of Half a Century* (1893), where he described the fishing on Keel Lough, Achill Island, Co. Mayo.

'We started on the sea side of the bridge, and in the first pool close to it I hooked, with a grey and silver fly, a nice peel, who bolted through one of the arches of the bridge and cut me. N.... was busy lower down, and had secured a fish of nearly 2 lbs. Fishing away with but little success, we arrived at the last pool before reaching the sea. I had fished half-way down it, when a big swirl of the water beneath my fly and a heavy tug told me I had got a big one; in a moment a fine salmon darted out of the water and made straight for the sea. I shouted to N.... to run and cut him off, but my fish beat him easy and soon disposed of my trout cast and some ten yards of line in that extensive pit, the Atlantic.

Returning to the lake, we saw somebody at one end fishing from a canoe. Tim informed us it was Captain Boycott, who resided about a mile off. Pulling to him, we found him fishing with a grasshopper, and with good success, his trout averaging larger than ours.

"I find I get the best trout with them," he said. This was our first introduction to one whose name, as applied to a vile system of coercion, became so notorious.

A few days afterwards we lunched with him and Mrs Boycott at his house, half-way up the side of a huge mountain.

It seemed pleasant enough in the sunny bright weather we had on our visit, and the view from it was grand – a combination of rocks, mountains, sea and lake one seldom sees; but Lord! What a place in winter, and for a lady! I pitied her. Capt. B. farmed several hundred acres of land, but from what he said I fancy it did not pay, and it was not long after our visit that he gave it up.'

the local angler, knowing this better than most, soon moves away from where other boats are drifting so as to be first over the new ground.

Most of the technique of brown trout dapping holds good for sea trout too, both in Ireland and Scotland, but there are some important differences.

Brown trout explore all regions of a fishery to exploit the feeding potential, whereas the (mainly) non-feeding sea trout tend to favour certain spots. It is essential for anglers to know these places before setting out, otherwise much precious leisure time will be wasted.

Except on rare occasions brown trout only rise to their natural food or to artificials representing it. Sea trout, on the other hand, take flies resembling small shaving brushes (see facing page 304 for a selection of these grotesquerie).

When brown trout fishing it usually pays to dap in a straight line ahead of the drifting boat. Sea trout are more likely to take a lure that is tripping from side to side *across* the line of drift.

Acidic fall-out can occur daily irrespective of the rainfall. In the absence of rain this fall-out is known as 'dry deposition', its acidic content being washed from the countryside into the river by later rainfall. In this it is akin to lime-spreading. The ill-effect of acidic deposits and the neutralising effect of lime both depend ultimately on rainfall.

Acid rain has been with us since the industrial revolution, its effects becoming more and more acute in many areas owing to the continuous leaching of alkaline elements in naturally boggy ground. Greatly to be regretted is the removal of the liming subsidy for hill farmland. This happened in September 1976, since when, in certain areas (e.g. the River Esk valley in Cumbria), the increase in acidic pollution has been devastating (see pages 292–3).

Acid fall-out is an illness we have neglected to our cost. Buildings, countryside, lakes and rivers are all suffering an accumulating damage. What can and should be done?

1. Fit desulphurization plants to coal and allied fuel-burning installations. (It is estimated that Europe alone produces in excess of thirty million tonnes of sulphur a year – equivalent to sixty million tonnes of sulphur dioxide.)

2. Re-design petrol and diesel engine exhausts to filter the toxic gases.

3. Re-design flue systems on oil- and gas-burning appliances, with the same object in view.

4. Improve the breakdown and disposal technology of toxic wastes.

5. Make alkaline replacement in areas where the alkali has been leached away (e.g. by lime-spreading).

ACID RAIN – AND HOW SOME OF ITS PROBLEMS MAY BE OVERCOME

Much of Britain, as well as Europe and Scandinavia, is suffering from the accelerating illness of acidic rainfall. Briefly, acid rain is caused by fossil fuel combustion. The resulting oxides of sulphur and nitrogen, formed when the 'gas' mixes with moisture in the atmosphere, travel with the airmasses of our weather system for hundreds or even thousands of miles, changing as they go into compounds that rain down as dilute but deadly solutions of sulphuric and nitric acid.

This acidic fall-out can be fatal to life forms in the soil which are the basis of all natural vegetation. It can also kill all forms of aquatic life, ultimately reducing fish stocks to nil.

During recent years the beautiful valley of the Cumbrian Esk – once one of Britain's most prolific little spate rivers – has suffered severely from chemical pollution caused by acid rain.

The Cumbrian Esk flows from the slopes of Sca Fell, England's highest mountain, and the estuary at Ravenglass, where two other rivers join to flow into the Irish Sea, forms its bottom reaches. The local geology is classified as 'Borrowdale volcanic series'. This is a complex mixture of rhyolitic and andesitic lava and ignibrite – which, because of their crystallation, are

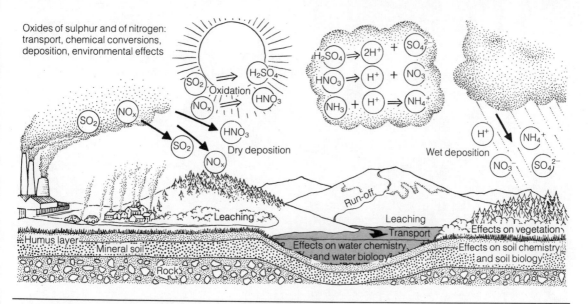

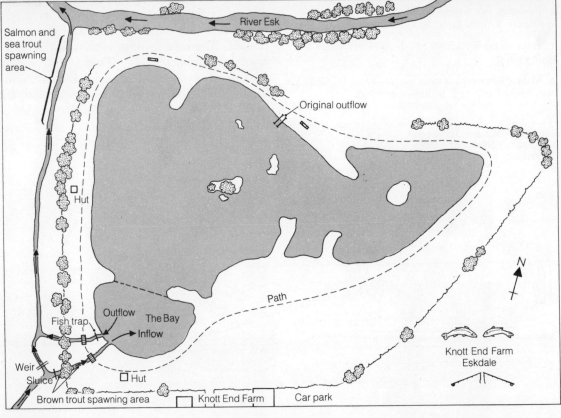

Salmon and
sea trout
spawning
area

River Esk

Original outflow

Hut

Path

Fish trap

Outflow   The Bay

Inflow

Weir

Sluice

Brown trout spawning area

Hut

Knott End Farm

Car park

Knott End Farm
Eskdale

N

known simply as 'granite' – together with a small amount of boulder clay. From the angler's point of view, the most important aspect of this 'granite' is that it contains aluminium.

Rainfall on Sca Fell is very heavy and, depending on wind direction (see figure 281) the resultant run-off into the River Esk can be highly toxic. Over many years this has so greatly reduced the alkaline elements in the river's naturally acidic watershed that now (in the absence of these elements as neutralizers) it can extract deadly compounds of aluminium from the granite rock. Results have been disastrous.

Unaware of acid rain, the previous owners of a riverside farm in Lower Eskdale excavated a field of swamp and rushes to make a small tarn for trout fishing. This was flooded from a nearby beck, which provides the farmhouse water supply and runs from the fellside into the river. Fifty brown trout and some rainbows weighing from $\frac{1}{2}$ lb to 2 lb were introduced.

At first all seemed well, but within a few months every fish had died. On investigation, mortality was found to be caused by the tarn's low pH values, together with a high level of aluminium.

This potentially lethal water was the problem facing a friend of ours, Bill Arnold, when he took over the property in 1983. In the hope that his experience may help other anglers confronted with a similar situation, or who are thinking of making their own fisheries in acidic hill country-side, Bill Arnold has very kindly written the following notes:

My first step towards solving the problem was to mix ground limestone with the tarn water. This was done from a boat with an outboard motor, to create as much turbulence as possible, and throwing the lime into the wake.

I had calculated the volume of water as approximately one-and-a-half million gallons. The first introduction of lime was 4 cwt, which raised the pH level from 4.0 to 5.3. A further addition of 3 cwt of lime raised the pH to the healthy figure of 6.6. This exercise was carried out over a period of ten days. The next step was to improve the tarn's food supply.

Investigation of the tarn's invertebrate life prior to liming revealed a distinct absence of Gammarus and Limnaea. Collection of freshwater shrimp (G. pulex) and wandering snail (L. peregra) from becks outside the River Esk catchment area corrected this deficiency.

At this stage I introduced fifty 12 in. brown trout and fifty 12 in. brook trout. This proved successful, and in the same year I made a further introduction of two hundred rainbows up to 3 lb.

During this period I continued to monitor the pH values regularly and found that $\frac{1}{2}$ cwt of lime, applied each month, kept the pH value to 6.5. The outflow from the tarn at this stage was diagonally opposite the inflow and a small but steady flow of water was passing straight through the tarn. (Later I was to change this.)

By now the tarn had become very popular with local anglers, to whom I let daily tickets, and encouraged by my success I decided to enlarge the tarn by excavating a further patch of boggy ground. Despite some poor weather this was accomplished in about a month, using heavy earth-moving plant.

Before flooding the new area I applied lime to the base in the proportion of 10 cwt to an estimated two-million gallons of water. During this exercise I constructed a new outflow in line with and about three feet away from the inflow (see sketch map). The object of this alteration was to draw the minimum amount of water from the feeder beck (so as to maintain the overall level of the tarn), while at the same time keeping undisturbed the main body of lime-treated water outside The Bay (see dotted line on the map).

Figure 278: Knott End Farm Fishery, Eskdale. The photograph of Knott End Tarn shows how well the fishery blends with the surrounding landscape. While the earth was still bare from bulldozing, a variety of wild seeds were swept from local barn floors before haytime. These were sown along the tarn sides and in the surrounding areas to create a varied flora. The resulting profusion of wild flowers and grasses has produced a summer scene of outstanding beauty.

During the first year twenty-five pairs of mallard were introduced. This was done chiefly because:

The duck droppings increase the phosphate and potash levels, which increase the plankton level which, in turn, increases the level of invertebrates on which the trout feed.

They help to control the pond weeds and save work in clearing.

They encourage the visits of migratory ducks.

The daily feeding attracts many other birds

Figure 279: Sketch plan

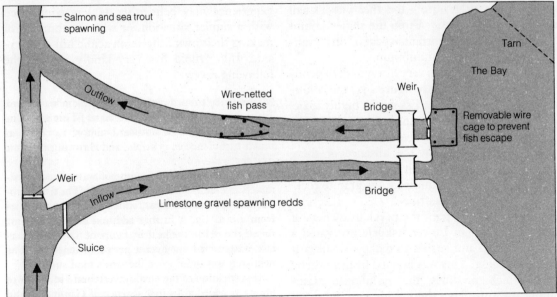

Salmon and sea trout spawning

Outflow

Wire-netted fish pass

Weir

Tarn

The Bay

Bridge

Removable wire cage to prevent fish escape

Weir

Inflow

Limestone gravel spawning redds

Bridge

Sluice

Figure 280: Knott End Tarn – inflow and outflow

This arrangement has made a dramatic reduction in the amount of lime required. Over the last sixteen months, although approximately two-and-a-half times the original volume of water was being treated, only ½ cwt of lime, applied every nine weeks on average, has been needed to maintain the pH at 6.5. This, it seems, is the amount of lime necessary to control both the wet precipitation and the dry deposition. Whether or not this will continue we shall find out by regular monitoring.

Over the past two years I have recorded daily the maximum and minimum temperatures, the barometric pressure, the wind direction and the volume and pH values of precipitation and deposition.

After completing the tarn enlargement I introduced in the first year, at various times, six hundred rainbow trout up to 5 lb. (Regrettably, owing to local hatchery problems, brown trout and brook trout were unavailable.) Like their predecessors, these fish thrived splendidly, staying in excellent condition and showing a slow increase in weight. Throughout the

Note: pH is a quantitative measure of the acidity (or basicity) of a solution on a reciprocal logarithmic scale. For example: pH 5 is ten times more acid than pH 6: pH 4 ten times more acid than pH 5.

past three years, with fish being introduced at various times, I have found only four fish dead from causes unknown.

The fishing, too, has been a great success. Anglers have had a marvellous time with nymph and, in particular, the dry-fly.

A point of interest is The Bay, where the feeder beck enters the tarn (inside the dotted line, see diagram).

The only water required in the main body of the tarn is compensation water, to replace the loss from evaporation or a fall in the water table during drought. This creates a unique situation in The Bay. The feeder beck at the sluice is only pH 4.5 to 4.8. When run over limestone chippings it rises to pH 5.0 to 5.3. As it flows round The Bay this water mixes with the main tarn water (pH 6.5) giving a value of about pH 5.6. (At this value a hybrid of the weed Nardus flourishes that doesn't survive in water of lower or higher pH.)

An exciting development is that, despite its comparatively low pH, the feeder offshoot is used by some of the tarn's brown trout for spawning. The young survive because they live in the limestone gravel as alevins and move into the tarn when they become fry.

We are also excited that at time of writing, sea trout and salmon are once again cutting redds in the main outflow beck within two hundred yards of the tarn. This beck was a spawning ground years ago, before the present-day pressures of acid rain.

Soon, we shall be introducing salmon and sea trout parr into the tarn. When they become smolts and congregate for migration in the outflow, they will be transported manually through the fish trap. If and when they return, the dream that Hugh Falkus and I have had – that the tarn should also develop into a wild salmon and sea trout fishery – may well become reality.

ACID RAIN DEVASTATION

Examples of how excessively acid conditions can kill not only juvenile but adult trout, sea trout and salmon, have occurred in the Cumbrian Esk. During a week of heavy spates in the period 16–22 September 1983, exceptionally high acidity caused a mass mortality of fish. This was exactly similar to an earlier disaster in June 1980, when the early run of sea trout and salmon was almost entirely destroyed.

The following extracts are from reports by the North West Water Authority Scientists' Department:

Although retrospective proof of the cause of the major Esk mortality in June 1980 is impossible, we feel that some tentative suggestions can be advanced in relation to recent work on physiological impact of acid stress on fish, and on the influences of aluminium.

Like extremely low pH stress, toxic levels of aluminium cause mucus clogging of the gills, and also induce ionic disequilibrium as measured by rapid loss of plasma salts. Regrettably, no aluminium data is available for the Esk at the time of the fish kill, but subsequent observations have shown a number of tributaries with total aluminium levels between 200 and 500 mg/litre and a negative correlation between pH and aluminium remarkably similar to that found for Swedish clearwater (i.e. non-dystrophic) lakes (Dickson, 1980). Aluminium toxicity is strongly pH dependent, being maximal around pH 5, and it may prove acutely lethal at levels as low as 200 mg/litre. ... It is suggested that pH depression to around 5 in the main river Esk, and elevated levels of mobilised aluminium from more acid tributaries, could account for the mortality in this clearwater system, under summer spate conditions.

R. F. Prigg, Biology Dept., Febuary 1983

The pH in the river Esk, having fallen to below 4.5 (16/9/83), spent several days between 5 and 5.5 which is the range when maximum toxicity due to aluminium may be expected. Brown (1983) found that year-old trout survived in the laboratory for only a few hours in a solution at pH 5.4, 0.5 mg/l, and it is quite likely that conditions very similar to these appertained during the mortality. Limited sampling on 16 and 19 September tend to support this view.

D. H. Crawshaw, River Management Group, July 1984

Bill Arnold writes:

These are just five examples of acidic pollution and its sources. Note the small amount of precipitation in each case. The more rain the higher the pH value, because of dilution. The total volume of pollution irrespective of volume of rain remains the same. The worst situation develops after a dry spell with just sufficient rain to pick up the dry deposition and put the river in spate; it then requires a large amount of neutralizing agents if it is not to act as a killer. It becomes a killer when it is so strong that it leaches aluminium, cadmium, magnesium, etc, from the soils and rocks.

Our Indian summer of 1985 lasted for 21 days from 11 October without any rain. The high pressure systems had established themselves over Europe and we had south and south-east winds. To measure dry deposition I wash the collecting vessels out with 100 milli-litres of ionized water which has a pH value of 5.7. On five days during this dry spell the 'washings' dropped as low as pH 4.5, which shows the acidity of dry deposition. Fortunately, when the rain came again, it came slowly at first and this diluted gradually the accumulated dry deposition before it got into the water courses, In fact it took four days of gentle rain and then a heavy downpour before the river was in spate. Our local fisheries staff and myself lived on tenterhooks because we had a nice stock of sea trout and salmon and we were dreading a repeat fish kill. The eventual heavy downpour helped the river from falling below pH 5.0, and also the fish had been acclimatized.

> According to wind speed and direction, meteorologists can calculate where a parcel of air has been. If it has passed over a densely populated or industrialized area it becomes contaminated and may deposit that contamination hundreds of miles away. These examples of lethal rainfall (as low as pH 3.4!) were recorded by Bill Arnold from his water gauge beside the River Esk. Sampling of the previous day's precipitation or deposition took place each morning at 0800 hours

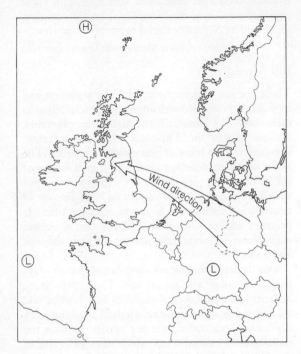

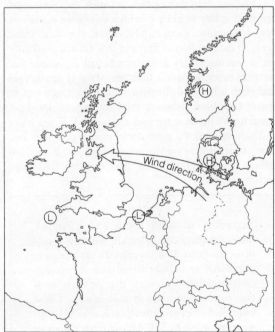

Figure 281: Acid Rain in Cumbria

1. 7 November 1984.
A small amount of rainfall: 5 mm with a pH value of 3.8 (pH 7.0 is regarded as neutral; below is acidic, above is alkali. Average rainfall is pH 5.7). Looking at the previous day's weather chart we found a complex depression with two low pressures to the south and one north-east of the British Isles. The pollution on this occasion came from West Germany and NE England

2. 17 January 1985.
A small amount of snow which, when melted and converted to rainfall, equalled 3 mm. It had a pH value of 3.7. The source of pollution was the same as the previous example. It had been reported on TV and in the press two days earlier, that the people in West Germany were having to wear smog-masks because the air was so polluted, there being no wind to disperse it. Then the east-bound depressions started to push the high pressure system eastwards, with the resultant winds bringing all the pollution our way. (Note: winds are clockwise on the high and anti-clockwise on the low)

3. 27 July 1985.
Rainfall of 7 mm with a value of pH 3.4. The centre of the depression on 26/7/85 was over the Bristol Channel with an air movement from south to north picking up pollution from the south-east, central and north-west of England and depositing it over Cumbria and SW Scotland

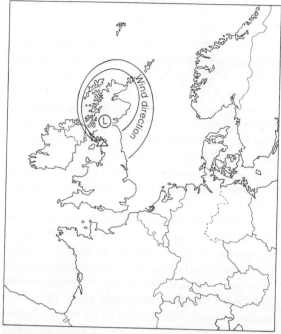

4. 17 August 1985.
Rainfall of 5 mm with a pH value of 3.5. The previous day's weather chart showed the depression situated over central Scotland. The air mass in this instance came from NW England, travelled out over the North Sea, round the north of Scotland and back down the North Channel to fall on Cumbria

5. 30 September 1985.
After the wet summer, there were two really hot days on 28 and 29 with winds from due south. On the early morning of the 30th we had 1.5 mm of rain with a pH value of 3.7. The pollution came from south and north Wales and NW England. On the same day we had a sand deposit which had come from N Africa, i.e. over 2,000 miles

Figure 282: (*below*) H. F. fishing the Cumbrian Esk in the days when it was one of Britain's most prolific little spate rivers

Since 1980, the River Esk has been systematically monitored by scientists of the North West Water Authority. Their research emphasizes that the excessively acidic rainfall becomes even more lethal when it leaches aluminium from the granite slopes of Sca Fell – the river's watershed.

It is significant that the catastrophe of 1980 followed close upon the cessation of lime-spreading four years earlier. Until September 1976, when the removal of the agricultural subsidy put an end to nearly all hill-farm liming, this amount of alkali may have just sufficed to keep the acidity in check.

In the case of the mortality recorded in 1983, the river's pH fell to below 4.5 and then lay there for several days between 5.0 and 5.5, before reverting to its normal low-flow level of pH 6.5. It is thought that the actual cause of fish deaths was the elevated concentration of aluminium (which is at its most toxic at pH 5.0–5.5) exacerbated by the reduction in calcium concentration.

Experimental liming by the NWWA was started in certain restricted areas of Eskdale in 1985. Results were encouraging (see opposite). In consequence, aided by funds from the EEC, liming was considerably increased in 1986.

THE RESULTS OF FIRST-PHASE LIMING PROJECTS (SPOTHOW GILL, R. ESK)

Spothow Gill was a fishless stream, with a poor invertebrate community symptomatic of acid-stress. In July 1982 trout placed in cages in Spothow Gill survived short-term exposures (two-day periods) but in subsequent trials over longer periods they died as a result of toxic concentrations of aluminium during episodes of high flows and low pHs. Similar results were obtained from a similarly acid-stressed unnamed tributary immediately downstream of Spothow Gill.

In June 1985, 13 tonnes of 15 mm limestone chippings were deposited in the upper catchment of Spothow Gill but not in the unnamed tributary. Both pH and Ca concentrations have increased, as a result of liming, in Spothow Gill. Spothow Gill has a geometric mean pH of 5.4 and a calcium concentration of 1.8 mg 1^{-1} before liming, rising to pH 5.7 and 2.2 mg 1^{-1} after liming.

Corresponding changes in the natural fish and invertebrate communities have not yet occurred and this is not surprising. Investigations covering the uplands of the whole north-west region indicate that a geometric mean pH of at least 5.9 is necessary for the long-term establishment of

Figure 283: Changes in the relationships between calcium and flow, and pH and flow before liming (solid circles) and after liming (open circles), Spothow Gill

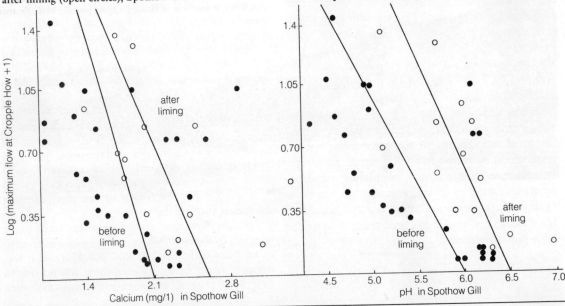

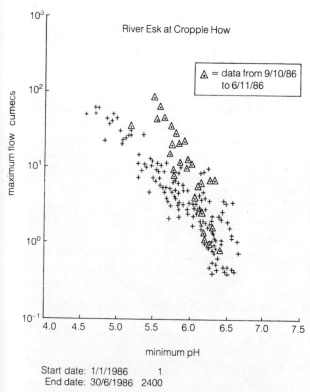

River Esk at Cropple How

△ = data from 9/10/86 to 6/11/86

maximum flow cumecs

minimum pH

Start date: 1/1/1986   1
End date: 30/6/1986   2400

Figure 284: Relationship between flow and pH during 1986

acid-intolerant fauna, i.e. mayflies, snails and freshwater shrimps. As these animals are the staple diet for salmonids in upland streams it is also unlikely that good quality fish populations will develop at geometric means below pH 5.9.

However, the increase in calcium concentration has apparently allowed trout fry to survive periods of high aluminium concentrations. In July 1985 trout fry were stocked in Spothow Gill and in the unnamed (unlimed) tributary downstream. At the end of September 1985 a high density of stocked trout fry remained in the lower reaches of Spothow Gill, but no trout could be found in the unnamed tributary. In summer 1986 a small population of slow-growing *stocked* trout still remained in Spothow Gill in which, prior to liming, no wild trout had been found and in which caged trout died under high flow conditions.

There have been many tales of big fish hooked with the first cast of the day, but the most charming we have read is by John Burroughs in *Locusts and Wild Honey* (1884):

It was a dull, rainy day; the fog rested low upon the mountains, and the time hung heavily on our hands. About three o'clock the rain slackened and we emerged from our den, Joe going to look after his horse, which had eaten but little since coming into the woods, the poor creature was so disturbed by the loneliness and the black flies; I, to make preparations for dinner, while my companion lazily took his rod and stepped to the edge of the big pool in front of camp. At the first introductory cast, and when his fly was not fifteen feet from him on the water, there was a lunge and a strike, and apparently the fisherman had hooked a boulder. I was standing a few yards below engaged in washing out the coffee pail, when I heard him call out:

I have got him now!

Yes, I see you have, said I, noticing his bending pole and moveless line. When I am through I will help you get loose.

No, but I'm not joking, said he. I have got a big fish.

I looked up again, but saw no reason to change my impression and kept on with my work.

It is proper to say that my companion was a novice at fly-fishing, he never having cast a fly until this trip.

Again he called out to me, but deceived by his coolness and nonchalant tones, and by the lethargy of the fish, I gave little heed. I knew very well that if I had struck a fish that held me down in that way I should have been going through a regular war-dance on that circle of boulder-tips, and should have scared the game into activity, if the hook had failed to wake him up. But as the farce continued I drew nearer.

Does that look like a stone or a log? said my friend, pointing to his quivering line, slowly cutting the current up towards the centre of the pool.

My scepticism vanished in an instant, and I could hardly keep my place on the top of the rock.

I can feel him breathe, said the now warming fisherman, just feel that pole.

I put my eager hand upon the butt and could easily imagine I felt the throb or pant of something alive down there in the black depths. But whatever it was it moved like a turtle. My companion was praying to hear his reel spin, but it gave out now and then

Figure 285: The distinguished octogenarian, the Reverend Edward Alston, sometime holder of two British angling records, fishing Glencullen Lough, Co. Galway, for sea trout on what proved to be his last angling holiday. Before his death this lovable cleric probably had a greater knowledge of ancient fishing tackle and early firearms than any contemporary. It was said of Alston that bereaved or sick parishioners could expect two visits in one day (to tide them over the following day) if the local spate stream seemed likely to receive a run of fish

only a few hesitating clicks. Still the situation was excitingly dramatic, and we were all actors. I rushed for the landing net, but being unable to find it, shouted desperately for Joe, who came hurrying back, excited before he had learned what the matter was.

The net had been left at the lake below, and must be had with the greatest despatch. In the meantime I skipped from boulder to boulder as the fish worked this way or that about the pool, peering into the water to catch a glimpse of him, for he had begun to yield a little to the steady strain that was kept upon him.

Presently I saw a shadowy, unsubstantial something just emerge from the black depths, then vanish. Then I saw it again, and this time the huge proportions of the fish were faintly outlined by the white facings of his fins.... I had been a fisher from my earliest boyhood. I came from a race of fishers; trout streams gurgled about the roots of the family tree, and there was a long accumulated and transmitted tendency and desire in me that that sight gratified. I did not wish the pole in my own hands; there was quite enough electricity overflowing from it and filling the air for me. The fish yielded more and more to the relentless pole, till, in about fifteen minutes, from the time he was struck, he came to the surface, then made a little whirlpool when he disappeared again. But presently he was up a second time and lashing the water into foam as the angler led him towards the rock upon which I was perched, net in hand. As I reached towards him, down he went again, and taking another circle of the pool, came up still more exhausted, when, between his paroxysms, I carefully ran the net under him and lifted him ashore, amid, it is needless to say, the wildest enthusiasm of the spectators.

What does he weigh? was the natural enquiry of each; and we took it in turns 'hefting' him. But gravity was less potent to us then than usual, and the fish seemed astonishingly light.

Four pounds, we said, but Joe said more. So we improvised a scale; a long strip of board was balanced across a stick, and our groceries served as weights. A four-pound package of sugar kicked the beam quickly; a pound of coffee was added; still it went up; then a pound of tea, and still the fish had a little the best of it. But we called it six pounds, not to drive too sharp a bargain with fortune, and were more than satisfied. Such a beautiful creature, marked in every respect like a trout of six inches. We feasted our eyes upon him for half an hour. We stretched him upon the ground and admired him, we laid him across a log and withdrew a few paces to admire him; we hung him against the shanty and turned our heads from side to side as women do when they are selecting dress-goods, the better to take in the full force of the effect.

He graced the board or stump that afternoon, and was the sweetest fish taken.

Figure 286: By the look of these Russian flies, purchased by F. B. in the USSR, it would seem that the ability to tie one's own flies is a prerequisite for the Russian fly-fisherman. Judging by the choice of tackle seen in two major cities, rod and fly-line making may also be necessary skills

Cooking the Trout

BAKED STUFFED TROUT

1 trout
2 tablespoonsful butter
Stuffing
Stale bread
$\frac{1}{2}$ stick celery
1 shallot
Parsley
Salt and pepper
Sauce
1 oz butter
1 oz flour
1 teaspoonful capers
1 teaspoonful lemon juice
$\frac{1}{3}$ teaspoonful anchovy essence
Salt and pepper

Make stuffing by grating bread, shallot, celery, parsley and mixing together with salt and pepper. Clean, scale and dry the fish and fill with stuffing.

Sew up. Melt butter in a baking dish, put in fish and bake in a moderate oven for about half an hour, basting frequently. Take fish out and keep hot.

Make sauce by heating butter, sieving in the flour and cooking for a few minutes. Strain in the liquor from the baking tray. If insufficient, make up with hot fish stock or milk. Stir until boiling and smooth, then add capers, lemon juice, anchovy essence, salt and pepper. Pour over fish and serve.

OVEN-COOKED TROUT AND BACON

Clean and dry the fish. Wrap each fish in a slice of bacon. Place fish on a rack inside a roasting tin. Cook in a hot oven for about twenty minutes. Serve with extra slices of bacon and slices of fried bread.

The
SEA TROUT
Salmo trutta trutta

Because of pronounced behavioural differences (as described on page 253 in the brown trout section), we have classified the sea trout as *Salmo trutta trutta* to distinguish it from *Salmo trutta fario*, the brown trout. It must be remembered, however, that physiologically the sea trout is an anadromous brown trout wearing its migratory coat. Sea trout eggs can be fertilized with milt from river trout and *vice versa*, and the offspring are fertile. Tate Regan recalls an experiment where members of a colony of sea trout, prevented from going to sea, subsequently lived and bred in freshwater. He cites a further example of river trout exported to New Zealand, which

became sea trout, finding their way to the sea and becoming an anadromous race. This has also happened in several other places, e.g. the Falkland Islands (see pages 322–3).

Why certain members of a species should migrate to sea whereas others of that species do not, is unknown. So is the origin of the Salmonoidei. The problem is summed up by Dr W. E. Frost and Dr M. E. Brown in their book, *The Trout* (1967):

The sub-order Salmonoidei includes species which live in freshwater, species which are marine and others which are anadromous (breeding in freshwater and feeding in the sea). The freshwater species, with the

---

A sea trout is a migratory brown trout; but there its likeness to a brown trout ends. It is similar in appearance to a salmon, but has very different habits. And before going any further it is necessary for the fisherman to appreciate that sea trout fishing is neither a branch of brown trout nor of salmon fishing: *it is a sport entirely of its own.*

Sea trout have acquired the reputation of being fickle and unpredictable. This is easily understood; few other fish are so sensitive to changes in weather and water. Nevertheless, a forecast of their reaction to these changes is far

from impossible, and it is a point of fundamental importance – on which our fishing philosophy should be based – that sea trout, while in the river on their return from sea, conform to a distinct pattern of behaviour. Failure to understand and take advantage of this pattern is to deny ourselves any real hope of successful fishing. Without understanding, we cannot fish with confidence – and confidence is the fingerpost to success.

Hugh Falkus,
Sea Trout Fishing

Freshwater Fishing

exception of *Retropinna* from New Zealand, are indigenous to the arctic and temperate zones of the Northern Hemisphere. The variety of habit among the Salmonoidei is shown by the following British species: the argentines (*Argentina silus* and *A. sphyraena*) are entirely marine. They are caught in deep waters off the west and south-west of Ireland and are sometimes sold in English fish markets. The smelt (*Osmerus eperlanus*) is a valuable food fish which lives in the sea but comes into estuaries to spawn. The salmon (*Salmo salar*) spawns in freshwater and spends the first two, three or four years of its life in freshwater, but then migrates to the sea from which it returns to spawn in freshwater. The trout (*Salmo trutta*) generally lives in freshwater but may feed in the sea. The British charrs (*Salvelinus alpinus*) are entirely freshwater, but in Scandinavia fish of this species may be anadromous. The British whitefish: the gwyniad, the schelly, the powan, the pollans and the vendace (all species of the genus *Coregonus*) are entirely freshwater and each species inhabits only one or a few lakes.

This gradation in habit from entirely marine through estuarine and anadromous forms to entirely freshwater species raises the question of the ancestry of the whole group – are the freshwater forms more primitive and the marine forms more advanced or

Figure 287: Sea trout, 13 lb, taken on Sunk Lure by H. F.

vice versa? There are two possible explanations for the present state of affairs. The ancestor could have been an entirely marine fish which developed the habit of laying its eggs in estuaries and then became more and more adapted to freshwater so that it bred farther and farther upstream until it lost the habit of returning to the sea even to feed. On the other hand, the ancestor could have been an entirely freshwater fish, living and breeding in freshwater, which began to forage in estuaries and then in the sea and at first returned to freshwater to breed, but then bred in estuaries and finally bred in the sea, losing all connection with freshwater.

The early life of the sea trout is so similar to that of the Atlantic salmon (already described) that there is little point in dealing with it in great detail. Sufficient to say that, like the salmon, the sea trout is born in freshwater where it spends the first two or three years of its life, going through the stages of alevin, fry and parr, finally assuming a silver coat and, as a smolt, migrating to sea.

The full story of the sea trout's life at sea is not known. It has often been said that sea trout travel little further than their local estuaries, but catches made by fishing vessels and fishery

Figure 288: F. B. with a $5\frac{1}{2}$ lb sea trout taken in H. F.'s stretch of fishing in the days before the onslaught of acid rain (see page 287)

research stations indicate that the distance can be substantially greater. In his excellent book *Child of the Tides*, Edward Fahy remarks:

Scottish investigations of sea trout migration suggest that the fish fan out from their natal river. There are numerous examples of individuals moving in excess of 65 miles (about 100 km) along the coast and some may even travel more than 300 miles (about 500 km).

In *Sea Trout Fishing*, H. F. records a sea trout kelt, tagged at the fish trap in the River Axe, south Devon, being recaptured 266 days after liberation. The place of recapture was the estuary of the River Tweed! The minimum distance this fish must have travelled (via the Straits of Dover) was approximately 580 miles. Via the Irish Sea, the distance would have been about 1,130 miles.

Whatever distance it travels, however, the sea trout (like the salmon) goes to sea in order to feed and grow, and while at sea it feeds avidly. Although its tastes are catholic its diet consists mainly of small fish. Sand eels and sprats contribute largely to this diet, together with the fry of herring and mackerel.

In most sea trout rivers there are two main seasonal runs of adult fish: the summer run, which may start as early as April or May in some rivers, but not until June or early July in others – with scatterings of earlier fish – and the autumn or 'harvest' run, which comes up in September.

The biggest fish tend to run early and late in the season. The shoals of young sea trout – known as herling, finnock, whitling, scurf, truff, school-peal or sprod according to the district – begin to appear in the bottom pools towards the end of July.

As many anglers have discovered to their cost, sea trout are extremely shy. No one is certain over exactly what range of the spectrum they are sensitive to colour (although they are certainly colour conscious), but there is no doubt that their vision is unusually acute and that being sensitive to vibration, both from movement on the bank and in the water, they are easily frightened. Disturb one fish and alarm can quickly spread through a shoal even though other fish in the shoal may be unaware of what has caused the disturbance.

Figure 289: Sea trout, $2\frac{1}{2}$ lb, caught at night by H. F. while fishing with F. B. in a Donegal sea lough, June 1970. The small fish underneath is a sparling, *Osmerus eperlanus*, taken from the sea trout's throat immediately after capture. In spite of having its mouth full, the sea trout took the sunk lure also pictured. A graphic example of sea trout behaviour when feeding in salt water

All fish possess otoliths, or earstones, which are located in the back of the brain. These not only assist a sense of balance but, as they are able to register vibration, form part of the warning system that transmits danger signals to the brain. A sea trout responds readily to the low frequencies, but not to the high frequencies. It will remain unaffected by an angler's conversation, but can become alarmed if he treads too heavily on the bank.

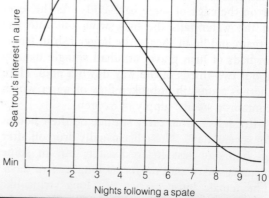

Figure 290: A graph roughly predicting sea trout behaviour

The point is academic, however. Although conversation may not affect the fish it will certainly affect the fisherman. Nothing destroys concentration so effectively as chatter, and concentration is essential to successful fishing; lack of it is one of the most common reasons for fishing failure.

THE ANGLING APPROACH

Sea trout that reach their destined pools during a spate seek shelter for a time from the turbulence and force of the current in the slacker water beside and underneath the bank, in little bays, or on the edge of some back-eddy. As the level of the water falls the fish swing out into the stream and lie in shoals, the larger fish in front, on beds of firm gravel or small shingle usually about two-thirds of the way down a pool. Here there is a smooth unbroken flow of water which contains a steady supply of oxygen.

Fresh fish often carry sea lice on their bodies for several days. These lice usually drop off after 48 hours or less in freshwater, but in some instances may stay on for as long as five days. The female louse carries two long string-like 'tails' or egg-sacs. These soon fall off in freshwater, so that lice with these 'tails' intact are evidence that a fish is very fresh run indeed.

Figure 291: Points of difference between a sea trout (*top*) and a salmon

A sea trout that has been for some time in the river takes a lure less readily than a fish fresh from the sea. This is probably because the longer a sea trout lies in the river the less susceptible it becomes to the sensation of hunger.

While in freshwater waiting to spawn, a sea trout eats very little – for the very good reason that in most rivers there is very little for it to eat. Many rivers which accommodate runs of sea trout are clear, rocky, acid, barren spate rivers that hold only a tiny proportion of the food necessary to support a sea trout population with normal appetites. While in the sea the fish feed greedily. Few rivers can supply such meals.

During their sojourn in freshwater following their return from sea, sea trout (like salmon) have no need for food. The supply of nourishment in their tissues is sufficient both to sustain them during a long fast, and to provide for the developing spawn. This is not to say that sea trout eat no food at all while in the river, but there is a considerable difference between the taking of occasional food items and feeding. If 'feeding' is defined as the taking of nourishment in order to sustain life, then most sea trout are non-feeders in freshwater.

This point is of the utmost importance to the fisherman, in particular to the fly-fisherman.

There are two fundamentally different forms of approach to sea trout fishing:

1. That the fish on their return from sea remain active feeders.

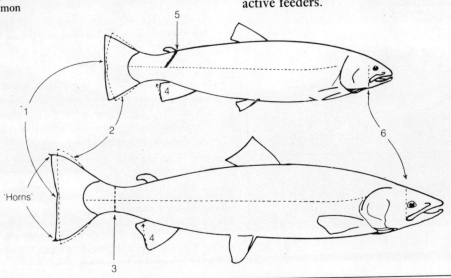

Freshwater Fishing

2. That the fish do not remain active feeders (in the sense already defined).

The fisherman who favours the first will take a bag of sea trout only at certain times and under certain conditions. He will be fishing a fly intended to simulate the natural fly on the water. When the hatch is over and fish have gone down he will lose hope, pack up and go home.

The fisherman who adopts the second approach has always a chance of catching fish. While taking advantage of any hatch that may materialize, he will know this to be merely a passing phase. When the fish are down he will change to a completely different form of lure and technique and continue fishing – with every hope of success.

Chances at sea trout are all too often missed because the angler is informed that 'the food situation is the decidedly dominant influence in the habits of the sea trout', or 'the sea trout has a big appetite and is an aggressive feeder'!

While in the sea the sea trout is certainly an aggressive feeder, its habits undoubtedly dominated by the search for food. But on its return to the river to spawn, nothing could be further from the truth.

Again, it has been said that '... rivers which hold large populations of migratory fish have to contain correspondingly large amounts of natural food'. Again, this is nonsense – simply because they don't. The fast, quick-rising, acid, spate

Sea trout/salmon identification

The main six points of difference are as follows:

1. *Tail*
When relaxed, the tail of a biggish sea trout is straight. When stretched it becomes convex. From being forked when relaxed, the salmon's tail straightens out when stretched – but notice the two 'horns'.

2. *Wrist*
The base of a salmon's tail (the caudal peduncle) has a pronounced 'wrist'. This enables an angler to tail a salmon, either with a mechanical tailer or by hand. The sea trout's broader-based tail has no wrist. Hence, a sea trout should be netted or beached, never tailed.

3. *Scale count*
The scales are counted from the front edge of the adipose fin backwards and downwards to the lateral line.
Sea trout count: 13–16, usually 14
Salmon count: 9–13, usually 11

4. *Anal fin*
With the anal fin *closed*, the *outermost* ray of a sea trout's fin is nearest to the tail. The *innermost* ray of the salmon's fin is nearest to the tail.

5. *Eye*
The sea trout's upper jaw reaches well past the hind edge of the eye. The salmon's upper jaw reaches only to the hind margin of the eye. (See figure 291.)

6. *Tongue*
The sea trout has up to eighteen teeth on the vomerine bone (or tongue) with two to six on the head of the vomer. The salmon has a staggered single row of vomerine teeth, but none on the vomer head.

Figure 292: Tail of $11\frac{1}{4}$ lb sea trout (*left*). Tail of $13\frac{1}{2}$ lb salmon (*right*). Although the trailing edge of a small sea trout's tail is forked, this fork becomes less and less pronounced as the fish increases in weight. At 4 lb to 5 lb the tail becomes square. Upwards of about 8 lb, the tail is convex. A salmon's tail is concave

river, which rises and falls several feet in as many hours, can seldom support more than a tiny population of diminutive brown trout in addition to supplying the needs of salmon and sea trout fry. The adult migrants populating a single pool in such a river would require more food during one summer's day than the river could supply in a year – if the fish were eating the meals to which they have become accustomed at sea. But of course they are not. Nor have they the appetites to do so. Were it otherwise they would, by preying on their own young, have eaten themselves out of existence long ago.

Naturally, not all sea trout waters present the same picture. Sea trout that run into those food-rich lakes contained between river systems often take more interest in food than their counterparts found in a spate river. In rivers containing a plentiful food supply, sea trout can sometimes be seen taking nymph or rising to a hatch of fly. But the reason for this interest in food is not because the fish have suddenly acquired an appetite, but because the food has suddenly appeared in front of them. Broadly speaking, the sea trout's interest in a food item (or, for that matter, the angler's lure) is similar to that well known mountaineer's interest in his mountain – because it is there!

If it is not there, sea trout make little or no effort to search for it. In many rivers sea trout stop hunting for food from the time they run from the sea, to their eventual return from the spawning redds. Sometimes, however, if a worm or maggot or a spinner or feathered lure is put in front of them they will take it. And the reason why they do so is probably because of habit – the feeding habit they have indulged so recently and so avidly at sea.

It would be folly to expect sea trout behaviour to conform to an exact pattern in all rivers. The behaviour of many species of animals depends largely on environment, and like salmon, sea trout are no exception. For generation after generation fish return to the rivers that bred them. This is so consistent that populations of migratory fish in rivers only a few miles apart undoubtedly follow slightly separate lines of evolution.

Nevertheless, sea trout, like salmon, are equipped to endure a fast while in freshwater, and although their behaviour may vary according to their environment, comparatively few can (by the terms of our definition) be called feeding fish.

This is the difference between the river behaviour of sea trout and brown trout. The difference between the behaviour of sea trout and salmon is that while the salmon tends to take a lure mainly by day, the sea trout tends to do so mainly by night.

Thus, the concept of a non-feeding fish, which is more active by night than by day and which takes a lure or bait because of habit rather than hunger, is a very sound basis from which to start thinking about how to catch sea trout.

Opposite (in colour)
H. F.'s SALMON AND SEA TROUT FLIES

These selections of river and loch flies, when fished in their correct context, will catch fish in almost any water conditions day or night. Further details of H. F.'s flies and his methods of using them will be found in his books: *Salmon Fishing* and *Sea Trout Fishing*.

Salmon box (left to right)
 1 Tubes, various (4)
 2 Sunk Lure
 3 Shrimp Fly
 4 Prawn Fly
 5 Falkus Fancies, various (2)
 6 Surface Riffler
 7 Stoat's Tail, various (3)
 8 Dee Specials, various (6)
 9 Yellow Esks (3)
 10 Yellow Dollies (dry flies) (3)
 11 Loch flies, various (9)
(including Black Buzz,
Silver Muddler
and Elverine)

Sea trout box (left to right)
 1 Surface Lures (2)
 2 Sunk Lures (3)
 3 Medicines (2)
 4 Flying Medicines (2)
 5 Tubes, various (2)
 6 Black Demon
 7 Secret Weapons, various (3)
 8 Moths (3)
 9 Silver Cowan
 10 Maggot Flies (2)
 11 Gold Cowan (dry fly)
 12 Worm Flies (2)
 13 Yellow Esks (3)
 14 Small Doubles, various (4)
 15 Loch flies, various (8)(including Flying Muddler, Loch Ordie and 3 dapping flies)

The dapper's reward – a beautiful wild 5 lb 5½ oz Mask trout, taken off 'Long Island' by F. B. on a dapped grasshopper

Sea trout lough at dusk,
Connemara

Right: 8 lb brown trout,
caught dapping on Lough
Curra with a double grasshopper by the Rev. Paddy
Whelan

At dusk, as the wind falls away leaving a lone angler standing on the rocky shore of Shintilla, an island in Lough Mask, the style of fishing must be changed. The traditional team of wet-flies give way to the dry-fly or to a small imitative nymph. Now the fly must be placed in the path of a single feeding fish

Below: Negley Farson in his classic *Going Fishing* (1942) propounded the mystique of the fishing rod '... I love rods – because of their associations, the places they have brought me to ... This magic wand has revealed to me some of the loveliest places on earth.' Your rod may take you to one of these places. The authors' rods have often taken them close (sometimes too close) to this outcrop of rock – the Shintillas – where great Lough Mask trout are waiting

SEA TROUT BY NIGHT

In the Night usually the best Trouts bite, and will rise ordinarily in the still deeps; but not so well in the Streams. And although the best and largest Trouts bite in the Night (being afraid to stir, or range about in the Daytime) yet I account this way of Angling both unwholsom, unpleasant and very ungentiel, and to be used by none but Idle pouching Fellows ... as for Damming, Groping, Spearing, Hanging, Twitcheling, Netting, or Firing by Night, I purposely omit them, and them esteem to be used only by disorderly and rascally Fellows, for whom this little Treatise is not in the least intended.

James Chetham, *The Angler's Vade-Mecum* (1681)

The sea trout madness is not quite so widespread as the salmon madness already described. But what the sea trout lunatics lack in number they make up for in degree. Salmon anglers, after all, are merely trying to tempt non-feeding fish to take something that vaguely represents food. But sea trout anglers are not only trying to hook fish, most of which have little or no appetite, they frequently elect to do it at night – and on very dark nights at that.

Sea trout can, of course, be caught on a variety of baits and lures at any hour of the day, and many are. But loch fishing apart and with the exception of a few rivers which particularly suit daylight fishing, most sea trout taken on fly are caught between the hours of dusk and dawn. For a steadily growing band of dedicated anglers, sea trout on the fly at night represents the very cream of freshwater fishing.

Night fly-fishing is a difficult sport and, naturally, it is not to everybody's taste. Indeed, anyone who does not derive a deep delight from spending long hours in the darkness with only the wind and water as his companions, should abandon any serious thought of it. It can, however, be a highly rewarding sport, for unless the river is in spate and coloured there is no night of the season when sea trout cannot be caught.

This is a view at variance with much that has been written on the subject. Many writers are of the opinion that sea trout night fly-fishing is a chancy sport, worthwhile only in certain favourable conditions, seldom profitable after midnight and that many blank nights can be expected: an opinion founded on ignorance, both of sea trout and of the best flies (or lures) with which to catch them.

Apart from the occasional big fish that remains apart from its fellows in its own carefully guarded lie, sea trout tend to herd together in shoals. And although during the hours of darkness they will accept a degree of disturbance not tolerated during daylight, mass alarm affects them just as it does porpoises, herring-gulls and other group species. For this reason, if for no other, the angler should cultivate stealth.

No matter how suitable his tackle and lures, no matter how skilfully he may cast, it is pointless if the fish have fled. He must learn to think and act like a hunter, move quietly both in and out of the water, know where sea trout are lying or are likely to be lying and, above all, understand at least some of the reasons why he fails to catch them.

There are anglers who arrive on a river bank in herds in broad daylight, thunder about against the skyline, wade in among the lies, thrash their lines across water from which every fish has vanished – and at the end of a fruitless hour make the night hideous with their wailing.

Starting to fish clear-water pools too soon before dusk is one of the most common sea trout fishing faults and probably results in more missed opportunities than any other. Unless the water is rippled sufficiently to obscure the angler and to 'absorb' the splash of his line, it is a golden rule never to start casting until well after the sun has set. Then, provided the water is fished stealthily, one pool is ample for a night's fishing.

When a river is well stocked with fish there is little to be gained by rushing about from place to place. If the angler has a good holding pool at his disposal to fish as he likes, he will do best to stay where he is. He knows he is covering fish. If sea trout are not taking in his pool they are unlikely to be doing so elsewhere. Better by far to become intimate with that piece of water, set up two rods and try the many variations of lure and technique available on both floating and sinking lines.

The exception to this occurs early in the season when the main sea trout run has yet to come and fish are spread very thinly throughout the beat. Then, mobility is more important than variety of method, and the best chance of taking fish is to choose one method, use one rod and cover as much water as possible.

Quite irrespective of any hatch of fly, there are three main taking periods:
1. From dusk until about midnight (the 'first-half').
2. From about 1.30 until daybreak (the 'second-half').
3. The hour of sunrise ('extra-time').

As may be expected, the period between first-half and second-half is known as 'half-time'. Although sport is often slack during this period, it is a useful break for the angler, allowing time for a rest and a change of tackle.

The angler who packs up at half-time, thinking the fish are down for the night, deprives himself of many chances, not least, the chance of catching a big sea trout. On average, more big fish are caught *after* midnight.

During the first-half, when sea trout are active and will take a fly swimming close to the surface, the angler will do well to fish a 'medicine' type lure on floating line. It is best fished fairly fast. But since this lure is supposed to simulate a little fish, the angler will be wise to present it at a speed possible for a creature of that size to attain.

Sometimes sea trout remain active all through the night. On these occasions the same fly can be fished, and an exceptional bag taken. But such nights are rare. A typical night usually starts with a taking period lasting perhaps from 45 minutes to an hour and a half. After this, fish usually stop taking and 'go down'. Quite suddenly the river seems utterly lifeless, the fly swings across the pool untouched, and at this point many anglers lose heart and go home.

Unless they have to be up early in the morning, or have no relish for late-night fishing, they are almost invariably wrong. The fish are certainly down, and the chances are they will stay down, but if the angler has the recommended lures and presents them correctly he can enjoy opportunities of catching fish throughout the night. He will, however, need to make considerable changes in technique during the second-half.

Now that the fish are inactive, a lure must be offered to them in such a way that it can be taken with the minimum of effort. This means sinking it close to the bottom and getting it to swing round in front of a fish's nose as slowly as possible. On most nights, unless fished for in this manner, very few sea trout will be caught.

Knowing this, the experienced angler will have equipped himself with the appropriate tackle: hence the second rod, set up ready with Wet-cel line and sunk lure.

Figure 293: The Steeple Cast: A very practical cast for the night fly-fisherman with a line of bushes behind

Position at start of back cast

Position at top of back cast. The line has been sent curling high in the air over the bushes

The cast is made with very fast acceleration. The rod raised with a stiff arm straight up above the head

Start of the forward cast

Figure 294: Record British sea trout – 28 lb 9 oz sea trout caught on 21 July 1987 at Wilford netting station at Northam on the River Tweed. Reputedly a 29-pounder was caught on the same day by fishers below Northam Castle

It is important that the principles of sunk lure fishing should be clearly understood. The angler who thinks that it consists merely of sinking the lure is deluding himself. A lure or fly will fish correctly only when its longitudinal axis forms a direct continuation of the leader and line. It is, then, the line that maintains the position of the lure close to the bottom.

The line must be fully sunk. A floating or semi-floating line will prevent the lure from swimming on an even keel and tend to lift its nose as soon as it is moved.

The use of a weighted lure is of value only in a strong current. But when the water is slack it is impossible to fish a heavy lure slowly enough, and it is in the slacker, deeper water that most sunk line fishing at night is carried out. True, the lure must fish deep, but it must also fish slowly without losing its trim. For this reason, a light iron or mount is more effective than a heavy one.

Everything relating to the Sunk Lure applies equally to fishing the small double, or maggot, or the Secret Weapon, often a deadly method of catching sea trout late at night. In both cases, the secret is to fish deep and slow.

Another lure that should be tried at regular intervals during the second-half is the Surface Lure (see page 311). This was exchanged for the Medicine on the first rod as soon as the first-half ended, and now stands ready for use. Indeed, it is now that it has its greatest chance of success. For reasons unknown, a sea trout that declines a fly fished just under the surface, or a sunk fly or maggot bounced off its nose, will sometimes rise furiously to a lure which is dragged across the surface.

That the period when the fish are down and sunk line fishing is in operation should also be suitable for surface fishing with floating line seems paradoxical. But on most nights – at least early in the season – it is never really dark until after midnight, and darkness is all-important for the Surface Lure.

Just beyond daybreak the Surface Lure is exchanged for a small Medicine, or a tiny double, which can be fished well into daylight.

During the magic hour of sunrise most sea trout fishermen, exhausted after an all-night session, are drinking a 'nightcap' and watching the sky catch fire behind the hills.

A pity, really. Now in the cool of the morning there is a splendid chance of hooking a salmon....

Sea trout night flies

A fish caught on a home-made fly is a greater satisfaction to the fisherman than one which has been tricked by a fly bought in a shop. Why? Because it better satisfies the fisherman's instinctive desire to re-create conditions in which he depends on himself alone in his voluntary contest with nature. There is no hostility in this contest.

Arthur Ransome, *Rod and Line*

With a little practice any angler can soon learn to tie successful flies provided he tries to avoid neatness and a polished finish. Like salmon, sea trout prefer something rather drab, straggly and well chewed.

One point must be made clear, however; presentation is all-important. No fly, however famous, will live up to its reputation if not fished attractively.

In common with most flies and lures, a variety of exotic materials may be added to the sea trout fly, and if the confidence of the angler depends on their addition they should, of course, be included. But simplicity is the keynote of success. The purpose of a lure is to entice, and a simple, sparsely dressed lure will entice more effectively than one that is lumpy and heavily dressed. In this context it is necessary to emphasize that, in common with salmon flies, most sea trout 'flies' are simply *lures*.

It is easy to allow fly dressing to become a complicated and esoteric art. The novice, faced with a list of fly dressings, may well despair not only of the mechanics of construction but the cost and difficulty of obtaining the supposedly vital materials.

It is all nonsense. Forget the name a fly has been given; think merely of what you want it to look like and use the most practical materials available. Christmas tinsels, coloured silks from ladies' knickers, hairs from the dog, silver and gold marker pens, nail varnish, feathers found at the waterside, wine bottle corks, sewing thread and pieces of wool are just a few of the items that have contributed to Hugh Falkus's sea trout and salmon flies over the years.

There are few rivers that do not possess some special fly patterns which, it is claimed, hold magic properties. Sometimes, indeed, they may, and if the locals catch fish on them so should the visitor. But he should not regard them as the only flies worth trying. Many local anglers are inclined to be conservative both in their choice of flies and methods of fishing.

The few lures we describe have proved their worth many times on many different rivers. Anyone fishing them on suitable tackle should seldom experience a blank night.

The Medicine

Dressing: Wing: wigeon, teal or brown mallard feather, badger, deer, dog or bear hair
Hackle: Blue
Body: Silver
Sizes: 3, 4, 5

Since in many rivers adult sea trout seldom show much interest in food, the angler's object is to tempt the fish and stimulate their feeding responses by presenting them with a lure that is tenuous and tantalizing.

A great variety of flies and lures will serve this purpose, but one that we can recommend, in the beaten way of experience, is the Medicine. This is a general purpose fly: good at night in clear water, and during the day when the river is in spate or slightly coloured. (It is also a good grilse fly – ideal for fishing the streamy, broken water at the neck of a pool.)

It should be tied in sizes 3, 4, 5, on the lightest low-water salmon hook procurable. The features of a good sea trout lure of this type – one intended to stimulate a little fish – are simplicity and slimness. A slim-line dressing on a low-water hook with silver-painted shank provides just that.

When sea trout are taking well at dusk, in streamy water, we have found nothing to beat the Medicine. A tube-fly, too, gives good results, but the slim-line body of a silver-painted low-water hook seems to get more offers.

The Medicine can, of course, be fished effectively all night, provided both floating line and sunk line techniques are used. But, generally speaking, the night fly-fisherman will get better results after midnight by using Sunk Lure, Surface Lure or Secret Weapon, especially if conditions become difficult: a sharp drop in temperature, ground mist, bright starlight, distant thunder, etc.

Note: The Medicine can also be tied Secret-Weapon style with tail treble (see colour picture of flies). This is very helpful when fish are 'coming short' and nipping at the fly.

The Falkus Sunk Lure

The Sunk Lure is a very lightweight lure, good for both sea trout and salmon. It is an excellent clear-water night fly-fishing lure for sea trout of all sizes – and especially good for hooking the really big fish. H. F. has taken a number of sea trout over 10 lb on this lure at night (one is pictured on page 299), in addition to the occasional salmon. Indeed, this is the only lure H. F. knows that will catch salmon with any consistency late on dark nights (see his book, *Salmon Fishing*, pages 85–89). It is also a successful daytime salmon lure for sunk line spring and autumn fishing.

The Sunk Lure seldom fails to catch fish. Except on those occasions when the river is in spate, and coloured, the night fly-fisherman armed with this lure should experience few blank nights. Its particular merit is to attract fish late on – usually after midnight – when so often the fish have 'gone down' and are refusing conventional flies. Provided the night is dark enough, it will catch fish when the river is at dead summer low; also when the water is running high but clear after successive spates – never good conditions for catching sea trout.

It should be fished slowly on a sunk line.

A weighted lure is often recommended for sunk line fishing, but the object of sunk line fishing for sea trout (and salmon, for that matter) is to fish the lure slowly. Except in a strong current a heavy lure will not 'work' so attractively as a light lure.

It is on the way in which the line is fished that the behaviour of the lure depends.

A fish is usually hooked on the tail hook. The advantage of having two hooks set well apart in tandem on a flexible mount is that when the fish turns and runs, the top hook sometimes catches in the underside of the fish's jaw, effecting a double hold. If the tail hook comes away (which often happens with a big sea trout early in the season) the fish is still held by the top hook.

CONSTRUCTION (see figure 295)

1. Put a seating of tying silk half-way along the shank of the tail hook.

2. Loop the nylon (22–24 lb BS) round to the hook and bring both ends out through the eye. The thickness of the nylon used will depend on the size of the hook and the intended length of the lure. It should be stiff enough to support the tail hook without drooping.

Note: The lure can be made in lengths of 2–3 in. The standard length recommended for sea trout night fly-fishing is $2\frac{1}{2}$ in.

3. Whip the nylon to the shank of the hook.

Freshwater Fishing

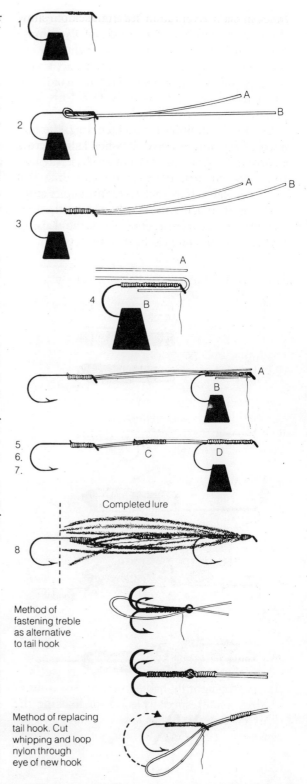

Figure 295: The Sunk Lure. *Dressing*: A blue hackle feather along either side of the mount with some strands of peacock herl overlaid. The dressing should not extend beyond the point of the tail hook. Fish on leader of 12–14 lb BS

4. Bring the longer strand B through the eye of the top hook and back along the shank. Cut off strand A level with the eye of the hook.

5. Whip the nylon to the shank of the top hook, taking care to maintain equal tension in the two strands. Put extra turns of tying silk round the hook at D to provide extra strength at this point.

6. Whip part of the link at C.

7. Varnish mount. Then coat with silver paint.

8. Apply dressing. It is important that the tail of the dressing should not extend past the point of the tail hook.

9. Touch off the head of the lure with red varnish.

Note: Don't overdress the lure. A tenuous dressing is more effective than something thick and bushy. Two blue hackle feathers, one tied either side, with a few strands of peacock herl on top is the standard dressing.

A small treble can be used at the tail, if preferred. Or the mount can be tied up with two small doubles (see colour picture); this swims well and is a good hooker.

When mounting the top hook on no account fail to bring the longer strand B up through the eye and back along the shank. This method of construction makes it virtually impossible for the mount to 'draw'.

Completed lure

Method of fastening treble as alternative to tail hook

Method of replacing tail hook. Cut whipping and loop nylon through eye of new hook

The Surface Lure

On a dark night, no matter how low the river, the drag caused by a floating lure or a big dry-fly moving across the surface of the water can provide a deadly attraction for sea trout (and, incidentally, for brown trout, too). Although the Surface Lure is of use only in darkness, it gives an angler the chance of hooking a really big fish and no night fisherman should ever be without one.

The principle underlying its attraction is different from that of any other type of lure.

Indeed, the technique of fishing it is the antithesis of all customary methods of fly-fishing. When an angler is fishing in daylight, the V-shaped drag caused by his fly skidding across the water is something he is careful to avoid; but when fishing at night with Surface Lure it is precisely this drag he is trying to create.

Obviously, in order to produce drag, the lure must be kept on the move. If, when fished across a current, the line is allowed to go slack, the lure will begin to drift downstream and drag will cease. Similarly, if in slack water the angler stops stripping-in line the lure will stay motionless, instantly losing its attraction. It is the wake of the lure, not the lure itself, that attracts fish.

Figure 296: The Surface Lure. Fish on a leader of 10–12 lb BS

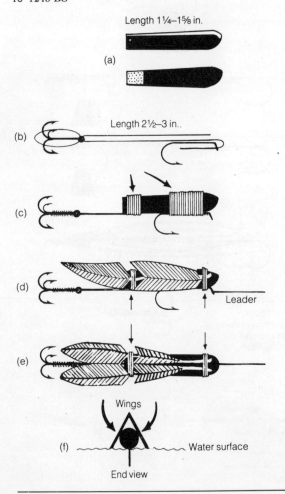

Length 1¼–1⅝ in.

(a)

Length 2½–3 in.

(b)

(c)

(d)

Leader

(e)

Wings

(f)

Water surface

End view

The lure *must* float. Provided it does so and provided it causes a wake, almost anything of reasonable size and shape will catch fish. A piece of cork or balsa wood trimmed to size will serve admirably. A length of quill plugged with cork can also be used.

The leader should be attached a short distance from the nose (as shown in figure 296 (d)). This keeps the lure cocked up slightly as it moves across the water and helps to prevent it from being dragged under. If the lure dips beneath the surface, drag ceases immediately and the lure becomes ineffective.

Strangely, the success of the Surface Lure varies from season to season. Some years it catches a lot of sea trout, in others very few; even so, it is capable of attracting the biggest fish in the pool on a night when all other methods fail.

MAKING A SURFACE LURE

1. Trim a wine cork or piece of balsa to the desired size and shape, or cut and plug a length of goose quill (figure 296 (a)).
2. Prepare a mount in exactly the same way as described for the Sunk Lure, using either an eyed or an eyeless treble on the tail (figure 296 (b)).
3. Whip the mount to the cork or quill body (see arrows, figure 296 (c)) and varnish.
4. Colour is unimportant but, if desired, the whole thing can be given a coat of silver paint.
5. Dressing, too, is unimportant. But when the silver paint is dry, two 'wings' can be attached (figure 296 (d) and (e)). These are by no means essential for catching fish, but have the merit of increasing the angler's confidence and making the lure more stable in the water (figure 296 (f)). Any small dark feathers will do, e.g. grouse.

FISHING THE SURFACE LURE

A still, warm, cloudy night is best, without moon or stars, but no conditions are hopeless. Provided the night is dark enough (as a rough guide the wake of the lure should not be visible to the angler) sea trout will take the Surface Lure at any hour. The most likely period, however, is between one and three in the morning. The best places to fish are unrippled runs, and pool tails where the water flows in a steady glide. All holding water is worth trying so long as the

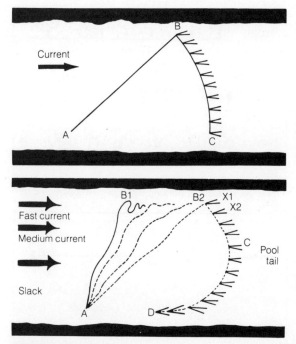

Figure 297: Fishing the Surface Lure

a fish will make a dash at the lure, just as it is about to be recovered, so it is essential that the speed of the lure should not decrease between C and D. If anything, it should increase.

It is important to remember that a fish will ignore a Surface Lure drifting with the current. Only when the lure 'comes to life' and begins to swim against and across the current are a fish's predatory instincts aroused. To take advantage of this is the reason for casting a loose line from A to B1. This sudden 'coming to life' of the lure at B2 (see figure 298) is very attractive.

This ruse may sometimes induce a fish to take after it has risen to but refused the lure at some other point of the cast. Mark the position of the fish and move slightly downstream. Then, cast above the fish and let the lure drift down, checking it at the right moment and bringing it across the fish's nose.

As the current tightens the line and the lure suddenly whips into action, a fish will often react by rushing straight at the lure and seizing it fiercely – a most exciting moment.

To attempt to fish the lure with a sticky line is a waste of time and effort. A considerable amount of line has to be shot at every cast, and this is impossible unless the line is running smoothly through the rod rings.

surface is calm enough for the lure to leave a wake.

During every cast, the lure must be kept skimming across the surface right up to the moment of recovery. It is not unusual for a fish to follow for some distance and take just as the lure is leaving the water; but if the lure falters and loses 'life', the fish will have nothing more to do with it.

A large Surface Lure is not an easy object to cast with a light trout rod. However, once this difficulty is overcome the tactics are simple enough.

When fishing down a 'run' or a pool tail (see figure 297), cast a loose line from A to B1, and then flick out a little more slack. Allow the lure to drift downstream with the current for three or four yards. At B2 the slack will take-up and the line tighten on the lure – which will immediately form a pronounced 'V' and begin to swing round on the arc B2C. Let it continue to fish round to C, then work it quickly and steadily towards you to D. Fish will take anywhere between B2 and D, usually at X1 and X2. Sometimes, however,

Figure 298: B2 shows the point at which the lure 'comes to life'

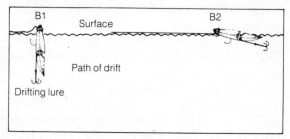

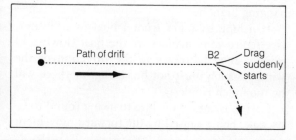

It is an advantage to use a heavier line than usual. This helps to punch the lure out against a wind, and to shoot the slack line that accumulates during the final 'work-in' – especially when stillwater is being fished.

In normal conditions use a leader of eight or nine feet; but if there is a head wind put on a heavier, shorter leader of not more than five or six feet.

In moonlight, or at dawn, fish fine. Sometimes fish will take in the half light – but only if you cast a slender, delicate lure on a fairly light leader.

In conditions of disturbed water, fish a tubby lure that causes sufficient drag to overcome the surface ripple. Generally speaking, use a larger lure on a 'run' than when fishing the smooth water of a pool tail.

Not infrequently one is faced with a piece of good holding water beyond casting range and impossible to cover by normal methods – an overgrown 'run' or glide (see figure 299), where depth of water, trees, bushes or other obstructions prevent the angler from going further downstream. Fish in these difficult pieces of water can be covered satisfactorily by carrying out the following procedure with a floating line and a much longer leader than normal.

Wade out to A, and let the lure drift downstream along the edge of the current by stripping off line. Work the lure in zig-zags across the stream (see the dotted lines in the diagram) by holding the rod parallel to the water on either side of you, at arm's length if necessary, and controlling the length of line by means of a coil in the non-casting hand.

Try 'hanging' the lure in the stronger parts of the current, and vary the path of the lure sometimes by drawing it upstream in the slacker water by the bank, perhaps underneath overhanging branches.

If fishing by night from a boat in stillwater, (see figure 300), manoeuvre the boat slowly and quietly at right-angles to the direction of the wind – which must not be strong, or there will be too much ripple.

Cast to B, and allow lure to swing round to C, its wake being caused by the forward movement

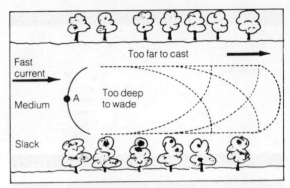

Figure 299: Reaching holding water beyond casting range

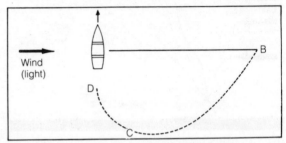

Figure 300: Boat fishing with the Floating Lure

of the boat. Work in from C to D. Fish may take at any point of the cast.

You can of course take fish by trailing the lure, but this method has one serious disadvantage: in the darkness long distances may be covered towing a streamer of weed. This wastes a good deal of time and exhausts patience.

Wherever you may be fishing don't let the lure slow down or stop at the end of a cast. When recovering, preparatory to casting again, do so with a steady, easy movement, speeding the lure up over its last yard or two.

A word of warning: the Surface Lure is not the easiest lure to cast, especially in anything of a wind. Any angler who has not previously fished it is advised to practise casting it in daylight.

The Secret Weapon

If you put a Cod-bait or Gentle, either natural or artificial, but Natural better, at point of your Dub-fly Hook,
they will take the Dub fly better, especially the Salmon
Smelt.

James Chetham, *The Angler's Vade-Mecum* (1681)

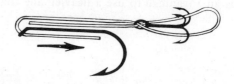

Figure 302: The Secret Weapon

There are times when the combination of fly
and maggot can be a very successful method of
catching sea trout at night. The conventional
lure is a small fly tied on a single hook, with one
or more maggots impaled on the bend of the
hook.

When a sea trout takes with gusto, this
arrangement is quite satisfactory, since (together
with the maggots) the hook is sucked inside the
fish's mouth. But sea trout do not always take in
such an obliging manner. Sometimes, using the
very front of the mouth, a fish will give the
maggots a little tweak (figure 301 (a)) and then
let them go again (rather in the same way that a
salmon will nip shrimp or prawn). It usually
occurs when rain is imminent, or when the night
turns cold in the small hours.

A fish behaving like this cannot be hooked on
conventional tackle because the hook is never
inside its mouth. All the angler feels is a series
of infuriating little tugs. Although he may strike
until his arm aches, his only reward is a slack
line.

The Secret Weapon puts an end to all this.
Now, when a sea trout tweaks a maggot
(figure 301 (b)) it finds itself lip-hooked by the
tiny treble lying astern of the main hook.

Fly/maggot fishing often provides good sport
late at night during the second-half when sea
trout have 'gone down'. In these conditions fish
are not inclined to race about in pursuit of a lure.
To ensure the best chance of its being taken,

therefore, the Secret Weapon must be placed
right in front of their noses. To achieve this it is
fished very slowly on a quick-sinking, smooth-
shooting line.

Fishing the Secret Weapon is delicate work
and very exciting. To avoid damaging the
maggots a special form of casting action should
be developed. It is quite impossible to describe
this cast, other than to say that it should be as
'soft' as possible, without jerkiness, all slack line
being shot first time with no false casting.

When they are in a tweaking mood, fish are
likely to be very lightly hooked through the skin
of the lip. Great care must be taken when playing
them. The tension of the reel should be slackened
and the fish handled as though on cotton.

CONSTRUCTION (see figure 302)

1. Lay a seating of fine tying silk along the shank
of a size 14 or 16 treble.

2. Loop a short length of 12 lb BS nylon round
the treble and bring both ends out through the
eye from opposite sides.

3. Whip the nylon to the shank of the treble.

4. Whip the two strands of nylon together just
above the eye of the treble.

5. Bring one strand of nylon through the eye of
a size 8 slender short-pointed hook and back
along the shank. Cut off the other strand level
with the eye of the hook.

Figure 301: The Secret Weapon. Fish on leader of 5–6 lb
BS

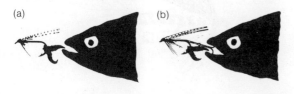

(a)   (b)

7. Varnish mount.
8. Apply dressing. Brown hackle, fluffed out, with a sparse 'wing' of brown mallard.
9. Varnish head of lure.

Avoid neatness in the dressing. The overall effect should be a small brown straggly-looking creature. It is a fiddly thing to make, but gloriously rewarding on the river in the small hours of a summer night.

Note: An example of re-discovery (see page 418). The sea trout Secret Weapon was designed by H. F. during a frustrating night's fishing in August 1962 (sixteen offers, three fish landed). The prototype was tied the following afternoon and fished later that night. Result: eleven offers; nine fish landed. Here was success. Here was an original type of lure: a new idea.

Not so. W. H. Lawrie had designed a lure on similar lines nearly twenty years earlier.

Like so many other examples quoted in this book, H. F.'s sea trout Secret Weapon was a re-discovery of an angling principle already published by the author of *Border River Angling*. By kind permission, we print the following extract:

As every angler of experience knows very well, there are nights, apparently perfect in regard to weather and water conditions, when trout appear to be 'rising

Figure 303: A simple, inexpensive but thoroughly practical fishing shelter. It is set with its back to the prevailing wind, and fenced against farm animals. A rain shelter of this type is of great value to the sea trout night fly-fisherman. Here he can sit out the heaviest shower in comparative comfort. During periods of really heavy rain, fishing is usually poor, but it can be very good immediately the rain stops. Sea trout often take furiously at night just after a thunderstorm has passed by, or during the intervals between heavy showers

Note: It is very important that the distance between treble and hook is not too great. As a guide, the eye of the treble should be about level with the bend of the hook.
6. Whip the nylon mount to the hook shank, taking care to maintain equal tension in the two strands. Put extra turns of tying silk round the mount at the end nearest the treble to provide maximum strength at this point.

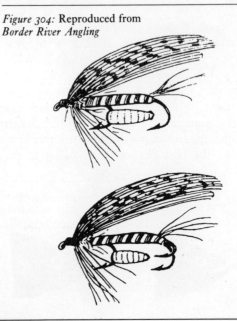

Figure 304: Reproduced from *Border River Angling*

short', or, as it is personally believed, to be devoting attention to the maggot alone. Nothing is more annoying than the constant failure to hook the author of repeated half-hearted offers, very often a good fish. On such occasions it is usually recommended that the line be shortened, and this is good advice up to a point, but does not greatly remedy matters. In an attempt to solve the problem the writer designed a hook which, while in no way interfering with dressing facilities, would greatly increase the probability of secure hooking. It has proved so successful in seasons past that the ordinary hook has now been abandoned entirely. The illustrations explain the idea, and it will be noted that the hackle effectively conceals the small hook.

The original consisted of two separate hooks, a size 16 being whipped to the usual night iron, dressing then being tied on as usual, but, as the idea has proved so successful, further efforts were made to perfect the design and double hooks were substituted for the single iron. It will be appreciated that any trout which is taking the maggot and disregarding the fly has little chance in avoiding the large hook(s).

W. H. Lawrie, *Border River Angling* (1939)

The Worm-Fly

Dressing: Brown or black hen hackles
Body: Peacock herl
Length: $1\frac{1}{4}$–$1\frac{1}{2}$ in.
This is a very good lure for sea trout on a late August night. A twist or two of green fluorescent silk showing through the body dressing of peacock herl seems to be effective, but whether its inclusion really makes any difference is questionable.

The Small Double

Dressing: Black hen hackle, with teal or brown mallard wing

Body: Silver
Size: 12/14 double iron
This little fly sometimes does well when sea trout are in a tweaking mood and being finicky. It is difficult for a fish to tweak such a tiny fly without being hooked (although some manage to do it!). When the angler has no opportunity or inclination to fish with maggot, the Small Double provides a good substitute for the Secret Weapon.

Fish taking it are usually well hooked.

Note: This size of double iron is just right for a salmon on a summer evening in low water.

Tackle

Together with the many other (more conventional) sea trout night fly-fishing lures, the few we recommend should give an angler good service on most rivers. He will, however, need certain items of tackle for a night's fishing:
Two rods (one set up with floating line, the other with sinking line)
A case of lures
Some spools of nylon of different thicknesses; or better, a case containing a selection of leaders ready looped and cut to length
A landing net
A 'priest'
A bag for carrying fish
A torch
A pair of scissors
A bottle of midge repellent

Flashlamp

Some sort of torch is essential at night. Needless to say, it should not be flashed on the water being fished. When you re-tie a fly, or unravel a tangle in cast or line, keep well back from the river.

The best place for a flashlamp when you wish to use it is in your mouth. This leaves both hands free and the beam can be directed exactly where you wish, so a light slender-bodied torch is the most practical.

To enable the teeth to maintain a grip, wrap a piece of Elastoplast round the base of the torch. To preserve your night vision, cover the lens with a piece of red cellophane.

Scissors

Scissors are essential. To avoid dropping them in the river or in long grass, especially at night, fasten them as shown in figure 305 and hang them round your neck. Blunt-ended scissors prevent any danger of getting proggled.

Rod carrying

A little dodge useful at night is the 'Pipe-Cleaner Safety Catch' (see figure 305). Twisted round rod and leader, as shown, it prevents a fly (or a spinner) from escaping and blowing into bushes or tree branches.

Leader carriers

To avoid tying knots in the darkness, some anglers prefer to carry spare leaders with flies attached, in which case a serviceable carrier can be made for nothing from old Christmas and invitation cards (see below).

Figure 306: Brigadier G. H. N. Wilson. Note the simple but practical methods of carrying and fastening a landing net. (See also page 400)

Figure 305

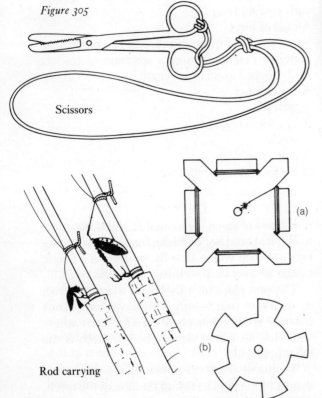

Scissors

Rod carrying

(a)

(b)

Leader carriers

Two loops

A very simple and neat method of joining casting line and leader (see below). Useful for the night fly-fisherman, since it facilitates the changing of a leader in the darkness. (The loop whipped in the end of the casting line should be renewed at the start of each season.) Another method is to loop the leader to the loop in a short length (say $1\frac{1}{2}$ ft) of stout nylon, needle knotted to the casting line. (For knots see pages 388—94.)

Two loops

THE WILSON FLY RETRIEVER

At last – a use for those little metal cylinders in which cigars are sold.

This little gadget - an invention of that splendid fisherman the late Brigadier G. H. N. Wilson – should live permanently in the tackle bag. It consists of a crook that can be lifted on the rod point to obtain a hold on a branch in which one's hook or fly is caught.

The crook is strapped on to the empty cigar cylinder with adhesive tape. A suitable length of light, strong cord is tied to the crook, with which to pull down the branch. For this purpose a piece of parachute cord is ideal.

1. Put the cylinder with crook attached on to the rod tip.
2. Reach up with your rod and place the crook over the offending branch.
3. Remove the rod and put it safely out of the way, stripping line off the reel in order to do so.
4. Take hold of the cord and pull down the branch.

It is surprising how easily a fly can be retrieved from seemingly inaccessible branches.

The crook should be light enough to be lifted vertically on the rod tip, but strong enough to take the strain of pulling down the branch. Friction is increased by winding a little adhesive tape round the bend of the hook, which prevents the crook from sliding down a branch when pressure is applied. This tendency to slip can, of course, be countered by the direction of the pull and by intelligent selection of the place where the crook is put over the branch. If possible, place it just above the junction of a lateral (see diagram).

This equipment can also be used to retrieve a hook, fly or spinner from certain underwater snags, when clarity of water, strength of current and other circumstances permit.

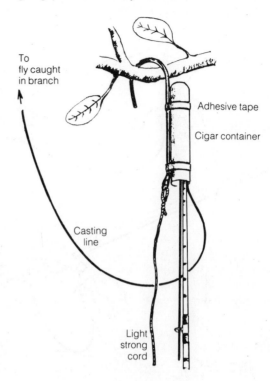

Figure 307: The Wilson fly-retriever

To fly caught in branch

Adhesive tape

Cigar container

Casting line

Light strong cord

THE FALKUS 'FINGER-RING' FIGURE-OF-EIGHT RETRIEVE

Having made a cast, anglers use various methods to 'work' and recover their flies. The most common method is to strip the line in and let it fall. There are times, however, when this technique is unsuitable.

1. In a strong wind.
2. When the angler is wading in a current.
3. When the slack line may become entangled with undergrowth.

In these cases, the line is gathered in tight coils inside the non-casting hand by what is known as the 'figure-of-eight' retrieve.

The conventional method is to draw the line straight from the butt ring, as shown in figure 308 (a), but a far better method is shown in (b). Here, the line is drawn not from the butt ring direct, but from a ring made by thumb and forefinger of the casting hand.

Having made a cast, grasp the rod only by the

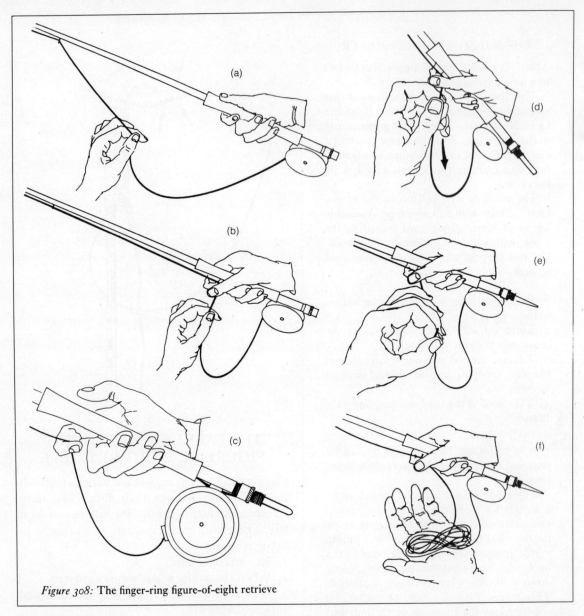

Figure 308: The finger-ring figure-of-eight retrieve

3rd, 4th and 5th fingers of the right (or casting) hand and pass the line over the crook of the index finger (c). Drop the thumb until it touches the ball of the index finger. Thumb and index finger now perform the role of an extra rod-ring.

Take hold of the fly line behind the thumb with thumb and index finger of the left hand (d) and draw about 4 inches of line through the 'finger ring'.

Grab the line with the remaining fingers of the left hand (e). Allow the loop that has formed over the tip of the left forefinger to slip off into the palm as the hand moves back to its former position.

Repeat the procedure over and over again, with the wrist pivoting in a smooth figure-of-eight movement. It is important to keep the hands very close together; indeed, the angler should be conscious of his left little finger brushing his right thumb with each backward stroke.

Gradually, as the fly is worked in towards the angler, coils of line are gathered up in the left hand. The gathered line is shown in (f) with the hand displayed in an open position. This has been done purposely to reveal the coiled line. In practice, the hand merely opens sufficiently to grab each succeeding coil of line.

The advantages of the 'finger-ring' figure-of-eight over the conventional method are considerable.

1. It is much easier to perform.
2. It is faster, thus permitting greater variation of fly speed during recovery.
3. When a fish is hooked, the line is under immediate control. One has simply to exert pressure with the right forefinger and trap the line against the rod butt.

Note: The figure-of-eight retrieve is made much easier (as indeed are all methods of retrieve) if the rod butt is kept anchored firmly against the groin. For this reason, it is advisable to fish with a rod that has a short extension below the reel.

PLAYING A SEA TROUT

Although its flesh hardens rapidly in freshwater, the mouth of a sea trout newly arrived from the sea is very soft. Many fish hooked early in the season are lost not because they are badly hooked or through any fault of the hook itself, but through this tenderness of the flesh. Normally the best hold is in the 'scissors' at the angle of the jaw. With many early fish hooked in this position, however, pressure on the hook while a fish is being played causes a slit to be torn in the thin flesh at the corner of the mouth (see figure 309). A momentary slackening of the line, especially when a fish jumps, allows the hook to lose its hold. It is said that the hook tears out.

More often than not, however, the chances are that it *drops* out. Examination of a fish from whose mouth the hook has come away on landing sometimes gives evidence of this.

Unless very fine tackle is being used, or the fish is exceptionally large, it is a good rule when playing a sea trout not to lower the rod point as the fish jumps. Instead, it is better to *increase* the

pressure on the fish as it leaves the water, thus tending to pull it sideways. This is contrary to the advice usually given on the subject, but any reader who has the confidence to try this ploy will undoubtedly land a higher proportion of early season fish.

Figure 309: Playing an early season sea trout
(a) A sea trout fresh from sea intercepts and takes the fly. He turns aways. As he does so the fly hooks him at the back of the jaw in the 'scissors' – in this case on the right-hand side.
(b) The fish runs hard downstream for a short distance, the shank of the hook working to and fro against his jaw as he zig-zags about.
(c) He turns and starts to come back upstream.
(d) He swims steadily past you. This is where you want him, but by now there is a big slit torn in the soft flesh at the corner of the mouth. If he suddenly turns towards you and jumps on a slack line you are very likely to lose him: the hook may simply fall out of the slit. As the fish jumps, *don't* drop the rod point and allow the line to go limp. Unless it is a big fish and likely to break the leader, *raise the rod and keep a tight line*.
(e) View of the fish's mouth showing slit

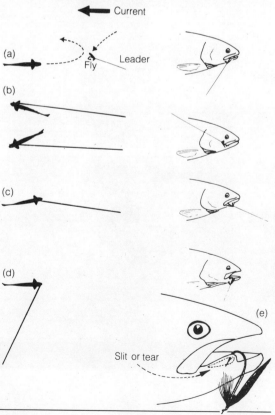

Bev Shutt with an $8\frac{1}{2}$ lb Falkland Islands sea trout caught in the Swan Inlet Pool, three miles from sea. Bev cast to this fish for over three hours, starting with a size 2 Black Fly and going down in size through seven different patterns to a size 14 Teal, Blue and Silver on a $2\frac{1}{2}$ lb leader. The fish, which in the clear water could be plainly seen, reacted to each fly in turn, but refused to take. Eventually, after it had 'hit' the size 14 twice without getting hooked, Bev filed off the hook-barb. The fish 'hit' again. This time, due perhaps to its better penetration, the hook secured a hold – precarious, but which lasted until the moment Bev slid the net underneath!

Swan Inlet Pool

Famous Falkland Islands sea trout pool: the Frying-pan – four miles from the sea

A catch of sea trout taken by Bev Shutt on his way upriver

(*Left*) Bev Shutt with two Falkland Islands sea trout caught on fly in saltwater

Cooking the Sea Trout

SEA TROUT WITH BACON AND FRIED BREAD

Clean and fillet a 2–3 lb sea trout.

Coat with oatmeal and fry in fairly hot bacon fat. Turn when golden brown.

Serve with slices of bacon and fried bread, and slices of cold tomato.

SEA TROUT COOKED WITH CUCUMBER

Clean several small sea trout.

Melt some butter in a pan. Add a tablespoonful of olive oil. Add cucumber rings. Fry for approximately one minute. Add the fish. Fry slowly until almost cooked, then crisp the skins by increasing heat. Lift out and place on a hot dish.

Clean pan. Add fresh butter. When butter bubbles, add fresh cucumber rings. Cook for about one minute, then pour the lot over the fish and serve.

Note: Also delicious with almonds instead of cucumber, cooked in the same way.

Knowing little about the finer points of cooking we were puzzled by the addition of olive oil, but are informed that this helps to prevent the butter from burning.

The
RAINBOW
TROUT

Salmo gairdneri

The rainbow is native only to north-west America, from the Bering Sea to California. But since 1880, on account of its fine sporting and culinary qualities, it has been exported to nearly every country in the world – at least to those that can offer cool, clean rivers, lakes or reservoirs.

In their native surroundings, rainbows – like brown trout – exploit both salt and freshwater. An anadromous variety (breeding in freshwater and feeding in the sea) is the steelhead. Another variety lives in lakes and spawns in the local feeder-streams. Yet a third spends its whole life in its natal river; whereas a fourth, known as the 'coastal' rainbow (an equivalent to our slob trout), is an estuarine feeder and river spawner.

The ancestry of these varieties is open to speculation, since some strains spawn in the autumn (*Shasta* type) and some in the spring (*Irideus* type).

The rainbow has managed to breed successfully in a few British rivers, for instance, the Buckinghamshire Chess and Misbourne, and the Derbyshire Wye. The breeding colonies of Chess and Misbourne, however, became extinct during the period 1945–70*. This was due partly to drought conditions in the headwaters brought on by a lowering of the water table, partly to sewage effluents and low water conditions in the middle reaches.

* These have re-established themselves in the 1980s.

From 1885, for some years, shipments of rainbow ova were sent every winter from the USA to hatcheries in Great Britain, but by 1890 quantities of eggs were also coming into this country from Herr Jaffe, who had been very successful in breeding rainbows in his hatchery at Osnabruck. Doubtless a certain number of fish were later distributed amongst a few owners of pools and lakes throughout England, yet it was not until about 1898 that there is any record of them being introduced into our waters in any substantial numbers. From that date onwards, many clubs and riparian owners purchased supplies from the English fish farms. Amongst them was King Edward VII who had some placed in the lake at Buckingham Palace, where, in 1903, Lord Denbigh took one on a fly – the first rainbow ever to be caught on rod and line in the heart of London.

A. Courtney Williams, *Angling Diversions* (1945)

Figure 311: Compare tail of rainbow (*below*) with that of brown trout (*middle*)

Figure 312: 'Wild' rainbows, like Peter Thomas's brace which grew quickly in a spacious reservoir, are handsome fish – unlike those that have spent too long in stews. Sadly, the ugliest of the latter, along with their captors, are often used to illustrate the sporting press. Not without irony such fish are often referred to as 'finless wonders'

Figure 313: Three pristine rainbows and one brown trout – catch shared by Peter Thomas (one of Britain's most versatile fishermen) and F. B.

Figure 314: So perfect is the shape of these two fish that they look like spring salmon – but see the tell-tale spotting on the tail fins

Figure 315: (right) A catch shared by Peter Thomas and F.B. – fifteen rainbows and one brown trout, taken 'loch style'

Figure 316: The spectacular fight of the rainbow trout. This $2\frac{1}{2}$-pounder in Hanningfield Reservoir jumped seven times before it was landed

Figure 317: Rainbows caught on a Muddler Minnow, an unlikely yet successful reservoir lure. A Muddler can be seen inside the mouth of the right-hand fish. The Muddler has also proved itself to be a first-rate lure for big white trout (sea trout) in the west of Ireland

The former reluctance to accept the presence of rainbow trout in Britain has steadily waned as more and more anglers have become aware of the rainbow's accommodating feeding habits and fighting prowess. Nowadays an increasing number of fishery owners stock with rainbows in order to enjoy the economic advantages accruing from a fast-growing and, by comparison with brown trout, disease-resistant species. In recent years some huge rainbows have been reared, and caught, notably at Avington Fishery, Hampshire.

Stocking a river with rainbows is quite another matter. Instant fishing on the 'put and take' basis can be created in rivers small enough to contain an efficient fish-barrier, but without a barrier rainbows move seawards and are lost. This seemingly instinctive tendency to move downstream is said to result from the mixing of migratory and non-migratory strains.

The normal four-year life span of the rainbow is shorter than that of the brown trout. Its habits, too, differ somewhat. Being a gregarious fish it tends to swim in shoals, whereas the brown trout is essentially territorial, having its own feeding territory which it will attempt to defend.

The fact that rainbows grow faster than browns and can withstand higher temperatures is sometimes reflected in an angler's catch, the rainbows' need for extra food to sustain their faster growth-rate making them slightly more vulnerable to the angler's fly. We have noticed that on occasion rainbows can provide good sport in the middle of a hot summer afternoon, a time when little response is usually expected from browns.

Since the normal four-year life cycle of the rainbow is shorter than that of the brown trout it is not surprising that, where both species thrive and where figures are available, the recovery rate for rainbows is better than that of browns, the rainbow being at risk from predators, disease and the ravages of winter for a shorter period. But the fact that it has to eat more food during its short life to sustain its faster growth, must also put it at greater risk from the angler.

The
BROOK
TROUT

Salvelinus fontinalis

A native of the north-eastern United States and Canada, this form of charr was introduced to Europe in the 1880s. It is not common in British waters, however, because although it can be reared successfully in hatcheries and thrives in cool, clean water, both river and lake, it has a slow growth-rate and costs roughly twice as much to stock as the rainbow trout.

Brook trout can grow to about six pounds; breed during winter and early spring and have a food range similar to that of brown trout, with which they are sometimes crossed to produce 'tiger' trout. H. F. has had capital sport with them in stillwater, using tiny imitation midge larvae tied on size 18 and 20 hooks, casting well out and leaving the fly to hang an inch or so beneath the surface and drift naturally with whatever breeze was blowing, but keeping the line as straight as possible to facilitate striking.

Despite the cost of stocking brook trout, it seems a shame that more of these beautiful and tasty fish are not available to British anglers. In his last book, *Bright Waters, Bright Fish*, Roderick Haig-Brown writes of the brook trout's eminence among Canadian anglers:

In the Maritimes and eastern Quebec, the Atlantic salmon is famous. A noble fish, certainly, of noble habits and the peak of ambition for most freshwater fishermen. But the fisherman's fish of the Maritimes, overwhelmingly popular, is the brook trout, the eastern speckled trout (*Salvelinus fontinalis*); in Quebec the speckled trout, *la truite mouchetée*, is 'the fish of the province' and the province may well be considered the centre of its abundance.

Figure 318: The brook trout can be recognized by dark, worm-like markings on the back and dorsal fin, red and whitish spots on the body, and white on the leading edge of the lower fins and bottom lobe of the tail fin (*Rodney Coldron*)

The
WHITEFISHES
Coregonidae

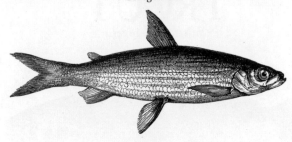

THE HOUTING
Coregonus lavaretus (powan, gwyniad, skelly)

THE VENDACE
Coregonus albula (vendace various, pollan)

As the years pass and angling continues to increase in popularity, it seems strange that there should be sport-fish of the highest quality that are seldom if ever fished for – the Whitefishes. Since these represent an angling resource of great potential, a discussion of their history and biology may help to stimulate interest in a rare but fascinating branch of angling.

The salmon, trout, charr, grayling and Whitefish found in British waters are related fishes. They belong to the order Isospondyli, one of the most primitive orders of the Teleosts (the bony fishes). Teleost fishes first came to prominence during the Cretaceous period, about 100 million years ago. Significantly, the Teleost fossil fishes found in the Cretaceous rocks resemble the modern herring.

The closeness of the relationship between salmon, trout, charr, grayling and Whitefish is further exemplified by the inclusion of whitefish in the same sub-order: Salmonoidei. This sub-order is represented by a number of genera, and it is at generic level that the fishes become separated. The salmon and trout belong to the genus *Salmo*, the charr to the genus *Salvelinus*, the grayling to the genus *Thymallus*, and the

Whitefishes to the genus *Coregonus*. All have the characteristic adipose fin, a small fleshy boneless fin situated on the back of the fish between dorsal fin and tail.

Until recently the genus *Coregonus* was represented by a considerable number of species. The common ones recognized in Britain were (with the exception of the marine houting) all freshwater fishes and included powan, pollan, vendaces, gwyniad and skelly. These were all regarded as distinct species.

Nowadays, however, opinion among taxonomists is divided as to whether certain of these Whitefishes should be recognized as different species, sub-species, or varieties of the same species. The matter remains to be settled. In the meantime we have followed the classification given by Alwyne Wheeler in *The Fishes of the British Isles and North-West Europe* (1969):

Houting – *Coregonus lavaretus*, including those fishes previously known as powan, gwyniad and skelly.

Vendace – *Coregonus albula*, including those fishes previously known as vendace (various) and pollan.

The freshwater houting and the vendace are probably surviving remnants of migratory stocks, part of which became isolated during a period when glaciation affected the northern land masses of Europe, Asia and North America. The remarkable diversity of the Whitefishes, which gives rise to a whole catalogue of visual and taxonomic differences among numerous isolated populations without creating new species, may be due to the relatively short stabilising period since glaciation. The inference being that the shaping hand of evolution will one day consolidate varieties into species.

HOUTING
Powan – *Coregonus clupeoides clupeoides*
(Loch Lomond, Loch Eck)

The powan is a herring-like fish. So like a herring in fact that in 1802, when first described in a scientific journal, it was given (by Lacépède, a Frenchman) its specific name *Clupeoides*, 'herring' in the Gallic tongue. Its distribution is confined to two British lakes: Loch Lomond and Loch Eck.

In summer, powan seek their food (plankton) near the surface. This habit gives rise to a peculiar characteristic known as 'finning'. At times large shoals of Loch Lomond powan swim so close to the surface that their dorsal fins are out

Figure 319: (below) Powan (houting) $11\frac{1}{4}$oz, caught by F. B. on Loch Lomond, February 1968

Figure 320: (bottom) Vendace, netted from Bassenthwaite Lake, Cumbria, February 1972. The Cumbrian vendace (*Coregonus gracilior*) is closely related to the Lochmaben vendace (*Coregonus vendesius*). Taxonomists now consider these and certain other British Whitefish to be varieties of one species: *Coregonus albula*. Note the projecting lower jaw, compared with the slightly projecting upper jaw of the powan (houting) shown in the top picture

H. F., who has feasted on both houting and vendace, finds it surprising that the delicious flavours of these fish are not more widely appreciated. He well remembers the lines of pollan nets hung out to dry by the fishermen of Lough Neagh when he flew regularly over the lough while serving with the Royal Air Force at Aldergrove before the war. More recently, while directing a wildlife film in Bavaria, he enjoyed a sumptuous lunch of locally caught houting in a pub on the banks of the Starnberger See.

of the water. Shoals thus engaged give a patch of otherwise calm water a disturbed look; and, strange to record, a patch of wind-rippled water, a smooth look.

Of great interest is the comment by Ian Wood, in his book *Loch Lomond and its Salmon*, that although visiting anglers cast their flies like mad among the 'finning' powan, mistaking them for rising trout, only three powan had to his knowledge been taken on the fly in twenty years.

In a somewhat confused account of the powan published in 1838, Dr Parnell noted that a few powan had been taken on the fly '... bait they have never been known to touch'. A strange statement when one remembers that in powan stomachs he found items such as '... small tough red worms' and '... a quantity of gravel which the fish had probably accumulated when in search of the larvae'.

Recent research has proved that in addition to grazing on plant life and foraging for insect larvae in submerged weed beds, powan feed actively on the bottom – particularly during the winter months. Professor Slack, head of the Glasgow University research team, while studying the flora and fauna of Loch Lomond, caught several powan on worm baits. Moreover, the former record powan was caught on fine ledger-tackle.

Powan spawn in January on gravelly shallows. Science has revealed that the young powan disappear from these shallows in spring shortly after hatching, and are never seen again until they are at least two years old. Considerable efforts have been made to obtain specimens of those young fish, but so far without success. For years it was thought that the myriads of fry frequenting the shallows in early summer were young powan. Nevertheless every sample caught by Professor Slack's team proved to be roach.

Not surprisingly, the powan has a reputation for being mysterious. Nor is this reputation diminished by the discovery of a few powan possessed of a supernumerary fin. This extra fin is found on the fish's back, just behind the head.

Thoughts on powan angling

At one time there was a ready market for powan. Nowadays, it seems, the economics of marketing fish would not support, as it once did, the cost of bringing over a team of professional pollan-netters from Ireland. That powan are no longer taken in their thousands by professional netsmen should encourage the angler. There is, moreover, little chance of his catching undersized fish – since these are not to be come by at all!

The curious coarse fisherman may like to know if he could catch powan using one of his deadly coarse-fishing methods. We think that he could, or at least that he could in winter, when the powan are bottom feeding. We would suggest the use of link-ledger or swimfeeder techniques, with maggot or small worm as bait.

Rather than ledger indiscriminately, we would select a deep swim within comfortable casting range of the bank – our selection depending to some extent on information derived from local boatmen who know something of the powan's movements.

Prior to fishing we would give the swim a thorough and heavy groundbaiting with chopped worms, maggots and pieces of turf. This would be done in the hope that the turf would provide a landmark for the roaming shoals of powan, and the groundbait an inducement to stay in the swim. In a few days, if our swim were well chosen, we would expect powan to be pre-occupied with our offerings, and to fall readily to the hookbait.

It has been said that powan are poor fighters. Like many other snap judgements on the fighting qualities of fish, often made by anglers least

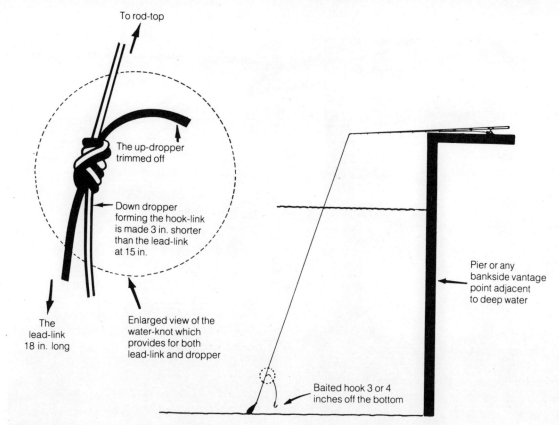

To rod-top

The up-dropper
trimmed off

Down dropper
forming the hook-link
is made 3 in. shorter
than the lead-link
at 15 in.

The
lead-link
18 in. long

Enlarged view of the
water-knot which
provides for both
lead-link and dropper

Pier or any
bankside vantage
point adjacent
to deep water

Baited hook 3 or 4
inches off the bottom

Figure 321: The Loch Lomond winter deep-water powan
paternoster

qualified to judge, this one is quite wrong. We
believe that when anglers 'discover' the powan
and fish for it with reasonably fine tackle – either
fly or bait – they will soon recognize the true
qualities of this sporting Whitefish.

Fishing for roach livebait near Balmaha, F. B.
hooked an 11¼ oz powan (once the British rod-
caught record) on suitably light tackle – and
thought he had hooked Loch Lomond's biggest
roach!

When cured of a mania to catch a 50-pound
Loch Lomond pike, F. B. intends to concentrate
on powan and charr. For powan he will trail a
tiny fly or nymph, behind a boat that is allowed
to drift with the breeze. The fly will be tied to a
number 16 or 18 hook, and the leader will be the
merest gossamer (1–1½ lb BS). The line will be a
floating (bubble) line, and the rod an ultra light
brook fly-rod. With this tackle (if he is fortunate
enough to drift through a shoal of powan) he

looks forward to enjoying sport-fishing as good
as any to be had in Britain.

Loch Lomond powan grow to a length
of 18 in. and a top weight of about 2 lb. A
rod-caught 2-pounder would be a wonderful
achievement. What more could any fisherman
wish for? Well, he could wish for his catch
to be worthy of cooking in wine. And his wish
would be granted, for the powan is delicious to
eat.

Very few powan have ever been caught on rod
and line, largely because very few anglers have
ever tried to catch them. Nevertheless, powan-
angling holds great possibilities; it also presents
a considerable challenge, since almost nothing is
known about it. We thought it would be interesting to ask our friend Richard Walker to speculate on how he would set about catching one of
these elusive little fish.

Speculation is held to constitute one of the attractions
of angling. Where powan are concerned, it is the only
course open to me, because I have never caught one,
nor have I ever seen one caught on rod and line.

Figure 322: Mill Loch, Lochmaben (see page 338). A lovely stretch of water that still holds vendace. This species was thought to have become extinct in Mill Loch until, in the 1960s, interest was re-kindled by an angler's discovery of a vendace inside a pike's stomach!

I can, therefore, only speculate about ways and means of catching them on a basis of what the books say about their food, and on the appearance of the fish, since I have been able to examine dead specimens.

The authorities say powan are plankton feeders, and that they also feed in the littoral shallows upon insects of various kinds. Certainly their mouths and digestive systems seem adapted to such a diet. Their mouths and indeed their faces bear a remarkable resemblance to those of grayling, the only noticeable difference being the larger eye of the powan. The shape, the scales and the general feel of the two species are also similar and I think the angler can regard the powan as a kind of stillwater grayling, with the advantage to his choice of angling methods.

I am pretty confident that if I could get within easy casting range of a shoal of feeding powan, I could catch them readily. I should use a fly rod, a long nylon leader tapered to about 2 lb BS, and an artificial nymph or midge pupa chosen to imitate such natural insects as I could capture and identify on that day, dressed on hooks from size 14 to 18 to match the size of the insects found.

Very successful dressings for insects of these kinds have been evolved for catching rainbow trout from reservoirs. Such trout are largely plankton feeders, as examination of stomach contents has shown. I am confident that these dressings, mainly of chironomid larvae, would also catch powan.

Various ephemerids, including Pond Olives, caenis and a rather large insect resembling a small mayfly* are common on Loch Lomond and I surmise that imitations of these, used when the natural insects were seen, would also account for powan.

I do not think that choosing the right artificial fly and fishing it with the right motion are the real problems. Much more important is the problem of putting the fly where a powan can see it.

Siphlonurus lacustris

In fly-fishing for trout on lakes and lochs, the methodical covering of likely areas usually brings some sort of success because trout, be they brown trout, sea trout or rainbow trout, are pretty widely distributed.

A series of drifts with the boat will be fairly sure to put the angler's flies within sight of at least some of the fish. Powan, however, seem to move in densely packed shoals covering a relatively small area. An angler might drift about on a big loch, like Lomond, all day for years without ever coming within casting range of a powan shoal.

With my friends, I have covered miles and miles on Loch Lomond, day after day, and have only twice seen shoals of powan. On neither occasion did I have a fly-rod fixed up.

In order to catch powan, I think it would be advisable to seek all possible information about the areas they frequent from local people, especially the commercial salmon and sea trout netsmen; and then to move the boat slowly about in these areas, keeping careful watch for shoals of powan, both visually and with a suitably arranged echo sounder, set up with its transducer looking ahead instead of downwards.

Figure 323: Well known Welsh angler, Moc Morgan, braves the wind and waves to fish Lake Bala on a cold January day

Powan shoals have a habit of coming to the surface which they break with their dorsal fins and upper tail lobes. This is known locally as 'finning' and is easy to observe, even in rough weather.

Very few powan have ever been caught on rod and line, but that need occasion no surprise, since anglers on Lomond do not try to catch them and do not employ tackle that is very likely to catch them accidentally. Local men fly-fish only for salmon and sea trout, using for the most part flies that are large and leaders that are stout by ordinary sea trout fishing standards, the idea being, I suppose, that if a salmon is hooked, an event for which they constantly hope, they will have a fair chance of boating it. When one considers the odds against such flies being cast where powan are, and also the odds against a powan taking a traditional wet-fly on a size 8 hook, tied to 8–12 lb nylon, one can readily see why the capture of powan is so rare.

There are lots of grayling in the River Tweed, but not many are caught on salmon and sea trout flies, though they can readily be caught on tiny nymphs and fine leader points as I have proved often enough. Grayling and powan are, as I have explained earlier, remarkably similar.

I expect that, like grayling, powan could also be caught with maggots or worms on float tackle; indeed F.B. caught one on a maggot off Balmaha pier. In

dealing with a powan shoal located out in the loch, however, I would expect fly-fishing methods to be more successful, since they would cause less disturbance than float and shot, and would allow an artificial to be fished only an inch or two below the surface. That is the method I would choose, until experience proved me wrong.

Gwyniad – *Coregonus clupeoides pennantii*
(Lake Bala)

The gwyniad of Lake Bala, Wales, and the skelly of Haweswater, Ullswater and Red Tarn in the English Lake District, are similar fishes; together with the powan they are collectively described as the freshwater houting, *Coregonus lavaretus*.

The gwyniad once swarmed in Lake Bala, but in 1803, according to Yarrel in *British Fishes*, the introduction of pike reduced their numbers considerably. The Ullswater variety, the skelly, was at one time netted by the local inhabitants. Unlike the charr of Windermere, which was preserved in butter, the skelly was preserved in salt. Like the Welsh gwyniads, the Ullswater skellies are now scarce.

Figure 324: Two gwyniad from Lake Bala

Skelly – *Coregonus clupeoides stigmaticus*
(Ullswater, Haweswater and Red Tarn)

The existence of skellies in Ullswater was first mentioned in 1686. John Watson, in his book *The English Lake District Fisheries* (1899), recorded their decline. Watson found an interesting reference to the skelly in Clarke's *Survey of the Lakes*: 'The skelly is remarkable for this, no bait has ever been found which they will take.' Watson brightens the picture, however, by telling us that he caught one in Haweswater on the fly.

It is interesting to note that once again the growing domination of another species is advanced as the reason for the decline of a Whitefish. On this occasion, Watson blamed an increasing perch population for the decline of the Ullswater skellies. If the perch were indeed responsible they seem to have derived no benefit. In Elizabethan times they were recorded as growing to a weight of 5 lb, whereas the Ullswater perch of today are very small indeed.

A Viking inheritance?

In South West Scotland and North West England, or more particularly in the country

Figure 325: Skelly, netted in February 1972, from Haweswater, Cumberland. Two other lakes in the Eden catchment area, Ullswater and Red Tarn, also hold skelly. The skelly (*Coregonus stigmaticus*), the powan (*Coregonus clupeoides*) and the gwyniad (*Coregonus pennantii*) are now considered to be one species: *Coregonus lavaretus*

bordering the Solway Firth, certain species of fish are given quaint names. These include 'sprod', 'smelt', 'herling', 'mort' – which refer to sea trout – and 'skelly', which is of particular interest since it describes two different species of fish.

Around the border town of Carlisle, 'skelly' refers to the chub (*Leuciscus cephalus*). South of Carlisle, in the heart of the Lake District, 'skelly' means the Whitefish (*Coregonus lavaretus*), an inhabitant of Haweswater, Ullswater and Red Tarn. Even Frank Buckland, the famous nineteenth-century naturalist, confused 'skelly' chub and 'skelly' Whitefish. This is not surprising since Whitefish are found in Ullswater and Haweswater, and chub are found in the rivers that flow out of these lakes. Occasionally, both species come 'face to face'. Dr Heysham, in *Hutchinson's History of Cumberland*, wrote: 'A few of them ['skellies' Whitefish] sometimes leave Ullswater, go down the river Eamont into the Eden, and now and then a solitary one is taken below the bay of Armathwaite.'

This is right in the middle of chub water.

Where does the name 'skelly' come from? Yarrell, in *British Fishes* (1841), thought that the 'skelly' Whitefish was so named on account of its large scales. So did that noted ichthyologist Tate

Regan, although in *British Freshwater Fishes* (1911), he referred to 'conspicuous' scales rather than large scales. J. J. Manley, in *Fish and Fishing* (1877), suggested that 'skelly' chub was a corruption of 'skully' or 'skull', since the specific name for the chub is *cephalus*, from cephalic: pertaining to the head, a reference to the size and breadth of the chub's head.

Referring to the tributaries of Ullswater in *The English Lake District Fisheries* (1899), Watson wrote: 'The chub occurs in some of them, and on account of its scales it is invariably called "skelly" by the natives.'

In *Excursion on the Banks of Ullswater* (1805) William Wordsworth wrote:

... The fishermen drew their net ashore, and hundreds of fish were leaping in the prison. They were all of the kind called skellies, a sort of freshwater herring, shoals of which may sometimes be seen dimpling or rippling the surface of the lake in calm weather. This species is not found, I believe, in any other of these lakes; nor, as far as I know, is the chevin, that spiritless fish (though I am loth to call it so, for it was a prime favourite with Izaak Walton), which must frequent Ullswater, as I have seen a large shoal passing into the lake from the river Eamont. . . .

It is of course possible that 'skelly' is a corruption of 'scaly', but we do not think it likely.

'Skalle', pronounced 'skelly' by the Danes, is used to describe the roach (*Rutilus rutilus*) and since the Solway area was settled by the Vikings (Danes, Norwegians and Swedes) in the ninth and tenth centuries, it would seem reasonable to suppose that the word has survived practically unchanged in both languages, like many other Viking words and place names.

The word 'mort', used by Cumbrians to describe large sea trout, is used in Sweden to describe an entirely different species of fish. Astonishingly, once again, it is the ubiquitous roach.

The word 'pickerel', used as the diminutive for pike in England during the Middle Ages, was taken by early British settlers to North America and used to describe similar fishes later identified as entirely different species: chain pickerel (*Esox niger*), red fin pickerel (*Esox americanus americanus*), grass pickerel (*Esox americanus vermiculatus*) and walleye (*Stizostedion vitreum*).

How likely it is, then, that the early Viking settlers in the Solway area used their native words to describe fishes that were *similar* (but not necessarily identical) to the fishes of their own lands. Roach, chub and whitefish are all silvery, herring-like fishes. Could it not be as simple as that?

Figure 326: Dr P. S. Maitland, who took this extremely rare picture of a Lochmaben vendace (*Coregonus vandesius*), estimates that only about 3,000 members of the species survive in their last known habitat – Mill Loch. He hopes to disperse the species by introducing it to other suitable waters in south-west Scotland. Maitland has already introduced powan fry into another Scottish loch and seen these fish grow to spawning size.

Note: The projecting *lower* jaw is characteristic of the vendace. A projecting *upper* jaw is characteristic of the powan

VENDACE

Vendace – *Coregonus vandesius vandesius*
(Mill Loch, near Lochmaben)

Vendace – *Coregonus vandesius gracilior*
(Derwentwater, Bassenthwaite)

The vendace of Mill Loch near Lochmaben (a town in Dumfriesshire), together with the vendace of Derwentwater and Bassenthwaite, are so closely related that they can be considered, with the pollan, as varieties of the same species: *Coregonus albula*.

Lochmaben vendace have had a long and unique association with fishermen. At one time this silvery, herring-like little fish (they rarely exceed nine inches) was the centre of activity of a small exclusive group of gentlemen who formed themselves into a vendace club. It was their practice to meet each July, net with sweepnets, and enjoy a great vendace feast.

In time the club became defunct. A second club, although bigger and more democratic, met the same fate. By the time the third club was formed (1910), the stock of fish was small and the club's annual catch was a mere half-dozen. Today, the 'club water', the beautiful Castle Loch, is empty of vendace. Fortunately, they still survive in nearby Mill Loch.

It is likely that the extinction of vendace in Castle Loch was due to a gradual change of character in the fish's environment. The present eutrophic nature of the water (rich in dissolved

Figure 327: Castle Loch, once famous for its vendace. The last vendace known to have been caught in Castle Loch on rod and line was taken with worm tackle near the tennis courts in 1937 by Francis Dummitt Dundas

Figure 328: Francis Dummitt Dundas

nutrient salts) favours roach and bream; whereas the previous oligotrophic nature (poor in dissolved nutrient salts) favoured the vendace. If the disappearance of Castle Loch's beloved little Whitefish is really due to the changed character of the water, it will almost certainly have been brought about by the introduction of sewage effluent – even though this may have been strictly controlled.

Pennant records the local belief that vendace were introduced into Lochmaben waters by the ill-fated Mary, Queen of Scots, when she visited the castle in 1565.

Figure 329: (*top*) Lough Neagh pollan. This fish was $11\frac{1}{2}$ in. long and weighed 9 oz. Dr D. Cragg-Hine of the Fisheries Research Laboratory, Coleraine, Co. Derry, very kindly arranged for this fish to be caught and photographed to enable us to complete the series of Whitefish photographs

Figure 330: (above) Vendace netted in February 1972, from Bassenthwaite Lake, Cumbria (E. Ramsbottam)

Braithwaite, in *Salmonidae of Westmorland* (1884), mentioned the vendace and noted the resemblance to the gwyniad (skelly) of Ullswater insofar as they swim in large shoals, retire to deep water in warm weather, and rarely take the angler's bait. The vendace, he claimed, often rises to the surface like a common herring, '... making a similar noise by their rise and fall to and from the surface'.

Describing the netting of vendace in the early nineteenth century, Sir W. Jardine, in *The Edinburgh Journal of Natural and Geographical Science*, wrote: 'They are most successfully taken during a dull day and sharp breeze, approaching near to the edges of the loch, and swimming in a direction contrary to the wind.'

Pollan – *Coregonus pollan pollan*
(Lough Neagh)
Coregonus pollan altior
(Lough Erne)
Coregonus pollan elegans
(Lough Derg, Lough Ree)

The pollan is generally associated with Ireland's Lough Neagh, although other varieties of pollan occur in Loughs Erne, Ree and Derg. The pollan, once so abundant in Ree and Derg, became rare after the Shannon was drained in 1845. Lough Neagh, the largest lake in the British Isles, has a long history of commercial pollan fishing. Thompson, the Irish naturalist who described the pollan in *History of British Fishes*, recorded a catch made in 1834 of over 17,000 fish with four draughts of the net.

Tate Regan, in *British Freshwater Fishes* (1911), states that the staple food of the pollan is plankton; although insect larvae, shrimps, small bivalves and *the fry of other fishes* are also taken (our italics). To digress for a moment, we should like to point out the fallacy of thinking that fish differentiate between their own fry and the fry of other species: it leads to the common mistake of calling certain species (or specimens, e.g. large brown trout) 'cannibals'. At times, *all* fish will eat smaller fish – trout included.

Pollan fishing

Writing in 1886, 'Hi-Regan' (Capt. J. J. Dunne), an authority on Irish fishing, made it clear that the capture of a Lough Neagh pollan was an ambition worthy of the best angler. To his everlasting credit he left us this dressing for a pollan fly: 'A very small silver-bodied gnat, hackled at shoulder; with blue-tip and a tiny ring of blue chatterer *and the whole disfigured with a gentle.*' (Our italics).

It seems that Hi-Regan's informant was a practical angler who killed his pollan either on this fly or on the 'wasp caddie – sunk and drawn up gently from the bottom'.

Pollan grow to about 13 inches in length. Although a weight of about $2\frac{1}{2}$lb has been recorded, a fish of this size would be exceptional.

The bank angler should have good chances to take pollan, for they are known to come into the shallows, not only during spring and summer, but when the autumn is far advanced. Thompson gives the spawning season as November and December. Judging by the results of netting, the pollan is very far from being generally distributed throughout the lough.

According to Thompson, the favourite resort of Lough Neagh pollan is between Six-Mile Water and Shane's Castle. We suggest that the area around Ram's Island would be a good starting point for an angler, for it was here that the record haul of pollan was taken.

There is no need to explain to any fisherman that the difference between a basket with a brace of fish in it and a basket containing none at all is an absolute, not a relative difference. Eight and ten brace of fish may be about the same thing, but between two fish and nothing no sort of comparison is possible.

Arthur Ransome

The authors and publishers would like to point out that since first publication of this book, the Whitefishes have been protected in Britain.

The
ZANDER
Stizostedion lucioperca

The zander is a member of the perch family (Percidae), which includes the common perch (*Perca fluviatilis*) and the ruffe (*Gymnocephalus cernua*).

An eastern European fish that has been widely introduced into western Europe, the zander was first brought to Britain in 1878 (at Woburn). Other introductions followed in 1910, 1947 and 1950. Today the zander is a breeding British species, notably in Woburn, Leighton Buzzard and Claydon Lakes, as well as in parts of the fens and the Great Ouse river system.

The name 'pike-perch', sometimes given both to the zander and the walleye, is a misnomer. The European zander (*Stizostedion lucioperca*) and the North American walleye (*Stizostedion vitreum*) are closely related. Both species display the 'family crest' of the perches – the spiked dorsal fin – and both possess large pike-like canine teeth. The combination of these features has led anglers to believe, quite erroneously, that zander and walleye are perch/pike crosses. They are not.

According to Alwyne Wheeler (*The Fishes of The British Isles and North-West Europe*) there is no breeding population of walleyes in Britain.

'My favourite among the freshwater fishes. Its capture with rod and line by means of spinning or livebaiting affords grand sport; he himself is an extremely beautiful, even a noble fish, and a very palatable eating indeed. In the Danube and its large tributaries, as well as in some of the Hungarian lakes, the pike-perch attains a weight of 40 lb and upwards. During the more than thirty years I have been devoted to angling I have caught several thousands of them, weighing from 2 lb up to 17 lb. The past month of September one of my fishermen, when netting, got one specimen in the River Thaya scaling 27 lb.

... I would highly recommend this fish to the attention of the National Fish Culture Association of Great Britain, and advise them not to spare any pains to attempt to naturalise the pike-perch in appropriate British waters, as by doing so the Association will not only increase the list of first-rate table fishes, but will also lay under an obligation the whole fellowship of English anglers, for he is a game fish and worth a challenge.'

From an account in *The Fishing Gazette*, 17 January 1885, by Emil Weeger

Zanders, like all the perches, are carnivorous. Indeed, when adult they are almost entirely fish-eaters. As a species they favour large lakes and large slow-moving rivers. Generally, angling methods are similar to those used for pike, although concessions in the form of smaller baits and lighter breaking-strain lines are made to the zander's smaller size. Most British zander fishermen, however, hold a poor opinion of the zander's fighting abilities compared with those of the pike.

Figure 331: The vivacity of the picture depicting a 37-inch zander (*below*) taken from Alkmaade contrasts with the dead cod-like look (*left*) of the larger zander caught by Dutchman Noel de Vries from Ijssel lake. Noel's fish took a 7-inch roach livebait and played for 45 minutes before being landed on what was obviously too light a line (6 lb BS)

The Zander

Figure 332: We like this picture (sent to us by Jan Eggers) not because the zander is particularly large (5–6 lb) but because of the artistry of its composition. As you look at this photograph every line (the captor's eye, the index finger of his left hand, two fingers of the right hand making a Churchillian gesture, the rod, the line and the body of the fish) points to the feature that the photographer wanted us to see – the dorsal fin of the zander. But there is more – the out-of-focus background of reeds and water tell you where the zander likes to live

Figure 333: 5 lb zander caught by Ken Sutton; Woburn Abbey lake, 1958

Cooking the Zander

Since few British anglers kill the zander they catch, only a few have discovered that the zander's delicious flavour compensates for its lack of gameness. A reluctance to kill fish for food is common among British coarse-fish anglers, unlike their eastern European counterparts, who fish for the table as well as for sport. This is somewhat ironic. Since the zander is very susceptible to injury and may die as a result of captivity in a keepnet, the zander fisherman may just as well kill his catch and eat it. Mortality due to angling is unlikely to make serious inroads on the zander population. The fecundity of this fish is astonishing: a 25-inch hen fish has been known to produce 685,000 eggs.

Part Two

TACKLE *&* TECHNIQUE

However delightful Angling may be, it ceases to
be innocent when used otherwise than as a mere
recreation.

Richard Brookes, *The Art of Angling* (1766)

Etruscan angler. Orvieto, *c.* 300 BC

Rods are most made to have the small canes thrust down into the wide canes, so that a man may walk with them as with a staffe, and when he pleaseth to draw them forth, and use them as occasion shall be offered: the only exception which is taken at these kinds of Rods, is the bright colour of the cane, which reflecting into the water offtimes feareth the Fish, and makes them afrayd to bite ... a Master in this Art will Umber and darken the Rod, by rubbing it over a gentle fire with a little Capons grease, and brown of Spaine mixt together.

Gervase Markham, *The Pleasures of Princes* (1614)

Figure 334: The earliest angling illustration, *c.* 2000 BC. From P. E. Newberry's *Beni Hasan* (1893)

RODS

Tackle development through the ages was painfully slow. It took about 4,000 years to advance from a *tight* line – that is, a line tied to the rod-tip – to a *loose* line, which slipped through a rod-ring, or rings. (For misuse of the term 'running-line' see page 443.) Even in medieval times there is no mention of a top ring. It is probable that a loose line came into use in Europe some time during the sixteenth or seventeenth centuries, although not until Barker's *The Art of Angling* (1651) was anything like a *reel* mentioned. Even in the seventeenth and eighteenth centuries, when reels of a sort were available, most anglers still fished with tight lines. The accepted drill on hooking a big fish was to throw the rod into the water and hope to retrieve it later, when the fish had tired itself out. But although they were poor inventors with a very limited choice of tackle, those early anglers were no fools when it came to presentation. Plutarch, writing 1,900 years ago, says:

Choose a rod which is slim, for fear lest if it cast a broad shadow it might move the doubt and suspicion that is naturally in fishes.

And on the choice of leader he says:

Take order that the hairs which reach to the hook should seem as white as possible, for the whiter they be the less they are seen in the water for their conformity and likeness to it.

It is important to note that Plutarch's advice refers specifically to the angler's *terminal* tackle. *Out* of the water the colour white was universally condemned both in tackle or dress. That excellent angler John Dennys summed it all up beautifully in *The Secrets of Angling* (1613):

So shalt thou have alwayes in store the best,
And fittest Rods to serve they turne aright;
For not the brittle Cane, nor all the rest,
I like so well, though it be long and light,
Since that the Fish are frighted with the least
Aspect of any glittering thing, or white:

Have twist likewise, so that it be not white
Your Rod to mend, or broken top to tye;
For all white colours doe the Fishes fright
And make them from the bayte away to flye.

He was right. There is no doubt whatever that the flash of glossy rod surfaces or white fly-lines can be as disturbing to fish as the flash of gun barrels can be to game, and it's a pity that tackle manufacturers continue to produce them. In fairness, however, it should be pointed out that these are what the buyer wants. Green or brown fly-lines are not so popular, and although some makers are able and indeed anxious to offer a matt finish to a rod, most anglers reject it.

ORIGIN AND MATERIALS

According to William Radcliffe's classic work *Fishing from the Earliest Times* (1921), at least four methods of fishing – spear, net, hand-line and rod – were being used *c.* 2000 BC by the ancient Egyptians. They were, indeed, responsible for the first known illustration of angling.

Figure 335: This engraving of a painting by R. Frain, entitled *Rob o' The Trows* (courtesy of the executors of the late Arthur Gilbey), is interesting because its details hold sufficient clues to enable a piscatorial historian to describe and date it.

The title and the Scotch pines suggest that the subject was almost certainly Scottish, and the big river in the background is surely the Tweed. The boat with its slim clinker-built construction has all the features of a Tweed boat, whereas River Tay 'cobbles' have a wider beam with characteristic hooped pin rowlocks.

The three joints of the rod (when measured against the boatman) indicate a salmon fly rod of 16–18 feet. The boatman's hat has two salmon flies stuck in it.

The type of reel, the lie-flat rings on the rod and the wrinkled gutta-percha waders with wading brogues suggest that the picture of this Scottish salmon fly-fisher was painted circa 1850

Judging by the tackle portrayed in the mural (page 345), the rod was in two pieces and tapered. Furthermore, since the fish is being lifted from the water by its mouth, one assumes that the fisherman has not snatched it but caught it on a baited hook. He is without doubt a true angler; the first on record. But what was his rod made of?

Natural fibrous materials have long been used in the making of rods, and it is likely that the earliest rods were fashioned from papyrus reeds growing beside the Nile. Even up to modern times, the reed has endured; in the late 1950s the best match rods were still being made from Spanish reed. But in the meantime, a variety of woods and other substances had been tried.

Gervase Markham, writing in 1614, advocated the use of special materials for different parts of a rod. His list included ground-wichen, sallow, beech, hazel, poplar, cane and whalebone.

Great care was taken to ensure a good rod action. For the upper length of a 'ground' (or bottom-fishing) rod, Robert Venables (1662) prescribed cane, into which was fitted a finer piece of blackthorne, into which was tucked an even finer piece of whalebone.

By the nineteenth century the most popular materials were ash, greenheart, hickory, cane and lancewood. Cuban lancewood, which was considered the best, was reserved for middle and top joints. Butts were mainly of white ash or hickory.

In *The Angler's Companion to the Rivers and Lochs of Scotland* (1847), Thomas Stoddart remarked:

Lance-wood is closer grained and somewhat heavier than hickory. It is a native of Cuba and other West India islands. For top-pieces, it is reckoned invaluable, possessing a spring and consistency, together with a capability of being highly wrought and polished, not found in any other wood. The great objection to lance-wood is its weight and consequent tendency, when used as a top-piece along with different woods, to injure or discompose the just and desirable balance of the rod.

('Just and desirable balance' – what a nice phrase; written with true feeling for a rod that should 'come alive' in the hand!)

Hickory was the first wood to fall out of general favour – although it was still a rodmaker's first choice for the handle of a big-game rod until as late as 1960.

Greenheart remained popular. Most of it came from Guyana. If the greenheart timbers were carefully selected, rods could be made that were both strong and elastic but unaffected by water. Greenheart was, and still is, a highly suitable rodmaking material. Treated with keen tools, it files, scrapes, turns and planes very well.

It has been said that although the idea of split-cane rods originated in Britain during the early part of the nineteenth century, the first serious attempt to construct rods from lengths of bamboo, split and glued together, was made by Samuel Phillippe of Easton, Pennsylvania, between 1846 and 1850. It seems, however, that William Blacker, the English rodmaker, was running him neck and neck. We quote from his *Art of Fly Making* (1855 edition):

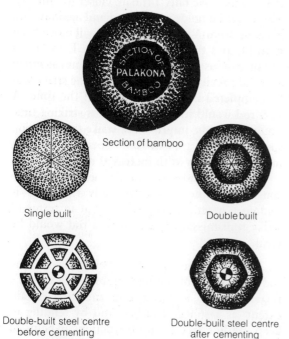

Section of bamboo

Single built

Double built

Double-built steel centre before cementing

Double-built steel centre after cementing

The beautiful rent and glued-up bamboo-cane fly-rods, which I turn out to the greatest perfection, are very valuable, as they are both light and powerful, and throw the line with great facility. The cane for these rods must be of the very best description, or they will not last any time. They will last for years if properly made, and of course the fisher must take care of them; they are best when made into pocket rods, in eight joints, with all the knots cut out, and the good pieces between each knot rent and glued up; these may be had in my shop of as good a balance as a three-joint rod, most superbly made of the lightest brazings. They make capital perch and roach rods with a bait top added to the extra fly top, with bored butt to hold all. These rods can be made to suit a lady's hand for either boat or fly-fishing.

Even when allowance is made for Blacker's salesmanship, it seems probable that his split-cane rods had been in production for a number of years. In Stoddart's book of 1847, already mentioned, we find:

Rod-makers are now in the habit of constructing the top-lengths, partly of lance-wood and partly of bamboo. The bamboo portion consists of a thin slit or slits detached from one of the jointed divisions of the cane. This is rounded off and otherwise cut and planed, so as to admit of being accurately glued on to the lance-wood section of the intended top-piece, the parts thus annexed being afterwards strengthened by a wrapping of waxed thread and coatings of varnish.

Although used only for a part of a rod and seemingly glued on to a lancewood core, this is undoubtedly what is known as 'split-cane', and it is almost certain that Blacker, working on his own, had started to follow the matter to its conclusion (a full-length rod) during the 1840s.

Although the notion of a split-cane fishing rod may have originated in Britain, split-cane had long been in use for other purposes. In *Angling Diversions* (1945), A. Courtney Williams writes:

Figure 336: Items from Hardy's *Angler's Guide*, 1909

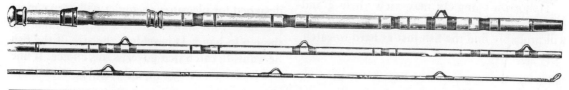

Built-cane seems to have been invented in China, first applied to fishing rods in England, and thereafter jointly developed by manufacturers in England and USA. Who first thought of splitting bamboo into strips and then gluing them together so as to obtain the full strength of the cane by eliminating its hollow centre, is likely to remain a matter of conjecture. It is, however, certain that it did not originate in either England or USA, but most probably in China. It seems to have been generally overlooked that the art was known in that country nearly 3,000 years ago. In the book of *Tchouang-Tseu* (950 BC) an explanation is given as to how to build split-cane 'rods', glued and bound.

Similar 'rods' are also mentioned in the *History* of *T'chou* and *T'au* (350 BC) Book 7, Chapter 71, which is now based in the National Museum in Paris.

It is true that in both cases the 'rods' are mentioned as being used by water-carriers to transport pails on their shoulders, but even though they were not fishing rods, the essence of the idea was there.

In 1925, a machine was devised to cut and plane the six triangular sections of bamboo that together made up a built-cane section; hitherto this job had been done by hand. Bamboo from the Tonkin region of China had been found to be the best, and it is interesting to note that when machines replaced the men who had previously split the Tonkin poles with a knife, the term 'split' cane was no longer used. Rodmakers now referred to their material as 'built' cane.

Since 1945, rodmaking developments have been spectacular: hollow-built cane rods; rods made from drawn-steel alloy tubes, and from aluminium alloy tubes (a failure, due to metal fatigue); rods of solid glass, fibre-glass and, recently, carbon-fibre and boron. The eclipse of natural fibrous materials is almost complete. Apart from a few individual craftsmen who, striving to keep old skills alive, still turn out split-cane rods of high quality, the rodmakers of the future will look to improved compounds that are man-made.

Tomorrow's anglers may view their grandfathers' rods with some amusement, but they will probably find the fish just as hard to catch.

CHOICE OF ROD

A fishing rod is a tool. It has four functions:

1. *Presentation.* A rod is an extension of the arm. By helping the angler to place his bait or lure inside the fishing area it increases his casting potential. Any lure can be presented by hand after a fashion, even a fly. A rod simply makes this presentation very much easier. It helps us to reach fish.

2. *Attraction.* A rod helps to control a lure; for instance, when a fly-line is 'mended' during salmon fishing (see page 210). Thus, it helps to attract fish.

3. *Striking.* A rod improves the efficiency of an angler's arm and helps him to hook fish. If an angler fishing a hand-line holds the line at A (see figure 337) and raises his arm to B, the baited hook – resting on the bottom eight yards away at E – will move only 1 ft 6 in. closer to him (F); whereas if he holds a $10\frac{1}{2}$ ft rod and again moves his hand from A to B, the rod-tip will move from C to D, and the baited hook from E to G – a distance of just over 5 ft 7 in., four times as much as it did previously. Furthermore, the strike will be completed in only a quarter of the time. A 14 ft rod would further reduce this striking time (in other words, improve the strike transmission speed). Strike transmission speed, therefore, increases directly with increased rod length.

There is, however, another design factor to consider: stiffness. A completely rigid rod is seldom a practical proposition, but in terms of strike transmission speed, such a rod would be ideal.

4. *Landing.* When a fish is being played, the rod takes some of the line strain off an angler's fingers. It also acts as a lever and, to a certain extent, as a shock absorber, and by tending to keep the line free from obstructions it helps to control and land fish.

It follows that since a fishing rod is a tool designed for pleasure, an angler will derive most pleasure from choosing a rod most suitable for the job in hand. It is seldom the size of the fish he wants to catch that governs this choice. If line and leader are strong enough, the biggest salmon

Freshwater Fishing

can be landed (in unobstructed water) on the smallest trout rod. Conversely, the smallest trout can be landed on the biggest salmon rod. Nevertheless, it would be as foolish to use a small trout rod for early spring salmon fishing, as it would be pointless to use a big salmon rod for trout fishing. What normally governs the choice of a rod is the method of fishing, the weight of bait or lure and the distance it has to be cast.

A salmon fly-fisherman casting in early spring with a sinking line and 3 in. tube-fly will need a powerful 14–16 ft double-handed rod to present and control his lure effectively. He can fish the same water for salmon in June or July with a $\frac{3}{4}$ in. tube-fly on floating line, using a 9–10 ft single-handed trout rod – and often will. It is his *approach* that dictates his choice of rod, not the size of the fish. Using a shooting-head the reservoir trout angler with no obstructions behind him can cast his 40 yards with an $8\frac{1}{2}$–9 ft rod. The sea trout fly-fisherman, wading in the darkness down a bushy run, needs a 10–11 ft rod to steeple-cast with rhythm, although the distance he casts is seldom more than 15–20 yards.

Generally speaking, a long rod (upwards of 12 ft) has a special if limited application. It is useful to the game angler when he wishes to keep as much line as possible out of the water – for instance, when playing a fish on a sinking line. Also, to the beach angler when it keeps his line clear of the first few breakers, thereby reducing false bites. The coarse angler uses a long rod for an altogether different reason.

Paradoxically, he uses it when float-fishing in deep water at *close range*. The long rod helps him to keep rod-tip, float and hook in a straight line, or nearly, thereby eliminating slack and helping him to strike more effectively.

Since the need to keep rod-tip, float and hook in a straight line is essential for quick striking, long rods (of up to 30 ft or over) are used for short-range float-fishing. As a swing rather than a cast is all that is needed for short-range work, long-rod anglers reject the flexible rod (its superior casting qualities are not needed) in favour of a stiff rod, which gives them the quickness required for a wristy strike.

Ideally, in the hands of a competent angler, the stiffer the rod the better for striking a fish, and the better for playing it. A too supple rod that bends nearly double when a fish is being played is of little use for keeping the line clear of the water, or controlling the fish when it is close to the angler's bank – where fish are frequently lost. It is for *casting* that a compromise must be found between extremes of flexibility.

Medium length rods, 9–12 ft, are the most versatile. Mainly, they are flexible throughout and have an 'all-through' action, that is, an action designed to withstand the strain of casting. No rod strain is more severe than that imposed by casting; so, of primary importance is the casting *weight*. Only with big-game rods, boat rods and

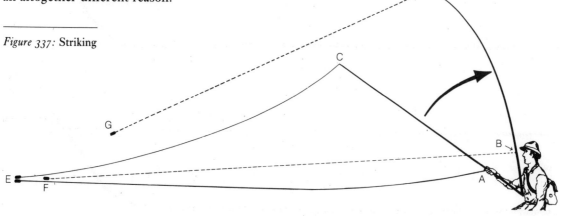

Figure 337: Striking

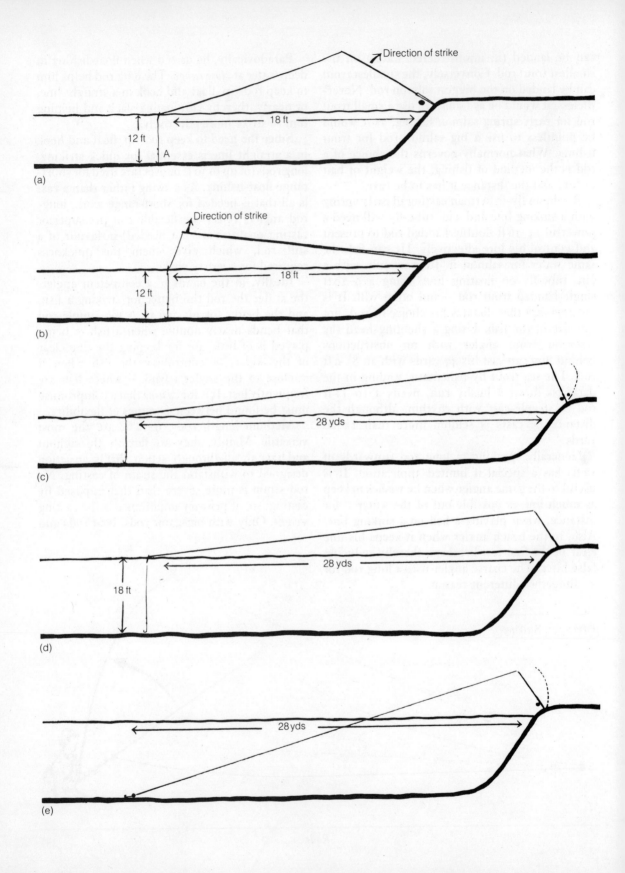

Figure 338: (a) A roach angler using a 9 ft rod is float-fishing at a point some six yards from the bank in twelve feet of water. In these circumstances, a strike that induces 12 in. of rod-tip movement merely flattens the angle between the rod-tip and the bait at A. $4\frac{1}{2}$ ft of slack line needs to be taken up before the hook can begin to penetrate. Hence, for many bites, very few fish will be hooked

(b) Here, an angler fishes the same swim with an 18 ft roach-pole. This time, a wristy strike inducing 12 in. of rod-tip movement will give immediate hook penetration, since there is almost no slack line. This style of fishing requires a stiff rod that will transmit the strike to the hook at maximum speed

The last three diagrams show a few situations anyone other than the fly-fisher has to deal with. If the principles involved are understood, the beginner will be able to decide what tackle and technique to use for fishing at any particular range or depth.

(c) An angler float-fishes a shallow swim about 28 yards from the bank. In these circumstances, a long forearm strike is needed to overcome nylon sag and stretch

(d) The angler is now fishing a swim about 18 ft deep. A strike with even a 6 ft rod-tip movement will hardly move the hook. With so much slack line to combat, float-fishing is almost impossible – unless a fish hooks itself!

(e) A simple answer to the problem: ledger fishing. Now, slack line is almost entirely eliminated and a strike is taken direct to the hook

Note: There is of course always a degree of sag, in the shape of a catinary curve, below a line drawn direct from rod-tip to lead

---

sometimes match rods, is this not the designer's first consideration. Most big-game and boat rod breakages occur during the playing of a fish, whereas with others it is casting (albeit through faulty technique) that causes most trouble. When made of Spanish reed, match rods often suffered damage when misused as casting rods.

Medium length all-action rods are suitable for long-range ledgering at any depth, and ideal for float-fishing at distance in shallow or medium depth water, especially in very clear streams where long-trotting is necessary to avoid frightening fish.

A short rod makes it difficult for the angler to lift his line clear of bushes and other obstructions, to control a sunk line, or to keep a fish away from obstructions close to his own bank. Except sometimes for boat fishing or fishing among overhanging branches, short rods should be avoided.

Choice of rod for the coarse-fish angler

The quarry may be divided conveniently into four categories:

1. Big carp and barbel
2. Bream, chub, tench, smaller carp, big perch
3. Roach, dace and rudd
4. Pike

For the first category, where the style of fishing will usually be ledgering, a 10 ft two-piece rod having a test-curve (see figure 339) of $1\frac{1}{2}$ lb is the best choice. Such a rod will take lines of from 6 lb to 12 lb BS (dry breaking strain) and cast leads of up to about $1\frac{1}{2}$ oz. It can thus be used for salmon and pike spinning, though it is not powerful enough for livebaiting with large baits, or deadbaiting with herrings or mackerel.

In recent years, it has been suggested that rods of 11 ft or 12 ft may have some advantage in carp fishing. In practice, such rods are generally held higher up the grip, so their effective length is not much greater; and if it is, there will be extra leverage against the angler's hand, which will the more quickly start to ache when a big fish is in play. A longer rod also reduces the pressure the angler can apply when that is necessary to keep a fish away from weed or snag. Consequently there is no reason for choosing a carp rod that is longer than 10 ft, except where fishing is to be done at extreme casting range.

It is important to choose one having correct tapers as well as a suitable test-curve, otherwise soft baits will not stay on the hook in casting.

For the second category, two kinds of rod are needed, for ledgering and float-fishing. For ledgering, a 10-ft two-piece rod with a test-curve of about 1 lb will usually do all that is required; a somewhat steeper taper than that of the $1\frac{1}{2}$ lb test-curve carp rod is advantageous. This will throw up to 1 oz, but for ledgering at extreme range as is sometimes necessary in lake fishing for bream and big perch, the carp rod can be used instead. The 1 lb test-curve rod will take lines from about $3\frac{1}{2}$ lb to 8 lb BS.

For float-fishing and for some aspects of lighter ledgering, there is a choice of lengths of three-piece rods, with test-curves of about $\frac{3}{4}$ lb,

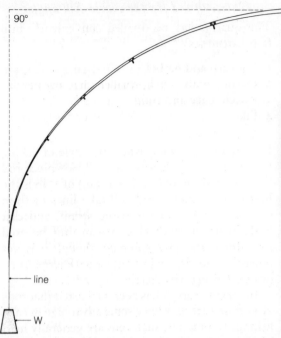

90°

line

W

Figure 339: (left) The test-curve rating of a rod is the load (W) needed to bend the rod to an approximate quarter-circle

Figure 340: (below) A blank is tested for correct deflection

though for long-trotting in fast water, where chub and barbel are found, a somewhat more powerful rod is needed with a 1 lb test-curve. For this, a rod of 11 ft to 12 ft is suitable. Ordinarily, a $\frac{3}{4}$ lb test-curve suffices and for easy, fatigue-free fishing a 12-footer is excellent. Only in special circumstances is there any advantage in a longer rod of 13 ft or even 14 ft. These longer rods are more tiring to use, but they are sometimes helpful in fishing over marginal weed beds or rush-growths.

For the third category, the same range of three-piece rods will do well. These rods will take a wide range of line-strengths, from about 2 lb to 7 lb BS, and cast up to $\frac{3}{4}$ oz, but they behave very well with lightly loaded tackle also.

For pike fishing, the 10 ft, $1\frac{1}{2}$ lb test-curve carp rod takes care of spinning with artificial lures, plugs, spoons and other spinners, up to $1\frac{1}{2}$ oz in weight, though the weight to consider is the combined weight of lure and lead, if any.

For much heavier baits, like live or dead fish, or outsize plugs, again a 10 ft two-piece rod is recommended, but with a test-curve of $3\frac{1}{2}$ to 4 lb.

Suitable lines run from 12 lb to 25 lb BS, and weights of up to $4\frac{1}{2}$ oz can be cast, using the full power of the rod. More important, by the use of a long, slow, sweeping, casting action, it is poss-

TEST CURVES

Manufacturers of experimental cane, glass, carbon and boron rod blanks, measure the power of assembled blanks by means of deflection tests, in order to arrive at what is known as a test-curve rating. Ratings are usually expressed in pounds (weight) to the nearest quarter-pound. If you know the manufacturer's rating, multiply the figure by six in order to arrive at the line-strength most suited to the rod (other than fly-

rods). To discover the rod's maximum casting weight, divide the figure by sixteen (other than fly-rods).

When no maker's figure is given anglers can rate their own rods by gradually filling a purse (which has been attached to the rod's top ring) with lead shot until the weight of the shot bends the rod to an approximate quarter circle (see figure 339).

Freshwater Fishing

ible to pitch baits weighing up to $\frac{1}{2}$ lb to sufficient distances, when these are needed to catch pike, and a rod of this power will pull home the larger hooks, or multiples of hooks, that are usually associated with these bigger baits.

Those then are the kinds of rod that the all-round coarse-fish angler will require to be basically well-equipped, though he may also wish to add more specialized rods to his armoury. The match angler may require rods that will take screw-in visual bite-indicators like swing-tips, spring-tips, or quiver-tips.

ROD-RINGS

Needless to say, the best rod-rings are expensive, since they are made with expensive materials, but over the lifetime of a rod their cost will be well worthwhile.

Before buying a rod (and you won't get the best unless you pay for it) ensure that all intermediate rings have been chromed. Any other finish is suspect, unless the material used (e.g.

Figure 341: The selection of rod-rings described in the text

tungsten-carbide) is harder than chrome. Also make sure that all rings are smoothly finished and jointed, otherwise the line will gradually suffer damage.

Since no single pattern of rod-ring is suitable for all rods, it is not surprising that anglers are faced with a bewildering choice. Nevertheless, the few patterns we describe cover the needs of most freshwater anglers.

1. *Snake ring.* An intermediate ring suitable for fly-rods, although not as good as a stand-off ring. Strong, light and unobtrusive.
2. *Cradle ring.* Popular intermediate ring for medium and heavy spinning and ledger rods.
3. *Semi stand-off intermediate ring.* Ideal for medium length float rods, 'Avon' type rods, and light spinning rods designed to cast very light baits. More susceptible to damage than the cradle ring, but less than the delicate, high, 'Bell's Life' ring. The importance of stand-off rings is that they reduce 'line-stick' and 'line-slap', which hinder casting efficiency, particularly with light baits. A wet line sticking to the underside of a rod increases the inertia that the casting stroke

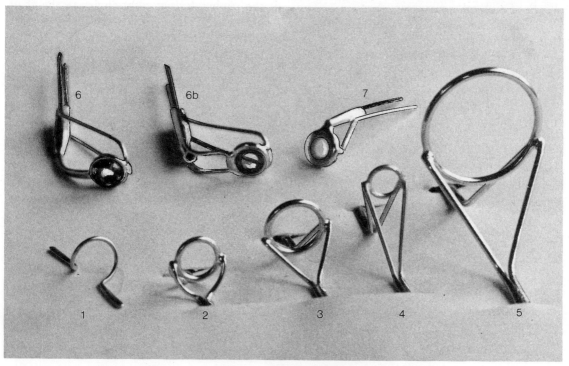

has to overcome; a wet line slapping against the underside of a rod increases the amount of drag. (Both are noticeable when a fly-line is being 'shot' through snake rings.)

4. *'Bell's Life' intermediate ring*. The classic pattern for a float-fishing rod. Line-slap and line-slip are almost entirely eliminated. The wire should be stiff and hard-chromed. Unfortunately, many rodmakers use soft wire which, as most coarse-anglers know to their cost, is an abomination: the long support legs being so easily damaged.

5. *Butt or 'gathering' ring*. Many anglers and rodmakers seem convinced that a large butt-ring is a vital feature on any rod used with a fixed-spool reel. As liquid has to be gathered in a funnel before it can be poured into the narrow neck of a bottle, so, it is thought, coils of line coming off a spool in spiral fashion need to be gathered by a large ring before they will 'pour' smoothly through the smaller-diameter intermediate rings. It seems plausible. Experience, however, teaches otherwise. Some tournament casters (and who should know better?) think that two smaller-diameter butt-rings placed within an inch of each other are more effective.

6. *Stand-off end ring*. This complements the 'Bell's Life' intermediate rings. It is usually finished with an agate or 'jewelled' centre. Although this is more groove resistant than most metals, a good tungsten-carbide ring is better still.

Note: There is also a stand-off end ring similar in design but screw-threaded to take a swing-tip (6b).

7. *Standard end ring*. The best are made of tungsten-carbide. Agate rings should be inspected frequently for cracks or roughness. Failure to notice cracks has lost a lot of fish.

All good end rings are fitted with a tube as well as two tangs. The tube accommodates the extreme tip of the rod and the tangs (when covered with binding) help to even out the bending strain at the wide end of the tube, where there is an unavoidable cutting edge.

ROD-RESTS

A. Welded metal rest, the cheapest available. Simply a superior forked stick.

B. A jointless metal rest, lighter and very slightly superior to type A.

C. Ideal for the angler who ledgers for carp and other fish that are allowed to run with a bait unhindered until the strike is made. The top of the 'V' supports the rod; the slot underneath permits the line to slip out through the rod-rings without being trapped between rod and rest, as it may be with a 'forked stick' rest.

D. Telescopic rest fitted with rubber fork. The height adjustment, similar to that of a shooting-stick, is a useful feature. To take advantage of his rod length while ledgering, the angler can re-fit the rubber fork at right-angles to the shaft (see diagram). This enables the rest to be set over the water while maintaining the fork in a vertical plane.

E. The Sheffield 'Match' rest is a favourite among competition anglers. The wide, shallow, rubber fork facilitates quick sideways striking when speed is all-important.

F. The 'Wilson Universal' is one of the best among many attempts to design a rest for use on ground too hard for a spike. All the joints can be swivelled and locked, to adjust for sloping banks and easy packing.

Figure 342: The selection of rod-rests described in the text

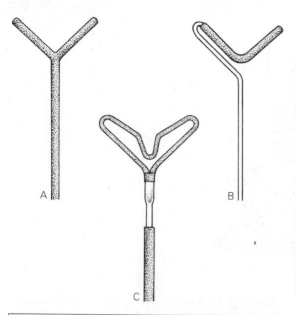

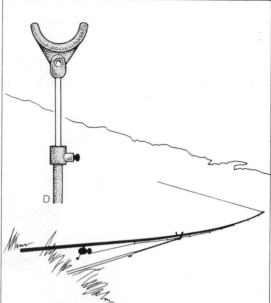

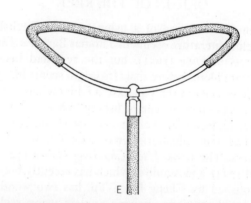

The manner of his Trouling was, with a Hazell Rod of twelve foot long, with a Ring of Wyre in the top of his Rod, for his line to run thorow: within two foot of the bottome of the Rod there was a hole made, for to put in a winde, to turne with a barrell, to gather up his Line, and loose at his pleasure.

Thomas Barker, *The Art of Angling* (1651)

Rods

REELS

ORIGIN OF THE REEL

The first mention of a fishing reel in English angling literature occurs in Thomas Barker's *The Art of Angling* (1651), but the reel had been invented long before that. Its origin seems likely to have been in the Far East: a Chinese painting of 1195 depicts a type of fishing 'wheele' in use five hundred years before *The Art of Angling*.

The 1195 illustration was soon followed by others. The book *T'ien Chu Ling Ch'ien* (1208 and 1224), a facsimile of which has recently been published by Cheng Chen-To, has two woodblock illustrations showing anglers using reels similar to the one painted by Ma Yuan.

A river landscape entitled *Fishermen*, painted by Wu Chen (1280–1354) (figure 347), shows two anglers fishing with what by now appears to be standard Chinese tackle. It is particularly interesting because one of the anglers seems to be holding the line in order to feel a bite – perhaps the earliest example of 'touch ledgering'. It also has a curious feature in that the lines fail to reach the end of the rods, although this of course could be ascribed to artistic licence.

Further evidence of an early reel comes in the form of an Armenian parchment Gospel of the thirteenth century – see G. Sarton's *Introduction to the History of Science* (1947) and Lynn White's *Medieval Technology and Social Change* (1962). Dr Joseph Needham in *Science and Civilisation in China* Vol. 2 (1965) sketches the historical links between China and Armenia, showing that techniques could have been transferred from one to the other.

In the book *San Tshai Thu Hui* (1609) there is a very clear illustration (figure 345) of a rod and reel being used for turtle fishing – a method still common in China today.

Figure 343: (above right) This picture, *Angler on a Wintry Lake*, painted by Ma Yuan c. 1195, contains the earliest known illustration* of a fishing reel. It was taken from O. Siren's *History of Early Chinese Painting* (1933) and *Chinese Painting: Leading Masters and Principles* (1956) *Figure 344: (below right)* These two illustrations from the facsimile edition of *T'ien Chu Ling Ch'ien*, were photographed for the authors by courtesy of the University Library, Cambridge

*On 18 December 1886 *The Fishing Gazette* published an extract from the *Japan Mail* reference an exhibition of antiquities which opened in Tokyo on 1 November 1885:

'There is one room, the contents of which alone will amply repay a visit. Its walls are entirely covered with pictures by the old Chinese masters. Two of them, gems from an antiquarian standpoint, hang inside a case which stands at the entrance. They are painters of the Sung period – Baian and Riushomen – and, apart from the merits as works of art, one of them established the fact that reels were used by Chinese Anglers in the *eleventh century*.' (Our italics.)

If there is substance in this report then the Chinese invention of the fishing reel is older than is presently conceded.

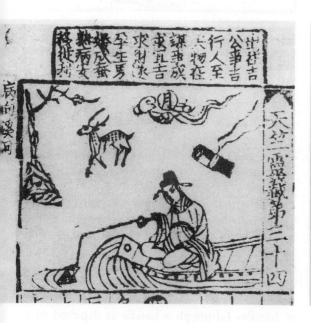

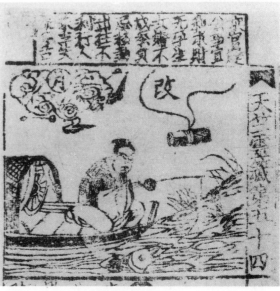

In *c.* 1850, according to Charles Chenevix Trench, in *A History of Angling* (1974) a certain Dabry de Thiersaut noticed the reel being used in China (the picture once more illustrates turtle fishing with a characteristic style Chinese 'spoke' reel – figure 346).

Chenevix Trench commented on the similarity of this reel to an earlier Chinese reel but made no comment on the obvious differences, viz:

(a) The 1850s reel possessed a winding handle whereas the older reels did not.

(b) The spindle of the newer reel did not pass through a hole in the rod handle as it must have done in the old models and certainly does in the reels currently used in China (see page 364). Instead, we can see from the illustration that the reel was either slung below the rod for a right-hander – or perched above the rod (like a multiplier) for a left-hander. We prefer the first option because five out of the six Chinese anglers so far depicted in this chapter are right-handers against the one left-hander.

(c) Notice the rod is fitted with two rings which are placed ideally for a left-handed fisherman using the reel on top of the rod!

(d) The rod button fitted to the rod is like the one depicted on the title page of *The Experienc'd Angler* (1662) (see page 366).

Throughout the centuries, Chinese fishing tackle has shown remarkably little change. Fred Buller, who toured China in March 1986 to discover more about early reels, was astonished to meet a Peking angler who was not only fishing during the bitter northern winter, but using an ancient handle-less 'spoke' reel similar in every respect to the one depicted in use over eight hundred years before. There follows a short account of his quest.

THE EARLIEST FISHING REELS

In March 1986 I went to Peking in the hope of studying the original paintings which depict Chinese using fishing reels nearly five centuries before the earliest illustration of the reel (1662) appeared in European angling literature.

In the event the location of these paintings,

Figure 345: This early seventeenth-century illustration shows a Chinese angler using a rod and reel for turtle fishing. For hundreds, perhaps even a thousand years, the Chinese have fished with seemingly identical rods and reels. The photograph is by courtesy of Dr Joseph Needham

some of which had been reproduced in various books on Chinese art and technology, proved elusive since I was to discover that many of them were now possessed by foreign museums and art galleries.

Throughout the centuries the classical Chinese drumless reel, hereon referred to as the 'spoke' reel, appeared to accommodate line around six to twelve 'cats cradles', each of which sat on the end of a spoke making up what looks like a miniature nine-spoke rimless cartwheel.

Since the reel was not provided with a handle or handles (although a handle is depicted in a nineteenth-century version (see figure 346 below), I had assumed that line-recovery was achieved by rotating the reel with the appropriate index finger poked between two spokes.

One morning all uncertainties as to how the reel functioned vanished after my companion Francis Plum spotted a group of Chinese, some of whom were fishing with reels which appeared to be identical (except for the materials used) to those shown in the early paintings.

As soon as we had recovered from the excitement of this discovery we settled down to watch and photograph the anglers fishing a match.

Whereas 20 ft roach-poles were used almost exclusively for float-fishing (a method not requiring a reel) the reels were used by anglers who

were ledgering, enabling them to make long and accurate casts; accuracy being a necessity in the case of one angler who was using five rods and casting out his baits in an impressive fan-like pattern.

Sure enough, as I had guessed, the index finger was used to wind in the line and playing fish presented no hazard. Hooked fish were dealt with in the traditional way – that is to say, the rod was moved upwards and backwards whenever the fish gave ground (or water) and then it was lowered quickly to facilitate line recovery by means of equally quick finger-winding of the reel.

After chatting to the Chinese fishermen through our interpreter (such assistance is really unnecessary in a country where English is taught as the second language) we discovered the whereabouts of Peking's best tackle shop where we were soon able to handle and purchase three versions of the classic 'spoke' reel.

Technically, the reel possesses two surprising features which may or may not have been present in the reels depicted in the old paintings. Firstly the reel – otherwise free-running and checkless – could, with a simple turn of a knurled nut, be locked so as to provide the facility of an anti-reverse. Secondly, to prevent overruns, hand-

Figure 346: Dabry de Thiersaut's picture of a reel

Figure 347: Fishermen. This part of Wu Chen's fine painting is reproduced by courtesy of the Freer Gallery of Art Library, Smithsonian Institution, Washington, DC

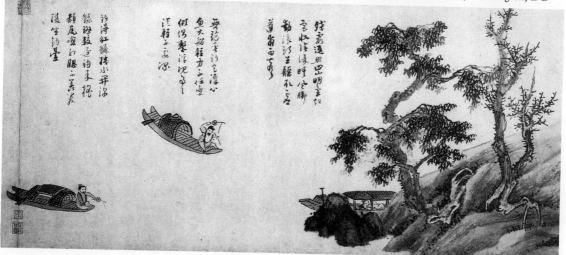

braking is achieved by applying thumb pressure to a special drum-shaped wooden extension of the spool (see page 364).

Casting with the 'spoke' reel is easy for all those able to cast with a single-action revolving drum or multiplying reel.

A special long-stemmed butt-ring has to be used in conjunction with the classic Chinese 'spoke' fishing reel. It is whipped on to the rod 15 in. above the reel axle.

The ring centre of $\frac{1}{8}$ in. bore is made of porcelain and is mounted on the end of a $2\frac{1}{2}$ in. stem thus ensuring that line, as it is recovered, is guided straight on to the reel.

Since the rest of the rings hug the rod in the normal way the porcelain ring at the end of the stem is slightly angled inwards so as to reduce line drag.

Figure 348: The 'roach-pole', which originated in China and was exported to the West; the fixed-spool reel, which originated in England but has now reached China (via Japan); and the Chinese 'spoke' reel, which originated in China and has so far stayed there, seemingly without causing even a ripple of interest elsewhere

A poem of silk and a fisherman

Foam resembling a thousand drifts of snow.
Soundless, the peach and pear trees form their
    battalions of spring.
With one jug of wine
And a fishing line,
On this earth how many are as happy as I?
I dip the oar – in the spring winds the boat drifts
    like a leaf.
A delicate hook on the end of a silk tassel,
An island covered with flowers,
A jugful of wine.
Among the ten thousand waves I wander in
    freedom!

Liyu (936–978): *Fisherman's Song.*
Translated from the Chinese by Hsiung Ting
(1947)

The poet reveals that anglers have used silk for a thousand years and since the technology of silk spinning in China is at least twice as old – we can only guess at the antiquity of the Chinese fishing reel.

Freshwater Fishing

Figure 349: (*above*) Ledgering with spoke reel in China – 1986 style. It might be thought that an angler is at a great disadvantage using such an instrument, but this is far from the case. F. B., who has cast with it, finds it a delight to use. Seemingly without change, the same design has been in use for many centuries – in all probability long before it was first illustrated – and so efficient was it that not until the late nineteenth century did it find an equal in the western world

Figure 350: The Chinese long-stemmed butt-ring

Figure 351: (*right*) This photograph taken by Dr Joseph Needham at Tunhuang in China (1943) depicts a working block-spoked driving-wheel, a form in which the ends of the spokes bear grooved blocks. In this instance the machinery was used for spinning hemp or flax. In his description of this and other inventions Dr Needham uses a most significant phrase: 'The Chinese never waste anything'

Figure 352: (*left*) One of the reels purchased from a Chinese tackle shop in 1986. On what technology is this long-lasting classic spoke reel based? In all probability it was Chinese sericulture or, more specifically, the technology of silk-spinning that inspired the invention of the fishing reel, just as the innovation of the fixed-spool reel is said to be based on Illingworth's knowledge of cotton-spinning machinery. As Dr Needham points out: 'Rimless driving-wheels are also common in Chinese textile technology. In one type the outwardly diverging spokes are connected by thin cords so as to form a bed or cats cradle (as in the "spoke" reel) which carries the driving-belt, while in others it passes over grooved blocks set at the end of spokes'

F. B. writes: This photograph (*far left*) shows the wooden drum-shaped extension of the spool used for hand-braking.

It also shows that the reel axle ($\frac{3}{16}$ in. diameter) goes through a hole in the rod handle before being secured with a wing nut. When the reel is fitted to the right-hand side of the rod (as in the photograph) the line needs to come off the top side of the spool. This way of fishing the line eliminates the tendency of the fast-revolving spool to turn the axle round – which would result in the loosening of the wing nut. Alternatively, line recovery by forward winding is achieved by fitting the reel on the left-hand side of the rod – in which case the line comes off from the bottom side of the reel

NOTES ON EARLY ENGLISH REELS

Since many accounts relating to the reel in English angling literature are inaccurate and confusing, we append a simple chronology.

First mention of the reel: Thomas Barker, *The Art of Angling* (1651) (strangely, it was used by a namesake of Barker's):

One of my name was the best Trouler for a Pike in this Realm. . . . The manner of his Trouling was, with a Hazel Rod of twelve foot long, with a ring of Wyre in the top of his rod, for his Line to run through; within two foot of the bottom of the Rod, there was a hole made for to put in a wind, to turn with a barrel, to gather up his Line and loose at his pleasure.

Repeat mention of the reel: Thomas Barker, in another edition of *The Art of Angling* (1653).

First mention of the reel in relation to salmon fishing: Izaak Walton, *The Compleat Angler* (2nd edition) 1655.

Note also, that many use to fish for a Salmon, with a ring of wyre on the top of their Rod, through which the line may run to as great a length as is needful when he is hook'd. And to that end, some use a wheele about the middle of their rod, or nearer their hand, which are to be observed better by seeing one of them than by a large demonstration of words.

Second mention of the reel in relation to salmon fishing was by Thomas Barker in a further edition of *The Art of Angling* – now re-titled *Barker's Delight* (1657). This edition also introduced a line drawing of the reel with the 'spring' fitting, which enabled the position of the reel to be varied:

. . . you must have your winder within two foot of the bottom to goe on your rod made in this manner, with a spring, that you may put it on as low as you please:

In *The Arte of Angling* (1577), attributed to William Samuel, there is an interesting remark. Piscator says:

My Master that taught me to angle could not abide to catch a Ruffe; for if he toke one, either he would remove or *wind up* and home for that time. (Our italics)

Figure 354: The early English reel – an interpretation

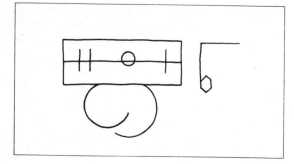

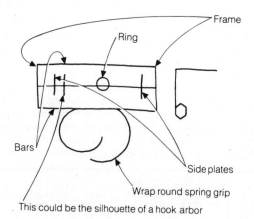

Figure 353: (*above*) Thomas Barker's illustration of a reel (1657) has never been clearly understood. We append our interpretation

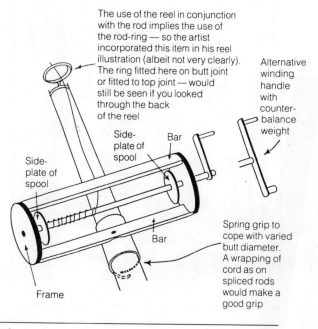

The use of the reel in conjunction with the rod implies the use of the rod-ring — so the artist incorporated this item in his reel illustration (albeit not very clearly). The ring fitted here on butt joint or fitted to top joint — would still be seen if you looked through the back of the reel

Alternative winding handle with counter-balance weight

Spring grip to cope with varied butt diameter. A wrapping of cord as on spliced rods would make a good grip

Now, what was meant by that? Did Piscator's Master wind up his line round his rod; or on a line-winder? Or was it a reference to an early reel? If so, it is certainly the first in English literature, preceding Barker's by seventy-four years.

That two of these proposals are not unreasonable can be seen from developments in other countries, viz: a Chinese painting by Tu Shu Chi Ch'ing (see page 367) depicts an angler fishing with a pole with spare line hooked round the rod, and in France (according to Charles Chenevix Trench) Liger's book *Amusements de Campagne* (1712) illustrates a hand-held bobbin round which spare line is wound. Indeed, we are told that even today some Japanese still favour the system of winding spare line round a cleat attached to the butt section of their rods.

Although not impossible, the proposals seem unlikely. One of the intermediate authors – Mascall, Dennys, Markham, Lauson – would surely have mentioned the reel had it been in use. According to the Shorter OED the first use of 'wind up' (*c.* 1205) referred to the hoisting of sails. It was subsequently used in the figurative sense: 'To sum up, or conclude'. In all probability Piscator meant simply that his Master would 'pack up and go home'.

All the same, it is worth remembering that before a reel could have been used there *must* have been a hole or a ring at the rod top for the line to pass through, doubtless to be taken up on a line-frame, similar to those shown in Dendy Sadler's painting (see page 12).

The use of a top ring in conjunction with a line-frame or 'winder', before the use of a reel, is not on record. Is Piscator's remark the first hint?

The first illustration of an identifiable reel is on the title page of Colonel Robert Venables's *The Experienc'd Angler* (1662). This, like most of those other early reels, had a 'pin and hole' fitting and was fastened with a wing nut.

The methods used in fastening the reel to the rod give the all-important clues to the age of reels: first the pin fastening through the rod butt (*c.* 1650–1700). Next the spring-clip and the spring-clip with leather padding (1657–1880). Finally, the modern type of reel seating with sliding bands on the rod butt. These dates are very rough, for it is impossible to establish an exact chronology and it seems clear that the various methods overlap considerably. The modern type of seating was illustrated by Daniel in 1807, but it seems that earlier versions were sometimes bound or nailed on.

Figure 355: The title page of Robert Venables's *The Experienc'd Angler* (1662) has caused much confusion. The left-hand rod has a knob on the butt resembling the recent screw-in button. The right-hand rod, however, has what seems to be a gun-butt. In fact, it is not part of the rod at all, but a *bait-horn* standing in front of the rod. Another bait-horn can be seen on the shelf, top-left

THE Experienc'd Angler; or Angling Improved.

Sold by Rich: Marriott in St Dunstans Churchyard. Vaughan sculp.

Figure 356: (right) Does this reproduction of an early Chinese painting by Tu Shu Chi Ch'ing show spare line looped round the rod, or does the artist's configuration of the wavelets create an optical illusion?

釣

Figure 357: The riddle of the reel

The frontispiece of Colonel Robert Venables's *The Experienc'd Angler* also contained the first identifiable illustration of a fishing reel, or 'winch'.

The reel is enlarged in (a) and the crudeness of the drawing calls for some textual support to convince the more sceptical reader that it really is intended to represent a fishing reel. This is provided on pages 44–5 of *The Experienc'd Angler*:

'The next way of Angling is with a Trowle for the Pike, which is very delightful, you may buy your trowle ready made, therefore I shall not trouble my self to describe it, only let it have a winch to wind it up withall. For this kind of fish your tackle must be strong, your Rod must not be very slender at the top, where you must place a small slender ring for your line to run through'

Ken Sutton's drawing of the Venables reel (b), which was published in *Fishing* (1965), shows what he thought to be the working principle: a barrel turned by a handle; a saddle, and a circular rod clamp. This was a most intelligent reconstruction and is probably very near to the truth. There is, however, one weakness: the way in which the reel is fastened to the rod. We find ourselves unable to endorse the practicability of the circular-sectioned rod-clamp.

The reel is redrawn in (c) to show the working principle: a barrel turned by a handle; a saddle, and an early pattern of wing nut screwing down on a vertical, threaded, reel-support pin that passed through a hole in the rod handle.

This method of fixing a reel to a rod was described eleven years earlier by Thomas Barker

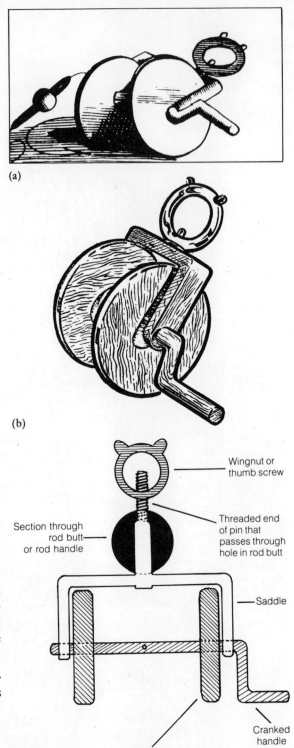

(a)

(b)

The idea of two sliding bands on the rod butt may seem a fairly simple engineering device, but it has to be remembered that in order to clasp the reel firmly the rings need to be on a slightly resilient surface, such as cork, and cork handles were not in use until much later. Cholmondeley-Pennell, in *Fishing* (1885), wrote:

Some reels are – or used to be – fitted with a circular clasp underneath. ... With butts such as are now the fashion, however, sloping rapidly away from the handle, these fastenings have naturally become obsolete.

So it can reasonably be assumed that the spring-clip, or 'circular clasp' as Pennell called it, was in use until about 1880.

Wingnut or thumb screw

Threaded end of pin that passes through hole in rod butt

Section through rod butt or rod handle

Saddle

Barrel or spool

Cranked handle

(c)

Figure 358: Early metal reels

All the very early brass reels had slender spindles, rarely more than a quarter of an inch in diameter, with spool diameters between one and two inches. As early as 1734 they were being advertised in London. It is surprising that so few have survived

Early metal reel. The pin fitted into a hole in the rod handle

Spring-clips to hold the reel securely on the ash or hickory poles used as rods succeeded the earlier 'pin' fastening. Some of the spring-clips were bound with leather to give a better grip

This early brass clip reel has a sliding pin which locks the handle, and a harbour for the hook when the reel was not in use. The small holes in the rim of the clip fastening are needle holes for stitching leather around the clip

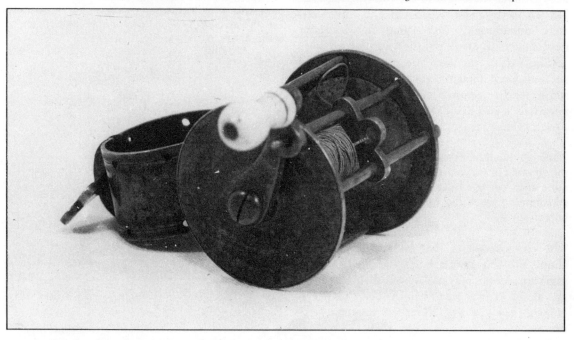

THE MULTIPLIER

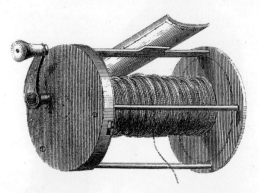

Figure 359: From the Rev. W. B. Daniel's *Rural Sports* (1801). The illustration shows the first known picture of a multiplying reel

Daniel's *Rural Sports* (1801) is doubly important because his reel is the first *multiplier* to be illustrated. A multiplying reel had already been mentioned by Onesimus Ustonson in an advertisement of 1770, which he added to his booklet *The True Art of Angling*. The Ustonson advertisement offered, amongst much else, 'The best Sort of Multiplying Brass Winches, both stop and plain'. (There has been much debate about the origin of the multiplying reel, but the truth is clear. Although the Americans were undoubtedly responsible for its later development, it was a British invention.)

The earlier models, however, were not a success. Even though Daniel, Best, Salter and some others recommended the multiplier, it was notoriously unreliable. Bainbridge, in *The Fly-Fisher's Guide* (1816), wrote:

Although the multiplying reel is now in general use, the advantages which are set forth in its favour are more than counter-balanced by the frequent disappointment which the Angler is liable to from its imperfections.

The construction of that early multiplier was simply not strong enough to stand any concerted pressure. As often as not the mechanism would fail at the critical moment. In *The Practice of Angling* (Vol. 1, 1845), O'Gorman was unequivocal:

I must say that I totally detest, abhor, and repudiate all click wheels, lock wheels, and multiplying wheels. ... A multiplying wheel is not worth a farthing for anything but small fish. You cannot get up a weight without breaking your machinery, or dropping your rod to the water. I have had sad experience of this kind of wheel, of which I may hereafter speak – having spoiled the work and lost an immense salmon through its means.

O'Gorman was, in fact, rather behindhand. T. Hofland, in his *British Angler's Manual* (1839), had already recorded the end of the multiplier's popularity:

The multiplying reel was formerly much used, but from its liability to be out of order, a plain reel, without a stop is now generally preferred.

In Britain during the rest of the nineteenth-century the multiplier was almost totally forgotten. It remained so until, towards the end of the century, its development by the famous Kentucky reel-makers of the United States gained it the reputation for workmanship and reliability it has subsequently never lost.

Figure 360: The early multiplier, like other early reel types variously known as wheeles, pirns or winches, was fitted underneath the rod handle, whereas today anglers universally adopt the reel-on-top position. We shall never know who caused the revolution, but it was probably a North American (see opposite)

Freshwater Fishing

Figure 361: (above) One of the earliest multiplying reels. Reels of this type were in use as early as 1770

Figure 363: (below) We are grateful to Mr Charles Bowen of Jacksonville, Illinois, for details of this seemingly modern multiplying reel. It was, in fact, made in 1883 by Benjamin F. Meek & Sons of Louisville, Kentucky. It has a gunmetal body with spiral gears, jewelled bearings and a takedown frame – all modern features. It represents a brilliant American development of a discarded British invention

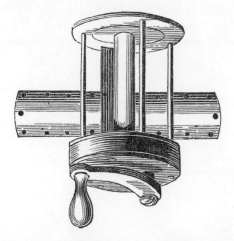

Figure 364: (below) This salmon fisher depicted in A. Mayer's book *Sport With Rod And Gun* (1883) shows that North Americans had no doubt 'which way up' the multiplier should be fixed to the rod

Figure 362: (above) If we remember that all the early multipliers were fitted under the rod and since it is likely that all these reels were made to accommodate right-handed anglers, the illustration, from Salter's *Anglers' Guide* (first published in 1814), is an anomaly. The reel position indicates that either (a) it was meant to be fitted on top of the rod for a right-handed operator, or (b) it was meant to be fitted under the rod for a left-handed operator, or (c) the illustrator fitted the reel the wrong way round on the handle prior to making his drawing.

We cannot dismiss the last option if we remember that an illustrator working for one of the biggest tackle companies (Millard Brothers) in the 1950s managed to print an image of a fixed-spool reel with the spool pointing towards the angler's groin on every page of the company catalogue!

Figure 365: The late William Hardy of Hardy Bros, Alnwick, coming ashore with a spring salmon. The use of a multiplier on Scotland's big rivers – now *de rigeur* for salmon spinning – is a comparatively recent development as is the almost universal adoption of the wooden rather than the metal Devon minnow

Figure 366: Some of the old reels we show, dated from 1650, come from the collection of Ken Sutton (*below*), while others come from the collection of David Beazley. We acknowledge our debt to them and for their opinions as to the provenance of those reels

Figure 367: In the 1930s the American-made Pflueger 'Supreme' reel was probably the first precision made multiplying reel to achieve worldwide acclaim. It featured (a) a lightweight one-piece spool; (b) an easily removable level-wind mechanism; (c) a wide-bearing line-guard; (d) an extra panel for level wind and (e) a dial regulator for anti-backlash

Figure 368: (*below*) In the 1960s the supremacy of American-made multipliers was successfully challenged by Abu of Sweden. Abu now (1987) make a whole range of multiplying reels of peerless quality and performance

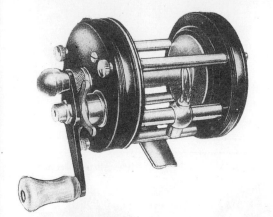

NOTTINGHAM-TYPE REELS

From about 1850 onwards, free-running centre-pin reels, mostly made of varnished wood, became very popular, especially among Nottingham anglers, who wanted to deliver heavy float tackle into the fast Trent current and control its progress throughout a chosen swim. These casting and tackle-control requirements prompted the development of a freely rotating reel of the sort publicized by Nottingham tackle-dealer William Bailey in *The Angler's Instructor*, 1857:

You cannot have a reel too light or that runs too free. The best is a four inch common wood reel, varnished to keep the rain from swelling the wood, the only brass about it being the hoop for fastening it to the rod. Brass inside and out adds to the weight and lessens its utility. To cast a long line you must have a free and easy running reel.

The invention of the 'Nottingham' reel was local, despite some attempts by London reel-makers to take the credit. Joseph Turner is said to have been the originator, whereas Samuel Lowkes and William Brailsford (*c.* 1850) developed the true centre-pin principle. In 1883, David Slater patented the first caged 'Nottingham'. In 1896, Henry Coxon invented the ultra-light drum design, which Allcock's took up and marketed initially as the 'Coxon-Aerial'; later as the 'Allcock-Aerial', the most famous centre-pin of all time. Further developments included the

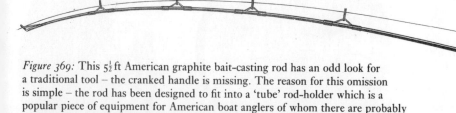

Figure 369: This 5½ ft American graphite bait-casting rod has an odd look for a traditional tool – the cranked handle is missing. The reason for this omission is simple – the rod has been designed to fit into a 'tube' rod-holder which is a popular piece of equipment for American boat anglers of whom there are probably several millions. This drawing is by courtesy of the *In-Fisherman* magazine whose editor has discerned (in 1986) an increasing interest among his readers for longer European-type rods

Figure 371: (*below*) A very heavy brass salmon fly reel with iron handle. The needle holes in the reel seating are for leather padding. Even in Hofland's day, reels were still made of brass. In *British Angler's Manual*, he wrote:

'A winch or reel is generally made of brass but I have seen them in Scotland made of wood, where they are called 'pirns'.

From 1800 on, salmon and trout reels were larger in capacity and spool size. Some weighed as much as $2\frac{1}{2}$lb. By then the reel seating with sliding rings was in use, but because of the weight and the smooth greenheart rod butts these old fly reels had pieces of leather stitched to the seat to achieve a tighter fit.

In the latter part of the nineteenth century, brass was combined with wood in some beautiful old salmon reels. Many of these have survived. Farlows were making them up to the turn of the present century

Figure 370: The ultimate model of the Allcock-Aerial spinning reel (this model figured in a 1941 catalogue), was marketed in $3\frac{1}{2}$in., 4in., and $4\frac{1}{2}$in. sizes and was represented as the 'high water mark of the reel makers' craft'

lighter 'Sheffield' style of fishing with the Homer 'Flick'em' reel (*c.* 1913), a design shown in the 'Eureka' and 'Rapidex'. Other 'Nottingham' type reels had casting and braking devices added, the best known being the 'Silex' (1896).

The better of the earlier centre-pins were 'star-backed', i.e. reinforced with crossed strips of brass. The larger wooden reels, which found equal popularity with sea anglers, were known as 'Scarborough' reels – and still are.

Figure 372: A selection of Nottingham reels   The Coxon-Aerial reel   The Allcock-Aerial reel

Nottingham centre-pin reel

THE FIXED-SPOOL REEL

In 1884 Peter Malloch introduced an all-metal reel in which the drum rotated through 90°, so that a cast could be made by having the line simply spill off the drum. A Mr G. R. Holding had already patented the idea of rotating a wooden Nottingham reel in 1878, but it was Malloch who made a commercial success of it once he had resolved the problem of line-twist.

To Alfred Holden Illingworth goes the credit for establishing the true threadline or 'fixed-spool' reel. He patented his design in 1905, crediting a Mr F. C. Moore for much of the engineering development. There is, however, evidence that John Ray of Belfast had made a fixed-spool prototype fifteen years earlier. This reel was discovered by John Piper, who photographed it. Unfortunately, the reel has since been destroyed in a bombing attack.

Following on Illingworth's ideas, some notable models were produced between the wars, but while lines were made of plaited silk, the fixed-spool was never widely used. When nylon monofilament became available cheaply in the late 1940s, however, it became immensely popular.

It is interesting to reflect how clearly Illingworth foresaw the deadly fish-catching potential of his reel. As early as 1907 he hoped that it would be 'used sparingly and with that discretion which the sportsmanlike instinct of fly-fishermen will dictate'. Later in life he wrote: 'I should like to see a curse fixed upon every evilly-disposed abuser of the terrible power it has placed in the hands of anglers.'

Nowadays the fixed-spool is used for almost every type of fishing in saltwater as well as fresh, and there is a wide variety of top-class reels available. Illingworth would be fascinated by their mechanical perfection. But as he so accurately predicted, the ease of use – and misuse – of the modern fixed-spool reel has caused bitter dissension. Perhaps it is just as well he is not with us today to witness it.

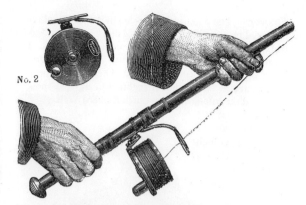

Figure 373: Malloch's patent casting reel was the forerunner of the fixed-spool. The cast was made with the reel in No. 2 position and the bait was retrieved simply by winding in after the spool was revolved 90° to the No. 2 position.

The one flaw to this design was that it caused the line to kink – a flaw that Malloch was to overcome when he made provision for the spool or drum to be reversed in its seating. The new version of the reel, marketed in the 1890s, thus eliminated kinks – provided that an equal number of casts was made with the drum facing forwards and backwards

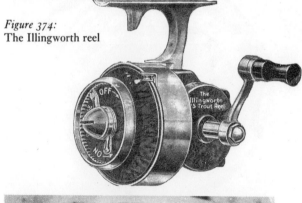

Figure 374:
The Illingworth reel

Figure 375: (right) John Ray's fixed-spool reel (1890)

Figure 376: The popular Allcock-Stanley fixed-spool reel marketed in 1926 (like the earlier Malloch and John Ray's reel) suffered a grave defect in that it made lines kink. It wasn't until the 'flier' type pick-up was invented that the bogey of kink was finally eliminated. The bale-arm pick-up invented by Hardy Bros (now fitted to all fixed-spool reels) and the bale-arm roller which Richard Walker campaigned for in order to reduce friction, has brought the invention (except for detail) up to date

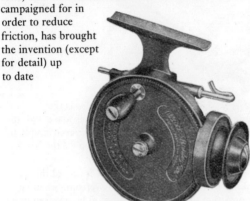

Figure 377: Mitchell – a modern fixed-spool that has received worldwide acclaim

Figure 378: (*above*) This centre-pin reel is used throughout the USSR. In 1984 it was practically the only reel available in that vast country

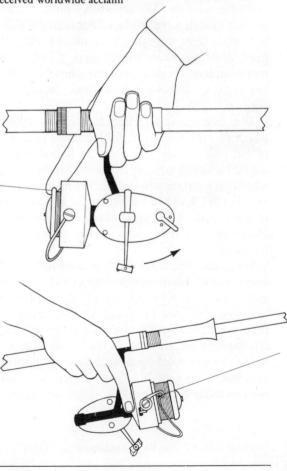

Figure 379: (*right*) The common method of playing a fish on a fixed-spool reel is by means of a lightly set clutch and finger pressure on the spool lip (*top*). The reel handle is *only* wound when line can be retrieved – never against a running fish

Although a slipping clutch is incorporated in almost every fixed-spool reel, some anglers (F. B.) much prefer to give line to a running fish by releasing the handle and allowing it to rotate backwards. During a run the bowl or pick-up carrier also rotates backwards allowing an angler to apply the appropriate finger pressure (*bottom*)

Figure 380: Russians have a very restricted choice of tackle, but this restriction, so far as reels are concerned, makes them masters of spinning, float-fishing, ledgering and livebaiting with a centre-pin – the only decent reel commonly available throughout the USSR. This Russian fishing in a gale of wind (photographed by F. B.) is touch-ledgering in a river that feeds the vast Vesjoloskoye Reservoir, a 200-mile-long feature of the Cossack homeland

LINES

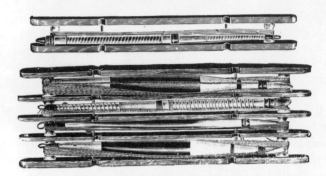

Then he shall have some fine smooth board of some curious wood for show sake, being as big as a trencher, and cut battlement-wise at each end; on which he shall fold his severall lines.

Gervase Markham, *The Pleasures of Princes* (1614)

Of all modern tackle developments, it is in the excellence and variety of lines that an angler may find some slight consolation for the damage industry has done to his fishing waters. Our angling forefathers, restricted to horsehair, would have given almost anything for the lines we can purchase today for a few pounds.

With the exception of fly-lines, the most popular line material is nylon monofilament. Many anglers may be surprised to learn that despite the many different brands of nylon there are very few different 'makes'. Nylon is produced by a few large chemical combines whose products are spooled-up for a host of smaller companies.

An angler's allegiance to one brand of nylon and his antipathy to another has often amused and sometimes embarrassed F. B., in his capacity as tackle-dealer, when he has known both brands to be one and the same nylon.

Before the days of the Trade Descriptions Act some brands of nylon were marked up at less than their true strength, with the result that some anglers were impressed if, say, it took a 5 lb pull to break a line marked 3 lb BS. Other brands of nylon were marked up at *more* than their true strength, which impressed anglers with the *fineness* of that particular brand when compared with others.

The only way to compare the relative strength of different brands of nylon is with a spring balance, first making sure that all samples to be tested are of the *same diameter*. (The gunmakers' balance once marketed by Messrs Parker-Hale and used for testing trigger-pulls on shotguns is ideal for testing nylon because it records the pressure at the moment of the line's fracture.)

Strength in relation to diameter, although important, is not the only quality to look for in nylon. Limpness is preferred for spinning reels. Because it sits neatly and tightly on a small diameter drum, limp nylon is less likely to spring off and cause overruns.

Stiffness in leaders is a quality appreciated by the fly caster. It helps him to lay the leader down in a straight continuation of the fly-line. Although it is always difficult for a fly caster to

Freshwater Fishing

get full turnover on his cast in the face of a head wind, stiff nylon helps.

A nylon less elastic than the average is useful in the hands of an expert angler, since a line with limited elasticity transmits the power of a strike with greater speed and impact. This lack of stretch, however, reduces the safety margin of the line, so that an inexperienced angler may well suffer more freak breaks when striking.

Many anglers are convinced that certain so-called 'strong' nylons break easily compared with their normal equivalents. In fact the dead-weight strength of a 4 lb BS 'strong' nylon is the same as the standard 4 lb BS product, but due to its limited elasticity it is less able to withstand the dynamic force of the strike.

The difference between dead-weight strength and dynamic force can be illustrated in the following manner. A 12-stone man leans against a door with all his weight. Nothing happens, the door resists the dead-weight (or pressure) of 12 stones. Taking a few steps back the same 12-

stone man throws himself at the door (applies a dynamic blow) and the door bursts open.

In the matter of choosing between 'standard' nylon and 'strong' nylon we advise the novice to buy 'strong' nylon of the *same diameter* as he normally chooses for any particular style of fishing, and thus take advantage of its higher strength. He should not (as many have done to their cost) purchase, say, a 3 lb 'strong' line to replace a 3 lb 'standard' line. The former will not be able to cushion a strike to the extent that the angler expects from a normal 3 lb line.

Braided nylon lines, though popular when they replaced braided silk lines, have not retained their popularity because, for most methods of angling, monofilament nylon has proved superior. Nevertheless, 'hot-stretched' braided nylon has remained popular with salmon fishermen owing to:

1. Its low elasticity, which helps to set a hook into a fish at long range.
2. Its suppleness, which makes for ease of handling on a multiplying reel. (Braided nylon is unsuitable for use on fixed-spool reels.)

Figure 381: An eighteenth-century line-winder. The tube on the left holds spare binding silks and twines

Figure 382: Front and back view of an early nineteenth-century machine for twisting horsehair lines. Horsehair was in use for fishing lines at least 1,800 years ago. Plutarch (*c.* AD 170) considered the hairs from a mare weaker than those from a stallion, due to her urination

Braided nylon also has the advantage of *buoyancy*. This makes it first choice for livebaiting and deadbait float-ledgering.

The last few yards of a nylon line suffer considerable wear and tear during a day's fishing. As a result its strength may be considerably reduced. At least five yards should be cut off before the angler tackles up.

Continued removal of line lowers the line level on the spool. With a fixed-spool reel the line must be 'set up' to proper level again, either by increasing the amount of backing, or by fitting a new line.

PUTTING LINE
ON A FIXED-SPOOL REEL

Most fixed-spool reels will carry considerably more monofilament nylon than is needed in actual fishing. The addition of backing to, say, 100 yards of casting line is a useful economy.

For maximum casting efficiency, the line level on the majority of fixed-spool reels should be fractionally less than $\frac{1}{8}$ in. below the lip.

Over-filling the spool causes tangles. Under-filling reduces casting range.

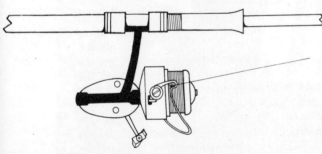

Figure 383: Filling a fixed-spool reel. Wind on nylon to within about $\frac{1}{8}$ in. below lip of spool

Freshwater Fishing

To ensure correct filling, carry out the following procedure:

1. Wind not less than 100 yards of new line on to the empty spool.

2. Join line to backing.

3. Wind backing on top of line until the correct level is reached, then cut off.

4. Reverse line and backing. This can be done either by running it off the spool across a field (or round and round the garden) or by winding on to another reel and thence on to a second reel. (Old centre-pin reels are useful for this job.) The end of the backing is now uppermost.

5. Tie end of backing to spool and wind on. The line will now finish up on top of the backing and the level will be exactly right.

FLY-LINES

Since it is important to good casting that rod and line should be in balance, rod manufacturers usually print the recommended line size for any rod just above the handle. This grading system was devised by the American Association of Tackle Manufacturers and is known as the 'AFTM' code.

As an example of this code, consider DT9F.

The *number* indicates the *weight* of the line in the scale 3 (very light) to 12 (very heavy). The last letter states whether the line is a floater or sinker. The first two letters give the *type* of line – whether double-tapered or weight-forward (forward-tapered). Thus, a line marked DT9F is a double-tapered No. 9 floater.

A line marked WF9S is a No. 9 forward-tapered sinker. It will be much thinner than the No. 9 floater, but the same weight, and both lines will fit the same rod.

Remember, in choosing a fly-line for any rod it is the *weight*, not the thickness of the line that matters. A sinking line – that is, one with a heavy coating – will be thinner than a floating line of the same AFTM number (because the floater has a less dense and therefore lighter coating), but the *weight* will be the same.

Fortunately, most modern fly-rods are fairly tolerant of line weight, so you don't have to be *too* fussy. Nevertheless, once you have found which AFTM number best suits a rod, you will know that whatever kind of line you need in the future – be it floater, sink-tip, neutral density, slow sinker, medium sinker, fast sinker or whatever – you can ask for that number in the tackle shop and be sure of getting a line that the rod will handle satisfactorily.

Time was when each angler made up his own lines. The following notes appear in the Sir John Hawkins (1784) edition of *The Compleat Angler*:

'I would recommend an engine lately invented, which is now to be had at almost any fishing-tackle shop in London; it consists of a large horizontal wheel, and three very small ones, inclosed in a brass box about a quarter of an inch thick, and two inches in diameter; the axis of each of the small wheels is continued through the under-side of the box, and is formed into a hook: by means of a strong screw it may be fixed in any post or partition, and is set in motion by a small winch in the centre of the box.

To twist links with this engine, take as many hairs as you intend each shall consist of, and, dividing them into three parts, tie each parcel to a bit of fine twine, about six inches long, doubled, and put through the aforesaid hooks; then take a piece of lead, of a conical figure, two inches high, and two in diameter at the base, with a hook at the apex, or point; tie your three parcels of hair into one knot, and to this, by the hook, hang the weight.

Lastly, take a quart or larger bottle-cork, and cut into the sides, at equal distances, three grooves; and placing it so as to receive each division of hair, begin to twist; you will find the link begin to twist with great evenness at the lead, as it grows tighter, shift the cork a little upwards; and when the whole is sufficiently twisted, take out the cork, and tie the link into a knot; and so proceed till you have twisted links sufficient for your line, observing to lessen the number of hairs in each link in such proportion as that the line may be taper.'

The AFTM code runs as follows:

DT	Double taper
WF	Weight forward, or forward taper
F	Floating
S	Sinking
FS	Floater with sink-tip
ST	Shooting taper, or shooting-head
3–12	Line size

Note: Weight-forward lines are useful for distance casting with an overhead cast, but *not* with a roll cast or either of the Spey casts. For these we need the heaviest part of the line close to the rod. Spey casting plays a big part in salmon fly-fishing and, in the absence of a special Spey casting line (no manufacturer has yet made one) the double-taper line is obligatory.

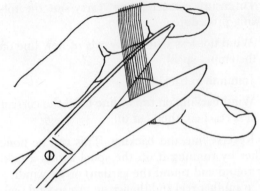

Figure 384: One way of disposing of unwanted nylon

DISCARDED NYLON – A WARNING!

Angling would be immeasurably poorer without the wild life that keep the angler company at the waterside. Although, like the fox and the otter, many animals stay out of sight during daylight, they tread the bank at night. Badger, water vole, stoat, squirrel and a host of others, furred and feathered, share the waterside with us. If an angler cares to use his eyes he will see the tracks and signs they leave, and 'read' stories of their activities that are as fascinating as anything the countryside has to offer. By learning to read both signs and stories an angler will sharpen his powers of observation. As a result he will become a better hunter and so, in the end, a better angler.

But *remember*, lengths of monofilament nylon left lying about can cause havoc. It gets wrapped round legs, bodies and wings of wild creatures, as well as injuring domestic animals. Cattle, sheep and dogs have all been known to suffer mutilation.

All too many anglers are guilty of this thoughtless behaviour.

Don't do it. Dispose of unwanted nylon by winding it round two fingers and cutting it with your scissors. This reduces it to a bundle of tiny ends that cannot possibly get wrapped round anything. Better still, take it home and burn it.

Figure 385: A few examples providing grisly evidence of what can happen when nylon is left lying about (*Angling Times*)

Freshwater Fishing

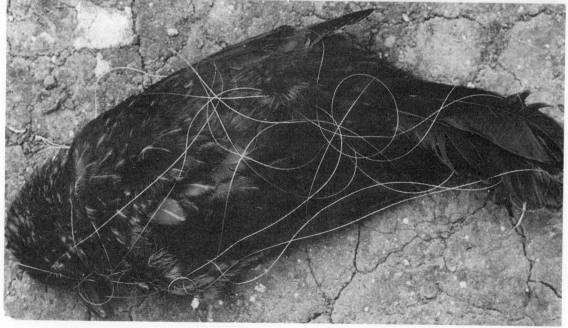

HOOKS

This is a hook with an eye in the shank. It is another Scotch invention, and as to its usefulness may be placed on a par with the newly invented mode of breeding salmon.

O'Gorman, *The Practice of Angling* (Vol. 2, 1845)

Together with the reel and nylon monofilament, the eyed-hook takes its place in history as one of the great angling inventions. It became popular during the latter part of the nineteenth century, and it is a sobering thought that the old eyed-hooks of years ago were stronger and more reliable than some being manufactured today.

Apart from the angler's incompetence, it is the hook that is responsible for most big-fish losses – and this in an age that boasts a 'scientific' approach to angling. The modern fly-fisherman can double-haul his shooting-head forty yards, but many of the hooks he casts are inferior to those in use a hundred years ago.

It would seem unnecessary to stress that tackle should be kept in good order. And yet the main reason why large fish so often break free (a constant topic of conversation when anglers meet) is because a hook is seldom replaced until lost on the bottom, or in weed, or in the fish itself!

Before using old hooks and tackles the angler should remind himself that big fish impose a greater strain on his tackle than small fish. Quite simply, they pull harder!

Remember: the loss of a fish due to breakage of any kind is almost always the fault of the angler.

HOOK DESIGN

Hookmakers are often remiss in the matter of hardening and tempering hooks. Hookwire is made of straight carbon steel with the following heat treatment.

First, hooks are hardened by heating and quenching. In this state they are very brittle indeed.

Secondly, the brittleness is reduced by tempering. This consists of re-heating the hooks to the correct temperature – much lower than that used in the hardening process – and again quenching, in water or oil.

If this is correctly done, a satisfactory compromise is obtained between a hard, stiff, but easily broken hook, and a soft, flexible, but easily bent hook. In practice this compromise is achieved far less often than anglers would like, and really good hooks are not easy to obtain.

Design *always* involves compromise. Consider the hook shown in figure 388.

Figure 386: (*right*) Kirkcudbright, at the mouth of the River Dee, and Risga by Loch Sunart, Argyllshire, are two of the places known to have been settled by Mesolithic or Middle Stone-Age men. From the evidence, it seems likely that they hunted seals, gathered shellfish and fished for a living. In 1895, William Pearson, fishing for sparling in the Dee opposite Cumstoun House in Kirkcudbright, dredged up a barbed harpoon (a) fashioned by one of those ancient hunters. Since the Kirkcudbrightshire Dee was once a prolific salmon river, it is likely that the harpoon was lost in an attempt to spear a salmon.

The bone fish-hook found at Risga (b) was probably used for sea fish or pike. It is interesting to note that H. Godwin (see *British Maglemose Harpoon Sites*, a paper in *Antiquary*, vol. 7, pp. 36–38, 1933) found pike remains together with harpoon heads at a peat site near North Atwick in Yorkshire – proving that pike were hunted in Britain in Mesolithic times. It is possible that those Mesolithic men of Kirkcudbrightshire once fished for pike in Loch Ken, home of Britain's most famous pike – the 72 lb Kenmure monster

Figure 387: (*right*) The oldest British metal hook: a spade-end found in the Thames at Grays, Essex. Now on view at Colchester Museum. Estimated age: 2,500 years. Ancient it may be, but in design as good as (if not superior to) some hooks being made today!

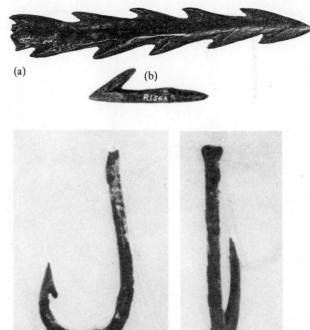

Directly the point P starts to penetrate, the line of pull is in the direction of P–E. It is not, as one might suppose, in line with the hook-shank, no matter what form of attachment of line to hook is used.

EPA is the angle at which the hook starts its penetration. As the hook 'bites', this angle decreases until, at B (the furthest point from E), the maximum penetration is achieved. Greater depth of penetration than this is impossible.

The greater the angle of penetration (EPA) the more force is needed to make the hook go in. This angle can be reduced by lengthening the shank in relation to the gape, but an increase in shank length over a certain amount reduces the suitability of the hook for some kinds of bait, fly or lure. Also, when a load comes on any hook that had been set in a fish, the shank tends to bend. The longer the shank, the greater this tendency will be. Compensation can be made by increasing the thickness of the wire, but the thicker the wire the greater the force needed to make the hook penetrate.

Practical experience indicates that a hook whose total length is from 2 to $2\frac{1}{2}$ times its gape, and whose point is parallel to its shank, is a good compromise for most kinds of fishing.

The design of point and barb is also important and there are few hooks that are not deficient in this. Figure 389 shows two hooks, A and B, with deliberately exaggerated points and barbs.

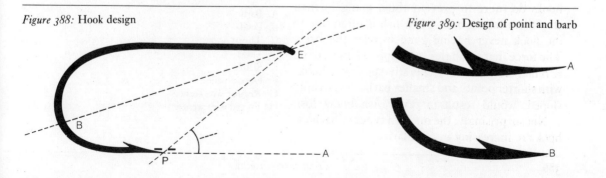

Figure 388: Hook design

Figure 389: Design of point and barb

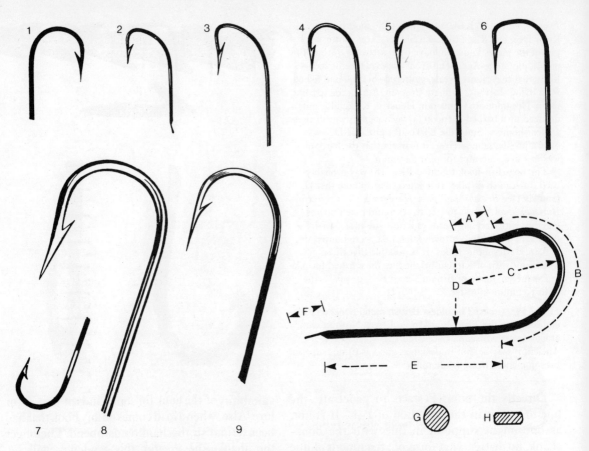

In A, the barb impedes penetration. It is too deeply cut; it is turned up too much; it is too far from the point. This hook will have to go in a long way before the barb is covered. The hook is weakened by the reduction in thickness brought about by cutting the barb. Nearly all hooks have these faults to some extent.

In B, the hook has a small barb, with only a shallow cut set nearer the point, and the smaller angle makes for easier penetration.

Only a very small barb is required to prevent a hook from coming out. The barbs on many hooks do more to prevent them going in than stop them falling out. A lost fish is often due to the hook never having gone in over the barb. The force that an angler can apply when striking is remarkably small. Generally speaking, hooks with shorter points and smaller barbs, less steeply sloped, would result in fewer fish being lost.

Not surprisingly, the modern types of barbless hook are increasing in popularity.

Figure 390: Hook patterns
A hook is generally recognized by the shape of its bend. The commonest types are:

1. The round bend
2. The crystal bend
3. The Limerick bend
4. The Kirby bend
5. The sproat bend
6. The sneck bend
7. The Kendal round bend
8. The round bend (deep throated)
9. The Model Perfect bend

The various parts of a fish hook are named:

A. Barb
B. Bend
C. Throat or bite
D. Gape
E. Shank
F. Eye or spade
G. Regular wire section
H. Forged wire section

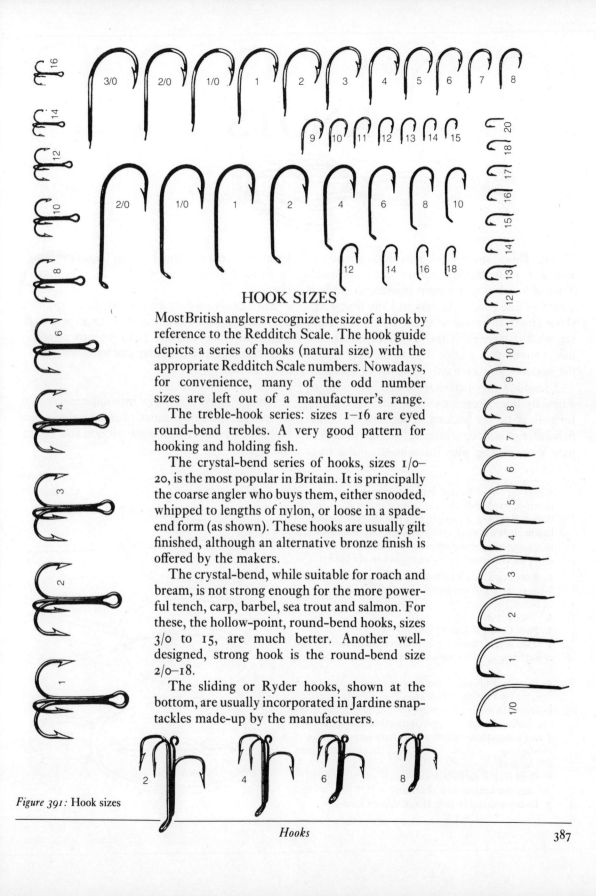

HOOK SIZES

Most British anglers recognize the size of a hook by reference to the Redditch Scale. The hook guide depicts a series of hooks (natural size) with the appropriate Redditch Scale numbers. Nowadays, for convenience, many of the odd number sizes are left out of a manufacturer's range.

The treble-hook series: sizes 1–16 are eyed round-bend trebles. A very good pattern for hooking and holding fish.

The crystal-bend series of hooks, sizes 1/0–20, is the most popular in Britain. It is principally the coarse angler who buys them, either snooded, whipped to lengths of nylon, or loose in a spade-end form (as shown). These hooks are usually gilt finished, although an alternative bronze finish is offered by the makers.

The crystal-bend, while suitable for roach and bream, is not strong enough for the more powerful tench, carp, barbel, sea trout and salmon. For these, the hollow-point, round-bend hooks, sizes 3/0 to 15, are much better. Another well-designed, strong hook is the round-bend size 2/0–18.

The sliding or Ryder hooks, shown at the bottom, are usually incorporated in Jardine snap-tackles made-up by the manufacturers.

Figure 391: Hook sizes

KNOTS

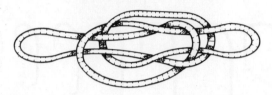

Never allow some well-meaning friend to assemble your tackle. *Always* do it yourself. Then if a rod-ring has been missed, or there is a turn of line round the rod and the line won't shoot (most irritating at night when you can't see what is wrong); if the reel falls off when a fish is running; if a knot slips in the best fish of the season – you have only yourself to blame.

A knot is a very personal matter. When fitting a new fly-line, never let anyone join the backing for you, or tie the backing to the reel. A salmon fisherman of our acquaintance lost thirty yards of new Wet-cel line, plus his tube-fly and a huge springer, because the backing knot (although professionally tied) drew while he was playing the fish.

Such grisly misfortune may happen only once, but that is once too often. Ask an experienced angler to show you the right way to assemble your tackle and tie the knots you need, and then – *do it all yourself.*

Note: Always lubricate monofilament nylon by moistening in the mouth before tightening a knot. This helps to overcome friction and to 'set' the knot.

Figure 392: The 'Bucket' Knot. A rather amusing knot for fastening two handles to any container that has a rim or sloping sides, e.g. a jam-jar, or a pail that has lost its handle. It is a knot of special interest to juvenile hunters of the minnow, or anglers who wish to fashion a make-shift portable livebait container from an old bucket.

1. Knot or splice a length of cord at A and arrange three loops as shown. *Note*: In the completed knot, loop A will be one of the two handles.
2. Place B over C.
3. Place C over B leaving hole D.
4. Take loop E down through loop A underneath C and B and bring it up through hole D to form the second handle.
5. Bring loops F and G together *underneath the knot* and turn the knot flat on its side away from you. It is important to *flatten* the knot as much as possible, so that the strands are running exactly as shown in the diagram. This can be done by untwisting the turns that have formed in the handle loops.   *Note*: The centre of the completed knot will be at H.
6. Bend loop F *backwards underneath and to the right.* Arrange the knot around the centre at H.
7. Place container in hole H and tighten knot

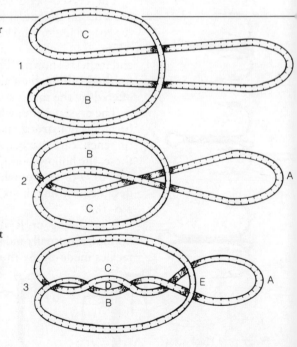

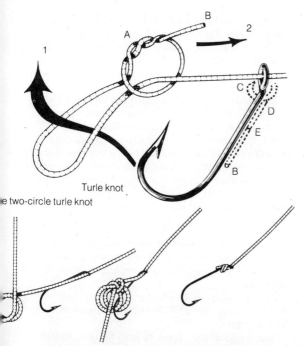

Turle knot

e two-circle turle knot

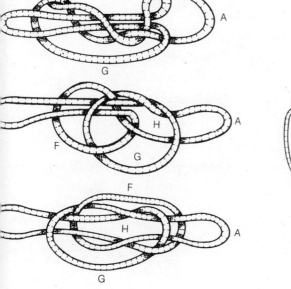

Figure 393: Turle knots. These knots grip the shank of a hook just behind the eye and leave nothing poking out in front – becoming, as it were, part of the fly dressing. In consequence, they are the dry-fly fisherman's first choice. They are particularly suited to hooks with pronounced up- or down-turned eyes

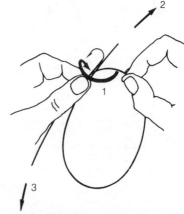

Figure 394: Spade-end knot. Put a $3\frac{1}{2}$ in. diameter loop in the end of the line (or a length of nylon) leaving a 2 in. overhang. Lay the loop along the hook shank (see diagram) gripping the nylon against the shank with thumb and index finger of the left hand. Start to wind turns clockwise round the shank (arrow No. 1), *keeping each turn hard up against the left thumb.* Make eight or ten turns, being careful not to wind them on too tightly. When the last turn is made, pull the end of the nylon in the direction of arrow No. 2, gently at first, then firmly. Since the knot forms on the shank some distance from the spade-end, it must be slid close up to the spade before being snugged down.

Tighten the knot by pulling on the opposite ends in direction of arrows 2 and 3.

The spade-end knot is equally effective for tying an eyed-hook to nylon, the bulge forming the eye being treated as the spade-end. If hooks with upturned or downturned eyes are used, the nylon can be passed through the eye before the knot is tied. But in the case of a *straight-eyed* hook the eye is by-passed – the hook treated as though it had a spade-end – otherwise it will stick out at an angle

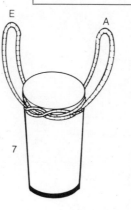

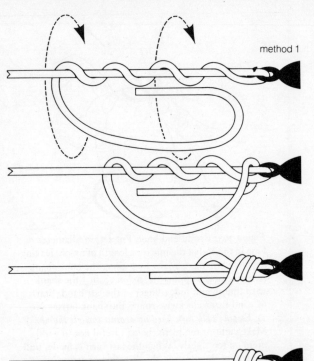

method 1

Figure 395: (*left*) The diagram shows two methods of tying a grinner knot. For tying on a bait-hook or any fly other than a simulated insect, this in our opinion is the best knot. Although popularized by Dick Walker some years ago, it is in fact the old Fisherman's Knot, only with three turns. It is safe, neat and very strong.

This knot also has a quality that makes it ideal for low-water salmon fly-fishing in the heat of summer, since it avoids the use of very light leaders when tiny flies are fished. It is a noose/lasso type of knot that will not undo, but will tighten under tension. Thus, if tied loosely so that there is a loop from which the fly can dangle (and articulate in a lifelike manner in the current, see bottom left), a tiny summer salmon fly, say, a size 12 or 14 double, can be fished attractively and safely on a leader of 14 or 15 lb BS.

Figure 396: (*below*) Double-grinner knot. Just as good as, if not better than the water knot for joining nylon, since it is slightly less bulky. It looks complicated, but is really very simple.

Tie one end and pull fairly tight. Turn the knot over and tie the other end. Pull the two knots together, snug down and trim.

Like the water knot, it can be used for tying droppers. As the grinner knot has superseded the half-blood knot for tying on hooks or swivels, so, in our opinion, have double-grinner and water knot superseded the blood-knot for joining nylon; making up tapered leaders; arranging droppers

method 2

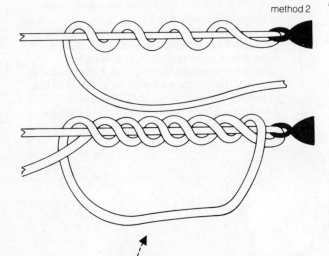

Articulated effect

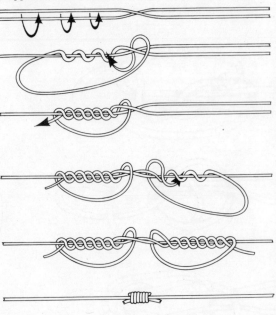

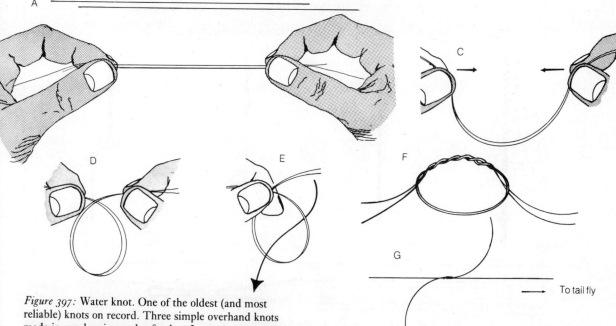

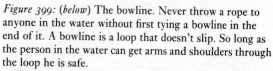

Figure 397: Water knot. One of the oldest (and most reliable) knots on record. Three simple overhand knots made in overlapping ends of nylon. It was recommended in *A Treatyse of Fysshynge wyth an Angle* for joining horsehairs. Nylon monofilament, a more slippery material, needs an extra turn.

When the water knot is used for making a dropper, the fly is fastened to the stalk running *away* from the rod. It is true that if tied on the other stalk the fly will stand out better from the leader, but this method is not so strong

Figure 398: Stewart and Pennell tackle knots. Stewart and Pennell worm tackles are simple to tie, indeed they can be made up at the waterside. Eyeless hooks whipped to nylon have an unfortunate habit of 'drawing'. Tackles made as shown will never draw

Figure 399: (*below*) The bowline. Never throw a rope to anyone in the water without first tying a bowline in the end of it. A bowline is a loop that doesn't slip. So long as the person in the water can get arms and shoulders through the loop he is safe.

The bowline is the best knot for tying a boat's painter to a ringbolt

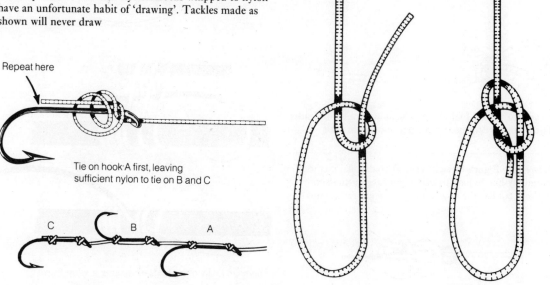

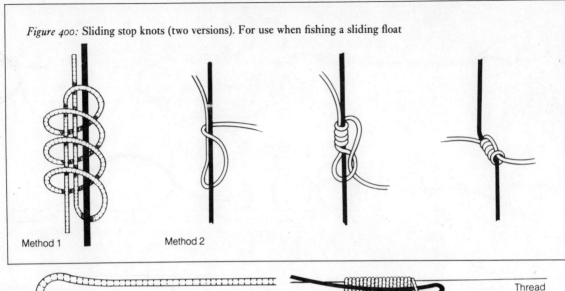

Figure 400: Sliding stop knots (two versions). For use when fishing a sliding float

Method 1   Method 2

Thread

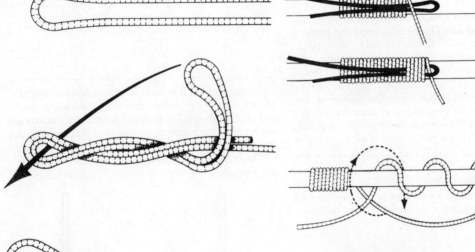

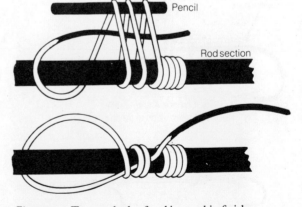

Pencil

Rod section

Figure 401: Blood bight loop. The loop for a nylon leader. The fly-line is attached with a figure-of-eight knot

Figure 402: Figure-of-eight knot. A traditional method for joining fly-line to loop in leader. An easy on-the-spot method, but has the disadvantage of being rather bulky

Figure 403: Two methods of making a whip finish

Needle knot (1)

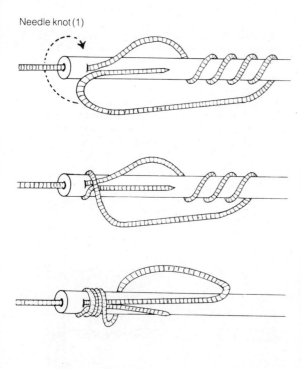

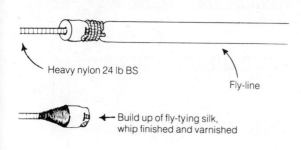

Heavy nylon 24 lb BS

Fly-line

← Build up of fly-tying silk, whip finished and varnished

Needle knot (2)

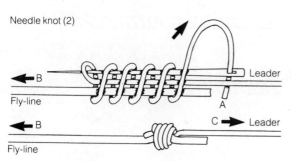

B →

Fly-line

Leader

A

C → Leader

B →

Fly-line

Figure 404: Needle knot (1). A much neater knot than the figure-of-eight to blood-bight loop. With a needle that is slightly thicker than the nylon, perforate the end of the fly-line so that the point comes out at the side of the line near to the end. Leave the needle stuck in the line with about $\frac{1}{4}$ in. of point emerging.

Apply the flame of a match or lighter to the eye end of the needle, until the line starts to bend.

Take the flame away and blow the needle cool.

Remove needle.

Take a yard or so of 20–24 lb BS nylon and point one end by cutting obliquely with a razor blade. Pass this end into the hole at the end of the fly-line and out at the side. Continue as shown in the diagram

Needle knot (2). The nylon does not *have* to pass through a hole in the end of the fly-line, it can simply lie alongside as shown above. A darning needle is a very convenient way of completing the knot. After four or five turns, the nylon is brought through the eye of the needle A and the needle pulled in the direction of B, so that the nylon end comes through the turns and fastens the knot. The completed knot is shown below. (Tighten by pulling strongly on the nylon from either end (B and C) before trimming.) This knot is easily tied at the waterside if a needle is kept in the fly-case

Figure 405: The half-blood stop knot. Pass the nylon through the eye of the swivel, then put a simple overhand knot in the end of the nylon before tying the half-blood as in A. Hold the stop-knot against the eye of the swivel before tightening in direction of arrow. The knot tightens as shown in B. Des Brennan, Ireland's famous sea angler, prefers this type of knot to any other. (His own version requires the nylon to be passed *twice* through the eye of the swivel.) The knot illustrated here is F. B.'s favourite knot for tying hooks and flies

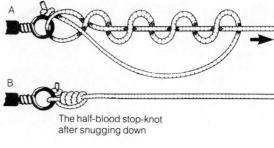

A

B

The half-blood stop-knot after snugging down

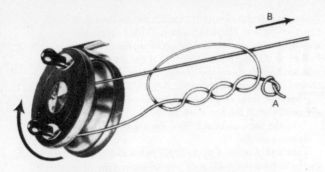

B →

A

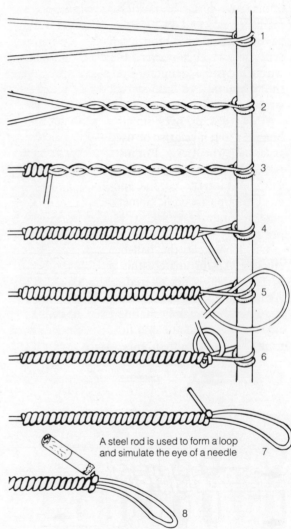

1

2

3

4

5

6

7

8

A steel rod is used to form a loop
and simulate the eye of a needle

Figure 408: (*below*) Hangman's jam knot. If one of the
popular monofilament knots is used when joining a line
of braided terylene or braided nylon to a swivel or tackle,
the line can break far below the maker's claimed strength,
usually an inch or so back from the knot. This is said to
be through 'strangulation' – because the strands within
the braid don't take an equal share of the load.

The pike fisherman often prefers a braided nylon line
because of its good floating qualities. Such a line will need
to be attached with a hangman's jam knot

Figure 406: A safe method of attaching a nylon line or
backing to a reel. Pull both parts of the knot tight and
trim at A. Wet the tightened knot before sliding it back
towards the reel. Finally, tighten the line firmly round the
drum of the reel by holding the reel handles firmly with
left hand and pulling the nylon in the direction of B

Figure 407: Tangles. The simplified diagram shows a
corner of a tangle. Tangles are a frequent occurrence.
Don't despair. Most tangles are caused by loops of line
getting caught up (see loop A). Work round the tangle
freeing these loops. Provided the line is not pulled too
tight, there is no tangle that will not unravel in a few
minutes. The golden rules are: patience; don't pull; find
the loops and free them one by one. When you have freed
all the loops, the tangle will be undone

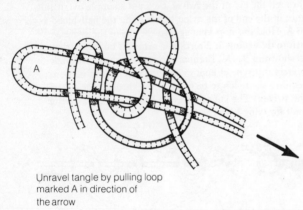

A

Unravel tangle by pulling loop
marked A in direction of
the arrow

SWIVELS

The swivel is an essential though sometimes underrated piece of tackle. Most swivels are made of brass and, in accordance with tradition, have a natural or a bronze finish. Two popular types of swivel, however, are made of rustless wire. One is the 'diamond-eye' swivel; the other, the 'diamond-eye link' swivel. Both are small, strong and efficient.

A swivel's primary function is to minimize line kink, but it can also be used as a link between separate parts of a rig. For instance, a wire leader is seldom joined direct to the mainline. Instead, a swivel is interposed; line and leader being fastened to opposite ends. Sometimes, to facilitate a quick change of tackle, a 'link' type swivel is preferred.

Of all swivels, the ball-bearing is the most efficient. Unfortunately this swivel, unlike the barrel swivel, is not offered in graded sizes. Its comparatively high cost tends to discourage the beginner, but we unhesitatingly recommend it to anyone who wants to spin for his fish—whether trout, sea trout, salmon, pike, perch or chub.

Fast-revolving baits often overload a barrel swivel. Even a ball-bearing swivel cannot cope with the revolutions caused by retrieving a spinner in a heavy current. In these circumstances a swivelled, celluloid anti-kink vane, or an anti-kink lead is efficient when deep water is being fished. (In shallow water the celluloid anti-kink vane is always better.)

Three-way swivels are popular for paternosting (see page 462). When using them, however, it is important that the bait link (the link that takes the strain when a big fish is hooked) is tied *opposite the mainline link*. The *middle* eye of the three-way swivel should always be used for the lead link. Failure to observe this rule will eventually result in a lost fish, due to fatigue fracture. The break is caused by the right-angle in the swivel being constantly strained to an obtuse angle, and as constantly bent back again by the angler.

Figure 409: A selection of swivels. The 'Diamond Eye' swivel (bottom) is an old favourite

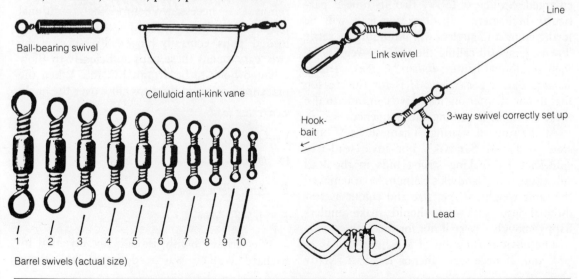

Ball-bearing swivel

Celluloid anti-kink vane

Barrel swivels (actual size)

Link swivel

Line

Hook-bait

3-way swivel correctly set up

Lead

LEADS

Your lynes must be plumbid wyth lede. And ye shall wyte yt the nexte plumbe unto
the hoke shall be therefro a large fote and more. And every plumbe of a quantyte to
the gretnes of the lyne. There be thre manere of plumbis for a grounde lyne rennynge.

Attrib. Dame Juliana Berners, *A Treatyse of Fysshynge wyth an Angle* (1496)

During recent years the spilling of anglers' lead
shot at the waterside has been blamed for a
decline in the population of mute swans. Birds,
it is claimed, have been poisoned through lead
ingestion.

Rightly or wrongly, this has resulted in legislation forcing anglers to replace lead (in certain
sizes) with non-toxic substitutes.

Despite a good deal of research into a suitable
replacement no coherent picture has yet
emerged. Sufficient to say that in time a particular high-merit substitute for lead will be
forthcoming and anglers will undoubtedly settle
down again, still calling the various weights by
their traditional names: *Bullets; Coffins; Arlesey
Bombs; Barrel Leads*, etc. It is for this reason
that in our chapter on 'leads' we continue to use
these names as if nothing had happened.

At the time of writing, Thamesley's 'Tungsten' shot and Sandvik's non-toxic lead-free
split-shot are making strong bids in the lead
substitute race. Sandvik's claim to have achieved
the same weight, shape, size and colour as traditional lead split-shot should make anglers
happy enough – were it not for the high cost.

The obvious function of a fishing lead is to
sink and, if necessary, anchor the bait. Many
leads, however, are designed for other functions
(see figure 412).

A. *The traditional plummet*. With this lead, the
depth can be measured when a floating rig is
assembled. The bare hook is run through the
wire loop and the hook-point housed in the strip
of cork underneath the lead. (To know the depth
of a swim, or pool, is all-important.)

B. *A more modern plummet*. Of French origin,
this plummet avoids delay caused by bait
removal – necessary before the traditional
plummet can be used. It consists of two spring-
loaded 'cups' centrally hinged. Pressure on the
two 'ears' opens these cups sufficiently to allow
a baited hook to be dropped inside. When the
pressure is released the cups close over the hook.

Ledgering leads

C. *Coffin lead*

D. *Drilled-bullet lead*

E. *Barleycorn or barrel lead*

F. *Arlesey bomb*

The Arlesey bomb, though not invented by
Richard Walker, was re-designed and popu-

Freshwater Fishing

larized by him in the early 1950s for long-distance casting: in particular, for reaching big perch that were almost out of casting range in Arlesey Lake, Bedfordshire. The bomb will not tumble in flight. As a result it is less likely to foul line and tackle during its passage through the air. The built-in swivel prevents kinks developing in the line. The bomb is also very useful when a lead is required to bounce over a river bed. The swivel almost entirely eliminates the chance of line kink.

G. *Arlesey bomb with flattened sides*. A useful lead for anchoring a bait in medium strength rivers. The more bulbous shape reduces casting range but improves anchoring efficiency.

Spinning leads

H. *Jardine lead*

I. *Wye lead*

J. *Half-moon lead*

K. *Hillman lead*

The Jardine is a quick-change lead that can be put on or removed from a leader without the tackle having to be broken down.

The Wye lead, too, can be removed easily if placed between two link-swivels (figure 410). It is a more secure lead than the Jardine, which occasionally falls off.

Both Wye and Hillman are practical anti-kink leads. The Hillman, also a quick-change lead, is used with a swivel (figure 411).

The Half-moon is a useful lead for light spinning, but sometimes comes adrift.

Figure 410: Link swivels on Wye lead

Figure 411: An anti-kink spinning lead (in this case the Hillman) is *always* fixed to the rod end of the swivel

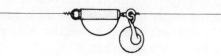

Figure 412: The selection of leads described in the text

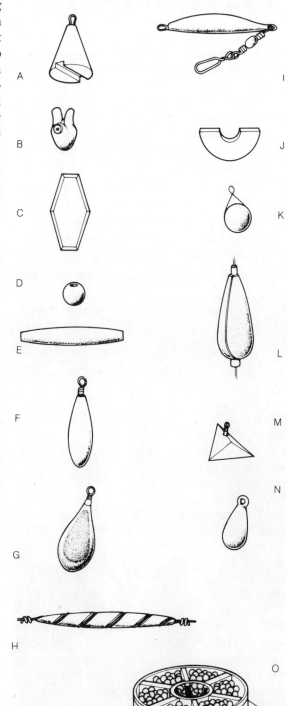

L. *Catherine lead*. Another quick-change lead that is particularly good for deadbaiting (with or without a float). The lead is slotted. So is the tapered, hollow, plastic peg that runs through its middle. The line passes through both slots into the bore of the plastic peg. Once the line is inside, the peg is revolved 10° or so to close the inner slot. Finally, the tapered peg is pushed tight into the lead, which is now free to be moved up or down the leader until located in the desired position by means of a stop-knot (see page 393). A fish picking up a bait is free to take line through the lead without feeling resistance.

M. *Capta lead*. This ledgering lead has leech-like qualities. It is an inferior casting lead, but will stay where it is on a river bottom when heavier leads would be swept away.

N. *Pear or Paternoster lead*. This, like the

Figure 413: Float-fishing for bream on Wroxham Broad c. 1880

Name or number	Pellets per ounce
Special SG	11
SSG	15
AAA	35
BB	70
1	100
3	140
4	170
5	220
6	270
7	340
8	450

Figure 414: Shot chart. A quantity of split-shot will be required. If sizes SSG, AAA, BB, No. 3 and No. 6 are chosen, every contingency is covered, since one SSG weighs the same as two AAAs, four BBs, eight No. 3s or 16 No. 6s

Arlesey bomb, stands nearly upright on the bottom.

O. *Split-shot dispenser*. A useful piece of equipment, provided refills of *any* size can be obtained.

Large shot should have the leading edges trimmed to form a 'V' entry to the split. This makes the putting-on or removal of shot much easier. Shot of any nominal size should be uniform in weight. This is very important, since it enables an angler to predetermine the number of shot a float will carry, thus eliminating the need for bankside experiment.

NETS

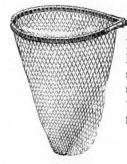

Lastly, you shall have a little fine wanded Pebbe to hang by your side, in which you shall put the Fish which you catch, and a small round net fastened to a poales end, wherewith you may land a Pike or other great Fish.

Gervase Markham, *The Pleasures of Princes* (1614)

LANDING NETS

According to A. Courtney Williams in *Angling Diversions* (1945), the first record of a landing net is to be found on one of the Leptic Magna mosaics of the first or second century AD, which were discovered in 1933, in Tripoli:

The picture depicts two Roman anglers, one baiting his hook, the other in the act of landing a fish; he is holding his 7 ft rod high above his shoulder in his left hand, whilst with the other he guides the fish towards his net.

As A. C. W. also points out, the triangular type of landing net was no modern invention; it was first described by François Fortin, in *Les Ruses Innocentes* (1660).

Figure 415: With a big fish safely in the net, Ken Taylor has shortened his grip of the net handle, so that he can lift the fish clear of the water

The first hint of a landing net in English literature is to be found in *The Arte of Angling* (1577), attributed to William Samuel. In this book – which was probably the model for Izaak Walton's *The Compleat Angler* – Piscator is teaching Viator how to fish. He hooks a good perch and, after playing it out, tells Viator to lie down on his belly, hold the bank with one hand and take the fish with the other by putting his forefinger into the gills and his thumb into its mouth.

As soon as the perch is landed, Viator, aglow with this sudden and unexpected justification for his presence, not unnaturally asks: 'How would you have done if I had not been here?' In a lengthy reply, Piscator tells his pupil that it had been his intention to fish the swim for roach, and he had brought only roach gear with him. He finishes thus:

I ... left one of my tooles at home for hast, whiche if I had brought I could have landed him without your help.

From this it is evident that a landing net (or something similar) was implied.

Described in the same little book (which we consider one of the most *practical* volumes of instruction among the early fishing books) is a piece of sixteenth-century equipment for snatching pike:

Figure 417: Salmon-tailer

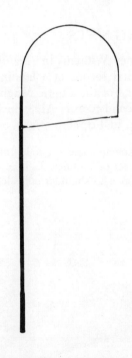

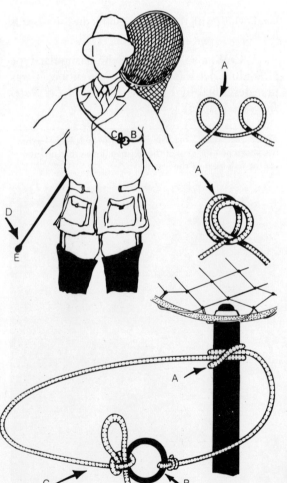

Figure 416: A simple method of carrying a landing net.

A. Clove hitch round net handle

B. Metal ring

C. Slip knot

D. A piece of lead sheet tacked round the end of the handle enables the net to be used as a wading staff – useful when fording a river

E. A rubber pad on the butt of the handle reduces noise when the net is used as wading staff

Figure 418: Netting a fish (see also next page)

It is surprising how inexpert many anglers are with a landing net. A net is never used on a fish in the manner of a butterfly net. Nor is it used to 'dig' the fish out of the water. It is used as a trap. And, as with all traps, it *must not be seen.*

A fish, when it is tired *and not before,* is drawn over the waiting net – which is completely submerged except for the handle end. When the fish is overhead the net is raised to encompass it. Once the fish is safely netted the rod can be put aside, since the net frame will need extra support (from the angler's rod hand) if the fish is a heavy one.

A long-handled net enables the angler to reach a fish from a high bank

The two corners of a triangular net cut off possible escape routes for a fish being landed in shallow water (see the shaded areas in diagram)

When the fish is lying on its side, the net is raised to encompass it

The fish is unhooked while still in the net, well back from the waterside

... he will be haltered [caught with a noose], and some men use that way very oft to kill him, for hee will lie glaring upon you, as the hare or larke, until you put the line with a snittle [noose] over his head, and so with a good stiff pole you may throw him to land.

This snittle evolved into the modern salmon-tailer (see below).

KEEPNETS

A keepnet is a receptacle for keeping fish alive. An angler should choose a net that will house the size and number of fish he hopes to catch.

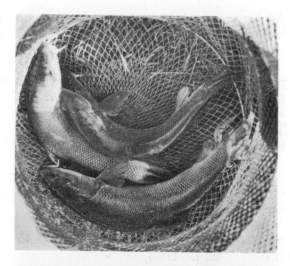

Figure 419: Round keepnets are bad for large fish, which get bent in the shape of the net – like this catch of barbel. The rectangular net allows fish to keep their noses to the stream and lie in a natural position

Figure 420: Since the first edition of this book was published, micromesh knotless keepnets (like the Church net, *below right*) have replaced the scale-damaging knotted nets. This change in keepnet material is a humanitarian advance but we hope that one more improvement will be embraced in keepnet design – namely, rectangular framing instead of round framing. This earliest known illustration of a keepnet appeared in a painting by Ma Yuan *c.* 1195. It is likely that the 'netting' was made of cane ribs and as such pre-dated the non-scale-damaging micromesh nets by 800 years!

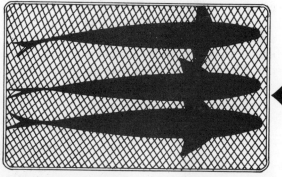

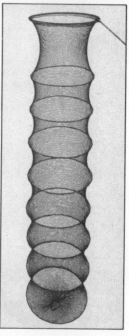

All keepnets today have knotless mesh. This helps to reduce injury to fish.

A keepnet should be able to accommodate the longest fish an angler is likely to catch, and be rectangular so that fish can lie side by side facing the stream in a natural position. It should have a long neck that can be used as a delivery funnel. This eliminates the need to raise the net from the water each time a fish is put in.

It should be fitted with a rope and bankstick-fitting so that it can be dangled to its plimsoll line even from a very high bank position.

The part of the net that houses fish should be fitted with a stretcher. This will eliminate the chances of the net failing to open out, if it gets caught on underwater obstruction.

F. B., who has had considerable experience as a match angler,* always carried two keepnets, one of which was held in reserve in case of a field day. The second net was also useful in the 'roving match' once popular in the south of England. It enabled him to move about without taking the bulk of his catch with him.

If an angler can allow himself the luxury of fishing in one swim and hanging his keepnet in another, he should do so, even if it necessitates carrying the fish a dozen yards to the net. It is possible that disturbance caused by fish in a keepnet is communicated to other fish and deters them from feeding (at least, it seems to deter the big ones!)

The reader who thinks this unlikely should remember that thousands of highly skilled match anglers fish every week-end – and rarely catch a two-pound roach between them during the whole season. Yet the waters they fish yield a number of two-pound roach when all is quiet. Although of course there are other reasons why big roach are not caught on match days, it is almost certain that the main reason is water disturbance.

* F. B. once held the record bag of dace taken in a match: 251 weighing 64 lb.

GAGS *and* DISGORGERS

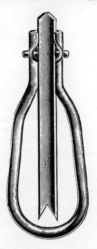

No angler can avoid the occasional hooking of undersized fish. Such fish are protected by legislation, but there is little point in having special size limits unless the angler takes special care when removing hooks. All too often, undersized fish returned to the water die as a result of rough handling.

For removing hooks, the 'V' prong (figure 425) is the disgorger often used. This is to be deplored, since the 'V' prong is both rough and ineffective. A much better instrument is the cross-cut slotted disgorger (used in figure 424). We cannot, alas, discover the name of its inventor and so cannot give him due credit. We can, however, assert that his invention is the most efficient available for use on small fish, and must have been responsible for saving many lives.

There are two patterns. One has a narrow slot and is designed to disgorge hooks whipped to nylon. The other has a wider slot and is intended for use with eyed or spade-end hooks.

Figure 421: The Buller pike gag (*above*) and the 'Hookout' disgorger

THE BULLER GAG AND BAKER 'HOOKOUT' DISGORGER

Nowadays the pike fisherman seldom wants to kill many of the fish he catches. He keeps one for the table, perhaps, and tries to return the others unharmed.

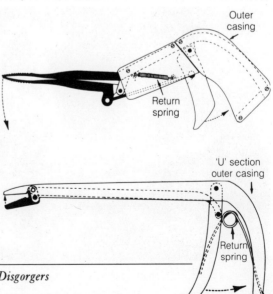

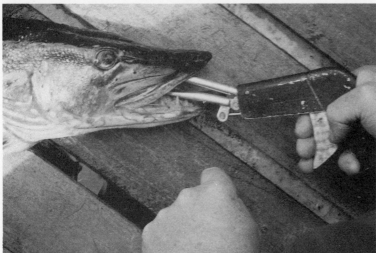

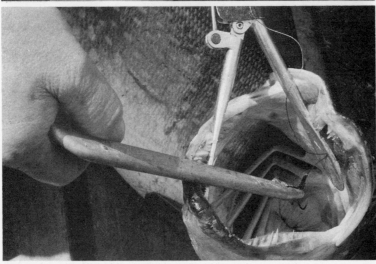

Figure 422: The photographs show a treble hook being extracted from the throat of a 15 lb Loch Lomond pike caught on ledgered deadbait. The authors have done a great deal of fishing together for many species of fish in many places. They have found the Buller gag and Baker 'Hookout' disgorger to be as useful in saltwater as in fresh

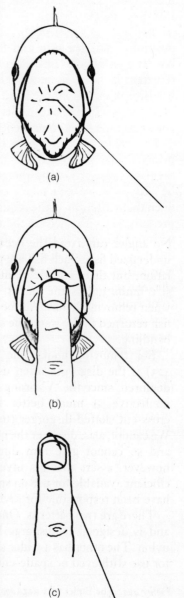

(a)

(b)

(c)

We write 'tries to' advisedly, because to return a pike unharmed is not as easy as it sounds. The hook is usually embedded behind rows of needle-sharp teeth.

Almost invariably the unhooking operation is performed with the aid of conventional gag and disgorger – both of which should long ago have been condemned to some angling museum. The gag has to be pushed sideways into the pike's mouth and then screwed round a full 90° before it can function as a gag. Inevitably, the forked ends – set nearly two inches apart in the closed position – tear the skin and flesh of the pike's jaw. It is extremely difficult to use on a live fish reluctant to open its mouth. Even after a pike has been knocked on the head the forcing open of its jaws can be hazardous – and many an angler has the scars to prove it!

The Buller gag (drawn to show the working principles for anglers who wish to make one for themselves) changes the picture. This gag can be slipped between a pike's clenched jaws and open them instantly to the required extent. While pressure is maintained on the trigger of the gag with one hand, the other hand is free to handle the disgorger. This disgorger – the 'Hookout' – is produced by an American company. It is both efficient and humane, and will remove a hook from a pike's mouth in a few seconds.

Figure 423: (*left*) The Finger Disgorger (for dead fish). If you have no disgorger handy when a fish has swallowed the hook, don't break the leader. Your finger will serve as a substitute.
(a) represents a view down the fish's throat. The hook is right at the back.
1. Having made sure the fish is dead, slide your forefinger down the leader into the bend of the hook (b) so that the point of the hook is on the finger nail.
2. Push your finger further down the fish's throat, taking the hook with it, and then ease backwards – still keeping the point of the hook on the fingernail and keeping the leader taut with the other fingers. The hook will come out as shown in (c).
Care must be taken to avoid ripping the back and sides of your finger on the fish's teeth. If you intend to make a habit of unhooking fish in this way, wrap your forefinger in adhesive tape

Figure 425: (*right*) The 'V' prong disgorger is rough and ineffective

Figure 424: Disgorging. Hold the hooked fish and tension the line coming to its mouth (a). Let the line drop in the cross cut before turning the disgorger 90° in the direction of the fish's mouth. The line now runs right through the disgorger. Slide the disgorger down the line into the fish's mouth until the nose of the disgorger creeps over the shank of the hook and touches the bend (b).
Now that the shank of the hook is regained by the disgorger a further push frees the barb, and the hook can be withdrawn

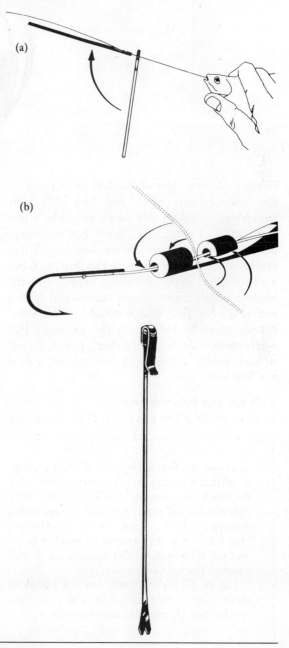

(a)

(b)

FLOATS

History does not record the first appearance of the float. Exactly when and how this little appendage found its way on to an angler's line is a matter of conjecture, but it certainly happened a long time ago. Since that far-off day evolution has had its way with the float, as it has with all other items of fishing tackle, and the modern angler finds himself confronted with a multiplicity of float design which, to the unin-itiated, must be baffling in the extreme. But whatever its style, be it long, short, round, fluted, slender, tubby, coloured or transparent, a float has four basic uses:

1. It acts as a bite indicator.
2. It suspends a bait at a given depth, or allows a calculated length of leader to rest, or drag, on the bottom.
3. When aided by current or wind it carries a bait to the fishing area.
4. It acts as a casting weight. A float, of course, contributes to the total casting weight at all times, but (apart from the hookbait) it becomes the sole casting weight when the chosen method of fishing requires an unshotted leader.

Float patterns are legion, and the angler's choice depends on his intended method of fishing and the prevailing conditions of light, weather and water. Generally speaking, when an angler wants to make a longer cast he puts on more lead. This extra lead demands a more buoyant float to

... to watch a float is the symbol of all angling, of all that recreates and is contemplative. Ask the man in the morning train if he angles. If he does not he will reply, perhaps apologetically, perhaps haughtily. 'I am afraid,' he will say, 'that I have not the patience to watch a float.' Not, mark you well, 'to flog a stream' or 'dangle a worm', but to 'watch a float'.

Yet, in all angling, there are few things of greater contenting than a float, and a red float (our brother Sheringham has written lovingly of a red float) is to be preferred before any other. What may it not, in certain waters cheerfully bobbing, indicate anon? A three-pound roach? A four-pound perch? A sixteen-pound carp? A twenty-pound pike? A float puts the whole subaqueous world at Fancy's disposal. A float may even foretell the accomplishment of a great trout – and blush no redder for man's sub-sequent ungrateful ignoring of its acquaintance in the tale of triumph.

Patrick Chalmers, *A Fisherman's Angles* (1931)

support it, so perhaps one may think of a float in terms of its shot-carrying capacity. But although shot-carrying capacity is related to the float's volume, the same volume can be represented by almost endless combinations of length and girth.

In normal conditions when choosing from a number of floats of different shape but roughly equal buoyancy, the most *sensitive* float is the best choice. A fish may become suspicious and drop a bait when it feels the resistance of a tubby float. The float designer, knowing this, puts a premium on slimness. A compromise, however, is obligatory with any float designed to carry a heavy shot load, otherwise its length would become excessive. Water conditions, too, dictate the shape of a float. In low, clear water a long float tends to 'rub the backs' of the fish and frighten them. In fast, swirling water a slim float is likely to be sucked under from time to time, whereas a short bulbous float will ride more smoothly and give fewer false bites.

There is a tendency for the unskilled angler to leave too much of his float showing. A fish will sometimes take a bait firmly but pull the float down very little. If a float dips $\frac{1}{2}$ in. when a full 2 or 3 in. are exposed above the surface, the bite often goes unnoticed. A float that dips the

same distance when only $\frac{1}{2}$ in. was showing goes out of sight, and the bite is noticed instantly.

The colour of a float is important if only for the confidence it inspires. A reed-stem green or yellowish brown are probably the best underwater colours, since these represent the colours of natural flotsam. The suggestion that a float should be painted white or blue to match the sky has little substance. To the fish a float is a solid object and will be seen as a dark silhouette as it passes overhead.

Figure 427: Richard Walker's choice of colours for the visible part of an antenna float (left) and a normal float (right)

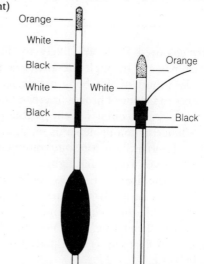

Figure 426: Pike-fishing, from *Dyalogus Creaturarum Moralizatus* – a Latin book published in 1480; cf. Turrell's *Ancient Angling Authors* (1910). The earliest known illustration of a float

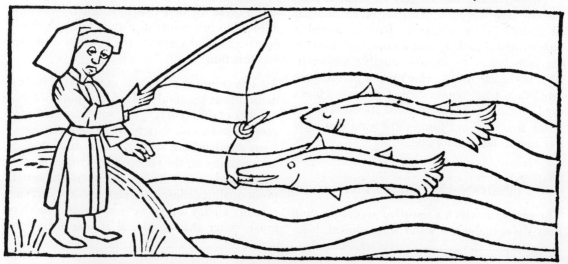

De lucio et trincha Dyalogus quadragefim̄ quartus

Piscator quidam piscabatur Unde escam inhamatam

An angler becomes aware of the need to make some adjustment to his tackle or technique through signals sent by float, rod-tip, lure or bait, or changing conditions of weather and water. The ability to receive and understand these signals and know how to act on them, separates the expert angler from the rest.

Unlike the participants in most other sports, anglers improve (or *should* improve) with age; their rate of improvement depending on:

(a) The extent of their angling experience.

(b) The ability to draw the right conclusions from that experience.

(c) A thirst for any information that will extend their knowledge of angling.

Since this book is something of a catalogue of thoroughly tested tackles and techniques we have used ourselves, it is in category (c) that we hope to be of assistance. We should point out, however, that the difference between success and failure often depends on some tiny variation. *Whatever rig or method is chosen, final adjustment must always be made at the waterside.*

Brightly coloured floats are likely to 'flash' during their passage through the air. (For this reason, both authors of this book have rejected white fly-lines in favour of brown or green lines.)

There is no 'best' colour for the visible part of a float. Choice of colour depends on the prevailing light. There is, however, one colour combination that serves well in any light.

The part of the float that shows above water when the float is properly trimmed with shot should be painted in three equal bands of colour: orange at the tip, then white, then black (see Fig. 427). A coloured float-cap is then placed on the appropriate band.

Few anglers can justify the multitude of floats that haunt their tackle bags. Yet they are justified in carrying them, for one day an unusual float pattern may meet the demands of an unusual situation. Walker admits to having carried a rather comical-looking float around with him for ten years before he found a suitable use for it. This particular float – which had a plastic vane fitted to its base, reminiscent of the paper flight used on darts – finally justified its existence at Tring Reservoir in a force-eight wind that blew any normal float on its side.

DESIGN AND FUNCTION

The ease with which a sensitive porcupine quill float slides under the water when pulled down by a biting fish can be described in terms of the float's *hydro-dynamic* qualities.

The reason why a fluted float moves downstream against an upstream wind better than any other float can be described in terms of the fluted float's *hydro-static* qualities.

It is, of course, quite unnecessary to remember these technical terms, but it *is* necessary to understand that they relate to two fundamentally different aspects of float behaviour. In the first example the float has been moved by a fish. In the second it has been moved by the water.

We believe that although most anglers 'know what they like' when it comes to choosing a float, many of them do not have a thorough understanding of float design, so that when selecting a float for a particular purpose they often fail to make the best choice. It might be helpful to look at the random display of floats shown in figure 428, and consider the relation of design and function.

A. The common porcupine quill float. The best natural float procurable. It can be obtained in a number of different lengths, with varying buoyancy, to suit a wide variety of fishing conditions – from canal fishing with a single dust shot, to long-trotting on the Hampshire Avon. The porcupine quill is very strong, and its natural waterproof qualities allow it to retain its shot-carrying capacity all day if need be (some floats absorb so much water that periodical adjustment of the

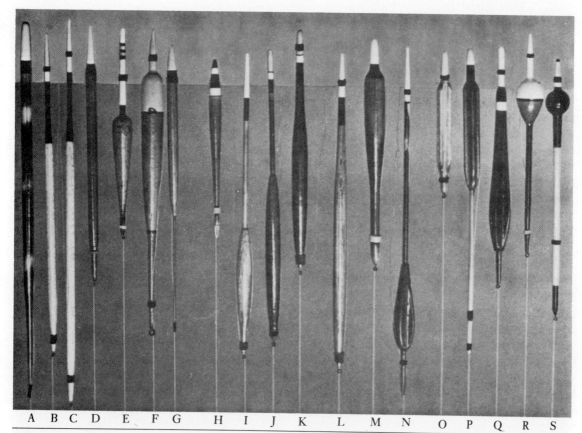

A B C D E F G H I J K L M N O P Q R S

Figure 428: Some characteristic design features (described in the text)

shotting is necessary). The inherent slimness of the porcupine quill, together with bird quills such as crow, puts it in a class of floats whose sensitivity has only recently been matched by manufactured floats.

B and C. Two examples of the 'wind' float (the larger one, of course, will carry more shot). This is an excellent pattern: a veritable iceberg of a float. Just a slim balsa stem (or antenna) shows above water, but underwater there is a long parallel balsa body of large shot-carrying capacity. As its name implies, this is a good float to use in windy conditions. It will be seen from the illustration that, despite the float's total volume, the wind has little to act upon. There are many floats that achieve the same end as the wind float.

D. The standard balsa float. Of medium length and thickness, it can carry a reasonable load of shot (considering its volume) because it is made from balsa wood. The exposed part of this float is thicker and therefore more visible than its counterpart on the wind float. This makes it a better proposition for long casting or long-trotting.

E. Some years ago this type of float was made in the south Midlands and called the 'Roach-Ideal'. It is a good float for a lively stream because of its shallow draught.

F. The conventional sliding float which has served generations of anglers. The line, instead of passing under the float cap before going down through the bottom ring, as with fixed floats, runs through a metal ring that sticks out of the side of the float on a level with the plimsoll line, thence through the ring on the submerged tip.

One snag with this type of slider is the loss of sliding efficiency due to friction of the line passing over the body of the float. To overcome friction, relatively heavy shotting has to be used. As a consequence the float often has to be larger than an angler would otherwise wish.

In the late 1950s, Billy Lane – a Midland tackle-dealer and master angler – discarded the upper ring and replaced the large bottom ring (which hitherto had been big enough to take a 50 lb BS line!) with a ring just big enough to allow a 3 lb BS line to slip through. These simple but all-important changes made the sliding float popular throughout coarse-fishing circles. With Lane's type of sliding float (I and J), friction is almost entirely eliminated since the line no longer passes over the body of the float.

With such a fine ring a small stop-knot suffices. Young anglers skilled in the use of modern sliding floats may be surprised to learn

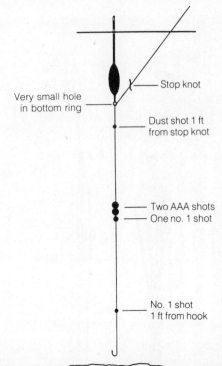

Figure 429: The sliding float, as described for the Welland by Austin Clissett. Note the distance between the dust shot and the stop-knot – about a foot – just enough to permit a clean strike and sure hooking

Figure 430: A selection of very modern floats

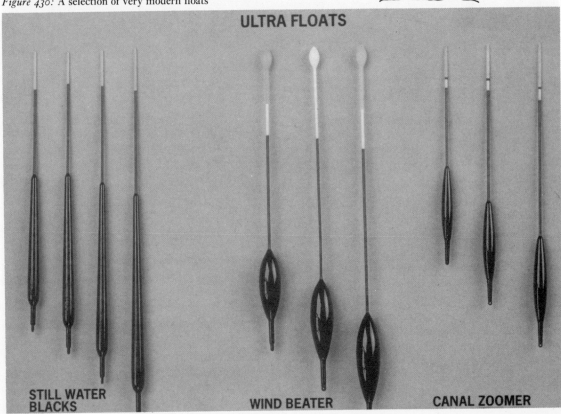

Freshwater Fishing

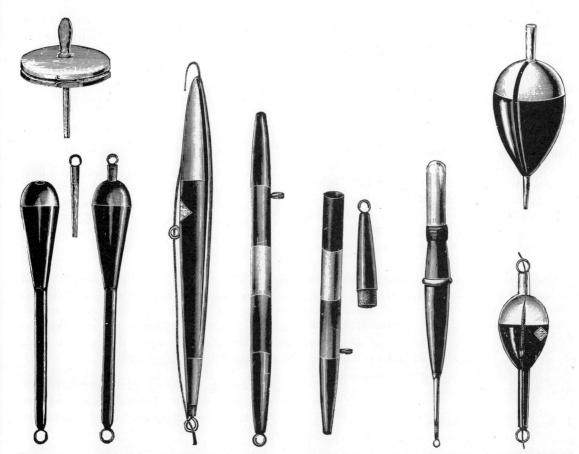

Figure 431: A selection of very old-fashioned floats from Allcocks' 1910 trade catalogue

that their fathers and grandfathers often tied float caps or matchsticks to their lines to act as stop-knots, even though a stiffish piece of gut would have worked perfectly well.

Austin Clissett, another Midland tackle dealer and master of the sliding-float technique, had some interesting comments on the make-up of the sliding rig:

I make rings for sliders from fine stainless steel wire; just a couple of turns around a sewing needle. A piece of nylon of about 5 lb breaking strain is used to form a stop-knot, and I always take the precaution of tying two knots to make sure I do not lose the depth. A single stop-knot can slip as it passes through the rod rings. Tying a stop-knot on the bank can prove awkward on a windy or wet day so I always tie my twin knots on the reel line at home. I use the 'needle-

knot' – the same knot that is used to tie spade-end hooks – and leave half inch 'tails'.

Lane's original sliding float was designed for use in deep, slow-moving rivers; waters too deep to fish with a fixed-float rig in conjunction with the favourite 12 or 13 ft match rod. Clissett and others subsequently realized that the advantage of a sliding float is not confined to deep-water fishing. Clissett, describing his match-fishing successes on the River Welland, said:

The reason I used a slider on the Welland had nothing to do with depth. You could have fished it just as easily with a fixed float because it's a comparatively shallow river. The advantage of the slider was that it did not impede the strike; you could hit your fish without having to drag the float a yard out of the water.

In situations where a sliding float is essential (e.g. deep, slow-moving rivers), the dust shot should be removed. This leaves the sliding float free to move between the main bunch of shots and the stop-knot. In practice it has been found beneficial to bunch the heavier shots on the leader midway between hook and float, and any small shot or shots between the hook and the heavy shots.

This method of shotting facilitates casting. It also gets the bait down to the fish quickly, thus increasing the amount of time that the bait is available to the fish. During the very last part of its fall, however, the bait is able to sink slowly and naturally. This natural movement often induces a fish to take the bait before it is finally suspended (unnaturally) on a tight line. When fish take a bait in this way the match angler describes their behaviour as 'taking on the drop'.

G. Because of the weight of its wire stem this float is semi self-cocking. Although only a shot or two is required to make it cock fully, it can still be cast a good distance because of its total 'load'. This can be an advantage if an angler wants to cast a long way and still have his bait sink gently in order to accommodate fish that will only take 'on the drop'.

H. Because of its shallow draught and dim-inutive size this float causes minimal disturbance when it is being retrieved over the heads of easily

---

Figure 432: A selection of modern pike floats. All of those shown are drilled centrally from end to end so that line can pass down their centres – facilitating their use as sliders. The fluted float (second from left) is unquestionably the best choice for river fishing for the reasons already given for other fluted floats

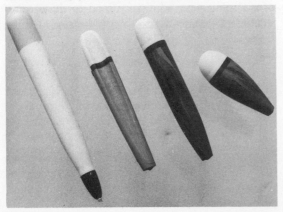

---

disturbed fish. Accordingly it is a useful float for fishing in clear streams in normal water conditions. A small version of this float carrying one BB shot is F. B.'s favourite float for trotting a single maggot to a shoal of wary sea trout in low-water conditions.

I and J. Billy Lane sliding floats. (See section F.)

K and L. Casting into wind is easier if a float carries the lead – or at least some of the lead needed to make it cock – inside its body. Floats so leaded are known as 'zoomers'. Zoomers can be used as fixed floats or (without the float cap) as sliders.

M. The balsa chub float. The designer scaled down the old Avon float without sacrificing its shot-carrying capacity, by using a more buoyant material – balsa. In addition, the balsa float has a shallower draught – which makes it less likely to frighten fish in shallow runs.

N, O, P and Q. These are versions of the famous fluted float. We cannot do better than quote Fred J. Taylor on this subject. Nobody has described it more succinctly:

It has been said that the fluted shape offers less resistance to a taking fish than a conventional round-bodied float, but this is not strictly true. Where the fluted float scores is in trotting downstream against an upstream wind. This I think was the purpose of its original design, as outlined by the late Major Smalley, its inventor.

A non-fluted float will not move downstream against a strong wind, but a fluted one will. The reason is the much greater surface area of the float to the current. The round-bodied float offers a stream-lined shape to the current and the current passes round it. The fluted float offers at least one of its concave depressions to the current and is therefore moved along by the flow of water which cannot pass round it.

R. The float that most boys buy the first time they visit a tackle shop. A shorter-stemmed version – the grayling float – is a design classic. Its bulbous body prevents its being sucked under in a lively gurgling stream.

S. A slightly more sophisticated version of float R. In our opinion this float would be improved if the lower stem were shortened to within half an inch of the body. The short-stemmed version would be less likely to get sucked under by the stream, and in shallow runs would not 'rub the backs' of the fish.

BITE INDICATORS

There are three types of bite indicator: tactile, auditory and visual. An angler can *feel* a bite, he can *hear* a bite and he can *see* a bite. An example of each is as follows:

Tactile   The touch-ledger
Auditory   The peg-bell
Visual   The float

Indication by touch is the classic method used by the boat angler at sea. He holds the line taut with his finger tips and *feels* for the bite. Barbel and chub anglers in particular make use of the same principle and call it touch-ledgering. Salmon fishermen depend on delicacy of touch when they fish the moving worm (although some

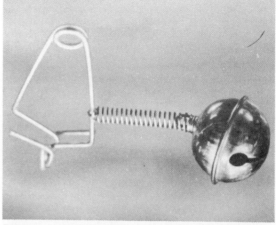

Figure 434: The rod bell (much beloved of sea anglers) is at least 250 years old. It was recommended as an aid to ledgering by Robert Howlett in *The Angler's Sure Guide* (1706)

fishermen, either from snobbery or ignorance, disdain this skilful salmon fishing technique).

The line can be tensioned by the rod alone: or (better) the rod can be held in one hand while the line is gripped between thumb and forefinger of the other hand. Apart from the lips, wetted finger-tips are more sensitive to touch than any other part of the body, as demonstrated in the photograph by Dick Walker.

Auditory bite indication in the shape of the rod-bell, also illustrated, has long been the pier and beach angler's delight.

For the ledger fisherman, bite indication until recent years was a simple matter of keeping an eye cocked for the slightest movement of the rod-tip or doughbobbin. Nowadays, the principle of the visual bite indicator is being adapted to numerous systems: slack-line fishing, swing-tipping, quiver-tipping and spring bite-indicator fishing are examples.

As its name implies, the doughbobbin method of bite indication offers:

1. An immediate visual warning of even the most tentative bite.

2. Time for a bite to develop – while the fish takes up the slack.

3. Time for the angler to 'read' the bite – again, while the fish takes up the slack.

Figure 433: This photograph demonstrates how that great angler Dick Walker practised what he had always advocated: that touch-ledgering – in the hands of an expert – was of all styles of ledgering the most sensitive

Figure 435: The doughbobbin rig, as used in 1662

Readers may be surprised to hear that the doughbobbin principle has been incorporated in a bite indicator for at least 300 years. There is a description of it in Robert Venables's book *The Experienc'd Angler: or Angling Improv'd,* first published in 1662:

Some use to lead their lines heavily, and to set their cork about a foot or more from the end of the rod, with a little lead to buoy it up, and thus in violent swift streams they avoid the offence of a flote, and yet perfectly discern the biting of the fish.

In spite of the extreme sensitivity of the doughbobbin rig – and in our opinion there is none better – it is easy to see why it has never been popular with the match-angler. Running up and down to fix on a doughbobbin would be an absurd waste of time. The match-angler largely ignored ledgering until Mr Jack Clayton, a celebrated Boston tackle dealer, created his now famous swing-tip.

Mechanically, the swing-tip and the doughbobbin are the same; but the swing-tip is an ever-precious time saver. Figure 437 illustrates the similarity between the two systems. Figure 438 shows the swing-tip in action over a streamy run, and displays the expected tip movement with normal and slack-line bites.

Sometimes this movement will be the merest twitch; at other times a dramatic swing. Delicacy of movement applies more particularly to roach

bites – for which the swing-tip was originally designed.

It should be remembered that the swing-tip is only a bite indicator, and will not compensate for inferior terminal tackle or technique. Care must be taken when setting up the rod-rest position for swing-tipping. Swing-tip movement should always be at right-angles to the wind, otherwise the more subtle tweaks (which at times may be the only bites) will go unnoticed.

One of the better swing-tip productions is illustrated in figure 439. This design allows a swing-tip to be removed at a moment's notice, so that an angler may, if he wishes, quickly change to float-fishing. The only drawback is a tendency for the tip to unscrew itself. This defect could easily be eliminated if the nose of the top ring projected about a quarter of an inch – sufficient to allow a piece of valve rubber to be slipped over the joint.

Cheap imitations are less efficient than Clayton's original swing-tip, and the angler is advised to choose the best he can afford. Generally speaking, it is better to swing-tip from the front rod-rest while maintaining a grip on the rod. In circumstances where two rests are used, the layout should ensure that the hand is free to hover over the rod butt, so that a quick strike can be made.

The spring bite-indicator is an extremely versatile instrument. It can be used in any ledgering situation where the ground is soft enough to take the stick. For normal ledgering the rig is set up as shown in the photograph. There are times, however, when an angler needs to make use of his rod length. On these occasions, a spring bite-indicator fitted to a 5 ft bankstick allows the rod to be rested right over the water.

The main advantages of the spring are as follows:

1. An angler is left free to choose a rod for its normal functions of casting for and playing a fish, without having to consider how well it can signal a bite.
2. An angler can remain seated, since there are no bits and pieces to fit up after each cast.
3. A slack-line bite is plainly registered.

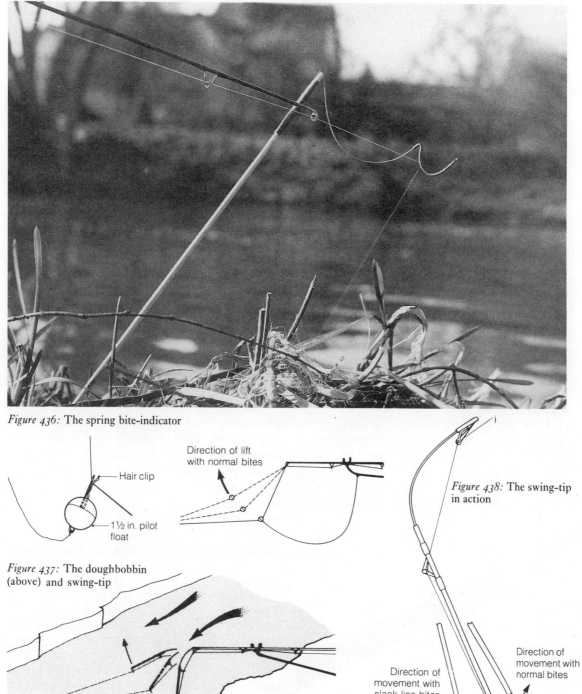

Figure 436: The spring bite-indicator

Hair clip

1½ in. pilot float

Direction of lift with normal bites

Figure 438: The swing-tip in action

Figure 437: The doughbobbin (above) and swing-tip

Direction of movement with slack-line bites

Direction of movement with normal bites

Threaded swing-tip

Knurled grip

Figure 439: Alternative swing-tip design

4. It will accommodate variations in current strength to a remarkable degree.

There is no commercial spring bite-indicator available, but for the angler who wishes to make his own we give the following instructions:

Take a 30 in. flat or round-sectioned piece of quarter-inch aluminium rod. Cut a slot down from the top about $\frac{1}{2}$ in. deep.

Take a 16 in. length of SWG spring-steel wire; bend one end round half a circle of $1\frac{1}{4}$ in. radius and bend the next section round half a circle of $2\frac{3}{4}$ in. radius.

The remaining straight section of wire is lashed to the back of the aluminium rod with water-proof 'Lassotape'.

See that the wire comes through the slot so as to obtain lateral support; cover the small half-circle (the 'dodger') with float-cap rubber, and paint it with contrasting colours. Choose the colours as if for a favourite float: it is the 'dodger' you will be staring at for long periods.

Directions for use

To get the best results from the indicator, set up two rod-rests. Cast out, take up the slack, and then lay the rod down in the rests.

Push the spring bite-indicator stick in the ground, so that the 'dodger' on the spring comes up under the line and tensions it about 10 in. or so from the rod-tip (the tension of the line actually depresses the spring). Note that the 'dodger' should always be pointing in the direction of the current flow.

Figure 440: The earliest known swing-tip first described in 1805

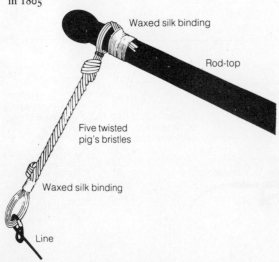

Waxed silk binding

Rod-top

Five twisted pig's bristles

Waxed silk binding

Line

Having discovered that the doughbobbin had been in use for hundreds of years, we looked closely for historical mention of the swing-tip. We were not disappointed. Strange to relate, this too is by no means a modern invention.

In the appendix of the third edition of a little book published in 1805, there is a description of *The Elastic or New Invented Superficial Float for a gentle Stream or Still Water Angling.*

On its cover, the book carries the following title: *Nobbs' Art of Trolling.* On the inside page, however, we find a different title: *The Angler's Pocket-Book: or Compleat English Angler: containing all that is necessary to be known in that Art. Also Nobbs' Celebrated Treatise on the Art of Trolling.*

Nobbes – this spelling of his name is given in Westwood and Satchell's *Bibliotheca Piscatoria* (1883) – the so-called 'father of trolling' (which he was not), published his celebrated book *The Compleat Troller, or The Art of Trolling* in 1682, and had no hand in the writing of the Appendix in the 1805 volume.

Although no author's name appears in the book other than Nobbs's it seems reasonable to conclude that the swing-tip was invented by the unknown author of *The Angler's Pocket Book.*

Because the author recommends the swing-tip primarily for bream fishing in still or slow waters, and because the first edition of the book was published in Norwich, we suspect that the author was a fensman. Be that as it may, here is his description of *The Elastic or New Invented Superficial Float* (the earliest recorded swing-tip (see left)):

Take five, six or more Pig's bristles, tie them together near the extremities of the thin end; bind as much of them with waxed silk as will make a loop about the size of a small ring of a trolling rod; twist the Bristles together with your finger and thumb, and tie the other ends, or they will untwist, leaving about an inch or more untied, that they may lay neat round the tip of your rod; divide the ends which are not tied, into two equal parts, placing the tip of your rod in the middle; bind them tight with waxed silk crossways, fastening the surplus as near the extremity of your rod as

Figure 441: (*right*) There are two super-modern versions of the doughbobbin, called the Doughbob and the Glowbobbin. They are provided with the best line-release clip that we have seen. The Doughbob has a screw-capped body which allows shot to be added, so that an adjustment can be made for different current strengths. With the Glowbobbin (illustrated here) extra weighting can be provided by pinching shot on the tethering string.

Where bites are expected to take the form of runs taking off many yards of line, as in carp fishing, a narrow strip of sheet plastic can be folded over the line between butt ring and reel, and its ends trapped in the clip of the Glowbobbin.

The light element in a Glowbobbin consists of what is known as a Beta-light. This is a tube coated on the inside with a material similar to that used in television tubes and filled with radioactive tritium gas. (Tritium gas has an active life of more than twenty years)

Figure 442: The Glowbobbin after dusk

Two alternative rigs for the Glowbobbin

Current

Close-up of the Glowbobbin

Spring leaves holding line

Coloured top

Glass tube filled with tritium gas (Beta light)

18 lb monofil secures Glowbobbin to rod-rest

possible, observing that the Float stands out horizontally, so that the loop hangs down towards the water, as in the Print.

This Float must not be made too stiff or you will not see when you have a bite, nor too weak, if it is, the weight of shot to your line will bend it, and will likewise prevent you seeing a bite; therefore to avoid either extreme, it must be made only stiff enough to remain quite horizontal as already explained; and this may be regulated by the number of shot, in the same manner as the common float, to make it stand higher or lower as the angler pleases; but above all it must remain quite horizontal to retain its elasticity.

Now your float is compleat and fastened to your rod, pass the loop of your line through the little loop of your float, and over the other end of your tip, and draw it tort, as you do when your tip has a common loop to it, when you begin to fish, let your line sink gently; you will feel when the shot touches the bottom, as it will give your float a visible check; then raise your line a little, that the bait may be near the bottom, but not touch it; when you have a bite, this float will have the same motion as the common float, although out of the water.

Among the many advantages this new float has above the common one, are these:

Your float will never frighten the fish; small fish will never play with it; nor will it disturb the water. In rough weather when you cannot see the common float, this remains unmolested; and if your line is long enough, you may fish a whole day without plumbing the depth. Amongst weeds you will find it answer beyond your expectation. When you strike, the rod, line, and fish has but one motion; but with the common float there is three if your line is long; the first motion is your rod, second the line, and third the float and fish, if the first motion has not frightened him away; but with this new elastic float, your line is infallibly perpendicular from the tip of your rod to the bait, and of course there can be but one motion when you strike, as the float is no impediment, it being one piece with the rod. Besides these advantages, with practice, you will find many more too tedious to mention. No float can equal this for Roach angling.

Instead of a loop, you may make a round knob of silk near the extremity of the float, of the same shape and size, as the knob at the end of a common rod, and fasten your line to it in the same manner.

For Smelt and Bleak fishing, this float will be found most useful, as well as at all mid-water angling.

BAITS *and* BAITING

BREADCRUST

Sometimes one angler will catch considerably more fish than other anglers fishing the same water. This may be due to his superior skill with a rod, but technical ability is not always the whole story. Attention to detail is the key to angling success, in whatever branch of the sport, and careful preparation of hookbaits ensures an advantage over all other anglers less well equipped. For instance, there are times when an angler will succeed simply because he has the 'taking bait' when others haven't.

If big roach happen to prefer breadcrust to maggots, as they so often do, it is clear that an angler of even moderate ability who has gone to the trouble to prepare some crusts prior to the fishing trip, will reap the major reward. More particularly is this so if he has bothered to *compress* his crust.

Whatever the bait size, compressed crust has three distinct advantages over normal crust, especially in fast water:

1. It survives longer when being cast.
2. It resists water erosion for longer periods.
3. It obtains a higher bite frequency and a higher ratio of fish hooked in relation to the number of strikes.

Small pieces of crust perform a special duty: they catch middling-sized roach as well as big roach, when this is the aim. They are obviously less selective than large pieces in the roach they produce, but even so the angler is unlikely to be plagued with undersized fish to the extent that he would be if using maggots.

Compressed breadcrust baits are prepared as follows:

Take a new, uncut loaf and cut off $\frac{3}{8}$ in. slices of crust from both ends and both sides. Lay the slices on one half of a dampened teacloth (figure 443) and use the other half to cover them.

Put the wrapped slices between two boards and place under a heavy weight. Leave overnight.

> Tis Hope that taketh birds with the snare, fish with the rod with fine Hooks well hidden in the bait.
>
> Tibullus

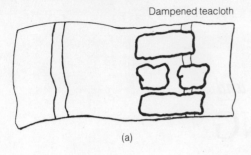

Dampened teacloth

(a)

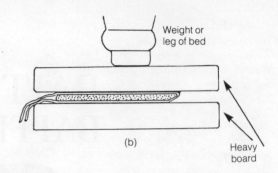

Weight or leg of bed

(b)

Heavy board

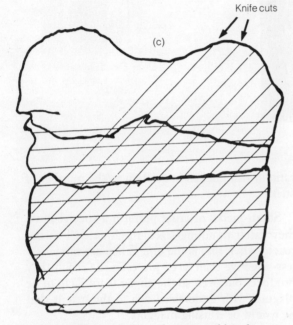

Knife cuts

(c)

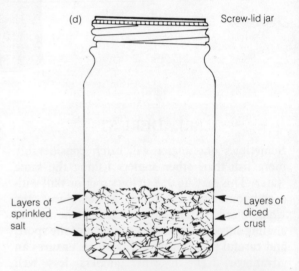

(d)

Screw-lid jar

Layers of sprinkled salt

Layers of diced crust

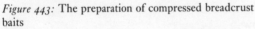

Figure 443: The preparation of compressed breadcrust baits

Next morning, remove the compressed slices of crust from the cloth and make a series of parallel cuts every quarter of an inch. Make a second series of cuts, so as to produce diamond-shaped pieces of varying size.

Keep the day's supply of crustbaits in a Kilner jar. This retains the moisture content of the bread, and will continue to do so if only a few hookbaits are removed at a time.

A spare supply can be preserved in the following manner:

Spread a layer of crustbaits on the bottom of a Kilner jar and shake a thin sprinkling of salt over them. Add another layer, and again cover with salt. Repeat the process until the jar is filled.

If the crusts are stored in polythene bags, refrigerators preserve them for an indefinite period. Refrigerated crusts need no salt preservative if the polythene bags are properly sealed.

Crust fishing

Although crust will account for larger roach than any other bait, many anglers avoid using it. They suspect that for much of the time they are fishing with baitless hooks! This is understandable. Crust softens quickly and an angler's suspicions that all is not well down below are seemingly confirmed each time he pulls up a bare hook.

We have gentles in a horn,
We have paste and worms too;
We can watch both night and morn,
Suffer rain and storms too.

> Izaak Walton, *The Compleat Angler* (1653)

... then he shall eyther have a close stopt horne, in which he shall keepe Maggots, Bobbes, Palmers, and such like, or a hollow Cane, in which he may put them, and Scarrabs.

> Gervase Markham, *The Pleasures of Princes* (1614)

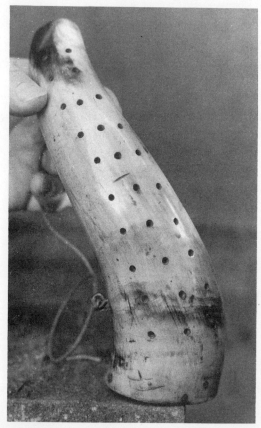

Figure 444: Bait horns

(*right*) A photograph of a 'yeoman's' bait-horn, taken by the authors when they were privileged to view the outstanding collection of sporting paraphernalia owned by the late Jos Milbourn of Carlisle

(*below*) An antique bait-horn with silver chain and fittings – the property of a wealthy *angler* – before those odious categories of fish and fishermen were defined, namely *coarse* and *game*. See also the illustrated title page of *The Experienc'd Angler* shown on page 366

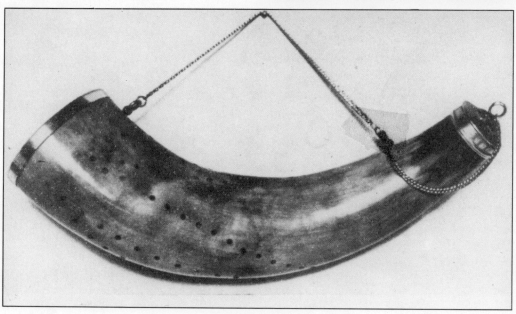

The chances are, however, that the bait was still on the hook – *until it was moved.*

Softened crust disintegrates when the hook is jerked, or if a fish gives it an exploratory knock. Even a slight touch will dislodge a crustbait that has been in the water for some time. Invariably, after striking, or an inconclusive bite, it is necessary to re-bait.

Successful crust fishing depends on four essentials:

1. Choice of bread.
2. Choice of hook.
3. Method of baiting the hook.
4. Confidence.

Clearly, an angler who lacks the confidence that his bread will stay on the hook until it is moved can never become a crust enthusiast. In consequence he will seldom give himself the best chance of hooking a really big roach.

Crustbait should be taken from a new loaf so that, when crust is torn off, a fair amount of white crumb remains adhering to it. Only the top and sides of the loaf are used. The choicest crustbaits usually come from the corners, which are golden, shining and rubbery. These parts are stored in a sealed tin or a slightly dampened cloth. Crust cracks easily when it begins to dry, soon becoming almost useless for hookbait. Many good fishing days have been ruined because crust slices were left out in the wind or sun.

A round-bend hook is best for crust fishing; crystal hooks should be avoided (see page 386). The round-bend cuts the truest arc through the crust and makes the smallest hole. It also provides a firmer hold.

The hookbait is held white-side up (figure 446). As the hook penetrates it is allowed to follow a natural course through the crust. The angler should be conscious of his right elbow being raised as the fingers holding the hook describe an arc. The illustration shows the changing angle of the hook as it finds its way through. Only the bend of the hook remains in the crust; the point and barb are left clear.

The baited hook can be tested by swinging it in the air like a conker on a string. If the bait comes off, the crust has been mounted wrongly,

Figure 445: A brace of river roach. A two-pound roach used to be a dream fish for an older generation of roach anglers. These two were taken on ledgered breadcrust

ROACH 2 lbs. 3 ozs. & 2 lbs. 1 oz

Caught by F.H.E. BULLER. Jan. 55. Suffolk Stour

Freshwater Fishing

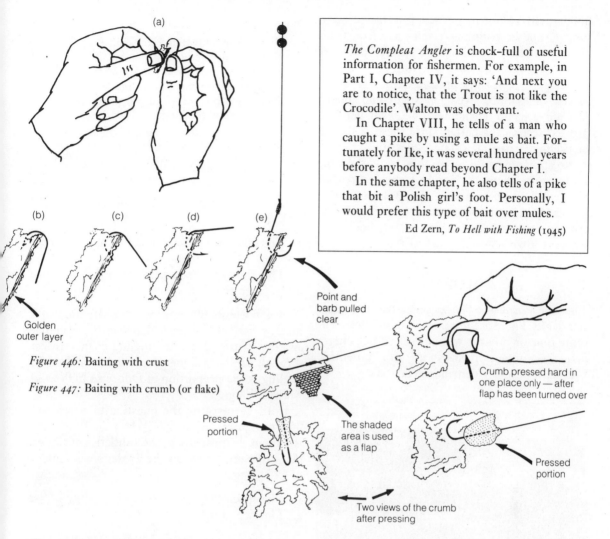

Golden outer layer

Figure 446: Baiting with crust

Figure 447: Baiting with crumb (or flake)

Point and barb pulled clear

Pressed portion

The shaded area is used as a flap

Crumb pressed hard in one place only — after flap has been turned over

Pressed portion

Two views of the crumb after pressing

the wrong sort of crust chosen, or the hook is too small. To make assurance double sure, experiment with a baited hook by dropping it into a bowl of water under a running tap. If the crust stays on for a time you can be confident that it will do so while you are fishing.

The size of the bait varies according to the species the angler is fishing for. Large pieces of crust are more selective than small pieces. This is helpful when we wish to avoid catching small fish. In strong currents, however, a large bait can be a drawback – especially when roach are the quarry. Even big roach have smallish mouths and in fast water a good bite indication is often obtained before the roach has sucked the bait

right in. By comparison, pieces of crust two or three inches across can be used effectively for chub.

BREADCRUMB

Baiting with crumb (or flake) is another method used by the experienced angler. Once again, a new loaf should be used and great care taken to prevent it from drying out.

The secret of crumb fishing is to use bread so new and soft that a single press of the finger turns it almost to paste.

When tearing off a piece of crumb, an angler should remember that the hook needs to reach about halfway down the bait (see figure 447). One part of the crumb is selected as a flap. With the minimum of handling the flap is bent over the hook-shank (but not over the bend or the point of the hook) and pressed hard. For larger pieces of crumb, eyed or spade-end hooks provide a good anchorage. The smaller the pressed section the better, since the bait should be used in as natural a state as possible.

No attempt should be made to 'tidy' the bait. Its irregular shape is thought to be one reason for its killing properties. Excessively hook-shy fish can sometimes be deceived by bringing the crumb round on both sides of the hook and securing it with a small pinch at the bend.

WORM

That the worm is a very popular bait is understandable. There are few species of fish which at some time or other it will not catch, but only a first-class angler realizes its full potential. Fishing it properly demands great skill.

Figure 448: F. J. Taylor, F. B. – and a lobworm

Tak Palma Christi and frankandsence, and medel hem togedir, and put hit in a fome clowte, and holde the pouder in thi finger that a gold ryng in upon, and wasch thy hond in every corner of the pont, fisches wolle come to thi honde.

From a MS on vellum, *c.* 1400, quoted by Robert Blakey, *Historical Sketches of the Angling Literature* (1856)

Broadly speaking, angling skill can be divided into two parts:

1. The ability to present a bait or lure in such a way that a fish will take it.
2. The ability to hook (and land) the fish once it has taken the bait.

It is not difficult to attract the attention of a hungry fish, but to hook that fish is altogether another matter. Many an angling chance is lost through faulty striking. And in no method of angling is the proportion of failure so high as in worm fishing.

It all devolves on the question of when and how to tighten on the fish. When the biting fish is unseen, as it usually is, the subtleties of timing the strike are based on the angler's assessment of two things:

1. The species of fish.
2. The size of fish.

The first is more important than the second, since each species has its own characteristic method of dealing with a worm. For instance, the 'taking' differences between, say, salmon, sea trout, brown trout, eel, chub and flounder, should be well known to any experienced angler. In the lower reaches of some rivers a worm fisher may hook any of these. He may even hook all of them on the same day. In each case the bite, and thus the timing of the strike, is quite different. And if the angler wishes to fish successfully, either to hook or (in the case of small eels) to *avoid* hooking the fish, he should be able to identify each species from the way in which it takes his worm. He should know this from the feel of the line, or movement of the rod-tip. And he should be able to do the same with other species.

The *size* of fish is also important, but perhaps not quite in the way that might be expected. A 3 lb chub may swallow a worm in a second. A 30 lb salmon may take ten seconds, or even longer – as many an angler who struck too soon has ruefully discovered. A large member of a species does not necessarily swallow a worm faster than a small member of that species. The reverse is often the case. As an example: a small sea trout can and often does swallow a whole lob-worm with great rapidity, whereas a big sea trout will usually bide its time and 'taste' the worm for several seconds before taking it properly.

It is clear, therefore, that although in some circumstances the worm may seem easy enough to fish, it is nevertheless difficult to fish well. The timing of the strike is subject to great variation, and it is the way in which he strikes that separates the good worm-fisher from the others.

Worm species

Twenty-seven species of earthworms are recorded from the British Isles. The following are those most commonly used by anglers:

1. Lobworm (*Lumbricus terrestris*). Also known as dew-worm, rain-worm, twachel, flat-tail, squirrel-tail and (in America) night-crawler.
2. Big blue-headed lobworm (*Allolobophora longa*). Also called blueys or roundtails.

Worm care

Take the Bones or Skull of a Dead Man, at the opening of a Grave, and beat the same into powder, and put of this powder into the Moss where in you keep your worms, but others like Grave-earth as well.

James Chetham, *The Angler's Vade-Mecum* (1681)

Amongst the old recipes for *scouring* worms, the putting them into a powder got from a dead man's *Skull*, by beating it to atoms, was deemed *super* excellent.

The Rev. W. B. Daniel, *Rural Sports* (1801)

---

3. Small blue-headed lobworm (*Allolobophora caliginosa*).
4. Brandling (*Eisenia foetida*). The bramble-worm, manure-worm, foetid-worm. The name is derived from the Scottish 'Brannit', meaning a reddish-brown colour as if singed by fire.
5. Gilt-tail (*Denrobaena rubida subrubicunda*). The cockspur, gold-tailed brandling or yellow-tail. There is a delightful reference to the gilt-tail by the eighteenth-century poet John Gay:

Those baits will best reward the fisher's pains,
Whose polished tails a shining yellow stains ...

6. Redworm (*Lumbricus rebellus*). A worm of rich organic soil with high moisture content.
7. Marshworm (*Lumbricus casaneus*).

Note: It should be remembered that colour alone is not a good guide to worm identification. Colour varies considerably according to the worm's habitat and food.

Worm collection

Worms can be bought from worm farms or (sometimes) from tackle shops. But many anglers collect brandlings from a manure dump, or compost heap, and lobworms from a lawn at night. Others dig desperately for lobs on the day they need them. This usually indicates a lack of foresight. In fairness, however, it should be stated that some anglers prefer to fish with freshly-dug worms. Although worms straight from the soil are less able to withstand the rigours of casting, they are, it is claimed, more attractive to fish.

It is not without good reason that the Americans call the lobworm the 'night-crawler'. On damp, dark nights, lobworms can be collected from the lawn or from any field of short grass. They are seldom picked up from dry ground, and never from frozen or even frosted ground. They are reluctant to surface on windy nights; when they do they tend to expose less of themselves above ground. In such conditions they are restless and easily disturbed.

All earthworms are sensitive to vibration and light (except red light), and both of these stimuli result in their retiring deep within their burrows.

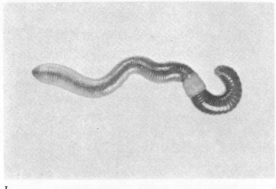

1

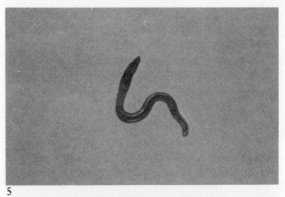

5

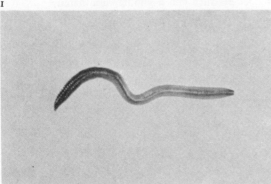

2

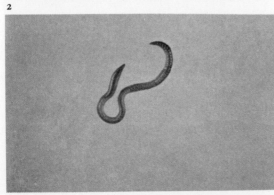

6

3

4

Figure 449: A selection of worms

1. The common lobworm; tail-end section oval or flat. Adult lobs are about six inches long when relaxed, not generally found in flower beds or well dug ground; found in more stable ground e.g. playing fields and meadows

2. The big blue-headed lobworm; tail-end section round. An adult blue-head, is the only other native worm to match the size of the lobworm; deep digging in rich soils e.g. in chicken runs, is the only way to collect numbers of them

3. The small blue-headed lobworm; tail-end section round; about 3–4 in. long. The common worm of well dug ground; the most common worm to find its way into an angler's bait can – if he digs his own

4. The common brandling; noticeable for its 'rugby shirt' skin pattern consisting of alternate hoops of reddish browns and yellows; the worm that anglers associate with a foetid yellow body fluid, and the rich smell of the dung heap

5. The gilt-tail; a smaller, striped brandling-type worm (but without the yellow hoops of the brandling); $1\frac{1}{2}$–2 in. long but more tapered in the body than the common brandling, and without its unpleasant smell

6. Marsh worms in a pot. Marsh worms and redworms are very similar in shape and size – $2\frac{1}{2}$–$3\frac{1}{2}$ in. in length with a practically uniform body thickness throughout. However, a marsh worm has a darker and a more iridescent hue than the redworm and is more active: it can actually jump if suddenly exposed to light

Only those persons who have observed it can appreciate the astonishing speed at which a disturbed lobworm can disappear down its hole. *A red light should be used for worm collecting at night*, since worms are blind to this part of the spectrum.

The collector should choose a damp, warm night; wear rubber shoes or wellingtons and move with great stealth. To have the use of both hands is an advantage, and the lobwormer will find it convenient to mount a torch on his head after the fashion of coal-miners or surgeons. An alternative method is to hold a small torch between the teeth (as recommended for night fly-fishing, see page 317).

Frequently only a small portion of worm is visible among the grass stems. It is this short length that the lobwormer searches for when he creeps about. Instantly, it is pinned down by a lightning movement of thumb and forefinger, or by both thumbs, one at either end. Next, the head of the worm is located and held firmly until the worm's peristaltic movement thins its body sufficiently to allow it to be withdrawn gently from the hole. Any attempt to drag a lobworm out too soon is disastrous; invariably it breaks in two. There is seldom any difficulty in locating the head of the worm, since it is always the tail that is in the hole. Sometimes, however, the whole worm is above ground – in which case it is unable to make a speedy escape.

Redworms are found in old manure sites (fresh manure sites favour the brandling) and under stones and cowpats resting on rich organic soil.

Wormcare

An Australian worm farmer, Don Ewers, who breeds the red compost worm, *Eisenia foetida*, has found that when packed in a peat moss and food mixture, the worms will live without weight-loss in cartons for between four and six weeks, unless exposed to direct sunlight or left in dead air space.

The worms live in a rich compost that supports 5,000 worms to the cubic foot, a hundred times as many as live in the finest soil.

This mixture, kept between 68° and 75°F, with summer cooling by mist sprays and winter

A man may fish with the worm that hath eat of a king, and eat of the fish that hath fed of that worm.

Hamlet, Act IV, scene 3

The first Fish you catch, take up his belly & you may then see his stomach; it is known by its largeness and place, lying from the Gills to the small Guts; take it out very tenderly (if you bruise it, your labour and design are lost) and with a sharp knife cut it open without bruising, and then you find his food in it, and thereby discover what bait the fish at that instant takes best, flies or ground baits, and so fit them accordingly.

Colonel Robert Venables,
The Experienc'd Angler (1662)

But Dame Juliana had beaten him to it:

When you have taken a grete fysshe, undo the maw and what ye find therein, make that your bayte, for it is your beste.

A Treatyse of Fysshynge wyth an Angle
(1496)

Oh – all right ...

Then go to Mother Gilberts, at the Flower-de-Luce at Clapton, near Hackney, and while you are drinking of a Pot of Ale, bid the maid make you two or three Penny-worth of Ground-bait, and some Paste (which they do very neatly, and well); and observing of them, you will know how to make it yourself for any other place; which is too tedious here to insert.

William Gilbert, *The Angler's Delight*
... 'the whole Art and Mystery of Clean, Neat, Gentile Angling, in a far more Plain, and Easie Way, than ever was yet in Print; All from Experience, and not Borrowed from other Books, and many things never before heard of, by most People.'
1676

Figure 450: Richard Walker fishing a tributary of the River Itchen

heating by special feed that generates heat, is basically composed of three types of manure – peat moss, lime, gypsum – and a powdered food made of meat-meal, sugar, lucernes and wheat.

Brandlings

Brandlings should be kept in bulb fibre, or peat, or compost from the actual worm bed – the top layer of compost being used. Brandlings kept in compost that is too moist will attempt to vacate their quarters at night.

Lobworms

The secret of keeping lobworms alive and in good condition is temperature. They must be kept cool during summer, and insulated against frost during the winter. The ideal temperature is 33–35°F.

Lobworms should be stored in shredded newspaper. They will survive far longer in newsprint than in the usually recommended moss.

Soak and squeeze enough shredded newspaper to fill a biscuit tin. Add worms. Place a piece of damp sacking on top of the newspaper. On top of the sacking put a plastic container full of ice. Have two containers on the go: one in the deep freeze, one on the worms. Change them round daily.

For this excellent advice on the care of worms (which we have thoroughly tested) we are indebted to those two great anglers F. J. and Ken Taylor. Using these methods, which they pioneered, they once kept 200 lobworms alive and well for twelve months.

Worm presentation

Worms can be presented to fish in many different ways. They can be ledgered, float-ledgered, float-fished, trotted, babbed, rolled, paternostered, sunk-and-drawn, or free-lined either upstream or down. First, however, the angler should give consideration to the various methods of attachment.

If long casting is necessary a worm will need maximum support from the hook. This is best achieved by using a slightly larger hook than would otherwise be required, and by putting several hookholds into the worm. One end of the worm should be left unhooked – or, as the ancients put it, 'un-armed' – so that it is free to wriggle.

This 'free' end of a worm is important for another reason: it provides an aiming point and, *ipso facto*, a starting end for the fish to take hold of. This ensures that when a worm is taken, the hook is automatically facing in the right direction.

A fish taking in fast water often grabs the worm and swings back to its lie before attempting to swallow. In these circumstances the drag caused by belly in the line either frightens the fish and makes it drop the bait, or pulls the bait away the moment the fish opens its mouth to swallow. The three-hook Stewart tackle helps to overcome this. This tackle is in effect a lobworming snap-tackle, since it ensures that at least one hook is in the fish's mouth when the worm

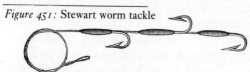
Figure 451: Stewart worm tackle

is grabbed, and allows the angler to strike immediately. For smaller worms the two-hook Pennell tackle can be used.

Lobworms fished on a single hook have a better chance of withstanding the exigencies of

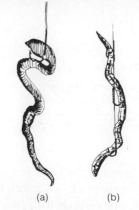

Figure 452: Properly hooked worms

(a)   (b)

casting if hooked in the area of the head rather than the tail. Brandlings can be mounted in ones, twos or threes. They remain more active when doubly supported at the quarter and three-quarter marks.

Bickerdyke claimed to have invented the two-

Figure 453: Pennell worm tackle

hook worm tackle (see *Angling for Coarse Fish,* 1899, page 58). It is Pennell, however, who should be given the credit.

In Bickerdyke's version, the bottom hook is larger than the top hook. His instructions for baiting-up are as follows:

The two-hook tackle I usually bait up by inserting the point of the large hook about the middle of the worm and threading it through to the tail, then catching the head of the worm on the top hook.

THE SLICED-SHANKED BAIT-HOOK

If sliced-shanked bait-hooks are not available whip a nylon bristle (or two bristles) to the hook-shank to prevent the worm, or worms, from slipping down the shank and bunching-up on the bend of the hook. Bunched-up worms often

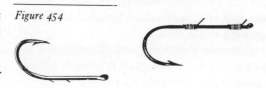
Figure 454

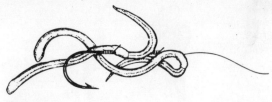

Figure 455

obscure the point of the hook and allow it to be pulled straight out of a fish's mouth on the strike.

The single hook baited with two lobworms is a suitable hooking arrangement for sea trout or salmon.

Or you may fasten some bristles under the silk, leaving the points above a straws breadth and half or almost half an inch standing out towards the line, which will keep him from slipping back.

Colonel Robert Venables, *The Experienc'd Angler* (1662)

THE STEWART 3-HOOK TACKLE

First described in 1857 by W. C. Stewart in his classic book *The Practical Angler:*

The advantages of this tackle are – that a trout can hardly take hold of the worm at all, without having one of the hooks in its mouth; that the worm lives much longer, and being free to wriggle itself into any shape, is more natural looking and consequently enticing; and lastly, that it is much more easily baited, particularly if the worms are fresh. Its disadvantages are, that it is more difficult to extricate from the trout's mouth; that it requires to be baited afresh every bite; and that the exposure of so many hooks is calculated to scare away some trout that would otherwise take the bait. But, upon the whole, the advantages preponderate considerably over the disadvantages, particularly when trout are biting shy.

For over a century Stewart's tackle has been popular with anglers. It can be purchased ready-made from a tackle shop or it can be made up with three-eyed hooks, together with a piece of nylon of suitable strength (i.e. slightly stronger than would normally be associated with a particular size of hook – so as to accommodate the harder pull that is required to set three hooks, as against a single hook).

It is worth observing that Stewart did *not* straighten the worm out – as it is often depicted – but hooked it so that it hung loosely.

MAGGOTS

The life of a maggot – after it has stopped feeding but before it pupates – can be extended by temperature control. For several weeks, maggots can be prevented from turning into chrysalids if kept at a low temperature (i.e. a few degrees above freezing point). An ordinary domestic refrigerator is ideal for this purpose.

Maggot care

The glazed pipe that protects a domestic water supply turn-cock – found in the grounds of most properties with a mains water supply – provides a site that will keep maggots in good condition for months. The bait should be placed in a dried-milk tin, fitted with a string handle, before being lowered down the pipe. The lid of the bait-tin should be punctured with tiny holes so that atmospheric humidity and the humidity inside the bait-tin can equalize. (Failure to ventilate a bait-tin may cause sweating, which will spoil the bait.)

If maggots are allowed to get too dry they tend to lose their body liquid. As a result, they shrink in size and their skins toughen. This toughness of skin makes a maggot more likely to burst when impaled on a hook. To prevent this, add three tablespoonfuls of water to each pint of sawdust mixture in which the maggots are kept.

Baiting with maggots

When attaching a maggot to a hook, care must be taken to ensure that the liveliness of the bait is retained. Use only fine, sharp hooks, and wherever you place the point of the hook make the smallest possible nick into the skin of the bait. If a maggot has a coarse, blunt hook pushed through its body it will burst and quickly lose its attraction.

There is no 'best' method of attaching a maggot, although the way illustrated in figure 456 (a) is usually described as such. The beginner's way (b) is useful as a change method, provided the hook just penetrates the skin.

The method illustrated in (c) leaves the point of the hook inside the maggot and provokes intense activity. Indeed, a maggot mounted in

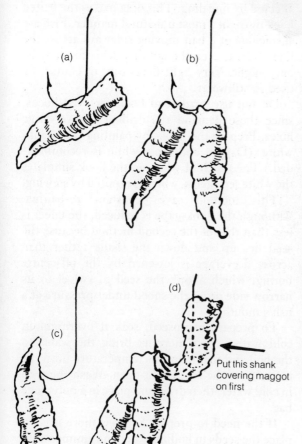

When hempseed is stewed it splits open. The usual method of mounting a seed is to push the bend of the hook into this split leaving point and barb exposed (figure 457(a)). This is a good method, but it entails frequent re-baiting since the seed is easily removed by a fish.

The point and barb are left exposed in the second method of baiting (b), but this time the point of the hook is inserted into the split and pulled out through the shell.

Mounted like this the hempseed is more secure, so that less re-baiting is necessary; but the position of the seed reduces the hook-gape, which in turn reduces the chance of a good hold. Moreover, a fish has a better chance of levering itself off the hook if the hempseed fails to budge.

The third method (c) is very good indeed, but like so many of the best fishing methods it requires a little more time and trouble. Select a large, partly-cooked seed that has not yet split

Figure 457: Different ways of attaching stewed hempseed

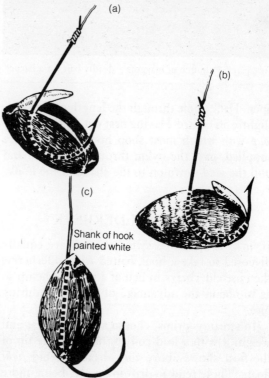

Shank of hook painted white

(a)
(b)
(c)

Put this shank covering maggot on first

Figure 456: Different ways of attaching maggots

this way often turns round and round on the hook like a propeller.

The method shown in (d) was the one used by Jack Harrigan, an outstandingly good Hampshire Avon barbel-angler. His method of mounting three large maggots hides the hook and presents the barbel with an attractive mouthful.

When fish become shy, try different methods of bait attachment. Vary the number of maggots. Try casters (chrysalids). Even a tiny change can help to deceive fish that might otherwise be suspicious of the same bait constantly presented in the same way.

Figure 458: A bunch of maggots – deadly bait for a barbel

open. Drill a hole through the length of the seed, slightly off centre. Having first cut off the snood-*loop* with which most shop hooks-to-nylon are supplied, pass the nylon through this hole and pull the seed down on to the shank of the hook.

HEMP AND ELDERBERRY

If, in a hemp-baited swim, the fish are equally disposed to take a hook baited with elderberry, then use elderberry in lieu of a grain of hemp so as to obtain the advantage of a more enduring bite.

In streamy swims, choose a *medium* float and weight it with a lead coil so that only the tip of the float shows above the surface. Avoid *light* floats. These tend to drift in an arc, being more affected by line drag. This drag makes the baited hook move in a most unnatural manner. Fish are suspicious of a bait moving sideways across the line of drift, even though that deviation may be only slight. Very light floats can, of course, be used in stillwater.

Do not use spade-end hooks or eyed-hooks, since these demand the drilling of over-large holes. Prepare the hooks by painting the shanks white. (Dayglo undercoat white is recommended.) The touch of white on the hook simulates the white seed germ, which is exposed by stewing.

This method saves constant re-baiting. Although the hook-gape is reduced, the effect is less than that of the second method because the seed lies up and down the shank rather than across. Leverage is lessened by the off-centre boring, which allows the seed to swivel to its narrow side or up the snood under pressure of a fish's mouth.

To prepare hempseed, soak it overnight in cold water. Next morning bring the water to the boil and maintain this temperature until the majority of the seeds split open. Wash the seed in cold water; then drain and place in a polythene bag.

If the need to prepare hemp is more urgent, place the seeds in boiling water and simmer until they begin to split open. Most novices tend to over-cook hemp, with the result that the seeds break up when an attempt is made to put them on a hook. Avoid this by keeping an eye on the pot and stirring frequently.

There is one other way of cooking hemp – the lazy way. Put the seeds into a vacuum flask, then fill with boiling water and leave standing overnight.

The best hemp obtainable is Chilean hemp. If you are lucky enough to get some, reserve it for hookbait. For groundbait, use a smaller, cheaper grade of hemp.

A bottle of preserved elderberries should always be included in a hemp angler's tackle bag, for there are days when fish take an elderberry just as eagerly as a hempseed. Such days are rewarding, since fish will hold on to a soft elderberry longer than they will a hempseed and more fish will be hooked for any given number of

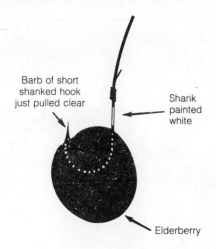

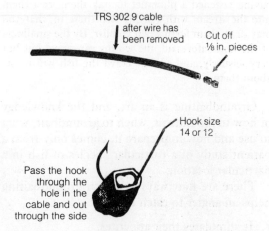

Figure 459: Hook-baiting: elderberry and cable-hemp

bites. Once again, a white-painted hook-shank is recommended. Apart from giving the elderberry the 'hemp-seed look', the white paint attracts a fish's attention and makes the bait visible at greater range.

Hempseed is a first-class bait for roach and dace. Sometimes, on hot, sunny days, it seems to be the only bait that will get a response. Roach and dace are not the only fish with a liking for this bait, however; chub, barbel and even bream will often invade a baited swim and provide a bonus for the hemp-fisherman.

Cable-hemp

Some hemp-fishers tire of having constantly to re-bait their hooks. An effective substitute for the natural seed, and one that will stay put, can be made from a small piece of special rubber known as TRS 302 9 cable.

For this technical description of the rubber, we are indebted to Mr Bourlet, a London hemp-angler of notable skill.

GROUNDBAITING

Nobody knows when groundbaiting devices were first used but the barrister William Hughes described one in his book *The Practical Angler* in 1842, that he and his cousin experimented with in *c.* 1815:

Then we were to have a small box with gimblet holes bored in it, in which a quantity of worms were to be placed, and when this box was sunk (a stone being put in for the first one) the worms, as a forlorn hope to escape drowning, it was supposed would crawl out through the holes, and so entice all the fish in the neighbourhood to the slot; to our certain benefit as to their just as certain destruction.

Hughes, of course, was doing what many anglers have done before and since – he re-invented an item of tackle which had been forgotten although described many years before.

The first groundbaiting device – the swimfeeder – was described in 1674 by Nicholas Cox, in *The Gentleman's Recreation …* 'Collected from Ancient and Modern Authors, Forrein and Domestick, Etc.'

If you will bait a stream, get some tin boxes made full of holes, no bigger than just fit for a worm to creep through; then fill these boxes with them, and

Figure 460: Cox's swimfeeder

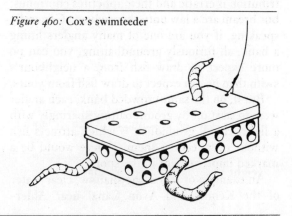

---

having fastened a plummet to sink them, cast them into the stream with a string tied there to, that you may draw them forth when you list. By the smallness of the holes aforesaid, the worms can crawl out but very leisurely, and as they crawl the fish will resort about them.

Groundbaiting is an art, and the knowledge of how to groundbait, when to groundbait, what to use and how to prepare it, comes only from a patient study of a particular species of fish in a particular location.

There are four ways in which groundbaiting helps an angler to catch fish:

1. It stimulates their appetites.
2. It attracts them into the fishing area.
3. Once they have been attracted into the fishing area, further groundbaiting will keep them there.
4. It tends to dull their protective mechanism and makes them less suspicious of the hookbait – especially when this resembles the groundbait, as it almost always should.

Since groundbaiting offers all these advantages, a novice might be forgiven for thinking that it automatically guarantees success. Experience soon teaches him otherwise. Usually the fault lies in himself, for like many beginners he thinks that the catching of fish depends on the lobbing-in of great quantities of groundbait.

Consider a river or canal bank crowded with anglers. If each angler satisfies the appetites of the fish in his swim, there will be few, if any, hungry fish about for anyone to catch. (Bream deserve special consideration, since their distribution is erratic and their appetites enormous; but bream are a law unto themselves.) Generally speaking, if you are one of many anglers lining a bank, all furiously groundbaiting, you can no more expect to draw fish from a neighbour's swim than he can expect to draw fish from yours.

But if, on the same crowded bank, each angler were to start off by groundbaiting sparingly with a light 'cloud' groundbait – which attracts fish without over-feeding them – there would be a marked improvement in the sport.

An example of this is the shallow, clear water of the Kennet and Avon Canal near Alder-

Figure 461: Match-fishermen at Stoke Weir on Trent care little about the weather. Snug under their umbrellas, like a row of mushrooms, they fish the hours away – intent only on beating the other fellow

maston. A study of this water reveals that most of the best bags of fish consist principally of dace. An angler with a good knowledge of this canal realizes that, in most swims, light or very light groundbaiting gives the best results. If the swim is a shallow one, the dace will respond well to a frequent light sprinkling of maggots, whereas heavy groundbaiting will make them vacate the swim altogether.

Roach, in the deeper swims, respond to small amounts of 'cloud' groundbait and sprinklings of maggots.

There are plenty of fine chub in this stretch of the canal. They often fall to bread-baits if a few walnut-sized lumps of bread groundbaiting are flicked out into the swim from time to time.

You must be first assured that the place where you Fish for Carps is provided therewith, which to know make use of these following Directions, not that they tend barely to make the Discovery and no more; for you must find other necessary uses made of them, for Instance, you Bait your Fish thereby, and make them bold; you also obtain a safe and sure place for your Hook to rest on, which is a good Convenience: and you are also assured that there are Carps in the place: the Figure shews the Form.

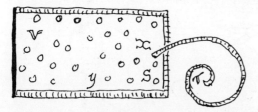

Frame some Bords together of such Length and Breadth; as you think fit, but for want of other Convenience, an old Door may serve the purpose, but the larger your Platform is, so much the better. The end Q is that which must be the Water side, at the Letter S make a hole to receive a good strong Cord, fastened with a knot on the inner side, then store over your Door with strong Earth or Clay about two Inches Thick; and so stiff, that it may not easily dissolve, nor work off with the Water, then stick the said Earth full of Beans (prepared as hereafter) at every four Inches Distance; the Letters VY denote them; they must be very gently put in, so as a Carp may easily Bite them out, yet so fast as not to be washed out by the Water, when all is fixed, let the end Q be put into the Water sloping downwards, then when the Hole is close; on the bottom fasten the cord T, at the Root of some Tree; the next Morning visit your Baits, pull out your Door Leasurely; if the Carps have eaten the Beans, tis a good sign of catchsome, but if not try it a second Day and night; if you then find the Beans unmoved, conclude there are no Carps. If you find the second time your Baits eaten, Replenish them, and think not your time lost. In case the bottom of the Water where you set your Door be clean and smooth, then remove your Door, casting in two or three Handfuls of the aforesaid Beans; but in case the Ground, be Muddy, Weedy, Rooty, or the like, let the Door be rebaited and returned to the place where it was, for there you may boldly let fall your Hook ... your Hook must have a Foot of line to Trail on the Water, and your Line must be of Green Silk, with a Device to let go store of it as you see occasion. When you perceive your Float to Sink, then strike him, but upright not slanting; and when once he is hit, let him have Line enough to tire himself.

Richard Blome, *The Gentleman's Recreation* (1686)

Groundbaiting devices

Anglers have ever been gadget-minded; and it is not surprising that attention has been paid to devices that make groundbaiting more sophisticated and precise.

Figure 462 (1) shows a twin-celled plastic pike float. The upper cell is air-filled to provide buoyancy; the lower cell is perforated, to allow a supply of maggots to escape gradually and attract small fish round the bait – an added attraction for pike.

A boat with a polythene bait-delivery tube rigged overside is shown in (2). The tube is designed to deliver groundbait close to the lake or river bed. This gives an angler the opportunity of swimming a baited hook just off the bottom in the middle of a groundbait trail. The bait-delivery tube can be adapted for bank fishing, and the tube combined with a hopper feed.

A bait-dropper is depicted in (3). Its object is two-fold:

1. It deposits a load of maggots on a selected part of the river or lake bed.
2. It carries the groundbait straight to the bottom, without attracting small fish on the way down.

The bait-dropper is an adaptable device which can be used for lift-fishing, laying-on, float-ledgering, or swimming the stream.

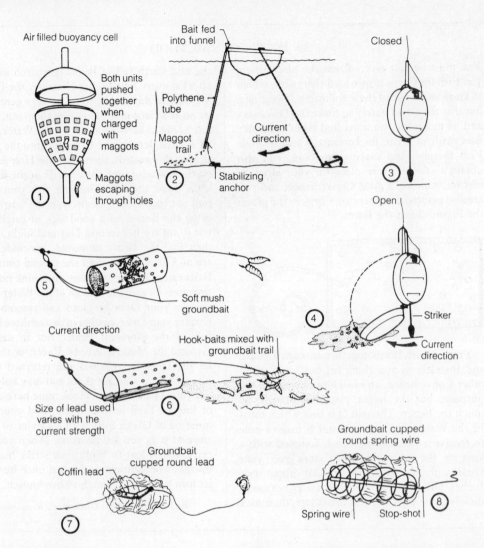

Figure 462: Groundbaiting devices

Most droppers have a cork fitted on one side to accommodate the angler's hook. This enables the angler to attach the bait-dropper to the end of his tackle without having to 'break-down'.

In (3) the loaded bait-dropper is shown before it hits bottom. Note how the striker releases the contents of the dropper as soon as it touches the river bed (4).

A bait-dropper must be swung out smoothly and easily with the rod, otherwise there is a danger of groundbait tipping out. Because of this, dropper techniques are associated with close-to-the-bank fishing.

One of the oldest and simplest methods of groundbaiting is shown in (7). A mash of bread/ bran (or similar groundbait), with or without a sprinkling of entombed maggots, is 'cupped' round the ledger lead. Although this method is simple in operation, the angler must take great care when mixing his mash. An over-sloppy mixture tends to come off during the cast, or when the lead hits the water; an over-stiff mixture may fail to break-up at all.

A natural development of the 'cupping' method of groundbaiting is the spring wire (8). This consists of a fine copper or brass tube soldered to a wire coil. Ledger anglers who fish at long range favour this method, because

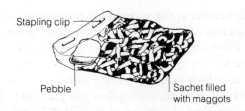

Stapling clip

Pebble

Sachet filled
with maggots

Figure 463: Another groundbaiting device

groundbait of any reasonable consistency readily adheres to a spring wire even during violent casting.

The spring wire can be used effectively in conjunction with float tackle provided the angler is fishing in deep water. The greater the depth, the less the disturbance caused by splash when the bait-loaded wire is cast.

Most anglers have a high opinion of the swimfeeder (5) and (6). Here is a device capable of depositing (at long range, if necessary) a quantity of maggots straight on the lake or river bed. The maggots, contained within a sandwich of soft mash, are prevented from escaping until the water has eroded the mash and freed them.

Seal one end of the feeder with mash. Fill the middle with maggots, and seal the other end with more mash.

Of all attractions, a crust-baited hook pitched on a carpet of similar pieces of groundbait crust is the deadliest for large capricious roach.

The swimfeeder also provides a means of getting pieces of breadcrust or breadcrumbs straight down to the bed of a river. Without wetting or pressing, the springy nature of the crust ensures a grip on the inside wall of the feeder.

One of the best methods of attachment is shown in (5).

The action of the stream emptying the feeder is shown in (6), and illustrates the effect of hook-bait mixed with groundbait.

A groundbaiting device that is capable of considerable development is depicted in figure 463: a transparent bag of soluble plastic (polyvinyl acetate) made by I.C.I.

Fill the sachet with maggots, and include a pebble to overcome the buoyancy of the trapped air. Staple-clip the end of the bag before throwing it into the swim.

The bag, with enclosed maggots, sinks to the bottom. Within minutes it dissolves – leaving a concentration of maggots on the bed of the swim. The value of putting groundbait straight on to the bottom, before small fish help themselves to it, is obvious.

In stillwater, the exact position of the groundbait can be marked by including a small quantity of sodium bicarbonate and citric acid in the sachet. As soon as water reaches the mixture, gas bubbles will be generated. These bubbles, rising to the surface, provide the angler with a target at which he can aim his baited hook.

The polycone (maggot) swimfeeder

Of all swimfeeder designs the polycone (figure 464) is the most advanced. The sharp nose of the cone cleaves the water like the bow of a ship, causing less disturbance than the conventional, blunt-nosed cylinder-shaped maggot-feeder. When stationary on the bottom, the cone-shaped body creates less drag, and during the strike reduces the stress on rod and line.

The feeder can be used either as a ledgering or a float-ledgering device. In both cases the mainline is passed through the hole in the sharp end and out through the hole in the blunt end. A stopshot prevents the feeder from running down to the hook.

Few anglers realize that most so-called modern fishing tackle and, for that matter, fishing techniques, are only modern in the sense that they represent the latest stage in the development of tackle and methods which have long been in use. An 'inventive' angler would be hard put to prove his claim to have devised something entirely new. John Waller Hills, in his classic book *A Summer on the Test* (1924), wrote:

'It is perhaps not surprising that I claim no wonderful discoveries. In fact I have made none. What I have learnt, very painfully, has been invented by others.'

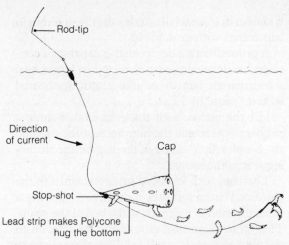

Rod-tip

Direction
of current

Cap

Stop-shot

Lead strip makes Polycone
hug the bottom

Figure 464: Float-ledgering with a polycone

The feeder is loaded with maggots by means of a removable cap that fits over the blunt end. When in position on the river bed the maggots crawl out of the holes and are carried in the direction of the hookbait. Removable caps are now fitted to the original swimfeeder (5). These are known as *block-end* feeders.

The groundbait marker-buoy

The consistently successful angler is the man who gives himself the best possible chance of catching a fish during every fishing moment. Part of his repertoire is the judicious use of groundbait – the purpose of which is to attract fish. But this in itself does not guarantee success. To be effective, his hookbait *must* fall inside his groundbait area otherwise the groundbait will merely tend to draw fish *away* from the hookbait.

Often, however, after throwing out his groundbait an angler becomes uncertain of its exact position, and can no longer ensure that his hookbait always falls in the right place. This is particularly evident when he is ledgering open sheets of water, such as lakes and reservoirs, devoid of local landmarks. In such waters, accurate pinpointing of the groundbaited area is very difficult and becomes progressively more difficult as the casting range increases.

This is easily overcome, if the groundbait is placed close to an anchored float acting as a marker-buoy, the subsequent positioning of the hookbait can be judged with complete accuracy.

First, ascertain the depth of water at the place you wish to groundbait. Do this by fitting up a float-fishing outfit consisting of rod, fixed-spool reel, 4 lb BS line, sliding float and plummet. The sliding float should be of the 'Billy Lane' type with a very small eye for the line to run through. Tie a special sliding stop-knot (see page 392) on the line above the float. Set the float at the estimated depth and cast to the desired area.

The depth has been over-estimated if the float lies on its side; under-estimated if it disappears. Adjust the stop-knot until the float just cocks. The distance between float and plummet now indicates the true depth.

From a reserve spool, cut off a length of 6 lb BS nylon exceeding the depth by about two feet. Tie one end to a $2\frac{1}{2}$ oz Arlesey bomb, the other end to the bottom eye of a medium pike-float (see figure 465 (b)). Anchored by the lead the pike-float will serve as a marker-buoy.

Hold the lead between thumb and forefinger; the top of the float between palm and little finger (figure 465 (a)). Throw the lead so that it pulls the float out behind it. When the float settles (point E in the diagram) its movement is restricted, since it has been allowed only two feet of spare anchor line.

Fit up a swimfeeder ledger rig (see page 438). Fill the feeder with groundbait and cast slightly beyond and to one side of the marker-buoy. The

Ointments to Allure Fish to the Bait ... Take Man's Fat and Cat's Fat, of each half an Ounce, Mummy finely powdred three Drams, Cummin-seed finely powdred one Dram, distill'd Oyl of Annise and Spike, of each six Drops, Civet two Grains, and Camphor four Grains, make an Ointment according to Art; and when you Angle anoint 8 inches of the Line next the Hook therewith, and keep it in a pewter box ...

James Chetham, *The Angler's Vade-Mecum* (1681)

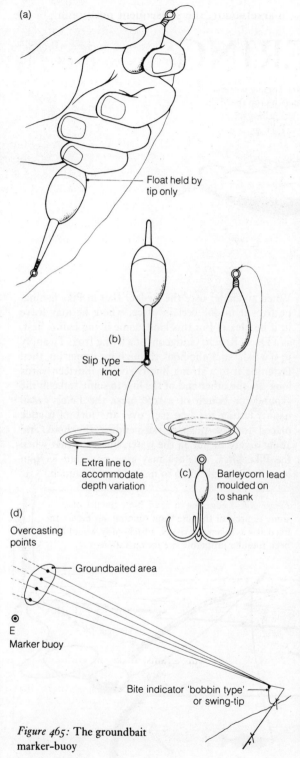

(a)

Float held by
tip only

(b)

Slip type
knot

Extra line to
accommodate
depth variation

(c) Barleycorn lead
moulded on
to shank

(d)
Overcasting
points

Groundbaited area

E
Marker buoy

Bite indicator 'bobbin type'
or swing-tip

Figure 465: The groundbait
marker-buoy

moment the feeder hits the water, retrieve it to
a point level with the float and allow it to sink.
As soon as the feeder touches bottom, give the
rod a fierce pull to eject the groundbait. Retrieve,
fill up the feeder and repeat the operation.
Twenty minutes of this will ensure that a carpet
of groundbait is accurately placed in position.

You are now ready to start fishing, and
knowing exactly where to place each cast, you
can fish with complete confidence.

The swimfeeder remains with the terminal
tackle of the ledger rig. Re-bait it fairly frequently during the first few hours of fishing.
This will entail more casting than you might
normally expect, but if carefully performed, this
activity will excite the fish rather than frighten
them.

Provided that the groundbaited area is within
accurate lobbing range, bream fishermen should
augment the supply of swimfeeder groundbait
with hand-thrown balls of heavier-texture
groundbaits e.g. a bread/bran mixture. Bream
have huge appetites and require more substantial
groundbaiting than other species.

At the end of the day's fishing, retrieve the
marker-buoy with a casting drag. The drag can
be fashioned from a piece of wire, or from a large
treble hook. *Don't* cast directly at the buoy. First
walk several paces along the bank either to right
or left, then cast across at an angle *beyond* the
buoy. Return to your original position before
retrieving, and the drag will catch the anchor
line first time.

It is interesting to reflect that in addition to
its material advantages, the marker-buoy method
offers a certain spiritual comfort. When lake or
reservoir fishing, the angler is easily over-
whelmed and dispirited by the great sheet of
water confronting him. With the marker-buoy,
a specific fishing area is defined. The angler is
no longer casting into a featureless expanse, but
concentrating on a piece of water which in his
imagination seems intimate and friendly. Far
from losing heart, he is made eager by a sense of
involvement – for in effect he has created a little
'swim'.

LEDGERING*

*During recent years, angling writers
and editors have tended to drop the 'd' in
ledger. We prefer the spelling offered
by the O.E.D.

As with many words, the meaning of 'ledger' has
changed with the centuries. 'Ledgering' today
means 'fishing at ground'; but in the early eighteenth century, to fish at ground was 'to lie upon
the grabble' – a term long fallen into desuetude.
Here is a description of it:

At six inches above the hook, a cut shot is to be fixed,
and next to this a small bored Bullet, thus the bullet
will be prevented from slipping, and the hook Link
have liberty to play in the water. If a Float be used,
let it lie flat on the surface; and when you see it move
along slowly, and presently stand upright, then strike.

So much for lying upo   .ie grabble, which to
modern anglers means ledgering or float-ledgering. 'Ledgering' to the eighteenth-century
angler meant something very different:

When an angler uses the Ledger Bait in Pike fishing,
he fixes it in one certain place, where he may leave
it; if he please. For this kind, some living bait is best,
as a Dace, Roach, Gudgeon, or a living frog. To apply
it; if a fish, stick the hook through his upper lip; then
fastening it to a strong line twelve or fourteen yards
long, tie the other end of the line to some stake in the
ground, or bough of a tree, near the Pike's usual
haunt, letting the line pass over the fork of a stick
placed for the purpose, suspending the hook and
about a yard of line in the water, but so as that when
the Pike bites, the fork may give way, and let him
have line enough to go to his hold, and paunch.

Figure 466: Ledgering in 1725. Note the use of a
stone to prevent the line from running out before the
livebait was taken. In rivers, a back-eddy would have
been found a profitable site for operations

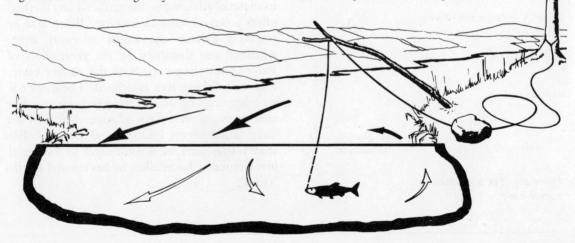

Nowadays, this method of setting a 'ledger bait' is seldom if ever used – except by poachers. Modern ledgering, float-ledgering and laying-on, however, are popular and skilled techniques, and the following pages are devoted to some of the rigs and methods used.

PIERCED-BULLET LEDGER

This rig has been with us for a very long time. A defect can be the tendency to roll – although this can be turned to advantage when we wish to move a bait towards fish lying underneath weed streamers, or on a gravel bottom. By this means, a direct fish-scaring cast is avoided. Rolling is prevented by the use of a coffin (or flat-sided) lead.

Figure 467: A famous angler: the late W. F. Hardy ledgering for roach from Balmaha Pier, Loch Lomond, in the 1960s. Bill Hardy had joined the authors on a pike hunting trip and was photographed in his attempt to catch his share of the baits

Figure 468: These are simply variations on the 'grounde lyne rennynge', or 'running line', one of the earliest recorded angling rigs. It should be remembered that the term 'running-line' as used by early angling writers, did *not* refer to a line running through the ring, or rings, of a rod (here William Radcliffe's *Fishing from the Earliest Times* is in error). It meant a line that ran unimpeded through a lead on the bottom – or, as they put it, 'at ground'

> Running-line: so-called, because it runs upon the bottom; it should be as long as the rod, or nearly so, and strong; about ten inches from the end fasten a small cleft shot, and through a hole made in a small or large bullet, according to the *current*, put the line, and draw the ball down to the shot; to the ·extremity of the line fasten a *grass* or silk-worm gut, with a large hook.
>
> The Rev. W. B. Daniel, *Rural Sports* (1801)

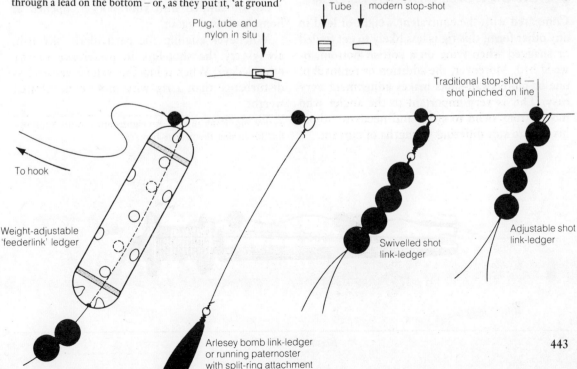

Plug, tube and nylon in situ ↓

The plug on a
↓ Tube ↓ modern stop-shot

To hook ←

Weight-adjustable 'feederlink' ledger

Arlesey bomb link-ledger or running paternoster with split-ring attachment

Swivelled shot link-ledger

Traditional stop-shot — shot pinched on line

Adjustable shot link-ledger

BOMB-LINK LEDGER

This is a typical variation on the Arlesey bomb theme. The shape of the weight helps with long-distance casting. It also prevents the lead from tumbling in flight, which so often causes the terminal tackle to snarl-up.

The lead-link is usually attached by means of a swivel, although some anglers prefer to use a barbel bead, or a split-ring. The link can vary between one inch and several feet in length. Use a long link when fishing from a high bank over deep water, otherwise excessive 'take-up' of line will be required during the strike.

VARIABLE SHOT-LINK LEDGER

Compared with the equivalent weight of lead in any other form, this rig is less likely to get fouled or snagged when lying on a softish bottom, or weed bed. Moreover, the addition or removal of one or more swan-shots makes adjustment very easy. This is very important to the angler who moves from swim to swim and needs to adjust his lead to suit differing strengths of current.

In ledgering, the calculation of weight can be critical; so critical, indeed, that frequently it makes the difference between success and failure. Users of the shot-link ledger soon appreciate the delicate weight adjustment provided by increments of $\frac{1}{15}$ oz, instead of by traditional leads graduated in quarter-ounces. With a little experience most anglers become expert at judging the number of shots required, either for anchoring the bait or allowing it to bounce along the bottom.

Prepare a stock of shot-loops holding varying numbers of shots, say from two to ten, so that you can start fishing with the loop you think correctly weighted for the prevailing conditions. This will save a lot of fiddling at the waterside.

Swan-shots pulled off a loop can be put into a tin, or slipped into your pocket, opened at home and used again.

Whenever angling for particularly shy fish, always try the shot-link in preference to any other ledger. When it hits the water it causes less disturbance than a rig with more concentrated weight.

Figure 469: Bank runner. An eighteenth-century running-line for fishing the 'ledger-bait'

FLOAT FISHING

The float is pleasing in appearance, and even
more pleasing in disappearance.

H. T. Sheringham, *An Angler's Hours* (1905)

FAST WATER TROTTING

The word 'fast' in the context of running water
is a relative term. It could be used to describe
the normal current speed of a river like the
Hampshire Avon, or it could be used to describe
the abnormal speed of flood or semi-flood water
in a normally sluggish river like the Thames or
the Great Ouse.

Of importance to the angler is the fact that
whereas the normal mainstream current in the
Avon causes no distress to an Avon fish, the same
speed of current in the Thames would cause a
Thames fish to vacate its usual mainstream swim
and seek a less rapid one.

An experienced angler instinctively recognizes
the maximum current that fish in a particular
swim are likely to tolerate. To deal with any
reasonable increase of current over the normal
flow, he will increase the amount of shot on his
line and use a larger float. With a further increase
in flow, he will stop fishing the mainstream swim

in favour of a more sheltered swim close to
the bank. There are other important aspects of
fishing in normally fast-flowing rivers. These
are best illustrated by recounting two actual
incidents.

A few years ago two anglers were sharing a
very fast weirpool swim in the course of a fishing
match (see figure 470). Angler No 1 stood on the
bank at the head of the weirpool close to the
apron. He faced downstream and trotted his float
down the current, so that after a trot of 20 yards
or so his float tripped through the swim of angler
No 2, who stood facing out towards the middle
of the pool. Because of the nature of the current
in the weirpool, both anglers could trot their
floats upstream or downstream according to
whether they cast into the main downstream
lasher or in the back-eddy, which carried the
float back to the apron. In practice it was more
convenient for both anglers to trot their floats
up and down the swim together, as shown by
the dotted line.

At first, when the fish were unwary, both anglers had plenty of bites. After a time, however, the 'apron' angler's sport declined, although angler No 2 continued to catch fish at the same rate.

After a few hours of frustration, the 'apron' angler stopped fishing and approached the other for a chat. The object of his visit was obvious: he was seeking an explanation for his failure to continue catching fish, even though he was fishing with a rig similar to that of his rival.

As the two anglers stood side by side exchanging pleasantries, more fish fell to the second angler's rod, and the fact that his float was not pulled under during these proceedings added to his companion's astonishment.

Quite simply, the 'apron' angler had failed to realize the significance of a slight increase in the speed of the current. Whereas the slacker current in the morning had given the fish time to take the bait 'out in front' as it were, the faster current of the afternoon forced the fish to chase the bait downstream. This change of behaviour made a great deal of difference to the behaviour of the float (see figure 471). In the morning, when fish were facing upstream as they took the bait, the float was pulled under by the drag of the stream. Later, when fish were obliged to turn downstream in order to take the bait, the only sign of a bite was a slight tipping backwards of the float – the result of a small degree of overshooting as the fish grabbed the bait. By this time, some

Figure 470: A Hampshire Avon weirpool. If the mainstream part of the diagram covered the next fifty yards upstream it would include the famous 'Armchair' swim, so-named by that great Avon fisherman Captain L. A. Parker. Parker considered it the best roach swim on the river. (It has produced six 2 lb roach for F. B. – all taken on crust). Although all these species could be caught in any of the weirpool swims, a pattern of distribution was always noticeable to anglers who fished there regularly

Key

C	Chub	R	Roach
D	Dace	ST	Small trout
G	Grayling	T	Trout
LG	Large Grayling		

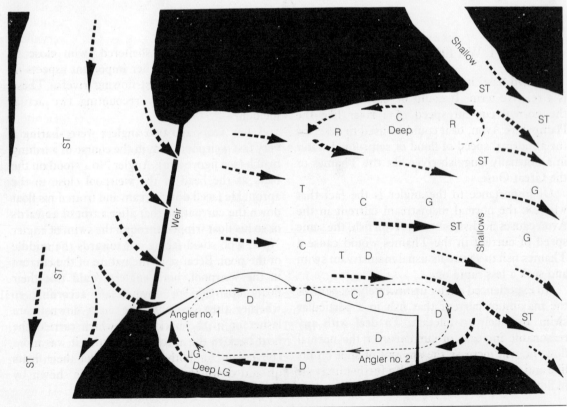

Freshwater Fishing

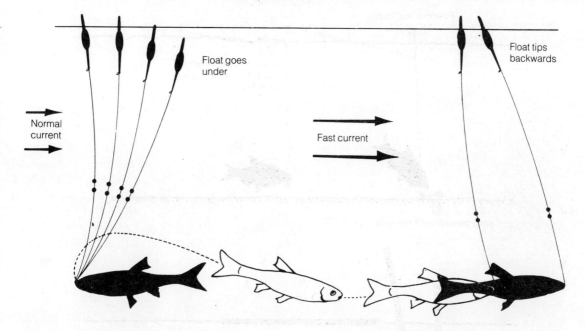

Float goes
under

Normal
current

Fast current

Float tips
backwards

Figure 471: Diagram showing how bite indication can vary
with the speed of the current

hours had elapsed and the fish remaining in
the swim had become more circumspect. Indeed
they were so suspicious that unless they were
struck on the first indication of a bite, the bait
was dropped.

In the second incident two anglers were float-
fishing from a punt moored above a fast run.
Both were trotting big Avon-type floats down
the run so close together as to be almost touching.
They were using identical tackle, and yet one
angler caught fish after fish while the other
caught nothing.

Again the answer, though simple, discloses a
fundamental truth. The unsuccessful angler had
been making a short cast down to the head of
the run, whereas the skilful angler had been
overcasting slightly and winding back before
letting his float join up with that of his
companion. The novice's baited hook tripped
along the bottom *behind* the float, whereas the
successful angler's baited hook *preceded* the
float – a killing combination.

THE LIFT METHOD OF FLOAT FISHING

Judging by their reluctance to use it, some
anglers must find the famous 'lift' method a bit
of a bogey. Although this method is very old, its
popularity suffered a decline until the persistence
of Fred J. Taylor brought it back into prominence (see page 448). Essentially of use in
stillwater, or a very slow stream, its principal
virtue lies in the visual exaggeration of a bite. As
can be been in figure 472, there is a dramatic
movement of the float the moment it is released
from tension through the lifting of bait, and
lead by a feeding fish. When more conventional
stillwater methods of float-fishing are used, such
pronounced bite indication can be expected only
when a fish actually moves off with the bait.

The lift method takes advantage of the changing postures of a feeding fish. From being nose
down and tail up (the near vertical position, as
shown at (a)), the fish moves into the horizontal
position (b) once it has picked up the bait.

Mount the rig as follows. Attach the float (in
this case a purposely overlong piece of peacock
quill) to the line by means of a half-inch rubber
float-band. This attachment should be made at
the base of the quill. Set the float somewhat

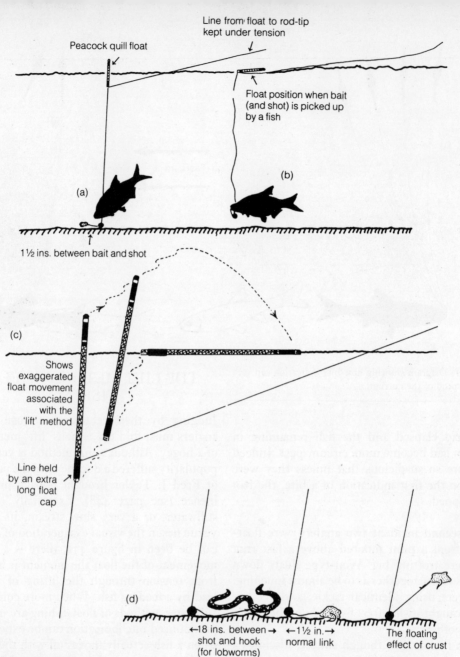

Peacock quill float

Line from float to rod-tip
kept under tension

Float position when bait
(and shot) is picked up
by a fish

(a)

(b)

1½ ins. between bait and shot

(c)

Shows
exaggerated
float movement
associated
with the
'lift' method

Line held
by an extra
long float
cap

(d)

←18 ins. between→
shot and hook
(for lobworms)

←1½ in.→
normal link

The floating
effect of crust

Figure 472: **The lift method**

deeper than the depth of the swim. Cast out, and draw the line tight with the rod seated in a rod-rest. After a preliminary cast, trim the peacock quill to a suitable length with a pair of scissors, leaving about 3/8 in. showing above the water.

Put the bait in the same spot each time by swinging out the tackle on a fixed length of line. Lay the rod in the rest while lead and bait are still sinking. As soon as the lead touches bottom, draw the rig tight until the float cocks.

A useful variation using the floating properties of crust is illustrated in (d). From the diagram it can be seen that the crustbait can be fished a predetermined distance off the bottom – to keep it clear of algal growth, debris or soft mud.

With worm baits, we recommend a longer

length of line between swan-shot and hook. This effectively dampens the immediate sensitivity of the rig and allows a fish more time to take a proper hold of the worm before feeling resistance. When lobworms are used, some 18 in. of line between shot and hook is desirable. Dampening the sensitivity of the rig does not hide bite-indication completely. A slight trembling of the float is enough to inform the angler that his bait is receiving attention.

With the lift method, it is normal practice to strike as soon as the float lies flat. Conditions prevailing at the waterside, however, always determine the course of action an angler should take. Apart from varying the timing of strike, anglers fishing canals and other waters where extreme delicacy of touch and tackle is required will prefer to use a smaller holding-shot and a correspondingly tiny float.

Lift fishing requires long and sturdy rod-rests.

Take great care to position them well, for they will in turn determine the fishing area of the float and hookbait. Once this area is established, groundbait it accurately.

THE ADJUSTABLE FLOAT-LINK RIG

Notwithstanding a float's natural uses, and its hundred and one different shapes and sizes, there are (trimmers apart) just two traditional methods of attachment.

1. *The fixed float*. Used when the distance between float and hook is less than the length of the rod.
2. *The sliding float*. Can be used for any depth, but *must* be used when the hook depth is greater than the rod length.

Figure 473: The adjustable float-link rig

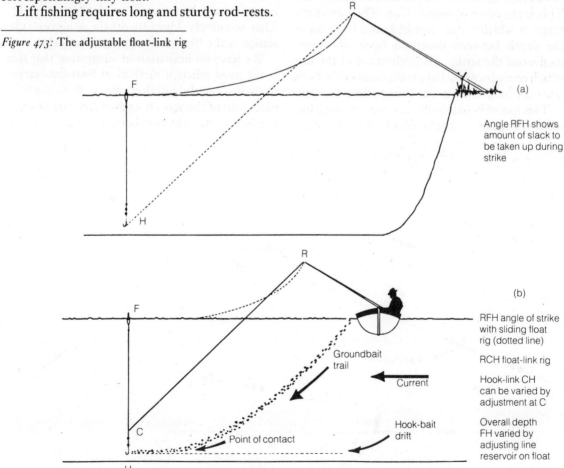

(a)

Angle RFH shows amount of slack to be taken up during strike

(b)

RFH angle of strike with sliding float rig (dotted line)

RCH float-link rig

Hook-link CH can be varied by adjustment at C

Overall depth FH varied by adjusting line reservoir on float

Groundbait trail

Current

Point of contact

Hook-bait drift

In both methods the float is attached to the mainline and operates somewhere between the rod-point and the hook. Although the first method is open to less criticism than the second, neither is entirely satisfactory. The trouble is that unless a float is fished with a very shallow hook-depth, or almost directly beneath the rod-point (as it is with roach-pole technique) it presents an angler with a problem of great complexity: how to strike effectively.

For a strike to be effective, the pull initiated by the sudden upward or sideways movement of the rod should be transferred instantaneously to the hook. But this is possible only when there is an absence of slack line between rod-point and hook. With conventional float tackle (figure 473 (a)), the angle between rod and hook represents a substantial amount of slack, which has to be taken up before the effect of a strike is felt. This is the curse of float-fishing. The longer the range at which a float is fished, and the greater the depth between float and hook, the more ineffectual the strike. The tightening of the line which precedes an incisive movement of the hook takes too long: the fish has time to drop the bait.

This loss of hooking efficiency due to slack line often frustrates an angler who is long-trotting a swim with fixed float. It is even more frustrating when he is fishing deep water with sliding float.

The traditional sliding-float technique is not without value. It permits an angler to float-fish in water of considerable depth. It enables him to cover a lot of ground. And by doing so it undoubtedly offers more chances of catching fish than any other method. *But*, the inevitable slack which accumulates between rod and hook inhibits him from taking these chances. Like those of the long-distance trotter, the sliding-float man's advantages are lost through ineffectual striking; and the ledger angler, with fewer bites but more fish, may be forgiven his gleeful grin.

No matter. Float enthusiasts can take heart. There is a third method of attaching a float: a method that not only allows the use of a smaller float and less lead to maximum range and depth, but offers the opportunity of an effective strike. This seemingly Utopian dream achieves substance in the 'float-link' rig (figure 473 (b)).

We have no hesitation in suggesting that this is the most efficient method of float-fishing yet devised – certainly in deep water. With the float nicely out of the way on its own separate linkage, the line is straightened between rod-point and

Figure 474: Examples of the 'float-link' rig

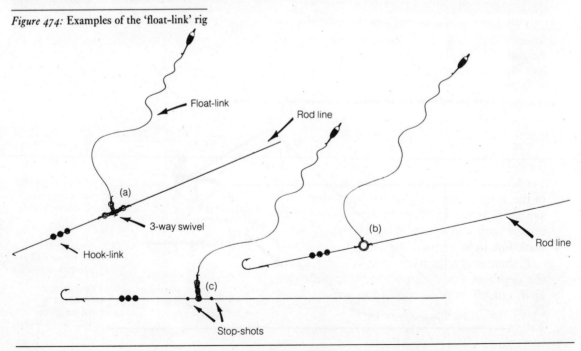

Float-link

Rod line

Rod line

(a)

3-way swivel

(b)

Hook-link

(c)

Stop-shots

Freshwater Fishing

hook, thus reducing that accursed slack which has always weakened the sting of an angler's strike. Nor is that all. Since the angler is now in direct contact with his hook, loss of power through striking against the float is almost entirely eliminated. By itself, no small advantage.

The full beauty of the method can be appreciated by referring to the diagram and comparing the direct route taken by a line when it travels to the hook via the float.

The rig has another distinct advantage over the sliding float. Virtually any float can be used. A sliding float has to be on the large side to support the extra lead needed to overcome the drag of the mainline pulling at right-angles to the eye of the float. Since this drag is non-existent in the float-link rig, less lead and a more delicate float can be used.

Although the float-link method has already been published (by F.B., in an earlier book), it is practised by very few anglers. And yet, with suitable modifications, it can be used for catching a wide variety of both fresh and salt water species and, compared with other methods, offers spectacular opportunities. It is a particularly effective method of float-fishing in any water – whether lake, reservoir, river or sea – which otherwise demands the use of a sliding-float.

Two ways of assembling the rig are shown in figure 474 (a) and (b). In each case the float has its own separate link, which is approximately 3 ft less than the depth of water.

In the first, the hook is attached to a separate link fastened to either a three-way swivel or a split-ring. The swivel, or ring, is used only when a wire leader is required for the hook-link.

When nylon will serve for the hook-line, tie the hook direct to the mainline as shown in figure 474 (c). The float-link slides on a tiny swivel held in the appropriate place by two split-shot. This simplifies and strengthens the rig by eliminating unnecessary knots, and allows the length of the hook-line to be adjusted instantly.

Fishing preparations are simple. First, plumb the depth of water. Supposing this to be, say, 20 ft, cut off 17 ft of nylon from a spare spool. (This can be much lighter than the mainline.) Tie one end to the float and the other to the

mainline, using one of the methods described, leaving 3 ft of hook-line below the join. Balance the float with the appropriate amount of lead.

The bait will now fish on, or just off, the bottom, but can be raised a few inches, if desired, by cutting off that amount from the hook-line.

When casting from a bank, wind up the rig until the connecting link is up to the top ring of the rod. Then, with the float-link dangling in a loop, hold the tip of the float between thumb and index finger of the left hand (figure 475 (a)).

Figure 475: Casting the float-link rig

(a)

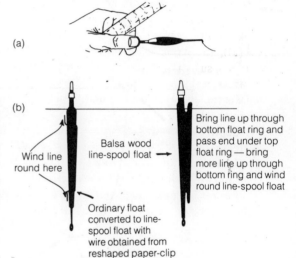

(b)

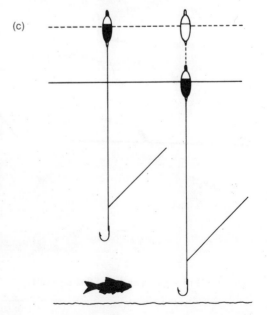

Wind line round here

Balsa wood line-spool float →

Bring line up through bottom float ring and pass end under top float ring — bring more line up through bottom ring and wind round line-spool float

Ordinary float converted to line-spool float with wire obtained from reshaped paper-clip

(c)

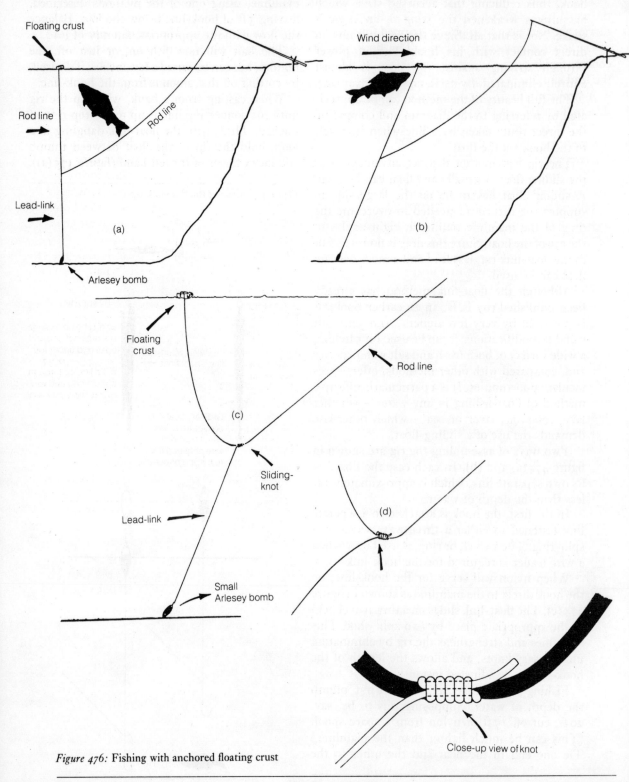

Figure 476: Fishing with anchored floating crust

The other hand controls the reel. Now, cast in the usual way. As soon as the lead is in flight, it carries the float out of the lightly-gripped fingers of the left (or non-casting) hand. The float, of course, lies flat on the surface until cocked by the lead sinking to its full extent.

A similar cast can be made from a boat when the angler is fishing in stillwater. In running water, no cast is necessary. The rig is simply lowered overside and allowed to drift away with the current.

Of importance to sea anglers is the Buller/Falkus design of float, shown in figure 475 (b). This device (known as the 'line-spool' float) incorporates a reservoir of link-line, which enables an angler to combat the rise and fall of the tide. The effect of a rising tide is shown at (c). It can be seen at once that float-link trotting in tidal water is impracticable without a simple method of regulating the depth at which the bait is fished.

On occasion, a line-spool float is very useful in freshwater. We do not pretend to have exhausted its possibilities. As with all other aspects of the rig, it offers opportunities of experiment and discovery that should appeal to thoughtful anglers.

The rig can, of course, be fished with the help of groundbait (see figure 473 (b)). The angler can be confident that his drifting hookbait will meet the groundbait trail regardless of the speed of the current. This meeting point can be described as the 'point of contact'. At sea, this point will be close to the boat during periods of slack water, but as much as 60 to 70 yards away when the tide is running strongly.

Most bites are obtained at the point of contact, but there are times when feeding fish start to work along the groundbait trail towards the source. If the angler suspects this, he should adjust the rig to fish at a shallower depth – and work it in shorter drifts. The use of a line-spool float makes this link adjustment very easy.

FLOATING CRUST LINK RIG

This is a variation of float-link fishing that may interest anglers who fish deep pits for carp. In certain circumstances, the thermocline forms in summer at depths of 15 to 20 feet. It occurs frequently when there are no shallows, and where the pits have deep-cut banks. In these conditions, bottom fishing is unlikely to be successful.

Baited with floating crust, the float-link rig (fished in reverse) offers splendid chances of catching fish (figure 476 (a) and (b)).

The rig is similar to the one already described, except that the float is exchanged for a crust-baited hook, and the hook for a small Arlesey bomb. The crust-hook is, of course, attached direct to the mainline, with the lead on a separate link. This link should be of very fine nylon. It has only a small lead to cast, and will easily break away from the mainline tackle if entangled in obstructions by a fighting carp.

The small Arlesey bomb not only facilitates casting, but anchors the crust in windy weather, as shown in the diagram. This is of paramount importance when the rig is fished against an onshore wind. Without an anchor, the crust is blown straight back to the bank.

Since the crust must be encouraged to float, there should be no weight of any sort between the hook and the Arlesey bomb. Hence, a sliding knot will be found useful for the lead-link attachment (figure 476 (c) and (d)).

FLOAT-LEDGERING, LAYING-ON *and* STRET-PEGGING

It is reasonable to assume that the use of a float in conjunction with a ledger rig dates from the earliest days of float-fishing. This assumption is based on the near certainty that the earliest float fishermen, whoever they were, must occasionally have over-estimated the depth of a swim – so that weight, hook and bait rested on the bottom, with the float, perhaps, lying flat on the surface. Thus, some ancient angler who failed to adjust his tackle became the first man in history to witness the mesmeric movement of a float suddenly coming to life before sliding out of sight. He was the first man to fish with a composite float-and-ledger rig. To put it more precisely, he was the first to *lay-on*.

The terms 'laying-on' and 'float-ledgering' may seem confusing, but the difference between them is simple enough. When a *fixed* lead is incorporated in a float-and-ledger rig, the method is termed 'laying-on'. When a *running* lead is used, the method is known as 'float-ledgering'.

There are two time-honoured precepts of coarse fishing:
1. Fish on the bottom and catch more fish.
2. Fish with a float and get more enjoyment from the sport.

It is to these precepts that float-ledgering and laying-on owe their popularity. Bottom fishing and float-fishing are combined.

FLOAT-LEDGERING

Float-ledgering as used in stillwater is a simple but highly effective method. If the float is to be attached in the normal manner, i.e. fixed at both ends, a pattern more buoyant at the base is advisable. This type of float will lean better than one with top buoyancy, and so help to reduce slack line (figure 477).

Most float-ledger anglers prefer to attach only the bottom end of a float – which reduces the float's resistance during the strike. This form of attachment helps in another way: an almost

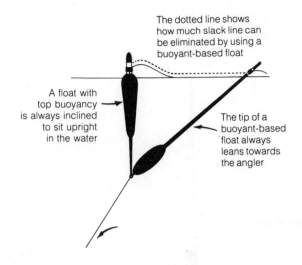

The dotted line shows how much slack line can be eliminated by using a buoyant-based float

A float with top buoyancy is always inclined to sit upright in the water

The tip of a buoyant-based float always leans towards the angler

Figure 477: Float-ledgering

Figure 478: Tackles for laying-on (float with fixed lead) and float-ledger (float with running lead)

imperceptible movement at the base of a float caused by a biting fish is signalled by a big, and therefore easily seen, movement at the float tip. (The windscreen wiper is an example of this: a small movement at the base of the blade; a very large movement at the tip.)

Without being 'broken down', an ordinary float rig can easily be adapted to a float-ledger rig by means of a slip-on lead. For example, the 'Ron' lead (figure 478 (f)). This type of lead is quickly removed if the angler wishes to revert to normal float-fishing.

In a fairly strong current float-ledgering can be a deadly method; but float-ledgering in fast water is, in our opinion, one of the most difficult of all fishing skills. It is also difficult to describe, in view of the many tiny but vital adjustments demanded by varying conditions.

Basically, float-ledgering in medium and fast

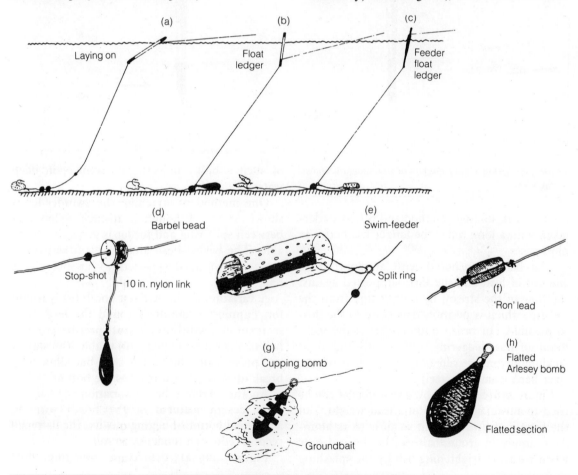

(a) Laying on

(b) Float ledger

(c) Feeder float ledger

(d) Barbel bead

Stop-shot — 10 in. nylon link

(e) Swim-feeder

Split ring

(f) 'Ron' lead

(g) Cupping bomb

Groundbait

(h) Flatted Arlesey bomb

Flatted section

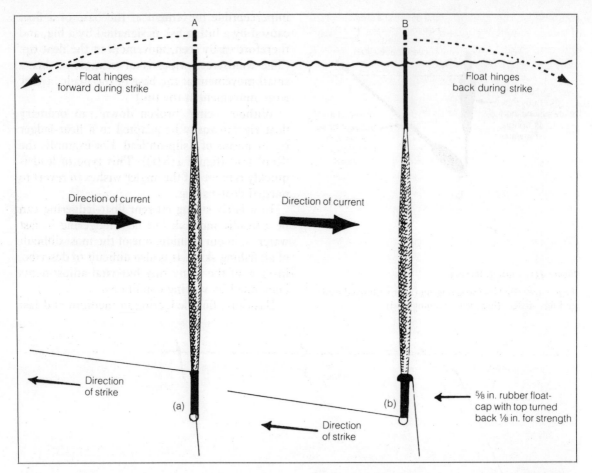

A

Float hinges
forward during strike

Direction of current

Direction
of strike

(a)

B

Float hinges
back during strike

Direction of current

Direction
of strike

(b)

⅝ in. rubber float-
cap with top turned
back ⅛ in. for strength

Figure 479: Arthur Cove's method of attachment is shown on the right

rivers is a close-range method and is best under-taken with a long rod – the longer the better in most cases.

The bait is anchored with an appropriate amount of lead and the float supported against the flow of the stream by a tight line from the rod-tip, which is positioned as close to the float as possible. (In broad outline, this is the tech-nique of float-ledgering; but the all-important tackle adjustments can only be learned on the river bank from a master.)

Figure 478 (c) shows how a swimfeeder can be used to advantage instead of a lead weight. But the benefit of fishing a bait so close to an abun-dant supply of groundbait can be derived only when we avoid frightening fish by the splashing

of such a bulky object: for instance, in deep water.

One method of attaching the swimfeeder is shown at (e), although a 10-inch nylon link between split-ring and feeder is generally desir-able. The barbel-bead attachment (d) carries a lead (or a swimfeeder) perfectly via a short nylon link.

A variation of the Arlesey bomb (g) is useful for 'cupping' groundbait round the lead. The secret of successful cupping is to prepare ground-bait of a consistency that will enable it to stay in one piece while the lead is cast, but allow it to break up soon after it reaches the bottom.

Another Arlesey bomb variation (h) has the good design features of the bomb with an additional bottom-hugging quality: the flattened section reduces a tendency to roll.

Figure 479 (a) depicts a swinging float

attached at the bottom end only. This method of attachment provides a sunk line to the float. On windy days this is a great advantage, since it reduces wind-drag on the line.

Usually associated with the float-ledger style of fishing, this is also a popular method of 'swimming the stream'; although when a fine line is used there is a danger of breakage as the float is struck against the current. Arthur Cove's ingenious 'reverse swing' float (figure 479(b)) reduces this danger. The line is passed *up* through the bottom float-cap instead of down, thus causing the float to swing *with* the current rather than against it.

Note: During their many expeditions together to Loch Lomond and other lakes, the authors have found float-ledgering with deadbait to be a highly successful method of catching pike.

LAYING-ON

Laying-on is usually practised with float tackle that is already rigged for normal float-fishing. There are times when an angler, having fished a swim successfully with ordinary float tackle, finds sport slackening off – even though he is pretty sure the water still holds plenty of feeding fish. In such cases, laying-on is well worth a try. The float is pulled higher up the line so that part of the shotted leader can lie on the bottom; the rod is placed along two rod-rests, and the float delicately tensioned by winding in a little line.

While waiting for fish to find the anchored bait, the angler should groundbait in small doses, making sure that it finds bottom close to the hookbait.

Fish tend to take a stationary bait quite boldly. Usually there is a warning vibration of the float, which gives the angler just enough time to grasp the rod handle preparatory to striking. Sometimes the float slides away; at other times (when the fish picks up the shot as well as the bait) the float lies flat on the surface. In both cases the angler should strike firmly.

Although primarily a method for stillwater or a sluggish river, laying-on can be employed along the edges of fast water. The rig is cast out and allowed to swing round with the current on a

Figure 480: Stret-pegging

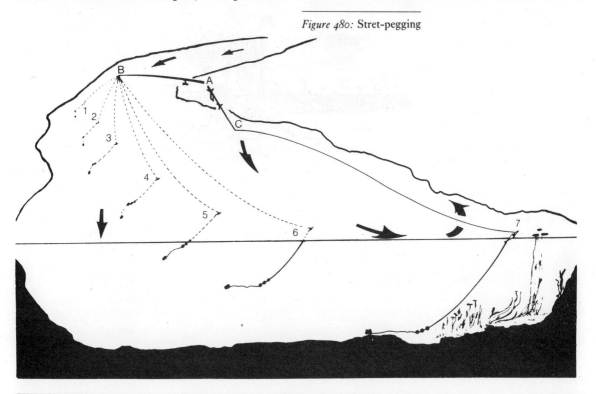

tight line until the lead comes to rest at a point between current and slack. When the float stops its swing, the rod is placed in the rod-rests with the tip pointing downstream.

STRET-PEGGING

Stret-pegging is a method of laying-on that can be used in running water at long range without the disturbance of long-range casting. The bait not only covers a wide area but reaches the prime feeding place without breaking the surface nearby.

Having set his float deeper than the true depth by some 12 in. to 18 in., the angler at A (see figure 480), makes a short cast at right-angles across the river to B. He then momentarily holds back his float on a tight line. This holding-back of the float induces the shotted leader to sweep the bottom. The float is then released and allowed to travel a yard or two downstream before, once again, being held back for a few seconds. And so on (see positions 1–6).

Each pause allows the shotted leader and the hookbait to cover ground, and even rest on the bottom for a moment or two wherever there are little pockets of deep underwater slack.

Gradually, in a crab-like fashion, the float moves over towards the angler's bank, ending up considerably farther downstream than when it started (see position 7). The rod – which up to now has been held at right-angles to the stream – is placed in a rod-rest so that it points downstream as close to the bank as possible (at C). This enables the float, bait and shot to make a final quiet approach to the slack water between current and bank.

As soon as the leader reaches the slack it will lie still. It is now that the angler has his best chance of catching the best fish in the swim.

Note: So far as we know, nobody has ever mentioned stret-pegging for salmon. And yet, when conditions are suitable, this method of presenting worm or shrimp is one of the most deadly of salmon fishing techniques (see page 227).

PATERNOSTERING

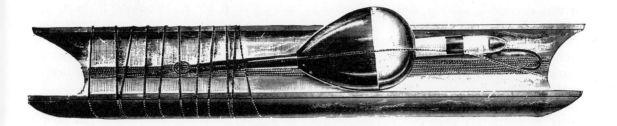

'The paternoster is a most deadly piece of tackle,' said Bickerdyke. 'Except in weirpools, there is rarely occasion to cast out the paternoster for any considerable distance in summer. Indeed to cast it out is a mistake; it should be swung out with the motion of a pendulum.'

If we add his third dictum from *The Book of the All-Round Angler* (1888) – 'One great advantage of this tackle is that it almost always puts the bait at about the right depth from the bottom, however much the depth may vary' – we have summed up a considerable combination of qualities.

There is a further quality, which Bickerdyke failed to mention: by reducing the need for casting to a minimum, an anchored rig has the merit of preserving the bait.

Even so, the beam and boom paternosters loved by old-time freshwater anglers would, through neglect, have long become obsolete but for the interest shown in them by sea anglers. The modern angler prides himself on a more subtle approach to his sport; he is inclined to treat any form of old-fashioned, crude-looking tackle with disdain. But in spite of a clumsy appearance, these old paternoster rigs were (and still are) very effective indeed.

The sliding bubble-float paternoster, how-ever, is both effective and suitably streamlined.

SLIDING BUBBLE-FLOAT PATERNOSTER

The rig is made up with a bubble-float, a split-ring, a barrel swivel, a three-way swivel, a Hillman lead and an Arlesey bomb. Once the principle of the rig is understood and its various parts remembered, its assembly can be varied to suit different situations.

An important feature of this rig is the bubble-float, which can be part-filled with water to provide additional casting weight. The float also provides the structure to which an additional bubble-float can be attached, should increased buoyancy be required.

The sliding stop-knot is positioned so as to make the distance between float and lead exceed the true depth by $1\frac{1}{2}$ ft to 2 ft. This latitude accommodates any small variation in depth. The remaining slack is taken up by drawing tight after the cast. The nylon link between the three-way swivel and the lead should be weaker than the mainline; thus, in the event of the rig's becoming snagged, only the lead is lost.

The sliding stop-knot should be made of thickish nylon. This will give the stub-ends the degree of stiffness that allows them to pass through the rod rings during the cast, but pre-vents them from passing through the eye of the

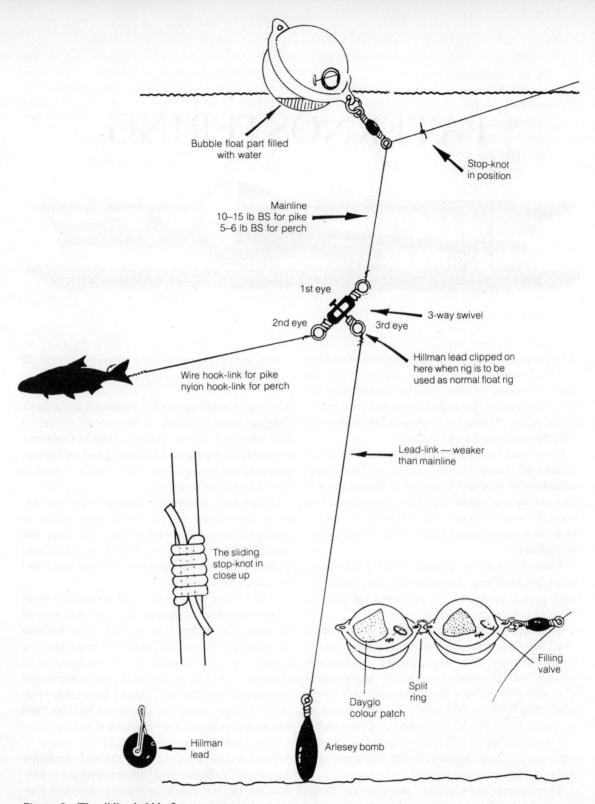

Bubble float part filled
with water

Stop-knot
in position

Mainline
10–15 lb BS for pike
5–6 lb BS for perch

1st eye

2nd eye

3rd eye

3-way swivel

Hillman lead clipped on
here when rig is to be
used as normal float rig

Wire hook-link for pike
nylon hook-link for perch

Lead-link — weaker
than mainline

The sliding
stop-knot in
close up

Filling
valve

Split
ring

Dayglo
colour patch

Hillman
lead

Arlesey bomb

Figure 481: **The sliding bubble-float paternoster**

small barrel swivel attached to the bubble-float. Use the knot illustrated opposite.

From the drawing it would seem difficult to prevent the lead-link and the hook-link becoming intertwined. In practice, the Arlesey bomb is retained in the left hand until the angler is ready to make his cast. As the rod is projected forward, the lead takes up the front position due to greater air-resistance operating on the bait and float.

If the rig is no longer required as a paternoster, the lead-link is removed. What remains is, with the addition of a Hillman lead, a live or dead-baiting float-rig. This has the special merit of being quickly adjustable to suit all conditions and bait sizes. The Hillman lead, available in graduated sizes, is readily clipped on the middle eye of the three-way swivel. To aid vision, patches of suitable paint can be dabbed on the bubble-float.

If perch are the quarry, the hook-link should be of nylon; but wire must be used for pike.

COUNT DE MOIRA'S BEAM PATERNOSTER

Numerous beam and boom paternosters have been advocated for pike fishing. This particular rig was described by John Bickerdyke in *The Book of the All-Round Angler*. The description is so clear that we give it verbatim. (The rig has been re-drawn in terms of modern materials, see figure 482.)

It is obviously important to have the cork just the right size to support the bait and the wire beam in horizontal position. With this tackle the bait has great freedom, pirouetting round the plumb which anchors it at the proper place and depth. It is altogether so novel, and apparently so complicated, that it is not likely to be viewed with much favour; but the Count de Moira says he kills more fish with it than his friends do on other tackle.

R. B. Marston wrote of this tackle: 'You often come across breaks and bays in beds of weeds and reeds which line the bank; they are often too small to try the ordinary livebait tackle in, because the bait would swim into the reeds at once. It is impossible to keep the bait on an ordinary paternoster at the exact depth, unless you are almost over the spot, and hold the line

taut all the time; directly the line slackens, the bait fouls the weeds at the bottom, and might remain there a month without attracting the notice of a fish. With Count de Moira's invention your bait must swim round, *supported* (at any depth you please) by the cork and anchored in one spot.

THE STANDING PIKE-PATERNOSTER

Most anglers are familiar with the beachcaster's style of setting his rod up almost vertically with a rod-rest. Strangely, the freshwater angler disdains to emulate him; yet the sea fisher's style, with certain modifications, is perfectly suitable for pike fishing. The standing pike-paternoster, which incorporates this style, has several advantages over most other rigs (figure 484).

1. It fishes a chosen spot effectively over an extended period without the disturbance of further casting.
2. The vigour of the bait is not dissipated by frequent retrieving and casting, as with other methods.
3. The bait can be fished at a calculated distance from the bottom, regardless of any variation in depth of water.
4. An anchored bait cannot foul up the tackle by swimming into weedbeds or other obstructions.
5. A bait is held out in position against the wind.
6. There is a close relationship between the number of baits used and the number of pike caught. This saving of baits is no small consideration.

Perhaps the greatest advantage of the standing paternoster is that the bait stays in position until the pike start to feed. This is very different from the usual practice of searching for fish that are already feeding.

It is a contemplative style of fishing, but deadly. It is, moreover, as effective on great pike rivers like the Dorset Stour and Hampshire Avon, as it is on the stillwaters of a Tring reservoir.

Choose a rod of 10 or 11 ft that will cast a bait weighing about $\frac{1}{2}$ lb. Important items are a 6 in. steel spike, threaded so as to screw into the rod-butt, and a beachfishing rod-rest.

Use a centre-pin reel of the Aerial or Silex type. Tie a 1 oz Arlesey bomb to the end of the line and introduce a three-way swivel into the line about 6 ft up from the bomb. To the second eye of the three-way swivel, tie, via a short link, any preferred type of hook tackle.

Select a swim and cast out the livebait with a long, slowly accelerated swing. As soon as the lead settles, stick the rod-spike into the ground and support the rod with the rod-rest in a near vertical position (see figure 484). Wind in the slack line until it is taut between rod-tip and lead. Maintain tension of the line by setting the drag on the reel to support the clutch.

Unless the sport is exceptionally fast, there is no need to sit behind the rod in a mood of tense concentration. Carry on fishing for bait if you wish, glancing at your rod-tip every minute or two. Sometimes, a pike will grab the bait and take line out in a smooth run, but when this happens the check will immediately give warning.

Figure 483 shows enlarged views of the three-way swivel: (a) the short link between three-way swivel and snap-tackle; (b) the link swivel; (c) the steel spike which screws into the rod-butt.

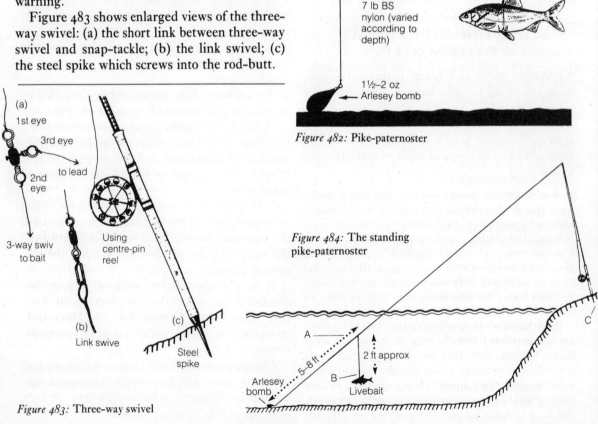

Fishing Gazette float
(floats on the surface
to give bite indication)

Stop-shot
fitted to
mainline a
foot or two
above beam

Common bottle-cork
supports beam and bait

Hole bored through cork

Mainline of 10–12 lb
BS nylon

8 in. twisted wire
crossbar of beam

7 in. length
of wire

2 feet or
more of
7 lb BS
nylon (varied
according to
depth)

1½–2 oz
Arlesey bomb

Figure 482: Pike-paternoster

(a)
1st eye

3rd eye

to lead

2nd
eye

3-way swiv
to bait

Using
centre-pin
reel

(b)
Link swive

(c)
Steel
spike

Figure 483: Three-way swivel

Figure 484: The standing
pike-paternoster

A

2 ft approx

5–8 ft

B

Arlesey
bomb

Livebait

C

Freshwater Fishing

SPINNING

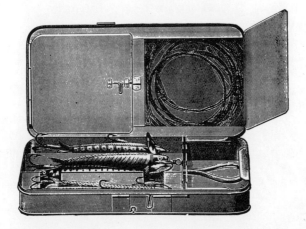

There is an old saying that goes: 'Those who keep their bait in the water catch the most fish.' This is true only up to a point. Certainly, unless it is fishing, no bait will hook a fish. But all baits need the help of enthusiasm and confidence.

By its very nature, spinning can so easily become repetitive and boring. You need spells of rest to rebuild your nervous energy. If you get the feeling that you're fishing empty water – stop and relax for a while. Don't flog yourself out and lose your enthusiasm, otherwise the chances are you'll be on your way home, tired and demoralized, just when the fish begin to take.

In no branch of angling is this approach more important than when you are salmon fishing.

Time after time I have seen novices catch fish because they were keen and hopeful, when the experienced rod comes back clean because he knew enough to be sure that the fish would be dour, and therefore spent his day flogging away mechanically or sitting on the bank in a hopeless frame of mind.

L. R. N. Gray, *Torridge Fishery* (1957)

Gray was right. In salmon fishing, the behaviour of these fish being what it is, a little learning is indeed a 'dangerous thing'. The would-be successful salmon angler is wise to 'taste not the Pierian Spring' until he has drunk deep from angling experience – and observation of the fish themselves!

SPINNING HISTORICAL

In *The Art of Angling* (1651) Thomas Barker described a new method of trolling for trout with minnow ('Trolling' then was what is known today as 'sink-and-draw'. A bait mounted on a leaded hook would be cast out, allowed to sink nose first, retrieved for a short distance tail first, allowed to sink again, then retrieved ... and so on. See page 479). But Barker, having given instructions for baiting the hook, recommends that *a swivel should be fixed to the line*. This, so far as we know, is the first mention of a swivel in angling literature. If the bait was intended to revolve, some sort of swivel was obligatory and it is likely that Barker's was the first reference to *spinning*, as it came to be known.

You must always be Angling with the poynt of your Rod down the stream, with drawing the menow up

The illustration above shows a nineteenth-century phantom bait and leader box

Figure 485: Taken from a cut in T. F. Salter's *The Angler's Guide* (8th edition, 1833)

the stream little by little nigh the top of the water. The Trout seeing the bait, cometh at it most fiercely, so give a little time before you strike.

There was a clear description of spinning in the 5th edition of *The Compleat Angler* (1676):

... and then you are to know, that your minnow must be so put on your hook, that it must run when 'tis drawn against the stream, and that it must turn nimbly ... the minnow shall be almost straight on your hook, this done, try how it will turn by drawing it cross the water or against a stream; and if it do not turn nimbly, then turn the tail a little to the right or left hand, and try again, till it turn quick; for if not, you are in danger to catch nothing; for know, that it is impossible that it should turn too quick.

The first edition also contained a reference to spinning, but not as detailed as this.

In the 5th edition of *The Experienc'd Angler* (1683), we find:

You must have a swivel or turn, placed about a yard or more above your hook; you need no lead on the line, you must continually draw your bait up the stream near to the top of the water.

There can be no doubt that this was spinning. By now, the element of 'sink' had been eliminated from the well-established method of sink-and-draw, leaving only the draw – which caused a suitably mounted bait to revolve.

During the eighteenth century, however, spinning seems to have been little practised. Like certain other methods and items of tackle, spinning fell into neglect until, during the early part of the nineteenth century, it was re-discovered.

Since the publication of *A Treatyse of Fysshynge wyth an Angle*, angling literature reveals many examples of re-discovery. Several are given in this book: the herring deadbait method of catching pike; the swing-tip bite indicator; the water-knot; the hook bristle for worm baiting; the tapered line; a maggot-tackle for sea trout night fly-fishing; the double fly-hook. Spinning was no exception. T. F. Salter said nothing about a revolving bait in the first edition of *The Angler's Guide* (1814); but in the 8th edition (1833) wrote:

Figure 486: (a) With its rigid tail-hook attachment, Pennell's original spoon was a much better hooker than any spoonbait marketed during the next century!
(b) The Toby lure – as you buy it from your tackle-dealer – with its dangling treble. Although the Toby is one of the best attractors ever made, like other spoons whose tail-hook hangs loose on a split-ring it loses a lot of the fish it hooks.

Taking into account the millions of anglers using such baits, the defect of split-ring and loose treble must have caused the loss of millions of fish – and yet bait manufacturers continue to ignore this ridiculous fault.
(c) The Toby lure fitted with Polyshrink tubing that has been shrunk (by dipping it in hot water) tightly round the back end of the lure, the split-ring and the upper part of the treble. We are grateful to Stephen Higgins for showing us this simple way of achieving our object – namely to make the treble hook and its attachment to the body of the Toby semi-rigid and 'in-line'
(d) An extremely well designed new bait, the Slyda, has its treble hook rigidly held in position by a slotted plastic bead, so that when a fish is hooked, the spoon is free to slide up the leader in much the same way as that proven good hooker, the Devon minnow

(a)

(b)

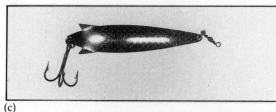

(c)

(d)

Anglers who will take the trouble to add a box swivel to the gorge hook, in the following manner, will find it assist much in spinning the bait and enticing the Jack or Pike to take it.

From this it is clear that he was adding spin to the action of sink-and-draw. He continues with:

After trying closely, make your next throw further in the water, and draw and sink the baited hook, by pulling and casting the line with your left hand, while raising and lowering the rod with your right, drawing it straight upwards, near the surface of the water, and also to the right and left, searching carefully every foot of water, and draw your bait against and across the stream *which causes it to twirl or spin*; [our italics], and then by its glistening in the water it is sure to attract and excite either Jack or Pike to seize it.

Salter had re-discovered an exciting new method – described nearly 200 years before!

ARTIFICIAL BAITS

Artificial baits have a long history. Apart from flies dressed to imitate natural insects, one of the earliest uses of an artificial bait in Britain is described in *The Compleat Angler*:

I have – which I will show you – an artificial minnow, that will catch a trout as well as an artificial fly and it was made by a handsome woman that had a fine hand and a live minnow lying by her, the body of cloth, the back of it of very sad French green silk and a paler green silk towards the belly, shadowed as perfectly as you can imagine, just as you see a minnow; the belly was wrought also with a needle, and it was a part of it white-silk, and another part of it of silver thread; the tail and fins were made of a quill, which was shaven thin; the eyes were of two little black beads, and the head was so shadowed, and all of it so curiously wrought, and so exactly dissembled, that it would beguile any sharp-sighted trout in a swift stream.

Walton neglected to give angling instructions, so it is not known if he ever used this bait himself. He assured his pupil, however, that an artificial minnow would be 'of excellent use: for note, that a large trout will come as fiercely at a minnow as the highest mettled hawk doth seize on a partridge, or a greyhound on a hare'.

Figure 487: A pike hooked on a plug leaps clear of the water (*Roy Shaw*)

Figure 488: (*above*) A Swedish lake, Lake Mälaren, known for its big perch and magnificent pike

Figure 489: (*left*) Much as the authors regret a photograph of a pike being held by the eyes (even a dead pike), this pike is a piece of history since, if authenticated, it is certainly the biggest pike landed on rod and line in modern times: *Weight* 58 lb 9¼ oz (*Olaf Wasland*)

PIKE ON SPINNING BAIT

In August 1986 Colin Dyson, the editor of *Coarse Angler*, gave F. B. details of a new Swedish Rod-Caught Record pike of 58 lb 9¼ oz. Later, contact was made with Mark Caldwell, an expatriate Englishman living in Sweden. In essence Fehmi Varli, a Swedish grocer of Turkish descent, caught the pike in 10 ft of water on a June afternoon (17 June 1986) at 3 p.m. while spinning from a boat at Ulvsundet* with his companion Anton.

In Caldwell's words: 'after Fehmi had hooked, played and finally, after fifty minutes, got the pike alongside, he gaffed it and managed to pull it halfway into the boat – at which point his companion whacked the fish on the head with a chair leg. Not surprisingly the pike leapt back into the water, breaking the line as it did so, which made Fehmi very angry with Anton.'

Notwithstanding the re-entry of the pike into the water, the two anglers decided to wait around in case the gaff wound, plus the blow on the pike's head with the chair leg, would take effect. Two hours later their patience was rewarded when the pike floated to the surface belly up. After the captor's and the witness's accounts were fully investigated by Lars Söderberg (Chairman of the Swedish Record Fish Committee) the pike was declared to be the new Swedish record.

* Ulvsundet, Jarnafjärden (Södertalje)

It seems likely that Walton was recounting somebody else's experience, but like all angling optimists, having heard about a super bait, had quickly obtained one for himself.

The use of a *hard* substance for making an artificial bait (in this case for pike) is given in Nobbes' *The Compleat Troller* (1682). 'Anything that may affect the eye, may be used at snap; some pike will take a piece of hard cheese, or pack-wax, a rasher of bacon, or sheep gut, or almost anything that is radiant and shining.'

Even though eighteenth century writers continued to describe artificial baits and spinners, the natural bait was still preferred in 1814 as evidenced by T. F. Salter's *The Angler's Guide*:

The shops keep artificial baits for trolling, both of fish and frogs, made of wood, pearl, and also of leather stuffed and painted, and which in form and colour, much resemble nature, but I should never think of using them while there was a possibility of getting a natural one; when they are used, it is with the snap, which I think shows judgement, for surely the most sanguine angler could hardly expect a pike to pouch either wood, pearl or leather even with the addition of stuffing.

Artificial *spinning* baits were not popular until much later; in fact, not until the principles of spinning with a natural bait had been established by four writers:

Captain T. Williamson, *The Complete Angler's Vade-Mecum* 1808

Robert Salter, *Modern Angler* (second edition) 1811

T. F. Salter, *The Angler's Guide* (eighth edition) 1833

Colonel P. Hawker, *Instructions to Young Sportsmen* (6th edition) 1844.

A plain spoon, it seems, was the first really successful all-metal bait and by the mid-nineteenth century was in common use on both sides of the Atlantic.

The origin of the spoon bait was investigated by H. Cholmondeley-Pennell in *The Book of the Pike* (1865). Seemingly the notion of catching pike on a metal spoon derived from an incident which took place in Devon (*c.* 1830) involving one of the Duke of Exeter's servants.

Pennell describes an incident in the mid-nineteenth century concerning one of the Duke of Exeter's servants. While emptying a pail of slops into the River Exe, this servant saw a pike dart out from under the bank and take a spoon that had been inadvertently left in the pail. Being a fisherman, he had a local tinsmith fashion a spoon bait with appropriate hooks.

Subsequently, a sample was given to Pennell –

the prototype for baits that were soon to be used by anglers throughout the world.

For an earlier mention of what might have been a spoon-bait see *The Angler's England* by Patrick Chalmers:

There was a nobleman in Denmark called Lodbroc, and his two young sons were Henguar and Hubba. Lodbroc was fond of fishing and of falconry. Indeed he was fond of all field sports. One day he took his boat and his fishing rods ... and he pulled out along the coast to make a mixed bag among the islands. But a storm came on and swept Lodbroc and his boat out to sea ... In due course Lodbroc was cast ashore on the Norfolk coast at the village of Redham to be exact.

King Edmund* [King of East Anglia] who happened to be passing Redham and who was fond of fishing and falconry as was Lodbroc, became Lodbroc's friend. Now one day the king's game warden, by name Berne, was advising his master as to the capture of a 30 lb pike which lay off a little holm (or eyot) of Hyckelyngge Broad. Berne's baits were not good baits, and it was only when Lodbroc produced a lure, one of his foreign contrivances (*'a trowling lure of bryte shel'*) that the pike came to hand. The King was delighted, but Berne hated Lodbroc for his knowledge of baits. [Our italics].

We do not know the origin of this passage, but 'a trowling lure of bryte shel' has the ring of truth: it indicates that the modern Scandinavian 'pirk' may be no new invention. Lodbroc's 'trowling lure' could have been an original Norse pirk, used with a 'trolling' (or sink-and-draw) action for cod and other fish.

THE McELRATH DEADBAIT (SPRAT) SPINNING MOUNT

Albert McElrath's mount is a superior piece of tackle. Uniquely, so far as a deadbait mount is concerned, it is not attached directly to the hooks, so that a salmon or any other fish for that matter, cannot use the mount and bait as a lever. Indeed, like the shell of a Devon Minnow, it can be blown right up the trace or leader (the Devon Minnow is known to be the best hooker of all artificial baits for this reason).

* The King Edmund of Patrick Chalmer's piece was murdered by a party of marauding Danes in the year 870. He was later canonized. The city of Bury St Edmunds commemorates his name and burial place.

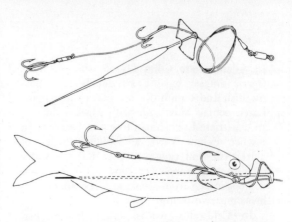

Figure 490: The McElrath (or Tweed) mount shows the leaded body of the mount and displays the feature which is at the heart of the mount's superior hooking efficiency, namely the double-coiled ring at the nose of the mount through which the wire leader (to one end of which is attached a team of treble hooks) passes to join up with the mainline

Since we have been unable to trace the inventor of this fine mount, henceforth we shall know it by the name of its most ardent advocate – Mr McElrath.

BAITS

When Captain Cook visited the Sandwich Islands (Hawaii) between 1772 and 1778 he made a note of 'the natives using a spoon-type lure, fashioned from shell'.

The New Fisherman's Encyclopaedia (1964)

The yellow belly

This bait was introduced by Herbert Hatton. It is a very good lure for early spring salmon fishing. Being made of wood it is much lighter than the traditional metal Devon, and can be fished slowly close to the bottom. In the original version the spinning fins were made from one piece of metal passed right through the bait, thus ensuring durability – a feature absent, alas, from most modern imitations.

The quill minnow

The direct descendant of Walton's artificial minnow. It is a wonderful brown-trout lure and, due to its lightness, better than the metal Devon when shallow waters are fished.

H. F. writes: 'I prefer to make these baits without the two flying trebles.'

The phantom bait

This killing bait is unfortunately out of production due to high cost – a much lamented loss. The larger phantoms were made of moleskin and accounted for many large pike, including Major W. H. Booth's 37 lb sometime record pike. Medium and small phantoms were made with silk bodies. Both materials produced 'soft body' baits that fish were likely to hold on to, thus enhancing the chances of a good hookhold.

The Devon minnow

Since the Devon's introduction during the last half of the eighteenth century, the total production of various types must have exceeded any other bait. In spite of changing fashions it is still one of the most popular spinners. Devons are made in sizes varying from $\frac{1}{2}$ in. to 4 in., and in almost every colour or combination of colours. Salmon fishermen usually prefer a blue-and-silver Devon during the early part of the season when the water temperature is low, and a brown-and-gold when the temperature begins to rise. In spring, some years ago (not far from the scene of that historic spoon-dropping incident), F. B.

fished the River Exe. Although during the previous days a number of salmon had been killed on blue-and-silver Devons, Buller and his two companions caught ten fish with brown-and-gold Devons – after trying the blue-and-silver without success.

The wagtail bait

Next to the Devon minnow, the wagtail bait has probably accounted for more predatory fish in British freshwater than any other bait. William Lunn, famous keeper of the Houghton club water, considered it the only artificial spinning bait of any use in removing pike from his beloved River Test. According to the manufacturers, its production is no longer economic. In truth, anglers will not pay the price for it, which is a pity. In an era that started during the last century and ended in the 1930s, the wagtail was the favourite bait of a long line of pike anglers – including such famous sportsmen as Payne-Gallwey, Lord Walsingham, Cholmondeley-Pennell, and the Rothschilds – who fished the great limestone loughs of Ireland: Conn, Mask, Derg and Corrib. These loughs were unique: they held huge trout as well as some of the biggest pike in Europe. As natural mixed fisheries they were unsurpassed. Today, only memories of their great pike remain. All of them, with the exception of Derg, have been extensively netted. For anglers (including both authors of this book) who loved those vast elemental lakes this is a matter of the utmost regret; the fascination and excitement of fishing them has almost vanished.

Note: Every wobbling bait shown whose tail treble is linked with a split-ring is defective.

The leather eel-tail

The kidney spoon

A development of that famous Irish pike and salmon bait, the natural eel-tail. Generations of Irishmen and visiting anglers have described its deadly qualities. It has a weighted head, the body consisting of two leather strips joined together for two-thirds of their length and free for one-third. It is usually made in 3 in., 4 in. and 5 in. sizes.

The slotted Devon and the kill devil Devon

Now extinct, these baits incorporate a design feature of doubtful merit. They were festooned with three or four treble hooks, presumably in the hope of improving their fish-hooking qualities. In fact, a single treble at the tail secures a more reliable hold. Not the largest, but certainly the most celebrated fish to fall for a slotted Devon was caught by the Rev. Tom Secombe Gray: a pike of 30 lb. (Gray wrote a very fine account of this incident.)

The River Runt spook
It floats at rest, dives a foot or two on retrieve. No imitations have ever surpassed the fish-catching potential of the original River Runt. F. B. writes: 'I am sure the River Runt's phenomenal success is due to the fact that the plastic content of the plug is standardized. With plastic material, once a killing pattern is established after testing in the field, it can be the model for any number of *true* copies.' H. F. writes: 'I have caught a lot of salmon on a River Runt.'

The original kidney spoon had a half-scaled copper finish outside and a silver finish inside. It was sometimes furnished with a single treble hook (as shown) and sometimes with a second treble attached by a split ring to the front swivel. The $2\frac{1}{2}$ in. or 2 in. kidney was considered to be one of the best baits for the big salmon of Norway. Latterly, it became more popular when made up as a bar-spoon (like the Canadian-bar). The kidney-bar-spoon has a red tassel and a different metal finish. Unlike the original kidney, it has a chrome finish outside and a red-painted finish inside. The action of this spoon is particularly attractive to pike.

The Toby spoon

This bait has become very popular. F. B. recalls a visit to the clubroom of the Vale of Leven Angling Society. From the large number of rods fitted up with Toby spoons it seemed that all Loch Lomond salmon and sea trout anglers – at least, all those who were spinning or trailing – were using this bait. This was in contrast to an earlier visit when the natural minnow was first choice.

H. F. writes: 'In my experience of spinning for salmon, sea trout and bass, the Toby spoon is a wonderful attractor but, like all similarly-mounted spoons, a poor hooker.' (See page 465.)

The Mepps spoon

During recent years the fame of the Mepps spinner has spread with the rapidity of a bush fire. It is modelled on a fly-spoon or bar-spoon action, and its popularity is well deserved. The basic improvement on earlier baits is the provision of a low friction bearing attachment to the blade of the spinner. This allows the blade to flutter even when fished at very low speeds.

The fly spoon

The fly spoon owes its popularity to a number of features:
(a) It is cheap.
(b) It catches fish.
(c) It continues to flutter attractively when retrieved at slow speeds.
(d) It can be fished conveniently on a fly-rod.

The Rapala

This Finnish plug bait was the cause of a mild sensation when it was introduced into the USA. Such was the demand for it that the Finnish manufacturers were unable to keep pace and American tackle dealers hired out baits on a daily basis. There was no such reaction to the Rapala in Britain, partly because its introduction came much later – when cheap copies of the bait could be purchased. These cheaper copies were inferior

fish-catchers and blunted the general enthusiasm. The genuine Rapala is excellent for both pike and salmon.

An interesting statistic has emerged from the annual big fish contests held by two American angling magazines with a vast circulation, namely *Field & Stream* and *Sports Afield*.

By far the most successful lures in these contests (where every item of tackle used by the successful participants is documented) over a thirteen-year period, have been Mepps with 399 wins and Rapalas with 154 wins.

Figure 491: F.B. caught this 22½lb River Tay salmon on a Toby spoon – and lost a few more which he probably wouldn't have, had he realized that a treble hanging from the back of a bait via a split-ring is a fish loser (see page 465)

The mackerel spoon

This cheap, mass-produced bait is equally attractive to salt and freshwater fish. It will kill charr for the visiting Lake District angler better than any other bait (in the absence of the local hand-made charr-baits). There is probably no predatory species of up to 20 lb or so in weight that has not at some time or other been taken on a mackerel spinner.

The Jim Vincent spoon

This famous pike spoon was named after the master pike angler Jim Vincent, who had copied an Indian-made spoon he brought back from Canada. Nowadays* made of chromed copper, it was originally made of hard-wood. The modern Canadian equivalent of the Vincent Spoon – also based on the Indian original – is called a William's Wabler. Being a quick sinker, the Vincent is effective in deep water, whereas the Wabler (which is made of light alloy) is a useful shallow-water bait.

The Norwich spoon

This spoon is an old favourite of Norfolk pike fishermen. As its name implies, it is closely associated with the Broads. It is finished in half-scaled gilt and half-polished nickel on the outside, and half nickel and half red on the inside. It is also furnished with a red glass-eye.

* Sadly, the Jim Vincent spoon is now out of production.

The Colorado spoon

First described in Cholmondeley-Pennell's *Pike and Coarse Fish* (1885), this spoon is a development of an old bait (recommended for perch spinning) known as the Comet bait. It is a popular pike spoon since:
(a) It flashes: the outside is chrome finished.
(b) It has a liberal dash of red about it: the inside is painted red and there is also a red wool tassel.
(c) Its leaded bar provides ample casting weight without the need for extra lead.
(d) It spins well.

The Canadian bar-spoon

The favourite spoon of a generation of successful Dorset Stour pike anglers.

The plain spoon

An excellent lightweight salmon spoon. Like others of its kind it would land more fish if the treble hook was prevented from waggling about.

The wooden Devon minnow

Probably the most popular of all British salmon baits, the wooden Devon is a reliable hooker. It has almost entirely replaced the scarab-mounted natural golden sprat.

HOUSING BAITS, PLUGS AND SPINNERS

There has always been a carrying and storage problem with artificial baits and mounts. If these are kept in tins or boxes, hooks become entangled and there is the ever-present problem of rusting when a wet bait is returned to the box. The American spinner and plug box, with its series of hinged trays honeycombed with individual compartments, solves the first problem, but does nothing to reduce the second – rust!

Nowadays, anglers can buy little hook-hoods in various sizes, to prevent trebles from becoming entangled, and our photograph shows F. B.'s improved, ventilated, spinner box that exposes one tray of baits at a time. The vertical packing of the spinners ensures perfect drainage and ventilation, thus eliminating the problem of rust.

A Devon-type bait presents a special problem since the hook mount is separate from the shell. We show the method we use to keep the component parts married: a simple paper-clip. But how effective!

Figure 494: The F. B. bait-box

Figure 492: The hook-hood

Figure 493: When not in use – use paper-clips to keep Devon flights and shells together

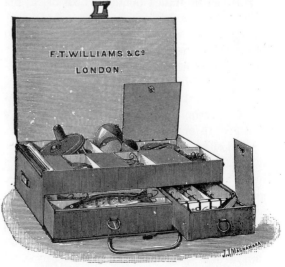

Figure 495: (*below*) A nineteenth-century spinner and tackle box

PLUG
FISHING

Although most species of freshwater fish are carnivorous sometime in their lives, those caught on plugs are almost exclusively pike, perch, zander, salmon and trout. Plugs come in all shapes and sizes – both single-bodied and jointed – and can be presented at varying depth and speed with considerable freedom of method.

In both still and running water a plug can be fished in any direction – from the bank or an anchored boat, from a drifting or slow moving boat. It can be trailed behind a boat or, in big rivers, used as a bait for 'harling' – when it is activated more by the pull of the current than the motion of the boat.

Plug fishing has several advantages over spinning. Perhaps the plug's most important advantage is that it can be fished successfully throughout the season, whereas, in summer, heavy weed growth often makes spinning impossible.

Areas of weedy water are usually highly productive. Sometimes these can be covered with a plug fished an inch or two below the surface (see figure 497).

Due to its buoyancy, a plug can be fished successfully in fast water over a lie that is upstream of the angler. All too often, a Devon minnow or a spoon (other than a Mepps type)

fished upstream in similar conditions has to be retrieved very fast – often too fast to attract a fish – otherwise owing to the speed of the current it drags on the bottom.

A floating plug can be used to cover a difficult lie underneath overhanging tree branches (figure 496). The angler stands at A, eight or ten yards upstream of the tree. The plug is cast to B, well beyond the branches, and allowed to drift down with the current – the rod being held well out over the water. When the plug has drifted to C, the rod-tip is dipped under the surface and the reel given a few quick turns to make the plug 'bite'. Once it is at the required depth the plug is retrieved with the rod-tip still held below the water level. The drag of the line will swing the plug in towards the bank and underneath the tree.

Patches of open water in a weedy swim may also be investigated with a floating plug (figure 497). The plug is cast from A to B just short of the far weed bed. It is made to dive sharply by means of a few quick turns of the reel, then retrieved at normal speed through the open water. When it reaches C it is allowed to surface. A fierce pluck retrieves it through the air in the manner of a retrieved fly.

If a fish is hooked, say at D, it is quickly 'walked' to more open water at E, and landed at F. (For notes on 'walking' a fish see page 214.)

The action of any plug design can be varied by: 1. Changing the direction of the cast relative to the stream.

2. Working the rod-tip during the retrieve.

3. Varying the speed of recovery.

Although American anglers favour a short rod and multiplier reel for plug fishing, we prefer a rod of not less than 9 ft. Within limits, the longer the rod the better an angler can control his lure.

The use of leads should be avoided whenever possible.

AN AFTERNOON WITH FLOATING PLUG

There is no consensus among pike anglers about which method is the most exciting; but, if it were more widely practised, plug fishing could well get the vote – especially the *floating* plug in conditions of shallow, weedy water. A splendid afternoon's sport enjoyed by F. B. in the west of Ireland illustrates how successful this technique can be in very difficult circumstances. He writes as follows:

Although I fish in Ireland every September for brown trout and sea trout and make no attempt to pike-fish until November, September 1985 was different. Due to the wet summer, Irish water levels were higher than I had ever known them. It occurred to me that a certain small weedy lough, which normally produces good fishing only after autumn floods have brought pike up from the river and frost has cleared the water for a spinning bait, might offer the chance of sport much earlier.

Forcing one's way by boat into this reed-covered, bog-fringed lough is difficult enough at any time of year. On the cloudy September afternoon in question, pushing our way through the two-hundred-yard jungle of lilies and reed beds that choked the access

Figure 496: Using a floating plug for a difficult lie

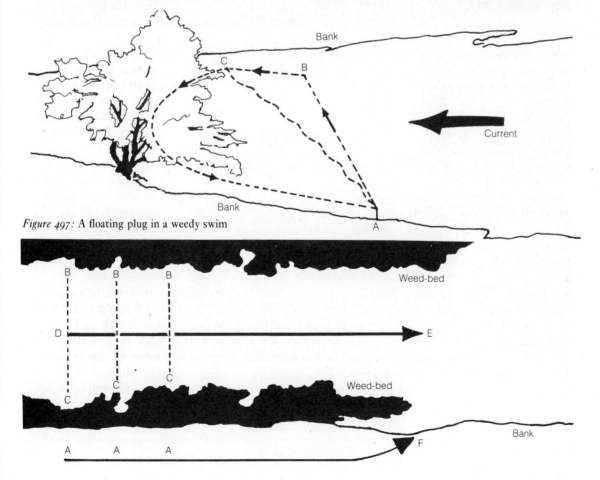

Figure 497: A floating plug in a weedy swim

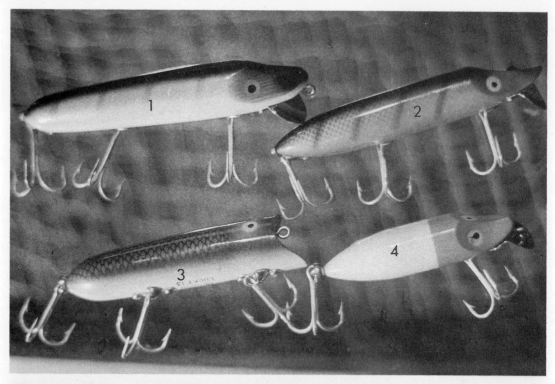

Figure 498: A selection of plugs (key opposite)

stream used up much adrenalin, and it was not until after two hours of perspiring effort that we found our way into patches of open water and began fishing the remembered pike-lies with large and medium spoons.

Hopes were high at first because most of the surface was clear of weed; but these soon faded as again and again swivel and bait were retrieved festooned with fronded pondweed. It was clear that fishing more than a few inches below the surface was impossible; that if pike *had* already come up from the river, our only chance lay in fishing a floating plug.

And so it proved. On my fifth or sixth cast, as the plug dipped below the surface in answer to my pull on the line, a big pike took the Heddon Vamp plug with a force that dragged the rod-tip down into the water.... That sudden eruptive take after a comparatively long period of inactivity with the spoons was quite unnerving!

Now we knew that pike were definitely in residence, we rowed the boat quietly through a succession of weed-free patches, following an old water course. During the next two hours as the sun sank behind the distant hills, six more pike, several of them heavy-

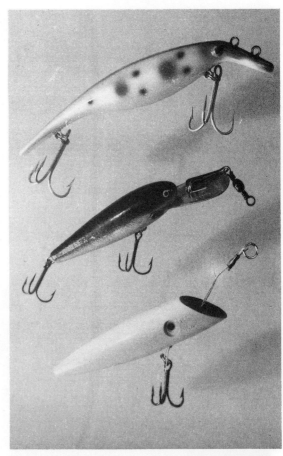

Figure 499: Swim wizz (*top*)   An excellent musky or pike plug. Two attaching eyes; top fixing makes the lure swim shallow. The inventor has caught over 5,000 muskies on this bait. A strawberry finish is the most killing if perch are present as forage bait. This information comes from my Canadian correspondent, John Tollady

Rapala (*middle*)   A deep diver. I have taken many pike on this plug in Irish waters

Kynoch killer (*bottom*)   Without doubt the deadliest bait of all for salmon on Scotland's River Tay. In June 1977 I was trailing this bait over the charr beds on Ireland's Lough Mask in the hope of connecting with a trout like the 13½ pounder my companion, Des Elliott of Dublin, had recently caught. Almost immediately I caught a small pike and on the next run connected with a fish that 'played' for almost twenty minutes on powerful salmon tackle before it was lost. Des Elliott, Robbie O'Grady (Lough Mask's finest fisherman) and I still argue about 'the fish that was never seen'. Was it, as O'Grady thinks, a huge trout, or was it, as I believe, a big Mask pike?

1. The original Heddon Vamp. The first floating/diving lure ever made – a pattern for hundreds of imitative baits. In an age of plastic, this is one of the few baits still made with wood. A great pike plug

2. Heddon Vamp Spook. One of the best plugs for pike and muskellunge. It floats at rest, dives about two feet below the surface on retrieve

3. The Heddon Lucky 13. An old favourite with pike fishermen. A good surface or shallow-diving plug for summer pike fishing

4. The most famous of all plug baits: the River Runt Spook. It floats at rest, dives a foot or two on retrieve. A great favourite with the Hampshire Avon salmon fishermen in the yellow shore colour. No imitations have ever surpassed the fish-catching qualities of the original River Runt. That this should be so is almost certainly due to the fact that the plastic material of its construction is standardized. With plastic, a killing pattern can be the model for any number of true copies

5. Heddon Commando. Patent plastic jointed plug having a rear section designed to spin. Once a fish is hooked, the bait slides up the line, making it impossible for the fish to lever itself free against the bait

6. Heddon Crazy Crawler. This has what can only be described as a 'violent' action. Nevertheless, this very action has given the bait a reputation for attracting big pike. It is essentially a surface lure, which makes it most effective for summer fishing in weedy waters

7. Heddon Deep Dive River Runt Spook (slow sinker). Note the outsize diving lip. It is the size of the lip, not the steepness of angle, that achieves a deep dive

weights, took the Vamp – while my companion, who had never before fished for pike, landed a splendid eleven-pounder, one of three that struck viciously at his rapala plug. These successes prompted me to predict that our next fish could well be over twenty pounds, since twelve years' experience on the lough had taught me that one in eight of the pike it produced was above this magic weight!

For a time the water seemed to have gone dead and although we fished hopefully on, the fading light began to warn us that fishing was nearly at an end. Then, as I retrieved my plug for the last time, a pike took it with the neatness of a brown trout sipping in a mayfly.

Unlike its predecessors, this pike was in no hurry to show itself and resisted all efforts to be brought close to the boat. For ten minutes or so, as the dusk closed around us, all that could be seen was the line cutting through the water, while adjacent water lilies shook or lifted themselves briefly into the air. It was a full twenty minutes before my companion slipped the net under him and lifted him aboard – a perfectly shaped twenty-four-and-a-half-pounder, forty-four inches in length.

This was just nine pounds lighter and two and a half inches shorter than the biggest pike ever landed on plug in British and Irish waters.* But although I

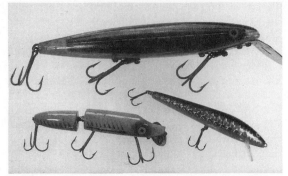

Figure 500: Top The Cisco Kid (9 in. long)
Bottom left The original Heddon Vamp, in all probability the finest pike plug ever made, i.e. the jointed model made in wood
Bottom right The Abu Killer, one of Europe's best pike baits

had a feeling of certainty that the remote lough we were fishing held bigger pike than that, we were faced with a long and arduous battle with those reed beds in the darkness and, regretfully, headed homewards.

* A bigger pike was recently caught by Peter Stone of Oxford.

Just before he died Richard Walker gave this drawing to F.B. The legend on the back reads 'From Reg Cooke to Dick Walker and from Dick Walker to Fred Buller'

TROLLING
and TRAILING

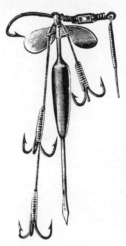

TROLLING

Since many anglers confuse 'trolling' with 'trailing' it would seem sensible to start by defining these two contrasting methods. Here is John Bickerdyke, in *The Book of the All Round Angler* (1888):

Dead-baits ... are either arranged so that they spin when drawn through the water, or are placed on trolling-tackle, in which case they do not spin. Spinning baits are either cast out some distance, and drawn back through the water to the angler, or are trailed at the back of a boat. This trailing is often called trolling in Scotland and Ireland, a misnomer which has doubtless caused some little confusion in the minds of anglers. Trolling proper is the use of a dead-bait which does not spin, and is worked with a *sink-and-draw* motion in the water. [Our italics.]

We have included this for the benefit of any reader who hitherto was unaware of the distinction and who may have been puzzled by references to trolling in angling literature of over a century ago. Authors of the past writing of 'the troll' meant sink-and-draw tackle such as the Gorge Deadbait Tackle or the Drop-Tackle (see

---

Trolling is the noblest branch of Angling, and is performed as follows: the Angler must have a very long and strong rod, with rings, as for Barble, and a winch or reel, properly fastened to the butt-end; a trolling line at least thirty or forty yards long, with a swivel at the end which receives the loop of the wire that the hook is fastened to; whether a double or single hook, it must be leaded. Thus equipped, begin to troll; let the bait fall in bold at first, close to the shore if deep. With your right hand hold the rod tight, keeping the top always in motion, by raising and lowering; in your left, hold your line, which keep continually pulling and letting go; this gives the bait a motion as if alive in the water. One gill-fin cut off, improves the motion of the bait. If a pike be near, he darts at the bait, and seizes it with incredible voracity, and runs off to his hole.

Anon. *The Angler's Pocket-Book* (third edition, 1805)

Figure 501: Trolling for Pike in the River Lea, '1831'. After the oil painting by James Pollard. By courtesy of the Executors of the late Arthur N. Gilbey's collection

figure 502). In the woodcut based on James Pollard's oil painting, it is clear how the angler is fishing his weighted 'Gorge' up and down by stripping-in and releasing line. Trolling (or sink-and-draw) was very well described by Alfred Jardine in his book *Pike and Perch* (1898):

When trolling it is best to fish upstream, and to work the bait down with the current through the weeds. If the contrary way is attempted it will result in many a hangup in the weeds; besides, there is this advantage in fishing up and bringing the bait down with the stream: it approaches the pike more naturally, and is better seen by them, as (except in gentle currents) they always lie, whether in ambush or not, with their heads up stream, on the lookout for small fish swimming past. It is not necessary to make long casts; in fact, it is better not to do so, for the bait being lifted and dropped almost perpendicularly in the openings between the weeds, trolls, or gyrates in a much more tempting way than when drawn slantwise through the water; and as the pike are usually among the weeds or in deep weedy holes, from whence they cannot readily see the angler, it is better to carefully fish all the nearest water than to make long shots with the bait. Raise the bait to the surface every two or three seconds and let it sink head foremost, giving a foot or so of slack line, and then it will have a darting rolling movement as it drops to the bottom.

Keep continuing this, and if a check is felt, slacken the line by paying off a few yards from the reel (if none is already unwound), and see that all is clear for a run, in case a fish has taken the bait, which will soon be known by the fish moving off, or by a few fierce little drags at the line; then allow the few minutes that are usually given the fish to pouch, wind up the slack line, give a firm draw with the rod, and play the fish on and off the reel, in preference to dropping the line in coils on the ground.

Figure 502: The Gorge, the snap-trolling and the drop-tackle

The Gorge Deadbait Tackle is the first tackle ever to be described in the English language. *A Treatyse of Fysshynge wyth an Angle* (1496) describes how the tackle is fitted to a deadbait (roach or fresh herring) for the purpose of taking a pike. This tackle survived practically unchanged until the early twentieth century and was mainly used for pike trolling (sink-and-draw)

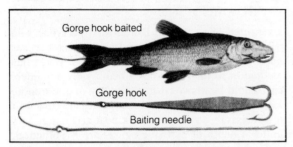

Gorge hook baited

Gorge hook

Baiting needle

John Bickerdyke's snap-trolling tackle invented in the 1880s was one of the most successful ever made. The leaded baiting-needle (B) was thrust down the deadbait's throat and gullet until the eyed pointed end emerged at the tail of the bait. The looped end (A) of the tackle was then pushed through the eye of the baiting needle before one hook from each of the trebles was pulled into the side of the bait. Bickerdyke reckoned that R. B. Marston's trolling snap-tackle (see below) was even better than his

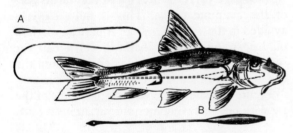

A

B

Hardy's Pike Drop-Tackle. This is a simplified version of R. B. Marston's Deadbait Flight, and was produced until quite recently. The spiked lead is pushed down the bait's throat and the single hook pulled right through the narrow fleshy part of the deadbait's tail. A twist of copper wire secures the bait

Trolling is a very old method. 'A trowling lure of bryte shel' is mentioned prior to the Norman conquest. William Gilbert in *The Angler's Delight* (1676) disdained to give much space to it (or perhaps he found a description of sink-and-draw beyond his powers):

'Many use to Troule for a Pike; but that is so easie, that I shall not spend time in giving Directions: For it will be far easier learnt; by once going with any Person that understands it, in one days time, than is possible to be taught by Printed Directions.'

At some moment in history an angler rowing across a lake allowed his bait to trail through the water astern of the boat. Doubtless encouraged by his success with this method, other anglers followed suit. And so started a new method of angling. Exactly when this happened is not recorded, but in Britain it is unlikely to have been prior to the seventeenth century. Robert Nobbes, in his book *The Complete Troller* (1682), mentions it as being something very unusual:

In some places they Troll without any Pole or any playing of the Bait, as I have seen them throw a Line out of a Boat, and so let it draw after them as they Row forward; but that must be a careless and unsafe way, for so they may have Bites and Offers so, yet it must certainly check the Fish so much that he will never Pouch it; I cannot tell what Art they may have at the Snap, though it is very improbable to have any as they go to work, without either Pole or Stick.

This, so far as we know, is the earliest description of *trailing* – a method to be considered next.

TRAILING

The four essential requirements needed for successful trailing are as follows:

1. The right location.
2. The right depth.
3. The right bait.
4. The right fishing speed for that bait.

As an angling method, trailing is often considered boring and lacking in finesse. But the fisherman who consistently takes good fish from the depths of what appears to be a featureless expanse of water is not, as many people seem to think, haphazardly dragging a bait about. On the contrary, he is being as calculating as the angler who fishes streamy water. His fish are caught by *design*, not accident. A skilful and imaginative angler who uses an echo sounder and tackle which fishes at a specified depth, gradually builds up a complex and fascinating picture of the loch bottom and the best 'taking' depths. As a result he will, in the long term, catch far bigger fish than the less imaginative angler who moves aimlessly about, never certain of the depth of water or the depth at which his lure is fishing.

In the early 1950s, when F. B. first made the acquaintance of that famous Loch Lomond angler the late Harry Britton of Balloch, he was puzzled by the local method of trailing for sea trout and salmon. This method, although popular on the loch, was restricted to fishing from a power-driven boat travelling at a uniform speed, a tactic which automatically causes the bait to fish at a uniform depth. The only important variables, it seemed, were in the type and size of bait (a freshly-killed natural minnow was preferred); the choice of locality; and, of course, the wind and weather conditions.

This choice of fishing depth – or, rather, this self-imposed *restriction* of depth, seemed to F. B. to be unnecessarily inhibiting and in conflict with his own trailing practice. From his experience of charr-trailing on Windermere, where six baits per line are fished at depths ranging from 6 ft to 50 ft (see page 54), he had learned the importance of varying the depth at which a bait is trailed. He had noted that brown trout and charr which had deserted the upper levels would sometimes take a bait avidly in deep water. In addition, his experience of trailing different baits for different species on many other waters had made him aware of the need to trail baits at varying speeds in order to find the best 'taking' speed for the day in question. (This speed varies from day to day.)

F. B. writes as follows:

I ventured to suggest to Britton that everyone who fished in the customary Loch Lomond manner was not making the most of his opportunities. When this method of fishing produced a blank, only one inference could be drawn: that on the day in question no sea trout was interested in taking that particular bait trailed (say) 35 yards behind a boat at 2 m.p.h. at a uniform depth of $2\frac{1}{2}$ ft (the figures are hypothetical, and used merely to illustrate the point). Britton was so impressed with my argument in favour of fishing at different depths and at different speeds that he lost no time in trying out a modified experimental charr-trailing rig himself. It met with immediate success. Alas, since this occurred only a short time before his final illness, he was unable to develop it further.

A disadvantage of the traditional charr-trailing rig (see page 54) is the heavy lead that forms part of the mainline tackle. This is most cleverly avoided in the *downrigger* – an American method of deep-water trailing that will get a bait (or baits) down to a considerable depth without the use of lead on the mainline.

Figure 503 shows the working principle of the rig with one or two homespun variations.

THE DOWNRIGGER

To prepare the downrigger, a Nottingham reel of large diameter (A), holding about 50 yards of

---

There is what may by courtesy be termed spinning, the practice of trailing (it is often erroneously called 'trolling') for big lake trout in Ireland and Scotland. The angler simply sits in the stern of a boat and lets his spinning bait trail thirty yards or more behind while somebody else rows. The tackle and rod must be strong, as a big pike or a salmon is sometimes a possibility. No overwhelming display of skill is demanded of the angler, but the oarsman must know something about the geography of the lake and the nature of the bottom. Trailing may, however, be made something of an art if the angler does his own rowing, and is alone; in fact, *there are few kinds of fishing which demand more promptitude and resource.*

H. T. Sheringham, *Elements of Angling* (1908)

60 lb BS terylene line, is secured with the usual winch fittings to the back of the rod-rest. The last 12 yards are marked at intervals of 3 ft with tags of wool (B). (2-inch tags of wool are passed through the braid of the terylene with the help of a coarse needle and then tied with a double knot, leaving an overhang of wool on each side. A colour code of wools is used so that an angler can tell precisely how much line is out at any time.)

The line is fed through the rod-rest and a 1 lb or $1\frac{1}{2}$ lb lead (C) is tied to the end.

A swivel (D) is tied into the line 3 ft above the lead.

When the downrigger is ready, sufficient line is pulled off to allow the lead to rest on the back seat of the boat.

The rod, reel and line are now assembled and the appropriate bait (E) attached.

The difference between this tackle and tackle normally used for trailing or bait casting, is that the former carries no lead and includes a three-way swivel (F) in lieu of the usual two-way swivel.

Finally, a line (G) of cotton, elastic or lead wire joins the third eye of the three-way swivel to the swivel of the downrigger.

The tackle is now ready for use and the rod is placed in the rest *with the reel-check on*.

Figure 503: The Downrigger

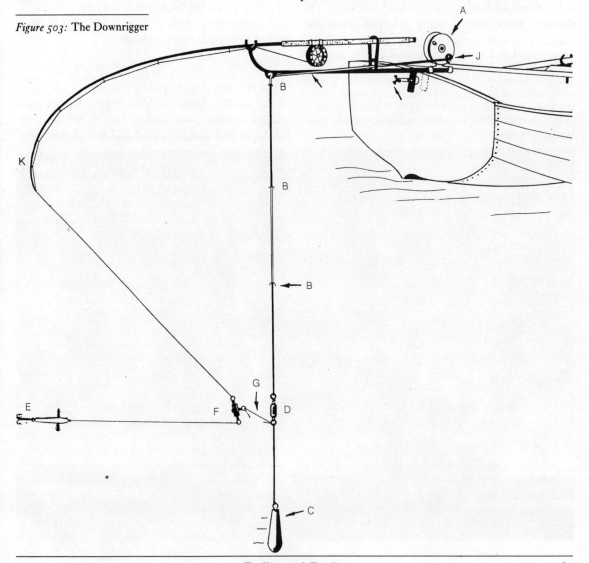

If two anglers are fishing together, one watches the rod, or rods, while the other rows the boat. The angler who fishes by himself will find it convenient to use a specially designed trailing electric-outboard-motor, otherwise he will need to clamp the downrigger rod-rest on to the gunwale within reach of the oars. (F. B. prefers the use of oars at all times owing to the greater variation of speed which rowing affords, but most anglers prefer to trail with the aid of a motor.)

As soon as the boat is in motion the lead-line is slowly released from the downrigger reel (A). Each coloured wool tag that passes the end of the rod-rest indicates that the lead is fishing 3 ft deeper. While line is being released from the

Figure 504: The downrigger layout used by F. B. in Canada. With hindsight he realizes that there are better 'quick strike' rod-holders than the one illustrated e.g. the tube-holder (see figure 510 the Cannon Downrigger) and the Scotty Rod-Holder (see figure 515). The fishing line in this photograph has been thickened to demonstrate the layout more clearly

downrigger reel the corresponding amount of line is being pulled off the rod reel – which is under the tension of its check.

When the required depth has been reached, the lead line is looped round the handle of the downrigger reel (J).

The angler now knows the exact depth at which his bait is fishing. An echo-sounder enables him to make any necessary adjustment to the depth of the downrigger lead to accommodate changes in depth of water, or any shoals of food-fish which the sounder may locate.

Some anglers make a point of tensioning the line until the rod dips slightly (K). Thus as soon as a fish takes the bait and breaks the cotton or lead connecting link (G), the rod straightens, giving immediate bite indication.

Downrigging – North American style

Since we first described the homespun variation of the North American downrigger in the first edition of this book (1975), one of the authors has been to Canada (1986) and fished with one

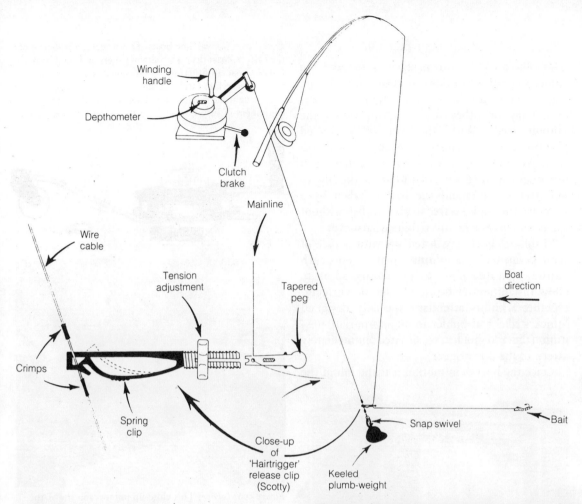

Winding
handle

Depthometer

Clutch
brake

Mainline

Wire
cable

Tension
adjustment

Tapered
peg

Boat
direction

Crimps

Spring
clip

Close-up
of
'Hairtrigger'
release clip
(Scotty)

Keeled
plumb-weight

Snap swivel

Bait

Figure 505: The downrigger and rod shown in the
photograph (left) are re-created in the drawing above to
reveal the layout at the unseen end of the rig. The vital
function of the tension-adjustable spring-clip (Scotty) and
the means by which the clip is attached to the cable, as
well as to the fisherman's line, is shown in the close-up
drawing

of the most refined professionally-made downriggers and found that it is a remarkably efficient
aid for fishing deep waters (100 ft or more).

It is mainly used for trailing baits or 'trolling',
as North Americans insist on calling the method,
in deep waters along the eastern sea-board and
among the islands which are the feeding grounds
for five species of Pacific Ocean salmon; a smaller
version is used on deep inland water like the
Great Lakes for salmon, trout, lake trout (charr),
pike and musky.

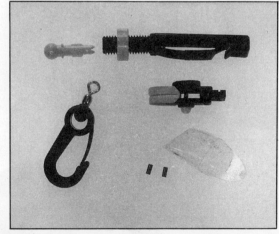

Figure 506: This photograph depicts (top left) the tapered
peg; (top right) release clip and immediately below an
alternative type release clip; (bottom left) the snap-swivel
which connects the cable to the plumbweight; (bottom
middle) crimps; (bottom right) a tiny-teaser

The downrigger in action

The object of the downrigger is to take the angler's line and bait down to the desired fishing depth, where the echo-sounder has located shoals of herring or other food-fish, on which the salmon feed. With the aid of a keeled plumbweight, suspended on a 90 or 150 lb BS stainless-steel cable – weighing as much as 10 lb but rigged in such a way as to allow the line to pull free the moment the bait is taken by a salmon – the angler is free to play his fish without the encumbrance of any weight whatsoever.

'Trolling' boats are fitted up with a pair of semi-permanent mounting plates on each gunwale (located close to the stern), so as to allow instant socket-fitting of each downrigger, together with its attendant specially designed 'quick strike' rod-holder in its appropriate position (the rod-holder is situated immediately astern of the downrigger).

Once the boat is in motion it is the job of the

Figure 507: (*below*) The Scotty Downrigger, a favourite of the eastern coast deep-sea salmon fishers and the Great Lakes Canadian fishermen; professional equipment for all those who seek to catch predatory fish in deep waters. F. B. caught his first two Canadian salmon using this equipment in July '86 – and greatly enjoyed the experience

Figure 508: (*above*) This close-up photograph shows the nose (in the form of a snap) of the release clip, clipped on to the plumbline between the two crimps – while the back of the release clip secures the fisherman's line via the peg

Figure 509: (*left*) Lowrance Computer Graph echo sounder

Figure 510: The Cannon Downrigger with 'combined tube' rod-holder

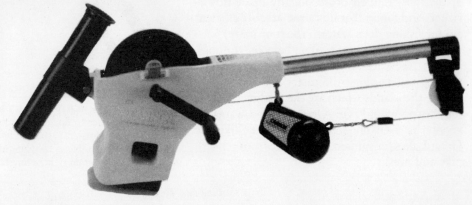

486

Figure 511: F. B., fishing off Bowen Island in British Columbia, is holding his first Pacific Salmon (Coho) caught on downrigger equipment; a small fish compared with the 56 lb chinook salmon caught on similar equipment off Lasqueti Island the same day – a fish which took three and a half hours to boat.

Another angler, Jim Chapman, fishing off Bowen Island had an extraordinary experience. He was reeling back a herring strip following an abortive take (a salmon had snatched at the bait 70 ft down, freeing the line from the downrigger but without getting hooked), when a seagull picked up the bait as it skipped over the wave tops and hooked itself.

Unknown to the angler and his companion Ron Lihou, the gull's struggles had attracted the attention of another predator. 'The next thing I knew, a Bald eagle stooped with its talons outstretched, grabbed the seagull and took off.' The eagle was soon 50 ft up and making towards the shore-line, pulling line off a screaming reel before Chapman (or Lord Jim, as he is known locally) could regain his composure and apply braking pressure to the drum – but not before bruising his knuckles on the flying handles.

Needless to say, the eagle broke the leader and was soon enjoying its meal perched on a shore-line tree in full view of the anglers.

Meantime Lord Jim and his companion had the doubtful pleasure of untangling the downrigger cable which had by now wrapped itself round the propeller (well, it would, wouldn't it!).

duty rodsman (while his companion drives what is usually a powerful outboard-engined cabin cruiser) to ensure that the downrigger's clutch-brake is operating in the 'brake' position before he attaches the cable, via a snap-swivel, to the plumbweight.

By resisting the pull of the plumbweight as the brake is released, the weight is allowed to pull off about 6 ft of cable until two crimps (these are permanently crimped on to the cable about an inch apart) are positioned midway between the guide-pulley and the water. The brake is then re-applied. The rodsman now places the first rod (ideally a powerful 10 ft salmon spinning rod) in the rod-holder – the rod having previously been fitted with a revolving-drum reel of one kind or another – loaded with 25 lb BS monofil line (or thereabouts). Prior to attaching the bait (either a sliver of fresh or frozen herring or an artificial bait, the favourite being a plastic squid bait called a Hoochy), a component part of the release clip, namely a tapered peg, is threaded on the line via a hole bored at the thinner end.

The rodsman now pulls line from the reel via

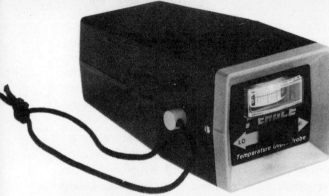

Figure 512: Eagle Electronics have produced an up-to-date thermometer that will, with the aid of a probe fitted to a cable marked in 1 ft increments, take temperatures down to 75 ft

Figure 513: (*below*) Frozen wedge-shaped herring strips are as freely available in western North American coastal tackle shops as maggots in the UK. The thicker ends of the strips are angle-cut to fit into Hastie nose-cones called 'tiny-teasers'. The strip is secured by pushing a toothpick through the side of the nose-cone until you get what old English gunmakers used to call a *wedgefast fit.* Amazingly, in the event of no action in the way of strikes, the bait will stay on all day

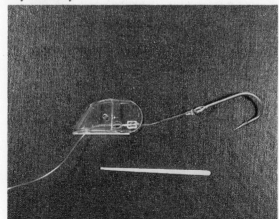

the top ring of the rod and, while still holding the tapered peg, tests the bait's action in the water. When the bait 'swims' properly in relation to the tide (or lack of tide), and the boat's speed, he pulls out a further 30 ft of line and pushes the pointed end of the tapered plug into a hole of a corresponding taper in the body of the release clip (thereby trapping the line) before attaching the clip on to the wire cable between the two crimps previously referred to.

The next task is to release the brake (under control), allowing the cable drum to rotate until the lead reaches the required depth.

Since the rod-line is attached to the cable (via the pushed-in plug) the fishing reel will have been revolving (with the check on to prevent over-runs) in unison with the cable drum, releasing fishing line until the bait reaches the depth selected on the cable drum's clearly calibrated depthometer. The whole sequence is then repeated until the second bait is fishing – probably at a different depth until a strike signals the 'taking' depth.

The salmon's strike pulls the plug out of the release-clip and as soon as the motion of the boat takes up the slack the take is indicated on the

Figure 514: (*below left*) Lowrance, at the forefront of sonar electronics in the USA, have produced a digital depth-sounder only 2 in. diameter which outdates, so far as the authors are concerned, all other 'small boat' sonar devices. It incorporates two major improvements, namely, back-lighted depth-indication visible even in bright sunlight and an alarm system which warns of approaching shallows or rocks

Figure 515: (*below*) A plan view of a quick-strike rod-holder (normally fitted to the gunwale of a 'trolling' boat via an instant socket fitting)

Freshwater Fishing

Figure 516: These Canadians, who probably trailed baits (or fished with live herring) to catch the bag of salmon seen in this picture, were in Cowichan Bay, Vancouver Island, B.C., in 1940 before downriggers were developed

Freshwater Fishing

rod-tip – visually by a violent backwards tug and audibly by the scream of the reel's check.

Salmon hooked in this way invariably swim up to the surface at great speed and within seconds show themselves by thrashing on the top or leaping clear of the water.

THE NOSE-CONE TRAILING TACKLE

Some time ago, while admiring the action of a plug as it burrowed its way into the water, we considered the question of making a natural bait behave likewise. It occurred to us that hitherto any life-like movement given to a non-revolving deadbait had always been imparted by the angler – by means of rod-tip movement, or an irregular retrieve. The well-known 'sink-and-draw' technique is an example.

The deadbait trailer always finds it difficult to get any sort of special action into his bait simply because so much of his time is taken up with handling the boat. With the intention of achieving a true *plug action* on a deadbait trailing rig we set about designing a fibre-glass nose-cone that would (a) fit over the head of a herring, (b) incorporate a plastic diving vane of the type fitted to the majority of plugs.

After experimenting with numerous patterns, we became even more convinced that the nose-cone was a practical proposition worthy of further development.

A chance conversation with a Canadian salmon angler, however, ended our quest for the perfect cone, for an American manufacturer with similar notions had anticipated our experiments. After trying out hundreds of different cones, involving thousands of comparative tests, his firm had finally developed a nose-cone that

would give a herring deadbait the true plug action.

This nose-cone is called *The Herring Magic, The Frantic Swimming Actionizer!* Purchasers are exhorted to: 'Fish it fast. Remember, you are simulating real, live, freshly-injured minnows trying to escape (herring, anchovy, sardine, mullet and freshwater shiners)!'

According to our Canadian informant, the *Herring Magic* nose-cone is used extensively and with great success in the famous 'Salmon Derby' – an annual competition for the biggest salmon, held off the west coast of Canada.

Since angling for salmon in British coastal waters with a trailed herring (or anything else, for the matter) is a waste of time, we suggest that the nose-cone should be used to catch pike. The large lochs of Scotland and Ireland are particularly suited to the trailing method, and we feel confident that if used intelligently the rig will open up opportunities for pike fishermen. As a result, more big loch pike will be caught than ever before.

Directions for use

Hold the herring in the left hand. Push the retaining spike into the back of the herring's head. Swing the herring's nose into the cone. Clip the end of the spike (which has penetrated right through the neck of the bait) into its retaining clip. Push the 'bend-over' wire clamp up through the belly of the herring to just behind the gills, and bend the emergent wire back towards the dorsal fin. The bend-over wire supports the hooks and hook-trace.

Figure 517: A brown trout, 17 lb 12 oz, length $32\frac{1}{4}$ in, girth 20 in., caught by Des Elliott trailing a copper and silver spoon in Lough Mask on 25 September 1983. The second largest rod-caught Mask trout on record. (The biggest, $18\frac{3}{4}$ lb, was caught by Thomas Malia in 1934.)

Nothing haphazard about this marvellous catch. Elliott (who already has two double-figure Mask trout to his credit) knew his location and fished accordingly

Figure 518: The nose-cone trailing tackle

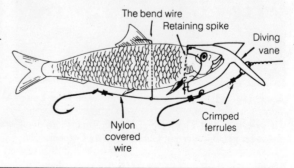

The bend wire
Retaining spike
Diving vane
Nylon covered wire
Crimped ferrules

Figure 519: (*left*) 16 lb 1 oz brown trout taken from Lough Mask on a trailed spoon – by the late William Keal in May 1971.

Figure 520: (*right*) This 55 lb $1\frac{3}{4}$ oz pike, some $33\frac{1}{2}$ in. long, was caught on a spoon by Lothar Louis from Bühl in a gravel pit near Greffern in Germany on 12 October 1986

CHANCE *and* MISCHANCE

ANGLING 'LUCK'

It is part of the charm of angling that success is not exclusive to the skilled angler. The novice may catch fish on his first outing – if he is lucky. It does not happen often, but it happens.

Such a feat sets angling apart from most other sports and games. One would hardly expect a novice batsman to score a hundred in his first innings, or a novice clay-shooter to break twenty-five straight at skeet. Of the greatest importance to his peace of mind, however, is the angling beginner's ability to rationalize this unexpected moment of triumph – when in the face of intense competition *his* rod lands more fish than any other.

The point is illustrated by the following example.

A comparative beginner who has joined a Midlands angling club and experienced blanks on two previous trips, is now taking a third coach-trip with his fellow members. At the waterside he draws an early number, which puts him near the head of the column of anglers winding along the river bank. Motivated only by fancy, he stops at a certain spot and, quite by chance, chooses to ledger the swim with cheese paste bait – perhaps because he is still too squeamish to use worms or maggots!

As it turns out, he has chosen the best swim in the whole section and, what is more, the water is full of chub. On this particular day the chub respond more readily to cheese than any other bait; furthermore, the best way of getting at them happens to be with a ledger rig. So, at the weigh-in, our novice finds himself the top rod!

Also in the group is a skilful angler. Had he been given first chance he would have stopped at the same place and, from experience, concluded that it could be fished best with a ledger rig. He would have known that chub were a likely prospect since, prior to the match, he had taken the trouble to enquire about the water. His sample of baits would have included cheese-paste by design, since he is aware of the excellence of this as a chub bait. With the minimum of experiment he would have started to catch chub. By the close he would undoubtedly have netted a larger bag of fish.

The illustration above demonstrates one way fish are lost. From A. Mayer's *Sport with Gun and Rod* (1883)

It takes little thought to place this example of the lucky novice in true perspective. For him, other winning days will be few, until he has reinforced the element of luck, which is common to all, with some hard-won experience.

At the same time, the incident underlines one of angling's main attractions: the beginner is always in with a chance. It is, after all, not impossible that the record roach or salmon could be hooked by a beginner at his first attempt!

TWENTY-SIX WAYS OF LOSING A FISH

Since the dawn of angling wild-eyed men have babbled of great fish hooked and lost. The literature is filled with stories of leviathans sometimes seen, sometimes unseen, that have escaped the record books. And yet in so many cases the loss could have been avoided if the angler had given a little more thought to the matter *in advance*; if he had spent just a little more time and care examining the water he was going to fish, and the tackle with which he was going to fish it. In other words, paying greater attention to detail. Time and again one's admiration of an angler's skill in hooking a fish is tempered by his stupidity in losing it.

Here for your consideration are various ways of losing a fish. They are compiled from experience. For each of them, except the first, the angler is mainly responsible – and even the first is not wholly free from suspicion. (There are, of course, other ways of losing a fish, but these will do to be going on with.)

1. Hook loses its hold

Unless the angler has mistimed the strike (in which case it is his own fault if the hook secures a poor hold), this is the only valid excuse for losing a fish. Once the angler has tightened on a fish nothing more can be done to improve the hold. If the fish is poorly hooked the chances are it will come off before it can be landed. Luck will always play a part in angling, and before he goes fishing the novice should realize that, through no fault of his own, he is destined to lose a proportion of the fish he hooks. To allow

> ### WEATHER
>
> Wenyng the ffissher suche fisshe to ffynde;
> Than comyth there a noyous north west wynde
> And dryveth the ffisshe into the depe,
> And causeth the draught nat worthe a leeke...
>
> Piers of Fulham, c. 1400
>
> Here ye shall wyte in what weder ye shall angle, as I sayd before ina derke lowrynge daye whanne the wynde blowyth softly. And in somer season whan it is brennynge hote thenne it is nought. From Septembre unto Apryll in a fayr sonny daye is ryght good to angle. And yf the wynde in that season have any parte of the Oryent: the wedyr thenne is nought. And whan it is a grete wynde. And whan it snowith reynyth or hayllyth, or is a grete tempeste as thondyr or lightenynge: or a swoly hote weder: thenne it is noughte for to angle.'
>
> Attrib. Dame Juliana Berners,
A Treatyse of Fysshynge wyth an Angle (1496)
>
> All windes are hurtful if too hard they blow,
> The worst of all is that out of the East,
> Whose nature makes the Fish to biting slow,
> And lets* the pastime most of all the rest;
> The next that comes from countries clad with Snow,
> And *Articque* pole is not offensive least,
> The Southern winde is counted best of all,
> Then, that which riseth where the sunne doth fall.
>
> John Dennys, The Secrets of Angling (1613)
>
> * Lets = Hinders.

such losses to upset him will simply reduce his confidence and concentration and detract from his future chances. He should, however, strive to ensure that the loss of a fish *is* due to plain chance – and not to his own carelessness.

2. Unsound tackle

No 'plain chance' about this. It is clearly the angler's fault. Every item of tackle should be overhauled and tested before fishing starts. Above all, it should be remembered that to buy cheap fishing tackle is nearly always false economy.

3. Hook failure

(a) *Broken* A broken hook is due either to poor casting or to poor-quality metal. In both cases the angler is at fault: in the former for clumsiness, in the latter for not testing the hook.

(b) *Straightened* A lot of fish are lost because a hook straightens out. Most modern hooks are suspect, trebles in particular. Every hook should be tested before use.

4. Knot slips

Another cause of misery. And whose fault is it? No one should go fishing who has not learned to tie *and to test* the right knot for the job in hand.

5. Failure to re-tie hook or fly

Impatience is usually the reason for this. A hook or fly should frequently be re-tied, and always after a big fish has been landed.

6. Wind knot

Wind or no wind, 'wind' knots appear in a fly leader as though by magic. They are usually due to indifferent casting, and considerably reduce the breaking strain of nylon. The only way of avoiding disaster is by frequent inspection of the leader.

7. Broken by fish

This may be due to unsound tackle, or clumsiness, or the fishing running into weed or round a snag. Whatever the reason, anyone who allows a fish to break him deserves to lose it. It is almost always the fault of the angler. All water should be examined before fishing starts. When the position of a snag is known a fish can usually be 'walked' away from it. The time to get on terms with a fish is the moment it is hooked. To wait until it has run halfway down a pool or gone to ground, or into a weed bed, before doing anything constructive, is the fault of many anglers on hooking a fish. Few people seem to know how to 'walk' a fish, or even that a fish *can* be walked. (For details of this, see page 214.)

Have pity on these holy maidens fair,
Resigned unto the Lord they bear their Cross.
Forbidden when they lose a fish to swear,
Or by a hair's breadth to exaggerate their loss.

David Jacques

8. Fishing too fine

Could have come under the previous heading, but deserves special mention since there is an unfortunate type of angler who boasts of fishing very fine to 'give the fish a chance'. He is a fool. There is nothing in the least sporting in giving a fish the chance to escape, taking with it a hook in its gullet and a length of nylon. A fish will refuse tackle that is too coarse and strong. It will break and swim away with tackle that is too fine. The sporting angler, knowing that he must use something in between, chooses the strongest tackle that will enable him to hook and land the species he is fishing for in the conditions existing at the time. *There are many reasons for being broken by a fish, but no excuses.*

9. Reel jams

This is due either to bad maintenance or lack of attention while fishing. To put the butt of a fly-rod down into dry earth or sand often results in the reel becoming clogged. An extension to the

Freshwater Fishing

rod butt helps to prevent this. It is a good habit (especially in the darkness) for an angler to place the rod butt on top of his foot. Another reason for a reel jamming is when tight coils of line bite down on loose coils underneath. A line should be stripped off and re-wound before fishing starts, and after a big fish has been played.

10. *Leader knot jams*

If, when a fish is being landed, the line is wound in too far – so that the knot joining leader and line jams in a rod ring – a sudden rush often enables the fish to break free. The use of a needle or nail knot (see page 393) avoids this altogether. If a figure-of-eight knot is used (see page 392), the angler should make sure that the leader is not too long for the rod.

11. *Striking too hard*

The most likely moment for a break is just as the fish is hooked. But striking usually consists of tightening on a fish, not giving it a great jerk.

12. *Holding a fish too hard*

Apart from the strike, this is the quickest and most certain way of suffering a straightened hook or getting broken. A fault common among beginners who, when they hook a fish, cannot bear to let it get further away from them. The only time a running fish should be 'held' is when the line (or backing) is almost exhausted, or when the fish is heading for an obvious snag: perhaps the middle arch of a bridge. But the mistake lies with the angler for allowing the fish to get into a position from which a disastrous run is likely. In most cases, prior action (such as 'walking' the fish) can prevent it. The angler should never be taken by surprise. The successful landing of any fish depends on careful thought before a line is cast.

Disaster through 'holding hard' is occasionally caused by what might be described as the 'military syndrome', an example of which became a favourite story of Colonel Crow, who, after his retirement, bailiffed a salmon beat on the Hampshire Avon. It was Crow's habit to keep an eye

Figure 521: The first cast at first-light: F. B. fishing for pike on Loch Ken – home of the legendary 72 lb monster

> ... perhaps as yet there has been no rain in the valley. A man from the hills has told us of it; we have seen it in the distance as a vast veil of greyness, hung in a moving heaven so that it swept gently over the screes, the bogs and mountain ploughland, the grateful upturned face of the earth. All we know of it and much more is already old news to the salmon. As soon as rain is in the offing, the salmon in the pools become restless and often will not look at a fly. Conversely, this persistent refusal to rise is frequently taken as a sign of the coming of rain.
>
> Eric Taverner, *Salmon Fishing* (1931)

on his anglers from a bridge near his house and assist whenever a salmon was hooked. Seeing a certain peppery old brigadier hook a fish and knowing him to be a novice, Crow covered three fields in short time – only to find the old man glaring balefully at a broken leader. Asked why he had held on to the fish rather than give it line, the brigadier drew himself up. 'Give it line?' he asked incredulously. 'This was no ordinary fish, Crow. This was a *big* fish. I stood my ground.'

13. *Rod top caught in branches*

This can happen very easily when a bushy run is being fished for sea trout at night.

14. *Trying to land a fish too soon*

A very common mistake. The angler has shortened line and, with net or gaff extended, hauls the fish towards him. The fish obligingly comes almost within reach; then, frightened by the sight of the fisherman, turns and dashes away in alarm. The reel fails to respond quickly enough or a handle gets hooked up, or the line knot jams in a rod ring and the leader snaps.

Wait until the fish has turned on its side. Even so, an angler should not use a landing net like a child catching tadpoles. A fish is not scooped out, but lifted out. The angler should conceal himself by crouching as low as possible, then sink the net to the bottom so that the fish cannot see it. When the fish is lying on its side, *and not before*, it is drawn steadily in, and the net raised to encircle it. (See page 402. Also *Lost at the gaff*, page 498.)

15. *Leader cut by gaff stroke*

Very easily done. (See page 230.)

16. *Leader nipped in joint of landing net*

A miserable business which can happen with a folding net, especially at night. Get yourself a strong net with a big wide mouth constructed on a solid frame.

17. *Nylon line or leader burned with cigarette end*

This is hardly likely to happen to a non-smoker. It once happened to H. F. when landing a large salmon – hence its inclusion.

18. *Fish knocked off hook by gaff or net*

This might be called the 'willing helper syndrome'. Invariably the bystander, anxious to help in landing a fish, goes into action too soon. Except in emergency, it is advisable for an angler to land his own fish. Then, if it gets knocked off the hook, he has only himself to blame.

19. *Line/backing splice draws* (see comment on page 388)

No fly fisherman should ever allow anyone else

Figure 522: Not one of the listed ways of losing a fish – but perhaps it should be!

No life so happy and so pleasant, as the life of a well-governed angler; for when the lawyer is swallowed up with business, and the statesman is preventing or contriving plots, then we sit on cowslip-banks, hear the birds sing, and possess ourselves in as much quietness as these silent silver streams...

Izaak Walton, *The Compleat Angler* (1653)

Today he might comment that it was just as well the lawyer and the lawmaker were about their business, and that the angler has been 'well-governed' because if they had not been there would now be precious little, if any, angling, cowslip-banks, birds, silver streams or fish.

Michael Gregory, LL. B *Angling and the Law* (1967)

to splice his fly-line and backing for him. If the splice draws he loses not only the fish but the line as well. If he does the job himself and tests it thoroughly it will *not* draw. A needle or nail knot is preferable to a splice if nylon backing is used.

20. *Hole in landing net*

Very irritating, but sheer carelessness. Having, as the angler thinks, been netted, the fish sets off with renewed vigour and leaves the angler trying to play it through the hole. Usually results in loss of fish; sometimes a broken rod-tip.

21. *Hole in keep net*

Really!

22. *Failure to cope with fish making off downstream*

Occasionally a fish is in danger of being lost because it makes a fast run downstream, with the angler unable to follow. This can be disastrous, but if he has plenty of backing (as he *should* have) and keeps his head, the angler is always in with a chance.

Only when the fish has run out all the line and backing is the situation hopeless; and in this instance the angler is wise to hold the fish *before* the last turn of backing has left the reel, otherwise he may lose the lot; fish, fly-line and backing – and doubtless his temper as well. By holding the fish in time (but after it has made a long run) he may turn it, or at least he may save his fly-line and backing.

It has been said that an angler can stop a fish running downstream by stripping line off the reel. He can't! Line cannot be stripped off quickly enough to affect a fast-running fish. This method of bringing a fish back upstream can, however, be used to good effect when a salmon, having gone some distance downstream, *has stopped and is lying there*. Now, if line is stripped off, a belly will form below the fish. The fish will soon feel the pressure of this bag of line from behind, and begin to swim upstream towards the rod.

The slack line method can also be used effectively when a fish is *beginning* to tire and is below the angler, stemming the current. But the danger of losing a fish downstream is greatest when the fish is very tired, because then it is unable to resist being carried off tail first. When this happens, no amount of slack line hanging below it will make it move upstream, for it is exhausted.

Think about all this before fishing starts, *not after a fish has been hooked.*

23. Hook caught in landing net

This loses a lot of fish. It happens when a fish is being landed on multi-hook tackle; fly leader with bob-fly and dropper; Stewart or Pennell tackles; spinning flight; prawn, livebait or dead-bait mounts; quill minnow with flying-treble, etc. As the fish is drawn to the net a hook attaches itself to a mesh, and the fish – now-held tantalizingly just outside the net's rim – can be brought no further. At this point it usually stages a rapid recovery, wrenches the hook out and departs.

24. Fish jumps back again

Every now and then a fish, having been landed successfully, slips out of the angler's hand, or

Figure 523: The twenty-seventh way of losing a fish? No – the fisherman has broken his rod but has still landed his fish. After all, he has merely exchanged a long rod for a short one

slithers down a bank and regains its freedom. A desperate business which (however unlikely it sounds) happens to most of us sooner or later. If a fish has to be handled when the angler is in or close to the water, it should be knocked on the head while still in the net. Otherwise it should be taken well back from the water's edge. For notes on beaching a salmon, see page 214. Remember: if you intend to kill the fish you catch, *always* carry a priest.

25. *Thieves*

Even when landed and killed, a fish is not always safe. Rats, cats, mink, otters, badgers and pigs have all been known to snitch fish from a river bank. Never leave a fish lying out on the grass. Always hang it up out of reach, or put it away in a bag.

Note: Plastic bags are not recommended for use in hot weather.

26. *Weakened nylon*

Some anglers hoard tackle like squirrels. Hoard by all means. But *never, never* hoard nylon. Many a fish has been lost by using old, weakened nylon. Unless you know how old it is – throw it away. And always put on a new leader at the start of fishing. Changing your leader at lunchtime will often avert disaster after casting continually into wind.

Figure 524: (*above*) This painting (courtesy of Walter Spencer) is entitled *Some Mishaps in The Pleasures of Angling* (1823) and was engraved by C. Turner. The painting illustrates one of the twenty-six ways of losing a fish – or is one that we missed, the twenty-seventh way, sitting on your rod

ANGLING SAFETY

WADING

The ability to wade deep is an asset to every fly fisherman. But rivers vary enormously. Some are gay, uncomplicated little streams with easily-waded gravel runs and glides. Others are awkward and treacherous, with slimy rocks and deep, sullen pools where a single false step may take the unsuspecting non-swimmer straight over a shallow, sunken ledge – into eternity.

On the river, wading is the most common cause of fishing accidents, and it is probable that accidents involving the use of body waders form the highest proportion. No denigration of body waders is intended; the point is simply that the higher his waders the deeper the angler is tempted to wade, until sooner or later the fatal step is taken. When this happens, the water is not up to his knees or thighs, but his chest, and in all probability he is swept off his feet by the current.

An experienced angler who knows the river can tell at a glance where he can wade safely and where he can't. Even so, mistakes are easily made. A place quite safe to wade when the river is, say, nine inches above summer level may be impossible after a further rise of two inches. In a lake, a two-inch rise means that your safe

wading depth is reduced by exactly that amount; but in the river there are two other factors involved. Two extra inches in the river mean not only two inches of extra depth, but a stronger current. This added pressure of water against your body increases the water level against your back. It also causes you to lean over at a greater angle against the current in order to maintain a footing – thus further reducing the safety margin of your waders. The combination of these two factors results in a loss of considerably more than two inches.

When wading for any distance downstream, always be sure of the depth of water between the bank and wherever you happen to be. Your path may be along an underwater ridge with deep water on either side, in which case the only possible retreat is straight back upstream. Wading against even a weak current is a great deal more difficult than wading with it. Your return will be even more difficult if, while you have been fishing, the river has begun to rise.

Such a rise may be entirely unexpected. It is not by any means unusual for a downpour further up the valley to affect the river, although not a drop of rain has fallen in your locality. The early stages of such a rise are not immediately evident to anyone intent on fishing. The water

---

level may creep up unnoticed – until the margin of safety is passed.

Before wading deep, make certain of the pool's underwater contours.

EMERGENCY

Most fishing accidents result in little more than a wetting. A fisherman gets his boots full, or stumbles and falls unhurt in shallow water. But

---

Figure 525: A fisherman wades in from A to B to cover salmon lying under the right bank. Wading along a shallow underwater ridge, he fishes down to point C. There he comes to deeper water and finds he can wade no farther downstream. He is unable to retrace his steps upstream owing to the strength of the current. Not realizing he is on the end of an underwater spit he starts to wade towards the bank along the line CD. Almost at once he steps into deep water (E) and is swept off his feet by the current. *Note:* When wading in a current, however gentle, *never* step up on top of a submerged rock. It is very difficult to keep your footing when stepping down again – particularly if you are not using a wading stick

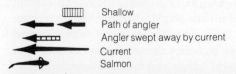

every so often comes news of a fatality. Someone has lost his balance or been swept off his feet while wading; a loose rock has toppled over; a piece of river bank has collapsed; a boat has capsized . . . a fisherman has drowned.

Accidents such as these can happen very suddenly; indeed, they usually do. Within seconds of being safe and sound, the unlucky man finds himself floundering out of his depth. Terrified, he throws up his arms and screams. Two involuntary actions. Both fatal.

Many lives would be saved if people would only think *beforehand* of the correct action to take in the event of an emergency.

It is the unexpectedness of most accidents that carries the greatest threat to safety; the shock of a sudden plunge into cold water, followed immediately by panic – panic caused by the thought of being heavily clothed and shod, and out of one's depth. It has been said – and a surprising number of people believe it – that if a fisherman wearing waders falls into deep water, his boots will drag him down.

They will do nothing of the sort.

It is a simple matter to swim for short distances fully clothed and wearing waders; their weight when submerged is negligible, and

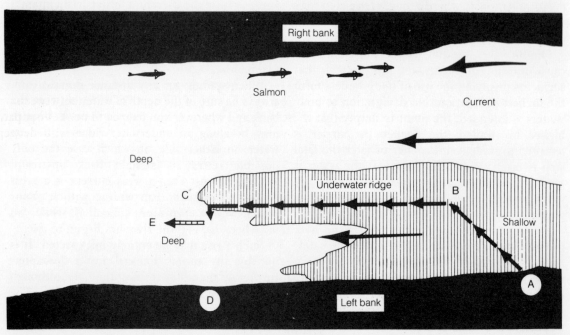

Freshwater Fishing

although they make swimming no easier they certainly don't make it impossible. It is not difficult to swim fully clothed while holding a fishing rod. Provided you can swim, no great danger need accompany a tumble into deep water.

In order to enjoy a feeling of security on or beside water – whether river or lake – you should be able to paddle about fully clothed when out of your depth. If you can't, practise until you can, paying particular attention to the back stroke. Most emergency swimming of this nature is (or should be) carried out on the back.

There is nothing difficult about it. On the contrary, it is very easy. And it is very, very important, for once you are able to swim on your back you will be armed with confidence, and the thought of falling into deep water will no longer be one of fear.

Remember: *it is panic that drowns most people.*

When the worst happens – perhaps an undermined river bank collapses, or a shingle bottom slides away beneath your feet – and you suddenly find yourself plunging fully clothed, rod in hand, into the deeps – *don't* open your mouth and shout. Pay no attention to those stories of drowning men coming up three times. If you ship enough water first time down, you won't come up at all. So – *keep your mouth shut.*

Provided you don't wave your arms about above your head you will soon bob up again. A living body is very buoyant. Even if you can't swim, there is sufficient air trapped in your various garments to keep you afloat for several minutes, if you only give yourself half a chance.

Float on your back, arms out in the 'crucifix' position, keep your head lying well back in the water and let your legs come to the surface. Once in this position you can start shouting for help.

If in a river, don't try to swim against the current. Let yourself drift downstream, feet first; then it will be your boots that may strike a rock, not your head. Paddle away with your hands and gradually edge in towards the bank (see picture sequence on pages 504 and 505).

BOAT FISHING ACCIDENTS

We make no apology for the elementary nature of the following advice. Some anglers who go afloat are astonishingly ignorant of boats and boat-handling and do the most stupid things. Each season we hear of boating accidents that could so easily have been avoided. Here are some 'don'ts'.

Don't step on the side of the boat, or on one of the seats, or on the bare planking between the ribs, when getting into a boat from a landing-stage. Always step on the floorboards as near the middle of the boat as possible. Having stepped into the boat, *sit down.*

Don't go out in any boat that is not provided with a baler, a spare oar, and spare rowlocks or thole-pins (whichever are used). If the boat normally relies on an engine, make sure it also has a pair of oars. Don't relax this rule however calm the day. The weather can change with frightening rapidity. In only a few hours a big lake (Lough Mask, for instance, or Loch Lomond) can become very dangerous.

Don't, if you are alone in a boat some distance from the bank on a hot day, succumb to the temptation of going in for a swim – unless the boat is anchored. A sudden breeze may spring up and blow the boat away from you faster than you can swim after it.

Don't try getting from the water into a small boat by clambering over the *side.* Pull yourself up over the stern (the blunt end).

If you decide to go overboard for a swim be quite sure you *can* pull yourself back on board. It isn't so easy as it sounds. (At one time or another we have had to assist quite a lot of people who hadn't considered this!)

Don't stand up in the boat without warning the other occupant or occupants. If you are inexperienced, don't stand up at all. If you want to pee, use the baler.

Don't attempt to change places with a companion without first planning exactly, move by move, where each of you is going to position himself.

Don't throw a rope to a person in the water without first tying a bowline in it (see page 391).

Figure 526:

ACTION IN EVENT OF
EMERGENCY

We are grateful to our friend
Frank Plum for his co-operation
in photographing the following
sequence

1.   A salmon fisherman wading
in a strong current on steep
shingle . . . takes a step too many

2.   The shingle slides away
underfoot; the current sweeps
him forward . . .

3.   . . . and down he goes, into
deep water. This type of accident
can happen in any river, whatever
the nature of the bottom. Within
seconds of being safe and sound
you may find yourself
floundering out of your depth. It
is the unexpectedness of such
accidents that carries the greatest
threat to safety – the shock of a
sudden plunge into cold water;
the fear that your waders may
drag you down. *They won't.*

Note: This picture story is similar
to the sequence shown in H. F.'s
TV film documentary *Salmo the
Leaper* – which, to date, has been
responsible for saving forty-one
lives

(1)

(2)

(3)

(4)

4. *Don't* try to swim back against the current. Turn on your back and let the stream take you with it. If you cannot swim and hold your rod too, let it go. With line out there should be a good chance of recovering it later. Float on your back, head upstream. Kick with your legs, paddle with your hands and *keep your head back*. The 'crucifix', the classic safe position – head well back, legs up, arms outstretched. Once in this position you can start shouting for help. Keep on your back. Float downstream feet first with the current and gradually edge in towards the bank by paddling with outstretched hands

5. But don't try to pull yourself up a steep bank out of deep water. The weight of sodden clothes and waders full of water will quickly exhaust you. Resist the temptation to cling on in a hopeless situation

6. Keep on down the pool! Head back, legs up. Don't drop your legs to feel for the bottom: a vertical body will sink at once

7. When you reach the shallows, don't try to stand up and walk out. Tired, suffering from shock and exposure, you may stumble and injure yourself. Roll over on to hands and knees . . . and crawl out

8. Having crawled out on to dry land, don't immediately get up and try to walk: lie on your back and empty your waders first!

(5)

(7)

(6)

(8)

Figure 527: Boat fishing accidents

Note: We have witnessed this accident on more than one occasion. Always remove rowlocks when not in use.
  (A mishap similar to this nearly drowned H. F.'s father – see *The Stolen Years*, Chapter 18)

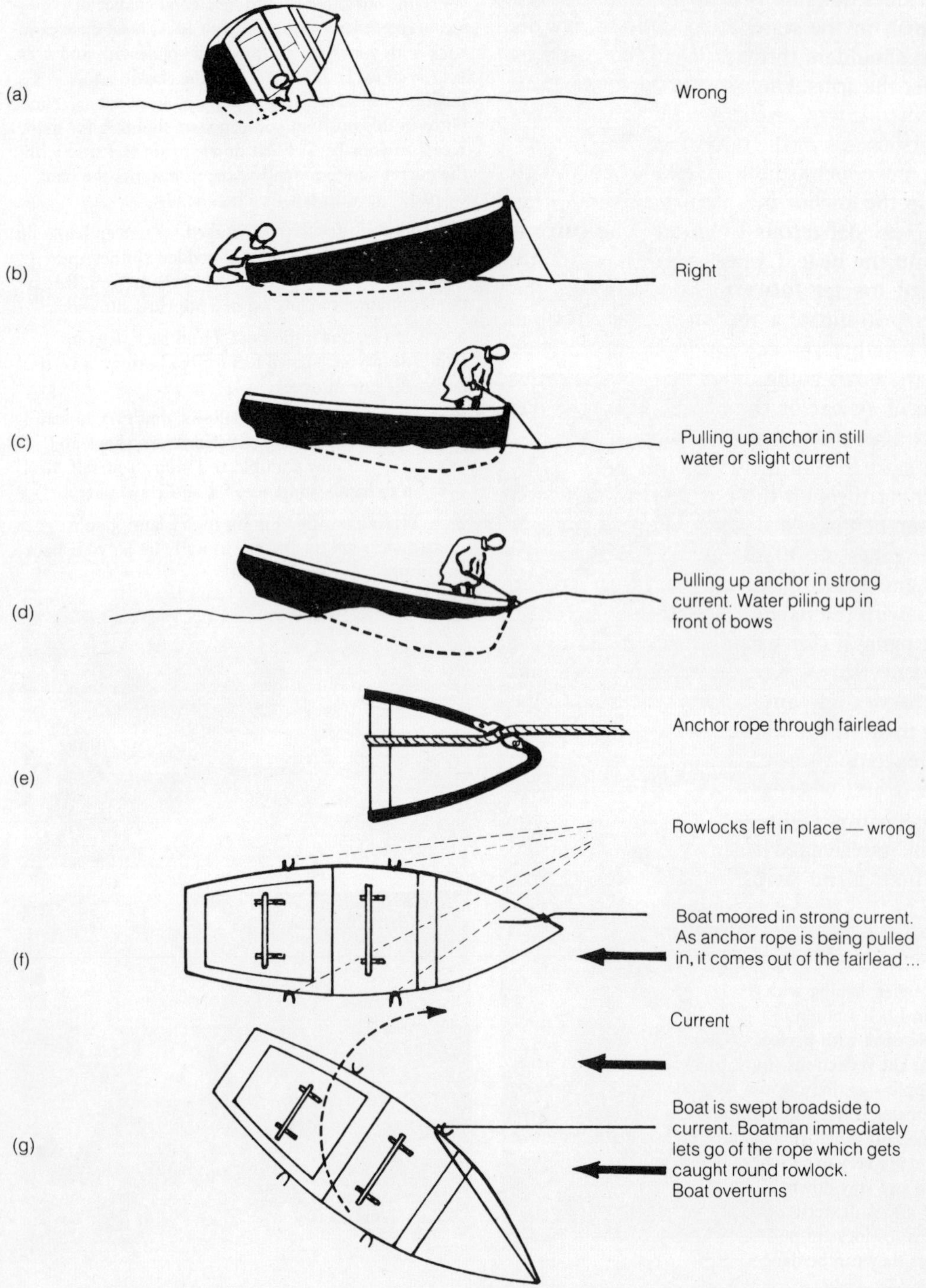

(a)   Wrong

(b)   Right

(c)   Pulling up anchor in still
water or slight current

(d)   Pulling up anchor in strong
current. Water piling up in
front of bows

(e)   Anchor rope through fairlead

Rowlocks left in place — wrong

(f)   Boat moored in strong current.
As anchor rope is being pulled
in, it comes out of the fairlead ...

Current

(g)   Boat is swept broadside to
current. Boatman immediately
lets go of the rope which gets
caught round rowlock.
Boat overturns

Failure to do this has cost a lot of lives. An exhausted person probably has numbed fingers and is unable to tie the knot. Without a loop in it, the rope is virtually useless. A bowline is a loop that does not slip. It must be large enough for the man in the water to be able to get his head and shoulders through it, so that it holds him under the arms. Once inside the loop he can be hauled to safety, even though he may have lost consciousness in the meantime.

Don't move forward too quickly when you go to pull up the anchor in a strong current. This can be a very dangerous situation. The current can swamp the boat if your weight is suddenly transferred too far forward. Edge towards the bows very carefully, a foot at a time. If it is doubtful whether you can reach the anchor rope without the bows going under, tie your knife to the loom of an oar or the handle of a landing-net, reach forward and cut the rope.

Don't start to pull in the anchor rope unless it is running through the fairlead on the bows. Keep your hands low down while you pull. If the rope comes out of the fairlead the chances are that the boat will swing broadside to the current – with the danger of a capsize.

Don't panic if (for whatever reason) the boat fills up or overturns. Keep your mouth shut and try not to swallow any water; you have some thinking to do. If the water is very cold you must quickly make up your mind whether to swim for the shore or stay where you are and wait for help. If help is coming you will naturally cling to the oars or the waterlogged hull and wait to be picked up. If there is no help forthcoming and you

Figure 528:

Top: An angler, fishing with deadbait float/ledger tackle for pike on Loch Lomond
Middle: He casts with perfect balance
Bottom: As the reflections show, there is hardly any extra surface ripple – as there would be if the boat were rocking wildly. But this is not a method we recommend the novice to try, especially when alone and in such a small boat. Unless you are very experienced, when you get into a boat, sit down – and stay down.
Note: For all his dexterity, this angler loses marks for keeping his rowlocks in position while at anchor. Even in slack water they can be dangerous

decide to swim for it, the sooner you start the better.

Don't undress if you only have a short distance to go. Air trapped in your clothes will help to keep you warm. But if you have far to go strip off all your clothes as quickly as you can and get started. When you want a rest, turn on your back; but don't just float, keep your legs and arms moving. Even when you reach the shore, force yourself to *keep moving* until you get help.

Remember: however strong a swimmer you may be it is the *cold* you are really up against.
Note: Most small boats that capsize or become swamped stay on the surface, waterlogged. One way of getting to safety is to swim the boat ashore (much easier than it sounds). Grip the boat's stern at arm's length with both hands and kick with your legs.

One advantage of this method is that you can rest from time to time by clinging to the hull when beginning to tire.

If the boat is anchored, remember to cut the rope or cast it off! This advice is not so unnecessary as it may seem. H. F. once forgot to check the anchor of a capsized sailing dinghy. It fell out and went to the bottom – automatically mooring the boat – and he swam hard pushing the boat for quite some time before realizing what had happened!

REMOVING HOOK FROM FLESH

Sooner or later most anglers get a hook stuck in their flesh. From our experience the most effective and least painful method of removal is as follows:

1. Press hard down on the hook shank, thus lessening the grip of the barb.
2. At the moment of maximum pressure, push the hook straight back in line with the shank with one, quick, powerful jerk. The barb will slide out cleanly with very little, if any, tearing of the flesh. If done within about two minutes of the accident, comparatively little pain will be felt.

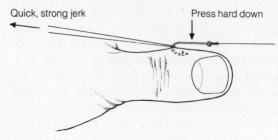

Figure 529: Removing hook from finger

Note: If a second person is available, the hook can be jerked out with a loop of string or nylon placed round the bend of the hook (see diagram).

RODS AND ELECTRICITY

Carbon fibre rods are wonderfully light and easy to handle, but carbon is a very efficient conductor of electricity! Some overhead power lines stretch well within reach of a 15 ft salmon fly-rod, or even a 10 ft rod. So – be careful when sea trout fishing at night. Split cane and fibreglass are dangerous; carbon fibre is very dangerous.

Remember, a rod doesn't have to *touch* a live wire to cause disaster. Electricity can arc across several feet.

Fishing lines, too, can cause shock when cast across power cables, particularly lead-cored fly-lines. And contrary to popular opinion, rubber waders offer no adequate protection.
Watch out for overhead power cables.

Figure 530: Power can arc across to rod-tip

INDEX

Note: Italicised page numbers refer to illustrations

(F) = fishery

(r) = river

Aarø (r) salmon in *200*
abdominal keel 189
Abramis brama see bream
Abri de Poisson, stone carving of salmon at *199*
Abu
  killer plug *478*
  multiplier reel *373*
Achill Island, Co. Mayo 286
acid rain pollution 287–95
  in Cumbria 287–94
  devastation of 291–4
  effects *287*
  first phase liming projects 294–5
  overcoming problems of 287–91
Acipenser sturio see sturgeon, common
Acipenser transmontanus see sturgeon, white
Acton, Eliza (*Modern Cookery for Private Families*) 115
Ade, Robin (*Fisher in the Hills*) on charr 52
adjustable float-link rig 449–53
  casting 450–3, *451*
  examples *450*
  methods of attachment 449–50

Aelfric the Abbot, on burbot 30
Aelian
  on artificial fly 262–3
  on sturgeon 243
Aerial reels 62, 373, *374*, 461
Age of Chivalry, The see Bryant, Arthur
age of fish, determining 38–9, 135–6
Aire (r) 200
Alburnus alburnus see bleak
alevin 192
Alkmaade, zander from *343*
Allcock
  Aerial reel 373, *374*
  floats (1910) *413*
  -Stanley fixed spool reel *376*
Allerton mill, sturgeon at 239
Alosa alosa see shad, allis
Alosa fallax see shad, twaite
Alston, Rev. E. C.
  big tench of *248*
  burbot catch of 31
  record rudd of 183
  trout fishing 296
Ambleside, charr in 53, 55
American Association of Fishing Tackle Manufacturers 381
  AFTM code 381–2
American catfish 48
Amia 132, 133
Amiurus lacustris see American catfish
Amphiperca 133
Amsterdam, big pike at canal near *158*
Amur (r) China, minnow in 110

Amur pike 124, 138
Amusements de la campagne see Liger
Ancient Angling Authors see Turrell, Dr W. J.
Angler in the Lake District, The see Davy, John
Angler in Wales, or Days and Nights of Sportsmen, The see Medwin, Thomas
Angler Naturalist see Cholmondeley-Pennell, H.
Angler on a Wintry Lake see Ma Yuan
Angler's Companion to the Rivers and Lochs of Scotland The see Stoddart, Thomas
Angler's Delight, The see Gilbert, William
Angler's Guide, The see Salter, T. F.
Angler's Hours, An see Sheringham, H. T.
Angler's Instructor, The see Bailey, William
Angler's Mail, The 111, 118
Angler's Museum, The see Shirley, Thomas
Angler's News, on carp 42
Angler's Pocket Book, The, on trolling 479
Angler's Souvenir, The, on chub 67
Angler's Sure Guide, The see Howlett, Robert
Angler's Vade Mecum, The see Chetham, James

Angling and the Law see Gregory, Michael
Angling Diversions see Williams, A. Courtney
Angling for Coarse Fish see Bickerdyke, John
Angling in All its Branches see Taylor, Samuel
Angling News Services 134
angling sportsmanship 255–62
Angling Times 77, 249
  on pike 133, *138*, 145, 157
Anguilla anguilla 73
Animal Behaviour see Tinbergen, Professor Niko
Annan (r) chub in 67
annuli see growth-checks
aphrodisiac, fish as 13
Archer deadbait spinning mount 147
Argentina silus see argentines
Argentina sphyraena see argentines
argentines 299
Arlesey bomb 396–7, *397*
  with flattened sides 397, *397*
  float-link fishing 453
  groundbaiting 440, 456
  link-ledger 174, 444
  paternostering 459–61
Arlesey Lake, big perch in 397
Armathwaite, skellies at 337
Arnold, Bill 289, 291
Arte of Angling, The see Samuel, William
artificial baits, 64, 98, 117, 262, 465–8

artificial caviare 242
Art of Angling see Barker,
Thomas
Art of Angling, The see
Brookes, Richard;
Mansfield, Kenneth
A Concise Treaty on see Best,
Thomas
Art of Fly Making see
Blacker, William
Arun (r) eel in 81
Asellus 166
Assem, J. van den (*Territory
in the Three-Spined
Stickleback*) 236
Astraeus (Roman r.), fly
fishing on 262
Athenaeum 128
Atlantic salmon *see* salmon,
Atlantic
Ausonius 234
Avington Fishery, rainbow
trout from 328
Avon (Hants)
barbel in 15, 16, 433
bream in 28
chub in 64, 67, *446*
current speed of 445
dace in 68, 70, *446*
fast water trotting in 446–7
floats 447
grayling in 95, *446*
perch in 118
pike in 461
roach in 173–5, 176, *446*
salmon in 477
tench in 245
trout in *446*
weirpool *446*
Avon (Wilts) (r), barbel in 15,
17, 19
Avon-Tyrell 19
Axe (r), sea trout in 300

babbing *see* eel-bobber
Bacon, Sir Francis (*A History
of Life and Death*), on pike
134–5
Baden, pike fossils in 124, 125
Bailey, William (*The Angler's
Instructor*) 373
Baillie-Grohman, W. A.
(*Sport in Art*) 218
Bainbridge, G. (*The Fly-
Fisher's Guide*), on
multiplier 370
baitdropper 437, *438*
and barbel 15, 16
and swimfeeder 439–50
bait-cans, for perch *121*
baited spoon, for flounder 89–
90
see also spoon baits
bait hooks 431–2, *431–2*

bait-horn *423*
baits and baiting 421–41
Baker 'Hookout' Disgorger
405–7, *405–7*
Baked Bream (recipe) 27
Bala, Lake, gwyniad of 336
Ballantine, Miss G. W. and
record salmon *217*
ball-bearing swivel 395, *395*
Baltic, flounder in 88
Balmaha (Loch Lomond)
pike at 145
powan at 333, 335
roach at *443*
Band, H., on pike 156
Bankes, Sir Joseph 192
bank-runner (running-line)
444
Barbeau (recipe) 21
barbel *15, 15–21, 17–19,* 97
baits 15–16
baked 21
boiled 20
British Record *16,* 16–18
catches 16–19
choice of rod 353
cooking 20–1
spawning 20
stuffed 21
young 21
Barbus barbus see barbel
Barbus tor 15
Barker's Delight see Barker,
Thomas
Barker, Thomas (*The Art of
Angling,* 2nd edn retitled
Barker's Delight)
on early reel 347, 358, 365,
365, 368
on trolling 357, 463
barleycorn (or barrel) lead
396, *397*
Barlow, Francis (*Salmon
Fishing* drawing) 216
Barnham (Norfolk) 69
Barrow (*Worcester Journal*) on
sturgeon 237
Bartas, Guillaume de Saluste
du (*La Semaine*) 20
Bassenthwaite, vendace in
331, 338
Bastard, Thomas
(*Chresteleros, Seven
Bookes of Epigrames*) 11
bâton fourchie 218
Bays, Lake of (Ontario), charr
in 56
Bazley, J. H. R., on perch's
panic in shoals 118
Beane (r), dace in 69, *70,* 70–
1
Beazley, David
and big trout 266
and charr-tackle *61,* 61–2

Beaufort, Duke of 238
Beddington, Roy 18
Beeton, Mrs
on barbel 21
Dictionary of Cookery 159
Family Cookery 93
on flounder 91, 93
*Mrs Beeton's Everyday
Cookery* 123
on perch 123
on pike 159
and roach 180
Belturbet, roach at 165
Bench, Frank (bream) 25
'Bell's Life' intermediate ring
356
Bendall, James, tench of *251*
Beni Hassan see Newberry,
P. E.
Berners, Dame Juliana (*A
Treatyse of Fysshynge
wyth an Angle*) 7, 262
on barbel 20
on carp 33
on deadbait for pike 140, 481
on dubbed hook 262
on running line 442
on stomach contents 429
on tench 245, 247, 248, 251
on water knot *391*
on weather 494
Berth-Jones, G., and big trout
279
Bertin, Leon, on eel migration
82, 84
Best, Thomas ([*A Concise
Treaty on*] *The Art of
Angling*)
on grayling 95
on gudgeon 99
on multiplier 370
Beta-light 175, *419*
Bibliotheca Piscatoria see
Westward and Satchell
Bickerdyke, John
Angling for Coarse Fish 317,
431
*The Book of the All-Round
Angler* 153, 247, 459, 461,
479
livebait tackle for pike *148*
on paternoster 459, 461
on pike 153
on rudd 182
snap-trolling tackle *481*
on tench 247
on trolling/trailing 479
and two-hook tackle 317, 431
Billingsgate market 198
Birds, Beasts and Flowers see
Lawrence, D. H.
bite alarm, for carp 36
bite indicators 415–18
basic types 415

doughbobbin 415–16, 419
Glowbobbin 36, *419*
Blaber, R., big tench of *247*
black eel 78
Blacker, William (*Art of Fly
Making*), split cane rods
of 349
Blackmore, R. 46
Blackwater (r)
dace in 68
roach in 165
Blagdon, trout at 254
Blake, William, on eels 87
Blakey, Robert (*Historical
Sketches of the Angling
Literature*) 426
Blandford stretch of Dorset
Stour, chub in 67
bleak 22, 22–3
cooking 23
fried 23
hybrids 184
Paste (recipe) 23
Blenham Tarn, pike in 127
Bletchley, Bucks, perch at 119
Blicca bjoerkna see silver
bream
Blome, Richard (*The
Gentleman's Recreation*),
on groundbaiting 437
Blundell, R. C. 18
Blunden, Edmund (*The Pike*)
127
boat-fishing 279–86
accidents 503, *506–7, 507–8*
cross-wind fly-fishing 282
dapping 282–6
Boeotians, eels as sacrificial
offerings for 74, 84
Boiled Barbel in Court
Bouillon (recipe) 21
bomb-link ledger 444
bone-pike (or gar-pike) 131–
3, *131–2*
Book of St Albans 27
*Book of the All-Round Angler,
The see* Bickerdyke, John
Book of the Pike, The see
Cholmondeley-Pennell, H.
*Booke of Fishing with Hooke
and Line, A see* Mascall,
Leonard
Boosey, Thomas (*Piscatorial
Reminiscences and
Gleanings*) on sturgeon
240
Booth, Major W. H., and
record pike 469
Border River Angling see
Lawrie, W. H.
Bourlet, Mr, and cable-hemp
435
Boutargue de mulet (mullet
recipe) 115

Bowen, Charles *371*
bowfin *132, 133*
Bowness, charr in 51
Brailsford, William 373
Braithwaite, G. F.
  (*Salmonidae of
  Westmorland*), on vendace
  340
brandlings (bait) 427, *428*, 431
  for bream 24
bran-paste (bait), for barbel 16
Brathay (r), charr in 50–1
Brazier's Pit, big perch in 119
bread
  paste, for chub 63
  Rye, for sturgeon 242
breadcrumb
  baiting with 425–6
  for barbel 16
  for chub 63
breadcrust
  baiting with 421–5, *425*
  for barbel 16
  diamond-shaped
    compressed 422, *422*
  fishing 422–5, *424*
  for roach 175, 177, 421
  for rudd 183
bream 24–6, *24–7, 186*
  angling methods 24
  baits 24
  baked 27
  British Record 26
  catches 25
  choice of rod 353–4
  cooking 27
  float fishing for *398*
  fossils *26, 125*
  hybrids 181, 184–9, *186*
  pharyngeal teeth *185*
  population pattern 25–6
  stuffed 27
  see also silver bream
Bremettis 28
Brème à la Mode du Pecheur
  (recipe) 27
Brennan, Des, half-blood stop
  knot of *393*
Bridge, Denis, and nymph
  fishing *265*
Bridge pool, Kelso, salmon at
  212
Bridges, Anthony, on cooking
  rudd 189
Bright Waters, Bright Fish see
  Haig-Browne, Roderick
Britannia's Pastorals see
  Browne, William
British Angler's Manual see
  Hofland, T.
British Fishes see Couch,
  Jonathan
*British Maglemose Harpoon
  Sites see* Godwin, H.

British Museum (Natural
  History Department) 131,
  183, 186
British Zoology see Pennant,
  Thomas
Britton, Harry, and Loch
  Lomond 145, 482
Broman, Arne, and big perch
  122
Bromley-Pennell flight 146,
  146
Brookes, Richard (*The Art of
  Angling*) 345
brook trout 329, *329*
Brown, Dr M. E. (*The Trout*)
  298–9
Browne, William (*Britannia's
  Pastorals*), on pike 136
brown trout *60*, 253–97, *253–
  97*
  acid-rain devastation 291–4
  acid-rain problems 287–91
  angling sportsmanship 255–
    62
  Baked Stuffed (recipe) 297
  boat-fishing 279–86
  casting the shooting-head
    271–6, *271–2*
  cooking 297
  crosswind fishing 282
  dapping 282–6, *284–5*
  distribution 253–4
  dry-fly fishing 264–7
  and first-phase liming
    projects 294
  fly fishing 262–86
  and grayling 276
  minnows 269–70, *270*, 463
  nymph fishing 269–70, *270*,
    463
  Oven-Cooked T. and Bacon
    (recipe) 297
  Permaflote 266–7
  rise-forms 277–9
  and sea trout 253
  sedge fishing at dusk 270,
    270, 276
  stillwater fly-fishing 267–9
  tail cf. rainbow trout *326*
  trailing *491, 492*
  trout stream 263–4, 274–6
Bryanston School, chub at 67
Bryant, Arthur (*The Age of
  Chivalry*), on carp 33
Buchan, John (*John MacNab*)
  215
Buckland, Frank (*The
  Natural History of British
  Fishes*)
  on burbot 30
  on catfish 45
  on eels 73, 78, 79, 81, 83
  *A Familiar History of British
    Fishes* 112, 235

  on minnows 112
  on pike 127, 135, 138
  Salmon Fishery report 106
  on skelly 337
  on stickleback 235
  on sturgeon 238
  on tench 245
Buckley, Albert, record carp
  of 36, 41, *42*
bucktail fly, for pike *154*
Buller, Fred (*Pike*)
  and big pike *161*
  on carp 38–9
  on Cepedian pike 131–3
  downrigger *484*
  *Falkus and Buller's
    Freshwater Fishing* (1st
    edn), on eels 87
  on growth record 38–9
  Pike and the Pike Angler 145,
    151
  pike fishing *496*
  on pike gag 405–7, *405–7*
  on plug fishing 475–8
  roach in Suffolk Stour *424*
  salmon of *196, 205, 211, 228*,
    229, *471*
  sea trout of *300*
  Universal Snap Tackle 149
  on visit to China and early
    reels 360–4
bullet lead 396, *397*
bullhead (a.k.a. Miller's
  Thumb) 29, *29*
  and chub 63
  and pike 29
burbot (a.k.a. pout; eel-pout)
  30–2, *30–1*
  cooking 32
  Meunière (recipe) 32
  Provençal Style (recipe) 32
  with Tomatoes and Wine
    (recipe) 32
Burgate, Hampshire Avon 64
Burr, Mr, and tench 245
Burroughs, John (*Locusts and
  Wild Honey*) 295–7
Bushley Meadows, big
  sturgeon at 239
Butler, Peter, on rudd 165
butt (or 'gathering') ring 356
  Chinese long-stemmed *363*

cable-hemp 435
Caine, William (*Fish, Fishing
  and Fishermen*),
  on dusk 264
Carassius carassius see crucian
  carp
Cairncross, D. (*Origin of the
  Silver Eel*),
  beetle theory of 78
Calder (r) 200
Caldwell, Mark, on Swedish

rod-caught record pike
  467
Cam (r), roach/bream hybrids
  in 189
Cambridgeshire, burbot in 30
Canada
  downriggers in 484–9, *484–
    9*
  salmon in *220*, 484–9, 491
  white sturgeon in 240
Canadian bar spoon 470, *472,
  472*
*Canadian Journal of Earth
  Sciences* 125
Capta lead 397, *398*
Carlisle, and skelly 337
carp 33–42, *33–5, 37–9, 41–2*
  catches *34, 35, 36*, 39–42
  choice of rod 353–4
  condition factor 35
  cooking 14, 44
  cf. crucian carp 43
  Delicious (recipe) 44
  determining age of 38–9
  fishing in temperate
    climate 36
  hibernation 34–5
  history 33
  hybrids 184
  pharyngeal teeth *185*
  spawning 34
  strength and cunning of 36
  Walton's (recipe) 44
  see also crucian c.; grass c.;
    leather c.; mirror c.; silver
    c.
Carra, Lough, dapping in 285
Caspian Sea, sturgeon from
  240
Cassey, C., big barbel of 19
casters *see* chrysalids
casting
  shooting-head 271–6
  steeple *305*
Castle Douglas 219
Castle Loch, vendace
  formerly in 338, *339*
Castor mill, sturgeon at 239
catfish 45–8, *45–8*
  catches 45, *46*
  cooking 48
  pre-baiting 46
  spawning 45
  see also American c.; wels c.;
    West African c.
Catherine lead 397, *398*
caviare from sturgeon roe 238,
  240, 242–4
  preparation of 244
Cepedian pike *see* pike,
  Cepedian
Chalmers, Patrick
  The Angler's England 51,
  467–8

Chalmers, Patrick – *cont.*
on charr 49, 51
A Fisherman's Angle 49, 51
on floats 408
on spoon bait 467–8
chance and mischance 493–500
angling luck 493–4
ways of losing fish 494–501
Chapman, Jim, and salmon 487
Charfy, Guiniad (*The Fisherman: or The Art of Angling Made Easy*, appropriation of Saunders *The Compleat Fisherman*)
on eel baits and tackle 85
on eels 77
on fish taken only by strategem 224
on lamprey (pride) 104
on roach 167
charr 49–62, 49–51, 53–62
cooking 62
habits 50–2
migration 49
pots 62
Potted (recipe) 62
spawning 49, 50
traditional tackle and techniques 52–62, 54, 55
Windermere 50–62, 50
see also brook trout
Chenevix Trench, Charles (*A History of Angling*), on early Chinese reels 360, 366
Cheng Chen-To 358
Chepstow fishery 238
Chertsey Bridge 16
Cherwell (r) 200
Chess (r)
grayling 95
rainbow trout 325
Chetham, James (*The Angler's Vade Mecum*)
on alluring ointments 440
on dub-fly hook baits 315
on sea trout by night 306
on worms 427
Child of the Tides see Fahy, Edward
Childs, Frank, and big pike 157
China
built-cane rods in 350
carp in *41*
early reels 358–64, *359–64*
sturgeon and caviare in 240
Chinese Painting: Leading Masters and Principles 359
Chironomids 166
Cholmondeley-Pennell, H. *Angler Naturalist* 128

on bleak 23
The Book of the Pike 153, 467
the Fisherman's Magazine 181
Fishing 74, 79, 368
Fishing Gossip, or Stray Leaves from the Note-books of Several Anglers 99, 102
on gudgeon 99, 102
Pennell tackle 431, *431*, 465
on pike 127–8, *146*, 146, *153*
on pike fry 467
Pike and other Coarse Fish 140, 472
on reels 368
on rudd 181
on spoon-bait 467, 469, 472
Chon, Loch, pike in 154
Chresteleros, Seven Bookes of Epigrames see Bastard, Thomas
Chronicles of the Houghton Fishing Club, The 84, 152, 263
chrysalids (or casters)
baiting with 433
for bleak 22
for bream 24
for dace 68
chub 63–7, 63–7
Annan (r) 67
baits 67
catches 67
choice of rod 353–4
cooking 67
dapping 63–4
fly-fishing 64
food of 63
hybrids 184
and minnows 66, 67
pharyngeal teeth *185*
small, and dace 65, 69
spawning 63
Cicero, on sturgeon 243
circuli 38
Cisco kid plug *478*
Clare, Co. rudd lough in 189
Clarke, Brian (*The Pursuit of Stillwater Trout*) 277
on pike 145
on rise forms 276–7, 277–9
Clarke, Michael 105
Clarke, W. H., dace of 69
Clarke, W. J., on sturgeon 238
Clarke (*Survey of the Lakes*), on skelly 336
Claydon lake
wels catfish in 45
zander in 342
Clayton, Jack, swing-tips of 416, *417*
Clere (r) 264

Clissett, Austen, sliding-float rig of *412*, 413–14
Clogher, Lake, sea trout in 324
Cloone, Lough, on pike growth-rate 135
Clupeidae see shads
Clupeiformes 124
Coarse Fish see Marshall-Hardy, E.
Coarse Angler 467
Coarse Fish 'Briefs' see 'Faddist'
Coarse Fishing see Sheringham, Hugh T.
Cobbledick, A. G. L., and big flounder 89
Cockburn, W. 67
cod, value in medieval England of 13
coffin lead 396, *397*
off Bowen Island, B. Columbia 487
coho salmon, in Lake Michigan 49
Colchester Museum 385
Coldstream, big pike in loch at 157
Coleraine Fisheries Research Laboratory, and pollan 340
Colne (r)
barbel in 15
tench in 247
Colorado spoon 472, *472*
colour
fishes' sense of 263
and identification of fishes 189
Colquhoun, Andrew, and lamprey on fly 105
Comet bait 472
Coming up for Air see Orwell, George
Compleat Angler, The see Walton, Izaak
Compleat Troller or the Art of Trolling, The see Nobbes, R.
Complete Angler's Vade Mecum, The see Williamson, Captain T.
Complete Sportsman, The see Jacob, Giles
condition factor 35
congers, and confusion with anguilla 78, 81
Coniston, Lake, charr in 58
Conn, Lough 105, 285, 469
Cook, Captain 468
Cooke, Reg, fishing drawing *478*
Cooper, A. *120*

Cooper, A. E. (*Sea Fishing*), on flounder 90
Cooper, J. & Sons (taxidermists)
of barbel 18
of burbot 31
of male pike 136
Copais Lake, eels in 74
Coregonidae see whitefishes
Coregonus albula see vendace
Coregonus clupeoides (cluheoides) see powan
Coregonus clupeoides pennantii see gwyniad
Coregonus clupeoides stigmaticus see skelly
Coregonus gracilior see Cumbria, vendace in
Coregonus lavaretus see houting
Coregonus pollan altior see Erne, Lough, pollan in
Coregonus pollan elegans see Derg, Lough, pollan in; Ree, Lough, pollan in
Coregonus pollan pollan see Neagh, Lough, pollan in
Coregonus vendesius see Lochmoben, vendace in
Coregonus vendesius gracilior see Bassenthwaite, vendace in; Derwentwater, vendace in
Corfe, R. C. Hardy, and rudd on dry fly 182
Cork, and Blackwater system, dace in 68
Corrib, Lough
big trout in *256*, 259, 469
dapping in 285
Permaflote in 266
pike in 138, *146*, 146, *152*, 469
Cotton, Charles, and dry-fly fishing 264
Cottus gobio 29
Couch, Jonathan (*British Fishes*)
on bream 28
on burbot 31
on eels 75
A History of British Fishes 103, 128, 237
on pike 128
on sea lamprey 103
on shad 234
on sturgeon 237, 238
on tench 251
Cove, Arthur, reverse swing float of 456, *456*
Cowichan Bay, Vancouver Island, salmon from *489*

Cox, Nicholas (*The Gentleman's Recreation*), on groundbaiting 435–6
Coxon, Henry 373
Coxon-Aerial reel 373, *374*
cradle ring 355
Cragg-Hine, Dr D., on pollan 340
Crane (r) chub in 67
Crawshaw, D. H. 291
Cromer, pike fossils in 124, *126*
Crosbie, R., back rod-rest of *172*
cross-wind fly-fishing 282
Crow, Col.
  big barbel of 19
  and broken leader 497
crucian carp 36n2, 43, *43*
  British Record 43
  hybrids 184
  see also carp
Cruikshank, D. 46
Crull, Dr (*Present State of Muscovy*), on pike 128
Crummock, Lake, charr in 58
crust fishing 422–5
Cumbria
  acid-rain effects on 287–94, *292–3*
  vendace in *331*
  see also Lake District; Windermere
Currane, Lough, charr in 58
current speed and bite indication *447*
Cut (r) 200
cuttyhunk 53
Cyprinidae 15, 52, 165
cyprinid hybrids *see* hybrids
Cyprinus carpio see carp
Czechoslovakia
  catfish in *47*
  roach in 167

dab 89
dabchick, pike and
dace *11*, 68–72
  Bouillabaisse (recipe) 72
  catches 69–70
  choice of rod 353, 354
  cooking 71–2
  hybrids 184
  migration 68
  record 68
  and small chub 65, 69
  spawning 68
Dagenham Breech, big perch in 117
Daniel, Rev. W. B. (*Rural Sports*) 12
  on bullhead 29
  on carp, keeping alive 33
  on dace 69

on lamprey 107
on multiplier 370, *370*
on perch 116, 117
on pike 151
on reel seating 366
on roach 166
on running line 443
on sturgeon 239
on tench 248
on worms 427
Danube (r)
  carp in 41
  'pike-perch' (zander or walleye) in 342
  world record catfish in 45
dapping
  chub 63–4
  trout 282–6, *284–5*
Darmstadt, bone-pike from *133*
Dart, Alan, record eel of *77*
Davies, A. G. 69
Davy, John (*The Angler in the Lake District*) 62
Dee (r), Kirkcudbrightshire
  big pike in 157, *213*
  early harpoon in *385*
  salmon in 213, 219
'Dee' otter *219*
Deekes, D. 67
Defoe, Daniel, on charr 62
Delph (r), eels in 85
Denbigh, Lord, and rainbow trout 325
Dennys, John (*The Secrets of Angling*) 179
  on bleak 22
  on dapping 282
  on rods 347
  on shad etc. 233
  on stealth 215
  on wind 494
Denver Sluice, big eel in 81
Derg, Lough
  big trout in 469
  dapping in 285
  pike in 153, *164*, 469
  pollan in 340
  rudd in 182
Derrick, Charles (*Coarse Fishing*) 95
Derwent (r), barbel in 15
Derwent (r), Cumberland, eels in 78
Derwentwater, vendace in 338
Deveron (r), big salmon in 216
Devon minnow 469, *469*
Dewdney, Canada, big white sturgeon at 240
'diamond-eye' swivel 395, *395*
Diary of an All-Round Angler, The see Smythe, Very Rev. Patrick Murray
Dick, Rev. C. H. (*Highways*

and Byways in Galloway and Carrick) 52
Dickens, Charles (*A Dictionary of the Thames*), on sturgeon 237, 243
Dictionary of the Thames see Dickens, Charles
disgorgers 405–7, *405–7*
Dixon, Albert, and Windermere charr 51–2, *53*, 58, *58*
DNA research on eel 82
Dobob, and roach 178
Docherty, Charles, and pike 145
Dodd, Major G. L. Ashley (*A Fisherman's Log*), on pike 155
dog-fish, as medicine 13
dolphin, as medicine 13
Don
  pollution of 200
  sturgeon in 238
Doncaster Museum, sturgeon in 238
Donegal lough, sea trout from 301
Doon, Loch 52, *52*
Dordogne
  stone carving of salmon in *199*
  sturgeon in 237
dorsal fin, in roach, rudd and hybrids 187, *187*
Double, C. E. 46
Dough-Bobbin 416, *417*, *419*
  and bream 24
  and early-rig *416*
  and roach 175, 178
Dove (r)
  barbel in 15
  grayling in 95
Dowdeswell Reservoir, big pike in *125*
downrigger 482–90, *483–9*
  in action *485*
  Cannon *486*
  for charr 59
  North American 484–5
  Scotty *486*
Drammen (r), world record salmon in 202
Driffield Angler, The see Mackintosh, Alexander
Driffield canal, grayling spawnings in 95, *96*
drilled-bullet lead 396, *397*
Drop-Tackle 479, *479*
Duborgel, Michel (*La Pêche et les Poissons de Rivière*) 20
Dundas, Francis Dummit, and vendace *339*
Dunkeld whisky pot *230*

Dunne, Capt. J. J. (Hi-Regan), and pollan fly 341
Dunne, J. W., black-gnat dressing of 179
Durham rivers, burbot in 30
Dutford Mill, big eel at 81
Dyalogus Creaturarum Moralizatus, on early float 409
Dyson, Colin 467

Eamont (r)
  eels in 83
  skellies in 337
echo-sounder 59, 60, *486*
Eck, Loch, powan from 331
Eden (r)
  dace in 68
  skellies in 337
Edinburgh Journal of Natural and Geographical Science, The see Jardine, Sir W.
Edward I 13
Edward II 238
Edward VII 325
ear bone *see* otolith
eel(s) 73–87, *73–87*
  adoration of by Egyptians 75, *84*
  Agatharchides on 74
  Antiphanes on 75
  Aristophanes, on raking the mud for 85
  Aristotle on 75
  in Athens 75
  -bobber *8*, 85
  British Record 81
  burnt, as medicine 13, 74
  chicken guts 85
  cooking 86
  denigration of 73
  'eye-to-eye' spawning theory 81
  fishing 85
  'glaives' *80*
  handling 86
  Jellied (recipe) 86
  killing 80
  life cycle 75, 84
  medicinal qualities attributed to 74
  migration of American 75, 82
  and minnows 85
  overland migration of 73, 74, *83–4*
  oxygen uptake 84
  -pout *see* burbot
  and pride (as bait) 104
  Roast (recipe) 86
  skinning 86–7, *87*, 146
  spearing 80–1
  stunning 86
  -tail bait 146, *146*, 470
  trap 79

Eel-Stank, eels at 83
Egville, Alan d' (*Calling All Sea-Fishers*), on mullet 113
elderberry
  baiting with 434–5, *435*
  for chub 63
Elements of Angling see Sheringham, Hugh T.
Elliott, Desmond, big trout of *266*, *281*, *477*, *490*
Elstree Reservoir, tench in 248, 249, 251
elvers 75, *76*, 78, 79, 80
Ely, and eels 84
emergency 502–3
Endrick (r), pike in 145
Engelgeer, Willem, big pike of *158*
English Lake District Fisheries see Watson, John
English Recipes and Others see Sheila Hutchins
English Recipes as They Appear in Eighteenth- and Nineteenth-century Cookery Books see Hutchins, Sheila
Eocene 94, 125, 133
'Ephemera' *see* Fitzgibbon, Edward
Ephemeroptera 166
epilimnion 60–1
Erne, Lough, big pike in 157
Erne (r), roach in 165
Escoffier, Georges Auguste
  A Guide to Modern Cookery 21, 31–2
  on barbel 21
  on burbot 31–2
  Ma Cuisine 115
  on mullet 115
  on pike 159
Esk (r)
  and acidic pollution 287–95, *293*
  lamprey from 104
  pike from 133
Eskdale 289, 294
Esocidae 124, 125, 183
Esox americanus see pickerel, redfin
Esox cepedianus 133
Esox lepidotus see 124, 125, *126*
Esox lucius see pike
Esox musquinongy see muskellunge
Esox niger see pickerel, chain
Esox papyraceus 124
Esox reicherti see Amur pike
Esox tiemani 125
Esox vermiculatus see pickerel, gross

Esthwaite Tarn
  roach at 165
  rudd in 184
Eureka reel 374
European catfish *see* wels catfish
eutrophic lakes 52, 165
Ewers, Don, on worms 429
Excursion on the Banks of the Ullswater see Wordsworth, William
Exe (r)
  and Devon minnow 469
  pike in 467
Exeter, Duke of 467
Experienc'd Angler, The. see Venables, Col. Robert
Eyzies, Les, stone carvings of salmon at *199*

Fahy, Edward (*Child of the Tides*), on sea trout 300
failure to cope with fish making off downstream 498–9
Falkland Islands *115*
  sea trout in 298, *322*, *323*
Falkus, Hugh
  'finger-ring' figure-of-eight retrieve 319–21, *320*
  and salmon *199*
  Salmon Fishing 195, 310
  Salmo the Leaper 504
  Sea-Trout Fishing 298, 300
  sea trout of *299*, *301*
  Secret Weapon 316
  The Stolen Years 90, 506
  Sunk Lure *see* sunk-lure fishing, Falkus
  on whitefishes 332
Falkus, Kathleen
Falkus and Buller's Freshwater Fishing (1st edn) *see* Buller, Fred
Far Away and Long Ago see Hudson, W. H.
Farlow's catalogue 79
Farson, Negley (*Going Fishing*) 274
fast water trotting 445–7
fens, zander in 342
Ferox and Char see Hardie, R. P.
Field, The
  on dace 71
  on pike 138, 153–4, 155
Field and Stream 154, 471
Findhorn (r)
  elver migration in 80
  sturgeon in 237
'Finger Disgorger' (for dead fish) 407
'finger-ring' figure-of-eight retrieve 319–21, *320*

Firle, pike at 152
'Fish' *see* Lawrence, D. H.
Fish and Fishing see Manley, Dr J. J.
Fisheries Inn, Elstree 251
Fisheries Research Laboratory, Coleraine 340
Fisher in the Hills 52
Fisherman's Angles, A see Chalmers, Patrick
Fisherman's Log, A see Dodd, Major G. L. Ashley
Fisherman's Magazine, The see Cholmondeley-Pennell, H.
Fisherman's Manual see Moreton, J. P. and Hunter, W. A.
Fisherman, The, or The Art of Angling made Easy see Charfy, Guiniad
Fishermen see Wu Chen
Fishery Commissioners 51
Fishes of the British Isles and N.W. Europe, The see Wheeler, Alwyn
Fish, Fishing and Fishermen see Caine, William
Fishing see Cholmondeley-Pennell, H.
Fishing Experiences of Half a Century see Powell, Major F.
Fishing for Beginners see Wiggin, Maurice
Fishing from the Earliest Times see Radcliffe, William
Fishing Gazette, The
  on charr *61*
  on early Chinese reels 358
  on gudgeon 100
  on lamprey 105
  on pike 129, 131, 153, 156, 157
  on 'pike-perch' (zander or walleye) 342
  on tench 248
  see also Weeger, Emil
Fishing Gossip, or Stray Leaves from the Notebooks of Several Anglers see Cholmondeley-Pennell, H.
Fishing, Its Cause, Treatment and Cure see Sheringham, H. T.
fishing manners 255–62
Fishing Pike and other Coarse Fish see Cholmondeley-Pennell, H.
fishing shelter *316*
fishing too fine 495

Fitzgibbon, Edward (*A Handbook of Angling*)
  on chub 67
  on pike 152, 156
Fitzmaurice, Patrick 58
Fitz-Stephen, on sturgeon 238
Fleming, Sir Daniel 62
flights, deadbait 146–7, *146–7*
float-fishing 445–53
  for bream *398*
  choice of rod 353–4
  fast-water trotting 445–7, *446–7*
  floating crust link rig *452*, 453
  float-link rig 449–53
  lift method 250, 447–9, *448*
  for tench 250
  see also laying-on; stret-pegging
float-ledgering 16, 143, 172, 442, 454–7, *455*
  with polycone 440
  see also ledgering
float-link, for flounder 89
float(s) 408–20
  basic uses of 408
  bite indicators 415–18
  for bream 24
  Buller/Falkus design *451*, 453
  colour *409*, 409–10
  cork, and tench 246
  Cove's reverse swing 456, *456*
  design and function 410–15, *411*
  early illustration *409*
  for flounder 89
  fluted 98, 414
  for gudgeon 99
  for pike *142*, 143–4, *414*
  sliding (Billy Lane's) 412, 440
  swing-tips 418–20
Floating Lure 314
flounder (or fluke) 88–93, *88–92*
  baited spoon for 89–90
  British Record 89
  cooking 91, 93
  feeding 91, *91–2*
  migration 88
  spawning 88
fludra 88
fluke *see* flounder
fly fishing in history 262–3
Fly-Fisher's Guide, The see Bainbridge
Fly Fishing see Grey, Sir Edward
Fly-Fishing in Salt and Fresh Water 157

fly-spoon bait 471, *471*
Foix, Gaston de (*Livre de Chasse*), on otters *218*
Fore-and-aft Glowstickle (fly dressing) 275, *275*
Fortin, François (*Les Ruses innocentes*), on landing net 399
Fowey, Cornwall, and flounder 89
Foyle (r), roach in 165
Francis, Francis (*A Month in the West*)
on bleak 23
on perch 123
Frain, R. (*Rob o' The Trows*) *348*
Franck, Richard, on pike 125
Frangipane Panada (pike recipe) 160
Fraser (r) Canada, white sturgeon in 240
Freshwater Biological Association 50, 128
freshwater mussels, catfish pre-baiting with 516
Friandaise, Manuel de la 44
Fried Bleak (recipe) 23
frogs (bait)
for chub 63
for pike 125
Froissart, Jean 218
Frost, Dr Winifred E.
on charr 50
on eels 81
on pike 127, 135–6, 138
The Trout 298–9
Frying-pan sea-trout pool, Falkland Islands *322*
Fuller, Thomas, on monks and eels 84

Gade (r), dace in 70
Gade, Lord, pike of 152
gags and disorders 405–7, *405–7*
Galen, on gudgeon 101
Game Birds and Wild Fowl see Knox
Gammarus 166
Gardyne, 'Jock' Bruce, salmon of *205*
Garonne (r) sturgeon in 237
gar-pike *see* bone-pike
Garrard, P. (*Sea Angling with Baited Spoon*), on flounder 89
Garvin, John, record Irish pike of 135
Gasterosteus aculeatus see three-spined stickleback
Gasterosteus pungitius 235
'gathering' (or butt) ring 356

Gay, John
on gilt-tail 437
on gudgeon 100
General Zoology Pisces see Shaw, George
Geneva, charr at 49–50
Genteel Recreation, The see Whitney, John
Gentleman's Recreation, The see Cox, Nicholas; Blome, Richard
Germany
introduction of catfish from 46
pike in *144*
gillies, salmon and 228–30
Gilbert, William (*The Angler's Delight*)
on paste 429
on trolling 481
Gilbey, Arthur *348*, *480*
Giles, William, pike of *136*
Gill, J. 71
gillaroo 254
gill bone *see* opercular
gill-maggots *197*
gilt-tail 427, *428*
Ginther, Garnet, and big white sturgeon 240
Glasgow University, Loch Lomond research at 332
Glasse, Mrs, flounder recipe 93
glass-eel *76*
Glencullen Lough, Co. Galway 296
Glendelvine on Tay (r), record salmon in *217*
glowbobbin 36
Gmelin (*Voyage en Sibérie*) 238
Gobio gobio see gudgeon
Godwin, H. (*British Maglemose Harpoon Sites*)
on pike remains 385
Going Fishing see Farson, Negley
golden mullet 113
Gollins, Will (big bream) 26
gorge deadbait tackle 479, *479*, *480*, *481*
Gorge d'Enfer, stone carving of salmon at *199*
grabble, to lie upon 85
Grafham Reservoir
big pike in 157–8
trout in *257*, *279*
'graining', and dace 68
Grant, Edwin *111*
grass carp 41
grasshoppers
for chub 63
for trout 286
Gray, L. R. N. (*Torridge*

Fishery), on enthusiasm 463
Gray, Rev. Tom Secombe, big pike of 470
Grayling see Righyni, R. V.
grayling 94–8, *94–7*
Baked (recipe) 98
British Record 94
and brown trout 276
cooking 98
Grilled (recipe) 98
spawning 94–5, *96*
tackle 98
Grays, Essex, early spade-end hook at 385
Great Lakes, Canada
downrigger in 485, *486*
salmon in 59, *486*
great lake trout 50, 254
Greeks, and love of eels 73–5
Greene, Harry Plunkett (*Where the Bright Waters Meet*), on trout 254
green sturgeon *see* sturgeon, common
Greffern gravel pit, Germany, big pike in *492*
Grey, Sir Edward (*Fly Fishing*) 17
grey mullets 113–15, *113–15*
Baked (recipe) 115
cooking 115
migration 113
Poached (recipe) 115
Roe (recipe) 115
spawning 113
tackle 114
thick/thin lipped 113, *114*
Greystoke, Cumbria eels at 83
Griggs, W. P. (taxidermist) 31
gross conversion rate of food, in pike, plaice, trout 130
groundbaiting 435–41
barbel 15–16
bream 24
chub 64
dace 68–9
devices 437–9
functions of 436
grayling 98, *276*
marker buoy 440–1
polycone (maggot) swimfeeder 439–40
roach 168, 174–5, 177, 182
rudd 182
growth-checks (annuli) 38, 136
growth record of fish 38
Guadalquivir (r), Spain, sturgeon in 237
gudgeon *11*, 99–102, *99–101*
bait and tackle 99
as bait for pike 127
and barbel 17

British Record 99
and chub 63
cooking 101–2
'Gudgeon Fishing, or He's Fairly Hook'd' *see* Wilson, T.
Guide to Modern Cookery see Escoffier, Georges Auguste
gulf stream, eels and 80
Gunther, Dr (of British Museum),
on eels 84
on tench 245
gwyniad 299, 330, 336
Gymnocephalus cernus see ruffe

Haig-Brown, Roderick (*Bright Waters, Bright Fish*) 329
Halls, G., record carp of 43
half-moon lead 397, *397*
Ham Mill Pool *18*
Hampshire Avon, The see Vesey-Fitzgerald, Brian
Handbook of Angling, A see Fitzgibbon, Edward
Hanningfield Reservoir
perch on the fly *121*
rainbow trout *327*
Hardie, R. P. (*Ferox and Char*), on charr 50
Harding, Mr (Stour fisherman) 67
Hardy, W. F.
ledgering for roach *443*
and multiplier *372*
Hardy Bros
Angler's Guide 349
bale-arm pick-up 376
multiplier *372*
pike drop-tackle *481*
Hargreaves, Barbara (*The Sporting Wife*)
bream (recipe) 27
carp (recipe) 44
Harlesden Angling Society *172*
Harrigan, Jack, and barbel baiting 433
Harvest, Rev. George 100
Hastings, Dr (*Natural History of Worcestershire*), on sturgeon 239
Hatton, Herbert, and yellow belly 468
Haweswater, skelly in 336, *337*, 337
Hawker, Col. Peter (*Instructions to Young Sportsmen*)
on angling 267
spinning with natural bait 467

Hawkins, Sir John (*The Compleat Angler*, 1754 ed.), on lines 381
Hayter, Mr (warden, Christchurch Royalty (F)) 17, 18
Heddon plugs (Commando, Crazy Crawler, Deep Dive River Runt Spook, Lucky 13, Vamp, Vamp Spook) 476–8
hempseed, stewed
  attaching *433*
  baiting with 433–4
  for barbel 15–16
  cable- 435
  for chub 63
  for dace 63
  and elderberry 434–5, *435*
Hendersyde (r), salmon in *201*
Henry I
  and sturgeon 237
  and surfeit of lampreys 107
herring bait
  for pike 140–1, *142*
  for salmon 488
  see also shads
'Herring Magic, The' 491
Hertford Museum, dace in 69
Heysham, Dr (*Hutchinson's History of Cumberland*), on skellies 337
Higgins, Stephen 465
Highways and Byways in Galloway and Carrick see Dick, Rev. C. H.
Hillman lead *397*, 397, 459–61
Hills, John Waller (*A Summer on the Test*), and 'inventive' angling 439
Hi-Regan *see* Dunne, Capt. J. J.
Historical Sketches of the Angling Literature see Blakey, Robert
History of Angling, A see Chenevix Trench, Charles
History of British Fishes see Thompson, J.
History of British Fishes, A see Yarrell, William
History of Earliest Chinese Painting see Siren, O.
History of Life and Death, A see Bacon, Sir Francis
History of the Fishes of the British Islands, A see Couch, Jonathan
Hoare, Sir Frederick *129*
Hofland, T. (*British Angler's Manual*)
  on brass reels 374

on multiplying reels 370
Hogg, Willie, on 'Dee' otter 219
Holding, G. R. 375
holding fish too hard 497
Holland, big pike in *158*
Hollar, W. (*Salmon Fishing* engraving) 216
Home, Lord, and big pike 157
Homer 'Flick 'em' reel 374
hooks
  barbel 15, 16
  broken 494–5
  carp straight-eyed 36
  catfish 46
  caught in landing net 498
  charr *55*
  for crumb 426
  for crust fishing 424
  design 384–6, *385–6*
  failure 494–5
  failure to retie 495
  grayling 98
  gudgeon 99
  hempseed 434
  historical 384, *385*
  hoods 473, *473*
  loses its hold 494
  patterns *386*
  powan 333
  sea-trout lures 310–17
  sharpness 384
  sizes 387, *387*
  straightened 495
  for worms 431–2
Hornsey Mere, big roach in *176*
hot-spots 282
Houghton Fishing Club 152, 469
Hougsund, world record salmon at 202
houting 330–8, *331,333,336–7*
  see also gwyniad; powan; skelly
How to Catch Coarse Fish see Matthews, A. R.
Howes, Colin 9
Howlett, Robert (*The Angler's Sure Guide*) 14
  on luminous float 175
  on pike 150, 159
  on rod bell *415*
  and salmon 202
Hsiung Ting 362
Hudson, W. H. (*Far Away and Long Ago*), on shads 234
Hughes, Gerry, big perch of 118–21
Hughes, Ted (*Pike*), 129
Hughes, William (*The Practical Angler*), on groundbaiting 435

Hull (r), minnows in 112
Humphrey, R. W., record dace of 69
Hunstrete Lake, record eel in 77
Hunter, W. A. *see* Moreton, J. P.
Hurley, roach-poling at *172*
Hutchins, Sheila
  English Recipes and Others 91, 93
  English Recipes as They Appear in Eighteenth- and Nineteenth-century Cookery Books 251
  on flounder 91, 93
  on tench 251
Hutchinson's History of Cumberland see Heysham, Dr
hybrids (bream/roach/rudd) 184–9
  pharyngeal teeth of *184*, *185*
hypolimnion 60

Ibbotson, Albert, and Yorkshire Specimen Group 133
Ibsley 19
ice-fishing of charr *56*
Ijssel lake, zander from *343*
Illingworth, Alfred Holden, early fixed-spool reel of 375, *375*
Illustrated Sporting and Dramatic News 164
In-Fisherman magazine 373
Ingham, Maurice (artist) 35
Inglemere Pond 128
Inland Fisheries Trust, Ireland 58, 127, *143*
Instructions to Young Sportsmen see Hawker, Col. Peter
Introduction to the History of Science see Sarton, G.
Ireland (lakes)
  charr in 49, 58
  dace in 68
  pike in 136
  roach in 165
  rudd in 181, 184
Isospondyli 330
Itchen (r)
  big grayling in 94, 95
  Richard Walker fishing in *430*
Ivel (r), Bedfordshire, dace in 70

Jacob, Giles (*The Compleat Sportsman*) 22
Jacques, David, on loss of fish 495

Jardine, Alfred (*Pike and Perch*)
  pike 127, 157
  snap tackle *148*, 387
  trolling 480
Jardine, Sir W. (*The Edinburgh Journal of Natural and Geographical Science*)
  on lampreys 103
  on vendace 340
Jardine lead 397, *397*
jaw-spear, for eels 81
Jeffries, Richard 217
Jim Vincent Spoon 472, *472*
John MacNab see Buchan, John
Johnsnon, Dr L., on food consumption of pike 128, 130
Jones, William (*May Fly Fishing*) 263
Jordan, Dr (curator, Tring Museum) 25
Journey Across Russia see McDowell, Bart
Junction Pool, salmon in 225
juxtaposition of lips 189
jumping back again, fish 499–500

Keal, William
  big trout of *492*
  carp catch of *34*
Keating, G. *117*
Keel Lough, Co. Mayo 286
keepnets 403–4, *403–4*
  hole in 498
Kelly, Martin *153*
Kelsey, W. (big barbel) 18
Kelso
  flounder at 90
  salmon at *212*
Ken, Loch
  pike in 151, 213, 385
  salmon from 229
Kendall, William, on pike 128
Kenmure monster (pike) 213, 385
Kennedy, Michael (*The Sea Angler's Fishes*) on pike 127, 135, *143*
Kennet (r)
  barbel in 15, *18*
  big eel in 81
  dace in 70
  grayling in 95
  tench in 247
Kennet and Avon Canal
  dace in 70
  groundbaiting in 436
kidney bar-spoon 147, 470, *470*
kill devil Devon bait 470, *470*

Killin, pike at *129*
kilner jar, compressed
  breadcrust 422
Kipling, Dr C., on pike 138
Kirkudbright and early
  harpoon *385*
Kirpichnikov, on carp
  condition factor 35
Kite, Major Oliver, artificial
  nymph of 265
kittens and pike 125
knots 388–95
  backing splice 388
  backing to reel 388, 394
  blood bight loop *392*
  bowline *391*
  bucket k. *388*
  double-grinner *390*
  figure-of-eight k. *392*
  grinner (Fisherman's k.) *390*
  half-blood k. *393*
  hangman's jam knot *394*
  needle k. *393*
  sliding stop k. *392*
  spade-end k. *389*
  Stewart and Pennell tackle k.
    391
  Turle k. *389*
  undoing a tangle *394*
  water k. *390, 391*
  whip finish *392*
  wind *495*
Knott End Farm Fishery,
  Eskdale 289
Knox (*Game Birds and Wild
  Fowl; their Friends and
  their Foes*), on pike 152
Konigsee, Lake, charr in 50
Krischker, Herr and father,
  world record catfish 45
Kunming Lake, China, carp
  in 41
Kynoch killer plug *477*

LaCépède 133, 331
Ladoga, Lake (Leningrad)
  ice fishing in 56
  sturgeon in 237
Lake and Loch Fishing see
  Lane, Jocelyn
Lake District
  charr in 49, 50–62, 472
  dace in 68
  roach in 165
  rudd in 184
  skelly in 336, 337
Lamond, Henry (*Loch
  Lomond*), on lampreys 105
lampern *see* lamprey, river
Lampetra fluviatilis see
  lamprey, river
Lampetra planeri see lamprey,
  brook
lamprey 103–9, *103, 104, 106*

Baked (recipe) 107
brook (or planer's) *104*, 105
  cooking 107
  pride 103, *104*
  river (or lampern) *104*, 104–
    5, *106*
  sea 103–4, *104*
  spawning 103
  Stewed (recipe) 107
Lancashire, dace in 68
landing net 399–402
  ancient 399–400
  carp *34*, 36
  design *400*
  function *401*
  hole in 498
  hook caught in 499
  modern 400–2
  simple method of carrying
    400
Lane, Billy, sliding float of
  412, 440
Lane, Jocelyn (*Lake and Loch
  Fishing*)
  on overland migration of eels
    83–4
Lasqueti Island, chinook
  salmon off 487
Lauson, William, on dapping
  282
Lawrence, D. H. ('Fish' from
  Birds, Beasts and Flowers),
  on pike 124
Lawrie, W. H. (*Border River
  Angling*) 316–17, *316*
laying-on 457
  of barbel 16
  of bream 24
  of roach 179
lazy-line, for charr 57, *58*
Lea (r)
  barbel in 15, 17
  deformed roach 134
  roach-poling in 170
  trolling for pike 480
leader
  burned with cigarette end
    498
  cut by gaff stroke 497
  knot jams 497
  nipped in joint of landing net
    498
Leaders, reservoir 267
leads 396–8
  Arlesey bomb 396–7, *397*
  charr-plumb-weight 53–5
  design *397*
  function 396–8
  Hillman 397, *397*, 459–61
  shot chart *398*
Leary, Dan, big pike of *142*
leather carp 40, *41*, 42
  see also carp
leather eel-tail bait 470, *470*

'ledger-bait', and eels 85
ledgering 442–4
  barbel 16
  bomb-link 444
  bream 24
  catfish 46
  choice of rod 353–4
  eels 85
  flounder 89
  historical 442–3, *442*
  pierced bullet 443–4
  roach 173–5
  rudd 184
  salmon 227
  shot-link 444
  with spoke-reel in China *363*
  tench 249
  see also float-ledgering
Leighton Buzzard lake,
  zander at 342
Leman, Lac, charr in 49–50,
  61, 62
Leptic Magna mosaics,
  landing net in 399
leptocephalus 75, *76*, 80
  brevirostris 79
Leuciscus cephalus see chub
Leuciscus leuciscus see dace
Leven, Loch, boat fishing in
  279
Life in Lakes and Rivers see
  Worthington, E. B. and
  Macan, T.
lift-fishing 179
  see also float fishing, lift
  method
Liger (*Amusements de la
  Campagne*) 366
Lihou, Ron 487
Likhvinsk inter-glacial
  deposits 26
Lilleymere, Lake, charr in
  52
Limanda limanda (dab) 89
liming projects in Spothow
  Gill 294–5
Lincolnshire
  burbot in 30
  pike in 130
line(s) 378–83, *378, 383*
  AFTM code 381–2
  braided nylon 379
  broken by fish 495
  discarded nylon, danger of
    382, *382–3*
  filling fixed-spool reel 380,
    380–1
  fly-l. 381–2
  horsehair *380*
  line/back splice draws 498
  line-winder 379
  monofilament nylon 378
link-ledger, for grayling 98
Linnaeus, Carl 88

Livre de Chasse see Foix,
  Gaston de
Liyu (*A Poem of Silk and a
  Fisherman*, from
  Fisherman's Song) 362
Llandogo, sturgeon at 238
lobworms
  baiting with *426*, 427–8, *428*
  for barbel 15, 16, 18
  for bream 24
  care of 430–1
  for eels *8*
  for perch 116
Loch Lomond see Lamond,
  Henry
*Loch Lomond and Its
  Salmon see* Wood, Ian
Lochmaben, vendace in 331,
  334, 338, 338–9
Locusts and Wild Honey see
  Burroughs, William
Loddon (r), barbel in 15
Lomond, Loch
  big perch in 117
  flounder in 90
  lamprey in 104–5
  pike in 141–4, *145, 406*, 457,
    507
  powan in *331*, 331–5
  roach in 165, *443*
  trailing in 470, *482*
London Angling Association
  43
London Zoo, carp in 39
long-blade spoons 147
Longfellow, Henry
  Wadsworth (*The Song of
  Hiawatha*), on sturgeon
  242
long-trotting
  bream 24
  choice of rod 354
  chub 64
Lota lota see burbot
Louis, Lothar, and big pike
  492
Low Shaw Pool, big salmon
  in *216*
Lowkes, Samuel 373
Lowrance
  Computer Graph echo
    sounder *486*
  digital depth-sounder *488*
Lucas-Tooth, Sir Hugh 64
luck 493–4
Lumbricus terrestris see
  lobworm
luncheon-meat (bait), for
  barbel 16
Lunn, William, and wagtail
  bait 469
Luss Water, lampreys in 105
lying on the grabble, for eels
  85

Lyng gravel pit, big pike from *142*

Macan, T. *see* Worthington, E. B.
macaroni, as food for chub 63
McDowell, bart (*Journey Across Russia*), on Kaluga sturgeon 242
McElrath, Albert, deadbait (sprat) spinning mount of 468, *468*
McElrath, Norman 205
McElrath family, and salmon 201
mackerel spoon 472, *472*
Mackintosh, Alexander (*The Driffield Angler*) 164
maggots
  attaching *433*
  baiting with 432–3, 439
  for barbel 16, *434*
  for bream 24
  care of 432
  for chub 63
  for dace 68–9
  for grayling 98
  polycone swimfeeder 439–40, *440*
  for roach 166
  for tench 248
mahseer 15, *19*
  see also barbel
Maidstone, big sturgeon near 239
Maitland, Dr P. S., and vendace *338*
Mälaren, Lake, pike and perch in *466*
Malia, Thomas, big trout of 491
Malloch, Peter, fixed spook reel of 375, *375*, 376
Manley, Dr J. J. (*Notes on Fish and Fishing*) 7
  on bleak 22
  on bream 28
  on dace 71
  on gudgeon 99, 100, 102
  on skelly 337
  on tench 245, 246, 249, 251
Man May Fish, A see Moore, T. C. Kingsmill
Mansfield, Kenneth (ed. *The Art of Angling*), on grayling 95
Manych (r), Som catfish in 48
Mapperley Reservoir, carp in *42*
margin-fishing
  for carp 36
  for rudd 183
marker-buoy, groundbait 440–1, *441*

Markham, Gervase (*The Pleasures of Princes*)
  on bait-horn 423
  on landing net 399
  on lines 378
  on rod material 346, 348
Marryat-Interfly tackle, charr *61, 62*
Marshall-Hardy, E. (*Coarse Fish*) 17
  on 'bread buoys' 183
  on chub 63
  on grayling 94, 98
  on rudd taking times 182
marshworm 427, *428*
Marson, Charles (*Super Flumina*)
  on dace 72
  on livebait, elastic support 148
Marston, R. B. 131, 248, 461, 481
Marsworth reservoir
  bream in 25
  catfish in *46*
Martial, on fly fishing 262
Martin, J. W. ('Trent Otter')
  deadbait flight 147
  roach fishing 165
Mary, Queen of Scots, and vendace 339
Mascall, Leonard (*A Booke of Fishing with Hooke and Line*), on carp 33
Mask, Lough
  big pike in 127, *141, 143*n, 469
  big trout in 55, 58, *266, 279–81, 469, 490, 492*
  charr in 58, *59*, 477
  dapping on *284, 285*
  pike cannibalism in 127
  pike growth rate in 135
Mason, David, deformed pike of 133
match fishermen 118, *436*
Matthews, A. R. (*How to Catch Coarse Fish*), big dace 70–1
Mayer, A. (*Sport with Gun and Rod*)
  on loss of fish *493*
  on multiplier *371*
mayflies and roach 166
May Fly Fishing see Jones, William
Ma Yuan (*Angler on a Wintry Lake*)
  early keepnet *403*
  early reel 358, *359*
medicine, fish as 13
Medicine (lure) 307–10, *308*
Medieval Technology and Social Change see White, Lynn

Medway (r)
  barbel in 15
  sturgeon in 239
Medway (r), Nova Scotia, salmon in 220
Medwin, Thomas (*The Angler in Wales, or Days and Nights of Sportsmen*), on chub 66
Meek, Benjamin F. & Sons, multiplying reel of *371*
Meiklejohn, Professor J. M. D. (*A New History of England and Great Britain*), on lampreys 107
Melvin, Lough, charr from *51*
Mepps spoon 471, *471*
Mersey (r) 200
Messel, bone pike from *131, 132, 133*
Messina, Straits of, *Leptocephalus brevirostris* in 79
Metropolitan Barn Elms reservoir, perch and ruffe disease 190
mice and pike 125
Michigan, Lake, coho salmon in 49
midge and roach 166
Milbourn, Jos *121, 423*
Mill Loch, vendace in *334, 338*
Miller, Jim, and salmon 199
Miller's Thumb *see* bullhead
minnows 110–12, *110–12*
  and barbel 17
  and chub 67
  cooking 112
  and eels 69, 85
  Muddler, and rainbow trout *328*
  and perch 117, 119
  and pike *146*
  spawning 110
Miocene, Upper 124, 125
Mirimichi (r), salmon in *204*
mirror carp 39, 40, 41, 42
  see also carp
Misbourne (r), rainbow trout in 325
Mitchell fixed-spool reel *376*
Modern Angler, The see Salter, Robert
Modern Cookery for Private Families see Acton, Eliza
Moira, Count de, paternoster of *461*
Mole (r), gudgeon in 100
Molesey Reservoir, record roach in *166*
Mollusca 166
Mona's Scale, and pike 133

Month in the West, A see Francis, Francis
Moor, Frank *146*
Moor, Thomas, and big pike *146*
Moore, F. C. 375
Moore, T. E. Kingsmill (*A Man May Fish*) 324
Mordaunt, H. J., big grayling of 95
Mordland, G. *118*
Moreton, J. P. and Hunter, W. A. (*Fisherman's Manual*), on grayling 98
Morgan, Pierpoint, big tench of 247
Morgan, Tommy, record pike of 145
'Morgan's Bay', Loch Lomond *145*
Morison, Mrs, big salmon of 216
Morris, Sean 29
Morton (*Natural History of Staffordshire*) 239
Moscow
  ice-fishing in 56
  University 125
Moser, Herr (taxidermist), of catfish *48*
Mossop, Samuel S. 105
mount, deadbait 146–7, *146–7*
mud-raking for eels 85
Mugilidae 113
Mugil capito see thin-lipped mullet
Mugil labrosus see thick-lipped mullet
mullet
  burnt as medicine 13
  grey *see* grey mullets
Mullins's tackle 148
multiple charr-tackle 61, *61*
Mundella, Mr 11
Murray, James 50
Murray and Hjört, on development of European eel 76
mussels, freshwater, and catfish pre-baiting 46
muskellunge 124

nacre 22
National Fish Culture Association of Great Britain 342
Natural History of British Fishes, The see Buckland, Frank
Natural History of Ireland see Thompson, W.
Natural History of Staffordshire see Morton

Naturalist 238
Naylor, Deryck, deformed
 pike of *134*
Nazeing, Essex, big perch at
 119
Neagh, Lough, pollan in 332,
 340, 340–1
Neave, Arnold, and
 Permaflote 266
Needham, Dr Joseph (*Science
 and Civilisation in China*)
 9, 358
 and Chinese fishing reels *360*
 on Chinese fishing 'wheel'
 364
Ness, Loch, charr in 50
nets 399–404, *399–404*
 see also keepnets; landing
 nets
netting a fish 401–2, *401–2*
Newberry, P. E. (*Beni
 Hassan*), earliest picture
 of angling *346*
New Brunswick salmon angler
 204
*New Fisherman's
 Encyclopaedia* 468
*New History of England and
 Great Britain, A see*
 Meiklejohn, Professor
 J. M. D.
New Scientist 202
New Sporting Magazine 120
Nicholsons of Bowness, charr
 of 53
Nidd (r), barbel in 15
Nikolsky, Professor G. V.
 (*The Ecology of Fishes*)
 on bream and perch fossils
 117, 125
 on perch 116
Nile (r) 348
Nobbes, R. (*The Compleat
 Troller, or The Art of
 Trolling*)
 on artificial bait 467
 on swing-tip 418–20
 on trailing 481
Norfolk, pike at 136
Norfolk Broads
 pike in *155*, 472
 rudd in 181
Normanton, Lord 19
North Atwick, pike remains
 and harpoon heads at 385
North Sea, big sturgeon in
 242
North Wales (lakes), charr in
 49
North West Water Authority
 Scientists' Department
 291, 294
northern pike (American) *see*
 pike

Norway
 dace in 68
 salmon in *200*
Norwich spoon 472, *472*
nose-cone trailing tackle 491
Notes on Fish and Fishing see
 Manley, Dr J. J.
Nottingham type reels *see*
 reels, Nottingham type
nylon
 discarded, dangers of 382,
 382–3
 line burned with cigarette
 end 498
 monofilament 328
 weakened 500
nymph fishing, stillwater 269–
 70, *270*
Nyn (r), sturgeon in 239

O'Connor, Terence 202–3
Oeningen, pike fossils at 124,
 125
O'Gorman (*The Practice of
 Angling*, Vols I and II)
 on eyed-hook 384
 on Irish eel-fishermen 80
 on lawyers as anglers 203
 on lobsters from fleas 192
 on multiplying reels 370
 on perch, effect of music on
 117
 on tadpole heresy 196
 on tench for the table 251
O'Grady, Robbie 477
oligotrophic lakes 52
olive dun *277*
on the drop, taking bream 24
Open Creel, An see
 Sheringham, H. L.
opercular (gill bone) reading
 of carp and pike 38–9, *38*,
 135–6
Oppian, on eels 75, 107
Opuszynski, on elver
 migration 80
Origin of the Silver Eel see
 Cairncross, D.
Orkney sea trout 254
Orrin Falls, salmon jumping
 in 196
Orvieto (Etruscan angler) *345*
Orwell, George (*Coming up for
 Air*), on carp 39–40
Osmerus eperlanus see sparling
Osnabruck hatchery, rainbow
 trout from 325
Ossiacher Lake, Austria,
 catfish in 48
otolith (ear bone) reading 38
otters *218*
 'Dee' *219*
Ouse, Great (r)
 barbel in 15

burbot in 31
 chub 67
 eel in 81
 pollution in 202–3
 rudd 181
 zander 342
Ouse, Little (r) 6
 dace in 69
Oxford Dictionary, on
 gudgeon 100
*Oxford English Dictionary of
 Etymology* 228
Oxford Scientific Films 29
oxygen content of water 58,
 60–1, 219

Pacific Ocean, salmon in 485
Palaeoperca 133
palm nuts, and catfish 46
Parker, Captain L. A., on
 Hampshire Avon *446*
Parks, Peter 29
Parnell, Dr, on powan 332
parr 192–3, 198
Parrett (r)
 pollution of 200
 sturgeon in 237
Parson, Grahame, big pike of
 138
Parsonstown, big pike in
 lough at *157*
'Party Angling, A' *118*
paste (bait), for bream 24
paternoster(ing) 459–62, *459*
 bleak 22
 Count de Moira's beam p.
 461
 for flounder 89
 for perch 117
 for pike 127, *148*
 for powan *333*
 sliding bubble-float 459–61,
 460
 standing pike p. 461–2, *462*
Patterson, Leo, big sturgeon
 of *241*
Payne-Gallwey, Sir R. 469
pear (or paternoster) lead *397*,
 398
Pearson, William, and barbed
 harpoon *385*
Pechum, John (enthronement
 feast) 99
peg-bell 415
Peking, and early Chinese
 reels 360–1
Pennant, Thomas (*British
 Zoology*)
 on perch 117
 on pike's age 135
 on sturgeon 237
 on vendace 339
Penney, W., British record
 roach of *166*

Penzance, grey mullet at 115
perca fluviatilis see perch
perch *11*, 116–23, *116–23*
 angling methods 117–21
 in Arlesey Lake 397
 and bleak 23
 and charr 51
 choice of rod 353–4
 cooking 123
 distribution 116
 feeding habits 116
 fossils *117*, 125
 Fried P. (recipe) 123
 Lakeside (recipe) 123
 and minnows 117, 119
 -ruffe hybrids 190
 spawning 116
 and worms 116
Permaflote 266–7, *266*
Percidae 342
Petromyzon marinus see
 lamprey, sea
Petterill (r), overland
 migration of eels in 83
Phantom bait 469, *469*
pharyngeal teeth *184–5*
Phillippe, Samuel, split cane
 rods of 349
pH values 289–95
Phoxinus phoxinus see
 minnow
pickerel 13, 338
 chain p., grass p. and redfin
 p. 124
pierced-bullet ledger 443–4
Piers of Fulham 13
 on eels 86
 Manuscript Poem 86
 on weather 494
pike *11*, 124–64, *124–64*
 age 134–8, *135*
 Amur 124
 in antiquity 124–5
 appetite 125–30
 and bleak 23
 and bullhead as food 29
 camouflage 133, *139*
 cannibalism in 127, *129*
 Cepedian p., riddle of *131*,
 131–3
 choice of rod 353, 354–5
 cooking 159–64
 deadbait flights and mounts
 146–7, *146–7*
 deadbait ledgering 140–7,
 143, *146–7*
 deformity 133–4
 diet 125–30
 fecundity 135–8
 feeding habits 138–40, 162
 filleting *163*
 Fishcakes (recipe) 162, 164
 fly fishing for 150–8, *153–7*
 fossils 124–5, *126*, 131–3, *132*

pike – *cont.*
gaffing 138
gags 405–7, *405–7*
à la Génevèse (recipe) *159*
gross conversion rate 130
livebaiting 139, 147–9, *150*
Loch Lomond rig 141–4
minnows *146*
northern 124
paternoster 461–2, *462*
plug fishing 475–8
record rod-caught 466, 467
rigs and tackles 147–9, *148–9*
saddle tackles 147–9, *148*
and salmon 213
senses 138–40
spawning 135–8
on spinning bait *466, 467*
and tench 147
trolling 480
Universal snap tackle 149, *149*
value in medieval England of 13–14
wobbling 147
Pike see Buller, Fred; Hughes, Ted
Pike, The see Blunden, Edmund
Pike and Other Coarse Fish see Cholmondeley-Pennell, H.
Pike and the Pike Angler see Buller, Fred
'Pike fishing at Killaloe' *164*
pin rowlocks, for charr fishing *57, 57*
pinched-crumb (bait), for bream 24
Piper, John
early fixed-spool reel 375
and perch 120
Piscatorial Reminiscences and Gleanings see Boosey, Thomas
Piscatorial Society 18, *51,* 70, 260
Pitchford, Denys Watkins, on roach 167
Pitsford Reservoir, record rudd in 183
plaice
and flounder 89
gross conversion rate 130
plain spoon 472, *472*
plankton
and charr 50–2
and perch 116
Platichthys flesus see flounder
Pleasures of Princes, The see Markham, Gervase
Pleuronecteo platessa see plaice

Pliny
on eels 76
on sturgeon 243
plug fishing 474–8
floating p. 475–8, *475*
selection of p. 476–8
Plum, Frank 361, 504
plumbline fishing, for charr 52, 53, 58, 59
Plumridge, T. *46*
Plutarch
on choice of horsehairs 380
on choice of rod 347
poaching implements *218*
Poem of Silk and a Fisherman, A see Liyu
Poland, wels catfish in 45
pollan 299, 330, 340–1
fishing 341
in Lough Ree 340
Pollard, James (*Trolling for Pike in the River Lea,* painting) 479, *480*
pollution *see* acid-rain pollution; river pollution
polycone (maggot) swimfeeder 439–40, *440*
pope *see* ruffe
pout *see* burbot
powan 299, 330–6, *331, 333*
angling 332–6
powdered beef, as bait for eels 78
Powell, Major F. (*Fishing Experiences of Half a Century*), on grasshopper 286
Practical Angler, The see Stewart, W. C.
Practice of Angling, The Vols I and II *see* O'Gorman
prawn fishing 223–6, *224–6*
Present State of Muscovy 128
prides
for chubs 63
for eels 85
of lampreys 103
Prigg, R. F. 291
Prince of Wales Hanwell Club 19
puppies and pike 125
Pursuit of Stillwater Trout, The see Clarke, Brian

Quebec, brook trout in 329
Quenelles de Brochet à la Lyonnaise (pike recipe) *159–60*
quick-strike rod-holder *488*
quill minnow 469, *469*
Quincey, Thomas de 7
quiver-tipping 415

rabbits (bait)

for catfish 47
for chub 63
Radcliffe, William (*Fishing from the Earliest Times*)
on early fishing methods 347
on running line 443
ragworm (bait) for flounder 89
rainbow trout 325–8, *325–8*
cross-wind fly fishing 282
and Muddle Minnow *328*
tail cf. brown trout *326*
'wild' *326*
raisins, and chub 63
raking the bottom
dace 69
eels 85
gudgeon 99
Ram's Island, record pollan at 341
Rannoch, Loch 153
Ransome, Arthur (*Rod and Line*)
on brace of fish 341
on carp 36
on catfish 48
on eels 73
on fashions in fish 14
on grayling 98
on home-made fly 309
ranunculus *177*
Rapala plug bait 471, *471, 477*
Rapidex reel 374
Rasputin fly dressing 275, *275*
rats
as fish thieves 500
as food for pike 125
Ravensthorpe Reservoir, rudd in 182
Rawling, Tom 258
Ray, John, early fixed-spool reel of 375, *375,* 376
Redditch Scale, hooks 387
Redi, Francisco, on eel immigration 78
Red Knab, Windermere 52
Redmire Pool, carp in *37, 39*
red rag as dace bait 71
Red Tarn, skelly in 336, 337
redworm 427, *428,* 429
reel(s) 358–7
Aerial 62, 373, 374
centre-pin 377
Chinese 358–64, *359–64*
earliest 360–9, *360–9*
fixed-spool *362,* 375–7, *375–6*
jams 495
multiplier 370–2, *370–3*
Nottingham-type 373–4, *374,* 482
origin 358–60, *359*
Scarborough-type 374
Sheffield-type 374

'spoke', Chinese *362, 363*
and 'tube' rod-holder *373*
Ree, Lough, pollan in 340
Regan, C. Tate (*British Freshwater Fishes*)
on charr 49
on flounder 89
on 'graining' 68
on lamprey 104
on pollan 341
on roach 165
on skelly 337
on tench 246
on trout 254, 298
Regents Park Canal, sticklebacks in 235
resting the swim, chub 64
Retropinna 299
reverse swing float 456, *456*
Rex cyprinorum see mirror carp
Rhone (r), pike in 128
Rib (r), dace in 70
Richardson, Rev. W., on eel migration 78, 81, 83
Rickmansworth (lake near), crucian carp in 43
Ringmere
big rudd at 183
big tench at *248*
Risga, bone fish-hook at *385*
river pollution 198–203
tenth-century 202–3
River Runt Spook bait 470
roach *11,* 165–70, *165–6, 168–78*
baited on breadcrust *424*
Baked (recipe) 180
Boiled (recipe) 180
British Record *166,* 167, 182
choice of rod 353–4
cooking 180
distribution 165
fly-fishing 179
food of 166
hybrids 181–2, 184–9, *185*
Irish match record 165
ledgering 173–5
migration 167
pharyngeal teeth *184*
pole-fishing 170–2, *362*
spawning 167
striking *352,* 353
swim-feeder technique 176–9
trotting 167–9, *168*
Rob o' The Trows see Frain, R.
Rochester, Bishop of, sturgeon of 239
Rod and Line see Ransome, Arthur
rod bell *415*
rod rest 356–7

roach pole 172, *172*
six patterns of 356, *357*
rod rings 355–6, *355*
rods 347–57
  attraction 350
  built-cane *349*, 350
  catfish ('R.W.' carp r.) 46
  charr 57
  choice 350–5
  coarse-fish 353–5
  development 347
  and electricity 508, *508*
  function 350
  Hardy 'R.W.' carp r. 36, 46
  history 347–50
  landing 350–3
  materials 347–50
  origin 347–50
  presentation 350
  sharing 261
  split-cane 349–50, *349*
  striking 350, *351–2*
  test-curve 354, *354*
  top caught in trees 497
Rolfe, H. L. 11
  on salmon *193*
Rolfe, R. 46
Romsey
  eels at 84
  tench at 245
Rondeletius
  on pike 128
  on tench 245
Rooper, George (*Thames and Tweed*) 152
Rothes, Lady, big barbel of 19
Rothschilds, the 469
Rott, pike fossils at 124
Rotter (r)
  chub in 67
  pollution of 200
Royalty (F)
  barbel in 16, 17, 18
  bream in 28
rubby-dubby bag 140
rudd 181–9, *181–4*, *186–8*
  choice of rod 353, 354
  cooking 189
  distribution 181
  groundbait 182–3
  hybrids 184–9, *186*
  record 183
ruffe (or pope) 190–1
  hybrids 190
  and substitute Pope 190
running line, historical 347, 443, *443*
Rural Sports see Daniel, Rev. W. B.
Ruses Innocentes, Les see Fortin, Françoise
Rutilus rutilus see roach
Russia see USSR

Russian Turkestan, roach in 165
Rydal (near Windermere) 62

Sachs, T. R., charr of 51
saddle tackles 147–8
Sadler, Dendy *12*, 366
safety 501–8
  action in event of emergency 504–5
  boat-fishing accidents 503, 506–7, 507–8
  emergency 502–3
  removing hook from flesh 508, *508*
  rods and electricity 508
  wading 501, *502*
St John, Charles, on elvers 80
St John, J., pike of 162
Salmo salar see salmon, Atlantic
salmon, Atlantic 192–231, *192–229*
  anatomy *195*
  ancestry 192
  angle of presentation 208–10, *209*
  British Record Rod-Caught 217
  choice and presentation of small fly 204–6, *206*
  camouflage 192
  colours 204–5, 224
  cooking 230–1
  cross-wind fly-fishing 282
  'Dee' otter *219*
  downrigger and Canadian s. 484–9, *484–9*
  early stone-carving *199*
  effective casting range 210–11, *210*
  fishing 202–21
  fly-fishing 203–17, *205–10*, 212, *216*
  fly-lines 206–8, *207*
  fly sizes 206
  Fresh Steaks (recipe) 230
  gaffing 212, 214
  gillies 214, 228–30
  hooking 211–12, *212*
  Kedgeree (recipe) 231
  kelts 198
  leaping 196
  leisters *218*
  life cycle 192–8
  low-water worm fishing 219–23
  lures for 203–4, 206, 223
  migration 193–6
  origin 192
  over-fishing of lies 221
  parasites *197*
  playing and landing 212–17
  and pike 213

Poached (recipe) 231
pollution 198–203
prawn fishing 223–6, *224–6*
presenting a worm 221–3, *222–3*
cf. sea trout 298–9, *302*, 303, *303*
sense of smell 224
shrimp fishing 226–7
spawning 194–8
and spinning 463
stealth 210, *215*, 215–17
tailing by hand 212, 214–15, *400*
temperature 194–5, 203, 206, 207
Thames 198
trailing 482
value in medieval England of 13
wading 210–11, *216*, 221, 222
'walking' 214
water sense 207, 210, 221, 222
waterside behaviour 217
world record 202
Salmo ferox see great lake trout
Salmo gairdneri see rainbow trout
Salmon Fishery Report see Buckland, Frank
Salmon Fishing see Taverner, Richard
Salmon Fishing (engraving) see Barlow, Francis; Hollar, W.
salmonid 192, *195*, 200
Salmonidae (Salmonoidei) 49, 52, 68, 94, 192, 253, 298, 330
  see also charr; salmon, Atlantic
Salmonidae of Westmorland see Braithwaite, G. F.
Salmo nigripinnis see Welsh black-finned trout
Salmo orcandensis see Orkney sea trout
Salmo stomachis see gillaroo
Salmo the Leaper see Falkus, Hugh
Salmo trutta fario see brown trout
Salmo trutta trutta see sea trout
Salter, Robert (*Modern Angler*), on spinning with natural bait 467
Salter, T. F. (*The Angler's Guide*)
  on artificial baits 467

on flounder 88
on multiplier 370, *371*
on perch 116
on rudd 181
saddle tackle 147–8, *148*
on spinning *464*, 464–5, 467
Salthouse Bay, pike at *152*
Salvelinus alpinus see charr
Salvelinus fontinalis see brook trout
Salvelinus namaycush 62
Samuel, William (*The Arte of Angling*)
  on burbot 30, 31
  on carp 36
  on chub 65
  on landing-net 399
  on ruffe 190–1
  on stealth 215
  on 'wind up' 365–6
San Tshai Thu Hui on early reel 358
Sanctuary, Dr T., record grayling of 94
sand-martins, and pike 156, *156*
Sandvik's non-toxic lead-free split-shot 396
Sandwich Islands, Hawaii, early spoon bait in 468
Saprolegnia *197*
Sargasso Sea, eels in 75, 79, 80, 82–3
Sarton, G. (*Introduction to the History of Science*) 358
Saunders, James (*The Compleat Fisherman*) see Charfy, Guiniad
sausage (bait), for barbel 16
Sca Fell (mountain) 287, 289
scale reading 38
Scandinavia, grayling in 94
Scarborough-type reel 374
Scardinius erythrophthalmus see rudd
schelly see skelly
Schliersee, Bavaria, big pike in *144*
Schmidt, Johannes, eel research of 79
Schrädler, Joseph, big pike of *144*
Science and Civilisation in China see Needham, Dr Joseph
Scotland (lakes), charr in 49
Scotty downrigger *59*, 484, *485*, 486
Sea Angler's Fishes see Kennedy, Michael
Sea Angling with Baited Spoon see Garrard, P.

Sea Fishing see Cooper, A.E.
sea-lice *197*
sea-trout 298–324
  angling approach 302–5
  with Bacon and Fried Bread
    (recipe) 325
  and brown trout 253
  Cooked with Cucumber
    (recipe) 325
  cooking 324–5
  cross-wind fly-fishing 282
  diet 300
  'finger-ring' figure-of-eight
    retrieve 319–21, *320*
  graph of behaviour *301*
  life-cycle 299–301
  migration 299–300, 309–10
  night-fishing and lures 306–
    18
  night fly-fishing 309–10
  playing 321, *321*
  rain shelter *316*
  cf. salmon 298–9, *302*, 303,
    303
  Secret Weapon 315–17
  sparling eaten by s.-t. *301*
  steeple cast *305*
  Sunk Lure *299*, 310–11
  Surface Lure 311–14
  tackle hints 317–19
  trailing 482
Sea-Trout Fishing see Falkus,
    Hugh
Secret Weapon 308–9, 310,
    315–17, *315*
Secrets of Angling, The see
    Dennys, John
Sedbergh, charr at 52
sedge-fishing 270, *270*
Semaine, Le see Bartas,
    Guillaume de Saluste du
semi stand-off intermediate
    ring 355–6
Serpentine
  big eel in 82
  perch in 117
  sturgeon in 237
Severn (r)
  barbel in 15
  chub in 67
  lampern in 106
  shad in 232, *233*, 233, 234
shads 232–4, *232–3*
  allis 232–3
  cooking 234
  Grilled (recipe) 234
  spawning 232
  twaite 232–3
Shakespeare, William
  on burbot 31
  Coriolanus 110
  Hamlet 243, 429
Shane's Castle, pollan at
    341

Shannon (r)
  allis shad in 232
  lamprey in 105
  pike in 153
  roach in 165
  shannon in 340
Sharpe, Dr Bowdler, on tench
    246
Shaw, George (*General
    Zoology Pisces*) 131
Shaw, Roy 20, *82*, *83*
  on grayling 96, 98
Sheffield-type reel 374
Sheringham, Hugh T.
  address to Piscatorial Society
    260, 262
  An Angler's Hours 445
  on careful baiting 249
  Coarse Fishing, on rudd 182
  and dace 69
  Elements of Angling 482
  *Fishing, Its Cause, Treatment
    and Cure* 190
  on floats 245, 408, 445
  on gudgeon 100
  An Open Creel 254
  on ruffe 190
  on trailing 482
Shirley, Thomas (*The
    Angler's Museum*)
  on alcohol 223
  on caviare 244
shooting-head, casting 271–6
Shorter Oxford English
    Dictionary, The
  def. caviare 243
  def. to wind up 366
shot-link ledger 444
shrimp
  fishing 226–7
  and roach 166
Shutt, Bev, sea trout of *322*,
    323
Siberia
  burbot in 31
  roach in 165
  rudd in 181
  sturgeon from 238
signals, angling 410
Silex reel 374, 461
Silurus glanis see catfish
silver bream 28, *28*
  hybrids 184
silver carp 41
silver eel 77, 78, *83*, 83–4
sink-and-draw, trolling for
    perch 117
Siren, O. (*History of Early
    Chinese Painting*) 359
Six-Mile Water, pollan at
    341
skelly (schelly) *60*, 299, 330,
    336–8, *337*
  houting and chub 64

Viking inheritance? 336–8
Slack, Professor H.D., on
    powan 332
slack-line fishing 415
Slapton Ley, rudd at 181
Slater, David 373
sleigh bell, and charr *54*, 57
sliced-shanked bait-hook
    431–2
sliding bubble-float
    paternoster 459–61, *460*
sliding float 411–14, *412*
slotted Devon bait 470, *470*
Small Double 317
smelt see sparling
Smith, J.R. *101*
Smith, Martin Tucker 263
Smythe, Very Rev. Patrick
    Murray (*The Diary of an
    All-Round Angler*) 111
snails, and roach 166
snake ring 355
soap (bait), for West African
    catfish 46
Söderberg, Lars 467
Solway Firth 337
*Some Mishaps in The Pleasures
    of Angling* see Turner, C.
Song of Hiawatha, The see
    Longfellow, Henry
    Wadsworth
Sonning-on-Thames, pike at
    127
sparling (smelt) *301*
Spencer, Walter 500
spinner box 473, *473*
spinning 463–73
  artificial baits 465–8
  baits 468–73
  historical 463–5
  housing spinners 473
  leads 397, *397*
  McElrath deadbait (sprat) s.
    mount 468
Spinning for Pike see Barder,
    Richard
split-shot dispenser 398
spoon baits 147
Sport in Art see Baillie-
    Grohman, W.A.
Sporting Wife, The see
    Hargreaves, Barbara
Sports Afield 471
Sportsman's Cookbook, The
    see Walker, E.M.
sportmanship and sporting
    angling methods
Sport with Gun and Rod see
    Mayer, A.
Spothow Gill, liming projects
    in 294–5
sprat, freshwater see bleak
spring-bite-indicator 415–17,
    416

Sproats (of Ambleside), charr
    of 53
Sprouston
  flounder at *90*
  salmon at *200*, *205*
Squires, Bruce (of
    Ambleside), charr of 55
Staines South Reservoir, pike
    in 129
Stamford Water
  burbot in 31
  roach in 183
  rudd in 183
standard end ring 356
standing pike-paternoster
    461–2, *462*
stand-off end ring 356
Stanley beat, Tay (r), salmon
    from *228*
Starnberger see houting in 332
Startops End reservoir, bream
    in 25
static fly 274–5
Stava, Jan *47*
stealth 210, *215*, 215–17
steeple cast *305*
Steinhart, E. 69
Steuart, Dave, on roach
    trotting *168*
Stewart, W.C. (*The Practical
    Angler*)
  on minnows 110
Stewart tackle 221, 431, *431*,
    432
  on worm fishing 221
stickleback
  ten-spined 235
  three-spined see three-
    spined stickleback
Still-Water Angling see
    Walker, Richard
Stizostedion lucioperca see
    zander
Stizostedion vitreum see
    walleye
Stoddart, Thomas Tod (*The
    Angler's Companion to the
    Rivers and Locks*)
  on pike 152
  on rods and materials 348
Stoke Weir on Trent *436*
Stone, Peter, big pike of *478*
Stour (Dorset) (r)
  barbel in 15–16
  bream, absence of 28
  chub in 67
  dace in 70
  pike 461, 472
  roach, swimfeeder
    techniques in 176–9, *177*
  stret-pegging 457–8, *457*
  roach 179
  salmon 227, *227*
  striking too hard 497

Stuffed Barbel (recipe) 21
Stuffed Bream (recipe) 27
sturgeon 237–44, *237–43*
  Baked (recipe) 244
  common (green) 237–9
  cooking 243–4
  Cutlets (recipe) 244
  distribution 237
  Kaluga 242
  preparation of caviare 244
  Roast (recipe) 244
  roe and caviare 238, 240,
    242–4
  white 240–2
Summer on the Test, A see
  Hills, John Waller
Sunart, Loch, bone fish-hook
  at *385*
Sunday Times, on pike 145
Sunk Lure 308–9
  Falkus 310–11, *311*
Super Flumina see Marson,
  Charles
Surface Lure 309–14, *312, 313*
  fishing 312–14
  making 312
Survey of the Lakes see Clarke
Sutton, Ken *372*
  reels *368, 372*
  zander *344*
Swale (r), barbel in 15
Swan Inlet Pool, Falkland
  Islands, sea trout at *323*
Sweden, perch in *122*
Swedish Record-Fish-
  Committee 467
Swift, Jonathan, on gudgeon
  100
Swim wizz plug *477*
swimfeeder 435
  bait-dropper 437, *438*
  and barbel 16
  Cox's *435*
  float-ledger *440, 455, 456*
  polycone 439–40
  and roach 176–9
swimming the stream
  and barbel 16
  and bream 24
  and roach 167
  see also trotting
swingtip 415
  ancient 418–20
  and bream 24
  modern 416, *417*
Switzerland, deep-water
  charr trailing in 61–2
swivels 395, *395*
Sybarites, addiction to eels 74,
  84

Tame (r) 200
Taverner, Eric (*Salmon
  Fishing*) 497

Tay, Loch, pike in 127, *129*
Tay (r), salmon in 197, *199*,
  217, 228, 471, 477
Taylor, F. J.
  on deadbait, pike 140
  on fluted float 414
  and fly-fishing for pike *156,
    157*
  and 'lift' method 447, *448*
  tackle 141
  and tench 250, *250*
  Tench 250
  and worms 426, 430–1
Taylor, Ken
  netting a fish *399*
  and pike 145, *156*, 157
  on worms 430–1
Taylor, Samuel (*Angling in
  All Its Branches*)
  on minnow 110
  on pike 150–1
Tchouang-Tseu, on split-
  cane rods 350
Teddington Lock, lamperns
  at 106
Tees (r) 200
Teifi (r), sturgeon from 238
Teith, Loch, roach in 165
Teleosts 330
tench 245–52, *245, 247–51*
  choice of rod 353–4
  colour 245
  cooking 251–2
  distribution 245
  and Eel Pie (recipe) 251, 252
  groundbaiting 247–9
  'lift' method 250
  pharyngeal teeth *185*
  and pike 147
  a la Poulette (recipe) 251
  spawning 245
  Stuffed (recipe) 252
  and tar 248
  see also carp
Tench see Taylor, F. J.
tenth-century river pollution
  202–3
*Territory in the Three-Spined
  Stickleback see* Assem, J.
  van den
Test (r)
  chub in 64, *67*
  dace in 70
  eels in 84
  grayling in 94, *95*, 95
  pike in 152, *469*
  salmon in *211*
  tench in 245
  trout in 17
test curves 354, *354*
Teviot (r), salmon in *225*
Thame (r) 200
Thames (r)
  barbel in 15, 17

crucian carp in 43
current speed in 445
dace in 69, 71
early spade-end hook in 385
eels in 77
flounder in 88
gudgeon 99, 102
lampern in 106
pike in 127
pollution of 232
roach-poling in 170, *172*
salmon in 198
sturgeon in 237
twaite shad in 232
whitebait in 233
Thames and Tweed see
  Rooper, George
Thamesley's 'Tungsten' shot
  396
Thaumaturas 133
Thaya (r), 'pike-perch'
  (zander or walleye) in 342
theft of fish by rats, cats, etc.
  500
Theocritus 160
thermocline 58, 60
Thetford
  burbot at 31
  dace at 69
  rudd at 183
Thiersaut, Dabry de, illus. of
  early reel *361*
thin/thick-lipped mullet 113,
  114
Thomas, Peter
  and carp catch *35*
  and pike *145*
  and 'wild' rainbow trout *326*
Thompson, J. (*History of
  British Fishes*), on pollan
  341
Thompson, Jackie, and record
  pike 145
Thompson, Mrs Louie *65*
Thompson, W. (*Natural
  History of Ireland*), on
  lampreys 103
Thomsett, Peter, and big pike
  157–8
Thornton, Col. T.
  big Loch Lomond perch of
  117
  big tench of *247*
three-spined stickleback (or
  tiddler) 235–6, *235–6*
  recommended reading 236
three-way swivel 395, *395*
Throop (F)
  barbel in 18
  bream in 28
Thymallus thymallus see
  grayling
Tibullus 421
tickling, barbel 16

Tieman, B. 125
T'ien Chu Ling Ch'ien 358
Tinbergen, Professor Niko
  (*Animal Behaviour*) 236
Tinca tinca see tench
toby spoon *465, 470, 470*
Tollady, John 477
Toner, Dr E. D., of pike
  cannibalism 127
torpedo fish 13
Torridge Fishery see Gray,
  L. R. N.
touch-ledgering 377, 415, *415*
Towi (r), sturgeon from 238
trailing, 481–2
  of charr 50–62
  see also trolling
*Treatyse of Fysshynge wyth an
  Angle, A see* Berners,
  Dame Juliana
Trent (r)
  barbel in 15
  lampern in 106
  match fishermen *436*
  and Nottingham anglers 373
  sturgeon in 237
'Trent Otter' *see* Martin,
  J. W.
Trichoptera 166
Tring lake
  bream in 24, 25
  pike in 461
  and Walker's float 410
  wels catfish in 45
Tring Museum 25
trolling 479–92
  downrigger 482–90
  historical 479–81, *479–81*
  sink-and-draw 479–81
  and trailing 481–2
  see also downrigger
*Trolling for Pike in the River
  Lea see* Pollard, James
trotting 167–9, *168*, 179
Troubled Waters see Wiggin,
  Maurice
trout *11*
  gross conversion rate 130
  see also brown t.; rainbow t.;
  sea-t.
trout, The see Brown,
  D. M. E.; Frost, Dr W. E.
True Art of Angling, The see
  Ustonson, Onesimus
Trueblood, Ted *154*
trying to land fish too soon
  497
Tryon, Aylmer; record barbel
  of 16–18
Tryon, G. C. 17, 18
Tu Shu Chi Ch'ing, of spare
  line looped around rod
  366, *367*
Tulla, Co. Clare, pike at *142*

Tummell, Loch, pike in 153
tunny, as medicine 13
turbot, value in medieval
England of 13
Turner, C. (*Some Mishaps in The Pleasures of Angling*), sitting on rod *500*
Turner, Joseph 373
Turrell, Dr W. J. (*Ancient Angling Authors*)
on burbot 30
on early float 409
Tweed (r)
flounder in 89
graylings in 335
19th c. painting *348*
salmon in *194*, 200, 205, 212, 229
sea trout in 300
Tweed (or McElrath) deadbait-spinning-mount 468, *468*
twenty-six ways of losing a fish 494–501
Twickenham, dace at 71
Tywi (r) 200

Ullswater
big eels in 83
perch in 336
skelly in 336, 337, 340
Ulvsundet, record pike at 467
Universal snap tackle *149*, 149
unsound tackle 494
Upton, T., and charr 52
Ure (r), barbel in 15
Usk (r)
dace in 70
sturgeon in 237
USSR
centre-pin reel *376*, *377*
fly-fishing in 297
ice-fishing in 56
roach in 165
sturgeon in 237, 240
wels catfish in 45, 48
Ustonson, Onesimus (*The True Art of Angling*), on multiplier 370

Vale of Leven Angling Society 470
variable shot-link ledger 444
Varli, Fehmi, and Swedish Rod-Caught Record Pike 467
Venables, Col. Robert (*The Experienc'd Angler*)
on bait-horn 423
on double hook 317
on early dough-bobbin 416
on early reel 360, 366, *366*, *368*
on fly fishing for pike 150

on hook and bristle 432
on recreation 193
on rod materials 348
on running line 444
on spinning 464
on stomach contents 429
on young salmon (or pike?) 214
vendace 299, 330, *331*, *334*, *338*, 338–41
see also pollan
Venner, T. (*Via Recta ad Vitam Longam*)
on barbel 21
on tench 252
Vesey-Fitzgerald, Brian (*The Hampshire Avon*)
on cooking pike 160
on perch 116
Vesjoloskoye Reservoir, USSR, touch ledgering in *377*
Via Recta ad Vitam Longam see Venner, T.
Vikings, and skelly 336–8
Vincent, Jim, spoon-bait of 472
voles, and pike 125
Volga (r), sturgeon from 240
Voorst, Van *192*
Voyage en Sibérie see Gmelin
Vranou Reservoir, Czechoslovakia, catfish in *47*
Vries, Noel de, zander of *343*

wading 210–11, *216*, 221, 222
and safety 501, *502*
Wagtail bait 469, *469*
Walker, A. *101*
Walker, Mrs E. M. (*The Sportsman's Cookbook*), on roach 180
Walker, Patricia 131
Walker, Richard (*Still-Water Angling*) Arlesey bomb of 396–7
on bag limit 258
and bale-arm roller 376
on bream 28
and carp catches 35, *37*, 38–9
and chub *65*, 67
colours for floats 409
exaggeration theory 265
fishing on Itchen 430
and flounder 90
grinner knot of 390
on hybrids 187
and 'leaded' nymph 268
on minnow-tansie 112
Permaflote of 266–7
on pharyngeal teeth 187
on pike 145

on powan fishing 333–6
on roach fly-fishing 179
on roach pole fishing *170*, 171, 187
on rudd 183, 187
touch ledgering 415, *415*
unusual float of 410
'walking' a fish 214
Waller, Edmund, on gudgeon 100
walleye 338, 342
Walsingham, Lord 469
Walton, Izaac (*The Compleat Angler*) 180, 400
on artificial minnow 465, 469
on baits 423
on bleak 23
on bream 24, 27
carp recipe of 14, 44
on charr 62
and chevin 337
on chubb 63–4, 67
on 'daping' (dapping) 282
on eels, origin and procreation 76–7, 78, 84
eel recipe 86
on fishing 'Wheels' 264
on grayling 95
on Isle of Ely 84
on loss of a fish 498
on Mannheim pike 134
on pike 130, 164, 246
on powdered beef 78
and rudd 181
on spinning 464
on tench 245, 246, 248
on Thames salmon 198
Zern's satire on 425
Warren, J. W. *120*
Waterford Marsh, dace in 69
waterfowl, as bait for pike 125
Waterhead, charr in 53
water louse, and roach 166
water-sense 207, 210, 221, 222, 260
Watson, John (*The English Lake District Fisheries*)
on big eels 81
on skelly 336, 337
Watts, Henry (Hank), big sturgeon of 240, *241*
weather 494
Weaver (r) 200
Webb, D., record rudd of 183
Weeger, Emil (*The Fishing Gazette*)
on carp 40, 41
on 'pike-perch' (zander or walleye) 342
Welland (r) sliding floats for *412*, 413
Wellington, Duke of, and livebait, elastic support 148

Wellow (r) 200
wels catfish (European catfish) 45, *47*
Welsh black-finned trout 254
West African catfish 46
Westminster Aquarium, tench in 246
Weston, R. 119
West Runton, pike fossils in 124, *126*
Westwood and Satchell (*Bibliotheca Piscatoria*) 418
Wey (r), barbel in 15
Wharfe (r), barbel in 15
Wheeler, Alwyne (*The Fishes of the British Isles and North-West Europe*) 9
on bleak 23
on bream 24
on charr 50
on pike 131, 133
on roach 165
on spawning temperatures of roach, rudd and bream 187
on tench 245
on walleye 342
on wels catfish 48
on whitefish 330
Where the Bright Waters Meet see Greene, Harry Plunkett
whiffing 233
White, Lynn (*Medieval Technology and Social Change*) 358
White, R. L., and rudd on dry-fly 182
whitebait 233
Whitefishes 299, 330–41
classification 330–1
see also houting (gwyniad; powan; skelly); vendace (vendace various; pollan)
white sturgeon *see* sturgeon, white
Whitney, John (*The Genteel Recreation*), on tar 248
Wiggin, Maurice
on dace 72
Fishing for Beginners 101
on fly fishing 275
on gudgeon 101
Troubled Waters 72
Wild Sports of the Highlands see St John, Charles
William of Wykeham, and minnows 112
Williams, A. Courtney (*Angling Diversions*)
a blank day 180
on chub 67

first record of landing-net
399
on rainbow trout caught in
London 325
on split cane rods 349–50
Williams, Phill, shad of *233*
William's Wabler bait 471
Williamson, Captain T. (*The
Complete Angler's Vade
Mecum*), on spinning with
natural bait 467
Wilson, Alan, and record rod-
caught tench *249*
Wilson, Brigadier G. H. N.
and fly-retriever 319
and landing net *318*
Wilson, T. ('Gudgeon
Fishing, or He's Fairly
Hook'd') *101*
Wilstone reservoir
bream in 24
catfish in 47
perch in 119
Winchester College, minnows
at 112
wind knot 495
Windermere, Lake
big eels 81
charr in 50–62, *53, 54, 336*

habits of charr 50–2
old charr recipe 62
pike 127, 128, 136, 139
traditional charr fishing 52–
62
trailing charr 482
trout 58
Windsor Park lake, pike in 135
Wisconsin scientists' research
on eel 82
Witham (r), deformed pike in
133–4, *134*
wobbling 147, 469
Woburn Abbey lake
catfish in 45, 46
zander in 342, *344*
Wood, Ian (*Loch Lomond and
Its Salmon*) 332
Wooden Devon minnow 472,
472
Worcester Journal see Barrow
Wordsworth, William
(*Excursion on the Banks of
Ullswater*), on skelly 337
worm-fly, and sea trout 317
worms 426–32, *426, 428*
bait-hooks 431–2, *431–2*
care of 429
collection 427–9

and perch 116
presentation 431
and salmon fishing 219–23
a selection *428*
sensitivity to light 427
species 427
Worthington, E. B. and
Macan, T. (*Life in Lakes
and Rivers*) 60
Wroxham Broad, bream in
398
Wu Chen (*Fishermen*) 358,
361
Wye (r)
allis shad in 232
barbel in 15
chub in 67
sturgeon in 237
Wye (r), Derbyshire, rainbow
trout in 325
Wye lead 397, *397*
Wylye (r)
record dace in 70
record grayling in 94

Xenocrates 13

Yarrell, William (*A History of
British Fishes*)

on barbel 17
on flounder 89
on 'graining' 68
on gwyniad 336
on hybrid fishes 182
on skelly 337
on sturgeon 237
yellow belly 77, 468, *468*
Yesselmeer lake, and flounder
88
Yorkshire Specimen Group
133
Young Barbel Baked in the
Oven (recipe) 21
Young Barbel Meuniere
(recipe) 21
Young Barbel with Shallots
and Mushrooms (recipe)
21

zander 342–4, *342–4*
cooking 344
Zern, Ed (*To Hell with
Fishing*), on Walton's
Compleat Angler 425
Zongouska (r), sturgeon from
238
zoo *see* London Zoo
Zuider Zee, and flounder 88